SAMUEL TAYLOR COLERIDGE

D1010100

# Samuel Taylor Coleridge

❧

# SELECTED POETRY AND PROSE

EDITED WITH AN INTRODUCTION AND NOTES

BY ELISABETH SCHNEIDER

❧

HOLT, RINEHART AND WINSTON

NEW YORK

Sixth Printing, August, 1962

Introduction and notes copyright, 1951, by Elisabeth Schneider
Typography Design by Stefan Salter
Printed in the United States of America
27741-0111

# INTRODUCTION

❧❧❧

The student who would take all knowledge for his province could do worse than begin with Coleridge. He had a mind, as Hazlitt said, "reflecting ages past"—a remark not intended to exclude ages present and future. Merely to trace his intellectual history would be a long task, for there is scarcely any extensive territory of man's knowledge that Coleridge had not at least dipped into. The literature and philosophy of Greece and Rome; church history; theology; what used to be called political economy; the literature of Germany and to a smaller extent that of Italy, France, Spain; the philosophical writers of Christian Europe; his own native literature, past and present; travel and exploration; chemistry, medicine, and natural history; psychology (scarcely yet differentiated from philosophy); the arts of painting and music: these were but some of the things that interested Coleridge. In some of them he was only a dabbler, in others much more than that. His literary interests were not, like those of Charles Lamb, confined largely to the "delicious" old folios of the sixteenth- and seventeenth-century writers. He kept up with the current *Monthly Magazine* and *Morning Post* and the latest publications of Schelling or Madame de Staël; and the books of his friends did not generally stand uncut on his shelves.

Perhaps more than any other English poet, Coleridge became a focus for the varied currents that together produced the Romantic Movement. Almost all the "romantic" impulses that found expression during the eighteenth century came to his capacious attention; they affected his development and he theirs. This is not the place to enter into the morass of definitions of Romanticism; but the main currents have been well enough charted—the medievalism, the general interest in what is dim and distant in time or place, democratic idealism, the "return to nature," the leaning toward introspection—all separate movements whose common ground seems to have been man's desire for infinite extension of experience. Coleridge had his finger in them all.

The accounts of travel and exploration that Coleridge read, a remarkable blend, most of them, of fantasy, history, and scientific observation, formed a material part of the romantic writers' mental furniture. Even the relatively stay-at-home Wordsworth, whose poetic themes rarely extended beyond the range of his own eyes, begged a friend to collect for him "any books of travel," as without them he could not carry on his work. Southey and Landor found in them material for their long romantic epics. Tales of voyagers to the Arctic and the Antarctic, of explorers in America and Africa, of travels into ancient regions of eastern Europe and Asia, all found their way into the writings of Coleridge, as the reader of *The Road to Xanadu* well knows. He found use also for the current popular fiction that stirred the imaginations, somewhat to our surprise today, of even the greatest Romantic writers—Mrs. Radcliffe, "Monk" Lewis, "Perdita" Robinson, and the rest. All this is but one strain in Coleridge's work; others will appear. For it was not only the dim and far-off that engaged him.

Coleridge entered into his young manhood as a political rebel. As a poet, however, he set out most conventionally. His early verse makes use of all the usual personified abstractions of eighteenth-century poetry. We find him imitating one after another fashionable writer of the preceding age. In some early lines on "Julia" his cramped and not very skillful heroic couplets take us back to *The Rape of the Lock,* even to the loss of lover and lap dog. But this is early indeed. More characteristic are fragments avowedly imitating Ossian and the obviously Radcliffean pieces that persist as late as 1800, when the *Morning Post* published his *Mad Monk* as "An Ode in Mrs. Ratcliff's Manner." And the somewhat sentimental influence of William Lisle Bowles will be seen everywhere.

A distinction to be noted, however, even in Coleridge's early poetry, is its music. Originality of thought and image, and the constructive power to produce an organic whole developed—insofar as the last developed at all—only afterward; but the melodious line and stanza came early. In this respect his work was from the start distinguished from that of his friend Southey, whose lines were often little more than prose, and even from Wordsworth, who could be musical when Milton's poetry was running in his mind but not always otherwise. The music of Coleridge's early verse is exceedingly graceful, but it is also a little too facile.

The meeting of Coleridge with Wordsworth hastened the poetic development of both men immeasurably. It did more than that, for by mutual sympathy each was enriched with some reflection of the other's genius. Each would seem almost to have talked the other into his native but scarcely awakened originality. To this exchange the influence of Wordsworth's sister Dorothy was added. It has often been remarked how the loving and delicate observations of nature, recorded freshly in Dorothy's journals, found their way into the poetry of both her brother and Coleridge. The conventional descriptive epithet inherited from eighteenth-century verse gave way in both poets to a more living vocabulary. Coleridge's early verse had been well padded with *countless hordes, fond hearts, unnumber'd sighs, sultry beams, vain resolves, feeble frames*—all the phrases that then came handy to the young writer. These were not dropped from his maturer poetry, but they were brought to life by keen observation, by the chosen word supplanting the accidental, by a conscious wish to be true to the observed facts.

In *The Road to Xanadu* Lowes took pains to show from notebooks Coleridge's persistent interest in the truth about natural phenomena, whether observed by himself or gleaned from his reading. *The Ancient Mariner* is filled with supernatural events and images. Yet in outline and descriptive detail it follows closely the factual accounts of voyages around Cape Horn to the Pacific. Coleridge was ready even to sacrifice poetic effect in favor of exactness: his first description of the ship's wake—"The furrow followed free"—he later altered to "The furrow streamed off free" because, he said, the former is the image only as seen by a spectator from a distance; seen from the ship itself, he had observed, the wake appears to fall away behind. In still later editions he very sensibly sacrificed truth to euphony by restoring the original line. Nevertheless, to a considerable degree this fidelity to fact gives Coleridge's best poetry its visual vividness. It may have been Lowes again who, commenting on the water snakes and the phosphorescent moonlit ocean of *The Ancient Mariner,* called attention to the precision with which Coleridge has visualized the scene. The poet was interested scientifically in the cause of the phenomenon, the "sundry rotten mackerel and other *smashy* matters," as he expresses it. But he also did not forget that a ship in moonlight casts a shadow and that colors in phosphorescent water become more vivid as the darkness increases. And so, "beyond the shadow" in full moonlight the phosphorescence shows "shining white" and "hoary," while "within the shadow" where the darkness is blacker, the colors are blue and green and gold and "a still and awful red." This eye for the truth we should take for granted in a painter. But the authors of oriental romances, the Radcliffeans, and later writers such as Poe were inclined to give us horrors or magnificences more verbal than visual. Coleridge's superiority in this respect partly explains why he rises above other poets who dealt in the same wild and fanciful romantic machinery. His pictures, as well as his language and music, take hold upon the imagination.

He was capable, however, of putting all his poetic powers to work without the aid of fantasy, mystery, or horror. *Frost at Midnight* opens with lines of beautiful movement that make a simple and factual, yet imaginative statement:

> The Frost performs its secret ministry,
> Unhelped by any wind.

The poem rounds to its conclusion with the help of a little Milton and a little Shakespeare, recreated into Coleridge's own.

> Therefore all seasons shall be sweet to thee,
> Whether the summer clothe the general earth
> With greenness, or the red breast sit and sing
> Betwixt the tufts of snow on the bare branch
> Of mossy apple-tree, while the nigh thatch
> Smokes in the sun-thaw; whether the eave-drops fall
> Heard only in the trances of the blast,
> Or if the secret ministry of frost
> Shall hang them up in silent icicles,
> Quietly shining to the quiet Moon.

We might have described this as finely Wordsworthian but for the fact that it preceded *Tintern Abbey* by several months.

The bulk of Coleridge's first-rate poetry is small. His second-rate and even his third-rate verse, however, deserves attention, partly for the grace that is rarely absent and partly for the lines and passages scattered throughout that Thomson at his best, or Cowper or Wordsworth might almost have written. The striking character of Coleridge's three most popular poems has tended to obscure for the general reader the quality of these quieter achievements. Yet in a poem not otherwise notable we come upon such lines as these:

> Through weeds and thorns, and matted underwood
> I force my way; now climb, and now descend
> O'er rocks, or bare or mossy, with wild foot
> Crushing the purple whorts; while oft unseen,
> Hurrying along the drifted forest-leaves,
> The scared snake rustles. Onward still I toil,
> I know not, ask not whither! A new joy,
> Lovely as light, sudden as summer gust,
> And gladsome as the first-born of the spring,
> Beckons me on, or follows from behind,
> Playmate, or guide! . . .
>
>          .    .    .    .    .
>
> And you, ye Earth-winds! you that make at morn
> The dew-drops quiver on the spiders' webs!
> You, O ye wingless Airs! that creep between
> The rigid stems of heath and bitten furze,
> Within whose scanty shade, at summer-noon,
> The mother-sheep hath worn a hollow bed—
> Ye, that now cool her fleece with dropless damp,
> Now pant and murmur with her feeding lamb.

Here Coleridge has his share in the "back to nature" strain of Romanticism.

Even of Coleridge's best work, however, much is fragmentary. He did not finish *Christabel,* he apparently scarcely more than began *Kubla Khan,* to mention only the most famous fragments. For this reason as well as others perhaps, critical estimates of

Coleridge's poetic achievement vary greatly today. Lowes obviously thought him one of the great poets of all time, and Professor Raysor marks him as "indubitably a poet of the first rank." Mr. T. S. Eliot, on the other hand, doles his praise rather more gingerly. *Dejection* he selects as "one piece of formal verse which in its passionate self-revelation rises almost to the height of great poetry." The shock here lies in the "almost."

Whatever we may think of Coleridge's poetry, it would be difficult to overestimate his importance to the history of criticism. Mr. Eliot's qualifying phrases are absent when he describes him as the greatest of English critics. To Mr. Herbert Read also, Coleridge is "head and shoulders above every other English critic." One great feature of his criticism is its scope. He busied himself with no one aspect of the subject to the exclusion of others. Gifted with a naturally theorizing and generalizing mind, he was concerned in the first place with general principles and wished to see literary judgment established on foundations more solid and more universal than English thought had known before. Impatient alike with eighteenth-century formalism, with the *de gustibus* critics and the beauty-blemish school, he sought the foundations for critical judgment in general aesthetic principles that should be applicable to other arts as well as to literature. And beyond this he wished to set the principles of aesthetics within the larger framework of a metaphysical system.

All this was a large order, and as an ambition for one man it had no doubt its comic aspect when at the age of twenty-eight, in a letter to his scientific friend Humphry Davy, Coleridge described his plan for a work that should ostensibly be "an essay on the elements of poetry" but that should be "in reality a disguised system of morals and politics." A few months later this had become, still in prospect only, a work "Concerning Poetry, and the nature of the Pleasures derived from it. I have faith," he wrote, "that I do understand the subject, and I am sure that if I write what I ought to do on it, the work would supersede all the books of metaphysics, and all the books of morals too." Absurd as this obviously is, it is perhaps less so coming from Coleridge than it would be from most other writers. The statement must not be taken too seriously, either, as representing Coleridge's settled views on the function of poetry in life. As will be seen in the *Biographia Literaria* and in some of the other selections presented in this volume, Coleridge was not a believer in the crude theory that great poetry must be a sugar-coated pill of morality. The "immediate" end of poetry, he held—almost, but not quite consistently—was "pleasure." Beyond this he believed there were other ultimate ends. But his views should be read in his own words rather than in an introductory summary.

Coleridge's criticism was not limited to the theoretical aesthetic and philosophical aspects of his subject. He delivered several series of lectures on poetry and drama. In these, philosophical criticism was mingled with discussions, often detailed, of individual works. It is a great pity that of all these lectures none was written out for publication by himself. Posterity has retrieved from limbo, however, a considerable bulk of the material. Coleridge left partial notes, some of them fairly full, others sketchy; friends or reporters took notes; one admirer, J. P. Collier, undertook to preserve complete shorthand reports of some of the lectures. Of all this material the most significant is the criticism of Shakespeare.

As the eighteenth century waned, the condescension of poets and critics toward Shakespeare had begun to wane also. The picture of Shakespeare as a rough diamond appeared less frequently; Shakespeare was less often taxed with ignorance of the dramatic unities or proprieties and more often praised for his "truth to nature" and his understanding of human character. However, in the early years of the new century, when Shakespeare's tragedies were played on the stage they were still played, not as Shakespeare had written them, but as one or another of his improvers had doctored them. In *Lear,* the part of the fool with all its significance of tragic irony was still omitted. Neoclassic taste retained its tyrannical hold on the stage versions of Shakespeare long after its influence upon critical thought had been weakened. It was Schlegel, Coleridge, Hazlitt, and Lamb who, by varying methods and in varying degrees, succeeded in completely overthrowing that hold.

This is not the place to discuss fully the complicated questions of priority, borrowing, even plagiarism among the Shakespearean critics of the nineteenth century, but the problem must be mentioned. Parallels between the criticism of Schlegel and Coleridge are at times close; and Schlegel's interpretations, so far as the evidence shows, were made public earlier. The problem resolves itself into the question whether the parallels occurred in consequence of the two critics' having followed similar paths in their previous reading and having thence arrived at strikingly similar conclusions independently, as Coleridge maintained, or whether they can be accounted for only on the assumption that Coleridge knew Schlegel's work before giving out his own views and that he used it without acknowledgment. Similar problems arise elsewhere in Coleridge's work, the question of debts to Schelling in certain philosophical writings in particular, and the question of unnamed sources for several poems. Perhaps the final word will prove to have been said by Henry James, who found in the personality of Coleridge a suggestion for Frank Saltram, the central character of his story *The Coxon Fund*. "He took whatever came," said James, "but he never plotted for it, and no man who was so much of an absorbent can ever have been so little of a parasite."

Approaching Coleridge's Shakespearean criticism for the first time, the modern reader sometimes finds himself surprised and even a trifle disappointed. He feels that he has met all that before. The feeling reflects Coleridge's strength, however, and not his weakness, for our generation has been brought up on Coleridge's Shakespeare, often without knowing it. His famous comments on the opening scene of Hamlet, analyzing in detail the effect upon dramatic illusion of each phrase and each attitude, have insensibly become our standard view of the play's opening. Hamlet to us is Coleridge's Hamlet, and only in a small degree is the latter being displaced by the Oedipus Hamlet or other post-Coleridge inventions.

Coleridge's greatest single work in prose is of course the *Biographia Literaria*, a quite unclassifiable combination of autobiography, philosophy, aesthetics, and literary criticism. Though there is much else that is of interest, its most notable feature is the elaborate critique, begun in the early chapters and resumed later, of

Wordsworth's poetic practice and theory. We have no other instance of a major poet-critic's exerting his full powers upon a considered analysis of the work of a great contemporary—a contemporary, too, with whose poetic and intellectual development his own has been intimately woven. Such an analysis could not fail to be of the greatest interest. Although the *Biographia Literaria* was written at a time when the tie had been weakened, the subject naturally drew Coleridge back to the earlier years. In criticizing the poetry and poetic theory of Wordsworth, he found himself debating with the worthiest and most significant (at least for him) antagonist he could possibly have had. His earlier interests and powers were reawakened and stimulated, and he found himself capable of a sustained constructive effort of writing such as he had not achieved before.

From a critical standpoint, possibly the most significant section of the work is its discussion of the language and meter of poetry. In the Preface to the *Lyrical Ballads* and elsewhere, Wordsworth had made illuminating statements about the creative processes of the poet. His attempt to give a philosophical explanation for the function of meter in poetry, however, was not satisfactory; he seemed to have gone little beyond the conception of meter as something "superadded" to poetry and not part of its essence. This position Coleridge attacked. He looked upon meter, as upon the other formal elements in the arts, from the standpoint of his fundamental insistence on "organic" form. Never tired of opposing the concept of organic to that of "mechanic" form, he illustrated the difference more than once by reference to the morphological development of the living plant from the apparently simple seed to its mature form with differentiated but organically unified parts, or to the organic "unity and diversity" of the human body. Although this conception of form and these illustrations of it did not originate with Coleridge, he was chiefly responsible for bringing them into the common currents of critical thought.

It is Coleridge's distinction to have been the only significant figure in English literature to unite the three or four professions of poet, critic, metaphysician, and theologian. Matthew Arnold and Mr. T. S. Eliot approach most nearly to his scope, but neither appears to have had Coleridge's speculative bent. They have written on social philosophy and religion. Coleridge wrote on these matters too, but did not stop there. Some admirers, no doubt, wish he had. Following his own suggestion in the *Dejection* ode, they have thought that his poetic inspiration drowned in the ocean of his speculative thought. We cannot here enter into a consideration of his philosophical writings; after all, he is not a major figure in the history of the world's philosophical thought. His influence, however, was materially felt by English thinkers throughout the nineteenth century.

However one estimates him as a writer—and I have already suggested how various these estimates can be—we must conclude that as a figure in literary history Coleridge, like Dr. Johnson, is greater than the sum of his parts. The fascination that he exerts derives perhaps mainly from the great complexity of the man, but it owes almost as much to his failures as to his successes. He lived, as Mr. Raysor has expressed it, "with an intermittent, discontinuous access to his own genius," and this fact arouses our curiosity about the constitution of genius. In Coleridge's own day almost all who knew him felt that his powers were practically unlimited, and yet all were in the end disappointed—the great man himself possibly not least. He "spawned plans like a herring," as Southey once told him. But the plans were only the beginning of a perpetually recurring cycle of procrastination, remorse, despair, and more plans. Now and then the turning wheel threw off something, an achievement often unrelated to any of the plans, but still a distinguished achievement. Coleridge himself was vividly aware of his weakness, and one of the more endearing features of his character was his quite humble and open admission of this failure of will. His preoccupation with the sense of guilt, notable even in his earliest writing, no doubt springs from this weakness. He attributed the inability to fulfill his hopes sometimes to one cause, sometimes to another. In *Dejection* it was his unhappy personal life that had deprived him of the inner joy essential to the creative spirit. At other times he thought it was ill-health, or opium, or a fatal "indolence" of character (a notebook records his idea for "A Poem on the endeavor to emancipate the mind from day-dreams"), or an entanglement among all these things that damped his powers.

It was probably something much deeper than any of them. Indolence itself is rather a symptom than a disease. Coleridge had the egotism that may, I think, be essential to men of genius—"poetry without egotism," he once noted, is "comparatively uninteresting"—but he seems to have lacked the fundamental belief in himself necessary to go with it. He made claims for himself and upon himself that could hardly be fulfilled by any human being. The man whose essay on poetry was to supersede all former works on morals and metaphysics had better not risk finishing it. To complete a work is to bring it to the test of one's own expectation; and Coleridge's standard was beyond almost any human range. Who could ever have completed—who could have perfected, that is—his treatise on the *logos?* The great projected Hymns to the Sun and Moon, had they satisfied Coleridge's intention for them, would very nearly have superseded the sun and moon of heaven. Coleridge asked of himself and claimed for himself almost superhuman powers, but—lacking the sublime blind confidence that occasionally drives human genius to the accomplishment of the impossible—the very extremity of his demand upon himself undermined his will. Hence the indolence and the opium, the nightmares of guilt and remorse. This is the Coleridge (though not thus explained) summed up by Sir Edmund Chambers at the close of his biography: "So Coleridge passed, leaving a handful of golden poems, an emptiness in the heart of a few friends, and a will-o'-the-wisp light for bemused thinkers."

To these bemused thinkers, however, and undoubtedly to some who are not entirely bemused, Coleridge was one of "the great seminal minds of the age." Hazlitt thought him the greatest man he had ever known, "the only one from whom I ever learnt anything." Yet he asked, "What is become of all this mighty heap of hope, of thought, of learning, and humanity?" Well, Coleridge was one of the most omnivorous readers in English literary history, and he read with an ever-restless and creative mind. He could not read without commenting, and if a listener were not at hand the margin of his book was, or one of his fabulous notebooks. At his death he left a tremendous mass of unpublished material, disorganized as only he could have left it, but containing much that should be known, and of bulk enough to furnish many volumes. As selections from this mass of writing have been made public from time to time during the past century, our view of Coleridge's indolence has altered somewhat. If it paralyzed his power to organize and finish, it evidently affected little the initial stages of his labor. William Butler Yeats had a theory that a poet must write out of his "antithetical self," that he is driven to complete in his writing what he lacks in his personal self. If this theory may be stretched a little to include criticism, we have it thoroughly illustrated in the phenomenon of Coleridge the formless preaching to the world organic form, and eloquently, too.

These posthumous volumes enable us to see something of what Coleridge's friends meant when they spoke of his unfulfilled promise—those brilliant gleams of comment, often so subtle as to be hardly rememberable afterward, that flashed from his talk. They could illuminate almost any subject—politics, economics, philosophy, natural beauty. Some of the fragmentary prose comments are unwritten and never-to-be written poems. Most of the best comments are either literary or psychological. In fact, it is his insight into human experience that gives Coleridge's criticism its greatest value. His observations sometimes read like anticipations of Freud. There were limitations to his understanding, it is true, rooted not in his intellect but in his character. Certain depths in himself, the profoundest depths of his own motives, he rarely faced and I think never explored; and these depths were for the most part sealed to him in others as well. It is noticeable even in his Shakespearean criticism that the finest passages rarely throw light on the foundations of individual character and motive. But Coleridge is supreme in his observation of "states of mind." He was capable of maintaining that split state in which one can be experiencer and observer simultaneously. In *Anima Poetae* there is the brief comment on "that perilous moment of a half reconciliation, when the coldness and the resentment have been sustained too long. Each is drawing toward the other, but like glass in the mid-state between fusion and compaction a single sand will splinter it." The subtlety of observation is there, and the poet's precision of image as well, an image drawn unexpectedly from the unpoetical region of chemistry or industry.

"One excellent use of communication of sorrow to a friend is this," he says, again in *Anima Poetae,* "that in relating what ails us, we ourselves first know exactly what the real grief is, and see it for itself in its own form and limits." The semanticists would like this. "Unspoken grief," he continues, "is a misty medley of which the real affliction only plays the first fiddle, blows the horn to a scattered mob of obscure feelings. Perhaps, at certain moments, a single, almost insignificant sorrow may, by association, bring together all the little relics of pain and discomfort, bodily and mental, that we have endured even from infancy." The thoughtless reader will stroll past this without knowing he has read anything. But let him sit down before it for a few moments and he will find that he knows something he did not know before, or that he now knows what he has only felt before. This is the Coleridge of the unbemused.

ELISABETH SCHNEIDER

*Philadelphia*
*April, 1951*

# CHRONOLOGY

1772   Samuel Taylor Coleridge was born October 21 in Ottery St. Mary, Devonshire, youngest of the large family of John Coleridge (Vicar of Ottery and master of the Grammar School) and his second wife, Anne Bowden.

1782   After his father's death in 1781, Coleridge entered Christ's Hospital in London.

1791   He was appointed to an Exhibition at Jesus College, Cambridge.

1793   He enlisted in the Fifteenth Light Dragoons in December.

1794   Rescued by family and friends, he returned to Cambridge in April. In June he left Cambridge for a walking tour

in Wales, met Robert Southey at Oxford, and formed the
scheme of "Pantisocracy," to be developed by emigrating
to America. At Bristol he met and later (though still attached to an earlier love, Mary Evans) became engaged
to Sarah Fricker. *The Fall of Robespierre,* a drama written
in collaboration with Southey, was published in September, and his first contributions of poetry appeared in the
*Morning Chronicle.* He left Cambridge for good in December.

1795   His political lectures, delivered at Bristol, were published
as *Conciones ad Populum. Or Addresses to the People.* He
met Wordsworth for the first time, and on October 4 was
married to Sarah Fricker.

1796   He published the short-lived periodical *The Watchman*
and *Poems on Various Subjects.* On September 19 his first
child, David Hartley, was born. In December the family
settled at Nether Stowey, near Thomas Poole.

1797   Intimacy developed between Coleridge and the Wordsworths, who settled for a time at Alfoxden to be near him.
In June appeared *Poems, by S. T. Coleridge, Second Edition.* He began *The Ancient Mariner,* completed his tragedy *Osorio,* and began to contribute to the *Morning Post.*

1798   While preaching at Shrewsbury, Coleridge made the acquaintance of Hazlitt. The Wedgwood brothers bestowed
on him an annuity of 150 pounds. A second son, Berkeley,
was born in May but died within a few months. About
September 1 the *Lyrical Ballads* was published, and on
September 16 Coleridge sailed, with William and Dorothy
Wordsworth, for Germany.

1799   He returned to England in July. In the autumn he visited
the Lake country for the first time, toured the district on
foot with Wordsworth, and met Sarah Hutchinson. He
returned to London to resume newspaper writing for the
*Morning Post* under Daniel Stuart. Here he revived his
early friendship with Charles Lamb and saw much of
Godwin.

1800   Coleridge settled with his family at Greta Hall, Keswick, in July. A third son, Derwent, was born in September. Intimacy with the Wordsworths was resumed through frequent visits to them at Grasmere.

1804-
1805 After several years of suffering from complications of ill health, opium, friction with his wife, and an attachment to Sarah Hutchinson, Coleridge journeyed to Malta in search of health, returning by way of Italy in 1806.

1808 He delivered his first lectures on poetry at the Royal Institution, then went north and settled with the Wordsworths at Allan Bank, which became his headquarters, for the most part, until spring, 1810.

1809-
1810 He published *The Friend,* a periodical.

1810 He went to London, where a quarrel with Basil Montagu resulted in estrangement from Wordsworth.

1810-
1815 Living for the most part in London with the Morgans, Coleridge wrote for the *Courier,* lectured in London and Bristol, and revised *Osorio,* which was produced at Drury Lane in 1813 as *Remorse.* Half of the Wedgwood annuity was withdrawn in 1812. In that year also there was a partial reconciliation with Wordsworth.

1816 In April Coleridge settled at Highgate with James Gillman and his wife, in the hope of controlling his use of opium. Though the arrangement began as a temporary one, it continued until Coleridge's death. During this year he published *Christabel* and *The Statesman's Manual; or The Bible the Best Guide to Political Skill and Foresight.*

1817 He published the second *Lay Sermon,* the *Biographia Literaria, Sibylline Leaves,* and *Zapolya.*

1818-
1825 Coleridge was engaged with lectures on literature and philosophy and the preparation of *Aids to Reflection* (1825). A revised edition of *The Friend* appeared in 1818.

1828 Three volumes of *Poetical Works* were collected and published. During the summer Coleridge traveled on the Continent with Wordsworth.

1830 *Constitution of Church and State* appeared.

1834 Coleridge died on July 25.

# TEXTUAL AND BIBLIOGRAPHICAL NOTE

As there is no definitive collected edition of Coleridge's works, the following texts have been followed here: for the poetry, the standard edition of E. H. Coleridge (*Complete Poetical Works*, 2 vols., London: Oxford University Press, 1912); for the *Biographia Literaria*, the edition of 1817, the only one published during Coleridge's lifetime; for the essay "On the Principles of Genial Criticism," the text printed by Mr. Shawcross from *Felix Farley's Bristol Journal* (*Biographia Literaria*, 2 vols., London: Oxford University Press, 1907); for the selections from *Table-Talk*, H. N. Coleridge's edition of 1835; for the *Anima Poetae*, the only text, E. H. Coleridge's (1895); for the lectures and notes on poetry and drama, T. M. Raysor's edition of the *Shakespearean Criticism* (Cambridge, Mass.: Harvard University Press, 1930); for the "Letter on Sir Thomas Browne," "Selden's Table-Talk," and the notes on Fielding, Raysor's edition of Coleridge's *Miscellaneous Criticism* (Cambridge, Mass.: Harvard University Press, 1936, originally published in *Literary Remains*, 1836). The "Allegoric Vision" is reprinted from *Miscellanies Aesthetic and Literary* (ed. T. Ashe, 1885). The Introductory Lecture from *Conciones ad Populum* follows the text of Sara Coleridge (*Essays on His Own Times*, 3 vols., 1850). Of the selections from the letters, eight are printed from *Letters of Samuel Taylor Coleridge* (ed. E. H. Coleridge, 1895), two from *Unpublished Letters of Samuel Taylor Coleridge* (ed. E. L. Griggs, New Haven: Yale University Press, 1933), and one from *Letters, Conversations and Recollections of S. T. Coleridge* (ed. T. Allsop, 3d ed., 1864).[1]

---

[1] I have taken no liberties with the texts used except for silent correction of a few obvious misprints. In the selections from the *Biographia Literaria* and in certain other instances I have printed Coleridge's footnotes. In his notes to poems, however, Coleridge changed his mind so often—adding, altering, or deleting in each new edition—that I have thought best to print them only when they are especially significant.

Other editions may be useful to the student: the *Complete Works* (7 vols., ed. W. G. T. Shedd, 1853, 1884), which is far from complete, despite the title, as is that of T. Ashe (8 vols., Bohn's Standard Library, 1858 and later reprints); E. H. Coleridge's one-volume edition of the *Poems* (London: Oxford University Press, 1912, reprinted frequently), which contains most of the material of the complete edition; Kathleen Coburn's edition of the *Philosophical Lectures* [1818-1819], (New York: Philosophical Library, 1949) and her *Inquiring Spirit* (London: Routledge and Kegan Paul, 1951); and the *Collected Letters, 1785-1806* (ed. E. L. Griggs, London: Oxford University Press, 1955).

There are three main biographical studies of Coleridge: J. Dykes Campbell's (*Samuel Taylor Coleridge: A Narrative of Events in His Life*), E. K. Chambers' (*Samuel Taylor Coleridge*, London: Oxford University Press, 1938), and Lawrence Hanson's *Life of Samuel Taylor Coleridge: The Early Years* (London: Oxford University Press, 1939). The most important critical work on Coleridge's poetry is still John Livingston Lowes's *The Road to Xanadu: A Study in the Ways of the Imagination* (Boston: Houghton Mifflin Company, 1927). Arthur H. Nethercot's *The Road to Tryermaine* (Chicago: University of Chicago Press, 1939), Robert Penn Warren's "A Poem of Pure Imagination: An Experiment in Reading" (in *The Rime of the Ancient Mariner*, New York: Reynal and Hitchcock, 1946), and my *Coleridge, Opium, and "Kubla Khan"* (Chicago: University of Chicago Press, 1953) are more recent studies. The notable studies of his ideas and his prose include J. Shawcross's critical introduction to his edition of the *Biographia Literaria*, T. M. Raysor's introduction to the *Shakespearean Criticism*, J. H. Muirhead's *Coleridge as Philosopher* (New York: The Macmillan Company, 1930), and I. A. Richards's *Coleridge on Imagination* (London: Routledge & Kegan Paul, 1934).

# ACKNOWLEDGMENT

I wish to acknowledge here my debts to Professor Thomas M.
Raysor and Miss Kathleen Coburn for their kindness in making
very helpful suggestions for this book, and to my mother, Mary R.
Schneider, for her kindness and patience in reading the proofs.
I am also greatly indebted, as anyone who works with Cole-
ridge must be, to previous editors, most especially the late E. H.
Coleridge.

I am also indebted to the following publishers for permission
to reproduce various parts of the book: the Harvard University
Press and the President and Fellows of Harvard College for
selections from T. M. Raysor, *Shakespearean Criticism*, 1930, and
*Miscellaneous Criticism*, 1936; Oxford University Press for selected
poetry from E. H. Coleridge, *Complete Poetical Works*, 1912, 2
vols., and the essay "On the Principles of Genial Criticism," from
*Felix Farley's Bristol Journal (Biographia Literaria*, 1907, 2 vols.);
Yale University Press for certain letters from E. L. Griggs's edition
of *Unpublished Letters of Samuel Taylor Coleridge*, 1933; and
the Houghton Mifflin Company for various material from *Letters
of Samuel Taylor Coleridge*, edited by E. H. Coleridge, 1895.

# CONTENTS

# POETRY

# SONNET

TO THE AUTUMNAL MOON

Mild Splendour of the various-vested Night!
    Mother of wildly-working visions! hail!
I watch thy gliding, while with watery light
    Thy weak eye glimmers through a fleecy veil;
And when thou lovest thy pale orb to shroud
    Behind the gather'd blackness lost on high;
And when thou dartest from the wind-rent cloud
    Thy placid lightning o'er the awaken'd sky.

Ah such is Hope! as changeful and as fair!
    Now dimly peering on the wistful sight;
Now hid behind the dragon-wing'd Despair:
    But soon emerging in her radiant might
She o'er the sorrow-clouded breast of Care
    Sails, like a meteor kindling in its flight.

1788.*                                              1796.

---

* The first date, here and elsewhere, is the known or supposed date of
composition; the second is that of the first publication. In general, but not
quite without exception, I have followed E. H. Coleridge's dates.

3

# THE COMPLAINT OF NINATHÓMA

[IMITATED FROM OSSIAN]

How long will ye round me be swelling,
    O ye blue-tumbling waves of the sea?
Not always in caves was my dwelling,
    Nor beneath the cold blast of the tree.
Through the high-sounding halls of Cathlóma
    In the steps of my beauty I strayed;
The warriors beheld Ninathóma,
    And they blesséd the white-bosom'd Maid!

A Ghost! by my cavern it darted!
    In moon-beams the Spirit was drest—
For lovely appear the Departed
    When they visit the dreams of my rest!
But disturb'd by the tempest's commotion
    Fleet the shadowy forms of delight—
Ah cease, thou shrill blast of the Ocean!
    To howl through my cavern by night.
1793.                                    1796.

# SONGS OF THE PIXIES

The Pixies, in the superstition of Devonshire, are a race of beings invisibly small, and harmless or friendly to man. At a small distance from a village in that county, half-way up a wood-covered hill, is an excavation called the Pixies' Parlour. The roots of old trees form its ceiling; and on its sides are innumerable cyphers, among which the author discovered his own cypher and those of his brothers, cut by the hand of their childhood. At the foot of the hill flows the river Otter.

To this place the Author, during the summer months of the year 1793, conducted a party of young ladies; one of whom, of stature elegantly small, and of complexion colourless yet clear, was proclaimed the Faery Queen. On which occasion the following Irregular Ode was written.

I

Whom the untaught Shepherds call
   Pixies in their madrigal,
Fancy's children, here we dwell:
   Welcome, Ladies! to our cell.
Here the wren of softest note
   Builds its nest and warbles well;
Here the blackbird strains his throat;
   Welcome, Ladies! to our cell.

II

When fades the moon to shadowy-pale,
And scuds the cloud before the gale,        10
Ere the Morn all gem-bedight
Hath streak'd the East with rosy light,
We sip the furze-flower's fragrant dews
Clad in robes of rainbow hues;
Or sport amid the shooting gleams
To the tune of distant-tinkling teams,
While lusty Labour scouting sorrow
Bids the Dame a glad good-morrow,
Who jogs the accustom'd road along,
And paces cheery to her cheering song.     20

III

   But not our filmy pinion
  We scorch amid the blaze of day,
When Noontide's fiery-tresséd minion
    Flashes the fervid ray.
   Aye from the sultry heat
   We to the cave retreat
O'ercanopied by huge roots intertwin'd
With wildest texture, blacken'd o'er with age:
Round them their mantle green the ivies bind,

    Beneath whose foliage pale 30
    Fann'd by the unfrequent gale
We shield us from the Tyrant's mid-day rage.


IV

    Thither, while the murmuring throng
    Of wild-bees hum their drowsy song,
    By Indolence and Fancy brought,
    A youthful Bard, "unknown to Fame,"
    Wooes the Queen of Solemn Thought,
And heaves the gentle misery of a sigh
      Gazing with tearful eye,
    As round our sandy grot appear 40
    Many a rudely-sculptur'd name
      To pensive Memory dear!
Weaving gay dreams of sunny-tinctur'd hue,
    We glance before his view:
O'er his hush'd soul our soothing witcheries shed
And twine the future garland round his head.


V

    When Evening's dusky car
    Crown'd with her dewy star
Steals o'er the fading sky in shadowy flight;
    On leaves of aspen trees 50
    We tremble to the breeze
Veil'd from the grosser ken of mortal sight.
    Or, haply, at the visionary hour,
Along our wildly-bower'd sequester'd walk,
We listen to the enamour'd rustic's talk;
Heave with the heavings of the maiden's breast,
Where young-eyed Loves have hid their turtle nest;
    Or guide of soul-subduing power
The glance that from the half-confessing eye
Darts the fond question or the soft reply. 60

VI

Or through the mystic ringlets of the vale
We flash our faery feet in gamesome prank;
Or, silent-sandal'd, pay our defter court,
Circling the Spirit of the Western Gale,
Where wearied with his flower-caressing sport,
Supine he slumbers on a violet bank;
Then with quaint music hymn the parting gleam
By lonely Otter's sleep-persuading stream;
Or where his wave with loud unquiet song
Dash'd o'er the rocky channel froths along;                    70
Or where, his silver waters smooth'd to rest,
The tall tree's shadow sleeps upon his breast.

VII

Hence thou lingerer, Light!
Eve saddens into Night.
Mother of wildly-working dreams! we view
The sombre hours, that round thee stand
With down-cast eyes (a duteous band!)
Their dark robes dripping with the heavy dew.
Sorceress of the ebon throne!
Thy power the Pixies own,                    80
When round thy raven brow
Heaven's lucent roses glow,
And clouds in watery colours drest
Float in light drapery o'er thy sable vest:
What time the pale moon sheds a softer day
Mellowing the woods beneath its pensive beam:
For mid the quivering light 'tis ours to play,
Aye dancing to the cadence of the stream.

VIII

Welcome, Ladies! to the cell
Where the blameless Pixies dwell:                    90
But thou, Sweet Nymph! proclaim'd our Faery Queen,

With what obeisance meet
Thy presence shall we greet?
For lo! attendant on thy steps are seen
Graceful Ease in artless stole,
And white-robed Purity of soul,
With Honour's softer mien;
Mirth of the loosely-flowing hair,
And meek-eyed Pity eloquently fair,
Whose tearful cheeks are lovely to the view,          100
As snow-drop wet with dew.

IX

Unboastful Maid! though now the Lily pale
Transparent grace thy beauties meek;
Yet ere again along the impurpling vale,
The purpling vale and elfin-haunted grove,
Young Zephyr his fresh flowers profusely throws,
We'll tinge with livelier hues thy cheek;
And, haply, from the nectar-breathing Rose
Extract a Blush for Love!
1793.                                          1796.

## SONNET

### TO THE RIVER OTTER

Dear native Brook! wild Streamlet of the West!
How many various-fated years have past,
What happy and what mournful hours, since last
I skimm'd the smooth thin stone along thy breast,
Numbering its light leaps! yet so deep imprest
Sink the sweet scenes of childhood, that mine eyes
I never shut amid the sunny ray,
But straight with all their tints thy waters rise,
Thy crossing plank, thy marge with willows grey,
And bedded sand that vein'd with various dyes

Gleam'd through thy bright transparence! On my way,
   Visions of Childhood! oft have ye beguil'd
Lone manhood's cares, yet waking fondest sighs:
   Ah! that once more I were a careless Child!
? 1793.                                   1796.


# IMITATIONS

## AD LYRAM

(CASIMIR, BOOK II. ODE 3)

The solemn-breathing air is ended—
   Cease, O Lyre! thy kindred lay!
From the poplar-branch suspended
   Glitter to the eye of Day!

On thy wires hov'ring, dying,
   Softly sighs the summer wind:
I will slumber, careless lying,
   By yon waterfall reclin'd.

In the forest hollow-roaring
   Hark! I hear a deep'ning sound—
Clouds rise thick with heavy low'ring!
   See! th' horizon blackens round!

Parent of the soothing measure,
   Let me seize thy wetted string!
Swiftly flies the flatterer, Pleasure,
   Headlong, ever on the wing.
1794.                                   1796.

## PANTISOCRACY

No more my visionary soul shall dwell
On joys that were; no more endure to weigh
The shame and anguish of the evil day,
Wisely forgetful! O'er the ocean swell
Sublime of Hope, I seek the cottag'd dell
Where Virtue calm with careless step may stray,
And dancing to the moonlight roundelay,
The wizard Passions weave an holy spell.
Eyes that have ach'd with Sorrow! Ye shall weep
Tears of doubt-mingled joy, like theirs who start
From Precipices of distemper'd sleep,
On which the fierce-eyed Fiends their revels keep,
And see the rising Sun, and feel it dart
New rays of pleasance trembling to the heart.
1794.                                          1849.

## TO THE AUTHOR OF "THE ROBBERS"

Schiller! that hour I would have wish'd to die,
If thro' the shuddering midnight I had sent
From the dark dungeon of the Tower time-rent
That fearful voice, a famish'd Father's cry—
Lest in some after moment aught more mean
Might stamp me mortal! A triumphant shout
Black Horror scream'd, and all her *goblin* rout
Diminish'd shrunk from the more withering scene!
Ah! Bard tremendous in sublimity!
Could I behold thee in thy loftier mood
Wandering at eve with finely-frenzied eye
Beneath some vast old tempest-swinging wood!

Awhile with mute awe gazing I would brood:
Then weep aloud in a wild ecstasy!
? 1794.                                                      1796.

## TO A YOUNG ASS

### ITS MOTHER BEING TETHERED NEAR IT

Poor little Foal of an oppresséd race!
I love the languid patience of thy face:
And oft with gentle hand I give thee bread,
And clap thy ragged coat, and pat thy head.
But what thy dulled spirits hath dismay'd,
That never thou dost sport along the glade?
And (most unlike the nature of things young)
That earthward still thy moveless head is hung?
Do thy prophetic fears anticipate,
Meek Child of Misery! thy future fate?                     10
The starving meal, and all the thousand aches
"Which patient Merit of the Unworthy takes"?
Or is thy sad heart thrill'd with filial pain
To see thy wretched mother's shorten'd chain?
And truly, very piteous is *her* lot—
Chain'd to a log within a narrow spot,
Where the close-eaten grass is scarcely seen,
While sweet around her waves the tempting green!

Poor Ass! thy master should have learnt to show
Pity—best taught by fellowship of Woe!                     20
For much I fear me that *He* lives like thee,
Half famish'd in a land of Luxury!
How *askingly* its footsteps hither bend!
It seems to say, "And have I then *one* friend?"
Innocent foal! thou poor despis'd forlorn!
I hail thee *Brother*—spite of the fool's scorn!
And fain would take thee with me, in the Dell

Of Peace and mild Equality to dwell,
Where Toil shall call the charmer Health his bride,
And Laughter tickle Plenty's ribless side!                    30
How thou wouldst toss thy heels in gamesome play,
And frisk about, as lamb or kitten gay!
Yea! and more musically sweet to me
Thy dissonant harsh bray of joy would be,
Than warbled melodies that soothe to rest
The aching of pale Fashion's vacant breast!
1794.                                             1794.


# SONNETS ON EMINENT CHARACTERS

### IV

#### LA FAYETTE

As when far off the warbled strains are heard
    That soar on Morning's wing the vales among;
    Within his cage the imprison'd Matin Bird
Swells the full chorus with a generous song:

He bathes no pinion in the dewy light,
    No Father's joy, no Lover's bliss he shares,
    Yet still the rising radiance cheers his sight—
His fellows' Freedom soothes the Captive's cares!

Thou, FAYETTE! who didst wake with startling voice
    Life's better Sun from that long wintry night,
    Thus in thy Country's triumphs shalt rejoice
And mock with raptures high the Dungeon's might:

For lo! the Morning struggles into Day,
And Slavery's spectres shriek and vanish from the ray!
1794.                                             1794.

## V

### KOSKIUSKO

O what a loud and fearful shriek was there,
　　As though a thousand souls one death-groan pour'd!
　　Ah me! they saw beneath a Hireling's sword
Their Koskiusko fall! Through the swart air
(As pauses the tir'd Cossac's barbarous yell
　　Of Triumph) on the chill and midnight gale
　　Rises with frantic burst or sadder swell
The dirge of murder'd Hope! while Freedom pale
Bends in such anguish o'er her destin'd bier,
　　As if from eldest time some Spirit meek
　　Had gather'd in a mystic urn each tear
That ever on a Patriot's furrow'd cheek

Fit channel found; and she had drain'd the bowl
In the mere wilfulness, and sick despair of soul!
1794.　　　　　　　　　　　　　　　　　　　1794.

## VII

### TO THE REV. W. L. BOWLES

[SECOND VERSION]

My heart has thank'd thee, Bowles! for those soft strains
　　Whose sadness soothes me, like the murmuring
　　Of wild-bees in the sunny showers of spring!
For hence not callous to the mourner's pains

Through Youth's gay prime and thornless paths I went:
　　And when the mightier Throes of mind began,
　　And drove me forth, a thought-bewilder'd man,
Their mild and manliest melancholy lent

A mingled charm, such as the pang consign'd
　　To slumber, though the big tear it renew'd;
　　Bidding a strange mysterious Pleasure brood
Over the wavy and tumultuous mind,

As the great SPIRIT erst with plastic sweep
Mov'd on the darkness of the unform'd deep.
? 1794.                                          1796.


# THE EOLIAN HARP

### COMPOSED AT CLEVEDON, SOMERSETSHIRE

My pensive Sara! thy soft cheek reclined
Thus on mine arm, most soothing sweet it is
To sit beside our Cot, our Cot o'ergrown
With white-flower'd Jasmin, and the broad-leav'd Myrtle,
(Meet emblems they of Innocence and Love!)
And watch the clouds, that late were rich with light,
Slow saddening round, and mark the star of eve
Serenely brilliant (such should Wisdom be)
Shine opposite! How exquisite the scents
Snatch'd from yon bean-field! and the world *so* hush'd!          10
The stilly murmur of the distant Sea
Tells us of silence.
                         And that simplest Lute,
Placed length-ways in the clasping casement, hark!
How by the desultory breeze caress'd,
Like some coy maid half yielding to her lover,
It pours such sweet upbraiding, as must needs
Tempt to repeat the wrong! And now, its strings
Boldlier swept, the long sequacious notes
Over delicious surges sink and rise,
Such a soft floating witchery of sound                              20
As twilight Elfins make, when they at eve
Voyage on gentle gales from Fairy-Land,
Where Melodies round honey-dropping flowers,
Footless and wild, like birds of Paradise,
Nor pause, nor perch, hovering on untam'd wing!
O! the one Life within us and abroad,

Which meets all motion and becomes its soul,
A light in sound, a sound-like power in light,
Rhythm in all thought, and joyance every where—
Methinks, it should have been impossible          30
Not to love all things in a world so fill'd;
Where the breeze warbles, and the mute still air
Is Music slumbering on her instrument.

   And thus, my Love! as on the midway slope
Of yonder hill I stretch my limbs at noon,
Whilst through my half-clos'd eye-lids I behold
The sunbeams dance, like diamonds, on the main,
And tranquil muse upon tranquillity;
Full many a thought uncall'd and undetain'd,
And many idle flitting phantasies,          40
Traverse my indolent and passive brain,
As wild and various as the random gales
That swell and flutter on this subject Lute!
   And what if all of animated nature
Be but organic Harps diversely fram'd,
That tremble into thought, as o'er them sweeps
Plastic and vast, one intellectual breeze,
At once the Soul of each, and God of all?
   But thy more serious eye a mild reproof
Darts, O belovéd Woman! nor such thoughts          50
Dim and unhallow'd dost thou not reject,
And biddest me walk humbly with my God.
Meek Daughter in the family of Christ!
Well hast thou said and holily disprais'd
These shapings of the unregenerate mind;
Bubbles that glitter as they rise and break
On vain Philosophy's aye-babbling spring.
For never guiltless may I speak of him,
The Incomprehensible! save when with awe
I praise him, and with Faith that inly *feels*;          60
Who with his saving mercies healéd me,
A sinful and most miserable man,

Wilder'd and dark, and gave me to possess
Peace, and this Cot, and thee, heart-honour'd Maid!
1795.                                          1796.


# REFLECTIONS ON HAVING LEFT

## A PLACE OF RETIREMENT

Sermoni propriora.—Hor.

Low was our pretty Cot: our tallest Rose
Peep'd at the chamber-window. We could hear
At silent noon, and eve, and early morn,
The Sea's faint murmur. In the open air
Our Myrtles blossom'd; and across the porch
Thick Jasmins twined: the little landscape round
Was green and woody, and refresh'd the eye.
It was a spot which you might aptly call
The Valley of Seclusion! Once I saw
(Hallowing his Sabbath-day by quietness)                    10
A wealthy son of Commerce saunter by,
Bristowa's citizen: methought, it calm'd
His thirst of idle gold, and made him muse
With wiser feelings: for he paus'd, and look'd
With a pleas'd sadness, and gaz'd all around,
Then eyed our Cottage, and gaz'd round again,
And sigh'd, and said, it was a Blesséd Place.
And we *were* bless'd. Oft with patient ear
Long-listening to the viewless sky-lark's note
(Viewless, or haply for a moment seen                        20
Gleaming on sunny wings) in whisper'd tones
I've said to my Belovéd, "Such, sweet Girl!
The inobtrusive song of Happiness,
Unearthly minstrelsy! then only heard
When the Soul seeks to hear; when all is hush'd,
And the Heart listens!"

But the time, when first
From that low Dell, steep up the stony Mount
I climb'd with perilous toil and reach'd the top,
Oh! what a goodly scene! *Here* the bleak mount,
The bare bleak mountain speckled thin with sheep;    30
Grey clouds, that shadowing spot the sunny fields;
And river, now with bushy rocks o'er-brow'd,
Now winding bright and full, with naked banks;
And seats, and lawns, the Abbey and the wood,
And cots, and hamlets, and faint city-spire;
The Channel *there,* the Islands and white sails,
Dim coasts, and cloud-like hills, and shoreless Ocean—
It seem'd like Omnipresence! God, methought,
Had built him there a Temple: the whole World
Seem'd *imag'd* in its vast circumference:    40
No *wish* profan'd my overwhelméd heart.
Blest hour! It was a luxury,—to be!

Ah! quiet Dell! dear Cot, and Mount sublime!
I was constrain'd to quit you. Was it right,
While my unnumber'd brethren toil'd and bled,
That I should dream away the entrusted hours
On rose-leaf beds, pampering the coward heart
With feelings all too delicate for use?
Sweet is the tear that from some Howard's eye
Drops on the cheek of one he lifts from earth:    50
And he that works me good with unmov'd face,
Does it but half: he chills me while he aids,
My benefactor, not my brother man!
Yet even this, this cold beneficence
Praise, praise it, O my Soul! oft as thou scann'st
The sluggard Pity's vision-weaving tribe!
Who sigh for Wretchedness, yet shun the Wretched,
Nursing in some delicious solitude
Their slothful loves and dainty sympathies!
I therefore go, and join head, heart, and hand,    60
Active and firm, to fight the bloodless fight
Of Science, Freedom, and the Truth in Christ.

Yet oft when after honourable toil
Rests the tir'd mind, and waking loves to dream,
My spirit shall revisit thee, dear Cot!
Thy Jasmin and thy window-peeping Rose,
And Myrtles fearless of the mild sea-air.
And I shall sigh fond wishes—sweet Abode!
Ah!—had none greater! And that all had such!
It might be so—but the time is not yet.                    70
Speed it, O Father! Let thy Kingdom come!
1795.                                              1796.

# RELIGIOUS MUSINGS

A DESULTORY POEM, WRITTEN ON THE CHRISTMAS EVE OF 1794

This is the time, when most divine to hear,
The voice of Adoration rouses me,
As with a Cherub's trump: and high upborne,
Yea, mingling with the Choir, I seem to view
The vision of the heavenly multitude,
Who hymned the song of Peace o'er Bethlehem's fields!
Yet thou more bright than all the Angel-blaze,
That harbingered thy birth, Thou Man of Woes!
Despiséd Galilaean! For the Great
Invisible (by symbols only seen)          10
With a peculiar and surpassing light
Shines from the visage of the oppressed good man,
When heedless of himself the scourgéd saint
Mourns for the oppressor. Fair the vernal mead,
Fair the high grove, the sea, the sun, the stars;
True impress each of their creating Sire!
Yet nor high grove, nor many-colour'd mead,
Nor the green ocean with his thousand isles,
Nor the starred azure, nor the sovran sun,
E'er with such majesty of portraiture          20
Imaged the supreme beauty uncreate,
As thou, meek Saviour! at the fearful hour
When thy insulted anguish winged the prayer
Harped by Archangels, when they sing of mercy!
Which when the Almighty heard from forth his throne
Diviner light filled Heaven with ecstasy!
Heaven's hymnings paused: and Hell her yawning mouth
Closed a brief moment.

          Lovely was the death
Of Him whose life was Love! Holy with power
He on the thought-benighted Sceptic beamed          30

Manifest Godhead, melting into day
What floating mists of dark idolatry
Broke and misshaped the omnipresent Sire:
And first by Fear uncharmed the drowséd Soul.
Till of its nobler nature it 'gan feel
Dim recollections; and thence soared to Hope,
Strong to believe whate'er of mystic good
The Eternal dooms for His immortal sons.
From Hope and firmer Faith to perfect Love
Attracted and absorbed: and centered there                    40
God only to behold, and know, and feel,
Till by exclusive consciousness of God
All self-annihilated it shall make
God its Identity: God all in all!
We and our Father one!

           And blest are they,
Who in this fleshly World, the elect of Heaven,
Their strong eye darting through the deeds of men,
Adore with steadfast unpresuming gaze
Him Nature's essence, mind, and energy!
And gazing, trembling, patiently ascend                       50
Treading beneath their feet all visible things
As steps, that upward to their Father's throne
Lead gradual—else nor glorified nor loved.
They nor contempt embosom nor revenge:
For they dare know of what may seem deform
The Supreme Fair sole operant: in whose sight
All things are pure, his strong controlling love
Alike from all educing perfect good.
Their's too celestial courage, inly armed—
Dwarfing Earth's giant brood, what time they muse             60
On their great Father, great beyond compare!
And marching onwards view high o'er their heads
His waving banners of Omnipotence.

Who the Creator love, created Might
Dread not: within their tents no Terrors walk.

For they are holy things before the Lord
Aye unprofaned, though Earth should league with Hell;
God's altar grasping with an eager hand
Fear, the wild-visag'd, pale, eye-starting wretch,
Sure-refug'd hears his hot pursuing fiends 70
Yell at vain distance. Soon refresh'd from Heaven
He calms the throb and tempest of his heart.
His countenance settles; a soft solemn bliss
Swims in his eye—his swimming eye uprais'd:
And Faith's whole armour glitters on his limbs!
And thus transfigured with a dreadless awe,
A solemn hush of soul, meek he beholds
All things of terrible seeming: yea, unmoved
Views e'en the immitigable ministers
That shower down vengeance on these latter days. 80
For kindling with intenser Deity
From the celestial Mercy-seat they come,
And at the renovating wells of Love
Have fill'd their vials with salutary wrath,
To sickly Nature more medicinal
Than what soft balm the weeping good man pours
Into the lone despoiléd traveller's wounds!

Thus from the Elect, regenerate through faith,
Pass the dark Passions and what thirsty cares
Drink up the spirit, and the dim regards 90
Self-centre. Lo they vanish! or acquire
New names, new features—by supernal grace
Enrobed with Light, and naturalised in Heaven.
As when a shepherd on a vernal morn
Through some thick fog creeps timorous with slow foot,
Darkling he fixes on the immediate road
His downward eye: all else of fairest kind
Hid or deformed. But lo! the bursting Sun!
Touched by the enchantment of that sudden beam
Straight the black vapour melteth, and in globes 100
Of dewy glitter gems each plant and tree;
On every leaf, on every blade it hangs!

Dance glad the new-born intermingling rays,
And wide around the landscape streams with glory!

There is one Mind, one omnipresent Mind,
Omnific. His most holy name is Love.
Truth of subliming import! with the which
Who feeds and saturates his constant soul,
He from his small particular orbit flies
With blest outstarting! From himself he flies,          110
Stands in the sun, and with no partial gaze
Views all creation; and he loves it all,
And blesses it, and calls it very good!
This is indeed to dwell with the Most High!
Cherubs and rapture-trembling Seraphim
Can press no nearer to the Almighty's throne.
But that we roam unconscious, or with hearts
Unfeeling of our universal Sire,
And that in His vast family no Cain
Injures uninjured (in her best-aimed blow          120
Victorious Murder a blind Suicide)
Haply for this some younger Angel now
Looks down on Human Nature: and, behold!
A sea of blood bestrewed with wrecks, where mad
Embattling Interests on each other rush
With unhelmed rage!
                    'Tis the sublime of man,
Our noontide Majesty, to know ourselves
Parts and proportions of one wondrous whole!
This fraternises man, this constitutes
Our charities and bearings. But 'tis God          130
Diffused through all, that doth make all one whole;
This the worst superstition, him except
Aught to desire, Supreme Reality!
The plenitude and permanence of bliss!
O Fiends of Superstition! not that oft
The erring Priest hath stained with brother's blood
Your grisly idols, not for this may wrath
Thunder against you from the Holy One!

But o'er some plain that steameth to the sun,
Peopled with Death; or where more hideous Trade          140
Loud-laughing packs his bales of human anguish;
I will raise up a mourning, O ye Fiends!
And curse your spells, that film the eye of Faith,
Hiding the present God; whose presence lost,
The moral world's cohesion, we become
An Anarchy of Spirits! Toy-bewitched,
Made blind by lusts, disherited of soul,
No common centre Man, no common sire
Knoweth! A sordid solitary thing,
Mid countless brethren with a lonely heart          150
Through courts and cities the smooth savage roams
Feeling himself, his own low self the whole;
When he by sacred sympathy might make
The whole one Self! Self, that no alien knows!
Self, far diffused as Fancy's wing can travel!
Self, spreading still! Oblivious of its own,
Yet all of all possessing! This is Faith!
This the Messiah's destined victory!

But first offences needs must come! Even now
(Black Hell laughs horrible—to hear the scoff!)          160
Thee to defend, meek Galilaean! Thee
And thy mild laws of Love unutterable,
Mistrust and Enmity have burst the bands
Of social peace: and listening Treachery lurks
With pious fraud to snare a brother's life;
And childless widows o'er the groaning land
Wail numberless; and orphans weep for bread!
Thee to defend, dear Saviour of Mankind!
Thee, Lamb of God! Thee, blameless Prince of Peace!
From all sides rush the thirsty brood of War!—          170
Austria, and that foul Woman of the North,
The lustful murderess of her wedded lord!
And he, connatural Mind! whom (in their songs
So bards of elder time had haply feigned)
Some Fury fondled in her hate to man,

Bidding her serpent hair in mazy surge
Lick his young face, and at his mouth imbreathe
Horrible sympathy! And leagued with these
Each petty German princeling, nursed in gore!
Soul-hardened barterers of human blood!                    180
Death's prime slave-merchants! Scorpion-whips of Fate!
Nor least in savagery of holy zeal,
Apt for the yoke, the race degenerate,
Whom Britain erst had blushed to call her sons!
Thee to defend the Moloch Priest prefers
The prayer of hate, and bellows to the herd,
That Deity, Accomplice Deity
In the fierce jealousy of wakened wrath
Will go forth with our armies and our fleets
To scatter the red ruin on their foes!                     190
O blasphemy! to mingle fiendish deeds
With blessedness!

          Lord of unsleeping Love,
From everlasting Thou! We shall not die.
These, even these, in mercy didst thou form,
Teachers of Good through Evil, by brief wrong
Making Truth lovely, and her future might
Magnetic o'er the fixed untrembling heart.

In the primeval age a dateless while
The vacant Shepherd wander'd with his flock,
Pitching his tent where'er the green grass waved.          200
But soon Imagination conjured up
An host of new desires: with busy aim,
Each for himself, Earth's eager children toiled.
So Property began, twy-streaming fount,
Whence Vice and Virtue flow, honey and gall.
Hence the soft couch, and many-coloured robe,
The timbrel, and arched dome and costly feast,
With all the inventive arts, that nursed the soul
To forms of beauty, and by sensual wants
Unsensualised the mind, which in the means                 210

Learnt to forget the grossness of the end,
Best pleasured with its own activity.
And hence Disease that withers manhood's arm,
The daggered Envy, spirit-quenching Want,
Warriors, and Lords, and Priests—all the sore ills
That vex and desolate our mortal life.
Wide-wasting ills! yet each the immediate source
Of mightier good. Their keen necessities
To ceaseless action goading human thought
Have made Earth's reasoning animal her Lord;                    220
And the pale-featured Sage's trembling hand
Strong as an host of arméd Deities,
Such as the blind Ionian fabled erst.

From Avarice thus, from Luxury and War
Sprang heavenly Science; and from Science Freedom.
O'er waken'd realms Philosophers and Bards
Spread in concentric circles: they whose souls,
Conscious of their high dignities from God,
Brook not Wealth's rivalry! and they, who long
Enamoured with the charms of order, hate                        230
The unseemly disproportion: and whoe'er
Turn with mild sorrow from the Victor's car
And the low puppetry of thrones, to muse
On that blest triumph, when the Patriot Sage
Called the red lightnings from the o'er-rushing cloud
And dashed the beauteous terrors on the earth
Smiling majestic. Such a phalanx ne'er
Measured firm paces to the calming sound
Of Spartan flute! These on the fated day,
When, stung to rage by Pity, eloquent men                       240
Have roused with pealing voice the unnumbered tribes
That toil and groan and bleed, hungry and blind—
These, hush'd awhile with patient eye serene,
Shall watch the mad careering of the storm;
Then o'er the wild and wavy chaos rush
And tame the outrageous mass, with plastic might
Moulding Confusion to such perfect forms,

As erst were wont,—bright visions of the day!—
To float before them, when, the summer noon,
Beneath some arched romantic rock reclined                    250
They felt the sea-breeze lift their youthful locks;
Or in the month of blossoms, at mild eve,
Wandering with desultory feet inhaled
The wafted perfumes, and the flocks and woods
And many-tinted streams and setting sun
With all his gorgeous company of clouds
Ecstatic gazed! then homeward as they strayed
Cast the sad eye to earth, and inly mused
Why there was misery in a world so fair.

Ah! far removed from all that glads the sense,                    260
From all that softens or ennobles Man,
The wretched Many! Bent beneath their loads
They gape at pageant Power, nor recognise
Their cots' transmuted plunder! From the tree
Of Knowledge, ere the vernal sap had risen
Rudely disbranchéd! Blessed Society!
Fitliest depictured by some sun-scorched waste,
Where oft majestic through the tainted noon
The Simoom sails, before whose purple pomp
Who falls not prostrate dies! And where by night,                    270
Fast by each precious fountain on green herbs
The lion couches: or hyaena dips
Deep in the lucid stream his bloody jaws;
Or serpent plants his vast moon-glittering bulk,
Caught in whose monstrous twine Behemoth yells,
His bones loud-crashing!

                    O ye numberless,
Whom foul Oppression's ruffian gluttony
Drives from Life's plenteous feast! O thou poor Wretch
Who nursed in darkness and made wild by want,
Roamest for prey, yea thy unnatural hand                    280
Dost lift to deeds of blood! O pale-eyed form,
The victim of seduction, doomed to know

Polluted nights and days of blasphemy;
Who in loathed orgies with lewd wassailers
Must gaily laugh, while thy remembered Home
Gnaws like a viper at thy secret heart!
O agéd Women! ye who weekly catch
The morsel tossed by law-forced charity,
And die so slowly, that none call it murder!
O loathly suppliants! ye, that unreceived                    290
Totter heart-broken from the closing gates
Of the full Lazar-house; or, gazing, stand,
Sick with despair! O ye to Glory's field
Forced or ensnared, who, as ye gasp in death,
Bleed with new wounds beneath the vulture's beak!
O thou poor widow, who in dreams dost view
Thy husband's mangled corse, and from short doze
Start'st with a shriek; or in thy half-thatched cot
Waked by the wintry night-storm, wet and cold
Cow'rst o'er thy screaming baby! Rest awhile                  300
Children of Wretchedness! More groans must rise,
More blood must stream, or ere your wrongs be full.
Yet is the day of Retribution nigh:
The Lamb of God hath opened the fifth seal:
And upward rush on swiftest wing of fire
The innumerable multitude of wrongs
By man on man inflicted! Rest awhile,
Children of Wretchedness! The hour is nigh
And lo! the Great, the Rich, the Mighty Men,
The Kings and the Chief Captains of the World,              310
With all that fixed on high like stars of Heaven
Shot baleful influence, shall be cast to earth,
Vile and down-trodden, as the untimely fruit
Shook from the fig-tree by a sudden storm.
Even now the storm begins: each gentle name,
Faith and meek Piety, with fearful joy
Tremble far-off—for lo! the Giant Frenzy
Uprooting empires with his whirlwind arm
Mocketh high Heaven; burst hideous from the cell

Where the old Hag, unconquerable, huge,          320
Creation's eyeless drudge, black Ruin, sits
Nursing the impatient earthquake.
                                    O return!
Pure Faith! meek Piety! The abhorréd Form
Whose scarlet robe was stiff with earthly pomp,
Who drank iniquity in cups of gold,
Whose names were many and all blasphemous,
Hath met the horrible judgment! Whence that cry?
The mighty army of foul Spirits shrieked
Disherited of earth! For she hath fallen
On whose black front was written Mystery;          330
She that reeled heavily, whose wine was blood;
She that worked whoredom with the Daemon Power,
And from the dark embrace all evil things
Brought forth and nurtured: mitred Atheism!
And patient Folly who on bended knee
Gives back the steel that stabbed him; and pale Fear
Haunted by ghastlier shapings than surround
Moon-blasted Madness when he yells at midnight!
Return pure Faith! return meek Piety!
The kingdoms of the world are your's: each heart          340
Self-governed, the vast family of Love
Raised from the common earth by common toil
Enjoy the equal produce. Such delights
As float to earth, permitted visitants!
When in some hour of solemn jubilee
The massy gates of Paradise are thrown
Wide open, and forth come in fragments wild
Sweet echoes of unearthly melodies,
And odours snatched from beds of Amaranth,
And they, that from the crystal river of life          350
Spring up on freshened wing, ambrosial gales!
The favoured good man in his lonely walk
Perceives them, and his silent spirit drinks
Strange bliss which he shall recognise in heaven.
And such delights, such strange beatitudes

Seize on my young anticipating heart
When that blest future rushes on my view!
For in his own and in his Father's might
The Saviour comes! While as the Thousand Years
Lead up their mystic dance, the Desert shouts!    360
Old Ocean claps his hands! The mighty Dead
Rise to new life, whoe'er from earliest time
With conscious zeal had urged Love's wondrous plan,
Coadjutors of God. To Milton's trump
The high groves of the renovated Earth
Unbosom their glad echoes: inly hushed,
Adoring Newton his serener eye
Raises to heaven: and he of mortal kind
Wisest, he first who marked the ideal tribes
Up the fine fibres through the sentient brain.    370
Lo! Priestley there, patriot, and saint, and sage,
Him, full of years, from his loved native land
Statesmen blood-stained and priests idolatrous
By dark lies maddening the blind multitude
Drove with vain hate. Calm, pitying he retired,
And mused expectant on these promised years.

O Years! the blest pre-eminence of Saints!
Ye sweep athwart my gaze, so heavenly bright,
The wings that veil the adoring Seraphs' eyes,
What time they bend before the Jasper Throne    380
Reflect no lovelier hues! Yet ye depart,
And all beyond is darkness! Heights most strange,
Whence Fancy falls, fluttering her idle wing.
For who of woman born may paint the hour,
When seized in his mid course, the Sun shall wane
Making noon ghastly! Who of woman born
May image in the workings of his thought,
How the black-visaged, red-eyed Fiend outstretched
Beneath the unsteady feet of Nature groans,
In feverous slumbers—destined then to wake,    390
When fiery whirlwinds thunder his dread name

And Angels shout, Destruction! How his arm
The last great Spirit lifting high in air
Shall swear by Him, the ever-living One,
Time is no more!

              Believe thou, O my soul,
Life is a vision shadowy of Truth;
And vice, and anguish, and the wormy grave,
Shapes of a dream! The veiling clouds retire,
And lo! the Throne of the redeeming God
Forth flashing unimaginable day                                    400
Wraps in one blaze earth, heaven, and deepest hell.

Contemplant Spirits! ye that hover o'er
With untired gaze the immeasurable fount
Ebullient with creative Deity!
And ye of plastic power, that interfused
Roll through the grosser and material mass
In organizing surge! Holies of God!
(And what if Monads of the infinite mind?)
I haply journeying my immortal course
Shall sometime join your mystic choir! Till then          410
I discipline my young and novice thought
In ministeries of heart-stirring song,
And aye on Meditation's heaven-ward wing
Soaring aloft I breathe the empyreal air
Of Love, omnific, omnipresent Love,
Whose day-spring rises glorious in my soul
As the great Sun, when he his influence
Sheds on the frost-bound waters—The glad stream
Flows to the ray and warbles as it flows.
1794–1796.                                                                  1796.

# MONODY ON THE DEATH

## OF CHATTERTON

O what a wonder seems the fear of death,
Seeing how gladly we all sink to sleep,
Babes, Children, Youths, and Men,
Night following night for threescore years and ten!
But doubly strange, where life is but a breath
To sigh and pant with, up Want's rugged steep.

Away, Grim Phantom! Scorpion King, away!
Reserve thy terrors and thy stings display
For coward Wealth and Guilt in robes of State!
Lo! by the grave I stand of one, for whom                    10
A prodigal Nature and a niggard Doom
(*That* all bestowing, *this* withholding all)
Made each chance knell from distant spire or dome
Sound like a seeking Mother's anxious call,
Return, poor Child! Home, weary Truant, home!

Thee, Chatterton! these unblest stones protect
From want, and the bleak freezings of neglect.
Too long before the vexing Storm-blast driven
Here hast thou found repose! beneath this sod!
Thou! O vain word! *thou* dwell'st not with the clod!        20
Amid the shining Host of the Forgiven
Thou at the throne of mercy and thy God
The triumph of redeeming Love dost hymn
(Believe it, O my Soul!) to harps of Seraphim.

Yet oft, perforce ('tis suffering Nature's call),
I weep that heaven-born Genius *so* should fall;
And oft, in Fancy's saddest hour, my soul
Averted shudders at the poison'd bowl.
Now groans my sickening heart, as still I view
        Thy corse of livid hue;                              30

Now Indignation checks the feeble sigh,
Or flashes through the tear that glistens in mine eye!

Is this the land of song-ennobled line?
Is this the land, where Genius ne'er in vain
　　　Pour'd forth his lofty strain?
Ah me! yet Spenser, gentlest bard divine,
Beneath chill Disappointment's shade,
His weary limbs in lonely anguish lay'd.
　　　And o'er her darling dead
　　　Pity hopeless hung her head,
While "mid the pelting of that merciless storm,"                    40
Sunk to the cold earth Otway's famish'd form!

Sublime of thought, and confident of fame,
From vales where Avon winds the Minstrel came.
　　　Light-hearted youth! aye, as he hastes along,
　　　He meditates the future song,
How dauntless Ælla fray'd the Dacyan foe;
　　　And while the numbers flowing strong
　　　In eddies whirl, in surges throng,
Exulting in the spirits' genial throe                               50
In tides of power his life-blood seems to flow.

And now his cheeks with deeper ardors flame,
His eyes have glorious meanings, that declare
More than the light of outward day shines there,
A holier triumph and a sterner aim!
Wings grow within him; and he soars above
Or Bard's or Minstrel's lay of war or love.
Friend to the friendless, to the sufferer health,
He hears the widow's prayer, the good man's praise;
To scenes of bliss transmutes his fancied wealth,                  60
And young and old shall now see happy days.
On many a waste he bids trim gardens rise,
Gives the blue sky to many a prisoner's eyes;
And now in wrath he grasps the patriot steel,
And her own iron rod he makes Oppression feel.

Sweet Flower of Hope! free Nature's genial child!
That didst so fair disclose thy early bloom,
Filling the wide air with a rich perfume!
For thee in vain all heavenly aspects smil'd;
From the hard world brief respite could they win—     70
The frost nipp'd sharp without, the canker prey'd within!
Ah! where are fled the charms of vernal Grace,
And Joy's wild gleams that lighten'd o'er thy face?
Youth of tumultuous soul, and haggard eye!
Thy wasted form, thy hurried steps I view,
On thy wan forehead starts the lethal dew,
And oh! the anguish of that shuddering sigh!

Such were the struggles of the gloomy hour,
    When Care, of wither'd brow,
Prepar'd the poison's death-cold power:     80
Already to thy lips was rais'd the bowl,
    When near thee stood Affection meek
    (Her bosom bare, and wildly pale her cheek)
Thy sullen gaze she bade thee roll
On scenes that well might melt thy soul;
Thy native cot she flash'd upon thy view,
Thy native cot, where still, at close of day,
Peace smiling sate, and listen'd to thy lay;
Thy Sister's shrieks she bade thee hear,
And mark thy Mother's thrilling tear;     90
    See, see her breast's convulsive throe,
    Her silent agony of woe!
Ah! dash the poison'd chalice from thy hand!

And thou hadst dashed it, at her soft command,
But that Despair and Indignation rose,
And told again the story of thy woes;
Told the keen insult of the unfeeling heart,
The dread dependence on the low-born mind;
Told every pang, with which thy soul must smart,
Neglect, and grinning Scorn, and Want combined!     100
Recoiling quick, thou badest the friend of pain

Roll the black tide of Death through every freezing vein!
        O spirit blest!
Whether the Eternal's throne around,
Amidst the blaze of Seraphim,
Thou pourest forth the grateful hymn,
Or soaring thro' the blest domain
Enrapturest Angels with thy strain,—
Grant me, like thee, the lyre to sound,
Like thee with fire divine to glow;—
But ah! when rage the waves of woe,             110
Grant me with firmer breast to meet their hate,
And soar beyond the storm with upright eye elate!

Ye woods! that wave o'er Avon's rocky steep,
To Fancy's ear sweet is your murmuring deep!
For here she loves the cypress wreath to weave;
Watching with wistful eye, the saddening tints of eve.
Here, far from men, amid this pathless grove,
In solemn thought the Minstrel wont to rove,
Like star-beam on the slow sequester'd tide
Lone-glittering, through the high tree branching wide.    120
And here, in Inspiration's eager hour,
When most the big soul feels the mastering power,
    These wilds, these caverns roaming o'er,
    Round which the screaming sea-gulls soar,
With wild unequal steps he pass'd along,
Oft pouring on the winds a broken song:
Anon, upon some rough rock's fearful brow
Would pause abrupt—and gaze upon the waves below.

Poor Chatterton! *he* sorrows for thy fate
Who would have prais'd and lov'd thee, ere too late.     130
Poor Chatterton! farewell! of darkest hues
This chaplet cast I on thy unshaped tomb;
But dare no longer on the sad theme muse,
Lest kindred woes persuade a kindred doom:
For oh! big gall-drops, shook from Folly's wing,
Have blacken'd the fair promise of my spring;

And the stern Fate transpierc'd with viewless dart
The last pale Hope that shiver'd at my heart!

Hence, gloomy thoughts! no more my soul shall dwell
On joys that were! no more endure to weigh                    140
The shame and anguish of the evil day,
Wisely forgetful! O'er the ocean swell
Sublime of Hope I seek the cottag'd dell
Where Virtue calm with careless step may stray;
And, dancing to the moon-light roundelay,
The wizard Passions weave an holy spell!

O Chatterton! that thou wert yet alive!
Sure thou would'st spread the canvass to the gale,
And love with us the tinkling team to drive
O'er peaceful Freedom's undivided dale;                       150
And we, at sober eve, would round thee throng,
Would hang, enraptur'd, on thy stately song,
And greet with smiles the young-eyed Poesy
All deftly mask'd as hoar Antiquity.

Alas, vain Phantasies! the fleeting brood
Of Woe self-solac'd in her dreamy mood!
Yet will I love to follow the sweet dream,
Where Susequehannah pours his untamed stream;
And on some hill, whose forest-frowning side
Waves o'er the murmurs of his calmer tide,                    160
Will raise a solemn Cenotaph to thee,
Sweet Harper of time-shrouded Minstrelsy!
And there, sooth'd sadly by the dirgeful wind,
Muse on the sore ills I had left behind.
1790–1834.                                    1794.

# VER PERPETUUM

**FRAGMENT**

From an unpublished poem.

The early Year's fast-flying vapours stray
In shadowing trains across the orb of day·
And we, poor Insects of a few short hours,
    Deem it a world of Gloom.
Were it not better hope a nobler doom,
Proud to believe that with more active powers
      On rapid many-coloured wing
      We thro' one bright perpetual Spring
Shall hover round the fruits and flowers,
Screen'd by those clouds and cherish'd by those showers!
1796.                                                    1796.

# ON OBSERVING A BLOSSOM ON THE

# FIRST OF FEBRUARY 1796

Sweet flower! that peeping from thy russet stem
Unfoldest timidly, (for in strange sort
This dark, frieze-coated, hoarse, teeth-chattering month
Hath borrow'd Zephyr's voice, and gazed upon thee
With blue voluptuous eye) alas, poor Flower!
These are but flatteries of the faithless year.
Perchance, escaped its unknown polar cave,
Even now the keen North-East is on its way.
Flower that must perish! shall I liken thee
To some sweet girl of too too rapid growth
Nipp'd by consumption mid untimely charms?
Or to Bristowa's bard, the wondrous boy!

An amaranth, which earth scarce seem'd to own,
Till disappointment came, and pelting wrong
Beat it to earth? or with indignant grief
Shall I compare thee to poor Poland's hope,
Bright flower of hope killed in the opening bud?
Farewell, sweet blossom! better fate be thine
And mock my boding! Dim similitudes
Weaving in moral strains, I've stolen one hour
From anxious Self, Life's cruel taskmaster!
And the warm wooings of this sunny day
Tremble along my frame and harmonize
The attempered organ, that even saddest thoughts
Mix with some sweet sensations, like harsh tunes
Played deftly on a soft-toned instrument.
1796.                                          1796.

# SONNET

~~~

COMPOSED ON A JOURNEY HOMEWARD; THE AUTHOR HAVING
RECEIVED INTELLIGENCE OF THE BIRTH OF A SON,
SEPT. 20, 1796

Oft o'er my brain does that strange fancy roll
    Which makes the present (while the flash doth last)
    Seem a mere semblance of some unknown past,
Mixed with such feelings, as perplex the soul
Self-questioned in her sleep; and some have said
    We liv'd, ere yet this robe of flesh we wore.
    O my sweet baby! when I reach my door,
If heavy looks should tell me thou art dead,
(As sometimes, through excess of hope, I fear)
I think that I should struggle to believe
    Thou wert a spirit, to this nether sphere
Sentenc'd for some more venial crime to grieve;

Did'st scream, then spring to meet Heaven's quick reprieve,
  While we wept idly o'er thy little bier!
1796.

1797.

## TO A YOUNG FRIEND

ON HIS PROPOSING TO DOMESTICATE WITH THE AUTHOR
*Composed in* 1796

A mount, not wearisome and bare and steep,
  But a green mountain variously up-piled,
Where o'er the jutting rocks soft mosses creep,
Or colour'd lichens with slow oozing weep;
  Where cypress and the darker yew start wild;
And, 'mid the summer torrent's gentle dash
Dance brighten'd the red clusters of the ash;
  Beneath whose boughs, by those still sounds beguil'd,
Calm Pensiveness might muse herself to sleep;
  Till haply startled by some fleecy dam,    10
That rustling on the bushy cliff above
With melancholy bleat of anxious love,
  Made meek enquiry for her wandering lamb:
  Such a green mountain 'twere most sweet to climb,
E'en while the bosom ach'd with loneliness—
How more than sweet, if some dear friend should bless
  The adventurous toil, and up the path sublime
Now lead, now follow: the glad landscape round,
Wide and more wide, increasing without bound!

O then 'twere loveliest sympathy, to mark    20
The berries of the half-uprooted ash
Dripping and bright; and list the torrent's dash,—
  Beneath the cypress, or the yew more dark,
Seated at ease, on some smooth mossy rock;
In social silence now, and now to unlock
The treasur'd heart; arm linked in friendly arm,

Save if the one, his muse's witching charm
Muttering brow-bent, at unwatch'd distance lag;
  Till high o'er head his beckoning friend appears,
And from the forehead of the topmost crag          30
  Shouts eagerly: for haply *there* uprears
That shadowing Pine its old romantic limbs,
  Which latest shall detain the enamour'd sight
Seen from below, when eve the valley dims,
  Tinged yellow with the rich departing light;
  And haply, bason'd in some unsunn'd cleft,
A beauteous spring, the rock's collected tears,
Sleeps shelter'd there, scarce wrinkled by the gale!
  Together thus, the world's vain turmoil left,
Stretch'd on the crag, and shadow'd by the pine,     40
  And bending o'er the clear delicious fount,
Ah! dearest youth! it were a lot divine
To cheat our noons in moralising mood,
While west-winds fann'd our temples toil-bedew'd:
  Then downwards slope, oft pausing, from the mount,
To some lone mansion, in some woody dale,
Where smiling with blue eye, Domestic Bliss
Gives *this* the Husband's, *that* the Brother's kiss!

  Thus rudely vers'd in allegoric lore,
The Hill of Knowledge I essayed to trace;        50
That verduous hill with many a resting-place,
And many a stream, whose warbling waters pour
  To glad, and fertilise the subject plains;
That hill with secret springs, and nooks untrod,
And many a fancy-blest and holy sod
  Where Inspiration, his diviner strains
Low-murmuring, lay; and starting from the rock's
Stiff evergreens, (whose spreading foliage mocks
Want's barren soil, and the bleak frosts of age,
And Bigotry's mad fire-invoking rage!)        60
O meek retiring spirit! we will climb,
Cheering and cheered, this lovely hill sublime;

And from the stirring world up-lifted high
(Whose noises, faintly wafted on the wind,
To quiet musings shall attune the mind,
  And oft the melancholy *theme* supply),
  There, while the prospect through the gazing eye
  Pours all its healthful greenness on the soul,
We'll smile at wealth, and learn to smile at fame,
Our hopes, our knowledge, and our joys the same,          70
  As neighbouring fountains image each the whole:
Then when the mind hath drunk its fill of truth
  We'll discipline the heart to pure delight,
Rekindling sober joy's domestic flame.
They whom I love shall love thee, honour'd youth!
  Now may Heaven realise this vision bright!
1796.                                                    1797.

# ODE TO THE DEPARTING YEAR

'Ιοὺ ἰού, ὢ ὢ κακά.
'Υπ' αὖ με δεινὸς ὀρθομαντείας πόνος
Στροβεῖ, ταράσσων φροιμίοις δυσφροιμίοις.

.    .    .    .    .    .

Τὸ μέλλον ἥξει. Καὶ σύ μ' ἐν τάχει παρὼν
"Αγαν ἀληθόμαντιν οἰκτείρας ἐρεῖς.

Aeschyl. *Agam.* 1173–75; 1199–1200.

### ARGUMENT

The Ode commences with an address to the Divine Providence
that regulates into one vast harmony all the events of time, however calamitous some of them may appear to mortals. The second
Strophe calls on men to suspend their private joys and sorrows,
and devote them for a while to the cause of human nature in general. The first Epode speaks of the Empress of Russia, who died
of an apoplexy on the 17th of November 1796; having just concluded a subsidiary treaty with the Kings combined against
France. The first and second Antistrophe describe the Image of
the Departing Year, etc., as in a vision. The second Epode proph-
esies, in anguish of spirit, the downfall of this country.

I

Spirit who sweepest the wild Harp of Time!
    It is most hard, with an untroubled ear
    Thy dark inwoven harmonies to hear!
Yet, mine eye fix'd on Heaven's unchanging clime
Long had I listen'd, free from mortal fear,
    With inward stillness, and a bowéd mind;
    When lo! its folds far waving on the wind,
I saw the train of the Departing Year!
    Starting from my silent sadness
    Then with no unholy madness,
Ere yet the enter'd cloud foreclos'd my sight,
I rais'd the impetuous song, and solemnis'd his flight.

10

41

## II

Hither, from the recent tomb,
From the prison's direr gloom,
From Distemper's midnight anguish;
And thence, where Poverty doth waste and languish;
Or where, his two bright torches blending,
Love illumines Manhood's maze;
Or where o'er cradled infants bending,
Hope has fix'd her wishful gaze;                    20
Hither, in perplexéd dance,
Ye Woes! ye young-eyed Joys! advance!
By Time's wild harp, and by the hand
Whose indefatigable sweep
Raises its fateful strings from sleep,
I bid you haste, a mix'd tumultuous band!
From every private bower,
And each domestic hearth,
Haste for one solemn hour;
And with a loud and yet a louder voice,              30
O'er Nature struggling in portentous birth,
Weep and rejoice!
Still echoes the dread Name that o'er the earth
Let slip the storm, and woke the brood of Hell:
And now advance in saintly Jubilee
Justice and Truth! They too have heard thy spell.
They too obey thy name, divinest Liberty!

## III

I mark'd Ambition in his war-array!
I heard the mailéd Monarch's troublous cry—
"Ah! wherefore does the Northern Conqueress stay!   40
Groans not her chariot on its onward way?"
Fly, mailéd Monarch, fly!
Stunn'd by Death's twice mortal mace,
No more on Murder's lurid face
The insatiate Hag shall gloat with drunken eye!

Manes of the unnumber'd slain!
   Ye that gasp'd on Warsaw's plain!
  Ye that erst at Ismail's tower,
When human ruin choked the streams,
  Fell in Conquest's glutted hour,        50
Mid women's shrieks and infants' screams!
   Spirits of the uncoffin'd slain,
   Sudden blasts of triumph swelling,
Oft, at night, in misty train,
   Rush around her narrow dwelling!
The exterminating Fiend is fled—
   (Foul her life, and dark her doom)
Mighty armies of the dead
   Dance, like death-fires, round her tomb!
Then with prophetic song relate,        60
Each some Tyrant-Murderer's fate!

### IV

Departing Year! 'twas on no earthly shore
  My soul beheld thy Vision! Where alone,
  Voiceless and stern, before the cloudy throne,
Aye Memory sits: thy robe inscrib'd with gore,
With many an unimaginable groan
  Thou storied'st thy sad hours! Silence ensued,
  Deep silence o'er the ethereal multitude,
Whose locks with wreaths, whose wreaths with glories shone.
   Then, his eye wild ardours glancing,      70
   From the choiréd gods advancing,
The Spirit of the Earth made reverence meet,
And stood up, beautiful, before the cloudy seat.

### V

  Throughout the blissful throng,
  Hush'd were harp and song:
Till wheeling round the throne the Lampads seven,
  (The mystic Words of Heaven)
  Permissive signal make:

The fervent Spirit bow'd, then spread his wings and spake!
   "Thou in stormy blackness throning        80
   Love and uncreated Light,
 By the Earth's unsolaced groaning,
   Seize thy terrors, Arm of might!
 By Peace with proffer'd insult scared,
     Masked Hate and envying Scorn!
   By years of Havoc yet unborn!
And Hunger's bosom to the frost-winds bared!
    But chief by Afric's wrongs,
    Strange, horrible, and foul!
   By what deep guilt belongs        90
To the deaf Synod, 'full of gifts and lies!'
By Wealth's insensate laugh! by Torture's howl!
      Avenger, rise!
For ever shall the thankless Island scowl,
 Her quiver full, and with unbroken bow?
Speak! from thy storm-black Heaven O speak aloud!
    And on the darkling foe
Open thine eye of fire from some uncertain cloud!
 O dart the flash! O rise and deal the blow!
The Past to thee, to thee the Future cries!    100
 Hark! how wide Nature joins her groans below!
  Rise, God of Nature! rise."

### VI

   The voice had ceas'd, the Vision fled;
   Yet still I gasp'd and reel'd with dread.
   And ever, when the dream of night
   Renews the phantom to my sight,
   Cold sweat-drops gather on my limbs;
     My ears throb hot; my eye-balls start;
   My brain with horrid tumult swims;
     Wild is the tempest of my heart;    110
   And my thick and struggling breath
   Imitates the toil of death!
   No stranger agony confounds

The Soldier on the war-field spread,
When all foredone with toil and wounds,
   Death-like he dozes among heaps of dead!
(The strife is o'er, the day-light fled,
   And the night-wind clamours hoarse!
See! the starting wretch's head
   Lies pillow'd on a brother's corse!)      120

### VII

Not yet enslaved, not wholly vile,
O Albion! O my mother Isle!
Thy valleys, fair as Eden's bowers
Glitter green with sunny showers;
Thy grassy uplands' gentle swells
   Echo to the bleat of flocks;
(Those grassy hills, those glittering dells
   Proudly ramparted with rocks)
And Ocean mid his uproar wild
Speaks safety to his Island-child!      130
Hence for many a fearless age
Has social Quiet lov'd thy shore;
Nor ever proud Invader's rage
Or sack'd thy towers, or stain'd thy fields with gore.

### VIII

Abandon'd of Heaven! mad Avarice thy guide,
At cowardly distance, yet kindling with pride—
Mid thy herds and thy corn-fields secure thou hast stood,
And join'd the wild yelling of Famine and Blood!
The nations curse thee! They with eager wondering
   Shall hear Destruction, like a vulture, scream!      140
   Strange-eyed Destruction! who with many a dream
Of central fires through nether seas up-thundering
   Soothes her fierce solitude; yet as she lies
   By livid fount, or red volcanic stream,
   If ever to her lidless dragon-eyes,
O Albion! thy predestin'd ruins rise,

The fiend-hag on her perilous couch doth leap,
Muttering distemper'd triumph in her charméd sleep.


IX

Away, my soul, away!
In vain, in vain the Birds of warning sing—                    150
And hark! I hear the famish'd brood of prey
Flap their lank pennons on the groaning wind!
Away, my soul, away!
I unpartaking of the evil thing,
    With daily prayer and daily toil
    Soliciting for food my scanty soil,
Have wail'd my country with a loud Lament.
Now I recentre my immortal mind
    In the deep Sabbath of meek self-content;
Cleans'd from the vaporous passions that bedim             160
God's Image, sister of the Seraphim.
1796.                                                        1796.


# THIS LIME-TREE BOWER MY PRISON

[ADDRESSED TO CHARLES LAMB, OF THE INDIA HOUSE, LONDON]

In the June of 1797 some long-expected friends paid a visit to the author's cottage; and on the morning of their arrival, he met with an accident, which disabled him from walking during the whole time of their stay. One evening, when they had left him for a few hours, he composed the following lines in the garden-bower.

Well, they are gone, and here must I remain,
This lime-tree bower my prison! I have lost
Beauties and feelings, such as would have been
Most sweet to my remembrance even when age
Had dimm'd mine eyes to blindness! They, meanwhile,
Friends, whom I never more may meet again,
On springy heath, along the hill-top edge,

Wander in gladness, and wind down, perchance,
To that still roaring dell, of which I told;
The roaring dell, o'erwooded, narrow, deep, 10
And only speckled by the mid-day sun;
Where its slim trunk the ash from rock to rock
Flings arching like a bridge;—that branchless ash,
Unsunn'd and damp, whose few poor yellow leaves
Ne'er tremble in the gale, yet tremble still,
Fann'd by the water-fall! and there my friends
Behold the dark green file of long lank weeds,
That all at once (a most fantastic sight!)
Still nod and drip beneath the dripping edge
Of the blue clay-stone. 20

            Now, my friends emerge
Beneath the wide wide Heaven—and view again
The many-steepled tract magnificent
Of hilly fields and meadows, and the sea,
With some fair bark, perhaps, whose sails light up
The slip of smooth clear blue betwixt two Isles
Of purple shadow! Yes! they wander on
In gladness all; but thou, methinks, most glad,
My gentle-hearted Charles! for thou hast pined
And hunger'd after Nature, many a year, 30
In the great City pent, winning thy way
With sad yet patient soul, through evil and pain
And strange calamity! Ah! slowly sink
Behind the western ridge, thou glorious Sun!
Shine in the slant beams of the sinking orb,
Ye purple heath-flowers! richlier burn, ye clouds!
Live in the yellow light, ye distant groves!
And kindle, thou blue Ocean! So my friend
Struck with deep joy may stand, as I have stood,
Silent with swimming sense; yea, gazing round 40
On the wide landscape, gaze till all doth seem
Less gross than bodily; and of such hues
As veil the Almighty Spirit, when yet he makes
Spirits perceive his presence.

                              A delight
Comes sudden on my heart, and I am glad
As I myself were there! Nor in this bower,
This little lime-tree bower, have I not mark'd
Much that has sooth'd me. Pale beneath the blaze
Hung the transparent foliage; and I watch'd                    50
Some broad and sunny leaf, and lov'd to see
The shadow of the leaf and stem above
Dappling its sunshine! And that walnut-tree
Was richly ting'd, and a deep radiance lay
Full on the ancient ivy, which usurps
Those fronting elms, and now, with blackest mass
Makes their dark branches gleam a lighter hue
Through the late twilight: and though now the bat
Wheels silent by, and not a swallow twitters,
Yet still the solitary humble-bee                              60
Sings in the bean-flower! Henceforth I shall know
That Nature ne'er deserts the wise and pure;
No plot so narrow, be but Nature there,
No waste so vacant, but may well employ
Each faculty of sense, and keep the heart
Awake to Love and Beauty! and sometimes
'Tis well to be bereft of promis'd good,
That we may lift the soul, and contemplate
With lively joy the joys we cannot share.
My gentle-hearted Charles! when the last rook                  70
Beat its straight path along the dusky air
Homewards, I blest it! deeming its black wing
(Now a dim speck, now vanishing in light)
Had cross'd the mighty Orb's dilated glory,
While thou stood'st gazing; or, when all was still,
Flew creeking o'er thy head, and had a charm
For thee, my gentle-hearted Charles, to whom
No sound is dissonant which tells of Life.
1797.                                        1800.

# THE RIME OF
# THE ANCIENT MARINER

## IN SEVEN PARTS

Facile credo, plures esse Naturas invisibiles quam visibiles in rerum universitate. Sed horum omnium familiam quis nobis enarrabit? et gradus et cognationes et discrimina et singulorum munera? Quid agunt? quae loca habitant? Harum rerum notitiam semper ambivit ingenium humanum, nunquam attigit. Juvat, interea, non diffiteor, quandoque in animo, tanquam in tabulà, majoris et melioris mundi imaginem contemplari: ne mens assuefacta hodiernae vitae minutiis se contrahat nimis, et tota subsidat in pusillas cogitationes. Sed veritati interea invigilandum est, modusque servandus, ut certa ab incertis, diem a nocte, distinguamus.

—T. Burnet, Archaeol. Phil. p. 68.

## ARGUMENT

How a Ship having passed the Line was driven by storms to the cold Country towards the South Pole; and how from thence she made her course to the tropical Latitude of the Great Pacific Ocean; and of the strange things that befell; and in what manner the Ancyent Marinere came back to his own Country.

### PART I

An ancient Mariner meeteth three Gallants bidden to a wedding-feast, and detaineth one.

It is an ancient Mariner,
And he stoppeth one of three.
"By thy long grey beard and glittering eye,
Now wherefore stopp'st thou me?

The Bridegroom's doors are opened wide,
And I am next of kin;
The guests are met, the feast is set:
May'st hear the merry din."

He holds him with his skinny hand,
"There was a ship," quoth he.                    10
"Hold off! unhand me, grey-beard loon!"
Eftsoons his hand dropt he.

The Wedding-
Guest is spell-
bound by the
eye of the old
seafaring man,
and con-
strained to
hear his tale.
He holds him with his glittering eye—
The Wedding-Guest stood still,
And listens like a three years' child:
The Mariner hath his will.

The Wedding-Guest sat on a stone:
He cannot choose but hear;
And thus spake on that ancient man,
The bright-eyed Mariner.                                    20

"The ship was cheered, the harbour cleared,
Merrily did we drop
Below the kirk, below the hill,
Below the lighthouse top.

The Mariner
tells how the
ship sailed
southward
with a good
wind and fair
weather, till it
reached the
line.
The Sun came up upon the left,
Out of the sea came he!
And he shone bright, and on the right
Went down into the sea.

Higher and higher every day,
Till over the mast at noon—"                               30
The Wedding-Guest here beat his breast,
For he heard the loud bassoon.

The Wedding-
Guest heareth
the bridal
music; but
the Mariner
continueth
his tale.
The bride hath paced into the hall,
Red as a rose is she;
Nodding their heads before her goes
The merry minstrelsy.

The Wedding-Guest he beat his breast,
Yet he cannot choose but hear;
And thus spake on that ancient man,
The bright-eyed Mariner.                                    40

The ship driven
by a storm
toward the
south pole.
"And now the STORM-BLAST came, and he
Was tyrannous and strong:
He struck with his o'ertaking wings,
And chased us south along.

With sloping masts and dipping prow,
As who pursued with yell and blow
Still treads the shadow of his foe,
And forward bends his head,
The ship drove fast, loud roared the blast,
And southward aye we fled. 50

And now there came both mist and snow,
And it grew wondrous cold:
And ice, mast-high, came floating by,
As green as emerald.

The land of ice, and of fearful sounds where no living thing was to be seen.

And through the drifts the snowy clifts
Did send a dismal sheen:
Nor shapes of men nor beasts we ken—
The ice was all between.

The ice was here, the ice was there,
The ice was all around: 60
It cracked and growled, and roared and howled,
Like noises in a swound!

Till a great sea-bird, called the Albatross, came through the snow-fog, and was received with great joy and hospitality.

At length did cross an Albatross,
Thorough the fog it came;
As if it had been a Christian soul,
We hailed it in God's name.

It ate the food it ne'er had eat,
And round and round it flew.
The ice did split with a thunder-fit;
The helmsman steered us through! 70

And lo! the Albatross proveth a bird of good omen, and followeth the ship as it returned northward through fog and floating ice.

And a good south wind sprung up behind;
The Albatross did follow,
And every day, for food or play,
Came to the mariner's hollo!

In mist or cloud, on mast or shroud,
It perched for vespers nine;
Whiles all the night, through fog-smoke white,
Glimmered the white Moon-shine."

*The ancient Mariner inhospitably killeth the pious bird of good omen.*

"God save thee, ancient Mariner!
From the fiends, that plague thee thus!—        80
Why look'st thou so?"—With my cross-bow
I shot the ALBATROSS.

PART II

The Sun now rose upon the right:
Out of the sea came he,
Still hid in mist, and on the left
Went down into the sea.

And the good south wind still blew behind,
But no sweet bird did follow,
Nor any day for food or play
Came to the mariners' hollo!        90

*His shipmates cry out against the ancient Mariner, for killing the bird of good luck.*

And I had done a hellish thing,
And it would work 'em woe:
For all averred, I had killed the bird
That made the breeze to blow.
Ah wretch! said they, the bird to slay,
That made the breeze to blow!

*But when the fog cleared off, they justify the same, and thus make themselves accomplices in the crime.*

Nor dim nor red, like God's own head,
The glorious Sun uprist:
Then all averred, I had killed the bird
That brought the fog and mist.        100
'Twas right, said they, such birds to slay,
That bring the fog and mist.

*The fair breeze continues; the ship enters the Pacific Ocean, and sails northward, even till it reaches the Line.*

The fair breeze blew, the white foam flew,
The furrow followed free;
We were the first that ever burst
Into that silent sea.

*The ship hath*

Down dropt the breeze, the sails dropt down,
'Twas sad as sad could be;
And we did speak only to break
The silence of the sea!        110

been suddenly
becalmed.

All in a hot and copper sky,
The bloody Sun, at noon,
Right up above the mast did stand,
No bigger than the Moon.

Day after day, day after day,
We stuck, nor breath nor motion;
As idle as a painted ship
Upon a painted ocean.

And the Alba-
tross begins to
be avenged.

Water, water, every where,
And all the boards did shrink;                    120
Water, water, every where,
Nor any drop to drink.

The very deep did rot: O Christ!
That ever this should be!
Yea, slimy things did crawl with legs
Upon the slimy sea.

About, about, in reel and rout
The death-fires danced at night;
The water, like a witch's oils,
Burnt green, and blue and white.                  130

A Spirit had
followed them;
one of the in-
visible inhabit-
ants of this
planet, neither

And some in dreams assuréd were
Of the Spirit that plagued us so;
Nine fathom deep he had followed us
From the land of mist and snow.

departed souls nor angels; concerning whom the learned Jew, Josephus, and
the Platonic Constantinopolitan, Michael Psellus, may be consulted. They
are very numerous, and there is no climate or element without one or more.

And every tongue, through utter drought,
Was withered at the root;
We could not speak, no more than if
We had been choked with soot.

The shipmates,
in their sore

Ah! well a-day! what evil looks
Had I from old and young!                          140

distress, would
fain throw the
whole guilt on
the ancient

Instead of the cross, the Albatross
About my neck was hung.

Mariner: in sign whereof they hang the dead sea-bird round his neck.


### PART III

There passed a weary time. Each throat
Was parched, and glazed each eye.
A weary time! a weary time!
How glazed each weary eye,

The ancient
Mariner be-
holdeth a sign
in the element
afar off.

When looking westward, I beheld
A something in the sky.

At first it seemed a little speck,
And then it seemed a mist;        150
It moved and moved, and took at last
A certain shape, I wist.

A speck, a mist, a shape, I wist!
And still it neared and neared:
As if it dodged a water-sprite,
It plunged and tacked and veered.

At its nearer
approach, it
seemeth him
to be a ship;
and at a dear
ransom he
freeth his
speech from
the bonds of
thirst.
A flash of joy;

With throats unslaked, with black lips baked,
We could nor laugh nor wail;
Through utter drought all dumb we stood!
I bit my arm, I sucked the blood,    160
And cried, A sail! a sail!

With throats unslaked, with black lips baked,
Agape they heard me call:
Gramercy! they for joy did grin,
And all at once their breath drew in,
As they were drinking all.

And horror
follows. For
can it be a
ship that
comes onward

See! see! (I cried) she tacks no more!
Hither to work us weal;
Without a breeze, without a tide,
She steadies with upright keel!    170

without wind<br>or tide?

The western wave was all a-flame.
The day was well nigh done!
Almost upon the western wave
Rested the broad bright Sun;
When that strange shape drove suddenly
Betwixt us and the Sun.

It seemeth him<br>but the skeleton<br>of a ship.

And straight the Sun was flecked with bars,
(Heaven's Mother send us grace!)
As if through a dungeon-grate he peered
With broad and burning face.                    18c

And its ribs are<br>seen as bars on<br>the face of the<br>setting Sun.<br>The Spectre-<br>Woman and<br>her Death-<br>mate, and no<br>other on board<br>the skeleton<br>ship.

Alas! (thought I, and my heart beat loud)
How fast she nears and nears!
Are those *her* sails that glance in the Sun,
Like restless gossameres?

Are those *her* ribs through which the Sun
Did peer, as through a grate?
And is that Woman all her crew?
Is that a DEATH? and are there two?
Is DEATH that woman's mate?

Like vessel,<br>like crew!<br><br>Death and<br>Life-in-Death<br>have diced for<br>the ship's<br>crew, and she<br>(the latter)<br>winneth the<br>ancient<br>Mariner.

*Her* lips were red, *her* looks were free,     190
Her locks were yellow as gold:
Her skin was as white as leprosy,
The Night-mare LIFE-IN-DEATH was she,
Who thicks man's blood with cold.

The naked hulk alongside came,
And the twain were casting dice;
"The game is done! I've won! I've won!"
Quoth she, and whistles thrice.

No twilight<br>within the<br>courts of the<br>Sun.

The Sun's rim dips; the stars rush out:
At one stride comes the dark;                    200
With far-heard whisper, o'er the sea,
Off shot the spectre-bark.

| | |
|---|---|
| At the rising of the Moon, | We listened and looked sideways up!<br>Fear at my heart, as at a cup,<br>My life-blood seemed to sip!<br>The stars were dim, and thick the night,<br>The steersman's face by his lamp gleamed white;<br>From the sails the dew did drip—<br>Till clomb above the eastern bar<br>The hornéd Moon, with one bright star    210<br>Within the nether tip. |
| One after another, | One after one, by the star-dogged Moon,<br>Too quick for groan or sigh,<br>Each turned his face with a ghastly pang,<br>And cursed me with his eye. |
| His shipmates drop down dead. | Four times fifty living men,<br>(And I heard nor sigh nor groan)<br>With heavy thump, a lifeless lump,<br>They dropped down one by one. |
| But Life-in-Death begins her work on the ancient Mariner. | The souls did from their bodies fly,—    220<br>They fled to bliss or woe!<br>And every soul, it passed me by,<br>Like the whizz of my cross-bow! |

**PART IV**

| | |
|---|---|
| The Wedding-Guest feareth that a Spirit is talking to him; | "I fear thee, ancient Mariner!<br>I fear thy skinny hand!<br>And thou art long, and lank, and brown,<br>As is the ribbed sea-sand. |
| | I fear thee and thy glittering eye,<br>And thy skinny hand, so brown."— |
| But the ancient Mariner assureth him of his bodily life, and proceedeth to relate his horrible penance. | Fear not, fear not, thou Wedding-Guest!    230<br>This body dropt not down. |
| | Alone, alone, all, all alone,<br>Alone on a wide wide sea!<br>And never a saint took pity on<br>My soul in agony. |

He despiseth
the creatures of
the calm,

The many men, so beautiful!
And they all dead did lie:
And a thousand thousand slimy things
Lived on; and so did I.

And envieth
that *they*
should live,
and so many
lie dead.

I looked upon the rotting sea,                    240
And drew my eyes away;
I looked upon the rotting deck,
And there the dead men lay.

I looked to heaven, and tried to pray;
But or ever a prayer had gusht,
A wicked whisper came, and made
My heart as dry as dust.

I closed my lids, and kept them close,
And the balls like pulses beat;
For the sky and the sea, and the sea and the
    sky                                           250
Lay like a load on my weary eye,
And the dead were at my feet.

But the curse
liveth for him
in the eye of
the dead men.

The cold sweat melted from their limbs,
Nor rot nor reek did they:
The look with which they looked on me
Had never passed away.

An orphan's curse would drag to hell
A spirit from on high;
But oh! more horrible than that
Is the curse in a dead man's eye!                 260
Seven days, seven nights, I saw that curse,
And yet I could not die.

In his loneliness
and fixedness he
yearneth to-
wards the
journeying
Moon, and the
stars that still
sojourn, yet still

The moving Moon went up the sky,
And no where did abide:
Softly she was going up,
And a star or two beside—

Her beams bemocked the sultry main,
Like April hoar-frost spread;

move onward;
and every
where the blue
sky belongs to
them, and is

But where the ship's huge shadow lay,
The charméd water burnt alway                    270
A still and awful red.

their appointed rest, and their native country and their own natural homes,
which they enter unannounced, as lords that are certainly expected and yet
there is a silent joy at their arrival.

By the light of
the Moon he
beholdeth
God's creatures
of the great
calm.

Beyond the shadow of the ship,
I watched the water-snakes:
They moved in tracks of shining white,
And when they reared, the elfish light
Fell off in hoary flakes.

Within the shadow of the ship
I watched their rich attire:
Blue, glossy green, and velvet black,
They coiled and swam; and every track       280
Was a flash of golden fire.

Their beauty
and their
happiness.

He blesseth
them in his
heart.

O happy living things! no tongue
Their beauty might declare:
A spring of love gushed from my heart,
And I blessed them unaware:
Sure my kind saint took pity on me,
And I blessed them unaware.

The spell
begins to break.

The self-same moment I could pray;
And from my neck so free
The Albatross fell off, and sank                290
Like lead into the sea.

PART V

Oh sleep! it is a gentle thing,
Beloved from pole to pole!
To Mary Queen the praise be given!
She sent the gentle sleep from Heaven,
That slid into my soul.

By grace of the
holy Mother,
the ancient
Mariner is
refreshed with
rain.

The silly buckets on the deck,
That had so long remained,
I dreamt that they were filled with dew;
And when I awoke, it rained.                    300

My lips were wet, my throat was cold,
My garments all were dank;
Sure I had drunken in my dreams,
And still my body drank.

I moved, and could not feel my limbs:
I was so light—almost
I thought that I had died in sleep,
And was a blesséd ghost.

He heareth
sounds and
seeth strange
sights and
commotions in
the sky and the
element.

And soon I heard a roaring wind:
It did not come anear;                          310
But with its sound it shook the sails,
That were so thin and sere.

The upper air burst into life!
And a hundred fire-flags sheen,
To and fro they were hurried about!
And to and fro, and in and out,
The wan stars danced between.

And the coming wind did roar more loud,
And the sails did sigh like sedge;
And the rain poured down from one black
       cloud;                                   320
The Moon was at its edge.

The thick black cloud was cleft, and still
The Moon was at its side:
Like waters shot from some high crag,
The lightning fell with never a jag,
A river steep and wide.

The bodies of
the ship's crew

The loud wind never reached the ship,
Yet now the ship moved on!

are inspired
and the ship
moves on;

Beneath the lightning and the Moon
The dead men gave a groan.      330

They groaned, they stirred, they all uprose,
Nor spake, nor moved their eyes;
It had been strange, even in a dream,
To have seen those dead men rise.

The helmsman steered, the ship moved on;
Yet never a breeze up-blew;
The mariners all 'gan work the ropes,
Where they were wont to do;
They raised their limbs like lifeless tools—
We were a ghastly crew.      340

The body of my brother's son
Stood by me, knee to knee:
The body and I pulled at one rope,
But he said nought to me.

But not by the
souls of the
men, nor by
dæmons of
earth or middle
air, but by a
blessed troop of
angelic spirits,
sent down by
the invocation
of the guardian
saint.

"I fear thee, ancient Mariner!"
Be calm, thou Wedding-Guest!
'Twas not those souls that fled in pain,
Which to their corses came again,
But a troop of spirits blest:

For when it dawned—they dropped their
     arms,      350
And clustered round the mast;
Sweet sounds rose slowly through their mouths,
And from their bodies passed.

Around, around, flew each sweet sound,
Then darted to the Sun;
Slowly the sounds came back again,
Now mixed, now one by one.

Sometimes a-dropping from the sky
I heard the sky-lark sing;

Sometimes all little birds that are,     360
How they seemed to fill the sea and air
With their sweet jargoning!

And now 'twas like all instruments,
Now like a lonely flute;
And now it is an angel's song,
That makes the heavens be mute.

It ceased; yet still the sails made on
A pleasant noise till noon,
A noise like of a hidden brook
In the leafy month of June,     370
That to the sleeping woods all night
Singeth a quiet tune.

Till noon we quietly sailed on,
Yet never a breeze did breathe:
Slowly and smoothly went the ship,
Moved onward from beneath.

*The lonesome Spirit from the south-pole carries on the ship as far as the Line, in obedience to the angelic troop, but still requireth vengeance.*

Under the keel nine fathom deep,
From the land of mist and snow,
The spirit slid: and it was he
That made the ship to go.     380
The sails at noon left off their tune,
And the ship stood still also.

The Sun, right up above the mast,
Had fixed her to the ocean:
But in a minute she 'gan stir,
With a short uneasy motion—
Backwards and forwards half her length
With a short uneasy motion.

Then like a pawing horse let go,
She made a sudden bound:     390
It flung the blood into my head,
And I fell down in a swound.

The Polar
Spirit's fellow-
dæmons, the
invisible in-
habitants of the
element, take
part in his
wrong; and two
of them relate,
one to the other,
that penance
long and heavy
for the ancient
Mariner hath
been accorded
to the Polar
Spirit, who
returneth
southward.

How long in that same fit I lay,
I have not to declare;
But ere my living life returned,
I heard and in my soul discerned
Two voices in the air.

"Is it he?" quoth one, "Is this the man?
By him who died on cross,
With his cruel bow he laid full low          400
The harmless Albatross.

The spirit who bideth by himself
In the land of mist and snow,
He loved the bird that loved the man
Who shot him with his bow."

The other was a softer voice,
As soft as honey-dew:
Quoth he, "The man hath penance done,
And penance more will do."

### PART VI

#### FIRST VOICE

"But tell me, tell me! speak again,          410
Thy soft response renewing—
What makes that ship drive on so fast?
What is the ocean doing?"

#### SECOND VOICE

"Still as a slave before his lord,
The ocean hath no blast;
His great bright eye most silently
Up to the Moon is cast—

If he may know which way to go;
For she guides him smooth or grim.
See, brother, see! how graciously          420
She looketh down on him."

### FIRST VOICE

"But why drives on that ship so fast,
Without or wave or wind?"

> *The Mariner hath been cast into a trance; for the angelic power causeth the vessel to drive northward faster than human life could endure.*

### SECOND VOICE

"The air is cut away before,
And closes from behind.

Fly, brother, fly! more high, more high!
Or we shall be belated:
For slow and slow that ship will go,
When the Mariner's trance is abated."

> *The supernatural motion is retarded; the Mariner awakes, and his penance begins anew.*

I woke, and we were sailing on                    430
As in a gentle weather:
'Twas night, calm night, the moon was high;
The dead men stood together.

All stood together on the deck,
For a charnel-dungeon fitter:
All fixed on me their stony eyes,
That in the Moon did glitter.

The pang, the curse, with which they died,
Had never passed away:
I could not draw my eyes from theirs,            440
Nor turn them up to pray.

> *The curse is finally expiated.*

And now this spell was snapt: once more
I viewed the ocean green,
And looked far forth, yet little saw
Of what had else been seen—

Like one, that on a lonesome road
Doth walk in fear and dread,
And having once turned round walks on,
And turns no more his head;
Because he knows, a frightful fiend            450
Doth close behind him tread.

But soon there breathed a wind on me,
Nor sound nor motion made:
Its path was not upon the sea,
In ripple or in shade.

It raised my hair, it fanned my cheek
Like a meadow-gale of spring—
It mingled strangely with my fears,
Yet it felt like a welcoming.

Swiftly, swiftly flew the ship,                    460
Yet she sailed softly too:
Sweetly, sweetly blew the breeze—
On me alone it blew.

And the ancient
Mariner be-
holdeth his na-
tive country.

Oh! dream of joy! is this indeed
The light-house top I see?
Is this the hill? is this the kirk?
Is this mine own countree?

We drifted o'er the harbour-bar,
And I with sobs did pray—
O let me be awake, my God!                    470
Or let me sleep alway.

The harbour-bay was clear as glass,
So smoothly it was strewn!
And on the bay the moonlight lay,
And the shadow of the Moon.

The rock shone bright, the kirk no less,
That stands above the rock:
The moonlight steeped in silentness
The steady weathercock.

And the bay was white with silent light,    480
Till rising from the same,
Full many shapes, that shadows were,
In crimson colours came.

The angelic
spirits leave

the dead bodies,
And appear in
their own
forms of light.

A little distance from the prow
Those crimson shadows were:
I turned my eyes upon the deck—
Oh, Christ! what saw I there!

Each corse lay flat, lifeless and flat,
And, by the holy rood!
A man all light, a seraph-man, 490
On every corse there stood.

This seraph-band, each waved his hand:
It was a heavenly sight!
They stood as signals to the land,
Each one a lovely light;

This seraph-band, each waved his hand,
No voice did they impart—
No voice; but oh! the silence sank
Like music on my heart.

But soon I heard the dash of oars, 500
I heard the Pilot's cheer;
My head was turned perforce away
And I saw a boat appear.

The Pilot and the Pilot's boy,
I heard them coming fast:
Dear Lord in Heaven! it was a joy
The dead men could not blast.

I saw a third—I heard his voice:
It is the Hermit good!
He singeth loud his godly hymns 510
That he makes in the wood.
He'll shrieve my soul, he'll wash away
The Albatross's blood.

PART VII

<table>
<tr><td>The Hermit of<br>the Wood,</td><td>This Hermit good lives in that wood<br>Which slopes down to the sea.<br>How loudly his sweet voice he rears!<br>He loves to talk with marineres<br>That come from a far countree.</td><td></td></tr>
</table>

He kneels at morn, and noon, and eve—
He hath a cushion plump:                        520
It is the moss that wholly hides
The rotted old oak-stump.

The skiff-boat neared: I heard them talk,
"Why, this is strange, I trow!
Where are those lights so many and fair,
That signal made but now?"

Approacheth
the ship with
wonder.

"Strange, by my faith!" the Hermit said—
"And they answered not our cheer!
The planks looked warped! and see those sails,
How thin they are and sere!                     530
I never saw aught like to them,
Unless perchance it were

Brown skeletons of leaves that lag
My forest-brook along;
When the ivy-tod is heavy with snow,
And the owlet whoops to the wolf below,
That eats the she-wolf's young."

"Dear Lord! it hath a fiendish look—
(The Pilot made reply)
I am a-feared"—"Push on, push on!"            540
Said the Hermit cheerily.

The boat came closer to the ship,
But I nor spake nor stirred;
The boat came close beneath the ship,
And straight a sound was heard.

The ship
suddenly
sinketh.

Under the water it rumbled on,
Still louder and more dread:
It reached the ship, it split the bay;
The ship went down like lead.

The ancient
Mariner is
saved in the
Pilot's boat.

Stunned by that loud and dreadful sound,        550
Which sky and ocean smote,
Like one that hath been seven days drowned
My body lay afloat;
But swift as dreams, myself I found
Within the Pilot's boat.

Upon the whirl, where sank the ship,
The boat spun round and round;
And all was still, save that the hill
Was telling of the sound.

I moved my lips—the Pilot shrieked        560
And fell down in a fit;
The holy Hermit raised his eyes,
And prayed where he did sit.

I took the oars: the Pilot's boy,
Who now doth crazy go,
Laughed loud and long, and all the while
His eyes went to and fro.
"Ha! ha!" quoth he, "full plain I see,
The Devil knows how to row."

And now, all in my own countree,        570
I stood on the firm land!
The Hermit stepped forth from the boat,
And scarcely he could stand.

The ancient
Mariner
earnestly en-
treateth the
Hermit to

"O shrieve me, shrieve me, holy man!"
The Hermit crossed his brow.
"Say quick," quoth he, "I bid thee say—
What manner of man art thou?"

shrieve him;
and the penance
of life falls on
him.

Forthwith this frame of mine was wrenched
With a woful agony,
Which forced me to begin my tale;                    580
And then it left me free.

And ever and
anon through-
out his future
life an agony
constraineth
him to travel
from land to
land;

Since then, at an uncertain hour,
That agony returns:
And till my ghastly tale is told,
This heart within me burns.

I pass, like night, from land to land;
I have strange power of speech;
That moment that his face I see,
I know the man that must hear me:
To him my tale I teach.                    590

What loud uproar bursts from that door!
The wedding-guests are there:
But in the garden-bower the bride
And bride-maids singing are:
And hark the little vesper bell,
Which biddeth me to prayer!

O Wedding-Guest! this soul hath been
Alone on a wide wide sea:
So lonely 'twas, that God himself
Scarce seeméd there to be.                    600

O sweeter than the marriage-feast,
'Tis sweeter far to me,
To walk together to the kirk
With a goodly company!—

To walk together to the kirk,
And all together pray,
While each to his great Father bends,
Old men, and babes, and loving friends
And youths and maidens gay!

And to teach,
by his own
example, love
and reverence
to all things
that God made
and loveth.

Farewell, farewell! but this I tell        610
To thee, thou Wedding-Guest!
He prayeth well, who loveth well
Both man and bird and beast.

He prayeth best, who loveth best
All things both great and small;
For the dear God who loveth us,
He made and loveth all.

The Mariner, whose eye is bright,
Whose beard with age is hoar,
Is gone: and now the Wedding-Guest        620
Turned from the bridegroom's door.

He went like one that hath been stunned,
And is of sense forlorn:
A sadder and a wiser man,
He rose the morrow morn.

1797–1798.                                 1798.

# CHRISTABEL

PREFACE

The first part of the following poem was written in the year 1797, at Stowey, in the county of Somerset. The second part, after my return from Germany, in the year 1800, at Keswick, Cumberland. It is probable that if the poem had been finished at either of the former periods, or if even the first and second part had been published in the year 1800, the impression of its originality would have been much greater than I dare at present expect. But for this I have only my own indolence to blame. The dates are mentioned for the exclusive purpose of precluding charges of plagiarism or servile imitation from myself. For there is amongst us a set of critics, who seem to hold, that every possible thought and image is traditional; who have no notion that there are such things as fountains in the world, small as well as great; and who would therefore charitably derive every rill they behold flowing, from a perforation made in some other man's tank. I am confident, however, that as far as the present poem is concerned, the celebrated poets whose writings I might be suspected of having imitated, either in particular passages, or in the tone and the spirit of the whole, would be among the first to vindicate me from the charge, and who, on any striking coincidence, would permit me to address them in this doggerel version of two monkish Latin hexameters.

> 'Tis mine and it is likewise yours;
> But an if this will not do;
> Let it be mine, good friend! for I
> Am the poorer of the two.

I have only to add that the metre of Christabel is not, properly speaking, irregular, though it may seem so from its being founded on a new principle: namely, that of counting in each line the accents, not the syllables. Though the latter may vary from seven to twelve, yet in each line the accents will be found to be only four. Nevertheless, this occasional variation in number of syllables is not introduced wantonly, or for the mere ends of convenience, but in correspondence with some transition in the nature of the imagery or passion.

## PART I

'Tis the middle of night by the castle clock,
And the owls have awakened the crowing cock;

Tu—whit!——Tu—whoo!
And hark, again! the crowing cock,
How drowsily it crew.

Sir Leoline, the Baron rich,
Hath a toothless mastiff bitch;
From her kennel beneath the rock
She maketh answer to the clock,
Four for the quarters, and twelve for the hour;          10
Ever and aye, by shine and shower,
Sixteen short howls, not over loud;
Some say, she sees my lady's shroud.

Is the night chilly and dark?
The night is chilly, but not dark.
The thin gray cloud is spread on high,
It covers but not hides the sky.
The moon is behind, and at the full;
And yet she looks both small and dull.
The night is chill, the cloud is gray:          20
'Tis a month before the month of May,
And the Spring comes slowly up this way.

The lovely lady, Christabel,
Whom her father loves so well,
What makes her in the wood so late,
A furlong from the castle gate?
She had dreams all yesternight
Of her own betrothéd knight;
And she in the midnight wood will pray
For the weal of her lover that's far away.          30

She stole along, she nothing spoke,
The sighs she heaved were soft and low,
And naught was green upon the oak
But moss and rarest mistletoe:
She kneels beneath the huge oak tree,
And in silence prayeth she.

The lady sprang up suddenly,
The lovely lady, Christabel!
It moaned as near, as near can be,
But what it is she cannot tell.—                    40
On the other side it seems to be,
Of the huge, broad-breasted, old oak tree.

The night is chill; the forest bare;
Is it the wind that moaneth bleak?
There is not wind enough in the air
To move away the ringlet curl
From the lovely lady's cheek—
There is not wind enough to twirl
The one red leaf, the last of its clan,
That dances as often as dance it can,               50
Hanging so light, and hanging so high,
On the topmost twig that looks up at the sky.

Hush, beating heart of Christabel!
Jesu, Maria, shield her well!
She folded her arms beneath her cloak,
And stole to the other side of the oak.
        What sees she there?

There she sees a damsel bright,
Drest in a silken robe of white,
That shadowy in the moonlight shone:               60
The neck that made that white robe wan,
Her stately neck, and arms were bare;
Her blue-veined feet unsandal'd were,
And wildly glittered here and there
The gems entangled in her hair.
I guess, 'twas frightful there to see
A lady so richly clad as she—
Beautiful exceedingly!

Mary mother, save me now!
(Said Christabel,) And who art thou?               70

The lady strange made answer meet,
And her voice was faint and sweet:—
Have pity on my sore distress,
I scarce can speak for weariness:
Stretch forth thy hand, and have no fear!
Said Christabel, How camest thou here?
And the lady, whose voice was faint and sweet,
Did thus pursue her answer meet:—

My sire is of a noble line,
And my name is Geraldine:                         80
Five warriors seized me yestermorn,
Me, even me, a maid forlorn:
They choked my cries with force and fright,
And tied me on a palfrey white.
The palfrey was as fleet as wind,
And they rode furiously behind.
They spurred amain, their steeds were white:
And once we crossed the shade of night.
As sure as Heaven shall rescue me,
I have no thought what men they be;               90
Nor do I know how long it is
(For I have lain entranced I wis)
Since one, the tallest of the five,
Took me from the palfrey's back,
A weary woman, scarce alive.
Some muttered words his comrades spoke:
He placed me underneath this oak;
He swore they would return with haste;
Whither they went I cannot tell—
I thought I heard, some minutes past,             100
Sounds as of a castle bell.
Stretch forth thy hand (thus ended she),
And help a wretched maid to flee.

Then Christabel stretched forth her hand,
And comforted fair Geraldine:

O well, bright dame! may you command
The service of Sir Leoline;
And gladly our stout chivalry
Will he send forth and friends withal
To guide and guard you safe and free                110
Home to your noble father's hall.

She rose: and forth with steps they passed
That strove to be, and were not, fast.
Her gracious stars the lady blest,
And thus spake on sweet Christabel:
All our household are at rest,
The hall as silent as the cell;
Sir Leoline is weak in health,
And may not well awakened be,
But we will move as if in stealth,                120
And I beseech your courtesy,
This night, to share your couch with me.

They crossed the moat, and Christabel
Took the key that fitted well;
A little door she opened straight,
All in the middle of the gate;
The gate that was ironed within and without,
Where an army in battle array had marched out.
The lady sank, belike through pain,
And Christabel with might and main                130
Lifted her up, a weary weight,
Over the threshold of the gate:
Then the lady rose again,
And moved, as she were not in pain.

So free from danger, free from fear,
They crossed the court: right glad they were.
And Christabel devoutly cried
To the lady by her side,
Praise we the Virgin all divine
Who hath rescued thee from thy distress!                140
Alas, alas! said Geraldine,

I cannot speak for weariness.
So free from danger, free from fear,
They crossed the court: right glad they were.

Outside her kennel, the mastiff old
Lay fast asleep, in moonshine cold.
The mastiff old did not awake,
Yet she an angry moan did make!
And what can ail the mastiff bitch?
Never till now she uttered yell                          150
Beneath the eye of Christabel.
Perhaps it is the owlet's scritch:
For what can ail the mastiff bitch?

They passed the hall that echoes still,
Pass as lightly as you will!
The brands were flat, the brands were dying,
Amid their own white ashes lying;
But when the lady passed, there came
A tongue of light, a fit of flame;
And Christabel saw the lady's eye,                       160
And nothing else saw she thereby,
Save the boss of the shield of Sir Leoline tall,
Which hung in a murky old niche in the wall.
O softly tread, said Christabel,
My father seldom sleepeth well.

Sweet Christabel her feet doth bare,
And jealous of the listening air
They steal their way from stair to stair,
Now in glimmer, and now in gloom,
And now they pass the Baron's room,                      170
As still as death, with stifled breath!
And now have reached her chamber door;
And now doth Geraldine press down
The rushes of the chamber floor.

The moon shines dim in the open air,
And not a moonbeam enters here.

But they without its light can see
The chamber carved so curiously,
Carved with figures strange and sweet,
All made out of the carver's brain,                    180
For a lady's chamber meet:
The lamp with twofold silver chain
Is fastened to an angel's feet.

The silver lamp burns dead and dim;
But Christabel the lamp will trim.
She trimmed the lamp, and made it bright,
And left it swinging to and fro,
While Geraldine, in wretched plight,
Sank down upon the floor below.

O weary lady, Geraldine,                               190
I pray you, drink this cordial wine!
It is a wine of virtuous powers;
My mother made it of wild flowers.

And will your mother pity me,
Who am a maiden most forlorn?
Christabel answered—Woe is me!
She died the hour that I was born.
I have heard the grey-haired friar tell
How on her death-bed she did say,
That she should hear the castle-bell                   200
Strike twelve upon my wedding-day.
O mother dear! that thou wert here!
I would, said Geraldine, she were!

But soon with altered voice, said she—
"Off, wandering mother! Peak and pine!
I have power to bid thee flee."
Alas! what ails poor Geraldine?
Why stares she with unsettled eye?
Can she the bodiless dead espy?
And why with hollow voice cries she,                   210
"Off, woman, off! this hour is mine—

Though thou her guardian spirit be,
Off, woman, off! 'tis given to me."

Then Christabel knelt by the lady's side,
And raised to heaven her eyes so blue—
Alas! said she, this ghastly ride—
Dear lady! it hath wildered you!
The lady wiped her moist cold brow,
And faintly said, " 'tis over now!"

Again the wild-flower wine she drank:            220
Her fair large eyes 'gan glitter bright,
And from the floor whereon she sank,
The lofty lady stood upright:
She was most beautiful to see,
Like a lady of a far countrée.

And thus the lofty lady spake—
"All they who live in the upper sky,
Do love you, holy Christabel!
And you love them, and for their sake
And for the good which me befel,            230
Even I in my degree will try,
Fair maiden, to requite you well.
But now unrobe yourself; for I
Must pray, ere yet in bed I lie."

Quoth Christabel, So let it be!
And as the lady bade, did she.
Her gentle limbs did she undress,
And lay down in her loveliness.

But through her brain of weal and woe
So many thoughts moved to and fro,            240
That vain it were her lids to close;
So half-way from the bed she rose,
And on her elbow did recline
To look at the lady Geraldine.

Beneath the lamp the lady bowed,
And slowly rolled her eyes around;

Then drawing in her breath aloud,
Like one that shuddered, she unbound
The cincture from beneath her breast:
Her silken robe, and inner vest,                               250
Dropt to her feet, and full in view,
Behold! her bosom and half her side——
A sight to dream of, not to tell!
O shield her! shield sweet Christabel!

Yet Geraldine nor speaks nor stirs;
Ah! what a stricken look was hers!
Deep from within she seems half-way
To lift some weight with sick assay,
And eyes the maid and seeks delay;
Then suddenly, as one defied,                                  260
Collects herself in scorn and pride,
And lay down by the Maiden's side!—
And in her arms the maid she took,
          Ah wel-a-day!
And with low voice and doleful look
These words did say:
"In the touch of this bosom there worketh a spell,
Which is lord of thy utterance, Christabel!
Thou knowest to-night, and wilt know to-morrow,
This mark of my shame, this seal of my sorrow;                 270
          But vainly thou warrest,
            For this is alone in
          Thy power to declare,
            That in the dim forest
          Thou heard'st a low moaning,
And found'st a bright lady, surpassingly fair;
And didst bring her home with thee in love and in charity,
To shield her and shelter her from the damp air."

### THE CONCLUSION TO PART I

It was a lovely sight to see
The lady Christabel, when she 280
Was praying at the old oak tree.
    Amid the jaggéd shadows
    Of mossy leafless boughs,
    Kneeling in the moonlight,
    To make her gentle vows;
Her slender palms together prest,
Heaving sometimes on her breast;
Her face resigned to bliss or bale—
Her face, oh call it fair not pale,
And both blue eyes more bright than clear, 290
Each about to have a tear.

With open eyes (ah woe is me!)
Asleep, and dreaming fearfully,
Fearfully dreaming, yet, I wis,
Dreaming that alone, which is—
O sorrow and shame! Can this be she,
The lady, who knelt at the old oak tree?
And lo! the worker of these harms,
That holds the maiden in her arms,
Seems to slumber still and mild, 300
As a mother with her child.

A star hath set, a star hath risen,
O Geraldine! since arms of thine
Have been the lovely lady's prison.
O Geraldine! one hour was thine—
Thou'st had thy will! By tairn and rill,
The night-birds all that hour were still.
But now they are jubilant anew,
From cliff and tower, tu—whoo! tu—whoo!
Tu—whoo! tu—whoo! from wood and fell! 310

And see! the lady Christabel
Gathers herself from out her trance;
Her limbs relax, her countenance
Grows sad and soft; the smooth thin lids
Close o'er her eyes; and tears she sheds—
Large tears that leave the lashes bright!
And oft the while she seems to smile
As infants at a sudden light!

Yea, she doth smile, and she doth weep,
Like a youthful hermitess,                                            320
Beauteous in a wilderness,
Who, praying always, prays in sleep.
And, if she move unquietly,
Perchance, 'tis but the blood so free
Comes back and tingles in her feet.
No doubt, she hath a vision sweet.
What if her guardian spirit 'twere,
What if she knew her mother near?
But this she knows, in joys and woes,
That saints will aid if men will call:                                330
For the blue sky bends over all!


### PART II

Each matin bell, the Baron saith,
Knells us back to a world of death.
These words Sir Leoline first said,
When he rose and found his lady dead:
These words Sir Leoline will say
Many a morn to his dying day!

And hence the custom and law began
That still at dawn the sacristan,
Who duly pulls the heavy bell,                                        340
Five and forty beads must tell
Between each stroke—a warning knell,
Which not a soul can choose but hear
From Bratha Head to Wyndermere.

Saith Bracy the bard, So let it knell!
And let the drowsy sacristan
Still count as slowly as he can!
There is no lack of such, I ween,
As well fill up the space between.
In Langdale Pike and Witch's Lair,                    350
And Dungeon-ghyll so foully rent,
With ropes of rock and bells of air
Three sinful sextons' ghosts are pent,
Who all give back, one after t'other,
The death-note to their living brother;
And oft too, by the knell offended,
Just as their one! two! three! is ended,
The devil mocks the doleful tale
With a merry peal from Borodale.

The air is still! through mist and cloud               360
That merry peal comes ringing loud;
And Geraldine shakes off her dread,
And rises lightly from the bed;
Puts on her silken vestments white,
And tricks her hair in lovely plight,
And nothing doubting of her spell
Awakens the lady Christabel.
"Sleep you, sweet lady Christabel?
I trust that you have rested well."

And Christabel awoke and spied                         370
The same who lay down by her side—
O rather say, the same whom she
Raised up beneath the old oak tree!
Nay, fairer yet! and yet more fair!
For she belike hath drunken deep
Of all the blessedness of sleep!
And while she spake, her looks, her air
Such gentle thankfulness declare,
That (so it seemed) her girded vests
Grew tight beneath her heaving breasts.                380

"Sure I have sinn'd!" said Christabel,
"Now heaven be praised if all be well!"
And in low faltering tones, yet sweet,
Did she the lofty lady greet
With such perplexity of mind
As dreams too lively leave behind.

So quickly she rose, and quickly arrayed
Her maiden limbs, and having prayed
That He, who on the cross did groan,
Might wash away her sins unknown,                   390
She forthwith led fair Geraldine
To meet her sire, Sir Leoline.

The lovely maid and the lady tall
Are pacing both into the hall,
And pacing on through page and groom,
Enter the Baron's presence-room.

The Baron rose, and while he prest
His gentle daughter to his breast,
With cheerful wonder in his eyes
The lady Geraldine espies,                          400
And gave such welcome to the same,
As might beseem so bright a dame!

But when he heard the lady's tale,
And when she told her father's name,
Why waxed Sir Leoline so pale,
Murmuring o'er the name again,
Lord Roland de Vaux of Tryermaine?

Alas! they had been friends in youth;
But whispering tongues can poison truth;
And constancy lives in realms above;                410
And life is thorny; and youth is vain;
And to be wroth with one we love
Doth work like madness in the brain.
And thus it chanced, as I divine,
With Roland and Sir Leoline.

Each spake words of high disdain
And insult to his heart's best brother:
They parted—ne'er to meet again!
But never either found another
To free the hollow heart from paining— 420
They stood aloof, the scars remaining,
Like cliffs which had been rent asunder;
A dreary sea now flows between;—
But neither heat, nor frost, nor thunder,
Shall wholly do away, I ween,
The marks of that which once hath been.

Sir Leoline, a moment's space,
Stood gazing on the damsel's face:
And the youthful Lord of Tryermaine
Came back upon his heart again. 430

O then the Baron forgot his age,
His noble heart swelled high with rage;
He swore by the wounds in Jesu's side
He would proclaim it far and wide,
With trump and solemn heraldry,
That they, who thus had wronged the dame,
Were base as spotted infamy!
"And if they dare deny the same,
My herald shall appoint a week,
And let the recreant traitors seek 440
My tourney court—that there and then
I may dislodge their reptile souls
From the bodies and forms of men!"
He spake: his eye in lightning rolls!
For the lady was ruthlessly seized; and he kenned
In the beautiful lady the child of his friend!

And now the tears were on his face,
And fondly in his arms he took
Fair Geraldine, who met the embrace,
Prolonging it with joyous look. 450
Which when she viewed, a vision fell

Upon the soul of Christabel,
The vision of fear, the touch and pain!
She shrunk and shuddered, and saw again—
(Ah, woe is me! Was it for thee,
Thou gentle maid! such sights to see?)

Again she saw that bosom old,
Again she felt that bosom cold,
And drew in her breath with a hissing sound:
Whereat the Knight turned wildly round,                          460
And nothing saw, but his own sweet maid
With eyes upraised, as one that prayed.

The touch, the sight, had passed away,
And in its stead that vision blest,
Which comforted her after-rest
While in the lady's arms she lay,
Had put a rapture in her breast,
And on her lips and o'er her eyes
Spread smiles like light!
                                   With new surprise,
"What ails then my belovéd child?"                              470
The Baron said—His daughter mild
Made answer, "All will yet be well!"
I ween, she had no power to tell
Aught else: so mighty was the spell.

Yet he, who saw this Geraldine,
Had deemed her sure a thing divine:
Such sorrow with such grace she blended,
As if she feared she had offended
Sweet Christabel, that gentle maid!
And with such lowly tones she prayed                            480
She might be sent without delay
Home to her father's mansion.
                                   "Nay!
Nay, by my soul!" said Leoline.
"Ho! Bracy the bard, the charge be thine!

Go thou, with music sweet and loud,
And take two steeds with trappings proud,
And take the youth whom thou lov'st best
To bear thy harp, and learn thy song,
And clothe you both in solemn vest,
And over the mountains haste along, 490
Lest wandering folk, that are abroad,
Detain you on the valley road.

"And when he has crossed the Irthing flood,
My merry bard! he hastes, he hastes
Up Knorren Moor, through Halegarth Wood,
And reaches soon that castle good
Which stands and threatens Scotland's wastes.

"Bard Bracy! bard Bracy! your horses are fleet,
Ye must ride up the hall, your music so sweet,
More loud than your horses' echoing feet! 500
And loud and loud to Lord Roland call,
Thy daughter is safe in Langdale hall!
Thy beautiful daughter is safe and free—
Sir Leoline greets thee thus through me!
He bids thee come without delay
With all thy numerous array
And take thy lovely daughter home:
And he will meet thee on the way
With all his numerous array
White with their panting palfreys' foam: 510
And, by mine honour! I will say,
That I repent me of the day
When I spake words of fierce disdain
To Roland de Vaux of Tryermaine!—
—For since that evil hour hath flown,
Many a summer's sun hath shone;
Yet ne'er found I a friend again
Like Roland de Vaux of Tryermaine.

The lady fell, and clasped his knees,
Her face upraised, her eyes o'erflowing; 520

And Bracy replied, with faltering voice,
His gracious Hail on all bestowing!—
"Thy words, thou sire of Christabel,
Are sweeter than my harp can tell;
Yet might I gain a boon of thee,
This day my journey should not be,
So strange a dream hath come to me,
That I had vowed with music loud
To clear yon wood from thing unblest,
Warned by a vision in my rest!            530
For in my sleep I saw that dove,
That gentle bird, whom thou dost love,
And call'st by thy own daughter's name—
Sir Leoline! I saw the same
Fluttering, and uttering fearful moan,
Among the green herbs in the forest alone.
Which when I saw and when I heard,
I wonder'd what might ail the bird;
For nothing near it could I see,
Save the grass and green herbs underneath the old tree.   540

"And in my dream methought I went
To search out what might there be found;
And what the sweet bird's trouble meant,
That thus lay fluttering on the ground.
I went and peered, and could descry
No cause for her distressful cry;
But yet for her dear lady's sake
I stooped, methought, the dove to take,
When lo! I saw a bright green snake
Coiled around its wings and neck.             550
Green as the herbs on which it couched,
Close by the dove's its head it crouched;
And with the dove it heaves and stirs,
Swelling its neck as she swelled hers!
I woke; it was the midnight hour,
The clock was echoing in the tower;
But though my slumber was gone by,

This dream it would not pass away--
It seems to live upon my eye!
And thence I vowed this self-same day 560
With music strong and saintly song
To wander through the forest bare,
Lest aught unholy loiter there."

Thus Bracy said: the Baron, the while,
Half-listening heard him with a smile;
Then turned to Lady Geraldine,
His eyes made up of wonder and love;
And said in courtly accents fine,
"Sweet maid, Lord Roland's beauteous dove,
With arms more strong than harp or song, 570
Thy sire and I will crush the snake!"
He kissed her forehead as he spake,
And Geraldine in maiden wise
Casting down her large bright eyes,
With blushing cheek and courtesy fine
She turned her from Sir Leoline;
Softly gathering up her train,
That o'er her right arm fell again;
And folded her arms across her chest,
And couched her head upon her breast, 580
And looked askance at Christabel——
Jesu, Maria, shield her well!

A snake's small eye blinks dull and shy;
And the lady's eyes they shrunk in her head,
Each shrunk up to a serpent's eye,
And with somewhat of malice, and more of dread,
At Christabel she looked askance!—
One moment—and the sight was fled!
But Christabel in dizzy trance
Stumbling on the unsteady ground 590
Shuddered aloud, with a hissing sound;
And Geraldine again turned round,
And like a thing, that sought relief,

Full of wonder and full of grief,
She rolled her large bright eyes divine
Wildly on Sir Leoline.

The maid, alas! her thoughts are gone,
She nothing sees—no sight but one!
The maid, devoid of guile and sin,
I know not how, in fearful wise,                                    600
So deeply had she drunken in
That look, those shrunken serpent eyes,
That all her features were resigned
To this sole image in her mind:
And passively did imitate
That look of dull and treacherous hate!
And thus she stood, in dizzy trance,
Still picturing that look askance
With forced unconscious sympathy
Full before her father's view——                                    610
As far as such a look could be
In eyes so innocent and blue!

And when the trance was o'er, the maid
Paused awhile, and inly prayed:
Then falling at the Baron's feet,
"By my mother's soul do I entreat
That thou this woman send away!"
She said: and more she could not say:
For what she knew she could not tell,
O'er-mastered by the mighty spell.                                  620

Why is thy cheek so wan and wild,
Sir Leoline? Thy only child
Lies at thy feet, thy joy, thy pride,
So fair, so innocent, so mild;
The same, for whom thy lady died!
O by the pangs of her dear mother
Think thou no evil of thy child!
For her, and thee, and for no other,
She prayed the moment ere she died:

Prayed that the babe for whom she died, 630
Might prove her dear lord's joy and pride!
   That prayer her deadly pangs beguiled,
      Sir Leoline!
   And wouldst thou wrong thy only child,
      Her child and thine?

Within the Baron's heart and brain
If thoughts, like these, had any share,
They only swelled his rage and pain,
And did but work confusion there.
His heart was cleft with pain and rage, 640
His cheeks they quivered, his eyes were wild,
Dishonoured thus in his old age;
Dishonoured by his only child,
And all his hospitality
To the wronged daughter of his friend
By more than woman's jealousy
Brought thus to a disgraceful end—
He rolled his eye with stern regard
Upon the gentle minstrel bard,
And said in tones abrupt, austere— 650
"Why, Bracy! dost thou loiter here?
I bade thee hence!" The bard obeyed;
And turning from his own sweet maid,
The agéd knight, Sir Leoline,
Led forth the lady Geraldine!

### THE CONCLUSION TO PART II

A little child, a limber elf,
Singing, dancing to itself,
A fairy thing with red round cheeks,
That always finds, and never seeks,
Makes such a vision to the sight 660
As fills a father's eyes with light;

And pleasures flow in so thick and fast
Upon his heart, that he at last
Must needs express his love's excess
With words of unmeant bitterness.
Perhaps 'tis pretty to force together
Thoughts so all unlike each other;
To mutter and mock a broken charm,
To dally with wrong that does no harm.
Perhaps 'tis tender too and pretty                      670
At each wild word to feel within
A sweet recoil of love and pity.
And what, if in a world of sin
(O sorrow and shame should this be true!)
Such giddiness of heart and brain
Comes seldom save from rage and pain,
So talks as it's most used to do.
? 1797–1801.

1816.

# LINES TO W. L.

❧❧

### WHILE HE SANG A SONG TO PURCELL'S MUSIC

While my young cheek retains its healthful hues,
    And I have many friends who hold me dear,
    L——! methinks, I would not often hear
Such melodies as thine, lest I should lose
All memory of the wrongs and sore distress
    For which my miserable brethren weep!
    But should uncomforted misfortunes steep
My daily bread in tears and bitterness;
And if at Death's dread moment I should lie
    With no belovéd face at my bed-side,
To fix the last glance of my closing eye,
    Methinks such strains, breathed by my angel-guide,

Would make me pass the cup of anguish by,
  Mix with the blest, nor know that I had died!
1797.                                 1800.

# FIRE, FAMINE, AND SLAUGHTER

### A WAR ECLOGUE

*The Scene a desolated Tract in La Vendée.* FAMINE *is discovered lying on
the ground; to her enter* FIRE *and* SLAUGHTER.

FAMINE.   Sisters! sisters! who sent you here?
SLAUGHTER. [*to* FIRE].   I will whisper it in her ear.
FIRE.   No! no! no!
Spirits hear what spirits tell:
'Twill make a holiday in Hell.
      No! no! no!
Myself, I named him once below,
And all the souls, that damnéd be,
Leaped up at once in anarchy,
Clapped their hands and danced for glee.           10
They no longer heeded me;
But laughed to hear Hell's burning rafters
Unwillingly re-echo laughters!
      No! no! no!
Spirits hear what spirits tell:
'Twill make a holiday in Hell!
FAMINE.   Whisper it, sister! so and so!
In a dark hint, soft and slow.
SLAUGHTER.   Letters four do form his name—
And who sent you?
BOTH.           The same! the same!         20
SLAUGHTER. He came by stealth, and unlocked my den,
And I have drunk the blood since then
Of thrice three hundred thousand men.

BOTH.   Who bade you do't?

SLAUGHTER.                    The same! the same!

Letters four do form his name.

He let me loose, and cried Halloo!

To him alone the praise is due.

FAMINE.   Thanks, sister, thanks! the men have bled,

Their wives and their children faint for bread.

I stood in a swampy field of battle;                          30

With bones and skulls I made a rattle,

To frighten the wolf and carrion-crow

And the homeless dog—but they would not go.

So off I flew: for how could I bear

To see them gorge their dainty fare?

I heard a groan and a peevish squall,

And through the chink of a cottage-wall—

Can you guess what I saw there?

BOTH.   Whisper it, sister! in our ear.

FAMINE.   A baby beat its dying mother:                       40

I had starved the one and was starving the other!

BOTH.   Who bade you do't?

FAMINE.                    The same! the same!

Letters four do form his name.

He let me loose, and cried, Halloo!

To him alone the praise is due.

FIRE.   Sisters! I from Ireland came!

Hedge and corn-fields all on flame,

I triumph'd o'er the setting sun!

And all the while the work was done,

On as I strode with my huge strides,                          50

I flung back my head and I held my sides,

It was so rare a piece of fun

To see the sweltered cattle run

With uncouth gallop through the night,

Scared by the red and noisy light!

By the light of his own blazing cot

Was many a naked Rebel shot:

The house-stream met the flame and hissed,

While crash! fell in the roof, I wist,
On some of those old bed-rid nurses, 60
That deal in discontent and curses.

   BOTH.   Who bade you do't?

   FIRE.                The same! the same!

Letters four do form his name.
He let me loose, and cried Halloo!
To him alone the praise is due.

   ALL.   He let us loose, and cried Halloo!

How shall we yield him honour due?

   FAMINE.   Wisdom comes with lack of food.

I'll gnaw, I'll gnaw the multitude,
Till the cup of rage o'erbrim: 70
They shall seize him and his brood—

   SLAUGHTER.   They shall tear him limb from limb!

   FIRE.   O thankless beldames and untrue!

And is this all that you can do
For him, who did so much for you?
Ninety months he, by my troth!
Hath richly catered for you both;
And in an hour would you repay
An eight years' work?—Away! away!
I alone am faithful! I 80
Cling to him everlastingly.

? 1798. 1798.

# FROST AT MIDNIGHT

The Frost performs its secret ministry,
Unhelped by any wind. The owlet's cry
Came loud—and hark, again! loud as before.
The inmates of my cottage, all at rest,
Have left me to that solitude, which suits
Abstruser musings: save that at my side
My cradled infant slumbers peacefully.

'Tis calm indeed! so calm, that it disturbs
And vexes meditation with its strange
And extreme silentness. Sea, hill, and wood,                    10
This populous village! Sea, and hill, and wood,
With all the numberless goings-on of life,
Inaudible as dreams! the thin blue flame
Lies on my low-burnt fire, and quivers not;
Only that film, which fluttered on the grate,
Still flutters there, the sole unquiet thing.
Methinks, its motion in this hush of nature
Gives it dim sympathies with me who live,
Making it a companionable form,
Whose puny flaps and freaks the idling Spirit                    20
By its own moods interprets, every where
Echo or mirror seeking of itself,
And makes a toy of Thought.

                              But O! how oft,
How oft, at school, with most believing mind,
Presageful, have I gazed upon the bars,
To watch that fluttering *stranger!* and as oft
With unclosed lids, already had I dreamt
Of my sweet birth-place, and the old church-tower,
Whose bells, the poor man's only music, rang
From morn to evening, all the hot Fair-day,                    30
So sweetly, that they stirred and haunted me
With a wild pleasure, falling on mine ear
Most like articulate sounds of things to come!
So gazed I, till the soothing things, I dreamt,
Lulled me to sleep, and sleep prolonged my dreams!
And so I brooded all the following morn,
Awed by the stern preceptor's face, mine eye
Fixed with mock study on my swimming book:
Save if the door half opened, and I snatched
A hasty glance, and still my heart leaped up,                    40
For still I hoped to see the *stranger's* face,

Townsman, or aunt, or sister more beloved,
My play-mate when we both were clothed alike!

   Dear Babe, that sleepest cradled by my side,
Whose gentle breathings, heard in this deep calm,
Fill up the interspersèd vacancies
And momentary pauses of the thought!
My babe so beautiful! it thrills my heart
With tender gladness, thus to look at thee,
And think that thou shalt learn far other lore,     50
And in far other scenes! For I was reared
In the great city, pent 'mid cloisters dim,
And saw nought lovely but the sky and stars.
But *thou*, my babe! shalt wander like a breeze
By lakes and sandy shores, beneath the crags
Of ancient mountain, and beneath the clouds,
Which image in their bulk both lakes and shores
And mountain crags: so shalt thou see and hear
The lovely shapes and sounds intelligible
Of that eternal language, which thy God     60
Utters, who from eternity doth teach
Himself in all, and all things in himself.
Great universal Teacher! he shall mould
Thy spirit, and by giving make it ask.

   Therefore all seasons shall be sweet to thee,
Whether the summer clothe the general earth
With greenness, or the redbreast sit and sing
Betwixt the tufts of snow on the bare branch
Of mossy apple-tree, while the nigh thatch
Smokes in the sun-thaw; whether the eave-drops fall   70
Heard only in the trances of the blast,
Or if the secret ministry of frost
Shall hang them up in silent icicles,
Quietly shining to the quiet Moon.
*February*, 1798.             1798.

# FRANCE: AN ODE

~~~~~~

### I

Ye Clouds! that far above me float and pause,
  Whose pathless march no mortal may controul!
  Ye Ocean-Waves! that, wheresoe'er ye roll,
Yield homage only to eternal laws!
Ye Woods! that listen to the night-birds singing,
  Midway the smooth and perilous slope reclined,
Save when your own imperious branches swinging,
  Have made a solemn music of the wind!
Where, like a man beloved of God,
Through glooms, which never woodman trod,       10
    How oft, pursuing fancies holy,
My moonlight way o'er flowering weeds I wound,
    Inspired, beyond the guess of folly,
By each rude shape and wild unconquerable sound!
O ye loud Waves! and O ye Forests high!
  And O ye Clouds that far above me soared!
Thou rising Sun! thou blue rejoicing Sky!
  Yea, every thing that is and will be free!
  Bear witness for me, wheresoe'er ye be,
With what deep worship I have still adored      20
  The spirit of divinest Liberty.

### II

When France in wrath her giant-limbs upreared,
  And with that oath, which smote air, earth, and sea,
  Stamped her strong foot and said she would be free,
Bear witness for me, how I hoped and feared!
With what a joy my lofty gratulation
  Unawed I sang, amid a slavish band:
And when to whelm the disenchanted nation,
  Like fiends embattled by a wizard's wand,

The Monarchs marched in evil day, 30
   And Britain joined the dire array;
Though dear her shores and circling ocean,
Though many friendships, many youthful loves
   Had swoln the patriot emotion
And flung a magic light o'er all her hills and groves;
Yet still my voice, unaltered, sang defeat
   To all that braved the tyrant-quelling lance,
And shame too long delayed and vain retreat!
For ne'er, O Liberty! with partial aim
I dimmed thy light or damped thy holy flame; 40
   But blessed the paeans of delivered France,
And hung my head and wept at Britain's name.

### III

"And what," I said, "though Blasphemy's loud scream
   With that sweet music of deliverance strove!
   Though all the fierce and drunken passions wove
A dance more wild than e'er was maniac's dream!
   Ye storms, that round the dawning East assembled,
The Sun was rising, though ye hid his light!"
   And when, to soothe my soul, that hoped and trembled,
The dissonance ceased, and all seemed calm and bright; 50
   When France her front deep-scarr'd and gory
   Concealed with clustering wreaths of glory;
     When, insupportably advancing,
   Her arm made mockery of the warrior's ramp;
     While timid looks of fury glancing,
   Domestic treason, crushed beneath her fatal stamp,
Writhed like a wounded dragon in his gore;
   Then I reproached my fears that would not flee;
"And soon," I said, "shall Wisdom teach her lore
In the low huts of them that toil and groan! 60
And, conquering by her happiness alone,
   Shall France compel the nations to be free,
Till Love and Joy look round, and call the Earth their own."

IV

Forgive me, Freedom! O forgive those dreams!
  I hear thy voice, I hear thy loud lament,
  From bleak Helvetia's icy caverns sent—
I hear thy groans upon her blood-stained streams!
  Heroes, that for your peaceful country perished,
And ye that, fleeing, spot your mountain-snows
  With bleeding wounds; forgive me, that I cherished     70
One thought that ever blessed your cruel foes!
    To scatter rage, and traitorous guilt,
    Where Peace her jealous home had built;
      A patriot-race to disinherit
Of all that made their stormy wilds so dear;
      And with inexpiable spirit
To taint the bloodless freedom of the mountaineer—
O France, that mockest Heaven, adulterous, blind,
    And patriot only in pernicious toils!
Are these thy boasts, Champion of human kind?     80
    To mix with Kings in the low lust of sway,
Yell in the hunt, and share the murderous prey;
To insult the shrine of Liberty with spoils
  From freemen torn; to tempt and to betray?

V

    The Sensual and the Dark rebel in vain,
    Slaves by their own compulsion! In mad game
    They burst their manacles and wear the name
      Of Freedom, graven on a heavier chain!
    O Liberty! with profitless endeavour
Have I pursued thee, many a weary hour;     90
  But thou nor swell'st the victor's strain, nor ever
Didst breathe thy soul in forms of human power.
    Alike from all, howe'er they praise thee,
    (Nor prayer, nor boastful name delays thee)
      Alike from Priestcraft's harpy minions,
    And factious Blasphemy's obscener slaves,

Thou speedest on thy subtle pinions,
The guide of homeless winds, and playmate of the waves!
And there I felt thee!—on that sea-cliff's verge,
   Whose pines, scarce travelled by the breeze above,    100
Had made one murmur with the distant surge!
Yes, while I stood and gazed, my temples bare,
And shot my being through earth, sea, and air,
   Possessing all things with intensest love,
     O Liberty! my spirit felt thee there.
*February,* 1798.                       1798.

# LEWTI*

∾∾∾

### OR THE CIRCASSIAN LOVE-CHAUNT

At midnight by the stream I roved,
To forget the form I loved.
Image of Lewti! from my mind
Depart; for Lewti is not kind.
The Moon was high, the moonlight gleam
   And the shadow of a star
Heaved upon Tamaha's stream;
   But the rock shone brighter far,
The rock half sheltered from my view
By pendent boughs of tressy yew.—         10
So shines my Lewti's forehead fair,
Gleaming through her sable hair.
Image of Lewti! from my mind
Depart; for Lewti is not kind.

I saw a cloud of palest hue,
   Onward to the moon it passed;
Still brighter and more bright it grew,

---

* This poem is founded on a fragment of Wordsworth's juvenile verse, "Beauty and Moonlight." Coleridge's first stanza follows Wordsworth quite closely; the rest has only an occasional resemblance.

With floating colours not a few,
  Till it reached the moon at last:
Then the cloud was wholly bright, 20
With a rich and amber light!
And so with many a hope I seek,
  And with such joy I find my Lewti;
And even so my pale wan cheek
  Drinks in as deep a flush of beauty!
Nay, treacherous image! leave my mind,
If Lewti never will be kind.

The little cloud—it floats away,
  Away it goes; away so soon!
Alas! it has no power to stay: 30
Its hues are dim, its hues are grey—
  Away it passes from the moon!
How mournfully it seems to fly,
  Ever fading more and more,
To joyless regions of the sky—
  And now 'tis whiter than before!
As white as my poor cheek will be,
  When, Lewti! on my couch I lie,
A dying man for love of thee.
Nay, treacherous image! leave my mind— 40
And yet, thou didst not look unkind.

I saw a vapour in the sky,
Thin, and white, and very high;
I ne'er beheld so thin a cloud:
  Perhaps the breezes that can fly
  Now below and now above,
Have snatched aloft the lawny shroud
  Of Lady fair—that died for love.
For maids, as well as youths, have perished
From fruitless love too fondly cherished. 50
Nay, treacherous image! leave my mind—
For Lewti never will be kind.

Hush! my heedless feet from under
  Slip the crumbling banks for ever:
Like echoes to a distant thunder,
  They plunge into the gentle river.
The river-swans have heard my tread,
And startle from their reedy bed.
O beauteous birds! methinks ye measure
  Your movements to some heavenly tune!       60
O beauteous birds! 'tis such a pleasure
  To see you move beneath the moon,
I would it were your true delight
To sleep by day and wake all night.

I know the place where Lewti lies,
When silent night has closed her eyes:
  It is a breezy jasmine-bower,
The nightingale sings o'er her head:
  Voice of the Night! had I the power
That leafy labyrinth to thread,       70
And creep, like thee, with soundless tread,
I then might view her bosom white
Heaving lovely to my sight,
As these two swans together heave
On the gently-swelling wave.

Oh! that she saw me in a dream,
  And dreamt that I had died for care;
All pale and wasted I would seem,
  Yet fair withal, as spirits are!
I'd die indeed, if I might see       80
Her bosom heave, and heave for me!
Soothe, gentle image! soothe my mind!
To-morrow Lewti may be kind.
? 1798.              1798.

# FEARS IN SOLITUDE

WRITTEN IN APRIL 1798, DURING THE ALARM OF AN INVASION

A green and silent spot, amid the hills,
A small and silent dell! O'er stiller place
No singing sky-lark ever poised himself.
The hills are heathy, save that swelling slope,
Which hath a gay and gorgeous covering on,
All golden with the never-bloomless furze,
Which now blooms most profusely: but the dell,
Bathed by the mist, is fresh and delicate
As vernal corn-field, or the unripe flax,
When, through its half-transparent stalks, at eve,    10
The level sunshine glimmers with green light.
Oh! 'tis a quiet spirit-healing nook!
Which all, methinks, would love; but chiefly he,
The humble man, who, in his youthful years,
Knew just so much of folly, as had made
His early manhood more securely wise!
Here he might lie on fern or withered heath,
While from the singing lark (that sings unseen
The minstrelsy that solitude loves best),
And from the sun, and from the breezy air,    20
Sweet influences trembled o'er his frame;
And he, with many feelings, many thoughts,
Made up a meditative joy, and found
Religious meanings in the forms of Nature!
And so, his senses gradually wrapt
In a half sleep, he dreams of better worlds,
And dreaming hears thee still, O singing lark,
That singest like an angel in the clouds!

My God! it is a melancholy thing
For such a man, who would full fain preserve    30
His soul in calmness, yet perforce must feel

For all his human brethren—O my God!
It weighs upon the heart, that he must think
What uproar and what strife may now be stirring
This way or that way o'er these silent hills—
Invasion, and the thunder and the shout,
And all the crash of onset; fear and rage,
And undetermined conflict—even now,
Even now, perchance, and in his native isle:
Carnage and groans beneath this blessed sun! 40
We have offended, Oh! my countrymen!
We have offended very grievously,
And been most tyrannous. From east to west
A groan of accusation pierces Heaven!
The wretched plead against us; multitudes
Countless and vehement, the sons of God,
Our brethren! Like a cloud that travels on,
Steamed up from Cairo's swamps of pestilence,
Even so, my countrymen! have we gone forth
And borne to distant tribes slavery and pangs, 50
And, deadlier far, our vices, whose deep taint
With slow perdition murders the whole man,
His body and his soul! Meanwhile, at home,
All individual dignity and power
Engulfed in Courts, Committees, Institutions,
Associations and Societies,
A vain, speech-mouthing, speech-reporting Guild,
One Benefit-Club for mutual flattery,
We have drunk up, demure as at a grace,
Pollutions from the brimming cup of wealth; 60
Contemptuous of all honourable rule,
Yet bartering freedom and the poor man's life
For gold, as at a market! The sweet words
Of Christian promise, words that even yet
Might stem destruction, were they wisely preached,
Are muttered o'er by men, whose tones proclaim
How flat and wearisome they feel their trade:
Rank scoffers some, but most too indolent

To deem them falsehoods or to know their truth.
Oh! blasphemous! the Book of Life is made                    70
A superstitious instrument, on which
We gabble o'er the oaths we mean to break;
For all must swear—all and in every place,
College and wharf, council and justice-court;
All, all must swear, the briber and the bribed,
Merchant and lawyer, senator and priest,
The rich, the poor, the old man and the young;
All, all make up one scheme of perjury,
That faith doth reel; the very name of God
Sounds like a juggler's charm; and, bold with joy,          80
Forth from his dark and lonely hiding-place,
(Portentous sight!) the owlet Atheism,
Sailing on obscene wings athwart the noon,
Drops his blue-fringèd lids, and holds them close,
And hooting at the glorious sun in Heaven,
Cries out, "Where is it?"

                      Thankless too for peace,
(Peace long preserved by fleets and perilous seas)
Secure from actual warfare, we have loved
To swell the war-whoop, passionate for war!
Alas! for ages ignorant of all                               90
Its ghastlier workings, (famine or blue plague,
Battle, or siege, or flight through wintry snows,)
We, this whole people, have been clamorous
For war and bloodshed; animating sports,
The which we pay for as a thing to talk of,
Spectators and not combatants! No guess
Anticipative of a wrong unfelt,
No speculation on contingency,
However dim and vague, too vague and dim
To yield a justifying cause; and forth,                     100
(Stuffed out with big preamble, holy names,
And adjurations of the God in Heaven,)
We send our mandates for the certain death

Of thousands and ten thousands! Boys and girls,
And women, that would groan to see a child
Pull off an insect's leg, all read of war,
The best amusement for our morning meal!
The poor wretch, who has learnt his only prayers
From curses, who knows scarcely words enough
To ask a blessing from his Heavenly Father,                110
Becomes a fluent phraseman, absolute
And technical in victories and defeats,
And all our dainty terms for fratricide;
Terms which we trundle smoothly o'er our tongues
Like mere abstractions, empty sounds to which
We join no feeling and attach no form!
As if the soldier died without a wound;
As if the fibres of this godlike frame
Were gored without a pang; as if the wretch,
Who fell in battle, doing bloody deeds,                120
Passed off to Heaven, translated and not killed;
As though he had no wife to pine for him,
No God to judge him! Therefore, evil days
Are coming on us, O my countrymen!
And what if all-avenging Providence,
Strong and retributive, should make us know
The meaning of our words, force us to feel
The desolation and the agony
Of our fierce doings?

              Spare us yet awhile,
Father and God! O! spare us yet awhile!                130
Oh! let not English women drag their flight
Fainting beneath the burthen of their babes,
Of the sweet infants, that but yesterday
Laughed at the breast! Sons, brothers, husbands, all
Who ever gazed with fondness on the forms
Which grew up with you round the same fire-side,
And all who ever heard the sabbath-bells
Without the infidel's scorn, make yourselves pure!

Stand forth! be men! repel an impious foe,
Impious and false, a light yet cruel race,                               140
Who laugh away all virtue, mingling mirth
With deeds of murder; and still promising
Freedom, themselves too sensual to be free,
Poison life's amities, and cheat the heart
Of faith and quiet hope, and all that soothes,
And all that lifts the spirit! Stand we forth;
Render them back upon the insulted ocean,
And let them toss as idly on its waves
As the vile sea-weed, which some mountain-blast
Swept from our shores! And oh! may we return             150
Not with a drunken triumph, but with fear,
Repenting of the wrongs with which we stung
So fierce a foe to frenzy!

                    I have told,
O Britons! O my brethren! I have told
Most bitter truth, but without bitterness.
Nor deem my zeal or factious or mistimed;
For never can true courage dwell with them,
Who, playing tricks with conscience, dare not look
At their own vices. We have been too long
Dupes of a deep delusion! Some, belike,                         160
Groaning with restless enmity, expect
All change from change of constituted power;
As if a Government had been a robe,
On which our vice and wretchedness were tagged
Like fancy-points and fringes, with the robe
Pulled off at pleasure. Fondly these attach
A radical causation to a few
Poor drudges of chastising Providence,
Who borrow all their hues and qualities
From our own folly and rank wickedness,                        170
Which gave them birth and nursed them. Others, meanwhile,
Dote with a mad idolatry; and all
Who will not fall before their images,

And yield them worship, they are enemies
Even of their country!

          Such have I been deemed.—
But, O dear Britain! O my Mother Isle!
Needs must thou prove a name most dear and holy
To me, a son, a brother, and a friend,
A husband, and a father! who revere
All bonds of natural love, and find them all        180
Within the limits of thy rocky shores.
O native Britain! O my Mother Isle!
How shouldst thou prove aught else but dear and holy
To me, who from thy lakes and mountain-hills,
Thy clouds, thy quiet dales, thy rocks and seas,
Have drunk in all my intellectual life,
All sweet sensations, all ennobling thoughts,
All adoration of the God in nature,
All lovely and all honourable things,
Whatever makes this mortal spirit feel        190
The joy and greatness of its future being?
There lives nor form nor feeling in my soul
Unborrowed from my country! O divine
And beauteous island! thou hast been my sole
And most magnificent temple, in the which
I walk with awe, and sing my stately songs,
Loving the God that made me!—

             May my fears,
My filial fears, be vain! and may the vaunts
And menace of the vengeful enemy
Pass like the gust, that roared and died away        200
In the distant tree: which heard, and only heard
In this low dell, bowed not the delicate grass.

   But now the gentle dew-fall sends abroad
The fruit-like perfume of the golden furze:
The light has left the summit of the hill,
Though still a sunny gleam lies beautiful,

Aslant the ivied beacon. Now farewell,
Farewell, awhile, O soft and silent spot!
On the green sheep-track, up the heathy hill,
Homeward I wind my way; and lo! recalled     210
From bodings that have well-nigh wearied me,
I find myself upon the brow, and pause
Startled! And after lonely sojourning
In such a quiet and surrounded nook,
This burst of prospect, here the shadowy main,
Dim-tinted, there the mighty majesty
Of that huge amphitheatre of rich
And elmy fields, seems like society—
Conversing with the mind, and giving it
A livelier impulse and a dance of thought!     220
And now, belovéd Stowey! I behold
Thy church-tower, and, methinks, the four huge elms
Clustering, which mark the mansion of my friend;
And close behind them, hidden from my view,
Is my own lowly cottage, where my babe
And my babe's mother dwell in peace! With light
And quickened footsteps thitherward I tend,
Remembering thee, O green and silent dell!
And grateful, that by nature's quietness
And solitary musings, all my heart     230
Is softened, and made worthy to indulge
Love, and the thoughts that yearn for human kind.

NETHER STOWEY, *April* 20, 1798.     1798.

# THE NIGHTINGALE

A CONVERSATION POEM, APRIL, 1798

No cloud, no relique of the sunken day
Distinguishes the West, no long thin slip
Of sullen light, no obscure trembling hues.
Come, we will rest on this old mossy bridge!

You see the glimmer of the stream beneath,
But hear no murmuring: it flows silently,
O'er its soft bed of verdure. All is still,
A balmy night! and though the stars be dim,
Yet let us think upon the vernal showers
That gladden the green earth, and we shall find      10
A pleasure in the dimness of the stars.
And hark! the Nightingale begins its song,
"Most musical, most melancholy" bird!
A melancholy bird? Oh! idle thought!
In Nature there is nothing melancholy.
But some night-wandering man whose heart was pierced
With the remembrance of a grievous wrong,
Or slow distemper, or neglected love,
(And so, poor wretch! filled all things with himself,
And made all gentle sounds tell back the tale      20
Of his own sorrow) he, and such as he,
First named these notes a melancholy strain.
And many a poet echoes the conceit;
Poet who hath been building up the rhyme
When he had better far have stretched his limbs
Beside a brook in mossy forest-dell,
By sun or moon-light, to the influxes
Of shapes and sounds and shifting elements
Surrendering his whole spirit, of his song
And of his fame forgetful! so his fame      30
Should share in Nature's immortality,
A venerable thing! and so his song
Should make all Nature lovelier, and itself
Be loved like Nature! But 'twill not be so;
And youths and maidens most poetical,
Who lose the deepening twilights of the spring
In ball-rooms and hot theatres, they still
Full of meek sympathy must heave their sighs
O'er Philomela's pity-pleading strains.

My friend, and thou, our Sister! we have learnt      40
A different lore: we may not thus profane

Nature's sweet voices, always full of love
And joyance! 'Tis the merry Nightingale
That crowds, and hurries, and precipitates
With fast thick warble his delicious notes,
As he were fearful that an April night
Would be too short for him to utter forth
His love-chant, and disburthen his full soul
Of all its music!

           And I know a grove
Of large extent, hard by a castle huge,         50
Which the great lord inhabits not; and so
This grove is wild with tangling underwood,
And the trim walks are broken up, and grass,
Thin grass and king-cups grow within the paths.
But never elsewhere in one place I knew
So many nightingales; and far and near,
In wood and thicket, over the wide grove,
They answer and provoke each other's song,
With skirmish and capricious passagings,
And murmurs musical and swift jug jug,       60
And one low piping sound more sweet than all—
Stirring the air with such a harmony,
That should you close your eyes, you might almost
Forget it was not day! On moonlight bushes,
Whose dewy leaflets are but half-disclosed,
You may perchance behold them on the twigs,
Their bright, bright eyes, their eyes both bright and full,
Glistening, while many a glow-worm in the shade
Lights up her love-torch.

           A most gentle Maid,
Who dwelleth in her hospitable home       70
Hard by the castle, and at latest eve
(Even like a Lady vowed and dedicate
To something more than Nature in the grove)
Glides through the pathways; she knows all their notes,
That gentle Maid! and oft, a moment's space,

What time the moon was lost behind a cloud,
Hath heard a pause of silence; till the moon
Emerging, hath awakened earth and sky
With one sensation, and those wakeful birds
Have all burst forth in choral minstrelsy,                    80
As if some sudden gale had swept at once
A hundred airy harps! And she hath watched
Many a nightingale perch giddily
On blossomy twig still swinging from the breeze,
And to that motion tune his wanton song
Like tipsy Joy that reels with tossing head.

Farewell, O Warbler! till to-morrow eve,
And you, my friends! farewell, a short farewell!
We have been loitering long and pleasantly,
And now for our dear homes.—That strain again!             90
Full fain it would delay me! My dear babe,
Who, capable of no articulate sound,
Mars all things with his imitative lisp,
How he would place his hand beside his ear,
His little hand, the small forefinger up,
And bid us listen! And I deem it wise
To make him Nature's play-mate. He knows well
The evening-star; and once, when he awoke
In most distressful mood (some inward pain
Had made up that strange thing, an infant's dream—)          100
I hurried with him to our orchard-plot,
And he beheld the moon, and, hushed at once,
Suspends his sobs, and laughs most silently,
While his fair eyes, that swam with undropped tears,
Did glitter in the yellow moon-beam! Well!—
It is a father's tale: But if that Heaven
Should give me life, his childhood shall grow up
Familiar with these songs, that with the night
He may associate joy.—Once more, farewell,
Sweet Nightingale! once more, my friends! farewell.          110
1798.                                              1798.

# THE BALLAD OF THE DARK LADIÉ

### A FRAGMENT

Beneath yon birch with silver bark,
And boughs so pendulous and fair,
The brook falls scatter'd down the rock:
    And all is mossy there!

And there upon the moss she sits,
The Dark Ladié in silent pain;
The heavy tear is in her eye,
    And drops and swells again.

Three times she sends her little page
Up the castled mountain's breast,          10
If he might find the Knight that wears
    The Griffin for his crest.

The sun was sloping down the sky,
And she had linger'd there all day,
Counting moments, dreaming fears—
    Oh wherefore can he stay?

She hears a rustling o'er the brook,
She sees far off a swinging bough!
" 'Tis He! 'Tis my betrothéd Knight!
    Lord Falkland, it is Thou!"         20

She springs, she clasps him round the neck,
She sobs a thousand hopes and fears,
Her kisses glowing on his cheeks
    She quenches with her tears.

\*      \*      \*      \*

"My friends with rude ungentle words
They scoff and bid me fly to thee!

O give me shelter in thy breast!
    O shield and shelter me!

"My Henry, I have given thee much,
I gave what I can ne'er recall,                              30
I gave my heart, I gave my peace,
    O Heaven! I gave thee all."

The Knight made answer to the Maid,
While to his heart he held her hand,
"Nine castles hath my noble sire,
    None statelier in the land.

"The Fairest one shall be my love's,
The fairest castle of the nine!
Wait only till the stars peep out,
    The fairest shall be thine:                              40

"Wait only till the hand of eve
Hath wholly closed yon western bars,
And through the dark we two will steal
    Beneath the twinkling stars!"—

"The dark? the dark? No! not the dark?
The twinkling stars? How, Henry? How?"
O God! 'twas in the eye of noon
    He pledged his sacred vow!

And in the eye of noon my love
Shall lead me from my mother's door,                         50
Sweet boys and girls all clothed in white
    Strewing flowers before:

But first the nodding minstrels go
With music meet for lordly bowers,
The children next in snow-white vests,
    Strewing buds and flowers!

And then my love and I shall pace,
My jet black hair in pearly braids,

Between our comely bachelors
And blushing bridal maids.                                        60

\*          \*          \*          \*

1798.                                        1834.

## KUBLA KHAN

~~~~~

OR, A VISION IN A DREAM. A FRAGMENT.

The following fragment is here published at the request of a poet of great
and deserved celebrity [Lord Byron], and, as far as the Author's own opinions are concerned, rather as a psychological curiosity, than on the ground
of any supposed *poetic* merits.

In the summer of the year 1797, the Author, then in ill health, had retired to a lonely farm-house between Porlock and Linton, on the Exmoor
confines of Somerset and Devonshire. In consequence of a slight indisposition, an anodyne had been prescribed, from the effects of which he fell
asleep in his chair at the moment that he was reading the following sentence, or words of the same substance, in "Purchas's Pilgrimage": "Here
the Khan Kubla commanded a palace to be built, and a stately garden
thereunto. And thus ten miles of fertile ground were inclosed with a wall."
The Author continued for about three hours in a profound sleep, at least
of the external senses, during which time he has the most vivid confidence,
that he could not have composed less than from two to three hundred lines;
if that indeed can be called composition in which all the images rose up
before him as *things,* with a parallel production of the correspondent expressions, without any sensation or consciousness of effort. On awaking he
appeared to himself to have a distinct recollection of the whole, and taking
his pen, ink, and paper, instantly and eagerly wrote down the lines that are
here preserved. At this moment he was unfortunately called out by a person
on business from Porlock, and detained by him above an hour, and on his
return to his room, found, to his no small surprise and mortification, that
though he still retained some vague and dim recollection of the general
purport of the vision, yet, with the exception of some eight or ten scattered
lines and images, all the rest had passed away like the images on the surface
of a stream into which a stone has been cast, but, alas! without the after
restoration of the latter!

Then all the charm
Is broken—all that phantom-world so fair
Vanishes, and a thousand circlets spread,
And each mis-shape['s] the other. Stay awhile,
Poor youth! who scarcely dar'st lift up thine eyes—
The stream will soon renew its smoothness, soon
The visions will return! And lo, he stays,
And soon the fragments dim of lovely forms
Come trembling back, unite, and now once more
The pool becomes a mirror.

Yet from the still surviving recollections in his mind, the Author has frequently purposed to finish for himself what had been originally, as it were, given to him. Σαμερον αδιον ασω: but the to-morrow is yet to come.

## KUBLA KHAN

In Xanadu did Kubla Khan
A stately pleasure-dome decree:
Where Alph, the sacred river, ran
Through caverns measureless to man
   Down to a sunless sea.
So twice five miles of fertile ground
With walls and towers were girdled round:
And there were gardens bright with sinuous rills,
Where blossomed many an incense-bearing tree;
And here were forests ancient as the hills,     10
Enfolding sunny spots of greenery.

But oh! that deep romantic chasm which slanted
Down the green hill athwart a cedarn cover!
A savage place! as holy and enchanted
As e'er beneath a waning moon was haunted
By woman wailing for her demon-lover!
And from this chasm, with ceaseless turmoil seething,
As if this earth in fast thick pants were breathing,
A mighty fountain momently was forced:
Amid whose swift half-intermitted burst     20
Huge fragments vaulted like rebounding hail,

Or chaffy grain beneath the thresher's flail:
And 'mid these dancing rocks at once and ever
It flung up momently the sacred river.
Five miles meandering with a mazy motion
Through wood and dale the sacred river ran,
Then reached the caverns measureless to man,
And sank in tumult to a lifeless ocean:
And 'mid this tumult Kubla heard from far
Ancestral voices prophesying war!                           30

    The shadow of the dome of pleasure
    Floated midway on the waves;
    Where was heard the mingled measure
    From the fountain and the caves.
It was a miracle of rare device,
A sunny pleasure-dome with caves of ice!

    A damsel with a dulcimer
    In a vision once I saw:
    It was an Abyssinian maid,
    And on her dulcimer she played,                    40
    Singing of Mount Abora.
    Could I revive within me
    Her symphony and song,
    To such a deep delight 'twould win me,
That with music loud and long,
I would build that dome in air,
That sunny dome! those caves of ice!
And all who heard should see them there,
And all should cry, Beware! Beware!
His flashing eyes, his floating hair!                        50
Weave a circle round him thrice,
And close your eyes with holy dread,
For he on honey-dew hath fed,
And drunk the milk of Paradise.

? 1797-? 1800.                                    1816.

# LINES

WRITTEN IN THE ALBUM AT ELBINGERODE,
IN THE HARTZ FOREST

I stood on Brocken's sovran height, and saw
Woods crowding upon woods, hills over hills,
A surging scene, and only limited
By the blue distance. Heavily my way
Downward I dragged through fir groves evermore,
Where bright green moss heaves in sepulchral forms
Speckled with sunshine; and, but seldom heard,
The sweet bird's song became a hollow sound;
And the breeze, murmuring indivisibly,
Preserved its solemn murmur most distinct                    10
From many a note of many a waterfall,
And the brook's chatter; 'mid whose islet-stones
The dingy kidling with its tinkling bell
Leaped frolicsome, or old romantic goat
Sat, his white beard slow waving. I moved on
In low and languid mood: for I had found
That outward forms, the loftiest, still receive
Their finer influence from the Life within;—
Fair cyphers else: fair, but of import vague
Or unconcerning, where the heart not finds                   20
History or prophecy of friend, or child,
Or gentle maid, our first and early love,
Or father, or the venerable name
Of our adoréd country! O thou Queen,
Thou delegated Deity of Earth,
O dear, dear England! how my longing eye
Turned westward, shaping in the steady clouds
Thy sands and high white cliffs!

                              My native Land!
Filled with the thought of thee this heart was proud,
Yea, mine eye swam with tears: that all the view          30
From sovran Brocken, woods and woody hills,
Floated away, like a departing dream,
Feeble and dim! Stranger, these impulses
Blame thou not lightly; nor will I profane,
With hasty judgment or injurious doubt,
That man's sublimer spirit, who can feel
That God is everywhere! the God who framed
Mankind to be one mighty family,
Himself our Father, and the World our Home.
*May 17, 1799.*                                  1799.


## THE DEVIL'S THOUGHTS *

### I

From his brimstone bed at break of day
A walking the Devil is gone,
To visit his snug little farm the earth,
And see how his stock goes on.

### II

Over the hill and over the dale,
And he went over the plain,
And backward and forward he switched his long tail
As a gentleman switches his cane.

### III

And how then was the Devil drest?
Oh! he was in his Sunday's best:                          10
His jacket was red and his breeches were blue,
And there was a hole where the tail came through.

---

* These satiric verses were a joint production of Coleridge and Southey.

#### IV

He saw a Lawyer killing a Viper
On a dunghill hard by his own stable;
And the Devil smiled, for it put him in mind
Of Cain and his brother, Abel.

#### V

He saw an Apothecary on a white horse
   Ride by on his vocations,
And the Devil thought of his old Friend
   Death in the Revelations.                    20

#### VI

He saw a cottage with a double coach-house,
   A cottage of gentility;
And the Devil did grin, for his darling sin
   Is pride that apes humility.

#### VII

He peep'd into a rich bookseller's shop,
   Quoth he! we are both of one college!
For I sate myself, like a cormorant, once
   Hard by the tree of knowledge.

#### VIII

Down the river did glide, with wind and tide,
   A pig with vast celerity;                    30
And the Devil look'd wise as he saw how the while,
It cut its own throat. "There!" quoth he with a smile,
   "Goes 'England's commercial prosperity.'"

#### IX

As he went through Cold-Bath Fields he saw
   A solitary cell;
And the Devil was pleased, for it gave him a hint
   For improving his prisons in Hell.

### X

He saw a Turnkey in a trice
  Fetter a troublesome blade;
"Nimbly," quoth he, "do the fingers move         40
  If a man be but used to his trade."

### XI

He saw the same Turnkey unfetter a man,
  With but little expedition,
Which put him in mind of the long debate
  On the Slave-trade abolition.

### XII

He saw an old acquaintance
  As he passed by a Methodist meeting;—
She holds a consecrated key,
  And the devil nods her a greeting.

### XIII

She turned up her nose, and said,         50
  "Avaunt! my name's Religion,"
And she looked to Mr. ——
  And leered like a love-sick pigeon.

### XIV

He saw a certain minister
  (A minister to his mind)
Go up into a certain House,
  With a majority behind.

### XV

The Devil quoted Genesis
  Like a very learnéd clerk,
How "Noah and his creeping things         60
  Went up into the Ark."

### XVI

He took from the poor,
   And he gave to the rich,
And he shook hands with a Scotchman,
   For he was not afraid of the ——

### XVII

General ——————— burning face
   He saw with consternation,
And back to hell his way did he take,
For the Devil thought by a slight mistake
   It was general conflagration.      70
1799.                             1799.

## LOVE

All thoughts, all passions, all delights,
Whatever stirs this mortal frame,
All are but ministers of Love,
   And feed his sacred flame.

Oft in my waking dreams do I
Live o'er again that happy hour,
When midway on the mount I lay,
   Beside the ruined tower.

The moonshine, stealing o'er the scene
Had blended with the lights of eve;      10
And she was there, my hope, my joy,
   My own dear Genevieve!

She leant against the arméd man,
The statue of the arméd knight;
She stood and listened to my lay,
   Amid the lingering light.

Few sorrows hath she of her own,
My hope! my joy! my Genevieve!
She loves me best, whene'er I sing
    The songs that make her grieve.          20

I played a soft and doleful air,
I sang an old and moving story—
An old rude song, that suited well
    That ruin wild and hoary.

She listened with a flitting blush,
With downcast eyes and modest grace;
For well she knew, I could not choose
    But gaze upon her face.

I told her of the Knight that wore
Upon his shield a burning brand;                          30
And that for ten long years he wooed
    The Lady of the Land.

I told her how he pined: and ah!
The deep, the low, the pleading tone
With which I sang another's love,
    Interpreted my own.

She listened with a flitting blush,
With downcast eyes, and modest grace;
And she forgave me, that I gazed
    Too fondly on her face!                        40

But when I told the cruel scorn
That crazed that bold and lovely Knight,
And that he crossed the mountain-woods,
    Nor rested day nor night;

That sometimes from the savage den,
And sometimes from the darksome shade,
And sometimes starting up at once
    In green and sunny glade,—

There came and looked him in the face
An angel beautiful and bright;                    50
And that he knew it was a Fiend,
    This miserable Knight!

And that unknowing what he did,
He leaped amid a murderous band,
And saved from outrage worse than death
    The Lady of the Land!

And how she wept, and clasped his knees;
And how she tended him in vain—
And ever strove to expiate
    The scorn that crazed his brain;—       60

And that she nursed him in a cave;
And how his madness went away,
When on the yellow forest-leaves
    A dying man he lay;—

His dying words—but when I reached
That tenderest strain of all the ditty,
My faultering voice and pausing harp
    Disturbed her soul with pity!

All impulses of soul and sense
Had thrilled my guileless Genevieve;              70
The music and the doleful tale,
    The rich and balmy eve;

And hopes, and fears that kindle hope,
An undistinguishable throng,
And gentle wishes long subdued,
    Subdued and cherished long!

She wept with pity and delight,
She blushed with love, and virgin-shame;
And like the murmur of a dream,
    I heard her breathe my name.               80

Her bosom heaved—she stepped aside,
As conscious of my look she stepped—
Then suddenly, with timorous eye
    She fled to me and wept.

She half enclosed me with her arms,
She pressed me with a meek embrace;
And bending back her head, looked up,
    And gazed upon my face.

'Twas partly love, and partly fear,
And partly 'twas a bashful art,          90
That I might rather feel, than see,
    The swelling of her heart.

I calmed her fears, and she was calm,
And told her love with virgin pride;
And so I won my Genevieve,
    My bright and beauteous Bride.
1799.                       1799.

## THE MAD MONK

I heard a voice from Etna's side;
    Where o'er a cavern's mouth
    That fronted to the south
A chestnut spread its umbrage wide:
A hermit or a monk the man might be;
    But him I could not see:
And thus the music flow'd along,
In melody most like to old Sicilian song:

"There was a time when earth, and sea, and skies,
    The bright green vale, and forest's dark recess,    10
With all things, lay before mine eyes
    In steady loveliness:
But now I feel, on earth's uneasy scene,
    Such sorrows as will never cease;—

I only ask for peace;
If I must live to know that such a time has been!"
A silence then ensued:
    Till from the cavern came
    A voice;—it was the same!
And thus, in mournful tone, its dreary plaint renew'd:   20

"Last night, as o'er the sloping turf I trod,
    The smooth green turf, to me a vision gave
Beneath mine eyes, the sod—
    The roof of Rosa's grave!

"My heart has need with dreams like these to strive,
    For, when I woke, beneath mine eyes I found
    The plot of mossy ground,
On which we oft have sat when Rosa was alive.—
Why must the rock, and margin of the flood,
    Why must the hills so many flow'rets bear,   30
Whose colours to a *murder'd* maiden's blood,
    Such sad resemblance wear?—

"*I struck the wound*,—this hand of mine!
For Oh, thou maid divine,
    I lov'd to agony!
The youth whom thou call'd'st thine
    Did never love like me!

"Is it the stormy clouds above
    That flash'd so red a gleam?
    On yonder downward trickling stream?—   40
'Tis not the blood of her I love.—
The sun torments me from his western bed,
    Oh, let him cease for ever to diffuse
    Those crimson spectre hues!
Oh, let me lie in peace, and be for ever dead!"

Here ceas'd the voice. In deep dismay,
Down thro' the forest I pursu'd my way.
1800.                        1800.

## TO ASRA

Are there two things, of all which men possess,
That are so like each other and so near,
As mutual Love seems like to Happiness?
Dear Asra, woman beyond utterance dear!
This Love which ever welling at my heart,
Now in its living fount doth heave and fall,
Now overflowing pours thro' every part
Of all my frame, and fills and changes all,
Like vernal waters springing up through snow,
This Love that seeming great beyond the power
Of growth, yet seemeth ever more to grow,
Could I transmute the whole to one rich Dower
Of Happy Life, and give it all to Thee,
Thy lot, methinks, were Heaven, thy age, Eternity!
1801.                                    1893.

## LOVE'S SANCTUARY

This yearning heart (Love! witness what I say)
Enshrines thy form as purely as it may,
Round which, as to some spirit uttering bliss,
My thoughts all stand ministrant night and day
Like saintly Priests, that dare not think amiss.
? 1801.                                  1893.

# DEJECTION: AN ODE

[WRITTEN APRIL 4, 1802]

> Late, late yestreen I saw the new Moon,
> With the old Moon in her arms;
> And I fear, I fear, my Master dear!
> We shall have a deadly storm.
> *Ballad of Sir Patrick Spence.*

## I

Well! If the Bard was weather-wise, who made
  The grand old ballad of Sir Patrick Spence,
  This night, so tranquil now, will not go hence
Unroused by winds, that ply a busier trade
Than those which mould yon cloud in lazy flakes,
Or the dull sobbing draft, that moans and rakes
Upon the strings of this Æolian lute,
    Which better far were mute.
  For lo! the New-moon winter-bright!
  And overspread with phantom light,          10
    (With swimming phantom light o'erspread
    But rimmed and circled by a silver thread)
I see the old Moon in her lap, foretelling
  The coming-on of rain and squally blast.
And oh! that even now the gust were swelling,
  And the slant night-shower driving loud and fast!
Those sounds which oft have raised me, whilst they awed,
    And sent my soul abroad,
Might now perhaps their wonted impulse give,
Might startle this dull pain, and make it move and live!  20

## II

A grief without a pang, void, dark, and drear,
  A stifled, drowsy, unimpassioned grief,

Which finds no natural outlet, no relief,
  In word, or sigh, or tear—
O Lady! in this wan and heartless mood,
To other thoughts by yonder throstle woo'd,
  All this long eve, so balmy and serene,
Have I been gazing on the western sky,
  And its peculiar tint of yellow green:
And still I gaze—and with how blank an eye!                    30
And those thin clouds above, in flakes and bars,
That give away their motion to the stars;
Those stars, that glide behind them or between,
Now sparkling, now bedimmed, but always seen:
Yon crescent Moon, as fixed as if it grew
In its own cloudless, starless lake of blue;
I see them all so excellently fair,
I see, not feel, how beautiful they are!

### III

  My genial spirits fail;
  And what can these avail                                      40
To lift the smothering weight from off my breast?
  It were a vain endeavour,
  Though I should gaze for ever
On that green light that lingers in the west:
I may not hope from outward forms to win
The passion and the life, whose fountains are within.

### IV

O Lady! we receive but what we give,
And in our life alone does Nature live:
Ours is her wedding garment, ours her shroud!
  And would we aught behold, of higher worth,                  50
Than that inanimate cold world allowed
To the poor loveless ever-anxious crowd,
  Ah! from the soul itself must issue forth
A light, a glory, a fair luminous cloud
    Enveloping the Earth—

And from the soul itself must there be sent
  A sweet and potent voice, of its own birth,
Of all sweet sounds the life and element!

### V

O pure of heart! thou need'st not ask of me
What this strong music in the soul may be!                 60
What, and wherein it doth exist,
This light, this glory, this fair luminous mist,
This beautiful and beauty-making power.
  Joy, virtuous Lady! Joy that ne'er was given,
Save to the pure, and in their purest hour,
Life, and Life's effluence, cloud at once and shower,
Joy, Lady! is the spirit and the power,
Which wedding Nature to us gives in dower
  A new Earth and new Heaven,
Undreamt of by the sensual and the proud—                  70
Joy is the sweet voice, Joy the luminous cloud—
    We in ourselves rejoice!
And thence flows all that charms or ear or sight,
  All melodies the echoes of that voice,
All colours a suffusion from that light.

### VI

There was a time when, though my path was rough,
  This joy within me dallied with distress,
And all misfortunes were but as the stuff
  Whence Fancy made me dreams of happiness:
For hope grew round me, like the twining vine,             80
And fruits, and foliage, not my own, seemed mine.
But now afflictions bow me down to earth:
Nor care I that they rob me of my mirth;
    But oh! each visitation
Suspends what nature gave me at my birth,
  My shaping spirit of Imagination.
For not to think of what I needs must feel,
  But to be still and patient, all I can;

And haply by abstruse research to steal
  From my own nature all the natural man—     90
  This was my sole resource, my only plan:
Till that which suits a part infects the whole,
And now is almost grown the habit of my soul.

VII

Hence, viper thoughts, that coil around my mind,
    Reality's dark dream!
I turn from you, and listen to the wind,
  Which long has raved unnoticed. What a scream
Of agony by torture lengthened out
That lute sent forth! Thou Wind, that rav'st without,
  Bare crag, or mountain-tairn, or blasted tree,     100
Or pine-grove whither woodman never clomb,
Or lonely house, long held the witches' home,
  Methinks were fitter instruments for thee,
Mad Lutanist! who in this month of showers,
Of dark-brown gardens, and of peeping flowers,
Mak'st Devils' yule, with worse than wintry song,
The blossoms, buds, and timorous leaves among.
  Thou Actor, perfect in all tragic sounds!
Thou mighty Poet, e'en to frenzy bold!
    What tell'st thou now about?     110
    'Tis of the rushing of an host in rout,
  With groans, of trampled men, with smarting wounds—
At once they groan with pain, and shudder with the cold!
But hush! there is a pause of deepest silence!
  And all that noise, as of a rushing crowd,
With groans, and tremulous shudderings—all is over—
  It tells another tale, with sounds less deep and loud!
    A tale of less affright,
    And tempered with delight,
As Otway's self had framed the tender lay,—     120
    'Tis of a little child
    Upon a lonesome wild,
Not far from home, but she hath lost her way:

And now moans low in bitter grief and fear,
And now screams loud, and hopes to make her mother hear.

### VIII

'Tis midnight, but small thoughts have I of sleep:
Full seldom may my friend such vigils keep!
Visit her, gentle Sleep! with wings of healing,
   And may this storm be but a mountain-birth,
May all the stars hang bright above her dwelling,       130
   Silent as though they watched the sleeping Earth!
     With light heart may she rise,
     Gay fancy, cheerful eyes,
  Joy lift her spirit, joy attune her voice;
To her may all things live, from pole to pole,
Their life the eddying of her living soul!
  O simple spirit, guided from above,
Dear Lady! friend devoutest of my choice,
Thus mayest thou ever, evermore rejoice.
1802.                                    1802.

# HYMN BEFORE SUN-RISE, IN THE VALE
## OF CHAMOUNI*

Besides the Rivers, Arve and Arveiron, which have their sources in the
foot of Mont Blanc, five conspicuous torrents rush down its sides; and within
a few paces of the Glaciers, the Gentiana Major grows in immense numbers,
with its "flowers of loveliest blue."

    Hast thou a charm to stay the morning-star
    In his steep course? So long he seems to pause
    On thy bald awful head, O sovran BLANC,
    The Arve and Arveiron at thy base
    Rave ceaselessly; but thou, most awful Form!
    Risest from forth thy silent sea of pines,

---

* This poem is founded on a much shorter German poem by Frederika Brun.

How silently! Around thee and above
Deep is the air and dark, substantial, black,
An ebon mass: methinks thou piercest it,
As with a wedge! But when I look again,                10
It is thine own calm home, thy crystal shrine,
Thy habitation from eternity!
O dread and silent Mount! I gazed upon thee,
Till thou, still present to the bodily sense,
Didst vanish from my thought: entranced in prayer
I worshipped the Invisible alone.

Yet, like some sweet beguiling melody,
So sweet, we know not we are listening to it,
Thou, the meanwhile, wast blending with my Thought,
Yea, with my Life and Life's own secret joy:           20
Till the dilating Soul, enrapt, transfused,
Into the mighty vision passing—there
As in her natural form, swelled vast to Heaven!

Awake, my soul! not only passive praise
Thou owest! not alone these swelling tears,
Mute thanks and secret ecstasy! Awake,
Voice of sweet song! Awake, my heart, awake!
Green vales and icy cliffs, all join my Hymn.

Thou first and chief, sole sovereign of the Vale!
O struggling with the darkness all the night,          30
And visited all night by troops of stars,
Or when they climb the sky or when they sink:
Companion of the morning-star at dawn,
Thyself Earth's rosy star, and of the dawn
Co-herald: wake, O wake, and utter praise!
Who sank thy sunless pillars deep in Earth?
Who filled thy countenance with rosy light?
Who made thee parent of perpetual streams?

And you, ye five wild torrents fiercely glad!
Who called you forth from night and utter death,       40
From dark and icy caverns called you forth,

Down those precipitous, black, jaggéd rocks,
For ever shattered and the same for ever?
Who gave you your invulnerable life,
Your strength, your speed, your fury, and your joy,
Unceasing thunder and eternal foam?
And who commanded (and the silence came),
Here let the billows stiffen, and have rest?

Ye Ice-falls! ye that from the mountain's brow
Adown enormous ravines slope amain—            50
Torrents, methinks, that heard a mighty voice,
And stopped at once amid their maddest plunge!
Motionless torrents! silent cataracts!
Who made you glorious as the Gates of Heaven
Beneath the keen full moon? Who bade the sun
Clothe you with rainbows? Who, with living flowers
Of loveliest blue, spread garlands at your feet?—
God! let the torrents, like a shout of nations,
Answer! and let the ice-plains echo, God!
God! sing ye meadow-streams with gladsome voice!  60
Ye pine-groves, with your soft and soul-like sounds!
And they too have a voice, yon piles of snow,
And in their perilous fall shall thunder, God!

Ye living flowers that skirt the eternal frost!
Ye wild goats sporting round the eagle's nest!
Ye eagles, play-mates of the mountain-storm!
Ye lightnings, the dread arrows of the clouds!
Ye signs and wonders of the element!
Utter forth God, and fill the hills with praise!

Thou too, hoar Mount! with thy sky-pointing peaks,  70
Oft from whose feet the avalanche, unheard,
Shoots downward, glittering through the pure serene
Into the depth of clouds, that veil thy breast—
Thou too again, stupendous Mountain! thou
That as I raise my head, awhile bowed low
In adoration, upward from thy base
Slow travelling with dim eyes suffused with tears,

Solemnly seemest, like a vapoury cloud,
To rise before me—Rise, O ever rise,
Rise like a cloud of incense from the Earth!                    80
Thou kingly Spirit throned among the hills,
Thou dread ambassador from Earth to Heaven,
Great Hierarch! tell thou the silent sky,
And tell the stars, and tell yon rising sun
Earth, with her thousand voices, praises GOD.
1802.                                                   1802.


# INSCRIPTION FOR A FOUNTAIN

## ON A HEATH

This Sycamore, oft musical with bees,—
Such tents the Patriarchs loved! O long unharmed
May all its agéd boughs o'er-canopy
The small round basin, which this jutting stone
Keeps pure from falling leaves! Long may the Spring,
Quietly as a sleeping infant's breath,
Send up cold waters to the traveller
With soft and even pulse! Nor ever cease
Yon tiny cone of sand its soundless dance,
Which at the bottom, like a Fairy's Page,
As merry and no taller, dances still,
Nor wrinkles the smooth surface of the Fount.
Here Twilight is and Coolness: here is moss,
A soft seat, and a deep and ample shade.
Thou may'st toil far and find no second tree.
Drink, Pilgrim, here; Here rest! and if thy heart
Be innocent, here too shalt thou refresh
Thy spirit, listening to some gentle sound,
Or passing gale or hum of murmuring bees!
1802.                                                   1802.

# THE PAINS OF SLEEP

Ere on my bed my limbs I lay,
It hath not been my use to pray
With moving lips or bended knees;
But silently, by slow degrees,
My spirit I to Love compose,
In humble trust mine eye-lids close,
With reverential resignation,
No wish conceived, no thought exprest,
Only a sense of supplication;
A sense o'er all my soul imprest                    10
That I am weak, yet not unblest,
Since in me, round me, every where
Eternal Strength and Wisdom are.

But yester-night I prayed aloud
In anguish and in agony,
Up-starting from the fiendish crowd
Of shapes and thoughts that tortured me:
A lurid light, a trampling throng,
Sense of intolerable wrong,
And whom I scorned, those only strong!                    20
Thirst of revenge, the powerless will
Still baffled, and yet burning still!
Desire with loathing strangely mixed
On wild or hateful objects fixed.
Fantastic passions! maddening brawl!
And shame and terror over all!
Deeds to be hid which were not hid,
Which all confused I could not know
Whether I suffered, or I did:
For all seemed guilt, remorse or woe,                    30
My own or others still the same
Life-stifling fear, soul-stifling shame.

So two nights passed: the night's dismay
Saddened and stunned the coming day.
Sleep, the wide blessing, seemed to me
Distemper's worst calamity.
The third night, when my own loud scream
Had waked me from the fiendish dream,
O'ercome with sufferings strange and wild,
I wept as I had been a child;                              40
And having thus by tears subdued
My anguish to a milder mood,
Such punishments, I said, were due
To natures deepliest stained with sin,—
For aye entempesting anew
The unfathomable hell within,
The horror of their deeds to view,
To know and loathe, yet wish and do!
Such griefs with such men well agree,
But wherefore, wherefore fall on me?                       50
To be beloved is all I need,
And whom I love, I love indeed.
1803.                                        1816.


## PHANTOM

All look and likeness caught from earth
All accident of kin and birth,
Had pass'd away. There was no trace
Of aught on that illumined face,
Uprais'd beneath the rifted stone
But of one spirit all her own;—
She, she herself, and only she,
Shone through her body visibly.
1805.                                        1834.

# WHAT IS LIFE?

Resembles life what once was deem'd of light,
   Too ample in itself for human sight?
An absolute self—an element ungrounded—
All that we see, all colours of all shade
    By encroach of darkness made?—
Is very life by consciousness unbounded?
And all the thoughts, pains, joys of mortal breath,
A war-embrace of wrestling life and death?
1805.                            1829.

# TO WILLIAM WORDSWORTH

COMPOSED ON THE NIGHT AFTER HIS RECITATION OF A POEM
ON THE GROWTH OF AN INDIVIDUAL MIND

Friend of the wise! and Teacher of the Good!
Into my heart have I received that Lay
More than historic, that prophetic Lay
Wherein (high theme by thee first sung aright)
Of the foundations and the building up
Of a Human Spirit thou hast dared to tell
What may be told, to the understanding mind
Revealable; and what within the mind
By vital breathings secret as the soul
Of vernal growth, oft quickens in the heart       10
Thoughts all too deep for words!—

                         Theme hard as high!
Of smiles spontaneous, and mysterious fears
(The first-born they of Reason and twin-birth),
Of tides obedient to external force,
And currents self-determined, as might seem,

Or by some inner Power; of moments awful,
Now in thy inner life, and now abroad,
When power streamed from thee, and thy soul received
The light reflected, as a light bestowed—
Of fancies fair, and milder hours of youth,                    20
Hyblean murmurs of poetic thought
Industrious in its joy, in vales and glens
Native or outland, lakes and famous hills!
Or on the lonely high-road, when the stars
Were rising; or by secret mountain-streams,
The guides and the companions of thy way!

Of more than Fancy, of the Social Sense
Distending wide, and man beloved as man,
Where France in all her towns lay vibrating
Like some becalméd bark beneath the burst        30
Of Heaven's immediate thunder, when no cloud
Is visible, or shadow on the main.
For thou wert there, thine own brows garlanded,
Amid the tremor of a realm aglow,
Amid a mighty nation jubilant,
When from the general heart of human kind
Hope sprang forth like a full-born Deity!
——Of that dear Hope afflicted and struck down,
So summoned homeward, thenceforth calm and sure
From the dread watch-tower of man's absolute self,    40
With light unwaning on her eyes, to look
Far on—herself a glory to behold,
The Angel of the vision! Then (last strain)
Of Duty, chosen Laws controlling choice,
Action and joy!—An Orphic song indeed,
A song divine of high and passionate thoughts
To their own music chaunted!

                              O great Bard!
Ere yet that last strain dying awed the air,
With stedfast eye I viewed thee in the choir
Of ever-enduring men. The truly great        50

Have all one age, and from one visible space
Shed influence! They, both in power and act,
Are permanent, and Time is not with them,
Save as it worketh for them, they in it.
Nor less a sacred Roll, than those of old,
And to be placed, as they, with gradual fame
Among the archives of mankind, thy work
Makes audible a linkéd lay of Truth,
Of Truth profound a sweet continuous lay,
Not learnt, but native, her own natural notes!                    60
Ah! as I listened with a heart forlorn,
The pulses of my being beat anew:
And even as Life returns upon the drowned,
Life's joy rekindling roused a throng of pains—
Keen pangs of Love, awakening as a babe
Turbulent, with an outcry in the heart;
And fears self-willed, that shunned the eye of Hope;
And Hope that scarce would know itself from Fear;
Sense of past Youth, and Manhood come in vain,
And Genius given, and Knowledge won in vain;                     70
And all which I had culled in wood-walks wild,
And all which patient toil had reared, and all,
Commune with thee had opened out—but flowers
Strewed on my corse, and borne upon my bier
In the same coffin, for the self-same grave!

   That way no more! and ill beseems it me,
Who came a welcomer in herald's guise,
Singing of Glory, and Futurity,
To wander back on such unhealthful road,
Plucking the poisons of self-harm! And ill                       80
Such intertwine beseems triumphal wreaths
Strew'd before thy advancing!

                              Nor do thou,
Sage Bard! impair the memory of that hour
Of thy communion with my nobler mind
By pity or grief, already felt too long!

Nor let my words import more blame than needs.
The tumult rose and ceased: for Peace is nigh
Where Wisdom's voice has found a listening heart.
Amid the howl of more than wintry storms,
The Halcyon hears the voice of vernal hours          90
Already on the wing.

                    Eve following eve,
Dear tranquil time, when the sweet sense of Home
Is sweetest! moments for their own sake hailed
And more desired, more precious, for thy song,
In silence listening, like a devout child,
My soul lay passive, by thy various strain
Driven as in surges now beneath the stars,
With momentary stars of my own birth,
Fair constellated foam, still darting off
Into the darkness; now a tranquil sea,               100
Outspread and bright, yet swelling to the moon.

And when—O Friend! my comforter and guide!
Strong in thyself, and powerful to give strength!—
Thy long sustainéd Song finally closed,
And thy deep voice had ceased—yet thou thyself
Wert still before my eyes, and round us both
That happy vision of belovéd faces—
Scarce conscious, and yet conscious of its close
I sate, my being blended in one thought
(Thought was it? or aspiration? or resolve?)         110
Absorbed, yet hanging still upon the sound—
And when I rose, I found myself in prayer.
*January,* 1807.                                 1817.


# PSYCHE

The butterfly the ancient Grecians made
The soul's fair emblem, and its only name—
But of the soul, escaped the slavish trade

Of mortal life!—For in this earthly frame
Ours is the reptile's lot, much toil, much blame,
Manifold motions making little speed,
And to deform and kill the things whereon we feed.
1808.                                                       1817


## A TOMBLESS EPITAPH

'Tis true, Idoloclastes Satyrane!
(So call him, for so mingling blame with praise,
And smiles with anxious looks, his earliest friends,
Masking his birth-name, wont to character
His wild-wood fancy and impetuous zeal,)
'Tis true that, passionate for ancient truths,
And honouring with religious love the Great
Of elder times, he hated to excess,
With an unquiet and intolerant scorn,
The hollow Puppets of a hollow Age,                           10
Ever idolatrous, and changing ever
Its worthless Idols! Learning, Power, and Time,
(Too much of all) thus wasting in vain war
Of fervid colloquy. Sickness, 'tis true,
Whole years of weary days, besieged him close,
Even to the gates and inlets of his life!
But it is true, no less, that strenuous, firm,
And with a natural gladness, he maintained
The citadel unconquered, and in joy
Was strong to follow the delightful Muse.                     20
For not a hidden path, that to the shades
Of the beloved Parnassian forest leads,
Lurked undiscovered by him; not a rill
There issues from the fount of Hippocrene,
But he had traced it upward to its source,
Through open glade, dark glen, and secret dell,
Knew the gay wild flowers on its banks, and culled

Its med'cinable herbs. Yea, oft alone,
Piercing the long-neglected holy cave,
The haunt obscure of old Philosophy,                    30
He bade with lifted torch its starry walls
Sparkle, as erst they sparkled to the flame
Of odorous lamps tended by Saint and Sage.
O framed for calmer times and nobler hearts!
O studious Poet, eloquent for truth!
Philosopher! contemning wealth and death,
Yet docile, childlike, full of Life and Love!
Here, rather than on monumental stone,
This record of thy worth thy Friend inscribes,
Thoughtful, with quiet tears upon his cheek.         40
? 1809.                                    1809.


# THE MADMAN AND THE LETHARGIST

### AN EXAMPLE

Quoth Dick to me, as once at College
We argued on the use of knowledge;—
"In old King Olim's reign, I've read,
There lay two patients in one bed.
The one in fat lethargic trance,
Lay wan and motionless as lead:
The other, (like the Folks in France),
Possess'd a different disposition—
In short, the plain truth to confess,
The man was madder than Mad Bess!         10
But both diseases, none disputed,
Were unmedicinably rooted;
Yet, so it chanc'd, by Heaven's permission,
Each prov'd the other's true physician.

"Fighting with a ghostly stare
Troops of Despots in the air,

Obstreperously Jacobinical,
The madman froth'd, and foam'd, and roar'd:
The other, snoring octaves cynical,
Like good John Bull, in posture clinical,        20
Seem'd living only when he snor'd.
The *Citizen* enraged to see
This fat Insensibility,
Or, tir'd with solitary labour,
Determin'd to convert his neighbour;
So up he sprang and to't he fell,
Like devil piping hot from hell,
With indefatigable fist
Belab'ring the poor Lethargist;
Till his own limbs were stiff and sore,        30
And sweat-drops roll'd from every pore:—
Yet, still, with flying fingers fleet,
Duly accompanied by feet,
With some short intervals of biting,
He executes the self-same strain,
Till the Slumberer woke for pain,
And half-prepared himself for fighting—
That moment that his mad Colleague
Sunk down and slept thro' pure fatigue.
So both were cur'd—and this example        40
Gives demonstration full and ample—
That *Chance* may bring a thing to bear,
Where *Art* sits down in blank despair."

"That's true enough, Dick," answer'd I,
"But as for the *Example*, 'tis a lie."
? 1809.                                    1912.

# THE VISIONARY HOPE

Sad lot, to have no Hope! Though lowly kneeling
He fain would frame a prayer within his breast,
Would fain entreat for some sweet breath of healing,
That his sick body might have ease and rest;
He strove in vain! the dull sighs from his chest
Against his will the stifling load revealing,
Though Nature forced; though like some captive guest,
Some royal prisoner at his conqueror's feast,
An alien's restless mood but half concealing,
The sternness on his gentle brow confessed,
Sickness within and miserable feeling:
Though obscure pangs made curses of his dreams,
And dreaded sleep, each night repelled in vain,
Each night was scattered by its own loud screams:
Yet never could his heart command, though fain,
One deep full wish to be no more in pain.

That Hope, which was his inward bliss and boast,
Which waned and died, yet ever near him stood,
Though changed in nature, wander where he would—
For Love's Despair is but Hope's pining Ghost!
For this one hope he makes his hourly moan,
He wishes and can wish for this alone!
Pierced, as with light from Heaven, before its gleams
(So the love-stricken visionary deems)
Disease would vanish, like a summer shower,
Whose dews fling sunshine from the noon-tide bower!
Or let it stay! yet this one Hope should give
Such strength that he would bless his pains and live.

? 1810.                                                    1817.

# TIME, REAL AND IMAGINARY

### AN ALLEGORY

On the wide level of a mountain's head,
(I knew not where, but 'twas some faery place)
Their pinions, ostrich-like, for sails out-spread,
Two lovely children run an endless race,
    A sister and a brother!
    This far outstripp'd the other;
  Yet ever runs she with reverted face,
  And looks and listens for the boy behind:
    For he, alas! is blind!
O'er rough and smooth with even step he passed,
And knows not whether he be first or last.
? 1812.                 1817.

# AN INVOCATION

### FROM *Remorse*

[Act III, Scene i. ll. 69–82.]

Hear, sweet Spirit, hear the spell,
Lest a blacker charm compel!
So shall the midnight breezes swell
With thy deep long-lingering knell.

And at evening evermore,
In a chapel on the shore,
Shall the chaunter, sad and saintly,
Yellow tapers burning faintly,
Doleful masses chaunt for thee,
    Miserere Domine!

Hush! the cadence dies away
   On the quiet moonlight sea:
The boatmen rest their oars and say,
    Miserere Domine!
1812.                                1813.

# HUMAN LIFE

## ON THE DENIAL OF IMMORTALITY

If dead, we cease to be; if total gloom
   Swallow up life's brief flash for aye, we fare
As summer-gusts, of sudden birth and doom,
   Whose sound and motion not alone declare,
But are their whole of being! If the breath
   Be Life itself, and not its task and tent,
If even a soul like Milton's can know death;
   O Man! thou vessel purposeless, unmeant,
Yet drone-hive strange of phantom purposes!
   Surplus of Nature's dread activity,
Which, as she gazed on some nigh-finished vase,
Retreating slow, with meditative pause,
   She formed with restless hands unconsciously.
Blank accident! nothing's anomaly!
   If rootless thus, thus substanceless thy state,
Go, weigh thy dreams, and be thy hopes, thy fears,
The counter-weights!—Thy laughter and thy tears
   Mean but themselves, each fittest to create
And to repay the other! Why rejoices
   Thy heart with hollow joy for hollow good?
   Why cowl thy face beneath the mourner's hood?
Why waste thy sighs, and thy lamenting voices,
   Image of Image, Ghost of Ghostly Elf,
That such a thing as thou feel'st warm or cold?
Yet what and whence thy gain, if thou withhold

These costless shadows of thy shadowy self?
Be sad! be glad! be neither! seek, or shun!
Thou hast no reason why! Thou canst have none;
Thy being's being is contradiction.
? 1815.                                    1817.


# SONG

~~~~

FROM *Zapolya*


A sunny shaft did I behold,
    From sky to earth it slanted:
And poised therein a bird so bold—
    Sweet bird, thou wert enchanted!

He sank, he rose, he twinkled, he trolled
    Within that shaft of sunny mist;
His eyes of fire, his beak of gold,
    All else of amethyst!

And thus he sang: "Adieu! adieu!
Love's dreams prove seldom true.
The blossoms they make no delay:
The sparkling dew-drops will not stay.
    Sweet month of May,
        We must away;
            Far, far away!
                To-day! to-day!"

1815.                                    1817.

# HUNTING SONG

from *Zapolya*

Up, up! ye dames, and lasses gay!
To the meadows trip away.
'Tis you must tend the flocks this morn,
And scare the small birds from the corn.
　　Not a soul at home may stay:
　　　For the shepherds must go
　　　With lance and bow
　　To hunt the wolf in the woods to-day.

Leave the hearth and leave the house
To the cricket and the mouse:
Find grannam out a sunny seat,
With babe and lambkin at her feet.
　　Not a soul at home may stay:
　　　For the shepherds must go
　　　With lance and bow
　　To hunt the wolf in the woods to-day.
1815.　　　　　　　　　　　　　　　　1817.

# TO NATURE

It may indeed be phantasy, when I
　Essay to draw from all created things
　Deep, heartfelt, inward joy that closely clings;
And trace in leaves and flowers that round me lie
Lessons of love and earnest piety.
　So let it be; and if the wide world rings
　In mock of this belief, it brings
Nor fear, nor grief, nor vain perplexity.
So will I build my altar in the fields,
　And the blue sky my fretted dome shall be,

And the sweet fragrance that the wild flower yields
    Shall be the incense I will yield to Thee,
Thee only God! and thou shalt not despise
Even me, the priest of this poor sacrifice.
? 1820.                       1836.

# LIMBO

\*      \*      \*      \*      \*

The sole true Something—This! In Limbo's Den
It frightens Ghosts, as here Ghosts frighten men.
Thence cross'd unseiz'd—and shall some fated hour
Be pulveris'd by Demogorgon's power,
And given as poison to annihilate souls—
Even now it shrinks them—they shrink in as Moles
(Nature's mute monks, live mandrakes of the ground)
Creep back from Light—then listen for its sound;—
See but to dread, and dread they know not why—
The natural alien of their negative eye.        10

'Tis a strange place, this Limbo!—not a Place,
Yet name it so;—where Time and weary Space
Fettered from flight, with night-mare sense of fleeing,
Strive for their last crepuscular half-being;—
Lank Space, and scytheless Time with branny hands
Barren and soundless as the measuring sands,
Not mark'd by flit of Shades,—unmeaning they
As moonlight on the dial of the day!
But that is lovely—looks like Human Time,—
An Old Man with a steady look sublime,        20
That stops his earthly task to watch the skies;
But he is blind—a Statue hath such eyes;—
Yet having moonward turn'd his face by chance,
Gazes the orb with moon-like countenance,
With scant white hairs, with foretop bald and high,
He gazes still,—his eyeless face all eye;—

As 'twere an organ full of silent sight,
His whole face seemeth to rejoice in light!
Lip touching lip, all moveless, bust and limb—
He seems to gaze at that which seems to gaze on him!        30
    No such sweet sights doth Limbo den immure,
Wall'd round, and made a spirit-jail secure,
By the mere horror of blank Naught-at-all,
Whose circumambience doth these ghosts enthral.
A lurid thought is growthless, dull Privation,
Yet that is but a Purgatory curse;
Hell knows a fear far worse,
A fear—a future state;—'tis positive Negation!
1817.        1893.


# NE PLUS ULTRA

    Sole Positive of Night!
    Antipathist of Light!
Fate's only essence! primal scorpion rod—
The one permitted opposite of God!—
Condenséd blackness and abysmal storm
    Compacted to one sceptre
    Arms the Grasp enorm—
    The Intercepter—
The Substance that still casts the shadow Death!—
    The Dragon foul and fell—
    The unrevealable,
And hidden one, whose breath
Gives wind and fuel to the fires of Hell!
    Ah! sole despair
    Of both th' eternities in Heaven!
Sole interdict of all-bedewing prayer,
    The all-compassionate!
Save to the Lampads Seven

Reveal'd to none of all th' Angelic State,
　　Save to the Lampads Seven,
　　That watch the throne of Heaven!
? 1826.　　　　　　　　　　　　　1834.


# THE KNIGHT'S TOMB

Where is the grave of Sir Arthur O'Kellyn?
Where may the grave of that good man be?—
By the side of a spring, on the breast of Helvellyn,
Under the twigs of a young birch tree!
The oak that in summer was sweet to hear,
And rustled its leaves in the fall of the year,
And whistled and roared in the winter alone,
Is gone,—and the birch in its stead is grown.—
The Knight's bones are dust,
And his good sword rust;—
His soul is with the saints, I trust.
? 1817.　　　　　　　　　　　　　1834.


# ON DONNE'S POETRY

With Donne, whose muse on dromedary trots,
Wreathe iron pokers into true-love knots;
Rhyme's sturdy cripple, fancy's maze and clue,
Wit's forge and fire-blast, meaning's press and screw.
? 1818.　　　　　　　　　　　　　1836.

## YOUTH AND AGE

Verse, a breeze mid blossoms straying,
Where Hope clung feeding, like a bee—
Both were mine! Life went a-maying
    With Nature, Hope, and Poesy,
        When I was young!

When I was young?—Ah, woful When!
Ah! for the change 'twixt Now and Then!
This breathing house not built with hands,
This body that does me grievous wrong,
O'er aery cliffs and glittering sands,
How lightly then it flashed along:—         10
Like those trim skiffs, unknown of yore,
On winding lakes and rivers wide,
That ask no aid of sail or oar,
That fear no spite of wind or tide!
Nought cared this body for wind or weather
When Youth and I lived in't together.

Flowers are lovely; Love is flower-like;
Friendship is a sheltering tree;
O! the joys, that came down shower-like,
Of Friendship, Love, and Liberty,
        Ere I was old!         20

Ere I was old? Ah woful Ere,
Which tells me, Youth's no longer here!
O Youth! for years so many and sweet,
'Tis known, that Thou and I were one,
I'll think it but a fond conceit—
It cannot be that Thou art gone!
Thy vesper-bell hath not yet toll'd:—
And thou wert aye a masker bold!
What strange disguise hast now put on,

To make believe, that thou art gone? 30
I see these locks in silvery slips,
This drooping gait, this altered size:
But Spring-tide blossoms on thy lips,
And tears take sunshine from thine eyes!
Life is but thought: so think I will
That Youth and I are house-mates still.

Dew-drops are the gems of morning,
But the tears of mournful eve!
Where no hope is, life's a warning
That only serves to make us grieve,
           When we are old: 40

That only serves to make us grieve
With oft and tedious taking-leave,
Like some poor nigh-related guest,
That may not rudely be dismist;
Yet hath outstay'd his welcome while,
And tells the jest without the smile.
1823–1832.         1834.


# FIRST ADVENT OF LOVE

O fair is Love's first hope to gentle mind!
As Eve's first star thro' fleecy cloudlet peeping;
And sweeter than the gentle south-west wind.
O'er willowy meads, and shadow'd waters creeping,
And Ceres' golden fields;—the sultry hind
Meets it with brow uplift, and stays his reaping.
? 1824.         1834.

# WORK WITHOUT HOPE

LINES COMPOSED 21ST FEBRUARY 1825

All Nature seems at work. Slugs leave their lair—
The bees are stirring—birds are on the wing—
And Winter slumbering in the open air,
Wears on his smiling face a dream of Spring!
And I the while, the sole unbusy thing,
Nor honey make, nor pair, nor build, nor sing.

Yet well I ken the banks where amaranths blow,
Have traced the fount whence streams of nectar flow.
Bloom, O ye amaranths! bloom for whom ye may,
For me ye bloom not! Glide, rich streams, away!
With lips unbrightened, wreathless brow, I stroll:
And would you learn the spells that drowse my soul?
Work without Hope draws nectar in a sieve,
And Hope without an object cannot live.
1825.                                                              1828.

# SONG

Though veiled in spires of myrtle-wreath,
Love is a sword which cuts its sheath,
And through the clefts itself has made,
We spy the flashes of the blade!

But through the clefts itself has made
We likewise see Love's flashing blade,
By rust consumed, or snapt in twain;
And only hilt and stump remain.
? 1825.                                                         1828.

# A CHARACTER

A bird, who for his other sins
Had liv'd amongst the Jacobins;
Though like a kitten amid rats,
Or callow tit in nest of bats,
He much abhorr'd all democrats;
Yet nathless stood in ill report
Of wishing ill to Church and Court,
Tho' he'd nor claw, nor tooth, nor sting,
And learnt to pipe God save the King;
Tho' each day did new feathers bring,                    10
All swore he had a leathern wing;
Nor polish'd wing, nor feather'd tail,
Nor down-clad thigh would aught avail;
And tho'—his tongue devoid of gall—
He civilly assur'd them all:—
"A bird am I of Phoebus' breed,
And on the sunflower cling and feed;
My name, good Sirs, is Thomas Tit!"
The bats would hail him Brother Cit,
Or, at the furthest, cousin-german.                      20
At length the matter to determine,
He publicly denounced the vermin;
He spared the mouse, he praised the owl;
But bats were neither flesh nor fowl.
Blood-sucker, vampire, harpy, goul,
Came in full clatter from his throat,
Till his old nest-mates chang'd their note
To hireling, traitor, and turncoat,—
A base apostate who had sold
His very teeth and claws for gold;—                      30
And then his feathers!—sharp the jest—
No doubt he feather'd well his nest!

"A Tit indeed! aye, tit for tat—
With place and title, brother Bat,
We soon shall see how well he'll play
Count Goldfinch, or Sir Joseph Jay!"
    Alas, poor Bird! and ill-bestarr'd—
Or rather let us say, poor Bard!
And henceforth quit the allegoric,
With metaphor and simile,              40
For simple facts and style historic:—
Alas, poor Bard! no gold had he;
Behind another's team he stept,
And plough'd and sow'd, while others reapt;
The work was his, but theirs the glory,
*Sic vos non vobis,* his whole story.
Besides, whate'er he wrote or said
Came from his heart as well as head;
And though he never left in lurch
His king, his country, or his church,      50
'Twas but to humour his own cynical
Contempt of doctrines Jacobinical;
To his own conscience only hearty,
'Twas but by chance he serv'd the party;—
The self-same things had said and writ,
Had Pitt been Fox, and Fox been Pitt;
Content his own applause to win,
Would never dash thro' thick and thin,
And he can make, so say the wise,
No claim who makes no sacrifice;—      60
And bard still less:—what claim had he,
Who swore it vex'd his soul to see
So grand a cause, so proud a realm,
With Goose and Goody at the helm;
Who long ago had fall'n asunder
But for their rivals' baser blunder,
The coward whine and Frenchified
Slaver and slang of the other side?—

Thus, his own whim his only bribe,
Our Bard pursued his old A. B. C. 70
Contented if he could subscribe
In fullest sense his name Ἔστησε;
('Tis Punic Greek for "he hath stood!")
Whate'er the men, the cause was good;
And therefore with a right good will,
Poor fool, he fights their battles still.
Tush! squeak'd the Bats;—a mere bravado
To whitewash that base renegado;
'Tis plain unless you're blind or mad,
His conscience for the bays he barters;— 80
And true it is—as true as sad—
These circlets of green baize he had—
But then, alas! they were his garters!

Ah! silly Bard, unfed, untended,
His lamp but glimmer'd in its socket;
He lived unhonour'd and unfriended
With scarce a penny in his pocket;—
Nay—tho' he hid it from the many—
With scarce a pocket for his penny!
1825.                              1834.


## CONSTANCY TO AN IDEAL OBJECT

Since all that beat about in Nature's range,
Or veer or vanish; why should'st thou remain
The only constant in a world of change,
O yearning Thought! that liv'st but in the brain?
Call to the Hours, that in the distance play,
The faery people of the future day——
Fond Thought! not one of all that shining swarm
Will breathe on thee with life-enkindling breath,
Till when, like strangers shelt'ring from a storm,
Hope and Despair meet in the porch of Death!

Yet still thou haunt'st me; and though well I see,
She is not thou, and only thou art she,
Still, still as though some dear embodied Good,
Some living Love before my eyes there stood
With answering look a ready ear to lend,
I mourn to thee and say—"Ah! loveliest friend!
That this the meed of all my toils might be,
To have a home, an English home, and thee!"
Vain repetition! Home and Thou are one.
The peacefull'st cot, the moon shall shine upon,
Lulled by the thrush and wakened by the lark,
Without thee were but a becalméd bark,
Whose Helmsman on an ocean waste and wide
Sits mute and pale his mouldering helm beside.

And art thou nothing? Such thou art, as when
The woodman winding westward up the glen
At wintry dawn, where o'er the sheep-track's maze
The viewless snow-mist weaves a glist'ning haze,
Sees full before him, gliding without tread,
An image with a glory round its head;
The enamoured rustic worships its fair hues,
Nor knows he makes the shadow, he pursues!

                                                    1828.


# EPITAPHIUM TESTAMENTARIUM

~~~

Τὸ τοῦ ΈΣΤΗΣΕ τοῦ ἐπιθανοῦς Epitaphium testamentarium αὐτόγραφον.

Quae linquam, aut nihil, aut nihili, aut vix sunt mea. Sordes Do Morti:
reddo caetera, Christe! tibi.
    1826.

### Έρως ἀεὶ λάλητρος ἑταῖρος

In many ways does the full heart reveal
The presence of the love it would conceal;
But in far more th' estrangéd heart lets know
The absence of the love, which yet it fain would shew.
1826.                                              1827.

## COLOGNE

In Köhln, a town of monks and bones,
And pavements fang'd with murderous stones
And rags, and hags, and hideous wenches;
I counted two and seventy stenches,
All well defined, and several stinks!
Ye Nymphs that reign o'er sewers and sinks,
The river Rhine, it is well known,
Doth wash your city of Cologne;
But tell me, Nymphs, what power divine
Shall henceforth wash the river Rhine?
1828.                                              1834.


## REASON

["Finally, what is Reason? You have often asked me: and this is my answer":—]

Whene'er the mist, that stands 'twixt God and thee,
Defecates to a pure transparency,
That intercepts no light and adds no stain—
There Reason is, and then begins her reign!

But alas!
——"tu stesso, ti fai grosso
Col falso immaginar, sì che non vedi
Ciò che vedresti, se l'avessi scosso."
                          Dante, *Paradiso*, Canto i.
1830.                                              1830.

# SELF-KNOWLEDGE

—E coelo descendit γνῶθι σεαυτόν.—Juvenal, xi. 27.

Γνῶθι σεαυτόν!—and is this the prime
And heaven-sprung adage of the olden time!—
Say, canst thou make thyself?—Learn first that trade;—
Haply thou mayst know what thyself had made.
What hast thou, Man, that thou dar'st call thine own?—
What is there in thee, Man, that can be known?—
Dark fluxion, all unfixable by thought,
A phantom dim of past and future wrought,
Vain sister of the worm,—life, death, soul, clod—
Ignore thyself, and strive to know thy God!
1832.                                                          1834.

# FORBEARANCE

Beareth all things.—1 Cor. xiii. 7.

Gently I took that which ungently came,
And without scorn forgave:—Do thou the same.
A wrong done to thee think a cat's-eye spark
Thou wouldst not see, were not thine own heart dark.
Thine own keen sense of wrong that thirsts for sin,
Fear that—the spark self-kindled from within,
Which blown upon will blind thee with its glare,
Or smother'd stifle thee with noisome air.
Clap on the extinguisher, pull up the blinds,
And soon the ventilated spirit finds
Its natural daylight. If a foe have kenn'd,
Or worse than foe, an alienated friend,
A rib of dry rot in thy ship's stout side,
Think it God's message, and in humble pride
With heart of oak replace it;—thine the gains—
Give him the rotten timber for his pains!
? 1832.                                                        1834.

# LOVE'S APPARITION AND EVANISHMENT

### AN ALLEGORIC ROMANCE

Like a lone Arab, old and blind,
Some caravan had left behind,
Who sits beside a ruin'd well,
Where the shy sand-asps bask and swell;
And now he hangs his agéd head aslant,
And listens for a human sound—in vain!
And now the aid, which Heaven alone can grant,
Upturns his eyeless face from Heaven to gain;—
Even thus, in vacant mood, one sultry hour,
Resting my eye upon a drooping plant,
With brow low-bent, within my garden-bower,
I sate upon the couch of camomile;
And—whether 'twas a transient sleep, perchance,
Flitted across the idle brain, the while
I watch'd the sickly calm with aimless scope,
In my own heart; or that, indeed a trance,
Turn'd my eye inward—thee, O genial Hope,
Love's elder sister! thee did I behold,
Drest as a bridesmaid, but all pale and cold,
With roseless cheek, all pale and cold and dim,
   Lie lifeless at my feet!
And then came Love, a sylph in bridal trim,
   And stood beside my seat;
She bent, and kiss'd her sister's lips,
   As she was wont to do;—
Alas! 'twas but a chilling breath
Woke just enough of life in death
   To make Hope die anew.

In vain we supplicate the Powers above;
There is no resurrection for the Love
That, nursed in tenderest care, yet fades away
In the chill'd heart by gradual self-decay.
1833.                                      1834.

# PROSE

# THE WANDERINGS OF CAIN

## PREFATORY NOTE

A prose composition, one not in metre at least, seems *primâ facie* to require explanation or apology. It was written in the year 1798, near Nether Stowey, in Somersetshire, at which place (*sanctum et amabile nomen!* rich by so many associations and recollections) the author had taken up his residence in order to enjoy the society and close neighbourhood of a dear and honoured friend, T. Poole, Esq. The work was to have been written in concert with another [Wordsworth], whose name is too venerable within the precincts of genius to be unnecessarily brought into connection with such a trifle, and who was then residing at a small distance from Nether Stowey. The title and subject were suggested by myself, who likewise drew out the scheme and the contents for each of the three books or cantos, of which the work was to consist, and which, the reader is to be informed, was to have been finished in one night! My partner undertook the first canto: I the second: and which ever had *done first,* was to set about the third. Almost thirty years have passed by; yet at this moment I cannot without something more than a smile moot the question which of the two things was the more impracticable, for a mind so eminently original to compose another man's thoughts and fancies, or for a taste so austerely pure and simple to imitate the Death of Abel? Methinks I see his grand and noble countenance as at the moment when having despatched my own portion of the task at full finger-speed, I hastened to him with my manuscript— that look of humourous despondency fixed on his almost blank sheet of paper, and then its silent mock-piteous admission of failure struggling with the sense of the exceeding ridiculousness of the whole scheme—which broke up in a laugh: and the Ancient Mariner was written instead.

Years afterward, however, the draft of the plan and proposed incidents, and the portion executed, obtained favour in the eyes of more than one person, whose judgment on a poetic work could not but have weighed with me, even though no parental partiality had been thrown into the same scale, as a make-weight: and I determined on commencing anew, and composing the whole in stanzas, and made some progress in realising this intention, when adverse gales drove my bark off the "Fortunate Isles" of the Muses: and then other and more momentous interests prompted a different voyage, to firmer anchorage and a securer port. I have in vain tried to recover the lines from the palimpsest tablet of my memory: and I can only offer the introductory stanza, which had been committed to writing for the purpose of procuring a friend's judgment on the metre, as a specimen:—

Encinctured with a twine of leaves,
That leafy twine his only dress!
A lovely Boy was plucking fruits,
By moonlight, in a wilderness.
The moon was bright, the air was free,
And fruits and flowers together grew
On many a shrub and many a tree:
And all put on a gentle hue,
Hanging in the shadowy air
Like a picture rich and rare.
It was a climate where, they say,
The night is more belov'd than day.
But who that beauteous Boy beguil'd,
That beauteous Boy to linger here?
Alone, by night, a little child,
In place so silent and so wild—
Has he no friend, no loving mother near?

I have here given the birth, parentage, and premature decease of the "Wanderings of Cain, a poem",—intreating, however, my Readers, not to think so meanly of my judgment as to suppose that I either regard or offer it as any excuse for the publication of the following fragment (and I may add, of one or two others in its neighbourhood) in its primitive crudity. But I should find still greater difficulty in forgiving myself were I to record pro *taedio* publico a set of petty mishaps and annoyances which I myself wish to forget. I must be content therefore with assuring the friendly Reader, that the less he attributes its appearance to the Author's will, choice, or judgment, the nearer to the truth he will be.

S. T. COLERIDGE (1828)

# THE WANDERINGS OF CAIN

### CANTO II

"A little further, O my father, yet a little further, and we shall come into the open moonlight." Their road was through a forest of fir-trees; at its entrance the trees stood at distances from each other, and the path was broad, and the moonlight and the moonlight shadows reposed upon it, and appeared quietly to inhabit that solitude. But soon the path winded and became narrow; the sun at high noon sometimes speckled, but never illumined it, and now it was dark as a cavern.

"It is dark, O my father!" said Enos, "but the path under our feet is smooth and soft, and we shall soon come out into the open moonlight."

"Lead on, my child!" said Cain; "guide me, little child!" And the innocent little child clasped a finger of the hand which had murdered the righteous Abel, and he guided his father. "The fir branches drip upon thee, my son." "Yea, pleasantly, father, for I ran fast and eagerly to bring thee the pitcher and the cake, and my body is not yet cool. How happy the squirrels are that feed on these fir-trees! they leap from bough to bough, and the old squirrels play round their young ones in the nest. I clomb a tree yesterday at noon, O my father, that I might play with them, but they leaped away from the branches, even to the slender twigs did they leap, and in a moment I beheld them on another tree. Why, O my father, would they not play with me? I would be good to them as thou art good to me: and I groaned to them even as thou groanest when thou givest me to eat, and when thou coverest me at evening, and as often as I stand at thy knee and thine eyes look at me?" Then Cain stopped, and stifling his groans he sank to the earth, and the child Enos stood in the darkness beside him.

And Cain lifted up his voice and cried bitterly, and said, "The Mighty One that persecuteth me is on this side and on that; he pursueth my soul like the wind, like the sand-blast he passeth through me; he is around me even as the air! O that I might be utterly no more! I desire to die—yea, the things that never had life, neither move they upon the earth—behold! they seem precious to mine eyes. O that a man might live without the breath of his nostrils. So I might abide in darkness, and blackness, and an empty space! Yea, I would lie down, I would not rise, neither would I stir my limbs till I became as the rock in the den of the lion, on which the young lion resteth his head whilst he sleepeth. For the torrent that roareth far off hath a voice: and the clouds in heaven look terribly on me; the Mighty One who is against me speaketh in the wind of the cedar grove; and in silence am I dried up." Then Enos spake to his father, "Arise, my father, arise, we are but a little way from the place where I found the cake and the pitcher." And Cain said, "How knowest thou!" and the child answered—"Behold the bare rocks are a few of thy strides distant from the forest; and while even now thou wert lifting up thy voice, I heard the echo." Then the child took hold of his father, as if he would raise him: and Cain being faint and feeble rose slowly on his knees and pressed himself against the trunk of a fir, and stood upright and followed the child.

The path was dark till within three strides' length of its termination, when it turned suddenly; the thick black trees formed a low arch, and the moonlight appeared for a moment like a dazzling portal. Enos ran before and stood in the open air; and when Cain, his father, emerged from the darkness, the child was affrighted. For the mighty limbs of Cain were wasted as by fire; his hair was as the matted curls on the bison's forehead, and so glared his fierce and sullen eye beneath: and the black abundant locks on either side, a rank and tangled mass, were stained and scorched, as though the grasp of a burning iron hand had striven to rend them; and his countenance told in a strange and terrible language of agonies that had been, and were, and were still to continue to be.

The scene around was desolate; as far as the eye could reach it was desolate: the bare rocks faced each other, and left a long and wide interval of thin white sand. You might wander on and look round and round, and peep into the crevices of the rocks and discover nothing that acknowledged the influence of the seasons. There was no spring, no summer, no autumn: and the winter's snow, that would have been lovely, fell not on these hot rocks and scorching sands. Never morning lark had poised himself over this desert; but the huge serpent often hissed there beneath the talons of the vulture, and the vulture screamed, his wings imprisoned within the coils of the serpent. The pointed and shattered summits of the ridges of the rocks made a rude mimicry of human concerns, and seemed to prophecy mutely of things that then were not; steeples, and battlements, and ships with naked masts. As far from the wood as a boy might sling a pebble of the brook, there was one rock by itself at a small distance from the main ridge. It had been precipitated there perhaps by the groan which the Earth uttered when our first father fell. Before you approached, it appeared to lie flat on the ground, but its base slanted from its point, and between its point and the sands a tall man might stand upright. It was here that Enos had found the pitcher and cake, and to this place he led his father. But ere they had reached the rock they beheld a human shape: his back was towards them, and they were advancing unperceived, when they heard him smite his breast and cry aloud, "Woe is me! woe is me! I must never die again, and yet I am perishing with thirst and hunger."

Pallid, as the reflection of the sheeted lightning on the heavy-sailing night-cloud, became the face of Cain; but the child Enos took hold of the shaggy skin, his father's robe, and raised his eyes to his father, and listening whispered, "Ere yet I could speak, I am sure, O my father, that I heard that voice. Have not I often said that I remembered a sweet voice? O my father! this is it": and Cain trembled exceedingly. The voice was sweet indeed, but it was thin and querulous, like that of a feeble slave in misery, who despairs altogether, yet can not refrain himself from weeping and lamentation. And, behold! Enos glided forward, and creeping softly round the base of the rock, stood before the stranger, and looked up into his face. And the Shape shrieked, and turned round, and Cain beheld him, that his limbs and his face were those of his brother Abel whom he had killed! And Cain stood like one who struggles in his sleep because of the exceeding terribleness of a dream.

Thus as he stood in silence and darkness of soul, the Shape fell at his feet, and embraced his knees, and cried out with a bitter outcry, "Thou eldest born of Adam, whom Eve, my mother, brought forth, cease to torment me! I was feeding my flocks in green pastures by the side of quiet rivers, and thou killedst me; and now I am in misery." Then Cain closed his eyes, and hid them with his hands; and again he opened his eyes, and looked around him, and said to Enos, "What beholdest thou? Didst thou hear a voice, my son?" "Yes, my father, I beheld a man in unclean garments, and he uttered a sweet voice, full of lamentation." Then Cain raised up the Shape that was like Abel, and said:—"The Creator of our father, who had respect unto thee, and unto thy offering, wherefore hath he forsaken thee?" Then the Shape shrieked a second time, and rent his garment, and his naked skin was like the white sands beneath their feet; and he shrieked yet a third time, and threw himself on his face upon the sand that was black with the shadow of the rock, and Cain and Enos sate beside him; the child by his right hand, and Cain by his left. They were all three under the rock, and within the shadow. The Shape that was like Abel raised himself up, and spake to the child, "I know where the cold waters are, but I may not drink, wherefore didst thou then take away my pitcher?" But Cain said, "Didst thou not find favour in the sight of the Lord thy God?" The Shape answered, "The Lord is God of the living only, the dead have another God." Then the child Enos lifted up his eyes and prayed; but Cain rejoiced secretly in his heart. "Wretched shall they be all the days of their mortal life," exclaimed the Shape, "who sacrifice worthy and acceptable sacrifices to the God of the dead; but after death their toil ceaseth. Woe is me, for I was well beloved by the God of the living, and cruel wert thou, O my brother, who didst snatch me away from his power and his dominion." Having uttered these words, he rose suddenly, and fled over the sands: and Cain said in his heart, "The curse of the Lord is on me; but who is the God of the dead?" and he ran after the Shape, and the Shape fled shrieking over the sands, and the sands rose like white mists behind the steps of Cain, but the feet of him that was like Abel disturbed not the sands. He greatly outrun Cain, and turning short, he wheeled round, and came again to the rock where they had been sitting, and where Enos still stood; and the child caught hold of his garment as he passed by, and he fell upon the ground. And Cain stopped, and beholding him not, said, "he has passed into the dark woods," and he walked slowly back to the rocks; and when he reached it the child told him that he had caught hold of his garment as he passed by, and that the man had fallen upon the ground: and Cain once more sate beside him, and said, "Abel, my brother, I would lament for thee, but that the spirit within me is withered, and burnt up with extreme agony. Now, I pray thee, by thy flocks, and by thy pastures, and by the quiet rivers which thou lovedst, that thou tell me all that thou knowest. Who is the God of the dead? where doth he make his dwelling? what sacrifices are acceptable unto him? for I have offered, but have not been received; I have prayed, and have not been heard; and how can I be afflicted more than I already am?" The Shape arose and answered, "O that thou hadst had pity on me as I will have pity on thee. Follow me, Son of Adam! and bring thy child with thee!"

And they three passed over the white sands between the rocks, silent as the shadows.

1798.                                                              1828.

# APOLOGETIC PREFACE TO

## "FIRE, FAMINE, AND SLAUGHTER"

~~~~

At the house of a gentleman who by the principles and cor-
responding virtues of a sincere Christian consecrates a cultivated
genius and the favourable accidents of birth, opulence, and splendid connexions, it was my good fortune to meet, in a dinner-party,
with more men of celebrity in science or polite literature than are
commonly found collected round the same table. In the course of
conversation, one of the party reminded an illustrious poet [Scott],
then present, of some verses which he had recited that morning,
and which had appeared in a newspaper under the name of a
War-Eclogue, in which Fire, Famine, and Slaughter were introduced as the speakers. The gentleman so addressed replied, that he
was rather surprised that none of us should have noticed or heard
of the poem, as it had been, at the time, a good deal talked of in
Scotland. It may be easily supposed that my feelings were at this
moment not of the most comfortable kind. Of all present, one only
[Sir H. Davy] knew, or suspected me to be the author; a man who
would have established himself in the first rank of England's
living poets, if the Genius of our country had not decreed that he
should rather be the first in the first rank of its philosophers and
scientific benefactors. It appeared the general wish to hear the
lines. As my friend chose to remain silent, I chose to follow his
example, and Mr. . . . . . [Scott] recited the poem. This he
could do with the better grace, being known to have ever been
not only a firm and active Anti-Jacobin and Anti-Gallican, but
likewise a zealous admirer of Mr. Pitt, both as a good man and a
great statesman. As a poet exclusively, he had been amused with
the Eclogue; as a poet he recited it; and in a spirit which made it
evident that he would have read and repeated it with the same
pleasure had his own name been attached to the imaginary object
or agent.

After the recitation our amiable host observed that in his opinion Mr. . . . . . had over-rated the merits of the poetry; but had they been tenfold greater, they could not have compensated for that malignity of heart which could alone have prompted sentiments so atrocious. I perceived that my illustrious friend became greatly distressed on my account; but fortunately I was able to preserve fortitude and presence of mind enough to take up the subject without exciting even a suspicion how nearly and painfully it interested me.

What follows is the substance of what I then replied, but dilated and in language less colloquial. It was not my intention, I said, to justify the publication, whatever its author's feelings might have been at the time of composing it. That they are calculated to call forth so severe a reprobation from a good man, is not the worst feature of such poems. Their moral deformity is aggravated in proportion to the pleasure which they are capable of affording to vindictive, turbulent, and unprincipled readers. Could it be supposed, though for a moment, that the author seriously wished what he had thus wildly imagined, even the attempt to palliate an inhumanity so monstrous would be an insult to the hearers. But it seemed to me worthy of consideration, whether the mood of mind and the general state of sensations in which a poet produces such vivid and fantastic images, is likely to co-exist, or is even compatible with, that gloomy and deliberate ferocity which a serious wish to realize them would pre-suppose. It had been often observed, and all my experience tended to confirm the observation, that prospects of pain and evil to others, and in general all deep feelings of revenge, are commonly expressed in a few words, ironically tame, and mild. The mind under so direful and fiend-like an influence seems to take a morbid pleasure in contrasting the intensity of its wishes and feelings with the slightness or levity of the expressions by which they are hinted; and indeed feelings so intense and solitary, if they were not precluded (as in almost all cases they would be) by a constitutional activity of fancy and association, and by the specific joyousness combined with it, would assuredly themselves preclude such activity. Passion, in its own quality, is the antagonist of action; though in an ordinary and natural degree the former alternates with the latter, and thereby revives and strengthens it. But the more intense and insane the passion is, the fewer and the more fixed are the correspondent forms and notions. A rooted hatred, an inveterate thirst of revenge, is a sort of madness, and still eddies round its favourite object, and exercises as it were a perpetual tautology of mind in thoughts and words which admit of no adequate substitutes. Like a fish in a globe of glass, it moves restlessly round and round the scanty circumference, which it cannot leave without losing its vital element.

There is a second character of such imaginary representations as spring from a real and earnest desire of evil to another, which we often see in real life, and might even anticipate from the nature of the mind. The images, I mean, that a vindictive man places before his imagination, will most often be taken from the realities of life: they will be images of pain and suffering which he has himself seen inflicted on other men, and which he can fancy himself as inflicting on the object of his hatred. I will suppose that we had heard at different times two common sailors, each speaking of some one who had wronged or offended him: that the first with apparent violence had devoted every part of his adversary's body and soul to all the horrid phantoms and fantastic places that ever Quevedo dreamt of, and this in a rapid flow of those outrageous and wildly combined execrations, which too often with our lower classes serve for escape-valves to carry off the excess of their passions, as so much superfluous steam that would endanger the vessel if it were retained. The other, on the contrary, with that sort of calmness of tone which is to the ear what the paleness of anger is to the eye, shall simply say, "If I chance to be made boatswain, as I hope I soon shall, and can but once get that fellow under my hand (and I shall be upon the watch for him), I'll tickle his pretty skin! I won't hurt him! oh no! I'll only cut the — — to the liver!" I dare appeal to all present, which of the two they would regard as the least deceptive symptom of deliberate malignity? nay, whether it would surprise them to see the first fellow, an hour or two afterwards, cordially shaking hands with the very man the fractional parts of whose body and soul he had been so charitably disposing of; or even perhaps risking his life for him? What language Shakespeare considered characteristic of malignant disposition we see in the speech of the good-natured Gratiano, who spoke "an infinite deal of nothing more than any man in all Venice";

> ——Too wild, too rude and bold of voice!

the skipping spirit, whose thoughts and words reciprocally ran away with each other;

> ———O be thou damn'd, inexorable dog!
> And for thy life let justice be accused!

and the wild fancies that follow, contrasted with Shylock's tranquil "I stand here for Law."

Or, to take a case more analogous to the present subject, should we hold it either fair or charitable to believe it to have been Dante's serious wish that all the persons mentioned by him (many recently departed, and some even alive at the time,) should actually suffer the fantastic and horrible punishments to which he has sentenced them in his Hell and Purgatory? Or what shall we say of the passages in which Bishop Jeremy Taylor anticipates the state of those who, vicious themselves, have been the cause of vice and misery to their fellow-creatures? Could we endure for a moment to think that a spirit, like Bishop Taylor's, burning with Christian love; that a man constitutionally overflowing with pleasurable kindliness; who scarcely even in a casual illustration introduces the image of woman, child, or bird, but he embalms the thought with so rich a tenderness, as makes the very words seem beauties and fragments of poetry from Euripides or Simonides;— can we endure to think, that a man so natured and so disciplined, did at the time of composing this horrible picture, attach a sober feeling of reality to the phrases? or that he would have described in the same tone of justification, in the same luxuriant flow of phrases, the tortures about to be inflicted on a living individual by a verdict of the Star-Chamber? or the still more atrocious sentences executed on the Scotch anti-prelatists and schismatics, at the command, and in some instances under the very eye of the Duke of Lauderdale, and of that wretched bigot who afterwards dishonoured and forfeited the throne of Great Britain? Or do we not rather feel and understand, that these violent words were mere bubbles, flashes and electrical apparitions, from the magic cauldron of a fervid and ebullient fancy, constantly fuelled by an unexampled opulence of language?

Were I now to have read by myself for the first time the poem in question, my conclusion, I fully believe, would be, that the writer must have been some man of warm feelings and active fancy; that he had painted to himself the circumstances that accompany war in so many vivid and yet fantastic forms, as proved that neither the images nor the feelings were the result of observation, or in any way derived from realities. I should judge that they were the product of his own seething imagination, and therefore impregnated with that pleasurable exultation which is experienced in all energetic exertion of intellectual power; that in the same mood he had generalized the causes of the war, and then personified the abstract and christened it by the name which he had been accustomed to hear most often associated with its management and measures. I should guess that the minister was in the author's mind at the moment of composition as completely ἀπαθὴς, ἀναιμόσαρκος, as Anacreon's grasshopper, and that he had as little notion of a real person of flesh and blood,

Distinguishable in member, joint, or limb,
[*Paradise Lost,* II. 668.]

as Milton had in the grim and terrible phantom (half person, half allegory) which he has placed at the gates of Hell. I concluded by observing, that the poem was not calculated to excite passion in any mind, or to make any impression except on poetic readers; and that from the culpable levity betrayed at the close of the eclogue by the grotesque union of epigrammatic wit with allegoric personification, in the allusion to the most fearful of thoughts, I should conjecture that the "rantin' Bardie," instead of really believing, much less wishing, the fate spoken of in the last line, in application to any human individual, would shrink from passing the verdict even on the Devil himself, and exclaim with poor Burns,

> But fare ye weel, auld Nickie-ben!
> Oh! wad ye tak a thought an' men!
> Ye aiblins might—I dinna ken—
>              Still hae a stake—
> I'm wae to think upon yon den,
>              Ev'n for your sake!

I need not say that these thoughts, which are here dilated, were in such a company only rapidly suggested. Our kind host smiled, and with a courteous compliment observed, that the defence was too good for the cause. My voice faltered a little, for I was somewhat agitated; though not so much on my own account as for the uneasiness that so kind and friendly a man would feel from the thought that he had been the occasion of distressing me. At length I brought out these words: "I must now confess, sir! that I am author of that poem. It was written some years ago. I do not attempt to justify my past self, young as I then was; but as little as I would now write a similar poem, so far was I even then from imagining that the lines would be taken as more or less than a sport of fancy. At all events, if I know my own heart, there was never a moment in my existence in which I should have been more ready, had Mr. Pitt's person been in hazard, to interpose my own body, and defend his life at the risk of my own."

I have prefaced the poem with this anecdote, because to have printed it without any remark might well have been understood as implying an unconditional approbation on my part, and this after many years' consideration. But if it be asked why I republished it at all, I answer, that the poem had been attributed at different times to different other persons; and what I had dared beget, I thought it neither manly nor honourable not to dare father. From the same motives I should have published perfect copies of two poems, the one entitled The Devil's Thoughts, and the other, The Two Round Spaces on the Tombstone, but that the three first stanzas of the former, which were worth all the rest of the poem, and the best stanza of the remainder, were written by a friend [Southey] of deserved celebrity; and because there are passages in both which might have given offence to the religious feelings of certain readers. I myself indeed see no reason why vulgar superstitions and absurd conceptions that deform the pure faith of a Christian should possess a greater immunity from ridicule than stories of witches, or the fables of Greece and Rome. But there are those who deem it profaneness and irreverence to call an ape an ape, if it but wear a monk's cowl on its head; and I would rather reason with this weakness than offend it.

The passage from Jeremy Taylor to which I referred is found in his second Sermon on Christ's Advent to Judgment; which is likewise the second in his year's course of sermons. Among many remarkable passages of the same character in those discourses, I have selected this as the most so. "But when this Lion of the tribe of Judah shall appear, then Justice shall strike, and Mercy shall not hold her hands; she shall strike sore strokes, and Pity shall not break the blow. As there are treasures of good things, so hath God a treasure of wrath and fury, and scourges and scorpions; and then shall be produced the shame of Lust and the malice of Envy, and the groans of the oppressed and the persecutions of the saints, and the cares of Covetousness and the troubles of Ambition, and the insolencies of traitors and the violences of rebels, and the rage of anger and the uneasiness of impatience, and the restlessness of unlawful desires; and by this time the monsters and diseases will be numerous and intolerable, when God's heavy hand shall press the sanies and the intolerableness, the obliquity and the unreasonableness, the amazement and the disorder, the smart and the sorrow, the guilt and the punishment, out from all our sins, and pour them into one chalice, and mingle them with an infinite wrath, and make the wicked drink off all the vengeance, and force it down their unwilling throats with the violence of devils and accursed spirits."

That this Tartarean drench displays the imagination rather than the discretion of the compounder; that, in short, this passage and others of the same kind are in a bad taste, few will deny at the present day. It would, doubtless, have more behoved the good bishop not to be wise beyond what is written on a subject in which Eternity is opposed to Time, and a Death threatened, not the negative, but the positive Opposite of Life; a subject, therefore, which must of necessity be indescribable to the human understanding in our present state. But I can neither find nor believe that it ever occurred to any reader to ground on such passages a charge against Bishop Taylor's humanity, or goodness of heart. I was not a little surprised therefore to find, in the Pursuits of Literature and other works, so horrible a sentence passed on Milton's moral character, for a passage in his prose writings, as nearly parallel to this of Taylor's as two passages can well be conceived to be. All his merits, as a poet, forsooth—all the glory of having written the Paradise Lost, are light in the scale, nay, kick the beam, compared with the atrocious malignity of heart, expressed in the offensive paragraph. I remembered, in general, that Milton had concluded one of his works on Reformation, written in the fervour of his youthful imagination, in a high poetic strain, that wanted metre only to become a lyrical poem. I remembered that in the former part he had formed to himself a perfect ideal of human virtue, a character of heroic, disinterested zeal and devotion for Truth, Religion, and public Liberty, in act and in suffering, in the day of triumph and in the hour of martyrdom. Such spirits, as more excellent than others, he describes as having a more excellent reward, and as distinguished by a transcendant glory: and this reward and this glory he displays and particularizes with an energy and brilliance that announced the Paradise Lost as plainly, as ever the bright purple clouds in the east announced the coming of the Sun. Milton then passes to the gloomy contrast, to such men as from motives of selfish ambition and the lust of personal aggrandizement should, against their own light, persecute truth and the true religion, and wilfully abuse the powers and gifts entrusted to them, to bring vice, blindness, misery and slavery, on their native country, on the very country that had trusted, enriched and honoured them. Such beings, after that speedy and appropriate removal from their sphere of mischief which all good and humane men must of course desire, will, he takes for granted by parity of reason, meet with a punishment, an ignominy, and a retaliation, as much severer than other wicked men, as their guilt and its consequences were more enormous. His description of this imaginary punishment presents more distinct pictures to the fancy than the extract from Jeremy Taylor; but the thoughts in the latter are incomparably more exaggerated and horrific. All this I knew; but I neither remembered, nor by reference and careful re-perusal could discover, any other meaning, either in Milton or Taylor, but that good men will be rewarded, and the impenitent wicked punished, in proportion to their dispositions and intentional acts in this life; and that if the punishment of the least wicked be fearful beyond conception, all words and descriptions must be so far true, that they must fall short of the punishment that awaits the transcendantly wicked. Had Milton stated either his ideal of virtue, or of depravity, as an individual or individuals actually existing? Certainly not! Is this representation worded historically, or only hypothetically? Assuredly the latter! Does he express it as his own wish that after death they should suffer these tortures? or as a general consequence, deduced from reason and revelation, that such will be their fate? Again, the latter only! His wish is expressly confined to a speedy stop being put by Providence to their power of inflicting misery on others! But did he name or refer to any persons living or dead? No! But the calumniators of Milton daresay (for what will calumny not dare say?) that he had Laud and Strafford in his mind, while writing of remorseless per-secution, and the enslavement of a free country from motives of selfish ambition. Now what if a stern anti-prelatist should daresay, that in speaking of the insolencies of traitors and the violences of rebels, Bishop Taylor must have individualised in his mind Hamp-den, Hollis, Pym, Fairfax, Ireton, and Milton? And what if he should take the liberty of concluding, that, in the after-description, the Bishop was feeding and feasting his party-hatred, and with those individuals before the eyes of his imagination enjoying, trait by trait, horror after horror, the picture of their intolerable agonies? Yet this bigot would have an equal right thus to criminate the one good and great man, as these men have to criminate the other. Milton has said, and I doubt not but that Taylor with equal truth could have said it, "that in his whole life he never spake against a man even that his skin should be grazed." He asserted this when one of his opponents (either Bishop Hall or his nephew) had called upon the women and children in the streets to take up stones and stone him (Milton). It is known that Milton repeatedly used his interest to protect the royalists; but even at a time when all lies would have been meritorious against him, no charge was made, no story pretended, that he had ever directly or indirectly engaged or assisted in their persecution. Oh! methinks there are other and far better feelings which should be acquired by the perusal of our great elder writers. When I have before me, on the same table, the works of Hammond and Baxter; when I reflect with what joy and dearness their blessed spirits are now loving each other; it seems a mournful thing that their names should be perverted to an occasion of bitterness among us, who are enjoying that happy mean which the human too-much on both sides was perhaps necessary to produce. "The tangle of delusions which stifled and distorted the growing tree of our well-being has been torn away; the parasite-weeds that fed on its very roots have been plucked up with a salutary violence. To us there remain only quiet duties, the constant care, the gradual improvement, the cautious unhazardous labours of the industrious though contented gardener—to prune, to strengthen, to engraft, and one by one to remove from its leaves and fresh shoots the slug and the caterpillar. But far be it from us to undervalue with light and senseless detraction the conscientious hardihood of our predecessors, or even to condemn in them that vehemence, to which the blessings it won for us leave us now neither temptation nor pretext. We antedate the feelings, in order to criminate the authors, of our present liberty, light and toleration." (*The Friend*, No. IV. Sept. 7, 1809.) [1818, i. 105.]

If ever two great men might seem, during their whole lives, to have moved in direct opposition, though neither of them has at any time introduced the name of the other, Milton and Jeremy Taylor were they. The former commenced his career by attacking the Church-Liturgy and all set forms of prayer. The latter, but far more successfully, by defending both. Milton's next work was against the Prelacy and the then existing Church-Government— Taylor's in vindication and support of them. Milton became more and more a stern republican, or rather an advocate for that religious and moral aristocracy which, in his day, was called republicanism, and which, even more than royalism itself, is the direct antipode of modern jacobinism. Taylor, as more and more sceptical concerning the fitness of men in general for power, became more and more attached to the prerogatives of monarchy. From Calvinism, with a still decreasing respect for Fathers, Councils, and for Church-antiquity in general, Milton seems to have ended in an indifference, if not a dislike, to all forms of ecclesiastic government, and to have retreated wholly into the inward and spiritual church-communion of his own spirit with the Light that lighteth every man that cometh into the world. Taylor, with a growing reverence for authority, an increasing sense of the insufficiency of the Scriptures without the aids of tradition and the consent of authorized interpreters, advanced as far in his approaches (not indeed to Popery, but) to Roman-Catholicism, as a conscientious minister of the English Church could well venture. Milton would be and would utter the same to all on all occasions: he would tell the truth, the whole truth, and nothing but the truth. Taylor would become all things to all men, if by any means he might benefit any; hence he availed himself, in his popular writings, of opinions and representations which stand often in striking contrast with the doubts and convictions expressed in his more philosophical works. He appears, indeed, not too severely to have blamed that management of truth (istam falsitatem dispensativam) authorized and exemplified by almost all the fathers: Integrum omnino doctoribus et coetus Christiani antistitibus esse, ut dolos versent, falsa veris intermisceant et imprimis religionis hostes fallant, dummodo veritatis commodis et utilitati inserviant.

The same antithesis might be carried on with the elements of their several intellectual powers. Milton, austere, condensed, imaginative, supporting his truth by direct enunciation of lofty moral sentiment and by distinct visual representations, and in the same spirit overwhelming what he deemed falsehood by moral denunciation and a succession of pictures appalling or repulsive. In his prose, so many metaphors, so many allegorical miniatures. Taylor, eminently discursive, accumulative, and (to use one of

his own words) agglomerative; still more rich in images than
Milton himself, but images of fancy, and presented to the common
and passive eye, rather than to the eye of the imagination. Whether
supporting or assailing, he makes his way either by argument or
by appeals to the affections, unsurpassed even by the schoolmen
in subtlety, agility, and logic wit, and unrivalled by the most
rhetorical of the fathers in the copiousness and vividness of his
expressions and illustrations. Here words that convey feelings, and
words that flash images, and words of abstract notion, flow together, and whirl and rush onward like a stream, at once rapid and
full of eddies; and yet still interfused here and there we see a
tongue or islet of smooth water, with some picture in it of earth
or sky, landscape or living group of quiet beauty.

Differing then so widely and almost contrariantly, wherein did
these great men agree? wherein did they resemble each other? In
genius, in learning, in unfeigned piety, in blameless purity of life,
and in benevolent aspirations and purposes for the moral and
temporal improvement of their fellow-creatures! Both of them
wrote a Latin Accidence, to render education more easy and less
painful to children; both of them composed hymns and psalms
proportioned to the capacity of common congregations; both,
nearly at the same time, set the glorious example of publicly recommending and supporting general toleration, and the liberty
both of the Pulpit and the press! In the writings of neither shall
we find a single sentence, like those meek deliverances to God's
mercy, with which Laud accompanied his votes for the mutilations
and loathsome dungeoning of Leighton and others!—nowhere such
a pious prayer as we find in Bishop Hall's memoranda of his own
life, concerning the subtle and witty atheist that so grievously perplexed and gravelled him at Sir Robert Drury's till he prayed to
the Lord to remove him, and behold! his prayers were heard: for
shortly afterward this Philistine-combatant went to London, and
there perished of the plague in great misery! In short, nowhere
shall we find the least approach, in the lives and writings of John
Milton or Jeremy Taylor, to that guarded gentleness, to that sigh-
ing reluctance, with which the holy brethren of the Inquisition

deliver over a condemned heretic to the civil magistrate, recommending him to mercy, and hoping that the magistrate will treat the erring brother with all possible mildness!—the magistrate who too well knows what would be his own fate if he dared offend them by acting on their recommendation.

The opportunity of diverting the reader from myself to characters more worthy of his attention, has led me far beyond my first intention; but it is not unimportant to expose the false zeal which has occasioned these attacks on our elder patriots. It has been too much the fashion first to personify the Church of England, and then to speak of different individuals, who in different ages have been rulers in that church, as if in some strange way they constituted its personal identity. Why should a clergyman of the present day feel interested in the defence of Laud or Sheldon? Surely it is sufficient for the warmest partisan of our establishment that he can assert with truth,—when our Church persecuted, it was on mistaken principles held in common by all Christendom; and at all events, far less culpable was this intolerance in the Bishops, who were maintaining the existing laws, than the persecuting spirit afterwards shewn by their successful opponents, who had no such excuse, and who should have been taught mercy by their own sufferings, and wisdom by the utter failure of the experiment in their own case. We can say that our Church, apostolical in its faith, primitive in its ceremonies, unequalled in its liturgical forms; that our Church, which has kindled and displayed more bright and burning lights of genius and learning than all other protestant churches since the reformation, was (with the single exception of the times of Laud and Sheldon) least intolerant, when all Christians unhappily deemed a species of intolerance their religious duty; that Bishops of our church were among the first that contended against this error; and finally, that since the reformation, when tolerance became a fashion, the Church of England in a tolerating age, has shewn herself eminently tolerant, and far more so, both in spirit and in fact, than many of her most bitter opponents, who profess to deem toleration itself an insult on the rights of mankind! As to myself, who not only know the Church-Establishment to be tolerant, but who see in it the greatest, if not the sole safe bulwark of toleration, I feel no necessity of defending or palliating oppressions under the two Charleses, in order to exclaim with a full and fervent heart, Esto perpetua!

1815.                                                                                     1817.

# BIOGRAPHIA LITERARIA

OR,

*Biographical Sketches of My*

# LITERARY LIFE AND OPINIONS

So wenig er auch bestimmt seyn mag, andure zu belehren, so wünscht
er doch sich denen mitzutheilen, die er sich gleichgesinnt weiss oder hofft,
deren Anzahl aber in der Breite der Welt zerstreut ist: er wünscht sein
Verhältniss zu den ältesten Freunden dadurch wieder anzuknüpfen, mit
neuen es fortzusetzen, und in der letzten Generation sich wieder andere
für seine übrige Lebenszeit zu gewinnen. Er wünscht der Jugend die
Umwege zu ersparen, auf denen er sich selbst verirrte.

(Goethe)

TRANSLATION. Little call as he may have to instruct others, he wishes
nevertheless to open out his heart to such as he either knows or hopes to
be of like mind with himself, but who are widely scattered in the world:
he wishes to knit anew his connexions with his oldest friends, to continue
those recently formed, and to win other friends among the rising generation for the remaining course of his life. He wishes to spare the young
those circuitous paths, on which he himself had lost his way.


## CHAPTER I

*The motives of the present work—Reception of the Author's first publica-
tion—The discipline of his taste at school—The effect of contemporary
writers on youthful minds—Bowles's sonnets—Comparison between the Poets
before and since Mr. Pope.*


It has been my lot to have had my name introduced, both in
conversation, and in print, more frequently than I find it easy
to explain, whether I consider the fewness, unimportance, and
limited circulation of my writings, or the retirement and distance
in which I have lived, both from the literary and political world.
Most often it has been connected with some charge which I could
not acknowledge, or some principle which I had never enter-

tained. Nevertheless, had I had no other motive or incitement, the reader would not have been troubled with this exculpation. What my additional purposes were, will be seen in the following pages. It will be found, that the least of what I have written concerns myself personally. I have used the narration chiefly for the purpose of giving a continuity to the work, in part for the sake of the miscellaneous reflections suggested to me by particular events, but still more as introductory to the statement of my principles in Politics, Religion, and Philosophy, and an application of the rules, deduced from philosophical principles, to poetry and criticism. But of the objects, which I proposed to myself, it was not the least important to effect, as far as possible, a settlement of the long continued controversy concerning the true nature of poetic diction; and at the same time to define with the utmost impartiality the real *poetic* character of the poet, by whose writings this controversy was first kindled, and has been since fuelled and fanned.

In 1794, when I had barely passed the verge of manhood, I published a small volume of juvenile poems. They were received with a degree of favor, which, young as I was, I well know was bestowed on them not so much for any positive merit, as because they were considered buds of hope, and promises of better works to come. The critics of that day, the most flattering equally with the severest, concurred in objecting to them obscurity, a general turgidness of diction, and a profusion of new coined double epithets.* The first is the fault which a writer is the least able to

---

* The authority of Milton and Shakespeare may be usefully pointed out to young authors. In the Comus, and other early Poems of Milton there is a superfluity of double epithets; while in the Paradise Lost we find very few, in the Paradise Regained scarce any. The same remark holds almost equally true of the Love's Labour's Lost, Romeo and Juliet, Venus and Adonis, and Lucrece, compared with the Lear, Macbeth, Othello, and Hamlet of our great Dramatist. The rule for the admission of double epithets seems to be this: either that they should be already denizens of our Language, such as blood-stained, terror-stricken, self-applauding: or when a new epithet, or one found in books only, is hazarded, that it, at least, be one word, not two words made one by mere virtue of the printer's hyphen. A language which, like the English, is almost without cases, is indeed in its very genius un-

detect in his own compositions: and my mind was not then sufficiently disciplined to receive the authority of others, as a substitute
for my own conviction. Satisfied that the thoughts, such as they
were, could not have been expressed otherwise, or at least more
perspicuously, I forgot to enquire, whether the thoughts themselves did not demand a degree of attention unsuitable to the
nature and objects of poetry. This remark however applies chiefly,
though not exclusively, to the *Religious Musings*. The remainder
of the charge I admitted to its full extent, and not without sincere
acknowledgments both to my private and public censors for their
friendly admonitions. In the after editions, I pruned the double
epithets with no sparing hand, and used my best efforts to tame
the swell and glitter both of thought and diction; though in truth,
these parasite plants of youthful poetry had insinuated themselves
into my longer poems with such intricacy of union, that I was
often obliged to omit disentangling the weed, from the fear of
snapping the flower. From that period to the date of the present
work I have published nothing, with my name, which could by
any possibility have come before the board of anonymous criticism.
Even the three or four poems, printed with the works of a friend,
as far as they were censured at all, were charged with the same or
similar defects, though I am persuaded not with equal justice:
with an EXCESS OF ORNAMENT, in addition to STRAINED AND ELABO-
RATE DICTION. (*Vide the criticisms on the* "Ancient Mariner" *in
the Monthly and Critical Reviews of the first volume of the Lyrical Ballads.*) May I be permitted to add, that, even at the early
period of my juvenile poems, I saw and admitted the superiority
of an austerer and more natural style, with an insight not less
clear, than I at present possess. My judgement was stronger, than

---

fitted for compounds. If a writer, every time a compounded word suggests
itself to him, would seek for some other mode of expressing the same sense,
the chances are always greatly in favor of his finding a better word. "Tanquam scopulum sic vites insolens verbum," is the wise advice of Cæsar to
the Roman Orators, and the precept applies with double force to the writers
in our own language. But it must not be forgotten, that the same Cæsar
wrote a grammatical treatise for the purpose of reforming the ordinary language by bringing it to a greater accordance with the principles of Logic
or universal Grammar.

were my powers of realizing its dictates; and the faults of my language, though indeed partly owing to a wrong choice of subjects, and the desire of giving a poetic colouring to abstract and metaphysical truths, in which a new world then seemed to open upon me, did yet, in part likewise, originate in unfeigned diffidence of my own comparative talent.—During several years of my youth and early manhood, I reverenced those, who had reintroduced the manly simplicity of the Greek, and of our own elder poets, with such enthusiasm as made the hope seem presumptuous of writing successfully in the same style. Perhaps a similar process has happened to others; but my earliest poems were marked by an ease and simplicity, which I have studied, perhaps with inferior success, to impress on my later compositions.

At school I enjoyed the inestimable advantage of a very sensible, though at the same time a very severe master. He* early moulded my taste to the preference of Demosthenes to Cicero, of Homer and Theocritus to Virgil, and again of Virgil to Ovid. He habituated me to compare Lucretius, (in such extracts as I then read) Terence, and above all the chaster poems of Catullus, not only with the Roman poets of the, so called, silver and brazen ages; but with even those of the Augustan era: and on grounds of plain sense and universal logic to see and assert the superiority of the former in the truth and nativeness, both of their thoughts and diction. At the same time that we were studying the Greek Tragic Poets, he made us read Shakespeare and Milton as lessons: and they were the lessons too, which required most time and trouble to *bring up*, so as to escape his censure. I learnt from him, that Poetry, even that of the loftiest and, seemingly, that of the wildest odes, had a logic of its own, as severe as that of science; and more difficult, because more subtle, more complex, and dependent on more, and more fugitive causes. In the truly great poets, he would say, there is a reason assignable, not only for every word, but for the position of every word; and I well remember that, availing himself of the synonimes to the Homer of Didymus, he made us attempt to show, with regard to each, *why* it would not have an-

---

* The Rev. James Bowyer, many years Head Master of the Grammar School, Christ's Hospital.

swered the same purpose; and *wherein* consisted the peculiar fitness of the word in the original text.

In our own English compositions, (at least for the last three years of our school education,) he showed no mercy to phrase, metaphor, or image, unsupported by a sound sense, or where the same sense might have been conveyed with equal force and dignity in plainer words. Lute, harp, and lyre, muse, muses, and inspirations, Pegasus, Parnassus, and Hippocrene were all an abomination to him. In fancy I can almost hear him now, exclaiming *"Harp? Harp? Lyre? Pen and ink, boy, you mean! Muse, boy, Muse? Your Nurse's daughter, you mean! Pierian spring? Oh aye! the cloister-pump, I suppose!"* Nay, certain introductions, similes, and examples, were placed by name on a list of interdiction. Among the similes, there was, I remember, that of the Manchineel fruit, as suiting equally well with too many subjects; in which however it yielded the palm at once to the example of Alexander and Clytus, which was equally good and apt, whatever might be the theme. Was it ambition? Alexander and Clytus!—Flattery? Alexander and Clytus!—Anger? Drunkenness? Pride? Friendship? Ingratitude? Late repentance? Still, still Alexander and Clytus! At length, the praises of agriculture having been exemplified in the sagacious observation, that, had Alexander been holding the plough, he would not have run his friend Clytus through with a spear, this tried and serviceable old friend was banished by public edict in secula seculorum. I have sometimes ventured to think, that a list of this kind, or an index expurgatorius of certain well known and ever returning phrases, both introductory, and transitional, including a large assortment of modest egoisms, and flattering illeisms, &c., &c., might be hung up in our law-courts, and both houses of parliament, with great advantage to the public, as an important saving of national time, an incalculable relief to his Majesty's ministers, but above all, as insuring the thanks of country attorneys, and their clients, who have private bills to carry through the house.

Be this as it may, there was one custom of our master's, which I cannot pass over in silence, because I think it imitable and worthy of imitation. He would often permit our exercises, under some pretext of want of time, to accumulate, till each lad had four or five to be looked over. Then placing the whole number *abreast* on his desk, he would ask the writer, why this or that sentence might not have found as appropriate a place under this or that other thesis: and if no satisfying answer could be returned, and two faults of the same kind were found in one exercise, the irrevocable verdict followed, the exercise was torn up, and another on the same subject to be produced, in addition to the tasks of the day. The reader will, I trust, excuse this tribute of recollection to a man, whose severities, even now, not seldom furnish the dreams, by which the blind fancy would fain interpret to the mind the painful sensations of distempered sleep; but neither lessen nor dim the deep sense of my moral and intellectual obligations. He sent us to the University excellent Latin and Greek scholars, and tolerable Hebraists. Yet our classical knowledge was the least of the good gifts, which we derived from his zealous and conscientious tutorage. He is now gone to his final reward, full of years, and full of honors, even of those honors, which were dearest to his heart, as gratefully bestowed by that school, and still binding him to the interests of that school, in which he had been himself educated, and to which during his whole life he was a dedicated thing.

From causes, which this is not the place to investigate, no models of past times, however perfect, can have the same vivid effect on the youthful mind, as the productions of contemporary genius. The Discipline, my mind had undergone, "Ne falleretur rotundo sono et versuum cursu, concinnis et floribus; sed ut inspiceret quidnam subesset, quæ sedes, quod firmamentum, quis fundus verbis; an figuræ essent mera ornatura et orationis fucus; vel sanguinis e materiæ ipsius corde effluentis rubor quidam nativus et incalescentia genuina"; removed all obstacles to the appreciation of excellence in style without diminishing my delight. That I was thus prepared for the perusal of Mr. Bowles's sonnets and earlier poems, at once increased *their* influence, and *my* enthusiasm. The great works of past ages seem to a young man things of another race, in respect to which his faculties must remain passive and submiss, even as to the stars and mountains. But the writings of a contemporary, perhaps not many years older than himself, surrounded by the same circumstances, and disciplined by the same manners, possess a *reality* for him, and inspire an actual friendship as of a man for a man. His very admiration is the wind which fans and feeds his hope. The poems themselves assume the properties of flesh and blood. To recite, to extol, to contend for them is but the payment of a debt due to one, who exists to receive it.

There are indeed modes of teaching which have produced, and are producing, youths of a very different stamp; modes of teaching, in comparison with which we have been called on to despise our great public schools, and universities

> in whose halls are hung
> Armoury of the invincible knights of old—

modes, by which children are to be metamorphosed into prodigies. And prodigies with a vengeance have I known thus produced! Prodigies of self-conceit, shallowness, arrogance, and infidelity! Instead of storing the memory, during the period when the memory is the predominant faculty, with facts for the after exercise of the judgement; and instead of awakening by the noblest models the fond and unmixed Love and Admiration, which is the natural and graceful temper of early youth; *these* nurselings of improved pedagogy are taught to dispute and decide; to suspect all, but their own and their lecturer's wisdom; and to hold nothing sacred from their contempt, but their own contemptible arrogance: boy-graduates in all the technicals, and in all the dirty passions and impudence of anonymous criticism. To such dispositions alone can the admonition of Pliny be requisite, "Neque enim debet operibus ejus obesse, quod vivit. An si inter eos, quos nunquam vidimus, floruisset, non solum libros ejus, verum etiam imagines conquireremus, ejusdem nunc honor præsentis, et gratia quasi satietate languescit? At hoc pravum, malignumque est, non admirari hominem admiratione dignissimum, quia videre, complecti, nec laudare tantum, verum etiam amare contingit." *Plin. Epist. Lib.* I.

I had just entered on my seventeenth year, when the sonnets of Mr. Bowles, twenty in number, and just then published in a

quarto pamphlet, were first made known and presented to me, by
a schoolfellow who had quitted us for the University, and who,
during the whole time that he was in our first form (or in our
school language a GRECIAN,) had been my patron and protector.
I refer to Dr. Middleton, the truly learned, and every way excellent Bishop of Calcutta:

> Qui laudibus amplis
> Ingenium celebrare meum, calamumque solebat,
> Calcar agens animo validum. Non omnia terræ
> Obruta; vivit amor, vivit dolor; ora negatur
> Dulcia conspicere; at flere et meminisse* relictum est.
> Petr. Ep., Lib. I, Ep. I.

It was a double pleasure to me, and still remains a tender recollection, that I should have received from a friend so revered the
first knowledge of a poet, by whose works, year after year, I was
so enthusiastically delighted and inspired. My earliest acquaint-
ances will not have forgotten the undisciplined eagerness and
impetuous zeal, with which I laboured to make proselytes, not
only of my companions, but of all with whom I conversed, of
whatever rank, and in whatever place. As my school finances did
not permit me to purchase copies, I made, within less than a year
and a half, more than forty transcriptions, as the best presents I
could offer to those, who had in any way won my regard. And
with almost equal delight did I receive the three or four following
publications of the same author.

Though I have seen and known enough of mankind to be well
aware, that I shall perhaps stand alone in my creed, and that it
will be well, if I subject myself to no worse charge than that of
singularity; I am not therefore deterred from avowing, that I
regard, and ever have regarded the obligations of intellect among
the most sacred of the claims of gratitude. A valuable thought, or
a particular train of thoughts, gives me additional pleasure, when

---

* I am most happy to have the necessity of informing the reader that, since
this passage was written, the report of Dr. Middleton's death on his voyage
to India has been proved erroneous. He lives and long may he live; for I
dare prophecy, that with his life only will his exertions for the temporal and
spiritual welfare of his fellow men be limited.

I can safely refer and attribute it to the conversation or correspondence of another. My obligations to Mr. Bowles were indeed important, and for radical good. At a very premature age, even before my fifteenth year, I had bewildered myself in metaphysicks, and in theological controversy. Nothing else pleased me. History, and particular facts, lost all interest in my mind. Poetry (though for a school-boy of that age, I was above par in English versification, and had already produced two or three compositions which, I may venture to say, without reference to my age, were somewhat above mediocrity, and which had gained me more credit than the sound, good sense of my old master was at all pleased with,) poetry itself, yea, novels and romances, became insipid to me. In my friendless wanderings on our *leave-days,** (for I was an orphan, and had scarcely any connections in London,) highly was I delighted, if any passenger, especially if he were drest in black, would enter into conversation with me. For I soon found the means of directing it to my favourite subjects

> Of providence, fore-knowledge, will, and fate,
> Fix'd fate, free will, fore-knowledge absolute,
> And found no end in wandering mazes lost.

This preposterous pursuit was, beyond doubt, injurious both to my natural powers, and to the progress of my education. It would perhaps have been destructive, had it been continued; but from this I was auspiciously withdrawn, partly indeed by an accidental introduction to an amiable family, chiefly however, by the genial influence of a style of poetry, so tender and yet so manly, so natural and real, and yet so dignified and harmonious, as the sonnets &c. of Mr. Bowles! Well were it for me, perhaps, had I never relapsed into the same mental disease; if I had continued to pluck the flower and reap the harvest from the cultivated surface, instead of delving in the unwholesome quicksilver mines of metaphysic depths. But if in after time I have sought a refuge from bodily pain and mismanaged sensibility in abstruse researches, which exercised the strength and subtlety of the understanding

---

* The Christ's Hospital phrase, not for holidays altogether, but for those on which the boys are permitted to go beyond the precincts of the school.

without awakening the feelings of the heart; still there was a long and blessed interval, during which my natural faculties were allowed to expand, and my original tendencies to develope themselves: my fancy, and the love of nature, and the sense of beauty in forms and sounds.

The second advantage, which I owe to my early perusal, and admiration of these poems, (to which let me add, though known to me at a somewhat later period, the Lewsdon Hill of Mr. CROW) bears more immediately on my present subject. Among those with whom I conversed, there were, of course, very many who had formed their taste, and their notions of poetry, from the writings of Mr. Pope and his followers: or to speak more generally, in that school of French poetry, condensed and invigorated by English understanding, which had predominated from the last century. I was not blind to the merits of this school, yet as from inexperience of the world, and consequent want of sympathy with the general subjects of these poems, they gave me little pleasure, I doubtless undervalued the *kind,* and with the presumption of youth withheld from its masters the legitimate name of poets. I saw that the excellence of this kind consisted in just and acute observations on men and manners in an artificial state of society, as its matter and substance: and in the logic of wit, conveyed in smooth and strong epigrammatic couplets, as its *form.* Even when the subject was addressed to the fancy, or the intellect, as in the Rape of the Lock, or the Essay on Man; nay, when it was a consecutive narration, as in that astonishing product of matchless talent and ingenuity, Pope's Translation of the Iliad; still a *point* was looked for at the end of each second line, and the whole was as it were a sorites, or, if I may exchange a logical for a grammatical metaphor, a *conjunction disjunctive,* of epigrams. Meantime the matter and diction seemed to me characterized not so much by poetic thoughts, as by thoughts *translated* into the language of poetry. On this last point, I had occasion to render my own thoughts gradually more and more plain to myself, by frequent amicable disputes concerning Darwin's BOTANIC GARDEN, which, for some years, was greatly extolled, not only by the *reading* public in general, but even by those, whose genius and natural robustness of understanding enabled them afterwards to act foremost in dissipating these "painted mists" that occasionally rise from the marshes at the foot of Parnassus. During my first Cambridge vacation, I assisted a friend in a contribution for a literary society in Devonshire: and in this I remember to have compared Darwin's work to the Russian palace of ice, glittering, cold and transitory. In the same essay too, I assigned sundry reasons, chiefly drawn from a comparison of passages in the Latin poets with the original Greek, from which they were borrowed, for the preference of Collins' odes to those of Gray; and of the simile in Shakespeare

> How like a younker or a prodigal,
> The skarfed bark puts from her native bay,
> Hugg'd and embraced by the strumpet wind!
> How like the prodigal doth she return,
> With over-weather'd ribs and ragged sails,
> Lean, rent, and beggar'd by the strumpet wind!

to the imitation in the Bard;

> Fair laughs the morn, and soft the zephyr blows,
> While proudly riding o'er the azure realm
> In gallant trim the gilded vessel goes,
> YOUTH at the prow and PLEASURE at the helm;
> Regardless of the sweeping whirlwind's sway,
> That hush'd in grim repose, expects its evening prey.

(In which, by the bye, the words "realm" and "sway" are rhymes dearly purchased.) I preferred the original on the ground, that in the imitation it depended wholly on the compositor's putting, or not putting, a *small Capital*, both in this, and in many other passages of the same poet, whether the words should be personifications, or mere abstractions. I mention this, because, in referring various lines in Gray to their original in Shakespeare and Milton; and in the clear perception how completely all the propriety was lost in the transfer; I was, at that early period, led to a conjecture, which, many years afterwards was recalled to me from the same thought having been started in conversation, but far more ably, and developed more fully, by Mr. Wordsworth; namely, that this style of poetry, which I have characterised above, as translations of prose thoughts into poetic language, had been kept up by, if it did not wholly arise from, the custom of writing Latin verses, and the great importance attached to these exercises, in our public schools. Whatever might have been the case in the fifteenth century, when the use of the Latin tongue was so general among learned men, that Erasmus is said to have forgotten his native language; yet in the present day it is not to be supposed, that a youth can *think* in Latin, or that he can have any other reliance on the force or fitness of his phrases, but the authority of the writer from whence he has adopted them. Consequently he must first prepare his thoughts, and then pick out, from Virgil, Horace, Ovid, or perhaps more compendiously from his* Gradus, halves and quarters of lines, in which to embody them.

I never object to a certain degree of disputatiousness in a young man from the age of seventeen to that of four or five and twenty, provided I find him always arguing on one side of the question. The controversies, occasioned by my unfeigned zeal for the honor of a favorite contemporary, then known to me only by his works, were of great advantage in the formation and establishment of my taste and critical opinions. In my defence of the lines running into each other, instead of closing at each couplet, and of natural language, neither bookish, nor vulgar, neither redolent of the lamp, nor of the kennel, such as *I will remember thee;* instead of the same thought tricked up in the rag-fair finery of

> ———Thy image on her wing
> Before my FANCY's eye shall MEMORY bring,

I had continually to adduce the metre and diction of the Greek Poets from Homer to Theocritus inclusive; and still more of our

---

* In the Nutricia of Politian there occurs this line:

> Pura coloratos interstrepit unda lapillos.

Casting my eye on a University prize-poem, I met this line:

> Lactea purpureos interstrepit unda lapillos.

Now look out in the Gradus for *Purus,* and you find as the first synonime, *lacteus;* for *coloratus,* and the first synonime is *purpureus.* I mention this by way of elucidating one of the most ordinary processes in the *ferrumination* of these centos.

elder English poets from Chaucer to Milton. Nor was this all. But as it was my constant reply to authorities brought against me from later poets of great name, that no authority could avail in opposition to TRUTH, NATURE, LOGIC, and the LAWS of UNIVERSAL GRAMMAR; actuated too by my former passion for metaphysical investigations; I laboured at a solid foundation, on which permanently to ground my opinions, in the component faculties of the human mind itself, and their comparative dignity and importance. According to the faculty or source, from which the pleasure given by any poem or passage was derived, I estimated the merit of such poem or passage. As the result of all my reading and meditation, I abstracted two critical aphorisms, deeming them to comprise the conditions and criteria of poetic style; first, that not the poem which we have *read*, but that to which we *return*, with the greatest pleasure, possesses the genuine power, and claims the name of *essential poetry*. Second, that whatever lines can be translated into other words of the same language, without diminution of their significance, either in sense, or association, or in any worthy feeling, are so far vicious in their diction. Be it however observed, that I excluded from the list of worthy feelings, the pleasure derived from mere novelty in the reader, and the desire of exciting wonderment at his powers in the author. Oftentimes since then, in pursuing French tragedies, I have fancied two marks of admiration at the end of each line, as hieroglyphics of the author's own admiration at his own cleverness. Our genuine admiration of a great poet is a continuous *under-current* of feeling; it is everywhere present, but seldom anywhere as a separate excitement. I was wont boldly to affirm, that it would be scarcely more difficult to push a stone out from the pyramids with the bare hand, than to alter a word, or the position of a word, in Milton or Shakespeare, (in their most important works at least,) without making the author say something else, or something worse, than he does say. One great distinction, I appeared to myself to see plainly, between, even the characteristic faults of our elder poets, and the false beauty of the moderns. In the former, from DONNE to COWLEY, we find the most fantastic out-of-the-way thoughts, but in the most pure and genuine mother English; in the latter, the most obvious thoughts, in language the most fantastic and arbitrary. Our faulty elder poets sacrificed the passion and passionate flow of poetry, to the subtleties of intellect, and to the starts of wit; the moderns to the glare and glitter of a perpetual, yet broken and heterogeneous imagery, or rather to an amphibious something, made up, half of image, and half of abstract * meaning. The one sacrificed the heart to the head; the other both heart and head to point and drapery.

The reader must make himself acquainted with the general style of composition that was at that time deemed poetry, in order to understand and account for the effect produced on me by the SONNETS, the MONODY at MATLOCK, and the HOPE, of Mr. Bowles; for it is peculiar to original genius to become less and less *striking*, in proportion to its success in improving the taste and judgement of its contemporaries. The poems of WEST, indeed, had the merit of chaste and manly diction, but they were cold, and, if I may so express it, only *dead-coloured*; while in the best of Warton's there is a stiffness, which too often gives them the appearance of imitations from the Greek. Whatever relation therefore of cause or impulse Percy's collection of Ballads may bear to the most *popular* poems of the present day; yet in the more sustained and elevated style, of the then living poets, Bowles and Cowper† were, to the

---

* I remember a ludicrous instance in the poem of a young tradesman:

> No more will I endure love's pleasing pain,
> Or round my *heart's leg* tie his galling chain.

† Cowper's Task was published some time before the Sonnets of Mr. Bowles; but I was not familiar with it till many years afterwards. The vein of satire which runs through that excellent poem, together with the sombre hue of its religious opinions, would probably, *at that time,* have prevented its laying any strong hold on my affections. The love of nature seems to have led Thompson to a chearful religion; and a gloomy religion to have led Cowper to a love of nature. The one would carry his fellow-men along with him into nature; the other flies to nature from his fellow-men. In chastity of diction however, and the harmony of blank verse, Cowper leaves Thompson immeasurably below him; yet still I feel the latter to have been the *born poet.*

best of my knowledge, the first who combined natural thoughts with natural diction; the first who reconciled the heart with the head.

It is true, as I have before mentioned, that from diffidence in my own powers, I for a short time adopted a laborious and florid diction, which I myself deemed, if not absolutely vicious, yet of very inferior worth. Gradually, however, my practice conformed to my better judgement; and the compositions of my twenty-fourth and twenty-fifth years (*ex. gr.* the shorter blank verse poems, the lines, which are now adopted in the introductory part of the Vision in the present collection, in Mr. Southey's Joan of Arc, 2nd book, 1st edition, and the Tragedy of REMORSE) are not more below my present ideal in respect of the general tissue of the style than those of the latest date. Their faults were at least a remnant of the former leaven, and among the many who have done me the honour of putting my poems in the same class with those of my betters, the one or two, who have pretended to bring examples of affected simplicity from my volume, have been able to adduce but one instance, and that out of a copy of verses half ludicrous, half splenetic, which I intended, and had myself characterized, as *sermoni propiora*.

Every reform, however necessary, will by weak minds be carried to an excess, that itself will need reforming. The reader will excuse me for noticing, that I myself was the first to expose *risu honesto* the three sins of poetry, one or the other of which is the most likely to beset a young writer. So long ago as the publication of the second number of the monthly magazine, under the name of NEHEMIAH HIGGINBOTTOM, I contributed three sonnets, the first of which had for its object to excite a good-natured laugh at the spirit of *doleful egotism,* and at the recurrence of favorite phrases, with the double defect of being at once trite and licentious. The second, on low, creeping language and thoughts, under the pretence of *simplicity*. And the third, the phrases of which were borrowed entirely from my own poems, on the indiscriminate use of elaborate and swelling language and imagery. The reader

will find them in the note\* below, and will I trust regard them
as reprinted for biographical purposes, and not for their poetic
merits. So general at that time, and so decided was the opinion
concerning the characteristic vices of my style, that a celebrated
physician (now, alas! no more) speaking of me in other respects

---

\* SONNET I.

Pensive at eve, on the *hard* world I mused,
And *my poor* heart was sad; so at the MOON
I gazed, and sighed, and sighed; for ah how soon
Eve saddens into night! mine eyes perused
With tearful vacancy the *dampy* grass
That wept and glitter'd in the *paly* ray:
And I *did pause me* on my lonely way
And *mused me* on the *wretched ones* that pass
O'er the bleak heath of sorrow. But alas!
Most of *myself* I thought! when it befel,
That the *soothe* spirit of the *breezy* wood
Breath'd in mine ear: "All this is very well,
But much of ONE thing, is for NO thing good."
Oh *my poor heart's* INEXPLICABLE SWELL!

SONNET II.

Oh I do love thee, meek SIMPLICITY!
For of thy lays the lulling simpleness
Goes to my heart, and soothes each small distress,
Distress tho' small, yet haply great to me.
'Tis true on Lady Fortune's gentlest pad
I amble on; and yet I know not why
So sad I am! but should a friend and I
Frown, pout and part, then I am *very* sad.
And then with sonnets and with sympathy
My dreamy bosom's mystic woes I pall;
Now of my false friend plaining plaintively,
Now raving at mankind in general;
But whether sad or fierce, 'tis simple all,
All very simple, meek SIMPLICITY!

SONNET III.

And this reft house is that, the which he built,
Lamented Jack! and here his malt he pil'd,
Cautious in vain! these rats, that squeak so wild,

with his usual kindness to a gentleman, who was about to meet me at a dinner party, could not however resist giving him a hint not to mention the *"House that Jack built"* in my presence, for "that I was *as sore as a boil* about that sonnet"; he not knowing, that I was myself the author of it.

## CHAPTER II

*Supposed irritability of men of Genius—Brought to the test of facts—Causes and Occasions of the charge—Its Injustice.*

I have often thought, that it would be neither uninstructive nor unamusing to analyze, and bring forward into distinct con-

---

> Squeak not unconscious of their father's guilt.
> Did he not see her gleaming thro' the glade!
> Belike 'twas she, the maiden all forlorn.
> What tho' she milk no cow with crumpled horn,
> Yet, *aye* she haunts the dale where *erst* she stray'd:
> And *aye,* beside her stalks her amorous knight!
> Still on his thighs their wonted brogues are worn,
> And thro' those brogues, still tatter'd and betorn,
> His hindward charms gleam an unearthly white.
> Ah! thus thro' broken clouds at night's high Noon
> Peeps in fair fragments forth the full-orb'd harvest-moon!

The following anecdote will not be wholly out of place here, and may perhaps amuse the reader. An amateur performer in verse expressed to a common friend a strong desire to be introduced to me, but hesitated in accepting my friend's immediate offer, on the score that "he was, he must acknowledge, the author of a confounded severe epigram on my *ancient mariner,* which had given me great pain." I assured my friend that, if the epigram was a good one, it would only increase my desire to become acquainted with the author, and begg'd to hear it recited: when, to my no less surprise than amusement, it proved to be one which I had myself some time before written and inserted in the Morning Post.

To the author of the Ancient Mariner.

> Your poem must eternal be,
> Dear sir! it cannot fail,
> For 'tis incomprehensible,
> And without head or tail.

sciousness, that complex feeling, with which readers in general take part against the author, in favor of the critic; and the readiness with which they apply to *all* poets the old sarcasm of Horace upon the scribblers of his time: "Genus irritabile vatum." A debility and dimness of the imaginative power, and a consequent necessity of reliance on the immediate impressions of the senses, do, we well know, render the mind liable to superstition and fanaticism. Having a deficient portion of internal and proper warmth, minds of this class seek in the crowd *circum-fana* for a warmth in common, which they do not possess singly. Cold and plegmatic in their own nature, like damp hay, they heat and inflame by co-acervation; or like bees they become restless and irritable through the increased temperature of collected multitudes. Hence the German word for fanaticism, (such at least was its original import,) is derived from the swarming of bees, namely, Schwärmen, Schwärmerei. The passion being in an inverse proportion to the insight, *that* the more vivid, as *this* the less distinct; anger is the inevitable consequence. The absense of all foundation within their own minds for that, which they yet believe both true and indispensable for their safety and happiness, cannot but produce an uneasy state of feeling, an involuntary sense of fear from which nature has no means of rescuing herself but by anger. Experience informs us that the first defence of weak minds is to recriminate.

> There's no Philosopher but sees,
> That rage and fear are one disease,
> Tho' that may burn, and this may freeze,
> They're both alike the ague.
>                                        MAD OX.

But where the ideas are vivid, and there exists an endless power of combining and modifying them, the feelings and affections blend more easily and intimately with these ideal creations than with the objects of the senses; the mind is affected by thoughts, rather than by things; and only then feels the requisite interest even for the most important events and accidents, when by means of meditation they have passed into *thoughts*. The sanity of the mind is between superstition with fanaticism on the one hand, and enthusiasm with indifference and a diseased slowness to action on the other. For the conceptions of the mind may be so vivid and adequate, as to preclude that impulse to the realizing of them, which is strongest and most restless in those, who possess more than mere *talent,* (or the faculty of appropriating and applying the knowledge of others,) yet still want something of the creative, and self-sufficing power of absolute *Genius.* For this reason therefore, they are men of *commanding* genius. While the former rest content between thought and reality, as it were in an intermundium of which their own living spirit supplies the *substance,* and their imagination the ever-varying *form;* the latter must impress their preconceptions on the world without, in order to present them back to their own view with the satisfying degree of clearness, distinctness, and individuality. These in tranquil times are formed to exhibit a perfect poem in palace, or temple, or landscape-garden; or a tale of romance in canals that join sea with sea, or in walls of rock, which, shouldering back the billows, imitate the power, and supply the benevolence of nature to sheltered navies; or in aqueducts that, arching the wide vale from mountain to mountain, give a Palmyra to the desert. But alas! in times of tumult they are the men destined to come forth as the shaping spirit of Ruin, to destroy the wisdom of ages in order to substitute the fancies of a day, and to change kings and kingdoms, as the wind shifts and shapes the clouds.* The records of biography seem to confirm this theory. The men of the greatest genius, as far as we can judge from their own works or from the accounts of their contemporaries, appear to have been of calm and tranquil temper in all that related to themselves. In the inward assurance of permanent fame, they seem to have been either indifferent or resigned,

---

* Of old things all are over old,
    Of good things none are good enough:—
    We'll show that we can help to frame
    A world of other stuff.

    I too will have my kings, that take
    From me the sign of life and death:
    Kingdoms shall shift about, like clouds,
    Obedient to my breath.
    WORDSWORTH'S ROB ROY.

with regard to immediate reputation. Through all the works of Chaucer there reigns a chearfulness, a manly hilarity, which makes it almost impossible to doubt a correspondent habit of feeling in the author himself. Shakespeare's evenness and sweetness of temper were almost proverbial in his own age. That this did not arise from ignorance of his own comparative greatness, we have abundant proof in his Sonnets, which could scarcely have been known to Mr. Pope,* when he asserted, that our great bard "grew immortal in his own despite." Speaking of one whom he had celebrated, and contrasting the duration of his works with that of his personal existence, Shakespeare adds:

> Your name from hence immortal life shall have,
> Tho' I once gone to all the world must die;
> The earth can yield me but a common grave,
> When you entombed in men's eyes shall lie.
> Your monument shall be my gentle verse,
> Which eyes not yet created shall o'er-read;
> And *tongues to be* your being shall rehearse,

---

* Mr. Pope was under the common error of his age, an error far from being sufficiently exploded even at the present day. It consists (as I explained at large, and proved in detail in my public lectures,) in mistaking for the *essentials* of the Greek stage certain rules, which the wise poets imposed upon themselves, in order to render all the remaining parts of the drama consistent with those, that had been forced upon them by circumstances independent of their will; out of which circumstances the drama itself arose. The circumstances in the time of Shakespeare, which it was equally out of his power to alter, were different, and such as, in my opinion, allowed a far wider sphere, and a deeper and more human interest. Critics are too apt to forget, that *rules* are but means to an end; consequently, where the ends are different, the rules must be likewise so. We must have ascertained what the end *is,* before we can determine what the rules *ought* to be. Judging under this impression, I did not hesitate to declare my full conviction, that the consummate judgement of Shakespeare, not only in the general construction, but in all the *detail,* of his dramas, impressed me with greater wonder, than even the might of his genius, or the depth of his philosophy. The substance of these lectures I hope soon to publish; and it is but a debt of justice to myself and my friends to notice, that the first course of lectures, which differed from the following courses only, by occasionally varying the illustrations of the same thoughts, was addressed to very numerous, and I need not add, respectable audiences at the royal institution, before Mr. Schlegel gave his lectures on the same subjects at Vienna.

When all the breathers of this world are dead:
You still shall live, such virtue hath my pen,
Where breath most breathes, e'en in the mouth of men.

SONNET 81st.

I have taken the first that occurred; but Shakespeare's readiness to praise his rivals, ore pleno, and the confidence of his own equality with those whom he deemed most worthy of his praise, are alike manifested in the 86th Sonnet.

Was it the proud full sail of his great verse,
Bound for the praise of all-too-precious you,
That did my ripe thoughts in my brain inhearse,
Making their tomb, the womb wherein they grew?
Was it his spirit, by spirits taught to write
Above a mortal pitch that struck me dead?
No, neither he, nor his compeers by night
Giving him aid, my verse astonished.
He, nor that affable familiar ghost,
Which nightly gulls him with intelligence,
As victors of my silence cannot boast;
I was not sick of any fear from thence!
But when your countenance fill'd up his line,
Then lack'd I matter, that enfeebled mine.

In Spenser, indeed, we trace a mind constitutionally tender, delicate, and, in comparison with his three great compeers, I had almost said, *effeminate;* and this additionally saddened by the unjust persecution of Burleigh, and the severe calamities, which overwhelmed his latter days. These causes have diffused over all his compositions "a melancholy grace," and have drawn forth occasional strains, the more pathetic from their gentleness. But no where do we find the least trace of irritability, and still less of quarrelsome or affected contempt of his censurers.

The same calmness, and even greater self-possession, may be affirmed of Milton, as far as his poems, and poetic character are concerned. He reserved his anger for the enemies of religion, freedom, and his country. My mind is not capable of forming a more august conception, than arises from the contemplation of this great man in his latter days: poor, sick, old, blind, slandered, persecuted,

Darkness before, and danger's voice behind,—

in an age in which he was as little understood by the party, *for* whom, as by that, *against* whom he had contended; and among men before whom he strode so far as to *dwarf* himself by the distance; yet still listening to the music of his own thoughts, or if additionally cheered, yet cheered only by the prophetic faith of two or three solitary individuals, he did nevertheless

> —Argue not
> Against Heaven's hand or will, nor bate a jot
> Of heart or hope; but still bore up and steer'd
> Right onward.

From others only do we derive our knowledge that Milton, in his latter day, had his scorners and detractors; and even in his day of youth and hope, that he had enemies would have been unknown to us, had they not been likewise the enemies of his country.

I am well aware, that in advanced stages of literature, when there exist many and excellent models, a high degree of talent, combined with taste and judgement, and employed in works of imagination, will acquire for a man the *name* of a great genius; though even that *analogon* of genius, which, in certain states of society, may even render his writings more popular than the absolute reality could have done, would be sought for in vain in the mind and temper of the author himself. Yet even in instances of this kind, a close examination will often detect, that the irritability, which has been attributed to the author's *genius* as its cause, did really originate in an ill conformation of body, obtuse pain, or constitutional defect of pleasurable sensation. What is charged to the *author,* belongs to the *man,* who would probably have been still more impatient, but for the humanizing influences of the very pursuit, which yet bears the blame of his irritability.

How then are we to explain the easy credence generally given to this charge, if the charge itself be not, as I have endeavoured to show, supported by experience? This seems to me of no very difficult solution. In whatever country literature is widely diffused, there will be many who mistake an intense desire to possess the reputation of poetic genius, for the actual powers, and original tendencies which constitute it. But men, whose dearest wishes are fixed on objects wholly out of their own power, become in all cases more or

less impatient and prone to anger. Besides, though it may be paradoxical to assert, that a man can know one thing and believe the
opposite, yet assuredly a vain person may have so habitually indulged the wish, and persevered in the attempt, to appear what he
is not, as to become himself one of his own proselytes. Still, as this
counterfeit and artificial persuasion must differ, even in the person's own feelings, from a real sense of inward power, what can be
more natural, than that this difference should betray itself in suspicious and jealous irritability? Even as the flowery sod, which
covers a hollow, may be often detected by its shaking and trembling.

But, alas! the multitude of books and the general diffusion of
literature, have produced other and more lamentable effects in the
world of letters, and such as are abundant to explain, though by no
means to justify, the contempt with which the best grounded complaints of injured genius are rejected as frivolous, or entertained
as matter of merriment. In the days of Chaucer and Gower, our
language might (with due allowance for the imperfections of a
simile) be compared to a wilderness of vocal reeds, from which the
favorites only of Pan or Apollo could construct even the rude
Syrinx; and from this the *constructors* alone could elicit strains of
music. But now, partly by the labours of successive poets, and in
part by the more artificial state of society and social intercourse,
language, mechanized as it were into a barrel-organ, supplies at
once both instrument and tune. Thus even the deaf may play, so
as to delight the many. Sometimes (for it is with similes, as it is
with jests at a wine table, one is sure to suggest another) I have
attempted to illustrate the present state of our language, in its relation to literature, by a press-room of larger and smaller stereotype
pieces, which, in the present Anglo-Gallican fashion of uncon-
nected, epigrammatic periods, it requires but an ordinary portion
of ingenuity to vary indefinitely, and yet still produce something,
which, if *not* sense, will be so like it as to do as well. Perhaps better; for it spares the reader the trouble of thinking; prevents vacancy, while it indulges indolence; and secures the memory from
all danger of an intellectual plethora. Hence of all trades, literature
at present demands the least talent or information; and, of all

modes of literature, the manufacturing of poems. The difference indeed between these and the works of genius is not less than between an egg and an egg-shell; yet at a distance they both look alike. Now it is no less remarkable than true, with how little examination works of polite literature are commonly perused, not only by the mass of readers, but by men of first rate ability, till some accident or chance* discussion have roused their attention,

---

* In the course of one of my Lectures, I had occasion to point out the almost faultless position and choice of words, in Mr. Pope's *original* compositions, particularly in his Satires and moral Essays, for the purpose of comparing them with his translation of Homer, which I do not stand alone in regarding as the main source of our pseudo-poetic diction. And this, by the bye, is an additional confirmation of a remark made, I believe, by Sir Joshua Reynolds, that next to the man who forms and elevates the taste of the public, he that corrupts it, is commonly the greatest genius. Among other passages, I analyzed sentence by sentence, and almost word by word, the popular lines,

> As when the moon, resplendent lamp of light, &c.

much in the same way as has been since done, in an excellent article on Chalmers's British Poets in the Quarterly Review. The impression on the audience in general was sudden and evident: and a number of enlightened and highly educated persons, who at different times afterwards addressed me on the subject, expressed their wonder, that truth so obvious should not have struck them *before;* but at the same time acknowledged (so much had they been accustomed, in reading poetry, to receive pleasure from the separate images and phrases successively, without asking themselves whether the collective meaning was sense or nonsense) that they might in all probability have read the same passage again twenty times with undiminished admiration, and without once reflecting, that "ἄστρα φαεινὴν ἀμφὶ σελήνην φαίνετ' ἀριπρεπέα" (i. e. the stars around, or near the full moon, shine pre-eminently bright) conveys a just and happy image of a moonlight sky: while it is difficult to determine whether, in the lines,

> Around *her throne* the vivid planets *roll,*
> And stars *unnumber'd gild* the *glowing pole,*

the sense or the diction be the more absurd. My answer was; that, though I had derived peculiar advantages from my school discipline, and though my *general* theory of poetry was the same then as now, I had yet experienced the same sensations myself, and felt almost as if I had been newly couched, when, by Mr. Wordsworth's conversation, I had been induced to re-examine with impartial strictness Gray's celebrated elegy. I had long before detected

and put them on their guard. And hence individuals below mediocrity not less in natural power than in acquired knowledge; nay, bunglers that had failed in the lowest mechanic crafts, and whose presumption is in due proportion to their want of sense and sensibility; men, who being first scribblers from idleness and ignorance, next become libellers from envy and malevolence; have been able to drive a successful trade in the employment of the booksellers, nay, have raised themselves into temporary name and reputation with the public at large, by that most powerful of all adulation, the appeal to the bad and malignant passions of mankind.* But as it is the nature of scorn, envy, and all malignant propensities to require a quick change of objects, such writers are sure, sooner or

---

the defects in "the Bard"; but "the Elegy" I had considered as proof against all fair attacks; and to this day I cannot read either without delight, and a portion of enthusiasm. At all events, whatever pleasure I may have lost by the clearer perception of the faults in certain passages, has been more than repaid to me by the additional delight with which I read the remainder.
* Especially "in this AGE OF PERSONALITY, this age of literary and political GOSSIPING, when the meanest insects are worshipped with a sort of Egyptian superstition, if only the brainless head be atoned for by the sting of personal malignity in the tail! When the most vapid satires have become the objects of a keen public interest, purely from the number of contemporary characters named in the patch-work notes, (which possess, however, the comparative merit of being more poetical than the text,) and because, to increase the stimulus, the author has sagaciously left his own name for whispers and conjectures! In an age, when even sermons are published with a double appendix stuffed with *names*—in a generation so transformed from the characteristic reserve of Britons, that from the ephemeral sheet of a London newspaper, to the everlasting Scotch Professorial Quarto, almost every publication exhibits or flatters the epidemic distemper; that the very "last year's rebuses" in the Ladies Diary, are answered in a serious elegy *"on my father's death,"* with the name and habitat of the elegiac Oedipus subscribed; and *"other ingenious solutions were likewise given"* to the said *rebuses*—not as heretofore by Crito, Philander, A, B, Y, &c., but by fifty or sixty plain English surnames at full length with their several places of abode! In an age, when a bashful *Philalethes,* or *Phileleutheros* is as rare on the title pages, and among the signatures, of our magazines, as a real name used to be in the days of our shy and notice-shunning grandfathers! When (more exquisite than all) I see an EPIC POEM (spirits of Mars and Mæonides, make ready to welcome your new compeer!) advertised with the special recommendation that the said EPIC POEM contains more than a hundred names of *living* persons."—FRIEND No. 10.

later, to awake from their dream of vanity to disappointment and neglect with embittered and envenomed feelings. Even during their short-lived success, sensible in spite of themsleves on what a shifting foundation it rests, they resent the mere refusal of praise, as a robbery, and at the justest censures kindle at once into violent and undisciplined abuse; till the acute disease changing into chronical, the more deadly as the less violent, they become the fit instruments of literary detraction, and moral slander. They are then no longer to be questioned without exposing the complainant to ridicule, because, forsooth, they are *anonymous* critics, and authorized as "synodical individuals" * to speak of themselves plurali majestatico! As if literature formed a caste, like that of the PARAS in Hindostan, who, however maltreated, must not dare to deem themselves wronged! As if that, which in all other cases adds a deeper dye to slander, the circumstance of its being anonymous, here acted only to make the slanderer inviolable! Thus, in *part,* from the accidental tempers of individuals (men of undoubted talent, but not men of genius) tempers rendered yet more irritable by their desire to *appear* men of genius; but still more effectively by the excesses of the mere *counterfeits* both of talent and genius; the number too being so incomparably greater of those who are *thought* to be, than of those who really *are* men of real genius; and in part from the natural, but not therefore the less partial and unjust distinction, made by the public itself between *literary* and all other property;— I believe the prejudice to have arisen, which considers an unusual irascibility concerning the reception of its products as characteristic of genius. It might correct the moral feelings of a numerous class of readers, to suppose a Review set on foot, the object of which should be to criticise all the chief works presented to the public by our ribbon-weavers, calico-printers, cabinet-makers, and china-manufacturers; a Review conducted in the same spirit, and which should take the same freedom with personal character, as our literary journals. They would scarcely, I think, deny their belief, not only that the "genus irritabile" would be found to include many other *species* besides that of bards; but that the irritability of *trade* would soon reduce the resentment of *poets* into mere shadow-fights

* A phrase of Andrew Marvel's.

(σκιομαχίας) in the comparison. Or is wealth the only rational object of human interest? Or even if this were admitted, has the poet no property in his works? Or is it a rare, or culpable case, that he who serves at the altar of the muses, should be compelled to derive his maintenance from the altar, when too he has perhaps deliberately abandoned the fairest prospects of rank and opulence in order to devote himself, an entire and undistracted man, to the instruction or refinement of his fellow-citizens? Or, should we pass by all higher objects and motives, all disinterested benevolence, and even that ambition of lasting praise which is at once the crutch and ornament, which at once supports and betrays, the infirmity of human virtue; is the character and property of the man, who labours for our intellectual pleasures, less entitled to a share of our fellow feeling, than that of the wine-merchant or milliner? Sensibility indeed, both quick and deep, is not only a characteristic feature, but may be deemed a component part, of genius. But it is not less an essential mark of true genius, that its sensibility is excited by any other cause more powerfully than by its own personal interests; for this plain reason, that the man of genius lives most in the ideal world, in which the present is still constituted by the future or the past; and because his feelings have been habitually associated with thoughts and images, to the number, clearness, and vivacity of which the sensation of *self* is always in an inverse proportion. And yet, should he perchance have occasion to repel some false charge, or to rectify some erroneous censure, nothing is more common than for the many to mistake the general liveliness of his manner and language, *whatever* is the subject, for the effects of peculiar irritation from its accidental relation to himself.*

---

* This is one instance among many of deception, by the telling the half of a fact, and omitting the other half, when it is from their mutual counteraction and neutralization, that the *whole* truth arises, as a tertium aliquid different from either. Thus in Dryden's famous line, "Great wit" (which here means genius) "to madness sure is near allied." Now as far as the profound sensibility, which is doubtless *one* of the components of genius, were alone considered, single and unbalanced, it might be fairly described as exposing the individual to a greater chance of mental derangement; but then a more than usual rapidity of association, a more than usual power of passing from thought to thought, and image to image, is a component equally

For myself, if from my own feelings, or from the less suspicious test of the observations of others, I had been made aware of any literary testiness or jealousy; I trust, that I should have been, however, neither silly nor arrogant enough to have burthened the imperfection on GENIUS. But an experience (and I should not need documents in abundance to prove my words, if I added) a tried experience of twenty years, has taught me, that the original sin of my character consists in a careless indifference to public opinion, and to the attacks of those who influence it; that praise and admiration have become yearly less and less desirable, except as marks of sympathy; nay that it is difficult and distressing to me, to think with any interest even about the sale and profit of my works, important as, in my present circumstances, such considerations must needs be. Yet it never occurred to me to believe or fancy, that the quantum of intellectual power bestowed on me by nature or education was in any way connected with this habit of my feelings; or that it needed any other parents or fosterers than constitutional indolence, aggravated into languor by ill-health; the accumulating embarrassments of procrastination; the mental cowardice, which is the inseparable companion of procrastination, and which makes us anxious to think and converse on any thing rather than on what concerns ourselves; in fine, all those close vexations, whether chargeable on my faults or my fortunes, which leave me but little grief to spare for evils comparatively distant and alien.

Indignation at literary wrongs I leave to men born under happier stars. I cannot *afford it*. But so far from condemning those who can, I deem it a writer's duty, and think it creditable to his heart, to feel and express a resentment proportioned to the grossness of the provocation, and the importance of the object. There is no profession on earth, which requires an attention so early, so long, or so unintermitting as that of poetry; and indeed as that of literary composition in general, if it be such as at all satisfies the demands both of

---

essential; and in the due modification of each by the other the GENIUS itself consists; so that it would be just as fair to describe the earth, as in imminent danger of exorbitating, or of falling into the sun, according as the assertor of the absurdity *confined* his attention either to the projectile or to the attractive force exclusively.

taste and of sound logic. How difficult and delicate a task even the mere mechanism of verse is, may be conjectured from the failure of those, who have attempted poetry late in life. Where then a man has, from his earliest youth, devoted his whole being to an object, which by the admission of all civilized nations in all ages is honorable as a pursuit, and glorious as an attainment; what of all that relates to himself and his family, if only we accept his moral character, can have fairer claims to his protection, or more authorize acts of self-defence, than the elaborate products of his intellect and intellectual industry? Prudence itself would command us to *show*, even if defect or diversion of natural sensibility had prevented us from *feeling*, a due interest and qualified anxiety for the offspring and representatives of our nobler being. I know it, alas! by woeful experience! I have laid too many eggs in the hot sands of this wilderness, the world, with ostrich carelessness and ostrich oblivion. The greater part indeed have been trod under foot, and are forgotten; but yet no small number have crept forth into life, some to furnish feathers for the caps of others, and still more to plume the shafts in the quivers of my enemies, of them that unprovoked have lain in wait against my soul.

Sic vos, non vobis, mellificatis, apes!

An instance in confirmation of the Note [p. 209], occurs to me as I am correcting this sheet, with the FAITHFUL SHEPHERDESS open before me. Mr. Seward first traces Fletcher's lines;

> More foul diseases than e'er yet the hot
> Sun bred thro' his burnings, while the dog
> Pursues the raging lion, throwing the fog
> And deadly vapour from his angry breath,
> Filling the lower world with plague and death.—

To Spenser's Shepherd's Calendar,

> The rampant lion hunts he fast
> With dogs of noisome breath;
> Whose baleful barking brings, in haste,
> Pyne, plagues, and dreary death!

He then takes occasion to introduce Homer's simile of the sight of Achilles' shield to Priam compared with the Dog Star, literally thus—

"For this indeed is most splendid, but it was made an evil sign, and brings many a consuming disease to wretched mortals." Nothing can be more simple as a description, or more accurate as a simile; which, (says Mr. S.) is thus *finely* translated by Mr. Pope:

> Terrific Glory! for his burning breath
> Taints the *red* air with fevers, plagues, and death!

Now here (not to mention the tremendous bombast) the *Dog Star,* so called, is turned into a *real* Dog, a very odd Dog, a Fire, Fever, Plague, and death-breathing, *red*-air-tainting Dog: and the whole *visual* likeness is lost, while the likeness in the *effects* is rendered absurd by the exaggeration. In Spenser and Fletcher the thought is justifiable; for the images are at least consistent, and it was the intention of the writers to mark the seasons by this allegory of visualized *Puns.*

# CHAPTER III

*The author's obligations to critics, and the probable occasion—Principles of modern criticism—Mr. Southey's works and character.*

To anonymous critics in reviews, magazines, and news-journals of various name and rank, and to satirists with or without a name in verse or prose, or in verse-text aided by prose-comment, I do seriously believe and profess, that I owe full two thirds of whatever reputation and publicity I happen to possess. For when the name of an individual has occurred so frequently, in so many works, for so great a length of time, the readers of these works (which with a shelf or two of BEAUTIES, ELEGANT EXTRACTS and ANAS, form nine-tenths of the reading of the reading public*) can-

---

* For as to the devotees of the circulating libraries, I dare not compliment their *pass-time,* or rather *kill-time,* with the name of *reading.* Call it rather a sort of beggarly day-dreaming, during which the mind of the dreamer furnishes for itself nothing but laziness, and a little mawkish sensibility; while the whole *materiel* and imagery of the dose is supplied *ab extra* by a sort of mental *camera obscura* manufactured at the printing office, which *pro tempore* fixes, reflects, and transmits the moving phantasms of one man's

not but be familiar with the name, without distinctly remembering whether it was introduced for an eulogy or for censure. And this becomes the more likely, if (as I believe) the habit of perusing periodical works may be properly added to Averrhoe's* catalogue of ANTI-MNEMONICS, or weakeners of the memory. But where this has not been the case, yet the reader will be apt to suspect, that there must be something more than usually strong and extensive in a reputation, that could either require or stand so merciless and long-continued a cannonading. Without any feeling of *anger* therefore (for which indeed, on my own account, I have no pretext) I may yet be allowed to express some degree of *surprize,* that, after having run the critical gauntlet for a certain class of faults which I *had,* nothing having come before the judgement-seat in the interim, I should, year after year, quarter after quarter, month after month (not to mention sundry petty periodicals of still quicker revolution, "or weekly or diurnal") have been, for at least

---

delirium, so as to people the barrenness of a hundred other brains afflicted with the same trance or suspension of all common sense and all definite purpose. We should therefore transfer this species of *amusement* (if indeed those can be said to retire *a musis,* who were never in their company, or relaxation be attributable to those, whose bows are never bent) from the genus, *reading,* to that comprehensive class characterized by the power of reconciling the two contrary yet co-existing propensities of human nature, namely, indulgence of sloth, and hatred of vacancy. In addition to novels and tales of chivalry in prose or rhyme, (by which last I mean neither rhythm nor metre), this genus comprises as its species, gaming, swinging, or swaying on a chair or gate; spitting over a bridge; smoking; snuff-taking; tête-à-tête quarrels after dinner between husband and wife; conning word by word all the advertisements of a daily newspaper in a public house on a rainy day, &c. &c. &c.

* Ex gr. Pediculos e capillis excerptos in arenam jacere incontusos: eating of unripe fruit; gazing on the clouds, and (in genere) on moveable things suspended in the air; riding among a multitude of camels; frequent laughter; listening to a series of jests and humorous anecdotes, as when (so to modernize the learned Saracen's meaning) one man's droll story of an Irishman inevitably occasions another's droll story of a Scotchman, which again, by the same sort of conjunction disjunctive, leads to some étouderie of a Welshman, and that again to some sly hit of a Yorkshireman; the habit of reading tombstones in church-yards, &c. By the bye, this catalogue, strange as it may appear, is not insusceptible of a sound psychological commentary.

17 years consecutively dragged forth by them into the foremost ranks of the *proscribed*, and forced to abide the brunt of abuse, for faults directly opposite, and which I certainly had not. How shall I explain this?

Whatever may have been the case with others, I certainly cannot attribute this persecution to personal dislike, or to envy, or to feelings of vindictive animosity. Not to the former, for with the exception of a very few who are my intimate friends, and were so before they were known as authors, I have had little other acquaintance with literary characters, than what may be implied in an accidental introduction, or casual meeting in a mixt company. And, as far as words and looks can be trusted, I must believe that, even in these instances, I had excited no unfriendly disposition.*

* Some years ago, a gentleman, the chief writer and conductor of a celebrated review, distinguished by its hostility to Mr. Southey, spent a day or two at Keswick. That he was, without diminution on this account, treated with every hospitable attention by Mr. Southey and myself, I trust I need not say. But one thing I may venture to notice; that at no period of my life do I remember to have received so many, and such high coloured compliments in so short a space of time. He was likewise circumstantially informed by what series of accidents it had happened, that Mr. Wordsworth, Mr. Southey, and I had become neighbours; and how utterly unfounded was the supposition, that we considered ourselves, as belonging to any common school, but that of good sense confirmed by the long-established models of the best times of Greece, Rome, Italy, and England; and still more groundless the notion, that Mr. Southey (for as to myself I have published so little, and that little of so little importance, as to make it ludicrous to mention my name at all) could have been concerned in the formation of a poetic sect with Mr. Wordsworth, when so many of his works had been published not only previously to any acquaintance between them; but before Mr. Wordsworth himself had written anything but in a diction ornate, and uniformly sustained; when too the slightest examination will make it evident, that between those and the after writings of Mr. Southey, there exists no other difference than that of a progressive degree of excellence from progressive development of power, and progressive facility from habit and increase of experience. Yet among the first articles which this man wrote after his return from Keswick, we were characterized as "the School of whining and hypochondriacal poets that haunt the Lakes." In reply to a letter from the same gentleman, in which he had asked me, whether I was in earnest in preferring the style of Hooker to that of Dr. Johnson; and Jeremy Taylor to Burke; I stated, somewhat at large, the comparative excellences and defects, which

Neither by letter, or in conversation, have I ever had dispute or controversy beyond the common social interchange of opinions. Nay, where I had reason to suppose my convictions fundamentally different, it has been my habit, and I may add, the impulse of my nature, to assign the grounds of my belief, rather than the belief itself; and not to express dissent, till I could establish some points of complete sympathy, some grounds common to both sides, from which to commence its explanation.

Still less can I place these attacks to the charge of envy. The few pages which I have published, are of too distant a date; and the extent of their sale a proof too conclusive against their having been popular at any time; to render probable, I had almost said possible, the excitement of envy on *their* account; and the man

---

characterized our best prose writers, from the reformation, to the first half of Charles 2nd; and that of those who had flourished during the present reign, and the preceding one. About twelve months afterwards, a review appeared on the same subject, in the concluding paragraph of which the reviewer asserts, that his chief motive for entering into the discussion was to separate a rational and qualified admiration of our elder writers, from the indiscriminate enthusiasm of a recent school, who praised what they did not understand, and caricatured what they were unable to imitate. And, that no doubt might be left concerning the persons alluded to, the writer annexes the names of Miss BAILIE, W. SOUTHEY, WORDSWORTH and COLE-RIDGE. For that which follows, I have only hearsay evidence; but yet such as demands my belief; viz. that on being questioned concerning this apparently wanton attack, more especially with regard to Miss Bailie, the writer had stated as his motives, that this lady, when at Edinburgh had declined a proposal of introducing him to her; that Mr. Southey had written against him; and Mr. Wordsworth had talked contemptuously of him; but that as to *Coleridge,* he had noticed him merely because the names of Southey and Wordsworth and Coleridge always went together. But if it were worth while to mix together, as ingredients, half the anecdotes which I either myself know to be true, or which I have received from men incapable of intentional falsehood, concerning the characters, qualifications, and motives of our anonymous critics, whose decisions are oracles for our reading public, I might safely borrow the words of the apocryphal Daniel, *"Give me leave,* O SOVEREIGN PUBLIC, *and I shall slay this dragon without sword or staff."* For the compound would be as the "Pitch, and fat, and hair which Daniel took, and did seethe them together, and made lumps thereof, and put into the dragon's mouth, and so the dragon burst in sunder; and Daniel said, 'Lo, THESE ARE THE GODS YE WORSHIP.' "

who should envy me on any *other,* verily he must be *envy-mad!*

Lastly, with as little semblance of reason, could I suspect any animosity towards me from vindictive feelings as the cause. I have before said, that my acquaintance with literary men has been limited and distant; and that I have had neither dispute nor controversy. From my first entrance into life, I have, with few and short intervals, lived either abroad or in retirement. My different essays on subjects of national interest, published at different times, first in the Morning Post and then in the Courier, with my courses of lectures on the principles of criticism as applied to Shakespeare and Milton, constitute my whole publicity; the only occasions on which I *could* offend any member of the republic of letters. With one solitary exception in which my words were first misstated and then wantonly applied to an individual, I could never learn, that I had excited the displeasure of any among my literary contemporaries. Having announced my intention to give a course of lectures on the characteristic merits and defects of English poetry in its different æras; first, from Chaucer to Milton; second, from Dryden inclusive to Thompson; and third, from Cowper to the present day; I changed my plan, and confined my disquisition to the two former æras, that I might furnish no possible pretext for the unthinking to misconstrue, or the malignant to misapply my words, and having stampt their own meaning on them, to pass them as current coin in the marts of garrulity or detraction.

Praises of the unworthy are felt by ardent minds as robberies of the deserving; and it is too true, and too frequent, that Bacon, Harrington, Machiavel, and Spinosa, are *not* read, because Hume, Condillac, and Voltaire *are.* But in promiscuous company no prudent man will oppugn the merits of a contemporary in his own supposed department; contenting himself with praising in his turn those whom *he* deems excellent. If I should ever deem it my duty at all to oppose the pretensions of individuals, I would oppose them in books which could be weighed and answered, in which I could evolve the whole of my reasons and feelings, with their requisite limits and modifications; not in irrecoverable conversation, where however strong the reasons might be, the feelings that prompted them would assuredly be attributed by some one or other to envy and discontent. Besides I well know, and I trust, have acted on that knowledge, that it must be the ignorant and injudicious who extol the unworthy; and the eulogies of critics without taste or judgement are the natural reward of authors without feeling or genius. "Sint unicuique sua præmia."

How then, dismissing, as I do, these three causes, am I to account for attacks, the long continuance and inveteracy of which it would require all three to explain? The solution may seem to have been given, or at least suggested, in a note to a preceding page. *I was in habits of intimacy with Mr. Wordsworth and Mr. Southey!* This, however, transfers, rather than removes the difficulty. Be it, that, by an unconscionable extension of the old adage, "noscitur a socio," my literary friends are never under the waterfall of criticism, but I must be wet through with the spray; yet how came the torrent to descend upon *them?*

First then, with regard to Mr. Southey. I well remember the general reception of his earlier publications: viz. the poems published with Mr. Lovell under the names of Moschus and Bion; the two volumes of poems under his own name, and the Joan of Arc. The censures of the critics by profession are extant, and may be easily referred to:—careless lines, inequality in the merit of the different poems, and (in the lighter works) a predilection for the strange and whimsical; in short, such faults as might have been anticipated in a young and rapid writer, were indeed sufficiently enforced. Nor was there at that time wanting a party spirit to aggravate the defects of a poet, who with all the courage of uncorrupted youth had avowed his zeal for a cause, which he deemed that of liberty, and his abhorrence of oppression by whatever name consecrated. But it was as little objected by others, as dreamt of by the poet himself, that he *preferred* careless and prosaic lines on rule and of forethought, or indeed that he pretended to any other art or theory of poetic diction, besides that which we may all learn from Horace, Quinctilian, the admirable dialogue de Causis Corruptae Eloquentiæ, or Strada's Prolusions; if indeed natural good sense and the early study of the best models in his own language had not infused the same maxims more securely, and, if I may venture the expression, more vitally. All that could have been fairly deduced was, that in his taste and estimation of writers Mr. Southey agreed far more with Warton, than with Johnson. Nor do I mean to deny, that at all times Mr. Southey was of the same mind with Sir Philip Sidney in preferring an excellent ballad in the *humblest* style of poetry to twenty indifferent poems that strutted in the *highest*. And by what have his works, published since then, been characterized, each more strikingly than the preceding, but by greater splendor, a deeper pathos, profounder reflections, and a more sustained dignity of language and of metre? Distant may the period be, but whenever the time shall come, when all his works shall be collected by some editor worthy to be his biographer, I trust that an excerpta of all the passages, in which his writings, name, and character have been attacked, from the pamphlets and periodical works of the last twenty years, may be an accompaniment. Yet that it would prove medicinal in after times I dare not hope; for as long as there are readers to be delighted with calumny, there will be found reviewers to calumniate. And such readers will become in all probability more numerous, in proportion as a still greater diffusion of literature shall produce an increase of sciolists, and sciolism bring with it petulance and presumption. In times of old, books were as religious oracles; as literature advanced, they next became venerable preceptors; they then descended to the rank of instructive friends; and, as their numbers increased, they sunk still lower to that of entertaining companions; and at present they seem degraded into culprits to hold up their hands at the bar of every self-elected, yet not the less peremptory, judge, who chuses to write from humour or interest, from enmity or arrogance, and to abide the decision (in the words of Jeremy Taylor) "of him that reads in malice, or him that reads after dinner."

The same gradual retrograde movement may be traced, in the relation which the authors themselves have assumed towards their readers. From the lofty address of Bacon: "these are the meditations of Francis of Verulam, which that posterity should be possessed of, he deemed *their* interest:" or from dedication to Monarch or Pontiff, in which the honor given was asserted in equipoise to the patronage acknowledged; from Pindar's

————ἐπ' ἄλλοι-
-σι δ' ἄλλοι μεγάλοι. τὸ δ' ἔσχατον κορυ-
φοῦται βασιλεῦσι. μηκέτι
πάπταινε πόρσιον.
εἴη σέ τε τοῦτον
ὑψοῦ χρόνον πατεῖν, ἐμέ
τε τοσσάδε νικαφόροις
ὁμιλεῖν, πρόφαντον σοφίᾳ καθ' Ἑλ-
-λανας ἐόντα παντᾷ.—OLYMP. OD. I.

there was a gradual sinking in the etiquette or allowed style of pretension.

Poets and Philosophers, rendered diffident by their very number, addressed themselves to "*learned* readers;" then, aimed to conciliate the graces of "the *candid* reader;" till, the critic still rising as the author sunk, the amateurs of literature collectively were erected into a municipality of judges, and addressed as THE TOWN! And now, finally, all men being supposed able to read, and all readers able to judge, the multitudinous PUBLIC, shaped into personal unity by the magic of abstraction, sits nominal despot on the throne of criticism. But, alas! as in other despotisms, it but echoes the decisions of its invisible ministers, whose intellectual claims to the guardianship of the muses seem, for the greater part, analogous to the physical qualifications which adapt their oriental brethren for the superintendence of the Harem. Thus it is said, that St. Nepomuc was installed the guardian of bridges, because he had fallen over one, and sunk out of sight; thus too St. Cecilia is said to have been first propitiated by musicians, because, having failed in her own attempts, she had taken a dislike to the art, and all its successful professors. But I shall probably have occasion hereafter to deliver my convictions more at large concerning this state of things, and its influences on taste, genius, and morality.

In the "Thalaba," the "Madoc," and still more evidently in the unique* "Cid," in the "Kehama," and, at last, so best, the "Don

---

* I have ventured to call it "unique;" not only because I know no work of the kind in our language (if we except a few chapters of the old translation of Froissart) none, which uniting the charms of romance and history, keeps

Roderick"; Southey has given abundant proof, "se cogitâsse quám sit magnum dare aliquid in manus hominum, nec persuadere sibi posse, non sæpe tractandum quod placere et semper et omnibus cupiat." Plin. Ep., Lib. 7, Ep. 17. But on the other hand, I guess, that Mr. Southey was quite unable to comprehend, wherein could consist the crime or mischief of printing half a dozen or more playful poems; or to speak more generally, compositions which would be enjoyed or passed over, according as the taste and humour of the reader might chance to be; provided they contained nothing immoral. In the present age "periturae parcere chartæ" is emphatically an unreasonable demand. The merest trifle, he ever sent abroad, had tenfold better claims to its ink and paper, than all the silly criticisms, which prove no more, than that the critic was not one of those, for whom the trifle was written; and than all the grave exhortations to a greater reverence for the public. As if the passive page of a book, by having an epigram or doggrel tale impressed on it, instantly assumed at once loco-motive power and a sort of ubiquity, so as to flutter and buz in the ear of the public to the sore annoyance of the said mysterious personage. But what gives an additional and more ludicrous absurdity to these lamentations is the curious fact, that if in a volume of poetry the critic should find poem or passage which he deems more especially worthless, he is sure to select and reprint it in the review; by which, on his own grounds, he wastes as much more paper than the author, as the copies of a fashionable review are more numerous than those of the original book; in some, and those the most prominent instances, as ten thousand to five hundred. I know nothing that surpasses the vileness of deciding on the merits of a poet or painter, (not by characteristic defects; for where there is genius, *these* always point to his characteristic *beauties*; but) by accidental failures or faulty passages; except the impudence of defending it, as the proper duty, and most instructive part, of

---

the imagination so constantly on the wing, and yet leaves so much for after reflection; but likewise, and chiefly, because it is a compilation which, in the various excellencies of translation, selection, and arrangement, required and proves greater genius in the compiler, as living in the present state of society, than in the original composers.

criticism. Omit or pass slightly over the expression, grace, and grouping of Raphael's *figures;* but ridicule in *detail* the knitting-needles and broom-twigs, that are to represent trees in his back grounds; and never let him hear the last of his *galli-pots!* Admit that the Allegro and Penseroso of Milton are not *without merit;* but repay yourself for this concession, by reprinting at length the *two poems on the University Carrier!* As a fair specimen of his Sonnets, quote *"A Book was writ of late called Tetrachordon;"* and, as characteristic of his rhythm and metre, cite his literal translation of the first and second psalm! In order to justify yourself, you need only assert, that had you dwelt chiefly on the beauties and excellencies of the poet, the admiration of these might seduce the attention of future writers from the objects of their love and wonder, to an imitation of the few poems and passages in which the poet was most unlike himself.

But till reviews are conducted on far other principles, and with far other motives; till in the place of arbitrary dictation and petulant sneers, the reviewers support their decisions by reference to fixed canons of criticism, previously established and deduced from the nature of man; reflecting minds will pronounce it arrogance in them thus to announce themselves to men of letters, as the guides of their taste and judgement. To the purchaser and mere reader it is, at all events, an injustice. He who tells me that there are *defects* in a new work, tells me nothing which I should not have taken for granted without his information. But he, who points out and elucidates the *beauties* of an original work, does indeed give me interesting information, such as experience would not have authorized me in anticipating. And as to compositions which the authors themselves announce with "Hæc ipsi novimus esse nihil," why should we judge by a different rule two printed works, only because the one author was alive, and the other in his grave? What literary man has not regretted the prudery of Spratt in refusing to let his friend Cowley appear in his slippers and dressing gown? I am not perhaps the only one who has derived an innocent amusement from the riddles, conundrums, trisyllable lines, &c., &c., of Swift and his correspondents, in hours of languor, when to have read his more finished works would have been useless to myself, and, in some sort, an act of injustice to the author. But I am at a loss to conceive by what perversity of judgement, these relaxations of his genius could be employed to diminish his fame as the writer of "Gulliver's Travels," and the "Tale of a Tub." Had Mr. Southey written twice as many poems of inferior merit, or partial interest, as have enlivened the journals of the day, they would have added to his honor with good and wise men, not merely or principally as proving the versatility of his talents, but as evidences of the purity of that mind, which even in its levities never wrote a line, which it need regret on any moral account.

I have in imagination transferred to the future biographer the duty of contrasting Southey's fixed and well-earned fame, with the abuse and indefatigable hostility of his anonymous critics from his early youth to his ripest manhood. But I cannot think so ill of human nature as not to believe, that these critics have already taken shame to themselves, whether they consider the object of their abuse in his moral or his literary character. For reflect but on the variety and extent of his acquirements! He stands second to no man, either as an historian or as a bibliographer; and when I regard him as a popular essayist, (for the articles of his composi-tions in the reviews are for the greater part essays on subjects of deep or curious interest rather than criticisms on particular works*) I look in vain for any writer, who has conveyed so much information, from so many and such recondite sources, with so many just and original reflections, in a style so lively and poig-nant, yet so uniformly classical and perspicuous; no one in short who has combined so much wisdom with so much wit; so much truth and knowledge with so much life and fancy. His prose is always intelligible and always entertaining. In poetry he has at-tempted almost every species of composition known before, and he has added new ones; and if we except the highest lyric, (in which how few, how very few even of the greatest minds have been fortunate) he has attempted every species successfully: from the political song of the day, thrown off in the playful overflow of

---

* See the articles on Methodism, in the Quarterly Review: the small volume on the New System of Education, &c.

honest joy and patriotic exultation, to the wild ballad;* from epistolary ease and graceful narrative, to the austere and impetuous moral declamation; from the pastoral claims and wild streaming lights of the "Thalaba," in which sentiment and imagery have given permanence even to the excitement of curiosity; and from the full blaze of the "Kehama," (a gallery of finished pictures in one splendid fancy piece, in which, notwithstanding, the moral grandeur rises gradually above the brilliance of the colouring and the boldness and novelty of the machinery) to the more sober beauties of the "Madoc"; and lastly, from the Madoc to his "Roderic," in which, retaining all his former excellencies of a poet eminently inventive and picturesque, he has surpassed himself in language and metre, in the construction of the whole, and in the splendour of particular passages.

Here then shall I conclude? No! The characters of the deceased, like the encomia on tombstones, as they are described with religious tenderness, so are they read, with allowing sympathy indeed, but yet with rational deduction. There are men, who deserve a higher record; men with whose characters it is the interest of their contemporaries, no less than that of posterity, to be made acquainted; while it is yet possible for impartial censure, and even for quick-sighted envy, to cross-examine the tale without offence to the courtesies of humanity; and while the eulogist detected in exaggeration or falsehood must pay the full penalty of his baseness in the contempt which brands the convicted flatterer. Publicly has Mr. Southey been reviled by men, who, (as I would fain hope for the honor of human nature) hurled fire-brands against a figure of their own imagination, publicly have his talents been depreciated, his principles denounced; as publicly do I therefore, who have known him intimately, deem it my duty to leave recorded, that it is SOUTHEY's almost unexampled felicity, to possess the best gifts of talent and genius free from all their characteristic defects. To those who remember the state of our public schools and universities some twenty years past, it will appear no ordinary praise in any man to have passed from innocence into virtue, not only

---

* See the incomparable "Return to Moscow" and the "Old Woman of Berkeley."

free from all vicious habit, but unstained by one act of intemperance, or the degradations akin to intemperance. That scheme of head, heart, and habitual demeanour, which in his early manhood, and first controversial writings, Milton, claiming the privilege of self-defence, asserts of himself, and challenges his calumniators to disprove; this will his school-mates, his fellow-collegians, and his maturer friends, with a confidence proportioned to the intimacy of their knowledge, bear witness to, as again realized in the life of Robert Southey. But still more striking to those, who by biography or by their own experience are familiar with the general habits of genius, will appear the poet's matchless industry and perseverance in his pursuits; the worthiness and dignity of those pursuits; his generous submission to tasks of transitory interest, or such as *his* genius alone could make otherwise; and that having thus more than satisfied the claims of affection or prudence, he should yet have made for himself time and power, to achieve more, and in more various departments than almost any other writer has done, though employed wholly on subjects of his own choice and ambition. But as Southey possesses, and is not possessed by, his genius, even so is he master even of his virtues. The regular and methodical tenor of his daily labours, which would be deemed rare in the most mechanical pursuits, and might be envied by the mere man of business, loses all semblance of formality in the dignified simplicity of his manners, in the spring and healthful chearfulness of his spirits. Always employed, his friends find him always at leisure. No less punctual in trifles, than stedfast in the performance of highest duties, he inflicts none of those small pains and discomforts which irregular men scatter about them, and which in the aggregate so often become formidable obstacles both to happiness and utility; while on the contrary he bestows all the pleasures, and inspires all that ease of mind on those around him or connected with him, which perfect consistency, and (if such a word might be framed) absolute *reliability*, equally in small as in great concerns, cannot but inspire and bestow: when this too is softened without being weakened by kindness and gentleness. I know few men who so well deserve the character which an antient attributes to Marcus Cato, namely, that he was likest virtue, in as much as he seemed to act aright, not in obedience to any law or outward motive, but by the necessity of a happy nature, which could not act otherwise. As son, brother, husband, father, master, friend, he moves with firm yet light steps, alike unostentatious, and alike exemplary. As a writer, he has uniformly made his talents subservient to the best interests of humanity, of public virtue, and domestic piety; his cause has ever been the cause of pure religion and of liberty, of national independence and of national illumination. When future critics shall weigh out his guerdon of praise and censure, it will be Southey the poet only, that will supply them with the scanty materials for the latter. They will likewise not fail to record, that as no man was ever a more constant friend, never had poet more friends and honorers among the good of all parties; and that quacks in education, quacks in politics, and quacks in criticism were his only enemies.*

---

* It is not easy to estimate the effects which the example of a young man as highly distinguished for strict purity of disposition and conduct, as for intellectual power and literary acquirements, may produce on those of the same age with himself, especially on those of similar pursuits and congenial minds. For many years, my opportunities of intercourse with Mr. Southey have been rare, and at long intervals; but I dwell with unabated pleasure on the strong and sudden, yet I trust not fleeting, influence, which my moral being underwent on my acquaintance with him at Oxford, whither I had gone at the commencement of our Cambridge vacation on a visit to an old school-fellow. Not indeed on my moral or religious principles, for *they* had never been contaminated; but in awakening the sense of the duty and dignity of making my actions accord with those principles, both in word and deed. The irregularities only not universal among the young men of my standing, which I always *knew* to be *wrong,* I then learned to feel as *degrading;* learnt to know that an opposite conduct, which was at that time considered by us as the easy virtue of cold and selfish prudence, might originate in the noblest emotions, in views the most disinterested and imaginative. It is not however from grateful recollections only, that I have been impelled thus to leave these my deliberate sentiments on record; but in some sense as a debt of justice to the man, whose name has been so often connected with mine for evil to which he is a stranger. As a specimen I subjoin part of a note, from "the Beauties of the Anti-jacobin," in which, having previously informed the public that I had been dishonour'd at Cambridge for preaching Deism, at a time when, for my youthful ardour in defence of Christianity, I was decried as a bigot by the proselytes of French

## CHAPTER IV

*The lyrical ballads with the preface—Mr. Wordsworth's earlier poems—On fancy and imagination—The investigation of the distinction important to the fine arts.*

I have wandered far from the object in view, but as I fancied to myself readers who would respect the feelings that had tempted me from the main road; so I dare calculate on not a few, who will warmly sympathize with them. At present it will be sufficient for my purpose, if I have proved, that Mr. Southey's writings no more than my own furnished the original occasion to this fiction of a *new school* of poetry, and to the clamors against its supposed founders and proselytes.

As little do I believe that "Mr. WORDSWORTH's Lyrical Ballads" were in *themselves* the cause. I speak exclusively of the two volumes so entitled. A careful and repeated examination of these confirms me in the belief, that the omission of less than an hundred lines would have precluded nine-tenths of the criticism on this work. I hazard this declaration, however, on the supposition, that the reader has taken it up, as he would have done any other collection of poems purporting to derive their subjects or interests from the incidents of domestic or ordinary life, intermingled with higher strains of meditation which the poet utters in his own person and character; with the proviso, that they were perused without knowledge of, or reference to, the author's peculiar opin-

---

Phi- (or to speak more truly, Psi-) losophy, the writer concludes with these words; "since this time he has left his native country, commenced citizen of the world, *left his poor children fatherless, and his wife destitute. Ex his disce his friends,* LAMB *and* SOUTHEY." With severest truth it may be asserted, that it would not be easy to select two men more exemplary in their domestic affections than those whose names were thus printed at full length as in the same rank of morals with a denounced infidel and fugitive, who had left his children *fatherless and his wife destitute!* Is it surprising, that many good men remained longer than perhaps they otherwise would have done, adverse to a party, which encouraged and openly rewarded the authors of such atrocious calumnies? "Qualis es, nescio; sed per quales agis, scio et doleo."

ions, and that the reader had not had his attention previously directed to those peculiarities. In these, as was actually the case with Mr. Southey's earlier works, the lines and passages which might have offended the general taste, would have been considered as mere inequalities, and attributed to inattention, not to perversity of judgement. The men of business who had passed their lives chiefly in cities, and who might therefore be expected to derive the highest pleasure from acute notices of men and manners conveyed in easy, yet correct and pointed language; and all those who, reading but little poetry, are most stimulated with that species of it, which seems most distant from prose, would probably have passed by the volume altogether. Others more catholic in their taste, and yet habituated to be most pleased when most excited, would have contented themselves with deciding, that the author had been successful in proportion to the elevation of his style and subject. Not a few perhaps, might by their admiration of "the lines written near Tintern Abbey," those "left upon a Seat under a Yew Tree," the "old Cumberland beggar," and "Ruth," have been gradually led to peruse with kindred feeling the "Brothers," the "Hart leap well," and whatever other poems in that collection may be described as holding a middle place between those written in the highest and those in the humblest style; as for instance between the "Tintern Abbey," and "the Thorn," or the "Simon Lee." Should their taste submit to no further change, and still remain unreconciled to the colloquial phrases, or the imitations of them, that are, more or less, scattered through the class last mentioned; yet even from the small number of the latter, they would have deemed them but an inconsiderable subtraction from the merit of the whole work; or, what is sometimes not unpleasing in the publication of a new writer, as serving to ascertain the natural tendency, and consequently the proper direction of the author's genius.

In the critical remarks, therefore, prefixed and annexed to the "Lyrical Ballads," I believe that we may safely rest, as the true origin of the unexampled opposition which Mr. Wordsworth's writings have been since doomed to encounter. The humbler passages in the poems themselves were dwelt on and cited to justify the rejection of the theory. What in and for themselves would have been either forgotten or forgiven as imperfections, or at least comparative failures, provoked direct hostility when announced as intentional, as the result of choice after full deliberation. Thus the poems, admitted by *all* as excellent, joined with those which had pleased the far *greater* number, though they formed two-thirds of the whole work, instead of being deemed (as in all right they should have been, even if we take for granted that the reader judged aright) an atonement for the few exceptions, gave wind and fuel to the animosity against both the poems and the poet. In all perplexity there is a portion of fear, which predisposes the mind to anger. Not able to deny that the author possessed both genius and a powerful intellect, they felt *very positive,* but were not *quite certain,* that he might not be in the right, and they themselves in the wrong; an unquiet state of mind, which seeks alleviation by quarrelling with the occasion of it, and by wondering at the perverseness of the man, who had written a long and argumentative essay to persuade them, that

Fair is foul, and foul is fair;

in other words, that they had been all their lives admiring without judgement, and were now about to censure without reason.*

---

* In opinions of long continuance, and in which we have never before been molested by a single doubt, to be suddenly *convinced* of an *error,* is almost like being *convicted* of a fault. There is a state of mind, which is the direct antithesis of that, which takes place when we *make a bull. The bull* namely consists in the bringing together two incompatible thoughts, with the *sensation,* but without the *sense,* of their connection. The psychological condition, or that which constitutes the possibility of this state, being such disproportionate vividness of two distant thoughts, as extinguishes or obscures the consciousness of the intermediate images or conceptions, or wholly abstracts the attention from them. Thus in the well known bull, "*I was a fine child, but they changed me;*" the first conception expressed in the word "*I,*" is that of personal identity—*Ego contemplans*: the second expressed in the word "*me,*" is the visual image or object by which the mind represents to itself its past condition, or rather, its personal identity under the form in which it imagined itself previously to have existed,—*Ego contemplatus*. Now the change of one visual image for another involves in itself no absurdity, and becomes absurd only by its immediate juxta-

That this conjecture is not wide from the mark, I am induced to believe from the noticeable fact, which I can state on my own knowledge, that the same general censure should have been grounded by almost every different person on some different poem. Among those, whose candour and judgement I estimate highly, I distinctly remember six who expressed their objections to the "Lyrical Ballads" almost in the same words, and altogether to the same purport, at the same time admitting, that several of the poems had given them great pleasure; and, strange as it might seem, the composition which one cited as execrable, another quoted as his favorite. I am indeed convinced in my own mind, that could the same experiment have been tried with these volumes, as was made in the well known story of the picture, the result would have been the same; the parts which had been covered by the number of the black spots on the one day, would be found equally *albo* lapide notatæ on the succeeding.

However this may be, it is assuredly hard and unjust to fix the attention on a few separate and insulated poems with as much aversion, as if they had been so many plague-spots on the whole work, instead of passing them over in silence, as so much blank paper, or leaves of a bookseller's catalogue; especially, as no one pretends to have found any immorality or indelicacy; and the poems, therefore, at the worst, could only be regarded as so many

---

position with the first thought, which is rendered possible by the whole attention being successively absorbed in each singly, so as not to notice the interjacent notion, "changed," which by its incongruity with the first thought, "I," constitutes the bull. Add only, that this process is facilitated by the circumstance of the words "I" and "me," being sometimes equivalent, and sometimes having a distinct meaning; sometimes, namely, signifying the act of self-consciousness, sometimes the external image in and by which the mind represents that act to itself, the result and symbol of its individuality. Now suppose the direct contrary state, and you will have a distinct sense of the connection between two conceptions, without that *sensation* of such connection which is supplied by habit. The man *feels* as if he were standing on his head, though he cannot but *see*, that he is truly standing on his feet. This, as a painful sensation, will of course have a tendency to associate itself with the person who occasions it; even as persons, who have been by painful means restored from derangement, are known to feel an involuntary dislike towards their physician.

light or inferior coins in a roleau of gold, not as so much alloy in
a weight of bullion. A friend whose *talents* I hold in the highest
respect, but whose *judgement* and strong sound sense I have had
almost continued occasion to *revere*, making the usual complaints
to me concerning both the style and subjects of Mr. Wordsworth's
minor poems; I admitted that there were some few of the tales and
incidents, in which I could not myself find a sufficient cause for
their having been recorded in metre. I mentioned the "Alice Fell"
as an instance; "nay," replied my friend with more than usual
quickness of manner, "I cannot agree with you *there!* that, I own,
*does* seem to me a remarkably pleasing poem." In the "Lyrical
Ballads," (for my experience does not enable me to extend the
remark equally unqualified to the two subsequent volumes,) I
have heard at different times, and from different individuals every
single poem *extolled* and *reprobated*, with the exception of those
of loftier kind, which as was before observed, seem to have won
universal praise. This fact of itself would have made me diffident
in my censures, had not a still stronger ground been furnished by
the strange contrast of the heat and long continuance of the opposition, with the nature of the faults stated as justifying it. The
seductive faults, the dulcia vitia of Cowley, Marini, or Darwin
might reasonably be thought capable of corrupting the public
judgement for half a century, and require a twenty years' war,
campaign after campaign, in order to dethrone the usurper and
re-establish the legitimate taste. But that a downright simpleness,
under the affectation of simplicity, prosaic words in feeble metre,
silly thoughts in childish phrases, and a preference of mean, degrading, or at best trivial associations and characters, should succeed in forming a school of imitators, a company of almost *religious*
admirers, and this too among young men of ardent minds, liberal
education, and not

with academic laurels unbestowed;

and that this bare and bald *counterfeit* of poetry, which is characterized as *below* criticism, should for nearly twenty years have
well-nigh *engrossed* criticism, as the main, if not the only, *butt* of
review, magazine, pamphlet, poem, and paragraph;—this is indeed

matter of wonder! Of yet greater is it, that the contest should still continue as* undecided as that between Bacchus and the frogs in Aristophanes; when the former descended to the realms of the departed to bring back the spirit of old and genuine poesy.—

    X.  βρεκεκεκὲξ, κοὰξ, κοάξ.

    Δ.  ἀλλ' ἐξόλοισθ' αὐτῷ κοάξ.
        οὐδὲν γάρ ἐστ' ἄλλ' ἢ κοάξ.
        οἰμώζετ'· οὐ γάρ μοι μέλει.

    X.  ἀλλὰ μὴν κεκραξόμεσθά
        γ', ὁπόσον ἡ φάρυγξ ἂν ἡμῶν
        χανδάνη, δι' ἡμέρας,
        βρεκεκεκὲξ, κοὰξ, κοάξ!

    Δ.  τούτῳ γὰρ οὐ νικήσετε.

    X.  οὐδὲ μὴν ἡμᾶς σὺ πάντως.

---

* Without however the apprehensions attributed to the *Pagan* reformer of the poetic republic. If we may judge from the preface to the recent collection of his poems, Mr. W. would have answered with Xanthias—

    σὺ δ' οὐκ ἔδεισας τὸν ψόφον τῶν ῥημάτων,
    καὶ τὰς ἀπειλάς; ΞΑΝ. οὐ μὰ Δί', οὐδ' ἐφρόντισα.

And here let me dare hint to the authors of the numerous parodies, and pretended imitations of Mr. Wordsworth's style, that at once to conceal and convey wit and wisdom in the semblance of folly and dulness, as is done in the Clowns and Fools, nay even in the Dogberry, of our Shakespeare, is doubtless a proof of genius, or at all events of satiric talent; but that the attempt to ridicule a silly and childish poem, by writing another still sillier and still more childish, can only prove (if it prove any thing at all) that the parodist is a still greater blockhead than the original writer, and, what is far worse a *malignant* coxcomb to boot. The talent for mimicry seems strongest where the human race are most degraded. The poor, naked, half human savages of New Holland were found excellent mimics: and, in civilized society, minds of the very lowest stamp alone satirize by *copying*. At least the difference, which must blend with and balance the likeness, in order to constitute a just imitation, existing here merely in caricature, detracts from the libeller's heart, without adding an iota to the credit of his understanding.

Δ.   οὐδὲ μὴν ὑμεῖς γε δή μ'
οὐδέποτε. κεκράξομαι γὰρ,
κἄν με δέη, δι' ἡμέρας,
ἕως ἂν ὑμῶν ἐπικρατήσω τοῦ κοάξ!

X.   βρεκεκεκὲξ, ΚΟΪΑΞ, ΚΟΑΪΞ!

During the last year of my residence at Cambridge, I became acquainted with Mr. Wordsworth's first publication entitled "Descriptive Sketches"; and seldom, if ever, was the emergence of an original poetic genius above the literary horizon more evidently announced. In the form, style, and manner of the whole poem, and in the structure of the particular lines and periods, there is an harshness and acerbity connected and combined with words and images all a-glow, which might recall those products of the vegetable world, where gorgeous blossoms rise out of the hard and thorny rind and shell, within which the rich fruit was elaborating. The language was not only peculiar and strong, but at times knotty and contorted, as by its own impatient strength; while the novelty and struggling crowd of images, acting in conjunction with the difficulties of the style, demanded always a greater closeness of attention, than poetry, (at all events, than descriptive poetry) has a right to claim. It not seldom therefore justified the complaint of obscurity. In the following extract I have sometimes fancied, that I saw an emblem of the poem itself, and of the author's genius as it was then displayed.

> 'Tis storm; and hid in mist from hour to hour,
> All day the floods a deepening murmur pour;
> The sky is veiled, and every cheerful sight:
> Dark is the region as with coming night;
> And yet what frequent bursts of overpowering light!
> Triumphant on the bosom of the storm,
> Glances the fire-clad eagle's wheeling form;
> Eastward, in long perspective glittering, shine
> The wood-crowned cliffs that o'er the lake recline;
> Wide o'er the Alps a hundred streams unfold,
> At once to pillars turn'd that flame with gold;
> Behind his sail the peasant strives to shun
> The West, that burns like one dilated sun,

> Where in a mighty crucible expire
> The mountains, glowing hot, like coals of fire.

The poetic PSYCHE, in its process to full development, under-
goes as many changes as its Greek name-sake, the butterfly.* And
it is remarkable how soon genius clears and purifies itself from
the faults and errors of its earliest products; faults which, in its
earliest compositions, are the more obtrusive and confluent, because as heterogeneous elements, which had only a temporary use,
they constitute the very *ferment,* by which themselves are carried
off. Or we may compare them to some diseases, which must work
on the humours, and be thrown out on the surface, in order to
secure the patient from their future recurrence. I was in my
twenty-fourth year, when I had the happiness of knowing Mr.
Wordsworth personally, and while memory lasts, I shall hardly
forget the sudden effect produced on my mind, by his recitation
of a manuscript poem, which still remains unpublished, but of
which the stanza, and tone of style, were the same as those of the
"Female Vagrant," as originally printed in the first volume of the
"Lyrical Ballads." There was here no mark of strained thought,
or forced diction, no crowd or turbulence of imagery; and, as the
poet hath himself well described in his lines "on re-visiting the
Wye," manly reflection, and human associations had given both
variety, and an additional interest to natural objects, which in
the passion and appetite of the first love they had seemed to him
neither to need or permit. The occasional obscurities, which had
risen from an imperfect controul over the resources of his native
language, had almost wholly disappeared, together with that worse

---

* The fact, that in Greek Psyche is the common name for the soul, and the
butterfly, is thus alluded to in the following stanzas from an unpublished
poem of the author:

> The butterfly the ancient Grecians made
> The soul's fair emblem, and its only name—
> But of the soul, escaped the slavish trade
> Of mortal life! For in this earthly frame
> Our's is the reptile's lot, much toil, much blame,
> Manifold motions making little speed,
> And to deform and kill the things, whereon we feed.
>                                        S. T. C.

defect of arbitrary and illogical phrases, at once hackneyed, and fantastic, which hold so distinguished a place in the *technique* of ordinary poetry, and will, more or less, alloy the earlier poems of the truest genius, unless the attention has been specifically directed to their worthlessness and incongruity.* I did not perceive anything particular in the mere style of the poem alluded to during its recitation, except indeed such difference as was not separable from the thought and manner; and the Spenserian stanza, which always, more or less, recalls to the reader's mind Spenser's own style, would doubtless have authorized, in my then opinion, a more frequent descent to the phrases of ordinary life, than could without an ill effect have been hazarded in the heroic couplet. It was not however the freedom from false taste, whether as to common defects, or to those more properly his own, which made so unusual an impression on my feelings immediately, and subsequently on my judgement. It was the union of deep feeling with profound thought; the fine balance of truth in observing, with the imaginative faculty in modifying the objects observed; and above all the original gift of spreading the tone, the *atmosphere*, and with it the depth and height of the ideal world around forms, incidents, and situations, of which, for the common view, custom had bedimmed all the lustre, had dried up the sparkle and the dew

---

* Mr. Wordsworth, even in his two earliest, "the Evening Walk and the Descriptive Sketches," is more free from this latter defect than most of the young poets his contemporaries. It may however be exemplified, together with the harsh and obscure construction, in which he more often offended, in the following lines:—

> 'Mid stormy vapours ever driving by,
> Where ospreys, cormorants, and herons cry;
> Where hardly given the hopeless waste to cheer,
> Denied the bread of life, the foodful ear,
> Dwindles the pear on autumn's latest spray,
> And *apple sickens* pale in summer's ray;
> *Ev'n here content has fixed her smiling reign*
> *With independence, child of high disdain.*

I hope, I need not say, that I have quoted these lines for no other purpose than to make my meaning fully understood. It is to be regretted that Mr. Wordsworth has not republished these two poems entire.

drops. "To find no contradiction in the union of old and new; to contemplate the ANCIENT of days and all his works with feelings as fresh, as if all had then sprang forth at the first creative fiat; characterizes the mind that feels the riddle of the world, and may help to unravel it. To carry on the feelings of childhood into the powers of manhood; to combine the child's sense of wonder and novelty with the appearances, which every day for perhaps forty years had rendered familiar;

> With sun and moon and stars throughout the year,
> And man and woman;

this is the character and privilege of genius, and one of the marks which distinguish genius from talents. And therefore is it the prime merit of genius and its most unequivocal mode of manifestation, so to represent familiar objects as to awaken in the minds of others a kindred feeling concerning them and that freshness of sensation which is the constant accompaniment of mental, no less than of bodily, convalescence. Who has not a thousand times seen snow fall on water? Who has not watched it with a new feeling, from the time that he has read Burns' comparison of sensual pleasure

> To snow that falls upon a river
> A moment white—then gone for ever!

In poems, equally as in philosophic disquisitions, genius produces the strongest impressions of novelty, while it rescues the most admitted truths from the impotence caused by the very circumstance of their universal admission. Truths of all others the most awful and mysterious, yet being at the same time of universal interest, are too often considered as *so* true, that they lose all the life and efficiency of truth, and lie bed-ridden in the dormitory of the soul, side by side with the most despised and exploded errors." —THE FRIEND,* p. 76, No. 5.

This excellence, which in all Mr. Wordsworth's writings is

---

* As "the Friend" was printed on stampt sheets, and sent only by the post to a very limited number of subscribers, the author has felt less objection to quote from it, though a work of his own. To the public at large indeed it is the same as a volume in manuscript.

more or less predominant, and which constitutes the character of his mind, I no sooner felt, than I sought to understand. Repeated meditations led me first to suspect, (and a more intimate analysis of the human faculties, their appropriate marks, functions, and effects matured my conjecture into full conviction,) that fancy and imagination were two distinct and widely different faculties, instead of being, according to the general belief, either two names with one meaning, or, at furthest, the lower and higher degree of one and the same power. It is not, I own, easy to conceive a more opposite translation of the Greek *Phantasia* than the Latin Imaginatio; but it is equally true that in all societies there exists an instinct of growth, a certain collective, unconscious good sense working progressively to desynonymize* those words originally of the same meaning, which the conflux of dialects had supplied to the more homogeneous languages, as the Greek and German: and which the same cause, joined with accidents of translation from original works of different countries, occasion in mixt lan-

---

* This is effected either by giving to the one word a general, and to the other an exclusive use; as "to put on the back" and "to indorse;" or by an actual distinction of meanings, as "naturalist," and "physician;" or by difference of relation, as "I" and "Me" (each of which the rustics of our different provinces still use in all the cases singular of the first personal pronoun). Even the mere difference, or corruption, in the *pronunciation* of the same word, if it have become general, will produce a new word with a distinct signification; thus "property" and "propriety;" the latter of which, even to the time of Charles II. was the *written* word for all the senses of both. Thus too "mister" and "master," both hasty pronunciations of the same word "magister," "mistress," and "miss," "if" and "give," &c. &c. There is a sort of *minim immortal* among the animalcula infusoria which has not naturally either birth, or death, absolute beginning, or absolute end: for at a certain period a small point appears on its back, which deepens and lengthens till the creature divides into two, and the same process recommences in each of the halves now become integral. This may be a fanciful, but it is by no means a bad emblem of the formation of words, and may facilitate the conception, how immense a nomenclature may be organized from a few simple sounds by rational beings in a social state. For each new application, or excitement of the same sound, will call forth a different sensation, which cannot but affect the pronunciation. The after recollection of the sound, without the same vivid sensation, will modify it still further; till at length all trace of the original likeness is worn away.

guages like our own. The first and most important point to be
proved is, that two conceptions perfectly distinct are confused
under one and the same word, and (this done) to appropriate that
word exclusively to one meaning, and the synonyme (should
there be one) to the other. But if (as will be often the case in
the arts and sciences) no synonyme exists, we must either invent
or borrow a word. In the present instance the appropriation has
already begun, and been legitimated in the derivative adjective:
Milton had a highly *imaginative,* Cowley a very *fanciful* mind.
If therefore I should succeed in establishing the actual existences
of two faculties generally different, the nomenclature would be
at once determined. To the faculty by which I had characterized
Milton, we should confine the term *imagination;* while the other
would be contra-distinguished as *fancy.* Now were it once fully
ascertained, that this division is no less grounded in nature, than
that of delirium from mania, or Otway's

> Lutes, lobsters, seas of milk, and ships of amber,

from Shakespear's

> What! have his daughters brought him to this pass?

or from the preceding apostrophe to the elements; the theory of
the fine arts, and of poetry in particular, could not, I thought, but
derive some additional and important light. It would in its immediate effects furnish a torch of guidance to the philosophical
critic; and ultimately to the poet himself. In energetic minds, truth
soon changes by domestication into power; and from directing in
the discrimination and appraisal of the product, becomes influ-
encive in the production. To admire on principle, is the only way
to imitate without loss of originality.

It has been already hinted, that metaphysics and psychology
have long been my hobby-horse. But to have a hobby-horse, and
to be vain of it, are so commonly found together, that they pass
almost for the same. I trust therefore, that there will be more good
humour than contempt, in the smile with which the reader chas-
tises my self-complacency, if I confess myself uncertain, whether
the satisfaction from the perception of a truth new to myself may

not have been rendered more poignant by the conceit, that it would be equally so to the public. There was a time, certainly, in which I took some little credit to myself, in the belief that I had been the first of my countrymen, who had pointed out the diverse meaning of which the two terms were capable, and analyzed the faculties to which they should be appropriated. Mr. W. Taylor's recent volume of synonymes I have not yet seen;* but his specifi-

* I ought to have added, with the exception of a single sheet which I accidentally met with at the printer's. Even from this scanty specimen, I found it impossible to doubt the talent, or not to admire the ingenuity of the author. That his distinctions were for the greater part unsatisfactory to *my* mind, proves nothing against their accuracy; but it may possibly be serviceable to him, in case of a second edition, if I take this opportunity of suggesting the query; whether he may not have been occasionally misled, by having assumed, as to me he appeared to have done, the non-existence of *any* absolute synonymes in our language? Now I cannot but think, that there are many which remain for our posterity to distinguish and appropriate, and which I regard as so much reversionary wealth in our mother-tongue. When two distinct meanings are confounded under one or more words, (and such must be the case, as sure as our knowledge is progressive and of course imperfect) erroneous consequences will be drawn, and what is true in one sense of the word will be affirmed as true in toto. Men of research, startled by the consequences, seek in the things themselves (whether in or out of the mind) for a knowledge of the fact, and having discovered the difference, remove the equivocation either by the substitution of a new word, or by the appropriation of one of the two or more words, that had before been used promiscuously. When this distinction has been so naturalized and of such general currency that the language itself does as it were *think* for us (like the sliding rule which is the mechanic's safe substitute for arithmetical knowledge) we then say, that it is evident to *common sense*. Common sense, therefore, differs in different ages. What was born and christened in the schools passes by degrees into the world at large, and becomes the property of the market and the tea-table. At least I can discover no other meaning of the term, *common sense,* if it is to convey any specific difference from sense and judgement in genere, and where it is not used scholastically for the *universal reason.* Thus in the reign of Charles II. the philosophic world was called to arms by the moral sophisms of Hobbs, and the ablest writers exerted themselves in the detection of an error, which a school-boy would now be able to confute by the mere recollection, that *compulsion* and *obligation* conveyed two ideas perfectly disparate, and that what appertained to the one, had been falsely transferred to the other by a mere confusion of terms.

cation of the terms in question has been clearly shown to be both insufficient and erroneous by Mr. Wordsworth in the Preface added to the late collection of his "Lyrical Ballads and other poems." The explanation which Mr. Wordsworth has himself given will be found to differ from mine, chiefly perhaps, as our objects are different. It could scarcely indeed happen otherwise, from the advantage I have enjoyed of frequent conversation with him on a subject to which a poem of his own first directed my attention, and my conclusions concerning which, he had made more lucid to myself by many happy instances drawn from the operation of natural objects on the mind. But it was Mr. Wordsworth's purpose to consider the influences of fancy and imagination as they are manifested in poetry, and from the different effects to conclude their diversity in kind; while it is my object to investigate the seminal principle, and then from the kind to deduce the degree. My friend has drawn a masterly sketch of the branches with their *poetic* fruitage. I wish to add the trunk, and even the roots as far as they lift themselves above ground, and are visible to the naked eye of our common consciousness.

Yet even in this attempt I am aware, that I shall be obliged to draw more largely on the reader's attention, than so immethodical a miscellany can authorize; when in such a work (the *Ecclesiastical Polity*) of such a mind as Hooker's, the judicious author, though no less admirable for the perspicuity than for the port and dignity of his language; and though he wrote for men of learning in a learned age; saw nevertheless occasion to anticipate and guard against "complaints of obscurity," as often as he was about to trace his subject "to the highest well-spring and fountain." Which, (continues he) "because men are not accustomed to, the pains we take are more needful a great deal, than acceptable; and the matters we handle, seem by reason of newness (till the mind grow better acquainted with them) dark and intricate." I would gladly therefore spare both myself and others this labour, if I knew how without it to present an intelligible statement of my poetic creed; not as my *opinions*, which weigh for nothing, but as deductions from established premises conveyed in such a form, as is calculated either to effect a fundamental conviction, or to receive a fundamental confutation. If I may dare on the words of Hooker, "they, unto whom we shall s are in no wise injured by us, because it is in their ow spare that labor, which they are not willing to endure. least, let me be permitted to add, who have taken so much pains to render me ridiculous for a perversion of taste, and have supported the charge by attributing strange notions to me on no other authority than their own conjectures, owe it to themselves as well as to me not to refuse their attention to my own statement of the theory, which I *do* acknowledge; or shrink from the trouble of examining the grounds on which I rest it, or the arguments which I offer in its justification.


## CHAPTER X

*A chapter of digression and anecdotes, as an interlude preceding that on the nature and genesis of the imagination or plastic power—On pedantry and pedantic expressions—Advice to young authors respecting publication—Various anecdotes of the author's literary life, and the progress of his opinions in religion and politics.*


"*Esemplastic. The word is not in Johnson, nor have I met with it elsewhere.*" Neither have I. I constructed it myself from the Greek words, εἰς ἓν πλάττειν, to shape into one; because, having to convey a new sense, I thought that a new term would both aid the recollection of my meaning, and prevent its being confounded with the usual import of the word, imagination. "*But this is pedantry!*" Not necessarily so, I hope. If I am not misinformed, pedantry consists in the use of words unsuitable to the time, place, and company. The language of the market would be in the schools as *pedantic*, though it might not be reprobated by that name, as the language of the schools in the market. The mere man of the world, who insists that no other terms but such as occur in common conversation should be employed in a scientific disquisition, and with no greater precision, is as truly a *pedant* as the man of letters, who either over-rating the acquirements of his auditors, or misled by his own familiarity with technical or scholastic terms, converses at the wine-table with his mind fixed on his musæum or laboratory; even though the latter pedant instead of desiring his wife to *make the tea* should bid her add to the quant. suff. of thea Sinensis the oxyd of hydrogen saturated with caloric. To use the colloquial (and in truth somewhat *vulgar*) metaphor, if the pedant of the cloyster, and the pedant of the lobby, both *smell equally of the shop,* yet the odour from the Russian binding of good old *authentic-looking* folios and quartos is less annoying than the steams from the tavern or bagnio. Nay, though the pedantry of the scholar should betray a little ostentation, yet a well-conditioned mind would more easily, methinks, tolerate the *fox brush* of learned vanity, than the *sans culotterie* of a contemptuous ignorance, that assumes a merit from mutilation in the self-consoling sneer at the pompous incumbrance of tails.

The first lesson of philosophic discipline is to wean the student's attention from the DEGREES of things, which alone form the vocabulary of common life, and to direct it to the KIND abstracted from *degree.* Thus the chemical student is taught not to be startled at disquisitions on the heat in ice, or on latent and fixible light. In such discourse the instructor has no other alternative than either to use old words with new meanings (the plan adopted by Darwin in his Zoonomia;) or to introduce new terms, after the example of Linnæus, and the framers of the present chemical nomenclature. The latter mode is evidently preferable, were it only that the former demands a twofold exertion of thought in one and the same act. For the reader, or hearer, is required not only to learn and bear in mind the new definition; but to unlearn, and keep out of his view, the old and habitual meaning; a far more difficult and perplexing task, and for which the mere *semblance* of eschewing pedantry seems to me an inadequate compensation. Where, indeed, it is in our power to recall an unappropriate term that had without sufficient reason become obsolete, it is doubtless a less evil to restore than to coin anew. Thus to express in one word, all that appertains to the perception, considered as passive, and merely recipient, I have adopted from our elder classics the word *sensuous;* because *sensual* is not at present used, except in a bad sense, or at least as a *moral* distinction; while *sensitive* and *sensible* would each convey a different meaning. Thus too I have followed Hooker, Sanderson, Milton, &c., in designating the *immediateness* of any act or object of knowledge by the word *intuition,* used sometimes subjectively, sometimes objectively, even as we use the word, thought, now as *the* thought, or act of thinking, and now as *a* thought, or the object of our reflection; and we do this without confusion or obscurity. The very words, *objective* and *subjective,* of such constant recurrence in the schools of yore, I have ventured to re-introduce, because I could not so briefly or conveniently by any more familiar terms distinguish the percipere from the percipi. Lastly, I have cautiously discriminated the terms, THE REASON, and THE UNDERSTANDING, encouraged and confirmed by the authority of our genuine divines and philosophers, before the revolution.

> ————both life, and sense,
> Fancy, and *understanding;* whence the soul
> *Reason* receives, and REASON is her *being,*
> DISCURSIVE or INTUITIVE: discourse\*

I say, that I was *confirmed* by authority so venerable: for I had previous and higher motives in my own conviction of the importance, nay, of the necessity of the distinction, as both an indispensable condition and a vital part of all sound speculation in metaphysics, ethical or theological. To establish this distinction was one main object of THE FRIEND; if even in a biography of my own literary life I can with propriety refer to a work, which was printed rather than published, or so published that it had been well for the unfortunate author, if it had remained in manuscript! I have even at this time bitter cause for remembering that, which a number of my subscribers have but a trifling motive for forget-

---

\* But for sundry notes on Shakespeare, &c., and other pieces which have fallen in my way, I should have deemed it unnecessary to observe, that *discourse* here, or elsewhere, does not mean what we *now* call discoursing; but the *discursion* of the *mind,* the processes of generalization and subsumption, of deduction and conclusion. Thus, Philosophy has *hitherto* been DISCURSIVE; while Geometry is *always* and *essentially* INTUITIVE.

> If oftest your's, the latter most is our's,
> Differing but in *degree,* in *kind* the same.
>                    PARADISE LOST, *Book* V.

ting. This effusion might have been spared; but I would feign flatter myself, that the reader will be less austere than an oriental professor of the bastinado, who during an attempt to extort per argumentum baculinum a full confession from a culprit, interrupted his outcry of pain by reminding him, that it was "*a mere digression!*" All this noise, Sir! is nothing to the point, and no sort of answer to my QUESTIONS! *Ah! but*, (replied the sufferer,) *it is the most pertinent reply in nature to your blows*.

An imprudent man of common goodness of heart cannot but wish to turn even his imprudences to the benefit of others, as far as this is possible. If therefore any one of the readers of this semi-narrative should be preparing or intending a periodical work, I warn him, in the first place, against trusting in the number of names on his subscription list. For he cannot be certain that the names were put down by sufficient authority; or, should that ʰe ascertained, it still remains to be known, whether they were not extorted by some over zealous friend's importunity; whether the subscriber had not yielded his name, merely from want of courage to answer, no! and with the intention of dropping the work as soon as possible. One gentleman procured me nearly a hundred names for THE FRIEND, and not only took frequent opportunity to remind me of his success in his canvas, but laboured to impress my mind with the sense of the obligation, I was under to the subscribers; for (as he very pertinently admonished me,) "*fifty-two shillings* a year was a large sum to be bestowed on one individual, where there were so many objects of charity with strong claims to the assistance of the benevolent." Of these hundred patrons ninety threw up the publication before the fourth number, without any notice; though it was well known to them, that in consequence of the distance, and the slowness and irregularity of the conveyance, I was compelled to lay in a stock of *stamped* paper for at least eight weeks beforehand; each sheet of which stood me in five pence previous to its arrival at my printer's; though the subscription money was not to be received till the twenty-first week after the commencement of the work; and lastly, though it was in nine cases out of ten impracticable for me to receive the money for two or three numbers without paying an equal sum for the postage.

In confirmation of my first caveat, I will select one fact among *many*. On my list of subscribers, among a considerable number of names equally flattering, was that of an Earl of Cork, with his address. He might as well have been an Earl of Bottle, for aught I knew of him, who had been content to reverence the peerage in abstracto, rather than in concretis. Of course THE FRIEND was regularly sent as far, if I remember right, as the eighteenth number: i. e. till a fortnight before the subscription was to be paid. And lo! just at this time I received a letter from his Lordship, reproving me in language far more lordly than courteous for my impudence in directing my pamphlets to him, who knew nothing of me or my work! Seventeen or eighteen numbers of which, however, his Lordship was pleased to retain, probably for the culinary or post-culinary conveniences of his servants.

Secondly, I warn all others from the attempt to deviate from the ordinary mode of publishing a work by *the trade*. I thought indeed, that to the purchaser it was indifferent, whether thirty per cent. of the purchase-money went to the booksellers or to the government; and that the convenience of receiving the work by the post at his own door would give the preference to the latter. It is hard, I own, to have been labouring for years, in collecting and arranging the materials; to have spent every shilling that could be spared after the necessaries of life had been furnished, in buying books, or in journies for the purpose of consulting them or of acquiring facts at the fountain head; then to buy the paper, pay for the printing, &c., all at least fifteen per cent. beyond what *the trade* would have paid; and then after all to give thirty per cent. not of the net profits, but of the gross results of the sale, to a man who has merely to give the books shelf or warehouse room, and permit his apprentice to hand them over the counter to those who may ask for them; and this too copy by copy, although if the work be on any philosophical or scientific subject, it may be years before the edition is sold off. All this, I confess, must seem an hardship, and one, to which the products of industry in no other mode of exertion are subject. Yet even this is better, far better, than to attempt in any way to unite the functions of author and publisher. But the most prudent mode is to sell the copy-right, at least of one or more editions, for the most that *the trade* will offer. By few only can a large remuneration be expected; but fifty pounds and ease of mind are of more real advantage to a literary man, than the *chance* of five hundred with the *certainty* of insult and degrading anxieties. I shall have been grievously misunderstood, if this statement should be interpreted as written with the desire of detracting from the character of booksellers or publishers. The individuals did not make the laws and customs of their trade, but, as in every other trade, take them as they find them. Till the evil can be proved to be removable, and without the substitution of an equal or greater inconvenience, it were neither wise or manly even to complain of it. But to use it as a pretext for speaking, or even for thinking, or feeling, unkindly or opprobriously of the tradesmen, as *individuals,* would be something worse than unwise or even than unmanly; it would be immoral and calumnious. My motives point in a far different direction and to far other objects, as will be seen in the conclusion of the chapter.

A learned and exemplary old clergyman, who many years ago went to his reward followed by the regrets and blessings of his flock, published at his own expense two volumes octavo, entitled, a new Theory of Redemption. The work was most severely handled in the Monthly or Critical Review, I forget which; and this unprovoked hostility became the good old man's favorite topic of conversation among his friends. Well! (he used to exclaim,) in the SECOND edition, I shall have an opportunity of exposing both the ignorance and the malignity of the anonymous critic. Two or three years however passed by without any tidings from the bookseller, who had undertaken the printing and publication of the work, and who was perfectly at his ease, as the author was known to be a man of large property. At length the *accounts* were written for; and in the course of a few weeks they were presented by the *rider* for the house, in person. My old friend put on his spectacles, and holding the scroll with no very firm hand, began—*Paper, so much:* O moderate enough—not at all beyond my expectation! *Printing, so much:* well! moderate enough! *Stitching, covers, advertisements, carriage, &c., so much.*—Still nothing amiss. *Selleridge* (for orthography is no necessary part of a bookseller's literary acquirements)

£3. 3s. Bless me! only three guineas for the what d'ye call it—the *selleridge?* No more, Sir! replied the rider. Nay, but that is *too* moderate! rejoined my old friend. Only three guineas for *selling* a thousand copies of a work in two volumes? O Sir! (cries the young traveller) you have mistaken the word. There have been none of them *sold;* they have been sent back from London long ago; and this £3. 3s. is for the cellaridge, or warehouse-room in our book *cellar.* The work was in consequence preferred from the ominous cellar of the publisher's to the author's garret; and, on presenting a copy to an acquaintance, the old gentleman used to tell the anecdote with great humour and still greater good nature.

With equal lack of worldly knowledge, I was a far more than equal sufferer for it, at the very outset of my authorship. Toward the close of the first year from the time, that in an inauspicious hour I left the friendly cloysters, and the happy grove of quiet, ever honored Jesus College, Cambridge, I was persuaded by sundry Philanthropists and Anti-polemists to set on foot a periodical work, entitled THE WATCHMAN, that, (according to the general motto of the work,) *all might know the truth, and that the truth might make us free!* In order to exempt it from the stamp-tax, and likewise to contribute as little as possible to the supposed guilt of a war against freedom, it was to be published on every eighth day, thirty-two pages, large octavo, closely printed, and price only FOUR-PENCE. Accordingly with a flaming prospectus, *"Knowledge is Power"* &c., *to cry the state of the political atmosphere,* and so forth, I set off on a tour to the North, from Bristol to Sheffield, for the purpose of procuring customers, preaching by the way in most of the great towns, as an hireless volunteer, in a blue coat and white waistcoat, that not a rag of the woman of Babylon might be seen on me. For I was at that time and long after, though a Trini-tarian (i.e. ad normam Platonis) in philosophy, yet a zealous Unitarian in Religion; more accurately, I was a *psilanthropist,* one of those who believe our Lord to have been the real son of Joseph, and who lay the main stress on the resurrection rather than on the crucifixion. O! never can I remember those days with either shame or regret. For I was most sincere, most disinterested! My opinions were indeed in many and most important points erroneous; but my heart was single. Wealth, rank, life itself then seemed cheap to me, compared with the interests of (what I believed to be) the truth, and the will of my maker. I cannot even accuse myself of having been actuated by vanity; for in the expansion of my enthusiasm I did not think of *myself* at all.

My campaign commenced at Birmingham; and my first attack was on a rigid Calvinist, a tallow-chandler by trade. He was a tall dingy man, in whom length was so predominant over breadth, that he might almost have been borrowed for a foundery poker. O that face! a face κατ' ἔμφασιν! I have it before me at this moment. The lank, black, twine-like hair, *pingui-nitescent,* cut in a straight line along the black stubble of his thin gunpowder eye-brows, that looked like a scorched *after-math* from a last week's shaving. His coat collar behind in perfect unison, both of colour and lustre, with the coarse yet glib cordage, that I suppose he called his hair, and which with a *bend* inward at the nape of the neck, (the only approach to flexure in his whole figure,) slunk in behind his waistcoat; while the countenance lank, dark, very *hard,* and with strong perpendicular furrows, gave me a dim notion of some one looking at me through a *used* gridiron, all soot, grease, and iron! But he was one of the *thorough-bred,* a true lover of liberty, and, (I was informed,) had proved to the satisfaction of many, that Mr. Pitt was one of the horns of the second beast in the Revelations, that *spoke like a dragon.* A person, to whom one of my letters of recommendation had been addressed, was my introducer. It was a new event in my life, my first *stroke* in the new business I had undertaken of an author, yea, and of an author trading on his own account. My companion after some imperfect sentences and a multitude of hums and haas abandoned the cause to his client; and I commenced an harangue of half an hour to Phileleutheros, the tallow-chandler, varying my notes, through the whole gamut of eloquence, from the ratiocinative to the declamatory, and in the latter from the pathetic to the indignant. I argued, I described, I promised, I prophesied; and beginning with the captivity of nations I ended with the near approach of the millennium, finishing the whole with some of my own verses describing that glorious state out of *the Religious Musings:*

———————— Such delights
As float to earth, permitted visitants!
When in some hour of solemn jubilee
The massive gates of Paradise are thrown
Wide open: and forth come in fragments wild
Sweet echoes of unearthly melodies,
And odors snatch'd from beds of Amaranth,
And they, that from the chrystal river of life
Spring up on freshen'd wing, ambrosial gales!
                                 *Religious Musings,* l. 356.

My taper man of lights listened with perseverant and praise-
worthy patience, though, (as I was afterwards told, on complaining of certain gales that were not altogether ambrosial,) it was a
*melting* day with him. And what, Sir, (he said, after a short
pause,) might the cost be? *Only* FOUR-PENCE, (O! how I felt the
anti-climax, the abysmal bathos of that *four-pence!*) *only four-
pence, Sir, each number, to be published on every eighth day.*
That comes to a deal of money at the end of a year. And how
much, did you say, there was to be for the money? *Thirty-two
pages, Sir! large octavo, closely printed.* Thirty and two pages?
Bless me! why except what I does in a family way on the Sabbath,
that's more than I ever reads, Sir! all the year round. I am as great
a one, as any man in Brummagem, Sir! for liberty and truth and
all them sort of things, but as to this, (no offence, I hope, Sir!) I
must beg to be excused.

So ended my first canvass: from causes that I shall presently
mention, I made but one other application in person. This took
place at Manchester to a stately and opulent wholesale dealer in
cottons. He took my letter of introduction, and, having perused it,
measured me from head to foot and again from foot to head, and
then asked if I had any bill or invoice of the thing; I presented my
prospectus to him; he rapidly skimmed and hummed over the first
side, and still more rapidly the second and concluding page;
crushed it within his fingers and the palm of his hand; then most
deliberately and *significantly* rubbed and smoothed one part
against the other; and lastly putting it into his pocket turned his
back on me with an *"over-run* with these articles!" and so without

another syllable retired into his counting-house. And, I can truly say, to my unspeakable amusement.

This, I have said, was my second and last attempt. On returning baffled from the first, in which I had vainly essayed to repeat the miracle of Orpheus with the Brummagen patriot, I dined with the tradesman who had introduced me to him. After dinner he importuned me to smoke a pipe with him, and two or three other illuminati of the same rank. I objected, both because I was engaged to spend the evening with a minister and his friends, and because I had never smoked except once or twice in my lifetime, and then it was herb tobacco mixed with Oronooko. On the assurance, however, that the tobacco was equally mild, and seeing too that it was of a yellow colour; (not forgetting the lamentable difficulty, I have always experienced, in saying, "No," and in abstaining from what the people about me were doing,) I took half a pipe, filling the lower half of the bole with salt. I was soon however compelled to resign it, in consequence of a giddiness and distressful feeling in my eyes, which, as I had drunk but a single glass of ale, must, I knew, have been the effect of the tobacco. Soon after, deeming myself recovered, I sallied forth to my engagement; but the walk and the fresh air brought on all the symptoms again, and, I had scarcely entered the minister's drawing-room, and opened a small pacquet of letters, which he had received from Bristol for me; ere I sunk back on the sofa in a sort of swoon rather than sleep. Fortunately I had found just time enough to inform him of the confused state of my feelings, and of the occasion. For here and thus I lay, my face like a wall that is whitewashing, *deathy* pale and with the cold drops of perspiration running down it from my forehead, while one after another there dropt in the different gentlemen, who had been invited to meet, and spend the evening with me, to the number of from fifteen to twenty. As the poison of tobacco acts but for a short time, I at length awoke from insensibility, and looked round on the party, my eyes dazzled by the candles which had been lighted in the interim. By way of relieving my embarrassment one of the gentlemen began the conversation, with *"Have you seen a paper to-day, Mr. Coleridge?"* "Sir!" (I replied, rubbing my eyes,) "I am far from convinced, that a christian is permitted to read either news-papers or any other works of merely political and temporary interest." This remark so ludicrously inapposite to, or rather, incongruous with, the purpose, for which I was known to have visited Birmingham, and to assist me in which they were all then met, produced an involuntary and general burst of laughter; and seldom indeed have I passed so many delightful hours, as I enjoyed in that room from the moment of that laugh to an early hour the next morning. Never, perhaps, in so mixed and numerous a party have I since heard conversation sustained with such animation, enriched with such variety of information, and enlivened with such a flow of anecdote. Both then and afterwards they all joined in dissuading me from proceeding with my scheme; assured me in the most friendly and yet most flattering expressions, that the employment was neither fit for me, nor I fit for the employment. Yet, if I had determined on persevering in it, they promised to exert themselves to the utmost to procure subscribers, and insisted that I should make no more applications in person, but carry on the canvas by proxy. The same hospitable reception, the same dissuasion, and, (that failing), the same kind exertions in my behalf, I met with at Manchester, Derby, Nottingham, Sheffield, indeed, at every place in which I took up my sojourn. I often recall with affectionate pleasure the many respectable men who interested themselves for me, a perfect stranger to them, not a few of whom I can still name among my friends. They will bear witness for me how opposite even then my principles were to those of Jacobinism or even of democracy, and can attest the strict accuracy of the statement which I have left on record in the 10th and 11th numbers of THE FRIEND.

From this rememberable tour I returned with nearly a thousand names on the subscription list of the Watchman; yet more than half convinced, that prudence dictated the abandonment of the scheme. But for this very reason I persevered in it; for I was at that period of my life so compleatly hag-ridden by the fear of being influenced by selfish motives, that to know a mode of conduct to be the dictate of *prudence* was a sort of presumptive proof to my feelings, that the contrary was the dictate of *duty*. Accordingly, I commenced the work, which was announced in London by long bills in letters larger than had ever been seen before, and which, (I have been informed, for I did not see them myself,) eclipsed the glories even of the lottery puffs. But, alas! the publication of the very first number was delayed beyond the day announced for its appearance. In the second number an essay against fast days with a most censurable application of a text from Isaiah for its motto, lost me near five hundred of my subscribers at one blow. In the two following numbers I made enemies of all my Jacobin and Democratic Patrons; for, disgusted by their infidelity, and their adoption of French morals with French *psilosophy;* and perhaps thinking, that charity ought to begin nearest home; instead of abusing the government and the Aristocrats chiefly or entirely, as had been expected of me, I levelled my attacks at *"modern patriotism,"* and even ventured to declare my belief, that whatever the motives of ministers might have been for the sedition, (or as it was then the fashion to call them, the *gagging*) bills, yet the bills themselves would produce an effect to be desired by all the true friends of freedom, as far as they should contribute to deter men from openly declaiming on subjects, the principles of which they had never bottomed, and from "pleading to the poor and ignorant, instead of pleading for them." At the same time I avowed my conviction, that national education and a concurring spread of the gospel were the indispensable condition of any true political amelioration. Thus by the time the seventh number was published, I had the mortification (but why should I say this, when in truth I cared too little for any thing that concerned my worldly interests to be at all mortified about it?) of seeing the preceding numbers exposed in sundry old iron shops for a penny a piece. At the ninth number I dropt the work. But from the London publisher I could not obtain a shilling; he was a ——— and set me at defiance. From other places I procured but little, and after such delays as rendered that little worth nothing: and I should have been inevitably thrown into jail by my Bristol printer, who refused to wait even for a month, for a sum between eighty and ninety pounds, if the money had not been paid for me by a man by no means affluent, a dear friend, who attached himself to me from my first arrival at

Bristol, who has continued my friend with a fidelity unconquered by time or even by my own apparent neglect; a friend from whom I never received an advice that was not wise, nor a remonstrance that was not gentle and affectionate.

Conscientiously an opponent of the first revolutionary war, yet with my eyes thoroughly opened to the true character and impotence of the favorers of revolutionary principles in England, principles which I held in abhorrence, (for it was part of my political creed, that whoever ceased to act as an *individual* by making himself a member of any *society* not sanctioned by his Government, forfeited the rights of a citizen)—a vehement anti-ministerialist, but after the invasion of Switzerland, a more vehement anti-gallican, and still more intensely an anti-jacobin, I retired to a cottage at Stowey, and provided for my scanty maintenance by writing verses for a London Morning Paper. I saw plainly, that literature was not a profession, by which I could expect to live; for I could not disguise from myself, that, whatever my talents might or might not be in other respects, yet they were not of the sort that could enable me to become a popular writer; and that whatever my opinions might be in themselves, they were almost equi-distant from all the three prominent parties, the Pittites, the Foxites, and the Democrats. Of the unsaleable nature of my writings I had an amusing memento one morning from our own servant girl. For happening to rise at an earlier hour than usual, I observed her putting an extravagant quantity of paper into the grate in order to light the fire, and mildly checked her for her wastefulness; "la, Sir!" (replied poor Nanny) "why, it is only WATCHMEN."

I now devoted myself to poetry and to the study of ethics and psychology; and so profound was my admiration at this time of Hartley's Essay on Man, that I gave his name to my first-born. In addition to the gentleman, my neighbour, whose garden joined on to my little orchard, and the cultivation of whose friendship had been my sole motive in choosing Stowey for my residence, I was so fortunate as to acquire, shortly after my settlement there, an invaluable blessing in the society and neighbourhood of one, to whom I could look up with equal reverence, whether I regarded him as a poet, a philosopher, or a man. His conversation extended to almost all subjects, except physics and politics; with the latter he never troubled himself. Yet neither my retirement nor my utter abstraction from all the disputes of the day could secure me in those jealous times from suspicion and obloquy, which did not stop at me, but extended to my excellent friend, whose perfect innocence was even adduced as a proof of his guilt. One of the many busy _sycophants_* of that day, (I here use the word sycophant in its original sense, as a wretch who _flatters_ the prevailing party by _informing_ against his neighbours, under pretence that they are exporters of prohibited _figs_ or fancies! for the moral application of the term it matters not which)—one of these sycophantic law-mongrels, discoursing on the _politics_ of the neighbourhood, uttered the following _deep_ remark: "As to _Coleridge_, there is not so much harm in _him_, for he is a whirl-brain that talks whatever comes uppermost; but that ———! he is the _dark_ traitor. _You never hear_ HIM _say a syllable on the subject._"

Now that the hand of providence has disciplined _all_ Europe into sobriety, as men tame wild elephants, by alternate blows and caresses; now that Englishmen of all classes are restored to their old English notions and feelings; it will with difficulty be credited, how great an influence was at that time possessed and exerted by the spirit of secret defamation, (the too constant attendant on party-zeal!) during the restless interim from 1793 to the commencement of the Addington administration, or the year before the truce of Amiens. For by the latter period the minds of the partizans, exhausted by excess of stimulation and humbled by mutual disappointment, had become languid. The same causes, that inclined the nation to peace, disposed the individuals to reconciliation. Both parties had found themselves in the wrong. The one had confessedly mistaken the moral character of the revolution, and the other had miscalculated both its moral and its physical resources. The experiment was made at the price of great, almost, we may say, of humiliating sacrifices; and wise men foresaw that it would fail, at least in its direct and ostensible object. Yet it was purchased cheaply, and realized an object of equal value, and, if

---

* Σύκους φαίνειν, to show or detect figs, the exportation of which from Attica was forbidden by the laws.

possible, of still more vital importance. For it brought about a national unanimity unexampled in our history since the reign of Elizabeth; and providence, never wanting to a good work when men have done their parts, soon provided a common focus in the cause of Spain, which made us all once more Englishmen by at once gratifying and correcting the predilections of both parties. The sincere reverers of the throne felt the cause of loyalty ennobled by its alliance with that of freedom; while the *honest* zealots of the people could not but admit, that freedom itself assumed a more winning form, humanized by loyalty and consecrated by religious principle. The youthful enthusiasts who, flattered by the morning rainbow of the French revolution, had made a boast of *expatriating* their hopes and fears, now, disciplined by the succeeding storms and sobered by increase of years, had been taught to prize and honour the spirit of nationality as the best safeguard of national independence, and this again as the absolute pre-requisite and necessary basis of popular rights.

If in Spain too disappointment has nipt our too forward expectations, yet all is not destroyed that is checked. The crop was perhaps springing up too rank in the stalk to *kern* well; and there were, doubtless, symptoms of the Gallican *blight* on it. If superstition and despotism have been suffered to let in their wolvish sheep to trample and eat it down even to the surface, yet the roots remain alive, and the second growth may prove all the stronger and healthier for the temporary interruption. At all events, to *us* heaven has been just and gracious. The *people* of England did their best, and have received their rewards. Long may we continue to deserve it! Causes, which it had been too generally the habit of former statesmen to regard as belonging to another world, are now admitted by all ranks to have been the main agents of our success. *"We fought from heaven; the stars in their courses fought against Sisera."* If then unanimity grounded on moral feelings has been among the least equivocal sources of our national glory, that man deserves the esteem of his countrymen, even as patriots, who devotes his life and the utmost efforts of his intellect to the preservation and continuance of that unanimity by the disclosure and establishment of *principles*. For by these all *opinions* must be ultimately tried; and, (as the feelings of men are worthy of regard only as far as they are the representatives of their fixed opinions), on the knowledge of these all unanimity, not accidental and fleeting, must be grounded. Let the scholar, who doubts this assertion, refer only to the speeches and writings of EDMUND BURKE at the commencement of the American war and compare them with his speeches and writings at the commencement of the French revolution. He will find the *principles* exactly the same and the deductions the same; but the practical inferences almost opposite in the one case from those drawn in the other; yet in both equally legitimate and in both equally confirmed by the results. Whence gained he this superiority of foresight? Whence arose the striking *difference,* and in most instances even, the discrepancy between the grounds assigned by *him,* and by those who voted *with* him, on the same questions? How are we to explain the notorious fact, that the speeches and writings of EDMUND BURKE are more interesting at the present day than they were found at the time of their first publication; while those of his illustrious confederates are either forgotten, or exist only to furnish proofs, that the same conclusion, which one man had deduced scientifically, *may* be brought out by another in consequence of errors that luckily chanced to neutralize each other. It would be unhandsome as a conjecture, even were it not, as it actually is, false in point of fact, to attribute this difference to deficiency of talent on the part of Burke's friends, or of experience, or of historical knowledge. The satisfactory solution is, that Edmund Burke possessed and had sedulously sharpened that eye, which sees all things, actions, and events, in relation to the *laws* that determine their existence and circumscribe their possibility. He referred habitually to *principles.* He was a *scientific* statesman; and therefore a *seer.* For every *principle* contains in itself the germs of a prophecy; and, as the prophetic power is the essential privilege of science, so the fulfilment of its oracles supplies the outward and, (to men in general), the *only* test of its claim to the title. Wearisome as Burke's refinements appeared to his parliamentary auditors, yet the cultivated classes throughout Europe have reason to be thankful, that

———he went on refining,
And thought of convincing, while they thought of dining.

Our very sign-boards, (said an illustrious friend to me), give evidence, that there has been a TITIAN in the world. In like manner, not only the debates in parliament, not only our proclamations and state papers, but the essays and leading paragraphs of our journals are so many remembrancers of EDMUND BURKE. Of this the reader may easily convince himself, if either by recollection or reference he will compare the opposition newspapers at the commencement and during the five or six following years of the French revolution with the sentiments, and grounds of argument assumed in the same class of Journals at present, and for some years past.

Whether the spirit of Jacobinism, which the writings of Burke exorcised from the higher and from the literary classes, may not, like the ghost in Hamlet, be heard moving and mining in the underground chambers with an activity the more dangerous because less noisy, may admit of a question. I have given my opinions on this point, and the grounds of them, in my letters to Judge Fletcher occasioned by his CHARGE to the Wexford grand jury, and published in the *Courier*. Be this as it may, the evil spirit of jealousy, and with it the Cerberean whelps of feud and slander, no longer walk their rounds, in cultivated society.

Far different were the days to which these anecdotes have carried me back. The dark guesses of some zealous Quidnunc met with so congenial a soil in the grave alarm of a titled Dogberry of our neighbourhood, that a SPY was actually sent down from the government *pour surveillance* of myself and friend. There must have been not only abundance, but *variety* of these "honorable men" at the disposal of Ministers: for this proved a very honest fellow. After three weeks' truly Indian perseverance in tracking us, (for we were commonly together,) during all which time seldom were we out of doors, but he contrived to be within hearing, (and all the while utterly unsuspected; how indeed *could* such a suspicion enter our fancies?) he not only rejected Sir Dogberry's request that he would try yet a little longer, but declared to him his belief, that both my friend and myself were as good subjects, for aught he could discover to the contrary, as any in His Majesty's dominions. He had repeatedly hid himself, he said, for hours together behind a bank at the sea-side, (our favorite seat), and overheard our conversation. At first he fancied, that we were aware of our danger; for he often heard me talk of one *Spy Nozy*, which he was inclined to interpret of himself, and of a remarkable feature belonging to him; but he was speedily convinced that it was the name of a man who had made a book and lived long ago. Our talk ran most upon books, and we were perpetually desiring each other to look at *this*, and to listen to *that*; but he could not catch a word about politics. Once he had joined me on the road; (this occurred, as I was returning home alone from my friend's house, which was about three miles from my own cottage), and, passing himself off as a traveller, he had entered into conversation with me, and talked of purpose in a *democrat* way in order to draw me out. The result, it appears, not only convinced him that I was no friend of Jacobinism; but, (he added), I had "plainly made it out to be such a silly as well as wicked thing, that he felt ashamed though he had only *put it on*." I distinctly remembered the occurrence, and had mentioned it immediately on my return, repeating what the traveller with his Bardolph nose had said, with my own answer; and so little did I suspect the true object of my "tempter ere accuser," that I expressed with no small pleasure my hope and belief, that the conversation had been of some service to the poor misled malcontent. This incident therefore prevented all doubt as to the truth of the report, which through a friendly medium came to me from the master of the village inn, who had been ordered to entertain the *Government Gentleman* in his best manner, but above all to be silent concerning such a person being in his house. At length he received Sir Dogberry's commands to accompany his guest at the final interview; and, after the absolving suffrage of the *gentleman honored with the confidence of Ministers*, answered, as follows, to the following queries? D. Well, landlord! and what do you know of the person in question? L. I see him often pass by with maister ———, my landlord, (i.e. *the owner of the house*), and sometimes with the new-comers at Holford; but I never said a word to him or he to me. D. But do you not know, that he has distributed papers and hand-bills of a seditious nature among the common people? L. No, your honor! I never heard of such a thing. D. Have you not seen this Mr. Coleridge, or heard of, his haranguing and talking to knots and clusters of the inhabitants?—What are you grinning at, Sir? L. Beg your honor's pardon! but I was only thinking, how they'd have stared at him. If what I have heard be true, your honor! they would not have understood a word he said. When our vicar was here, Dr. L. the master of the great school and Canon of Windsor, there was a great dinner party at maister ——'s; and one of the farmers, that was there, told us that he and the Doctor talked real Hebrew Greek at each other for an hour together after dinner. D. Answer the question, Sir! Does he ever harangue the people? L. I hope your honor an't angry with me. I can say no more than I know. I never saw him talking with any one, but my landlord, and our curate, and the strange gentleman. D. Has he not been seen wandering on the hills towards the Channel, and along the shore, with books and papers in his hand, taking charts and maps of the country? L. Why, as to that, your honor! I own, I have heard; I am sure, I would not wish to say ill of any body; but it is certain, that I have heard—D. Speak out, man! don't be afraid, you are doing your duty to your King and Government. What have you heard? L. Why, folks do say, your honor! as how that he is a *Poet,* and that he is going to put Quantock and all about here in print; and as they be so much together, I suppose that the strange gentleman has some *consarn* in the business.—So ended this formidable inquisition, the latter part of which alone requires explanation, and at the same time entitles the anecdote to a place in my literary life. I had considered it as a defect in the admirable poem of the TASK, that the subject, which gives the title to the work, was not, and indeed could not be, carried on beyond the three or four first pages, and that, throughout the poem, the connections are frequently awkward, and the transitions abrupt and arbitrary. I sought for a subject, that should give equal room and freedom for description, incident, and impassioned reflections on men, nature, and society, yet supply in itself a natural connection to the parts, and unity to the whole. Such a subject I conceived myself to have found in a stream, traced from its source in the hills among the

yellow-red moss and conical glass-shaped tufts of bent, to the first
break or fall, where its drops become audible, and it begins to form
a channel; thence to the peat and turf barn, itself built of the same
dark squares as it sheltered; to the sheepfold; to the first cultivated
plot of ground; to the lonely cottage and its bleak garden won
from the heath; to the hamlet, the villages, the market-town, the
manufactories, and the seaport. My walks therefore were almost
daily on the top of Quantock, and among its sloping combes. With
my pencil and memorandum book in my hand, I was *making studies,* as the artists call them, and often moulding my thoughts into
verse, with the objects and imagery immediately before my senses.
Many circumstances, evil and good, intervened to prevent the
completion of the poem, which was to have been entitled "THE
BROOK." Had I finished the work, it was my purpose in the heat
of the moment to have dedicated it to our then committee of public
safety as containing the charts and maps, with which I was to have
supplied the French Government in aid of their plans of invasion.
And these too for a tract of coast that, from Clevedon to Minehead,
scarcely permits the approach of a fishing-boat!

All my experience from my first entrance into life to the present
hour is in favor of the warning maxim, that the man, who opposes
in toto the political or religious zealots of his age, is safer from their
obloquy than he who differs from them but in one or two points,
or perhaps only in degree. By that transfer of the feelings of private
life into the discussion of public questions, which is the *queen bee*
in the hive of party fanaticism, the partisan has more sympathy
with an intemperate Opposite than with a moderate Friend. We
now enjoy an intermission, and long may it continue! In addition
to far higher and more important merits, our present Bible societies
and other numerous associations for national or charitable objects,
may serve perhaps to carry off the superfluous activity and fervour
of stirring minds in innocent hyperboles and the bustle of management. But the poison-tree is not dead, though the sap may for a
season have subsided to its roots. At least let us not be lulled into
such a notion of our entire security, as not to keep watch and
ward, even on our best feelings. I have seen gross intolerance
shewn in support of toleration; sectarian antipathy most obtru-

sively displayed in the promotion of an undistinguishing comprehension of sects; and acts of cruelty, (I had almost said,) of treachery, committed in furtherance of an object vitally important to the cause of humanity; and all this by men too of naturally kind dispositions and exemplary conduct.

The magic rod of fanaticism is preserved in the very adyta of human nature; and needs only the re-exciting warmth of a master hand to bud forth afresh and produce the old fruits. . . .

## FROM CHAPTER XII

*A Chapter of requests and premonitions concerning the perusal or omission of the chapter that follows.*

. . . I shall now proceed to the nature and genesis of the imagination; but I must first take leave to notice, that after a more accurate perusal of Mr. Wordsworth's remarks on the imagination, in his preface to the new edition of his poems, I find that my conclusions are not so consentient with his as, I confess, I had taken for granted. In an article contributed by me to Mr. Southey's Omniana, on the soul and its organs of sense, are the following sentences. "These (the human faculties) I would arrange under the different senses and powers: as the eye, the ear, the touch, &c.; the imitative power, voluntary and automatic; the imagination, or shaping and modifying power; the fancy, or the aggregative and associative power; the understanding, or the regulative, substantiating and realizing power; the speculative reason, *vis theoretica et scientifica,* or the power by which we produce or aim to produce unity, necessity, and universality in all our knowledge by means of principles a priori;* the will, or practical reason; the faculty of

---

* This phrase, *a priori,* is in common, most grossly misunderstood, and an absurdity burdened on it, which it does not deserve. By knowledge, *a priori,* we do not mean, that we can know anything previously to experience, which would be a contradiction in terms; but that having once known it by occasion of experience (that is, something acting upon us from without) we then know, that it must have pre-existed, or the experience itself would have been impossible. By experience only I know, that I have eyes; but

choice (*Germanice*, Willkür) and (distinct both from the moral will and the choice,) the *sensation* of volition, which I have found reason to include under the head of single and double touch." To this, as far as it relates to the subject in question, namely the words (*the aggregative and associative power*) Mr. Wordsworth's "only objection is that the definition is too general. To aggregate and to associate, to evoke and to combine, belong as well to the imagination as to the fancy." I reply, that if, by the power of evoking and combining, Mr. Wordsworth means the same as, and no more than, I meant by the aggregative and associative, I continue to deny, that it belongs at all to the imagination; and I am disposed to conjecture, that he has mistaken the copresence of fancy with imagination for the operation of the latter singly. A man may work with two very different tools at the same moment; each has its share in the work, but the work effected by each is distinct and different. But it will probably appear in the next Chapter, that deeming it necessary to go back much further than Mr. Wordsworth's subject required or permitted, I have attached a meaning to both fancy and imagination, which he had not in view, at least while he was writing that preface. He will judge. Would to Heaven, I might meet with many such readers. I will conclude with the words of Bishop Jeremy Taylor: he to whom all things are one, who draweth all things to one, and seeth all things in one, may enjoy true peace and rest of spirit. (*J. Taylor's* Via Pacis).

# FROM CHAPTER XIII

*On the imagination, or esemplastic power.*

. . . Thus far had the work been transcribed for the press, when I received the following letter from a friend, whose practical judgement I have had ample reason to estimate and revere, and whose taste and sensibility preclude all the excuses which my self-love might possibly have prompted me to set up in plea against the

---

then my reason convinces me, that I must have had eyes in order to the experience.

decision of advisers of equal good sense, but with less tact and feeling.

Dear C.

You ask my opinion concerning your Chapter on the Imagination, both as to the impressions it made on myself, and as to those which I think it will make on the PUBLIC, i.e. that part of the public, who, from the title of the work and from its forming a sort of introduction to a volume of poems, are likely to constitute the great majority of your readers.

As to myself, and stating in the first place the effect on my *understanding,* your opinions and method of argument were not only so *new* to me, but so directly the reverse of all I had ever been accustomed to consider as truth, that even if I had comprehended your premises sufficiently to have admitted them, and had seen the necessity of your conclusions, I should still have been in that state of mind, which in your note p. 231, 232, you have so ingeniously evolved, as the antithesis to that in which a man is, when he makes a *bull.* In your own words, I should have felt as if I had been standing on my head.

The effect on my *feelings,* on the other hand, I cannot better represent, than by supposing myself to have known only our light airy modern chapels of ease, and then for the first time to have been placed, and left alone, in one of our largest Gothic cathedrals in a gusty moonlight night of autumn. "Now in glimmer, and now in gloom;" often in palpable darkness not without a chilly sensation of terror; then suddenly emerging into broad yet visionary lights with coloured shadows of fantastic shapes, yet all decked with holy insignia and mystic symbols; and ever and anon coming out full upon pictures and stone-work images of great men, with whose *names* I was familiar, but which looked upon me with countenances and an expression, the most dissimilar to all I had been in the habit of connecting with those names. Those whom I had been taught to venerate as almost super-human in magnitude of intellect, I found perched in little fret-work niches, as grotesque dwarfs; while the grotesques, in my hitherto belief, stood guarding the high altar with all the characters of Apotheosis. In short, what

I had supposed substances were thinned away into shadows, while everywhere shadows were deepened into substances:

> If substance may be call'd what shadow seem'd,
> For each seem'd either!

MILTON

Yet after all, I could not but repeat the lines which you had quoted from a MS. poem of your own in the FRIEND, and applied to a work of Mr. Wordsworth's though with a few of the words altered:

> ————An orphic tale indeed,
> A tale *obscure* of high and passionate thoughts
> To *a strange* music chaunted!

Be assured, however, that I look forward anxiously to your great book on the CONSTRUCTIVE PHILOSOPHY, which you have promised and announced: and that I will do my best to understand it. Only I will not promise to descend into the dark cave of Trophonius with you, there to rub my own eyes, in order to *make* the sparks and figured flashes, which I am required to see.

So much for myself. But as for the PUBLIC, I do not hesitate a moment in advising and urging you to withdraw the Chapter from the present work, and to reserve it for your announced treatises on the Logos or communicative intellect in Man and Deity. First, because, imperfectly as I understand the present Chapter, I see clearly that you have done too much, and yet not enough. You have been obliged to omit so many links, from the necessity of compression, that what remains, looks (if I may recur to my former illustration) like the fragments of the winding steps of an old ruined tower. Secondly, a still stronger argument (at least one that I am sure will be more forcible with you) is, that your readers will have both right and reason to complain of you. This Chapter, which cannot, when it is printed, amount to so little as an hundred pages, will of necessity greatly increase the expense of the work; and every reader who, like myself, is neither prepared nor perhaps calculated for the study of so abstruse a subject so abstrusely treated, will, as I have before hinted, be almost entitled to accuse you of a sort of imposition on him. For who, he might truly observe, could from your title-page, viz. **My Literary Life and Opinions,** published too as introductory to a volume of miscellaneous poems, have anticipated, or even conjectured, a long treatise on ideal Realism which holds the same relation in abstruseness to Plotinus, as Plotinus does to Plato. It will be well, if already you have not too much of metaphysical disquisition in your work, though as the larger part of the disquisition is historical, it will doubtless be both interesting and instructive to many to whose *unprepared* minds your speculations on the esemplastic power would be utterly unintelligible. Be assured, if you do publish this Chapter in the present work, you will be reminded of Bishop Berkley's Siris, announced as an Essay on Tar-water, which beginning with Tar ends with the Trinity, the omne scibile forming the interspace. I say in the *present* work. In that greater work to which you have devoted so many years, and study so intense and various, it will be in its proper place. Your prospectus will have described and announced both its contents and their nature; and if any persons purchase it, who feel no interest in the subjects of which it treats, they will have themselves only to blame.

I could add to these arguments one derived from pecuniary motives, and particularly from the probable effects on the *sale* of your present publication; but they would weigh little with you compared with the preceding. Besides, I have long observed, that arguments drawn from your own personal interests more often act on you as narcotics than as stimulants, and that in money concerns you have some small portion of pig-nature in your moral idiosyncracy, and, like these amiable creatures, must occasionally be pulled backward from the boat in order to make you enter it. All success attend you, for if hard thinking and hard reading are merits, you have deserved it.

Your affectionate, &c.

In consequence of this very judicious letter, which produced complete conviction on my mind, I shall content myself for the present with stating the main result of the Chapter, which I have reserved for that future publication, a detailed prospectus of which the reader will find at the close of the second volume.

͢AGINATION then, I consider either as primary, or second-
͢rimary IMAGINATION I hold to be the living Power and
prime Agent of all human Perception, and as a repetition in the
finite mind of the eternal act of creation in the infinite I AM.
The secondary Imagination I consider as an echo of the former,
co-existing with the conscious will, yet still as identical with the
primary in the *kind* of its agency, and differing only in *degree,*
and in the *mode* of its operation. It dissolves, diffuses, dissipates,
in order to recreate; or where this process is rendered impossible,
yet still at all events it struggles to idealize and to unify. It is
essentially *vital,* even as all objects (*as* objects) are essentially
fixed and dead.

FANCY, on the contrary, has no other counters to play with, but
fixities and definites. The Fancy is indeed no other than a mode of
Memory emancipated from the order of time and space; while it
is blended with, and modified by that empirical phenomenon of
the will, which we express by the word CHOICE. But equally with
the ordinary memory the Fancy must receive all its materials ready
made from the law of association.

Whatever more than this, I shall think it fit to declare concerning the powers and privileges of the imagination in the present
work, will be found in the critical essay on the uses of the Supernatural in poetry, and the principles that regulate its introduction:
which the reader will find prefixed to the poem of **The Ancient
Mariner.**

## CHAPTER XIV

*Occasion of the Lyrical Ballads, and the objects originally proposed—Preface
to the second edition—The ensuing controversy, its causes and acrimony—
Philosophic definitions of a poem and poetry with scholia.*

During the first year that Mr. Wordsworth and I were neighbours, our conversations turned frequently on the two cardinal
points of poetry, the power of exciting the sympathy of the reader
by a faithful adherence to the truth of nature, and the power of
giving the interest of novelty by the modifying colors of imagina-

tion. The sudden charm, which accidents of light and shade, which moon-light or sun-set diffused over a known and familiar landscape, appeared to represent the practicability of combining both. These are the poetry of nature. The thought suggested itself (to which of us I do not recollect) that a series of poems might be composed of two sorts. In the one, the incidents and agents were to be, in part at least, supernatural; and the excellence aimed at was to consist in the interesting of the affections by the dramatic truth of such emotions, as would naturally accompany such situations, supposing them real. And real in *this* sense they have been to every human being who, from whatever source of delusion, has at any time believed himself under supernatural agency. For the second class, subjects were to be chosen from ordinary life; the characters and incidents were to be such, as will be found in every village and its vicinity, where there is a meditative and feeling mind to seek after them, or to notice them, when they present themselves.

In this idea originated the plan of the "Lyrical Ballads"; in which it was agreed, that my endeavours should be directed to persons and characters supernatural, or at least romantic; yet so as to transfer from our inward nature a human interest and a semblance of truth sufficient to procure for these shadows of imagination that willing suspension of disbelief for the moment, which constitutes poetic faith. Mr. Wordsworth, on the other hand, was to propose to himself as his object, to give the charm of novelty to things of every day, and to excite a feeling analogous to the supernatural, by awakening the mind's attention from the lethargy of custom, and directing it to the loveliness and the wonders of the world before us; an inexhaustible treasure, but for which, in consequence of the film of familiarity and selfish solicitude we have eyes, yet see not, ears that hear not, and hearts that neither feel nor understand.

With this view I wrote "The Ancient Mariner," and was preparing among other poems, "The Dark Ladie," and the "Christabel," in which I should have more nearly realized my ideal. than I had done in my first attempt. But Mr. Wordsworth's industry had proved so much more successful, and the number of his poems so much greater, that my compositions, instead of forming a balance, appeared rather an interpolation of heterogeneous matter. Mr. Wordsworth added two or three poems written in his own character, in the impassioned, lofty, and sustained diction, which is characteristic of his genius. In this form the "Lyrical Ballads" were published; and were presented by him, as an *experiment*, whether subjects, which from their nature rejected the usual ornaments and extra-colloquial style of poems in general, might not be so managed in the language of ordinary life as to produce the pleasureable interest, which it is the peculiar business of poetry to impart. To the second edition he added a preface of considerable length; in which, notwithstanding some passages of apparently a contrary import, he was understood to contend for the extension of this style to poetry of all kinds, and to reject as vicious and indefensible all phrases and forms of style that were not included in what he (unfortunately, I think, adopting an equivocal expression) called the language of *real* life. From this preface, prefixed to poems in which it was impossible to deny the presence of original genius, however mistaken its direction might be deemed, arose the whole long-continued controversy. For from the conjunction of perceived power with supposed heresy I explain the inveteracy and in some instances, I grieve to say, the acrimonious passions, with which the controversy has been conducted by the assailants.

Had Mr. Wordsworth's poems been the silly, the childish things, which they were for a long time described as being; had they been really distinguished from the compositions of other poets merely by meanness of language and inanity of thought; had they indeed contained nothing more than what is found in the parodies and pretended imitations of them; they must have sunk at once, a dead weight, into the slough of oblivion, and have dragged the preface along with them. But year after year increased the number of Mr. Wordsworth's admirers. They were found too not in the lower classes of the reading public, but chiefly among young men of strong sensibility and meditative minds; and their admiration (inflamed perhaps in some degree by opposition) was distinguished by its intensity, I might almost say, by its *religious* fervor.

These facts, and the intellectual energy of the author, which was more or less consciously felt, where it was outwardly and even boisterously denied, meeting with sentiments of aversion to his opinions, and of alarm at their consequences, produced an eddy of criticism, which would of itself have borne up the poems by the violence, with which it whirled them round and round. With many parts of this preface, in the sense attributed to them, and which the words undoubtedly seem to authorize, I never concurred; but on the contrary objected to them as erroneous in principle, and as contradictory (in appearance at least) both to other parts of the same preface, and to the author's own practice in the greater number of the poems themselves. Mr. Wordsworth in his recent collection has, I find, degraded this prefatory disquisition to the end of his second volume, to be read or not at the reader's choice. But he has not, as far as I can discover, announced any change in his poetic creed. At all events, considering it as the source of a controversy, in which I have been honored more than I deserve by the frequent conjunction of my name with his, I think it expedient to declare once for all, in what points I coincide with his opinions, and in what points I altogether differ. But in order to render myself intelligible I must previously, in as few words as possible, explain my ideas, first, of a POEM; and secondly, of POETRY itself, in *kind*, and in *essence*.

The office of philosophical *disquisition* consists in just *distinction;* while it is the privilege of the philosopher to preserve himself constantly aware, that distinction is not division. In order to obtain adequate notions of any truth, we must intellectually separate its distinguishable parts; and this is the technical *process* of philosophy. But having so done, we must then restore them in our conceptions to the unity, in which they actually co-exist; and this is the *result* of philosophy. A poem contains the same elements as a prose composition; the difference therefore must consist in a different combination of them, in consequence of a different object being proposed. According to the difference of the object will be the difference of the combination. It is possible, that the object may be merely to facilitate the recollection of any given facts or observations by artificial arrangement; and the composition will be a poem, merely because it is distinguished from prose by metre, or by rhyme, or by both conjointly. In this, the lowest sense, a man might attribute the name of a poem to the well-known enumeration of the days in the several months;

> Thirty days hath September,
> April, June, and November, &c.

and others of the same class and purpose. And as a particular pleasure is found in anticipating the recurrence of sounds and quantities, all compositions that have this charm super-added, whatever be their contents, *may* be entitled poems.

So much for the superficial *form*. A difference of object and contents supplies an additional ground of distinction. The immediate purpose may be the communication of truths; either of truth absolute and demonstrable, as in works of science; or of facts experienced and recorded, as in history. Pleasure, and that of the highest and most permanent kind, may *result* from the *attainment* of the end; but it is not itself the immediate end. In other works the communication of pleasure may be the immediate purpose; and though truth, either moral or intellectual, ought to be the *ultimate* end, yet this will distinguish the character of the author, not the class to which the work belongs. Blest indeed is that state of society, in which the immediate purpose would be baffled by the perversion of the proper ultimate end; in which no charm of diction or imagery could exempt the Bathyllus even of an Anacreon, or the Alexis of Virgil, from disgust and aversion!

But the communication of pleasure may be the immediate object of a work not metrically composed; and that object may have been in a high degree attained, as in novels and romances. Would then the mere superaddition of metre, with or without rhyme, entitle *these* to the name of poems? The answer is, that nothing can permanently please, which does not contain in itself the reason why it is so, and not otherwise. If metre be superadded, all other parts must be made consonant with it. They must be such, as to justify the perpetual and distinct attention to each part, which an exact correspondent recurrence of accent and sound are calculated to excite. The final definition then, so deduced, may be thus worded. A poem is that species of composition, which is opposed to works of science, by proposing for its *immediate* object pleasure, not truth; and from all other species (having *this* object in common with it) it is discriminated by proposing to itself such delight from the *whole*, as is compatible with a distinct gratification from each component *part*.

Controversy is not seldom excited in consequence of the disputants attaching each a different meaning to the same word; and in few instances has this been more striking, than in disputes concerning the present subject. If a man chooses to call every composition a poem, which is rhyme, or measure, or both, I must leave his opinion uncontroverted. The distinction is at least competent to characterize the writer's intention. If it were subjoined, that the whole is likewise entertaining or affecting, as a tale, or as a series of interesting reflections, I of course admit this as another fit ingredient of a poem, and an additional merit. But if the definition sought for be that of a *legitimate* poem, I answer, it must be one, the parts of which mutually support and explain each other; all in their proportion harmonizing with, and supporting the purpose and known influences of metrical arrangement. The philosophic critics of all ages coincide with the ultimate judgement of all countries, in equally denying the praises of a just poem, on the one hand, to a series of striking lines or distiches, each of which, absorbing the whole attention of the reader to itself, disjoins it from its context, and makes it a separate whole, instead of an harmonizing part; and on the other hand, to an unsustained composition, from which the reader collects rapidly the general result, unattracted by the component parts. The reader should be carried forward, not merely or chiefly by the mechanical impulse of curiosity, or by a restless desire to arrive at the final solution; but by the pleasureable activity of mind excited by the attractions of the journey itself. Like the motion of a serpent, which the Egyptians made the emblem of intellectual power; or like the path of sound through the air; at every step he pauses and half recedes, and from the retrogressive movement collects the force which again carries him onward. "Præcipitandus est *liber* spiritus," says Petronius Arbiter most happily. The epithet, *liber*, here balances the preceding verb; and it is not easy to conceive more meaning condensed in fewer words.

But if this should be admitted as a satisfactory character of a poem, we have still to seek for a definition of poetry. The writings of PLATO, and Bishop TAYLOR, and the "Theoria Sacra" of BURNET, furnish undeniable proofs that poetry of the highest kind may exist without metre, and even without the contra-distinguishing objects of a poem. The first chapter of Isaiah (indeed a very large portion of the whole book) is poetry in the most emphatic sense; yet it would be not less irrational than strange to assert, that pleasure, and not truth, was the immediate object of the prophet. In short, whatever *specific* import we attach to the word, poetry, there will be found involved in it, as a necessary consequence, that a poem of any length neither can be, or ought to be, all poetry. Yet if an harmonious whole is to be produced, the remaining parts must be preserved *in keeping* with the poetry; and this can be no otherwise effected than by such a studied selection and artificial arrangement, as will partake of *one,* though not a *peculiar* property of poetry. And this again can be no other than the property of exciting a more continuous and equal attention than the language of prose aims at, whether colloquial or written.

My own conclusions on the nature of poetry, in the strictest use of the word, have been in part anticipated in the preceding disquisition on the fancy and imagination. What is poetry? is so nearly the same question with, what is a poet? that the answer to the one is involved in the solution of the other. For it is a distinction resulting from the poetic genius itself, which sustains and modifies the images, thoughts, and emotions of the poet's own mind.

The poet, described in *ideal* perfection, brings the whole soul of man into activity, with the subordination of its faculties to each other, according to their relative worth and dignity. He diffuses a tone and spirit of unity, that blends, and (as it were) *fuses,* each into each, by that synthetic and magical power, to which we have exclusively appropriated the name of imagination. This power, first put in action by the will and understanding, and retained under their irremissive, though gentle and unnoticed, controul

(*laxis effertur habenis*) reveals itself in the balance or reconciliation of opposite or discordant qualities: of sameness, with difference; of the general, with the concrete; the idea, with the image;
the individual, with the representative; the sense of novelty and
freshness, with old and familiar objects; a more than usual state
of emotion, with more than usual order; judgement ever awake
and steady self-possession, with enthusiasm and feeling profound
or vehement; and while it blends and harmonizes the natural and
the artificial, still subordinates art to nature; the manner to the
matter; and our admiration of the poet to our sympathy with the
poetry. "Doubtless," as Sir John Davies observes of the soul (and
his words may with slight alteration be applied, and even more
appropriately, to the poetic IMAGINATION)

> Doubtless this could not be, but that she turns
>   Bodies to spirit by sublimation strange,
> As fire converts to fire the things it burns,
>   As we our food into our nature change.
>
> From their gross matter she abstracts their forms,
>   And draws a kind of quintessence from things;
> Which to her proper nature she transforms,
>   To bear them light on her celestial wings.
>
> Thus does she, when from individual states
>   She doth abstract the universal kinds;
> Which then re-clothed in divers names and fates
>   Steal access through our senses to our minds.

Finally, GOOD SENSE is the BODY of poetic genius, FANCY its
DRAPERY, MOTION its LIFE, and IMAGINATION the SOUL that is
everywhere, and in each; and forms all into one graceful and
intelligent whole.

## CHAPTER XV

*The specific symptoms of poetic power elucidated in a critical analysis of
Shakespeare's Venus and Adonis, and Lucrece.*

In the application of these principles to purposes of practical
criticism as employed in the appraisal of works more or less im-

perfect, I have endeavoured to discover what the qualities in a poem are, which may be deemed promises and specific symptoms of poetic power, as distinguished from general talent determined to poetic composition by accidental motives, by an act of the will, rather than by the inspiration of a genial and productive nature. In this investigation, I could not, I thought, do better, than keep before me the earliest work of the greatest genius, that perhaps human nature has yet produced, our *myriad-minded* * Shakespeare. I mean the "Venus and Adonis," and the "Lucrece"; works which give at once strong promises of the strength, and yet obvious proofs of the immaturity, of his genius. From these I abstracted the following marks, as characteristics of original poetic genius in general.

1. In the "Venus and Adonis," the first and most obvious excellence is the perfect sweetness of the versification; its adaptation to the subject; and the power displayed in varying the march of the words without passing into a loftier and more majestic rhythm than was demanded by the thoughts, or permitted by the propriety of preserving a sense of melody predominant. The delight in richness and sweetness of sound, even to a faulty excess, if it be evidently original, and not the result of an easily imitable mechanism, I regard as a highly favourable promise in the compositions of a young man. "The man that hath not music in his soul" can indeed never be a genuine poet. Imagery (even taken from nature, much more when transplanted from books, as travels, voyages, and works of natural history); affecting incidents; just thoughts; interesting personal or domestic feelings; and with these the art of their combination or intertexture in the form of a poem; may all by incessant effort be acquired as a trade, by a man of talents and much reading, who, as I once before observed, has mistaken an intense desire of poetic reputation for a natural poetic genius; the love of the arbitrary end for a possession of the peculiar means. But the sense of musical delight, with the power of producing it, is a gift

---

* Ἀνὴρ μυριόνους, a phrase which I have borrowed from a Greek monk, who applies it to a Patriarch of Constantinople. I might have said, that I have *reclaimed,* rather than borrowed it: for it seems to belong to Shakespeare, "de jure singulari, et ex privilegio naturæ."

of imagination; and this together with the power of reducing multitude into unity of effect, and modifying a series of thoughts by
some one predominant thought or feeling, may be cultivated and
improved, but can never be learned. It is in these that "poeta
nascitur non fit."

2. A second promise of genius is the choice of subjects very
remote from the private interests and circumstances of the writer
himself. At least I have found, that where the subject is taken
immediately from the author's personal sensations and experiences, the excellence of a particular poem is but an equivocal
mark, and often a fallacious pledge, of genuine poetic power. We
may perhaps remember the tale of the statuary, who had acquired
considerable reputation for the legs of his goddesses, though the
rest of the statue accorded but indifferently with ideal beauty; till
his wife, elated by her husband's praises, modestly acknowledged
that she herself had been his constant model. In the "Venus and
Adonis" this proof of poetic power exists even to excess. It is
throughout as if a superior spirit more intuitive, more intimately
conscious, even than the characters themselves, not only of every
outward look and act, but of the flux and reflux of the mind in
all its subtlest thoughts and feelings, were placing the whole before
our view; himself meanwhile unparticipating in the passions, and
actuated only by that pleasureable excitement, which had resulted
from the energetic fervor of his own spirit in so vividly exhibiting,
what it had so accurately and profoundly contemplated. I think,
I should have conjectured from these poems, that even then the
great instinct, which impelled the poet to the drama, was secretly
working in him, prompting him by a series and never broken chain
of imagery, always vivid and, because unbroken, often minute; by
the highest effort of the picturesque in words, of which words are
capable, higher perhaps than was ever realized by any other poet,
even Dante not excepted; to provide a substitute for that visual
language, that constant intervention and running comment by
tone, look and gesture, which in his dramatic works he was entitled to expect from the players. His "Venus and Adonis" seem
at once the characters themselves, and the whole representation
of those characters by the most consummate actors. You seem to

be told nothing, but to see and hear everything. Hence it is, that from the perpetual activity of attention required on the part of the reader; from the rapid flow, the quick change, and the playful nature of the thoughts and images; and above all from the alienation, and, if I may hazard such an expression, the utter *aloofness* of the poet's own feelings, from those of which he is at once the painter and the analyst; that though the very subject cannot but detract from the pleasure of a delicate mind, yet never was poem less dangerous on a moral account. Instead of doing as Ariosto, and as, still more offensively, Wieland has done, instead of degrading and deforming passion into appetite, the trials of love into the struggles of concupiscence; Shakespeare has here represented the animal impulse itself, so as to preclude all sympathy with it, by dissipating the reader's notice among the thousand outward images, and now beautiful, now fanciful circumstances, which form its dresses and its scenery; or by diverting our attention from the main subject by those frequent witty or profound reflections, which the poet's ever active mind has deduced from, or connected with, the imagery and the incidents. The reader is forced into too much action to sympathize with the merely passive of our nature. As little can a mind thus roused and awakened be brooded on by mean and indistinct emotion, as the low, lazy mist can creep upon the surface of a lake, while a strong gale is driving it onward in waves and billows.

3. It has been before observed that images, however beautiful, though faithfully copied from nature, and as accurately represented in words, do not of themselves characterize the poet. They become proofs of original genius only as far as they are modified by a predominant passion; or by associated thoughts or images awakened by that passion; or when they have the effect of reducing multitude to unity, or succession to an instant; or lastly, when a human and intellectual life is transferred to them from the poet's own spirit,

> Which shoots its being through earth, sea, and air.

In the two following lines for instance, there is nothing objectionable, nothing which would preclude them from forming, in their proper place, part of a descriptive poem:

> Behold yon row of pines, that shorn and bow'd
> Bend from the sea-blast, seen at twilight eve.

But with a small alteration of rhythm, the same words would be equally in their place in a book of topography, or in a descriptive tour. The same image will rise into semblance of poetry if thus conveyed:

> Yon row of bleak and visionary pines,
> By twilight glimpse discerned, mark! how they flee
> From the fierce sea-blast, all their tresses wild
> Streaming before them.

I have given this as an illustration, by no means as an instance, of that particular excellence which I had in view, and in which Shakespeare even in his earliest, as in his latest, works surpasses all other poets. It is by this, that he still gives a dignity and a passion to the objects which he presents. Unaided by any previous excitement, they burst upon us at once in life and in power.

> Full many a glorious morning have I seen
> *Flatter* the mountain tops with sovereign eye.
> Shakespeare, Sonnet 33rd.
> Not mine own fears, nor the prophetic soul
> Of the wide world dreaming on things to come—
> \*　　　\*　　　\*　　　\*　　　\*　　　\*　　　\*
> \*　　　\*　　　\*　　　\*　　　\*　　　\*　　　\*
>
> The mortal moon hath her eclipse endur'd,
> And the sad augurs mock their own presage;
> Incertainties now crown themselves assur'd,
> And Peace proclaims olives of endless age.
> Now with the drops of this most balmy time
> My Love looks fresh, and DEATH to me subscribes!
> Since spite of him, I'll live in this poor rhyme,
> While he insults o'er dull and speechless tribes.
> And thou in this shalt find thy monument,
> When tyrants' crests, and tombs of brass are spent.
> Sonnet 107.

As of higher worth, so doubtless still more characteristic of poetic genius does the imagery become, when it moulds and colors itself to the circumstances, passion, or character, present and foremost in the mind. For unrivalled instances of this excellence, the reader's own memory will refer him to the LEAR, OTHELLO, in short to which not of the *"great, ever living, dead man's"* dramatic works? "Inopem me copia fecit." How true it is to nature, he has himself finely expressed in the instance of love in Sonnet 98.

> From you have I been absent in the spring,
> When proud pied April drest in all its trim
> Hath put a spirit of youth in every thing,
> That heavy Saturn laugh'd and leap'd with him.
> Yet nor the lays of birds, nor the sweet smell
> Of different flowers in odour and in hue,
> Could make me any summer's story tell,
> Or from their proud lap pluck them, where they grew:
> Nor did I wonder at the lilies white,
> Nor praise the deep vermilion in the rose;
> They were, tho' sweet, but figures of delight,
> Drawn after you, you pattern of all those.
> Yet seem'd it winter still, and, you away,
> *As with your shadow I with these did play!*

Scarcely less sure, or if a less valuable, not less indispensable mark

> Γονίμου μὲν ποιητοῦ——
> ——ὅστις ῥῆμα γενναῖον λάχοι,

will the imagery supply, when, with more than the power of the painter, the poet gives us the liveliest image of succession with the feeling of simultaneousness!

> With this, he breaketh from the sweet embrace
> Of those fair arms, that held him to her heart,
> And homeward through the dark lawns runs apace:
> *Look! how a bright star shooteth from the sky,*
> *So glides he in the night from Venus' eye.*

4. The last character I shall mention, which would prove indeed but little, except as taken conjointly with the former; yet without which the former could scarce exist in a high degree, and (even if this were possible) would give promises only of transitory flashes and a meteoric power; is DEPTH, and ENERGY of THOUGHT. No man was ever yet a great poet, without being at the same time a profound philosopher. For poetry is the blossom and the fra-

grancy of all human knowledge, human thoughts, human passions, emotions, language. In Shakespeare's *poems* the creative power and the intellectual energy wrestle as in a war embrace. Each in its excess of strength seems to threaten the extinction of the other. At length in the DRAMA they were reconciled, and fought each with its shield before the breast of the other. Or like two rapid streams, that, at their first meeting within narrow and rocky banks, mutually strive to repel each other and intermix reluctantly and in tumult; but soon finding a wider channel and more yielding shores blend, and dilate, and flow on in one current and with one voice. The "Venus and Adonis" did not perhaps allow the display of the deeper passions. But the story of Lucretia seems to favor and even demand their intensest workings. And yet we find in *Shakespeare's* management of the tale neither pathos, nor any other *dramatic* quality. There is the same minute and faithful imagery as in the former poem, in the same vivid colors, inspirited by the same impetuous vigor of thought, and diverging and contracting with the same activity of the assimilative and of the modifying faculties; and with a yet larger display, a yet wider range of knowledge and reflection; and lastly, with the same perfect dominion, often *domination,* over the whole world of language. What then shall we say? even this; that Shakespeare, no mere child of nature; no automaton of genius; no passive vehicle of inspiration possessed by the spirit, not possessing it; first studied patiently, meditated deeply, understood minutely, till knowledge, become habitual and intuitive, wedded itself to his habitual feelings, and at length gave birth to that stupendous power, by which he stands alone, with no equal or second in his own class; to that power which seated him on one of the two glory-smitten summits of the poetic mountain, with Milton as his compeer, not rival. While the former darts himself forth, and passes into all the forms of human character and passion, the one Proteus of the fire and the flood; the other attracts all forms and things to himself, into the unity of his own IDEAL. All things and modes of action shape themselves anew in the being of MILTON; while SHAKESPEARE becomes all things, yet for ever remaining himself. O what great men hast thou not produced, England! my country! truly indeed—

Must *we* be free or die, who speak the tongue,
Which SHAKESPEARE spake; the faith and morals hold,
Which MILTON held. In every thing we are sprung
Of earth's first blood, have titles manifold!

WORDSWORTH.

# CHAPTER XVI

*Striking points of difference between the Poets of the present age and those of the 15th and 16th centuries—Wish expressed for the union of the characteristic merits of both.*

Christendom, from its first settlement on feudal rights, has been so far one great body, however imperfectly organized, that a similar spirit will be found in each period to have been acting in all its members. The study of Shakespeare's *poems* (I do not include his dramatic works, eminently as they too deserve that title) led me to a more careful examination of the contemporary poets both in this and in other countries. But my attention was especially fixed on those of Italy, from the birth to the death of Shakespeare; that being the country in which the fine arts had been most sedulously, and hitherto most successfully cultivated. Abstracted from the degrees and peculiarities of individual genius, the properties common to the good writers of each period seem to establish one striking point of difference between the poetry of the fifteenth and sixteenth centuries, and that of the present age. The remark may perhaps be extended to the sister art of painting. At least the latter will serve to illustrate the former. In the present age the poet (I would wish to be understood as speaking generally, and without allusion to individual names) seems to propose to himself as his main object, and as that which is the most characteristic of his art, new and striking IMAGES; with INCIDENTS that interest the affections or excite the curiosity. Both his characters and his descriptions he renders, as much as possible, specific and individual, even to a degree of portraiture. In his diction and metre, on the other

hand, he is comparatively careless. The measure is either constructed on no previous system, and acknowledges no justifying
principle but that of the writer's convenience; or else some mechanical movement is adopted, of which one couplet or stanza is
so far an adequate specimen, as that the occasional differences
appear evidently to arise from accident, or the qualities of the language itself, not from meditation and an intelligent purpose. And
the language from Pope's "Translation of Homer" to Darwin's
"Temple of Nature," may, notwithstanding some illustrious exceptions, be too faithfully characterized, as claiming to be poetical
for no better reason, than that it would be intolerable in conversation or in prose. Though alas! even our prose writings, nay even
the style of our more set discourses, strive to be in the fashion, and
trick themselves out in the soiled and over-worn finery of the
meretricious muse. It is true that of late a great improvement in
this respect is observable in our most popular writers. But it is
equally true, that this recurrence to plain sense and genuine
mother English is far from being general; and that the composition of our novels, magazines, public harangues, &c., is commonly
as trivial in thought, and yet enigmatic in expression, as if ECHO
and SPHINX had laid their heads together to construct it. Nay,
even of those who have most rescued themselves from this con-
tagion, I should plead inwardly guilty to the charge of duplicity
or cowardice, if I withheld my conviction, that few have guarded
the purity of their native tongue with that jealous care, which the
sublime Dante in his tract "De la nobile volgare eloquenza" declares to be the first duty of a poet. For language is the armoury
of the human mind; and at once contains the trophies of its past,
and the weapons of its future conquests. "Animadverte, quam sit
ab improprietate verborum pronum hominibus prolabi in errores
circa res!" HOBBES: *Exam. et Exmend. hod. Math.*—"Sat vero, in
hâc vitæ brevitate et naturæ obscuritate, rerum est, quibus cog-
noscendis tempus impendatur, ut confusis et multivocis sermoni-
bus intelligendis illud consumere non opus sit. Eheu! quantas
strages paravere verba nubila, quæ tot dicunt, ut nihil dicant—
nubes potius, e quibus et in rebus politicis et in ecclesiâ turbines

et tonitrua erumpunt! Et proinde recte dictum putamus a Platone in Gorgia: ὃς ἂν τὰ ὀνόματα εἰδῇ, εἴσεται καὶ τὰ πράγματα: et ab Epicteto, ἀρχὴ παιδεύσεως ἡ τῶν ὀνομάτων ἐπίσκεψις: et prudentissime Galenus scribit, ἡ τῶν ὀνομάτων χρῆσις ταραχθεῖσα καὶ τὴν τῶν πραγμάτων ἐπιταράττει γνῶσιν, Egregie vero J. C. Scaliger, in Lib. I. de Plantis: Est *primum,* inquit, *sapientis officium, bene sentire, ut sibi vivat: proximum, bene loqui, ut patriæ vivat."* SENNERTUS *de Puls: Differentiâ.*

Something analogous to the materials and structure of modern poetry I seem to have noticed (but here I beg to be understood as speaking with the utmost diffidence) in our common landscape painters. Their foregrounds and intermediate distances are comparatively unattractive: while the main interest of the landscape is thrown into the background, where mountains and torrents and castles forbid the eye to proceed, and nothing tempts it to trace its way back again. But in the works of the great Italian and Flemish masters, the front and middle objects of the landscape are the most obvious and determinate, the interest gradually dies away in the background, and the charm and peculiar worth of the picture consists, not so much in the specific objects which it conveys to the understanding in a visual language formed by the substitution of figures for words, as in the beauty and harmony of the colors, lines and expression, with which the objects are represented. Hence novelty of subject was rather avoided than sought for. Superior excellence in the manner of treating the same subjects was the trial and test of the artist's merit.

Not otherwise is it with the more polished poets of the 15th and 16th century, especially with those of Italy. The imagery is almost always general: sun, moon, flowers, breezes, murmuring streams, warbling songsters, delicious shades, lovely damsels cruel as fair, nymphs, naiads, and goddesses, are the materials which are common to all, and which each shaped and arranged according to his judgement or fancy, little solicitous to add or to particularize. If we make an honourable exception in favour of some English poets, the thoughts too are as little novel as the images; and the fable of their narrative poems, for the most part drawn from mythology, or sources of equal notoriety, derive their chief attractions from the manner of treating them; from impassioned flow, or picturesque arrangement. In opposition to the present age, and perhaps in as faulty an extreme, they placed the essence of poetry in the *art*. The excellence, at which they aimed, consisted in the exquisite polish of the diction, combined with perfect simplicity. This, their prime object, they attained by the avoidance of every word, which a *gentleman* would *not* use in dignified conversation, and of every word and phrase, which none but a *learned* man *would* use; by the studied position of words and phrases, so that not only each part should be melodious in itself, but contribute to the harmony of the whole, each note referring and conducing to the melody of all the foregoing and following words of the same period or stanza; and lastly with equal labor, the greater because unbetrayed, by the variation and various harmonies of their metrical movement. Their measures, however, were not indebted for their variety to the introduction of new metres, such as have been attempted of late in the "Alonzo and Imogen," and others borrowed from the German, having in their very mechanism a specific overpowering tune, to which the generous reader humours his voice and emphasis, with more indulgence to the author than attention to the meaning or quantity of the words; but which, to an ear familiar with the *numerous* sounds of the Greek and Roman poets, has an effect not unlike that of galloping over a paved road in a German stage-waggon without springs. On the contrary, our elder bards both of Italy and England produced a far greater as well as more charming variety by countless modifications and subtle balances of sound in the common metres of their country. A lasting and enviable reputation awaits that man of genius, who should attempt and realize a union; who should recall the high finish, the appropriateness, the facility, the delicate proportion, and above all, the perfusive and omnipresent grace, which have preserved, as in a shrine of precious amber, the "Sparrow" of Catullus, the "Swallow," the "Grasshopper," and all the other little loves of Anacreon: and which, with bright, though diminished glories, revisited the youth and early manhood of

Christian Europe, in the vales of * Arno, and the groves of Isis and of Cam; and who with these should combine the keener interest, deeper pathos, manlier reflection, and the fresher and more various imagery, which give a value and a name that will not pass away to the poets who have done honor to our own times, and to those of our immediate predecessors.

---

* These thoughts were suggested to me during the perusal of the Madrigals of GIOVAMBATISTA STROZZI published in Florence (nella Stamperia del Sermartelli) 1st May 1593, by his sons Lorenzo and Filippo Strozzi, with a dedication to their deceased paternal uncle, "Signor Leone Strozzi, Generale delle battaglie di Santa Chiesa." As I do not remember to have seen either the poems or their author mentioned in any English work, or have found them in any of the common collections of Italian poetry; and as the little work is of rare occurrence; I will transcribe a few specimens. I have seldom met with compositions that possessed, to my feelings, more of that satisfying *entireness,* that complete adequateness of the manner to the matter which so charms us in Anacreon, join'd with the tenderness, and more than the *delicacy* of Catullus. Trifles as they are, they were probably elaborated with great care; yet in the perusal we refer them to a spontaneous energy rather than to voluntary effort. To a cultivated taste there is a delight in *perfection* for its own sake, independent of the material in which it is manifested, that none but a cultivated taste can understand or appreciate.

After what I have advanced, it would appear presumption to offer a translation; even if the attempt were not discouraged by the different genius of the English mind and language, which demands a denser body of thought as the condition of a high polish, than the Italian. I cannot but deem it likewise an advantage in the Italian tongue, in many other respects inferior to our own, that the language of poetry is more distinct from that of prose than with us. From the earlier appearance and established primacy of the Tuscan poets, concurring with the number of independent states, and the diversity of written dialects, the Italians have gained a poetic idiom, as the Greeks before them had obtained it from the same causes with greater and more various discriminations—ex. gr. the ionic for their heroic verses; the attic for their iambic; and the two modes of the doric, the lyric or sacerdotal, and the pastoral, the distinctions of which were doubtless more obvious to the Greeks themselves than they are to us.

I will venture to add one other observation before I proceed to the transcription. I am aware, that the sentiments which I have avowed concerning the points of difference between the poetry of the present age, and that of the period between 1500 and 1650, are the reverse of the opinion commonly entertained. I was conversing on this subject with a friend, when

# CHAPTER XV

*Examination of the tenets peculiar to Mr. Wordswortn.*
*all, low and rustic life) especially unfavorable to the formath.*
*diction—The best parts of language the product of philosophe.*
*clowns or shepherds—Poetry essentially ideal and generic—The langua*
*Milton as much the language of real life, yea, incomparably more so than*
*that of the cottager.*

As far then as Mr. Wordsworth in his preface contended, and most ably contended, for a reformation in our poetic diction, as far as he has evinced the truth of passion, and the *dramatic* propriety of those figures and metaphors in the original poets, which, stripped of their justifying reasons, and converted into mere artifices of connection or ornament, constitute the characteristic falsity in the poetic style of the moderns; and as far as he was, with equal acuteness and clearness, pointed out the process by which this change was effected, and the resemblances between that state into which the reader's mind is thrown by the pleasure-

---

the servant, a worthy and sensible woman, coming in, I placed before her two engravings, the one a pinky-colored plate of the day, the other a masterly etching by Salvator Rosa from one of his own pictures. On pressing her to tell us, which she preferred, after a little blushing and flutter of feeling, she replied—"Why, that, Sir! to be sure!" (pointing to the *ware* from the Fleet-street print shops); "it's so *neat* and elegant. T'other is such a *scratchy* slovenly thing." An artist, whose writings are scarcely less valuable than his works, and to whose authority more deference will be willingly paid, than I could even wish should be shown to mine, has told us, and from his own experience too, that good taste must be *acquired,* and like all other good things, is the result of thought, and the submissive study of the best models. If it be asked, "But what shall I deem such?" the answer is; *presume* those to be the best, the *reputation* of which has been matured into *fame* by the consent of ages. For wisdom always has a final majority, if not by conviction, yet by acquiescence. In addition to Sir J. Reynolds I may mention Harris of Salisbury; who in one of his philosophical disquisitions has written on the means of acquiring a just taste with the precision of Aristotle, and the elegance of Quinctilian. . . . [The Italian poems quoted by Coleridge are omitted here.]

fusion of thought from an unaccustomed train of words
nages; and that state which is induced by the natural lan-
ge of empassioned feeling; he undertook a useful task, and
serves all praise, both for the attempt and for the execution.
The provocations to this remonstrance in behalf of truth and
nature were still of perpetual recurrence before and after the publication of this preface. I cannot likewise but add, that the comparison of such poems of merit, as have been given to the public
within the last ten or twelve years, with the majority of those produced previously to the appearance of that preface, leave no doubt
on my mind, that Mr. Wordsworth is fully justified in believing
his efforts to have been by no means ineffectual. Not only in the
verses of those who have professed their admiration of his genius,
but even of those who have distinguished themselves by hostility
to his theory, and depreciation of his writings, are the impressions
of his principles plainly visible. It is possible, that with these principles others may have been blended, which are not equally evident; and some which are unsteady and subvertible from the nar-
rowness or imperfection of their basis. But it is more than possible,
that these errors of defect or exaggeration, by kindling and feeding
the controversy, may have conduced not only to the wider propa-
gation of the accompanying truths, but that, by their frequent
presentation to the mind in an excited state, they may have won
for them a more permanent and practical result. A man will borrow a part from his opponent the more easily, if he feels himself
justified in continuing to reject a part. While there remain important points in which he can still feel himself in the right, in which
he still finds firm footing for continued resistance, he will gradually adopt those opinions, which were the least remote from his
own convictions, as not less congruous with his own theory than
with that which he reprobates. In like manner with a kind of
instinctive prudence, he will abandon by little and little his weak-
est posts, till at length he seems to forget that they had ever belonged to him, or affects to consider them at most as accidental
and "petty annexments," the removal of which leaves the citadel
unhurt and unendangered.

My own differences from certain supposed parts of Mr. Words-

worth's theory ground themselves on the assumption, that his
words had been rightly interpreted, as purporting that the proper
diction for poetry in general consists altogether in a language
taken, with due exceptions, from the mouths of men in real life,
a language which actually constitutes the natural conversation of
men under the influence of natural feelings. My objection is, first,
that in *any* sense this rule is applicable only to *certain* classes of
poetry; secondly, that even to these classes it is not applicable,
except in such a sense, as hath never by any one (as far as I know
or have read) been denied or doubted; and lastly, that as far as,
and in that degree in which it is *practicable*, yet as a *rule* it is
useless, if not injurious, and therefore either need not, or ought
not to be practised. The poet informs his reader, that he had generally chosen *low and rustic* life; but not *as* low and rustic, or in
order to repeat that pleasure of doubtful moral effect, which persons of elevated rank and of superior refinement oftentimes derive
from a happy *imitation* of the rude unpolished manners and discourse of their inferiors. For the pleasure so derived may be traced
to three exciting causes. The first is the naturalness, in *fact*, of the
things represented. The second is the apparent naturalness of the
*representation*, as raised and qualified by an imperceptible infusion of the author's own knowledge and talent, which infusion
does, indeed, constitute it an *imitation* as distinguished from a
mere *copy*. The third cause may be found in the reader's conscious
feeling of his superiority awakened by the contrast presented to
him; even as for the same purpose the kings and great barons of
yore retained sometimes *actual* clowns and fools, but more frequently shrewd and witty fellows in that *character*. These, however, were not Mr. Wordsworth's objects. *He* chose low and rustic
life, "because in that condition the essential passions of the heart
find a better soil, in which they can attain their maturity, are less
under restraint, and speak a plainer and more emphatic language;
because in that condition of life our elementary feelings co-exist
in a state of greater simplicity, and consequently may be more
accurately contemplated, and more forcibly communicated; because the manners of rural life germinate from those elementary
feelings; and from the necessary character of rural occupations are

more easily comprehended, and are more durable; and lastly, because in that condition the passions of men are incorporated with the beautiful and permanent forms of nature."

Now it is clear to me, that in the most interesting of the poems, in which the author is more or less dramatic, as "the Brothers," "Michael," "Ruth," "the Mad Mother," &c., the persons introduced are by no means taken *from low or rustic life* in the common acceptation of those words; and it is not less clear, that the sentiments and language, as far as they can be conceived to have been really transferred from the minds and conversation of such persons, are attributable to causes and circumstances not necessarily connected with "their occupations and abode." The thoughts, feelings, language, and manners of the shepherd-farmers in the vales of Cumberland and Westmoreland, as far as they are actually adopted in those poems, may be accounted for from causes, which will and do produce the same results in *every* state of life, whether in town or country. As the two principal I rank that INDEPENDENCE, which raises a man above servitude, or daily toil for the profit of others, yet not above the necessity of industry and a frugal simplicity of domestic life; and the accompanying unambitious, but solid and religious, EDUCATION, which has rendered few books familiar, but the Bible, and the liturgy or hymn book. To this latter cause, indeed, which is so far *accidental*, that it is the blessing of particular countries and a particular age, not the product of particular places or employments, the poet owes the show of probability, that his personages might really feel, think, and talk with any tolerable resemblance to his representation. It is an excellent remark of Dr. Henry More's, (Enthusiasmus triumphatus, Sec. XXXV.), that "a man of confined education, but of good parts, by constant reading of the Bible will naturally form a more winning and commanding rhetoric than those that are learned; the intermixture of tongues and of artificial phrases debasing *their* style."

It is, moreover, to be considered that to the formation of healthy feelings, and a reflecting mind, *negations* involve impediments not less formidable than sophistication and vicious intermixture. I am convinced, that for the human soul to prosper in rustic life a certain vantage-ground is pre-requisite. It is not every man that is likely to be improved by a country life or by country labors. Education, or original sensibility, or both, must pre-exist, if the changes, forms, and incidents of nature are to prove a sufficient stimulant. And where these are not sufficient, the mind contracts and hardens by want of stimulants: and the man becomes selfish, sensual, gross, and hard-hearted. Let the management of the Poor Laws in Liverpool, Manchester, or Bristol be compared with the ordinary dispensation of the poor rates in agricultural villages, where the *farmers* are the overseers and guardians of the poor. If my own experience have not been particularly unfortunate, as well as that of the many respectable country clergymen with whom I have conversed on the subject, the result would engender more than scepticism concerning the desireable influences of low and rustic life in and for itself. Whatever may be concluded on the other side, from the stronger local attachments and enterprising spirit of the Swiss, and other mountaineers, applies to a particular mode of pastoral life, under forms of property that permit and beget manners truly republican, not to rustic life in general, or to the absence of artificial cultivation. On the contrary the mountaineers, whose manners have been so often eulogized, are in general better educated and greater readers than men of equal rank elsewhere. But where this is not the case, as among the peasantry of North Wales, the ancient mountains, with all their terrors and all their glories, are pictures to the blind, and music to the deaf.

I should not have entered so much into detail upon this passage, but here seems to be the point, to which all the lines of difference converge as to their source and centre. (I mean, as far as, and in whatever respect, my poetic creed *does* differ from the doctrines promulged in this preface.) I adopt with full faith the principle of Aristotle, that poetry as poetry is essentially* *ideal*, that it

---

* Say not that I am recommending abstractions; for these class-characteristics which constitute the instructiveness of a character, are so modified and particularized in each person of the Shakespearean Drama, that life itself does not excite more distinctly that sense of individuality which belongs to real existence. Paradoxical as it may sound, one of the essential properties of Geometry is not less essential to dramatic excellence; and Aristotle has

avoids and excludes all *accident;* that its apparent individualities
of rank, character, or occupation must be *representative* of a class;
and that the *persons* of poetry must be clothed with *generic* attributes, with the *common* attributes of the class: not with such
as one gifted individual might *possibly* possess, but such as from
his situation it is most probable before-hand that he *would* possess.
If my premises are right and my deductions legitimate, it follows
that there can be no *poetic* medium between the swains of Theocritus and those of an imaginary golden age.

The characters of the vicar and the shepherd-mariner in the
poem of "THE BROTHERS," that of the shepherd of Greenhead
Ghyll in the "MICHAEL," have all the verisimilitude and representative quality, that the purposes of poetry can require. They
are persons of a known and abiding class, and their manners and
sentiments the natural product of circumstances common to the
class. Take "MICHAEL" for instance:

> An old man stout of heart, and strong of limb:
> His bodily frame had been from youth to age
> Of an unusual strength: his mind was keen,

---

accordingly required of the poet an involution of the universal in the individual. The chief differences are, that in Geometry it is the universal truth,
which is uppermost in the consciousness; in poetry the individual form, in
which the truth is clothed. With the ancients, and not less with the elder
dramatists of England and France, both comedy and tragedy were considered as kinds of poetry. They neither sought in comedy to make us laugh
merely; much less to make us laugh by wry faces, accidents of jargon, *slang*
phrases for the day, or the clothing of common-place morals drawn from
the shops or mechanic occupations of their characters. Nor did they con-
descend in tragedy to wheedle away the applause of the spectators, by representing before them facsimiles of their own mean selves in all their existing
meanness, or to work on the sluggish sympathies by a pathos not a whit
more respectable than the maudlin tears of drunkenness. Their tragic scenes
were meant to *affect* us indeed; but yet within the bounds of pleasure, and
in union with the activity both of our understanding and imagination. They
wished to transport the mind to a sense of its possible greatness, and to
implant the germs of that greatness, during the temporary oblivion of the
worthless "thing we are," and of the peculiar state in which each man
*happens* to be, suspending our individual recollections and lulling them to
sleep amid the music of nobler thoughts.

Intense, and frugal, apt for all affairs,
And in his shepherd's calling he was prompt
And watchful more than ordinary men.
Hence he had learnt the meaning of all winds,
Of blasts of every tone; and oftentimes
When others heeded not, he heard the South
Make subterraneous music, like the noise          10
Of bagpipers on distant Highland hills.
The shepherd, at such warning, of his flock
Bethought him, and he to himself would say,
The winds are now devising work for me!
And truly at all times the storm, that drives
The traveller to a shelter, summon'd him
Up to the mountains. He had been alone
Amid the heart of many thousand mists,
That came to him and left him on the heights.
So liv'd he, till his eightieth year was pass'd.          20
And grossly that man errs, who should suppose
That the green vallies, and the streams and rocks,
Were things indifferent to the shepherd's thoughts.
Fields, where with chearful spirits he had breath'd
The common air; the hills, which he so oft
Had climb'd with vigorous steps; which had impress'd
So many incidents upon his mind
Of hardship, skill or courage, joy or fear;
Which, like a book, preserved the memory
Of the dumb animals, whom he had sav'd,          30
Had fed or shelter'd, linking to such acts,
So grateful in themselves, the certainty
Of honorable gain; these fields, these hills
Which were his living being, even more
Than his own blood—what could they less? had laid
Strong hold on his affections, were to him
A pleasureable feeling of blind love,
The pleasure which there is in life itself.

On the other hand, in the poems which are pitched at a lower note, as the "HARRY GILL," "IDIOT BOY," the *feelings* are those of human nature in general; though the poet has judiciously laid the *scene* in the country, in order to place *himself* in the vicinity of interesting images, without the necessity of ascribing a sentimental perception of their beauty to the persons of his drama. In the "Idiot Boy," indeed, the mother's character is not so much a real and native product of a "situation where the essential passions of the heart find a better soil, in which they can attain their maturity and speak a plainer and more emphatic language," as it is an impersonation of an instinct abandoned by judgement. Hence the two following charges seem to me not wholly groundless: at least, they are the only plausible objections, which I have heard to that fine poem. The one is, that the author has not, in the poem itself, taken sufficient care to preclude from the reader's fancy the disgusting images of *ordinary morbid idiocy,* which yet it was by no means his intention to represent. He has even by the "burr, burr, burr," uncounteracted by any preceding description of the boy's beauty, assisted in recalling them. The other is, that the idiocy of the *boy* is so evenly balanced by the folly of the *mother,* as to present to the general reader rather a laughable burlesque on the blindness of anile dotage, than an analytic display of maternal affection in its ordinary workings.

In the "Thorn" the poet himself acknowledges in a note the necessity of an introductory poem, in which he should have pourtrayed the character of the person from whom the words of the poem are supposed to proceed: a superstitious man moderately imaginative, of slow faculties and deep feelings, "a captain of a small trading vessel, for example, who, being past the middle age of life, had retired upon an annuity, or small independent income, to some village or country town of which he was not a native, or in which he had not been accustomed to live. Such men having nothing to do become credulous and talkative from indolence." But in a poem, still more in a lyric poem (and the Nurse in Shakespeare's Romeo and Juliet alone prevents me from extending the remark even to dramatic *poetry,* if indeed the Nurse itself can be deemed altogether a case in point) it is not possible to imitate truly a dull and garrulous discourser, without repeating the effects of dullness and garrulity. However this may be, I dare assert, that the parts (and these form the far larger portion of the whole) which might as well or still better have proceeded from the poet's own imagination, and have been spoken in his own character, are those which have given, and which will continue to give, universal delight; and that the passages exclusively appropriate to the supposed narrator, such as the last couplet of the third stanza;* the seven last lines of the tenth;† and the five following stanzas, with the exception of the four admirable lines at the commencement of the fourteenth, are felt by many unpreju-

---

\* I've measured it from side to side;
'Tis three feet long, and two feet wide.

† Nay, rack your brain—'tis all in vain,
I'll tell you every thing I know;
But to the Thorn, and to the Pond
Which is a little step beyond,
I wish that you would go:
Perhaps when you are at the place,
You something of her tale may trace.

I'll give you the best help I can:
Before you up the mountain go,
Up to the dreary mountain-top,                                    10
I'll tell you all I know.
'Tis now some two-and-twenty years
Since she (her name is Martha Ray)
Gave, with a maiden's true good will,
Her company to Stephen Hill;
And she was blithe and gay,
And she was happy, happy still
Whene'er she thought of Stephen Hill.

And they had fix'd the wedding-day,
The morning that must wed them both;                              20
But Stephen to another maid
Had sworn another oath;
And, with this other maid, to church
Unthinking Stephen went—
Poor Martha! on that woeful day
A pang of pitiless dismay
Into her soul was sent;
A fire was kindled in her breast,
Which might not burn itself to rest.

They say, full six months after this,                            30
While yet the summer leaves were green,
She to the mountain-top would go,
And there was often seen.
'Tis said a child was in her womb,

diced and unsophisticated hearts, as sudden and unpleasant sink-
ings from the height to which the poet had previously lifted them,
and to which he again re-elevates both himself and his reader.

If then I am compelled to doubt the theory, by which the choice
of *characters* was to be directed, not only *à priori,* from grounds of
reason, but both from the few instances in which the poet himself
*need* be supposed to have been governed by it, and from the comparative inferiority of those instances; still more must I hesitate
in my assent to the sentence which immediately follows the former
citation; and which I can neither admit as particular fact, or as
general rule. "The language too of these men is adopted (purified
indeed from what appear to be its real defects, from all lasting and
rational causes of dislike or disgust) because such men hourly
communicate with the best objects from which the best part of
language is originally derived; and because, from their rank in

As now to any eye was plain;
She was with child, and she was mad;
Yet often she was sober sad
From her exceeding pain.
Oh me! ten thousand times I'd rather
That he had died, that cruel father!          40
\*     \*     \*     \*     \*     \*

Last Christmas when we talked of this,
Old farmer Simpson did maintain,
That in her womb the infant wrought
About its mother's heart, and brought
Her senses back again:
And, when at last her time drew near,
Her looks were calm, her senses clear.

No more I know, I wish I did,
And I would tell it all to you:
For what became of this poor child          50
There's none that ever knew:
And if a child was born or no,
There's no one that could ever tell;
And if 'twas born alive or dead,
There's no one knows, as I have said:
But some remember well,
That Martha Ray about this time
Would up the mountain often climb.

society and the sameness and narrow circle of their intercourse, being less under the action of social vanity, they convey their feelings and notions in simple and unelaborated expressions." To this I reply; that a rustic's language, purified from all provincialism and grossness, and so far reconstructed as to be made consistent with the rules of grammar (which are in essence no other than the laws of universal logic, applied to psychological materials) will not differ from the language of any other man of commonsense, however learned or refined he may be, except as far as the notions, which the rustic has to convey, are fewer and more indiscriminate. This will become still clearer, if we add the consideration (equally important though less obvious) that the rustic, from the more imperfect developement of his faculties, and from the lower state of their cultivation, aims almost solely to convey *insulated facts,* either those of his scanty experience or his traditional belief; while the educated man chiefly seeks to discover and express those *connections* of things, or those relative *bearings* of fact to fact, from which some more or less general law is deducible. For *facts* are valuable to a wise man, chiefly as they lead to the discovery of the indwelling *law,* which is the true *being* of things, the sole solution of their modes of existence, and in the knowledge of which consists our dignity and our power.

As little can I agree with the assertion, that from the objects with which the rustic hourly communicates the best part of language is formed. For first, if to communicate with an object implies such an acquaintance with it, as renders it capable of being discriminately reflected on; the distinct knowledge of an uneducated rustic would furnish a very scanty vocabulary. The few things, and modes of action, requisite for his bodily conveniences, would alone be individualized; while all the rest of nature would be expressed by a small number of confused general terms. Secondly, I deny that the words and combinations of words derived from the objects, with which the rustic is familiar, whether with distinct or confused knowledge, can be justly said to form the *best* part of language. It is more than probable, that many classes of the brute creation possess discriminating sounds, by which they can convey to each other notices of such objects as concern their food, shelter, or safety. Yet we hesitate to call the aggregate of such sounds a language, otherwise than metaphorically. The best part of human language, properly so called, is derived from reflection on the acts of the mind itself. It is formed by a voluntary appropriation of fixed symbols to internal acts, to processes and results of imagination, the greater part of which have no place in the consciousness of un-educated man; though in civilized society, by imitation and passive remembrance of what they hear from their religious instructors and other superiors, the most uneducated share in the harvest which they neither sowed or reaped. If the history of the phrases in hourly currency among our peasants were traced, a person not previously aware of the fact would be surprised at finding so large a number, which three or four centuries ago were the exclusive property of the universities and the schools; and, at the commence-ment of the Reformation, had been transferred from the school to the pulpit, and thus gradually passed into common life. The ex-treme difficulty, and often the impossibility, of finding words for the simplest moral and intellectual processes of the languages of uncivilized tribes has proved perhaps the weightiest obstacle to the progress of our most zealous and adroit missionaries. Yet these tribes are surrounded by the same nature as our peasants are; but in still more impressive forms; and they are, moreover, obliged to *particularize* many more of them. When, therefore, Mr. Words-worth adds, "accordingly, such a language" (meaning, as before, the language of rustic life purified from provincialism) "arising out of repeated experience and regular feelings, is a more permanent, and a far more philosophical language, than that which is fre-quently substituted for it by poets, who think they are conferring honor upon themselves and their art in proportion as they indulge in arbitrary and capricious habits of expression:" it may be an-swered, that the language, which he has in view, can be attributed to rustics with no greater right, than the style of Hooker or Bacon to Tom Brown or Sir Roger L'Estrange. Doubtless, if what is pecul-iar to each were omitted in each, the result must needs be the same. Further, that the poet, who uses an illogical diction, or a style fitted to excite only the low and changeable pleasure of won-der by means of groundless novelty, substitutes a language of *folly* and *vanity*, not for that of the *rustic*, but for that of *good sense* and *natural feeling*.

Here let me be permitted to remind the reader, that the positions, which I controvert, are contained in the sentences—"*a selection of the* REAL *language of men;*"—"*the language of these men*" (i.e. men in low and rustic life) "*I propose to myself to imitate, and, as far as is possible, to adopt the very language of men.*" "*Between the language of prose and that of metrical composition, there neither is, nor can be any essential difference.*" It is against these exclusively that my opposition is directed.

I object, in the very first instance, to an equivocation in the use of the word "real." Every man's language varies, according to the extent of his knowledge, the activity of his faculties, and the depth or quickness of his feelings. Every man's language has, first, its *individualities;* secondly, the common properties of the *class* to which he belongs; and thirdly, words and phrases of *universal* use. The language of Hooker, Bacon, Bishop Taylor, and Burke differs from the common language of the learned class only by the superior number and novelty of the thoughts and relations which they had to convey. The language of Algernon Sidney differs not at all from that, which every well-educated gentleman would wish to write, and (with due allowances for the undeliberateness, and less connected train, of thinking natural and proper to conversation) such as he would wish to talk. Neither one nor the other differ half so much from the general language of cultivated society, as the language of Mr. Wordsworth's homeliest composition differs from that of a common peasant. For "real" therefore, we must substitute *ordinary*, or *lingua communis*. And this, we have proved, is no more to be found in the phraseology of low and rustic life than in that of any other class. Omit the peculiarities of each, and the result of course must be common to all. And assuredly the omissions and changes to be made in the language of rustics, before it could be transferred to any species of poem, except the drama or other professed imitation, are at least as numerous and weighty, as would be required in adapting to the same purpose the ordinary language of tradesmen and manufacturers. Not to mention, that the language so highly extolled by Mr. Wordsworth varies in every county, nay in every village, according to the accidental character of the clergyman, the existence or non-existence of schools; or even, perhaps, as the exciseman, publican, or barber, happen to be, or not to be, zealous politicians, and readers of the weekly newspaper *pro bono publico*. Anterior to cultivation, the lingua communis of every country, as Dante has well observed, exists every where in parts, and no where as a whole.

Neither is the case rendered at all more tenable by the addition of the words, *in a state of excitement*. For the nature of a man's words, where he is strongly affected by joy, grief, or anger, must necessarily depend on the number and quality of the general truths, conceptions and images, and of the words expressing them, with which his mind had been previously stored. For the property of passion is not to *create*; but to set in increased activity. At least, whatever new connections of thoughts or images, or (which is equally, if not more than equally, the appropriate effect of strong excitement) whatever generalizations of truth or experience, the heat of passion may produce; yet the terms of their conveyance must have pre-existed in his former conversations, and are only collected and crowded together by the unusual stimulation. It is indeed very possible to adopt in a poem the unmeaning repetitions, habitual phrases, and other blank counters, which an unfurnished or confused understanding interposes at short intervals, in order to keep hold of his subject, which is still slipping from him, and to give him time for recollection; or in mere aid of vacancy, as in the scanty companies of a country stage the same player pops backwards and forwards, in order to prevent the appearance of empty spaces, in the procession of Macbeth, or Henry VIIIth. But what assistance to the poet, or ornament to the poem, these can supply, I am at a loss to conjecture. Nothing assuredly can differ either in origin or in mode more widely from the *apparent* tautologies of intense and turbulent feeling, in which the passion is greater and of longer endurance than to be exhausted or satisfied by a single representation of the image or incident exciting it. Such repetitions I admit to be a beauty of the highest kind; as illustrated by Mr. Wordsworth himself from the song of Deborah. *"At her*

feet he bowed, he fell, he lay down; at her feet he bowed, he fell;
where he bowed, there he fell down dead."


## CHAPTER XVIII

*Language of metrical composition, why and wherein essentially different
from that of prose—Origin and elements of metre—Its necessary consequences, and the conditions thereby imposed on the metrical writer in the
choice of his diction.*


I conclude, therefore, that the attempt is impracticable; and that,
were it not impracticable, it would still be useless. For the very
power of making the selection implies the previous possession of
the language selected. Or where can the poet have lived? And by
what rules could he direct his choice, which would not have enabled him to select and arrange his words by the light of his own
judgement? We do not adopt the language of a class by the mere
adoption of such words exclusively, as that class would use, or at
least understand; but likewise by following the *order,* in which
the words of such men are wont to succeed each other. Now this
order, in the intercourse of uneducated men, is distinguished from
the diction of their superiors in knowledge and power, by the
greater *disjunction* and *separation* in the component parts of that,
whatever it be, which they wish to communicate. There is a want
of that prospectiveness of mind, that *surview,* which enables a
man to foresee the whole of what he is to convey, appertaining to
any one point; and by this means so to subordinate and arrange the
different parts according to their relative importance, as to convey
it at once, and as an organized whole.

Now I will take the first stanza, on which I have chanced to
open, in the Lyrical Ballads. It is one the most simple and the
least peculiar in its language.

> In distant countries have I been,
> And yet I have not often seen
> A healthy man, a man full grown,
> Weep in the public roads alone.

> But such a one, on English ground,
> And in the broad highway, I met;
> Along the broad highway he came,
> His cheeks with tears were wet:
> Sturdy he seem'd, though he was sad;
> And in his arms a lamb he had.

The words here are doubtless such as are current in all ranks of life; and of course not less so in the hamlet and cottage than in the shop, manufactory, college, or palace. But is this the *order,* in which the rustic would have placed the words? I am grievously deceived, if the following less *compact* mode of commencing the same tale be not a far more faithful copy. "I have been in a many parts, far and near, and I don't know that I ever saw before a man crying by himself in the public road; a grown man I mean, that was neither sick nor hurt," &c., &c. But when I turn to the following stanza in "The Thorn":

> At all times of the day and night
> This wretched woman thither goes,
> And she is known to every star,
> And every wind that blows:
> And there, beside the thorn, she sits,
> When the blue day-light's in the skies;
> And when the whirlwind's on the hill,
> Or frosty air is keen and still;
> And to herself she cries,
> Oh misery! Oh misery!
> Oh woe is me! Oh misery!

and compare this with the language of ordinary men; or with that which I can conceive at all likely to proceed, in *real* life, from *such* a narrator, as is supposed in the note to the poem; compare it either in the succession of the images or of the sentences; I am reminded of the sublime prayer and hymn of praise, which MILTON, in opposition to an established liturgy, presents as a fair *specimen* of common extemporary devotion, and such as we might expect to hear from every self-inspired minister of a conventicle! And I reflect with delight, how little a mere theory, though of his own workmanship, interferes with the processes of genuine imagination in a man of true poetic genius, who possesses, as Mr. Wordsworth, if ever man did, most assuredly does possess,

## "THE VISION AND THE FACULTY DIVINE."

One point then alone remains, but that the most important; its examination having been, indeed, my chief inducement for the preceding inquisition. *"There neither is or can be any essential difference between the language of prose and metrical composition."* Such is Mr. Wordsworth's assertion. Now prose itself, at least in all argumentative and consecutive works, differs, and ought to differ, from the language of conversation; even as* reading ought to differ from talking. Unless therefore the difference denied be that of the mere *words,* as materials common to all styles of writing, and not of the *style* itself in the universally admitted sense of the term, it might be naturally presumed that there must exist a still greater between the ordonnance of poetic composition and that of prose, than is expected to distinguish prose from ordinary conversation.

---

* It is no less an error in teachers, than a torment to the poor children, to inforce the necessity of reading as they would talk. In order to cure them of *singing* as it is called, that is, of too great a difference, the child is made to repeat the words with his eyes from off the book; and then, indeed, his tones resemble talking, as far as his fears, tears and trembling will permit. But as soon as his eye is again directed to the printed page, the spell begins anew; for an instinctive sense tells the child's feelings, that to utter its own momentary thoughts, and to recite the written thoughts of another, as of another, and a far wiser than himself, are two widely different things; and as the two acts are accompanied with widely different feelings, so must they justify different modes of enunciation. Joseph Lancaster, among his other sophistications of the excellent Dr. Bell's invaluable system, cures this fault of *singing,* by hanging fetters and chains on the child, to the music of which one of his school-fellows, who walks before, dolefully chaunts out the child's last speech and confession, birth, parentage, and education. And this soul-benumbing ignominy, this unholy and heart-hardening burlesque on the last fearful infliction of outraged law, in pronouncing the sentence to which the stern and familiarized judge not seldom bursts into tears, has been extolled as a happy and ingenious method of remedying—what? and how?—why, one extreme in order to introduce another, scarce less distant from good sense, and certainly likely to have worse moral effects, by enforcing a semblance of petulant ease and self-sufficiency, in repression, and possible after-perversion of the natural feelings. I have to beg Dr. Bell's pardon for this connection of the two names, but he knows that contrast is no less powerful a cause of association than likeness.

There are not, indeed, examples wanting in the history of literature, of apparent paradoxes that have summoned the public wonder as new and startling truths, but which on examination have
shrunk into tame and harmless *truisms;* as the eyes of a cat, seen
in the dark, have been mistaken for flames of fire. But Mr. Wordsworth is among the last men, to whom a delusion of this kind
would be attributed by anyone, who had enjoyed the slightest opportunity of understanding his mind and character. Where an
objection has been anticipated by such an author as natural, his
answer to it must needs be interpreted in some sense which either
is, or has been, or is capable of being controverted. My object then
must be to discover some other meaning for the term *"essential
difference"* in this place, exclusive of the indistinction and com-
munity of the words themselves. For whether there ought to exist
a class of words in the English, in any degree resembling the poetic
dialect of the Greek and Italian, is a question of very subordinate
importance. The number of such words would be small indeed, in
our language; and even in the Italian and Greek, they consist not
so much of different words, as of slight differences in the *forms*
of declining and conjugating the same words; forms, doubtless,
which having been, at some period more or less remote, the common grammatic flexions of some tribe or province, had been accidentally appropriated to poetry by the general admiration of certain master intellects, the first established lights of inspiration, to
whom that dialect happened to be native.

Essence, in its primary signification, means the principle of *in-
dividuation,* the inmost principle of the possibility of any thing, as
that particular thing. It is equivalent to the *idea* of a thing, when
ever we use the word, idea, with philosophic precision. Existence,
on the other hand, is distinguished from essence, by the super-
induction of *reality.* Thus we speak of the essence, and essential
properties of a circle; but we do not therefore assert, that any thing,
which really exists, is mathematically circular. Thus too, without
any tautology we contend for the *existence* of the Supreme Being;
that is, for a reality correspondent to the idea. There is, next, a
*secondary* use of the word essence, in which it signifies the point

or ground of contra-distinction between two modifications of the
same substance or subject. Thus we should be allowed to say, that
the style of architecture of Westminster Abbey is *essentially* different from that of St. Paul's, even though both had been built with
blocks cut into the same form, and from the same quarry. Only
in this latter sense of the term must it have been *denied* by Mr.
Wordsworth (for in this sense alone is it *affirmed* by the general
opinion) that the language of poetry (i.e. the formal construction,
or architecture, of the words and phrases) is *essentially* different
from that of prose. Now the burthen of the proof lies with the
oppugner, not with the supporters of the common belief. Mr.
Wordsworth, in consequence, assigns as the proof of his position,
"that not only the language of a large portion of every good poem,
even of the most elevated character, must necessarily, except with
reference to the metre, in no respect differ from that of good prose,
but likewise that some of the most interesting parts of the best
poems will be found to be strictly the language of prose, when
prose is well written. The truth of this assertion might be demonstrated by innumerable passages from almost all the poetical writings even of Milton himself." He then quotes Gray's sonnet—

> In vain to me the smiling mornings shine,
> And redding Phœbus lifts his golden fire;
> The birds in vain their amorous descant join,
> Or chearful fields resume their green attire.
> These ears, alas! for other notes repine;
> *A different object do these eyes require;*
> *My lonely anguish melts no heart but mine;*
> *And in my breast the imperfect joys expire.*
> Yet morning smiles the busy race to cheer,
> And newborn pleasure brings to happier men:
> The fields to all their wonted tribute bear,
> To warm their little loves the birds complain.
> *I fruitless mourn to him that cannot hear,*
> *And weep the more because I weep in vain,*

and adds the following remark:—"It will easily be perceived, that
the only part of this Sonnet, which is of any value, is the lines
printed in italics. It is equally obvious, that, except in the rhyme,

and in the use of the single word 'fruitless' for 'fruitlessly,' which is so far a defect, the language of these lines does in no respect differ from that of prose."

An idealist defending his system by the fact, that when asleep we often believe ourselves awake, was well answered by his plain neighbour, "Ah, but when awake do we ever believe ourselves asleep?"—Things identical must be convertible. The preceding passage seems to rest on a similar sophism. For the question is not, whether there may not occur in prose an order of words, which would be equally proper in a poem; nor whether there are not beautiful lines and sentences of frequent occurrence in good poems, which would be equally becoming as well as beautiful in good prose; for neither the one nor the other has ever been either denied or doubted by any one. The true question must be, whether there are not modes of expression, a *construction,* and an *order* of sentences, which are in their fit and natural place in a serious prose composition, but would be disproportionate and heterogeneous in metrical poetry; and, vice versa, whether in the language of a serious poem there may not be an arrangement both of words and sentences, and a use and selection of (what are called) *figures of speech,* both as to their kind, their frequency, and their occasions, which on a subject of equal weight would be vicious and alien in correct and manly prose. I contend that in both cases this unfitness of each for the place of the other frequently will and ought to exist.

And first from the *origin* of metre. This I would trace to the balance in the mind effected by that spontaneous effort which strives to hold in check the workings of passion. It might be easily explained likewise in what manner this salutary antagonism is assisted by the very state, which it counteracts; and how this balance of antagonists became organized into *metre* (in the usual acceptation of that term) by a supervening act of the will and judgement, consciously and for the foreseen purpose of pleasure. Assuming these principles, as the data of our argument, we deduce from them two legitimate conditions, which the critic is entitled to expect in every metrical work. First, that, as the *elements* of metre owe their existence to a state of increased excitement, so the metre itself should be accompanied by the natural language of excitement. Secondly, that as these elements are formed into metre *artificially*, by a *voluntary* act, with the design and for the purpose of blending *delight* with emotion, so the traces of present *volition* should throughout the metrical language be proportionately discernible. Now these two conditions must be reconciled and co-present. There must be not only a partnership, but a union; an interpenetration of passion and of will, of *spontaneous* impulse and of *voluntary* purpose. Again, this union can be manifested only in a frequency of forms and figures of speech (originally the offspring of passion, but now the adopted children of power) greater than would be desired or endured, where the emotion is not voluntarily encouraged and kept up for the sake of that pleasure, which such emotion, so tempered and mastered by the will, is found capable of communicating. It not only dictates, but of itself tends to produce, a more frequent employment of picturesque and vivifying language, than would be natural in any other case, in which there did not exist, as there does in the present, a previous and well understood, though tacit, *compact* between the poet and his reader, that the latter is entitled to expect, and the former bound to supply, this species and degree of pleasureable excitement. We may in some measure apply to this union the answer of POLIXENES, in the Winter's Tale, to PERDITA's neglect of the streaked gilly-flowers, because she had heard it said,

> There is an art which, in their piedness, shares
> With great creating nature.
> > *Pol:* Say there be;
> Yet nature is made better by no mean,
> But nature makes that mean; so, ev'n that art,
> Which, you say, adds to nature, is an art,
> That nature makes. You see, sweet maid, we marry
> *A gentler scyon to the wildest stock;*
> And make conceive a bark of ruder kind
> By bud of nobler race. This is an art,
> Which does mend nature—change it rather; but
> The art itself is nature.

Secondly, I argue from the EFFECTS of metre. As far as metre acts in and for itself, it tends to increase the vivacity and susceptibility both of the general feelings and of the attention. This effect it produces by the continued excitement of surprize, and by the quick reciprocations of curiosity still gratified and still re-excited, which are too slight indeed to be at any one moment objects of distinct consciousness, yet become considerable in their aggregate influence. As a medicated atmosphere, or as wine during animated conversation; they act powerfully, though themselves unnoticed. Where, therefore, correspondent food and appropriate matter are not provided for the attention and feelings thus roused, there must needs be a disappointment felt; like that of leaping in the dark from the last step of a stair-case, when we had prepared our muscles for a leap of three or four.

The discussion on the powers of metre in the preface is highly ingenious and touches at all points on truth. But I cannot find any statement of its powers considered abstractly and separately. On the contrary Mr. Wordsworth seems always to estimate metre by the powers, which it exerts during (and, as I think, in *consequence of*) its combination with other elements of poetry. Thus the previous difficulty is left unanswered, *what* the elements are, with which it must be combined in order to produce its own effects to any pleasureable purpose. Double and tri-syllable rhymes, indeed, form a lower species of wit, and, attended to exclusively for their own sake, may become a source of momentary amusement; as in poor Smart's distich to the Welsh 'Squire who had promised him a hare:

> Tell me, thou son of great Cadwallader!
> Hast sent the hare? or hast thou swallow'd her?

But for any *poetic* purposes, metre resembles (if the aptness of the simile may excuse its meanness) yeast, worthless or disagreeable by itself, but giving vivacity and spirit to the liquor with which it is proportionally combined.

The reference to the "Children in the Wood," by no means satisfies my judgement. We all willingly throw ourselves back for awhile into the feelings of our childhood. This ballad, therefore, we read under such recollections of our own childish feelings, as would equally endear to us poems, which Mr. Wordsworth himself would regard as faulty in the opposite extreme of gaudy and technical ornament. Before the invention of printing, and in a still greater degree, before the introduction of writing, metre, especially *alliterative* metre (whether alliterative at the beginning of the words, as in "Pierce Plouman," or at the end as in rhymes) possessed an independent value as assisting the recollection, and consequently the preservation, of *any* series of truths or incidents. But I am not convinced by the collation of facts, that the "Children in the Wood" owes either its preservation, or its popularity, to its metrical form. Mr. Marshal's repository affords a number of tales in prose inferior in pathos and general merit, some of as old a date, and many as widely popular. "TOM HICKATHRIFT," "JACK THE GIANT-KILLER," "GOODY TWO-SHOES," and "LITTLE RED RIDING-HOOD" are formidable rivals. And that they have continued in prose, cannot be fairly explained by the assumption, that the comparative meanness of their thoughts and images precluded even the humblest forms of metre. The scene of GOODY TWO-SHOES in the church is perfectly susceptible of metrical narration; and, among the Θαύματα θαυμαστότατα even of the present age, I do not recollect a more astonishing image than that of the *"whole rookery, that flew out of the giant's beard,"* scared by the tremendous voice, with which this monster answered the challenge of the heroic TOM HICKATHRIFT!

If from these we turn to compositions universally, and independently of all early associations, beloved and admired; would "THE MARIA," "THE MONK," or "THE POOR MAN'S ASS" of Sterne, be read with more delight, or have a better chance of immortality, had they without any change in the diction been composed in rhyme, than in their present state? If I am not grossly mistaken, the general reply would be in the negative. Nay, I will confess, that, in Mr. Wordsworth's own volumes, the "ANECDOTE FOR FATHERS," "SIMON LEE," "ALICE FELL," "THE BEGGARS," and "THE SAILOR'S MOTHER," notwithstanding the beauties which are to be found in each of them where the poet interposes the music of his own thoughts, would have been more delightful to me in prose, told and managed, as by Mr. Wordsworth they would have been, in a moral essay, or pedestrian tour.

Metre in itself is simply a stimulant of the attention, and there-

fore excites the question: Why is the attention to be thus stimulated? Now the question cannot be answered by the pleasure of
the metre itself: for this we have shown to be *conditional,* and
dependent on the appropriateness of the thoughts and expressions,
to which the metrical form is superadded. Neither can I conceive
any other answer that can be rationally given, short of this: I write
in metre, because I am about to use a language different from that
of prose. Besides, where the language is not such, how interesting
soever the reflections are, that are capable of being drawn by a
philosophic mind from the thoughts or incidents of the poem, the
metre itself must often become feeble. Take the last three stanzas
of "THE SAILOR'S MOTHER," for instance. If I could for a moment
abstract from the effect produced on the author's feelings, as a man,
by the incident at the time of its real occurrence, I would dare appeal to his own judgement, whether in the *metre* itself he found
a sufficient reason for *their* being written *metrically?*

> And, thus continuing, she said,
> I had a son, who many a day
> Sailed on the seas; but he is dead;
> In Denmark he was cast away:
> And I have travelled far as Hull, to see
> What clothes he might have left, or other property.

> The bird and cage they both were his:
> 'Twas my son's bird; and neat and trim
> He kept it: many voyages
> This singing-bird hath gone with him;
> When last he sailed he left the bird behind;
> As it might be, perhaps, from bodings of his mind.

> He to a fellow-lodger's care
> Had left it, to be watched and fed,
> Till he came back again; and there
> I found it when my son was dead;
> And now, God help me for my little wit!
> I trail it with me, Sir! he took so much delight in it.

If disproportioning the emphasis we read these stanzas so as
to make the rhymes perceptible, even *tri-syllable* rhymes could
scarcely produce an equal sense of oddity and strangeness, as we
feel here in finding *rhymes at all* in sentences so exclusively collo-

quial. I would further ask whether, but for that visionary state, into which the figure of the woman and the susceptibility of his own genius had placed the poet's imagination, (a state, which spreads its influence and coloring over all, that co-exists with the exciting cause, and in which

> The simplest, and the most familiar things
> Gain a strange power of spreading awe around * them,)

I would ask the poet whether he would not have felt an abrupt downfall in these verses from the preceding stanza?

> The ancient spirit is not dead;
> Old times, thought I, are breathing there;
> Proud was I that my country bred
> Such strength, a dignity so fair:
> She begged an alms, like one in poor estate;
> I looked at her again, nor did my pride abate.

It must not be omitted, and is besides worthy of notice, that those stanzas furnish the only fair instance that I have been able to discover in all Mr. Wordsworth's writings, of an *actual* adoption, or true imitation, of the *real* and *very* language of *low and rustic life,* freed from provincialisms.

Thirdly, I deduce the position from all the causes elsewhere assigned, which render metre the proper form of poetry, and poetry imperfect and defective without metre. Metre therefore having been connected with *poetry* most often and by a peculiar fitness, whatever else is combined with *metre* must, though it be not itself *essentially* poetic, have nevertheless some property in common with poetry, as an intermedium of affinity, a sort (if I may dare

---

* Altered from the description of Night-Mair in the "Remorse."

> Oh Heaven! 'twas frightful! Now run down and stared at
> By hideous shapes that cannot be remembered;
> Now seeing nothing and imagining nothing;
> But only being afraid—stifled with fear!
> While every goodly or familiar form
> Had a strange power of spreading terror round me!

N.B. Though Shakespeare has, for his own *all-justifying* purposes, introduced the Night-*Mare* with her own foals, yet Mair means a Sister, or perhaps a Hag.

borrow a well-known phrase from technical chemistry) of *mor-daunt* between it and the super-added metre. Now poetry, Mr. Wordsworth truly affirms, does always imply PASSION: which word must be here understood in its general sense, as an excited state of the feelings and faculties. And as every passion has its proper pulse, so will it likewise have its characteristic modes of expression. But where there exists that degree of genius and talent which entitles a writer to aim at the honors of a poet, the very *act* of poetic composition *itself* is, and is *allowed* to imply and to produce, an unusual state of excitement, which of course justifies and demands a correspondent difference of language, as truly, though not perhaps in as marked a degree, as the excitement of love, fear, rage, or jealousy. The vividness of the descriptions or declamations in DONNE or DRYDEN is as much and as often derived from the force and fervor of the describer, as from the reflections, forms or incidents, which constitute their subject and materials. The wheels take fire from the mere rapidity of their motion. To what extent, and under what modifications, this may be admitted to act, I shall attempt to define in an after remark on Mr. Wordsworth's reply to this objection, or rather on his objection to this reply, as already anticipated in his preface.

Fourthly, and as intimately connected with this, if not the same argument in a more general form, I adduce the high spiritual instinct of the human being impelling us to seek unity by harmonious adjustment, and thus establishing the principle, that *all* the parts of an organized whole must be assimilated to the more *important* and *essential* parts. This and the preceding arguments may be strengthened by the reflection, that the composition of a poem is among the *imitative* arts; and that imitation, as opposed to copying, consists either in the interfusion of the SAME throughout the radically DIFFERENT, or of the different throughout a base radically the same.

Lastly, I appeal to the practice of the best poets, of all countries and in all ages, as *authorizing* the opinion (*deduced* from all the foregoing) that in every import of the word ESSENTIAL, which would not here involve a mere truism, there may be, is, and ought to be an *essential* difference between the language of prose and of metrical composition.

In Mr. Wordsworth's criticism of Gray's Sonnet, the readers' sympathy with his praise or blame of the different parts is taken for granted rather perhaps too easily. He has not, at least, attempted to win or compel it by argumentative analysis. In *my* conception at least, the lines rejected as of no value do, with the exception of the two first, differ as much and as little from the language of common life, as those which he has printed in italics as possessing genuine excellence. Of the five lines thus honourably distinguished, two of them differ from prose, even more widely than the lines which either precede or follow, in the *position* of the words.

> *A different object do these eyes require;*
> My lonely anguish melts no heart but mine;
> *And in my breast the imperfect joys expire.*

But were it otherwise, what would this prove, but a truth, of which no man ever doubted? Videlicet, that there are sentences, which would be equally in their place both in verse and prose. Assuredly it does not prove the point, which alone requires proof; namely, that there are not passages, which would suit the one and not suit the other. The first line of this sonnet is distinguished from the ordinary language of men by the epithet to morning. (For we will set aside, at present, the consideration, that the particular word *"smiling"* is hackneyed and (as it involves a sort of personification) not quite congruous with the common and material attribute of *shining*.) And, doubtless, this adjunction of epithets for the purpose of additional description, where no particular attention is demanded for the quality of the thing, would be noticed as giving a poetic cast to a man's conversation. Should the sportsman exclaim, *"Come boys! the rosy morning calls you up,"* he will be supposed to have some song in his head. But no one suspects this, when he says, "A wet morning shall not confine us to our beds." This then is either a defect in poetry, or it is not. Whoever should decide in the *affirmative*, I would request him to re-peruse any one poem of any confessedly great poet from Homer to Milton, or from Æschylus to Shakespeare; and to strike out (in thought I mean) every instance of this kind. If the number of these fancied erasures did not startle him; or if he continued to deem the work improved by their total omission; he must advance reasons of no ordinary strength and evidence, reasons grounded in the essence of human nature. Otherwise, I should not hesitate to consider him as a man not so much *proof against* all authority, as *dead to* it.

The second line,

> And reddening Phœbus lifts his golden fire;

has indeed almost as many faults as words. But then it is a bad line, not because the language is distinct from that of prose; but because it conveys incongruous images, because it confounds the cause and the effect, the real *thing* with the personified *representative* of the thing; in short, because it differs from the language of GOOD SENSE! That the "Phœbus" is hackneyed, and a school-boy image, is an *accidental* fault, dependent on the age in which the author wrote, and not deduced from the nature of the thing. That it is part of an exploded mythology, is an objection more deeply grounded. Yet when the torch of ancient learning was re-kindled, so cheering were its beams, that our eldest poets, cut off by Christianity from all *accredited* machinery, and deprived of all *acknowledged* guardians and symbols of the great objects of nature, were naturally induced to adopt, as a *poetic* language, those fabulous personages, those forms of the* supernatural in nature, which had given them such dear delight in the poems of their great masters. Nay, even at this day what scholar of genial taste will not so far sympathize with them, as to read with pleasure in PETRARCH, CHAUCER, or SPENSER, what he would perhaps condemn as puerile in a modern poet?

I remember no poet, whose writings would safelier stand the test of Mr. Wordsworth's theory, than SPENSER. Yet will Mr. Words-

---

\* But still more by the mechanical system of philosophy which has needlessly infected our theological opinions, and teaching us to consider the world in its relation to God, as of a building to its mason, leaves the idea of omnipresence a mere abstract notion in the state-room of our reason.

worth say, that the style of the following stanza is either undistinguished from prose, and the language of ordinary life? Or that it is vicious, and that the stanzas are *blots* in the "Faery Queen"?

> By this the northern waggoner had set
> His sevenfold teme behind the steadfast starre,
> That was in ocean waves yet never wet,
> But firme is fixt, and sendeth light from farre
> To all that in the wild deep wandering are:
> And chearful chanticleer with his note shrill
> Had warned once that Phœbus' fiery carre
> In haste was climbing up the easterne hill,
> Full envious that night so long his roome did fill.
> > *Book I. Can. 2. St. 2.*

> At last the golden orientall gate
> Of greatest heaven gan to open fayre,
> And Phœbus fresh, as brydegrome to his mate,
> Came dauncing forth, shaking his deawie hayre,
> And hurl'd his glist'ring beams through gloomy ayre:
> Which when the wakeful elfe perceived, streightway
> He started up, and him selfe prepayre
> In sun-bright armes and battailous array;
> For with that pagan proud he combat will that day.
> > *B. I. Can. 5. St. 2.*

On the contrary to how many passages, both in hymn books and in blank verse poems, could I, (were it not invidious), direct the reader's attention, the style of which is most *unpoetic, because,* and only because, it is the style of *prose?* He will not suppose me capable of having in my mind such verses, as

> I put my hat upon my head
> And walk'd into the Strand;
> And there I met another man,
> Whose hat was in his hand.

To such specimens it would indeed be a fair and full reply, that these lines are not bad, because they are *unpoetic;* but because they are empty of all sense and feeling; and that it were an idle attempt to prove that an ape is not a Newton, when it is evident that he is not a man. But the sense shall be good and weighty, the language correct and dignified, the subject interesting and treated with feeling; and yet the style shall, notwithstanding all these merits, be justly blamable as *prosaic,* and solely because the words and the order of the words would find their appropriate place in prose, but are not suitable to *metrical* composition. The "Civil Wars" of Daniel is an instructive, and even interesting work; but take the following stanzas (and from the hundred instances which abound I might probably have selected others far more striking):

> And to the end we may with better ease
> Discern the true discourse, vouchsafe to shew
> What were the times foregoing near to these,
> That these we may with better profit know.
> Tell how the world fell into this disease;
> And how so great distemperature did grow;
> So shall we see with what degrees it came;
> How things at full do soon wax out of frame.
>
> Ten kings had from the Norman conqu'ror reign'd
> With intermixt and variable fate,
> When England to her greatest height attain'd
> Of power, dominion, glory, wealth, and state;
> After it had with much ado sustain'd
> The violence of princes, with debate
> For titles and the often mutinies
> Of nobles for their ancient liberties.
>
> For first, the Norman, conqu'ring all by might,
> By might was forc'd to keep what he had got;
> Mixing our customs and the form of right
> With foreign constitutions he had brought;
>
> Mast'ring the mighty, humbling the poorer wight,
> By all severest means that could be wrought;
> And, making the succession doubtful, rent
> His new-got state, and left it turbulent.
>                         *B. I. St. VII. VIII. & IX.*

Will it be contended on the one side, that these lines are mean and senseless? Or on the other, that they are not prosaic, and for *that* reason unpoetic? This poet's well-merited epithet is that of the *"well-languaged Daniel;"* but likewise, and by the consent of his contemporaries no less than of all succeeding critics, the "prosaic Daniel." Yet those, who thus designate this wise and amiable writer, from the frequent incorrespondency of his diction to his metre in the majority of his compositions, not only deem them valuable and interesting on other accounts; but willingly admit, that there are to be found throughout his poems, and especially in his *Epistles* and in his *Hymen's Triumph,* many and exquisite specimens of that style which, as the *neutral ground* of prose and verse, is common to both. A fine and almost faultless extract, eminent, as for other beauties, so for its perfection in this species of diction, may be seen in LAMB's Dramatic Specimens, &c., a work of various interest from the nature of the selections themselves, (all from the plays of Shakespeare's contemporaries), and deriving a high additional value from the notes, which are full of just and original criticism, expressed with all the freshness of originality.

Among the possible effects of practical adherence to a theory, that aims to *identify* the style of prose and verse, (if it does not indeed claim for the latter a yet nearer resemblance to the average style of men in the vivâ voce intercourse of real life) we might anticipate the following as not the least likely to occur. It will happen, as I have indeed before observed, that the metre itself, the sole acknowledged difference, will occasionally become metre to the eye only. The existence of *prosaisms,* and that they detract from the merit of a poem, *must* at length be conceded, when a number of successive lines can be rendered, even to the most delicate ear, unrecognizable as verse, or as having even been intended for verse, by simply transcribing them as prose; when, if the poem be in blank verse, this can be effected without any alteration, or at most by merely restoring one or two words to their proper places, from which they have been* transplanted for no assignable cause

---

* As the ingenious gentleman under the influence of the Tragic Muse contrived to dislocate, "I wish you a good morning, Sir! Thank you, Sir, and I wish you the same," into two blank-verse heroics:—

> To you a morning good, good Sir! I wish.
> You, Sir! I thank: to you the same wish I.

In those parts of Mr. Wordsworth's works which I have thoroughly studied, I find fewer instances in which this would be practicable than I have met in many poems, where an approximation of prose has been sedulously and on system guarded against. Indeed excepting the stanzas already quoted from "THE SAILOR'S MOTHER," I can recollect but one

or reason but that of the author's convenience; but, if it be in rhyme, by the mere exchange of the final word of each line for some other of the same meaning, equally appropriate, dignified, and euphonic.

The answer or objection in the preface to the anticipated remark "that metre paves the way to other distinctions," is contained in the following words. "The distinction of rhyme and metre is voluntary and uniform, and not, like that produced by (what is called) poetic diction, arbitrary, and subject to infinite caprices, upon which no calculation whatever can be made. In the one case the reader is utterly at the mercy of the poet respecting what imagery or diction he may choose to connect with the passion." But is this a *poet,* of whom a poet is speaking? No surely! rather of a fool or madman: or at best of a vain or ignorant phantast! And might not brains so wild and so deficient make just the same havock with rhymes and metres, as they are supposed to effect with modes and figures of speech? How is the reader at the *mercy* of such men? If he continue to read their nonsense, is it not his own fault? The ultimate end of criticism is much more to establish the principles of writing, than to furnish *rules* how to pass judgement

---

instance: viz. a short passage of four or five lines in "THE BROTHERS," that model of English pastoral, which I have never yet read with unclouded eye.—"James, pointing to its summit, over which they had all purposed to return together, informed them that he would wait for them there. They parted, and his comrades passed that way some two hours after, but they did not find him at the appointed place, *a circumstance of which they took no heed:* but one of them, going by chance into the house, which at this time was James's house, learnt *there,* that nobody had seen him all that day." The only change which has been made is in the position of the little word *there* in two instances, the position in the original being clearly such as is not adopted in ordinary conversation. The other words printed in *italics* were so marked because, though good and genuine English, they are not the phraseology of common conversation either in the word put in apposition, or in the connection by the genitive pronoun. Men in general would have said, "but that was a circumstance they paid no attention to, or took no notice of," and the language is, on the theory of the preface, justified only by the narrator's being the *Vicar.* Yet if any ear *could* suspect, that these sentences were ever printed as metre, on these very words alone could the suspicion have been grounded.

on what has been written by others; if indeed it were possible that
the two could be separated. But if it be asked, by what principles
the poet is to regulate his own style, if he do not adhere closely
to the sort and order of words which he hears in the market, wake,
high-road, or plough-field? I reply; by principles, the ignorance or
neglect of which would convict him of being no *poet,* but a silly
or presumptuous usurper of the name! By the principles of grammar, logic, psychology! In one word by such a knowledge of the
facts, material and spiritual, that most appertain to his art, as, if it
have been governed and applied by *good sense,* and rendered instinctive by habit, becomes the representative and reward of our
past conscious reasonings, insights, and conclusions, and acquires
the name of TASTE. By what *rule* that does not leave the reader at
the poet's mercy, and the poet at his own, is the latter to distinguish
between the language suitable to *suppressed,* and the language,
which is characteristic of *indulged,* anger? Or between that of rage
and that of jealousy? Is it obtained by wandering about in search
of angry or jealous people in uncultivated society, in order to copy
their words? Or not far rather by the power of imagination proceeding upon the *all in each* of human nature? By *meditation,*
rather than by *observation?* And by the latter in consequence only
of the former? As eyes, for which the former has pre-determined
their field of vision, and to which, as to *its* organ, it communicates
a microscopic power? There is not, I firmly believe, a man now
living, who has, from his own inward experience, a clearer intuition, than Mr. Wordsworth himself, that the last mentioned are
the true sources of *genial* discrimination. Through the same process
and by the same creative agency will the poet distinguish the
degree and kind of the excitement produced by the very act of
poetic composition. As intuitively will he know, what differences
of style it at once inspires and justifies; what intermixture of conscious volition is natural to that state; and in what instances such
figures and colors of speech degenerate into mere creatures of an
arbitrary purpose, cold technical artifices of ornament or connection. For, even as truth is its own light and evidence, discovering at
once itself and falsehood, so is it the prerogative of poetic genius
to distinguish by parental instinct its proper offspring from the

changelings, which the gnomes of vanity or the fairies of fashion may have laid in its cradle or called by its names. Could a rule be given from *without,* poetry would cease to be poetry, and sink into a mechanical art. It would be μόρφωσις, not ποίησις. The *rules* of the IMAGINATION are themselves the very powers of growth and production. The *words,* to which they are reducible, present only the outlines and external appearance of the fruit. A deceptive counterfeit of the superficial form and colors may be elaborated; but the marble peach feels cold and heavy, and *children* only put it to their mouths. We find no difficulty in admitting as excellent, and the legitimate language of poetic fervor self-impassioned, DONNE's apostrophe to the Sun in the second stanza of his "Progress of the Soul:"

> Thee, eye of heaven! this great soul envies not:
> By thy male force is all, we have, begot.
> In the first East thou now beginn'st to shine,
> Suck'st early balm and island spices there,
> And wilt anon in thy loose-rein'd career
> At Tagus, Po, Seine, Thames, and Danow dine,
> And see at night this western world of mine:
> Yet hast thou not more nations seen than she,
> Who before thee one day began to be,
> And, thy frail light being quench'd, shall long, long outlive thee!

Or the next stanza but one:

> Great destiny, the commissary of God,
> That hast mark'd out a path and period
> For ev'ry thing! Who, where we offspring took,
> Our ways and ends see'st at one instant: thou
> Knot of all causes! Thou, whose changeless brow
> Ne'er smiles or frowns! O! vouchsafe thou to look,
> And shew my story in thy eternal book, &c.

As little difficulty do we find in excluding from the honors of unaffected warmth and elevation the madness prepense of pseudo-poesy, or the startling *hysteric* of weakness over-exerting itself, which bursts on the unprepared reader in sundry odes and apostrophes to abstract terms. Such are the Odes to Jealousy, to Hope, to Oblivion, and the like, in Dodsley's collection and the magazines

of that day, which seldom fail to remind me of an Oxford copy
of verses on the two SUTTONS, commencing with

> INOCULATION, heavenly maid! descend!

It is not to be denied that men of undoubted talents, and even
poets of true, though not of first-rate, genius, have from a mistaken
theory deluded both themselves and others in the opposite extreme.
I once read to a company of sensible and well-educated women the
introductory period of Cowley's preface to his *"Pindaric Odes,*
*written in imitation of the style and manner of the odes of Pindar."*
"If, (says Cowley), a man should undertake to translate Pindar,
word for word, it would be thought that one madman had translated another; as may appear, when he, that understands not the
original, reads the verbal traduction of him into Latin prose, than
which nothing seems more raving." I then proceeded with his own
free version of the second Olympic, composed for the charitable
purpose of *rationalizing* the Theban Eagle.

> Queen of all harmonious things,
> Dancing words and speaking strings,
> What God, what hero, wilt thou sing?
> What happy man to equal glories bring?
> Begin, begin thy noble choice,
> And let the hills around reflect the image of thy voice.
> Pisa does to Jove belong,
> Jove and Pisa claim thy song.
> The fair first-fruits of war, th' Olympic games,
> Alcides offer'd up to Jove;
> Alcides too thy strings may move!
> But, oh! what man to join with these can worthy prove?
> Join Theron boldly to their sacred names;
> Theron the next honor claims;
> Theron to no man gives place,
> Is first in Pisa's and in Virtue's race;
> Theron there, and he alone,
> Ev'n his own swift forefathers has outgone.

One of the company exclaimed, with the full assent of the rest,
that if the original were madder than this, it must be incurably
mad. I then translated the ode from the Greek, and as nearly as

possible, word for word; and the impression was, that in the general movement of the periods, in the form of the connections and transitions, and in the sober majesty of lofty sense, it appeared to them to approach more nearly, than any other poetry they had heard, to the style of our Bible in the prophetic books. The first strophe will suffice as a specimen:

> Ye harp-controuling hymns! (or) ye hymns the sovereigns of harps!
> What God? what Hero?
> What Man shall we celebrate?
> Truly Pisa indeed is of Jove,
> But the Olympiad (or the Olympic games) did Hercules establish,
> The first-fruits of the spoils of war.
> But Theron for the four-horsed car,
> That bore victory to him,
> It behoves us now to voice aloud:
> The Just, the Hospitable,
> The Bulwark of Agrigentum,
> Of renowned fathers
> The Flower, even him
> Who preserves his native city erect and safe.

But are such rhetorical caprices condemnable only for their deviation from the language of real life? and are they by no other means to be precluded, but by the rejection of all distinctions between prose and verse, save that of metre? Surely good sense, and a moderate insight into the constitution of the human mind, would be amply sufficient to prove, that such language and such combinations are the native produce neither of the fancy nor of the imagination; that their operation consists in the excitement of surprise by the juxta-position and *apparent* reconciliation of widely different or incompatible things. As when, for instance, the hills are made to reflect the image of a *voice*. Surely, no unusual taste is requisite to see clearly, that this compulsory juxta-position is not produced by the presentation of impressive or delightful forms to the inward vision, nor by any sympathy with the modifying powers with which the genius of the poet had united and in-spirited all the objects of his thought; that it is therefore a species of *wit*, a pure work of the *will*, and implies a leisure and self-possession both of thought and of feeling, incompatible with the steady fervor of a mind possessed and filled with the grandeur of its subject. To sum up the whole in one sentence. When a poem, or a part of a poem, shall be adduced, which is evidently vicious in the figures and contexture of its style, yet for the condemnation of which no reason can be assigned, except that it differs from the style in which men actually converse, then, and not till then, can I hold this theory to be either plausible, or practicable, or capable of furnishing either rule, guidance, or precaution, that might not, more easily and more safely, as well as more naturally, have been deduced in the author's own mind from considerations of grammar, logic, and the truth and nature of things, confirmed by the authority of works, whose fame is not of ONE country nor of ONE age.

## CHAPTER XIX

*Continuation—Concerning the real object which, it is probable, Mr. Words-worth had before him in his critical preface—Elucidation and application of this—The neutral style, or that common to Prose and Poetry, exemplified by specimens from Chaucer, Herbert, and others.*

It might appear from some passages in the former part of Mr. Wordsworth's preface, that he meant to confine his theory of style, and the necessity of a close accordance with the actual language of men, to those particular subjects from low and rustic life, which by way of experiment he had purposed to naturalize as a new species in our English poetry. But from the train of argument that follows; from the reference to Milton; and from the spirit of his critique on Gray's sonnet; those sentences appear to have been rather courtesies of modesty, than actual limitations of his system. Yet so groundless does this system appear on a close examination; and so strange and * over-whelming in its consequences, that I

---

* I had in my mind the striking but untranslatable epithet, which the celebrated Mendelssohn applied to the great founder of the Critical Philosophy *"Der alleszermalmende* KANT," i. e. the all-becrushing, or rather the *all-to-nothing-crushing* KANT. In the facility and force of compound epithets, the German from the number of its cases and inflections approaches to the Greek: that language so

cannot, and I do not, believe that the poet did ever himself adopt
it in the unqualified sense, in which his expressions have been
understood by others, and which, indeed, according to all the common laws of interpretation they seem to bear. What then did he
mean? I apprehend, that in the clear perception, not unaccom-
panied with disgust or contempt, of the gaudy affectations of a style
which passed current with too many for poetic diction, (though in
truth it had as little pretensions to poetry, as to logic or common
sense), he narrowed his view for the time; and feeling a justifiable
preference for the language of nature and of good sense, even in
its humblest and least ornamented forms, he suffered himself to
express, in terms at once too large and too exclusive, his predilection for a style the most remote possible from the false and showy
splendour which he wished to explode. It is possible, that this predilection, at first merely comparative, deviated for a time into direct
partiality. But the real object which he had in view, was, I doubt
not, a species of excellence which had been long before most happily characterized by the judicious and amiable GARVE, whose
works are so justly beloved and esteemed by the Germans, in his
remarks on GELLERT, (see Sammlung einiger Abhandlungen von
Christian Garve), from which the following is literally translated.
"The talent, that is required to make excellent verses, is perhaps
greater than the philosopher is ready to admit, or would find it in
his power to acquire: the talent to seek only the apt expression of
the thought, and yet to find at the same time with it the rhyme
and the metre. Gellert possessed this happy gift, if ever any one of
our poets possessed it; and nothing perhaps contributed more to
the great and universal impression which his fables made on their
first publication, or conduces more to their continued popularity.
It was a strange and curious phenomenon, and such as in Germany
had been previously unheard of, to read verses in which everything
was expressed just as one would wish to talk, and yet all dignified,
attractive, and interesting; and all at the same time perfectly correct as to the measure of the syllables and the rhyme. It is certain,
that poetry when it has attained this excellence makes a far greater

---

Bless'd in the happy marriage of sweet words.

It is in the woeful harshness of its sounds alone that the German need
shrink from the comparison.

impression than prose. So much so indeed, that even the gratification which the very rhymes afford, becomes then no longer a contemptible or trifling gratification."

However novel this phenomenon may have been in Germany at
the time of Gellert, it is by no means new, nor yet of recent existence in our language. Spite of the licentiousness with which
Spenser occasionally compels the orthography of his words into a
subservience to his rhymes, the whole "Faery Queen" is an almost
continued instance of this beauty. Waller's song "Go, lovely Rose,"
is doubtless familiar to most of my readers; but if I had happened
to have had by me the Poems of COTTON, more but far less deservedly celebrated as the author of the "Virgil travestied," I should
have indulged myself, and I think have gratified many, who are
not acquainted with his serious works, by selecting some admirable
specimens of this style. There are not a few poems in that volume,
replete with every excellence of thought, image, and passion,
which we expect or desire in the poetry of the milder muse; and
yet so worded, that the reader sees no one reason either in the
selection or the order of the words, why he might not have said
the very same in an appropriate conversation, and cannot conceive
how indeed he could have expressed such thoughts otherwise,
without loss or injury to his meaning.

But in truth our language is, and from the first dawn of poetry
ever has been, particularly rich in compositions distinguished by
this excellence. The final *e*, which is now mute, in Chaucer's age
was either sounded or dropt indifferently. We ourselves still use
either *beloved* or *belov'd* according as the rhyme, or measure, or
the purpose of more or less solemnity may require. Let the reader
then only adopt the pronunciation of the poet and of the court, at
which he lived, both with respect to the final *e* and to the accen-
tuation of the last syllable; I would then venture to ask, what even
in the colloquial language of elegant and unaffected women,
(who are the peculiar mistresses of "pure English and undefiled,")
what could we hear more natural, or seemingly more unstudied,
than the following stanzas from Chaucer's "Troilus and Creseide"?

> And after this forth to the gate he wente,
> Ther as Creseide out rode a full gode paas,
> And up and doun there made he many a wente,

And to himselfe ful oft he said, Alas!
Fro hennis rode my blisse and my solas:
As wouldè blisful God now for his joie,
I might her sene agen come in to Troie!
    And to the yondir hil I gan her guide,
Alas! and there I toke of her my leve:
And yond I saw her to her fathir ride;               10
For sorrow of which mine hearte shall to-cleve;
And hithir home I came whan it was eve,
And here I dwel, out-cast from allè joie,
And shal, til I maie sene her efte in Troie.
    "And of himselfe imaginid he ofte
To ben defaitid, pale and waxen lesse
Than he was wonte, and that men saidin softe,
What may it be? who can the sothè gesse,
Why Troilus hath al this hevinesse?
And al this n' as but his melancolie,               20
That he had of himselfe suche fantasie.
    Another time imaginin he would
That every wight, that past him by the wey,
Had of him routhe, and that they saien should,
I am right sorry, Troilus wol dey!
And thus he drove a daie yet forth or twey,
As ye have herde: suche life gan he to lede
As he that stode betwixin hope and drede:
    For which him likid in his songis shewe
Th' encheson of his wo as he best might,               30
And made a songe of wordis but a fewe,
Somwhat his woful hertè for to light,
And whan he was from every mannis sight,
With softé voice he of his lady dere,
That absent was, gan sing as ye may hear:

\*    \*    \*    \*    \*    \*

    This song when he thus songin had, ful soon
He fell agen into his sighis olde:
And every night, as was his wonte to done,
He stodè the bright moonè to beholde
And all his sorrowe to the moone he tolde,               40
And said: I wis, whan thou art hornid newe,
I shall be glad, if al the world be trewe!

Another exquisite master of this species of style, where the scholar and the poet supplies the material, but the perfect well-bred gentleman the expressions and the arrangement, is George

Herbert. As from the nature of the subject, and the too frequent quaintness of the thoughts, his "Temple: or Sacred Poems and Private Ejaculations" are comparatively but little known, I shall extract two poems. The first is a Sonnet, equally admirable for the weight, number, and expression of the thoughts, and for the simple dignity of the language. (Unless indeed a fastidious taste should object to the latter half of the sixth line.) The second is a poem of greater length, which I have chosen not only for the present purpose, but likewise as a striking example and illustration of an assertion hazarded in a former page of these sketches: namely, that the characteristic fault of our elder poets is the reverse of that, which distinguishes too many of our more recent versifiers; the one conveying the most fantastic thoughts in the most correct and natural language; the other in the most fantastic language conveying the most trivial thoughts. The latter is a riddle of words; the former an enigma of thoughts. The one reminds me of an odd passage in Drayton's IDEAS:

### SONNET IX.

> As other men, so I myself do muse,
> Why in this sort I wrest invention so;
> And why these *giddy metaphors* I use,
> Leaving the path the greater part do go!
> I will restolve you: *I am lunatic!*

The other recalls a still odder passage in the "SYNAGOGUE: *or The Shadow of the Temple,*" a connected series of poems in imitation of Herbert's "TEMPLE," and, in some editions, annexed to it.

> O how my mind
>                 Is gravell'd!
>                           Not a thought,
>         That I can find,
>                 But's ravell'd
>                           All to nought!
>         Short ends of threds,
>                 And narrow shreds
>                           Of lists,
>                 Knots, snarled ruffs,
>                           Loose broken tufts
>                                   Of twists,
> Are my torn meditation's ragged clothing,
> Which, wound and woven, shape a sute for nothing:

One while I think, and then I am in pain
To think how to unthink that thought again!

Immediately after these burlesque passages I cannot proceed to
the extracts promised, without changing the ludicrous tone of feeling by the interposition of the three following stanzas of Herbert's.

### VIRTUE.

Sweet day, so cool, so calm, so bright,
The bridal of the earth and sky,
The dew shall weep thy fall to-night;
    For thou must dye.

Sweet rose, whose hue angry and brave
Bids the rash gazer wipe his eye:
Thy root is ever in its grave,
    And thou must dye.

Sweet spring, full of sweet days and roses,
A nest, where sweets compacted lie:
My musick shews, ye have your closes,
    And all must dye.

### THE BOSOM SIN:

#### A SONNET BY GEORGE HERBERT.

Lord, with what care hast thou begirt us round,
Parents first season us; then schoolmasters
Deliver us to laws; they send us bound
To rules of reason, holy messengers,
Pulpits and Sundays, sorrow dogging sin,
    Afflictions sorted, anguish of all sizes,
    Fine nets and stratagems to catch us in,
Bibles laid open, millions of surprizes;
Blessings beforehand, ties of gratefulness,
    The sound of glory ringing in our ears:
    Without, our shame; within, our consciences;
Angels and grace, eternal hopes and fears!
    Yet all these fences and their whole array
    One cunning BOSOM-SIN blows quite away.

### LOVE UNKOWN.

Dear friend, sit down, the tale is long and sad:
And in my faintings, I presume, your love
Will more comply than help. A Lord I had,
And have, of whom some grounds, which may improve,

I hold for two lives, and both lives in me.
To him I brought a dish of fruit one day,
And in the middle placed my HEART. But he
(I sigh to say)

Look't on a servant, who did know his eye,
Better than you knew me, or (which is one)        10
Than I myself. The servant instantly,
Quitting the fruit, seiz'd on my *heart* alone,
And threw it in a font, wherein did fall
A stream of blood, which issued from the side
Of a great rock: I well remember all
And have good cause: there it was dipt and dyed,
And washt, and wrung! the very wringing yet
Enforceth tears. *Your heart was foul, I fear.*
Indeed 'tis true. I did and do commit
Many a fault, more than my lease will bear;        20
Yet still ask'd pardon, and was not deny'd.
But you shall hear. After my heart was well,
And clean and fair, as I one eventide
(I sigh to tell)

Walk'd by myself abroad, I saw a large
And spacious furnace flaming, and thereon
A boiling caldron, round about whose verge
Was in great letters set AFFLICTION.
The greatness shew'd the owner. So I went
To fetch a sacrifice out of my fold,        30
Thinking with that, which I did thus present,
To warm his love, which, I did fear, grew cold.
But as my heart did tender it, the man
Who was to take it from me, slipt his hand,
And threw my *heart* into the scalding pan;
My heart that brought it (do you understand?)
The *offerer's* heart. *Your heart was hard, I fear.*
Indeed 'tis true. I found a callous matter
Began to spread and to expatiate there:
But with a richer drug than scalding water        40
I bath'd it often, ev'n with holy blood,
Which at a board, while many drank bare wine,
A friend did steal into my cup for good,
Ev'n taken inwardly, and most divine
To supple hardnesses. But at the length
Out of the caldron getting, soon I fled
Unto my house, where to repair the strength
Which I had lost, I hasted to my bed;
But when I thought to sleep out all these faults,

(I sigh to speak)                     50
I found that some had stuffed the bed with thoughts,
I would say *thorns*. Dear, could my heart not break,
When with my pleasures ev'n my rest was gone?
Full well I understood who had been there:
For I had given the key to none but one:
It must be he. *Your heart was dull, I fear.*
*Indeed a slack and sleepy state of mind*
*Did oft possess me; so that when I pray'd,*
*Though my lips went, my heart did stay behind.*
*But all my scores were by another paid,*                     60
*Who took my guilt upon him. Truly, friend,*
*For aught I hear, your master shews to you*
*More favor than you wot of. Mark the end!*
*The font did only what was old renew:*
*The caldron suppled what was grown too hard:*
*The thorns did quicken what was grown too dull:*
*All did but strive to mend what you had marr'd.*
*Wherefore be cheer'd, and praise him to the full*
*Each day, each hour, each moment of the week*
*Who fain would have you be new, tender, quick!*                     70


# CHAPTER XX

### *The former subject continued.*

I have no fear in declaring my conviction, that the excellence
defined and exemplified in the preceding Chapter is not the characteristic excellence of Mr. Wordsworth's style; because I can add
with equal sincerity, that it is precluded by higher powers. The
praise of uniform adherence to genuine, logical English is undoubtedly his; nay, laying the main emphasis on the word *uniform,* I will dare add that, of all contemporary poets, it is *his
alone.* For in a less absolute sense of the word, I should certainly
include Mr. Bowles, Lord Byron, and, as to all his later writings,
Mr. Southey, the exceptions in their work being so few and
unimportant. But of the specific excellence described in the quotation from Garve, I appear to find more, and more undoubted
specimens in the works of others; for instance, among the minor
poems of Mr. Thomas Moore, and of our illustrious Laureate. To

me it will always remain a singular and noticeable fact; that a theory which would establish this *lingua communis,* not only as the best, but as the only commendable style, should have proceeded from a poet, whose diction, next to that of Shakespeare and Milton, appears to me of all others the most *individualized* and characteristic. And let it be remembered too, that I am now interpreting the controverted passages of Mr. W's. critical preface by the purpose and object, which he may be supposed to have intended, rather than by the sense which the words themselves must convey, if they are taken without this allowance.

A person of any taste, who had but studied three or four of Shakespeare's principal plays, would without the name affixed scarcely fail to recognise as Shakespeare's a quotation from any other play, though but of a few lines. A similar peculiarity, though in a less degree, attends Mr. Wordsworth's style, whenever he speaks in his own person; or whenever, though under a feigned name, it is clear that he himself is still speaking, as in the different dramatis personæ of the "Recluse." Even in the other poems, in which he purposes to be most dramatic, there are few in which it does not occasionally burst forth. The reader might often address the poet in his own words with reference to the persons introduced:

> It seems, as I retrace the ballad line by line,
> That but half of it is theirs, and the better half is thine.

Who, having been previously acquainted with any considerable portion of Mr. Wordsworth's publications, and having studied them with a full feeling of the author's genius, would not at once claim as Wordsworthian the little poem on the rainbow?

> The child is father of the man, &c.

Or in the "Lucy Gray?"

> No mate, no comrade Lucy knew;
> She dwelt on a wide moor;
> *The sweetest thing that ever grew*
> *Beside a human door.*

Or in the "Idle Shepherd-boys"?

> Along the river's stony marge
> The sand-lark chaunts a joyous song;
> The thrush is busy in the wood,
> And carols loud and strong.
> A thousand lambs are on the rocks,
> All newly born! both earth and sky
> Keep jubilee, and more than all,
> Those boys with their green coronal;
> They never hear the cry,
> That plaintive cry! which up the hill
> Comes from the depth of Dungeon Gill.

Need I mention the exquisite description of the Sea Loch in the "Blind Highland Boy"? Who but a poet tells a tale in such language to the little ones by the fire-side as—

> Yet had he many a restless dream
> Both when he heard the eagle's scream,
> And when he heard the torrents roar,
> And heard the water beat the shore
>     Near where their cottage stood.
>
> Beside a lake their cottage stood,
> Not small like ours, a peaceful flood,
> But one of mighty size, and strange,
> That, rough or smooth, is full of change,
>     And stirring in its bed.
>
> For to this lake, by night and day,
> The great sea-water finds its way
> Through long, long windings of the hills,
> And drinks up all the pretty rills
>     And rivers large and strong:
>
> Then hurries back the road it came—
> Returns on errand still the same;
> This did it when the earth was new;
> And this for evermore will do,
>     As long as earth shall last.
>
> And with the coming of the tide,
> Come boats and ships that sweetly ride,
> Between the woods and lofty rocks;
> And to the shepherds with their flocks
>     Bring tales of distant lands.

I might quote almost the whole of his "Ruth," but take the following stanzas:

> But, as you have before been told,
> This stripling, sportive, gay, and bold,
> And with his dancing crest,
> So beautiful, through savage lands
> Had roamed about with vagrant bands
>     Of Indians in the West.
>
> The wind, the tempest roaring high,
> The tumult of a tropic sky,
> Might well be dangerous food
> For him, a youth to whom was given
> So much of earth, so much of heaven,
>     And such impetuous blood.
>
> Whatever in those climes he found
> Irregular in sight or sound,
> Did to his mind impart
> A kindred impulse, seemed allied
> To his own powers, and justified
>     The workings of his heart.
>
> Nor less, to feed voluptuous thought,
> The beauteous forms of nature wrought,
> Fair trees and lovely flowers;
> The breezes their own langour lent;
> The stars had feelings, which they sent
>     Into those magic bowers.
>
> Yet, in his worst pursuits, I ween
> That sometimes there did intervene
> Pure hopes of high intent:
> For passions, linked to forms so fair
> And stately, needs must have their share
>     Of noble sentiment.

But from Mr. Wordsworth's more elevated compositions, which
already form three-fourths of his works; and will, I trust, constitute hereafter a still larger proportion;—from these, whether in
rhyme or blank-verse, it would be difficult and almost superfluous
to select instances of a diction peculiarly his own, of a style which
cannot be imitated, without its being at once recognised as originating in Mr. Wordsworth. It would not be easy to open on any

one of his loftier strains, that does not contain examples of this;
and more in proportion as the lines are more excellent, and most
like the author. For those, who may happen to have been less
familiar with his writings, I will give three specimens taken with
little choice. The first from the lines on the "BOY OF WINANDER-
MERE,"—who

> Blew mimic hootings to the silent owls,
> That they might answer him. And they would shout
> Across the watery vale, and shout again,
> With long halloos and screams, and echoes loud
> Redoubled and redoubled; concourse wild
> Of mirth and jocund din. And when it chanced,
> That pauses of deep silence mock'd his skill,
> *Then sometimes in that silence, while he hung*
> *Listening, a gentle shock of mild surprize*
> *Has carried far into his heart the voice*
> *Of mountain-torrents; or the visible scene* \*

---

\* Mr. Wordsworth's having judiciously adopted *"concourse wild"* in this
passage for *"a wild scene"* as it stood in the former edition, encourages me
to hazard a remark, which I certainly should not have made in the works
of a poet less austerely accurate in the use of the words, than he is, to his
own great honor. It respects the propriety of the word *"scene,"* even in the
sentence in which it is retained. DRYDEN, and he only in his more careless
verses, was the first, as far as my researches have discovered, who for the
convenience of rhyme used this word in the vague sense, which has been
since too current even in our best writers, and which (unfortunately, I
think) is given as its first explanation in Dr. Johnson's Dictionary, and
therefore would be taken by an incautious reader as its proper sense. In
Shakespeare and Milton the word is never used without some clear reference, proper or metaphorical, to the theatre. Thus Milton:

> Cedar, and pine, and fir, and branching palm,
> A sylvan *scene;* and, as the ranks ascend,
> Shade above shade, a woody *theatre*
> Of stateliest view.

I object to any extension of its meaning, because the word is already more
equivocal than might be wished; inasmuch as in the limited use, which I
recommend, it may still signify two different things; namely, the scenery,
and the characters and actions presented on the stage during the presence
of particular scenes. It can therefore be preserved from *obscurity* only by
keeping the original signification full in the mind. Thus Milton again:

> Prepare thou for another scene.

> *Would enter unawares into his mind*
> *With all its solemn imagery, its rocks,*
> *Its woods, and that uncertain heaven, received*
> *Into the bosom of the steady lake."*

The second shall be that noble imitation of Drayton\* (if it was not rather a coincidence) in the "JOANNA."

> When I had gazed perhaps two minutes' space,
> Joanna, looking in my eyes, beheld
> That ravishment of mine, and laughed aloud.
> The rock, like something starting from a sleep,
> Took up the lady's voice, and laughed again!
> That ancient woman seated on HELM-CRAG
> Was ready with her cavern; HAMMAR-SCAR
> And the tall steep of SILVER-How sent forth
> A noise of laughter; southern LOUGHRIGG heard,
> And FAIRFIELD answered with a mountain tone.
> HELVELLYN far into the clear blue sky
> Carried the lady's voice!—old SKIDDAW blew
> His speaking trumpet!—back out of the clouds
> From GLARAMARA southward came the voice:
> And KIRKSTONE tossed it from his misty head!

The third, which is in rhyme, I take from the "Song at the feast of Brougham Castle, upon the restoration of Lord Clifford the shepherd to the estates of his ancestors."

> Now another day is come,
> Fitter hope, and nobler doom;
> He hath thrown aside his crook,
> And hath buried deep his book;
> *Armour rusting in the halls*

---

\* Which COPLAND scarce had spoke, but quickly every hill,
Upon her verge that stands, the neighbouring vallies fill;
HELVILLON from his height it through the mountains threw,
From whom as soon again the sound DUNBALRASE drew,
From whose stone-trophied head it on the WENDROSS went,
Which tow'rds the sea again resounded it to DENT.
That BROADWATER, therewith within her banks astound,
In sailing to the sea, told it to EGREMOUND,
Whose buildings, walks, and streets, with echoes loud and long,
Did mightily commend old COPLAND for her song.
DRAYTON'S POLYOLBION: *Song XXX.*

*On the blood of Clifford calls;*
*"Quell the Scot," exclaims the lance!*
*"Bear me to the heart of France,"*
*Is the longing of the shield—*
*Tell thy name, thou trembling field!—*
*Field of death, where'er thou be,*
*Groan thou with our victory!*
Happy day, and mighty hour,
When our shepherd, in his power,
Mailed and horsed, with lance and sword,
To his ancestors restored,
Like a re-appearing star,
Like a glory from afar,
*First shall head the flock of war!*

Alas! the fervent harper did not know
That for a tranquil soul the lay was framed,
Who, long compelled in humble walks to go,
Was softened into feeling, soothed, and tamed.

Love had he found in huts where poor men lie:
His daily teachers had been woods and rills;
*The silence that is in the starry sky,*
*The sleep that is among the lonely hills.*

The words themselves, in the foregoing extracts, are no doubt sufficiently common for the greater part. (But in what poem are they not so, if we except a few misadventurous attempts to translate the arts and sciences into verse?) In the "Excursion" the number of polysyllabic (or what the common people call, *dictionary*) words is more than usually great. And so must it needs be, in proportion to the number and variety of an author's conceptions, and his solicitude to express them with precision. But are those words *in those places* commonly employed in real life to express the same thought or outward thing? Are they the style used in the ordinary intercourse of spoken words? No! nor are the modes of connections; and still less the breaks and transitions. Would any but a poet—at least could any one without being conscious that he had expressed himself with noticeable vivacity—have described a bird singing loud by, "The thrush is *busy* in the wood?" —or have spoken of boys with a string of club-moss round their rusty hats, as the boys *"with their green coronal?"*—or have translated a beautiful May-day into *"Both earth and sky keep jubilee?"* or have brought all the different marks and circumstances of a sea-loch before the mind, as the actions of a living and acting power? Or have represented the reflection of the sky in the water, as *"That uncertain heaven received into the bosom of the steady lake?"* Even the grammatical construction is not unfrequently peculiar; as *"The wind, the tempest roaring high, the tumult of a tropic sky,* might well be dangerous food *to him, a youth* to whom was given, &c."* There is a peculiarity in the frequent use of the ἀσυνάρτητον (i. e. the omission of the connective particle before the last of several words, or several sentences used grammatically as single words, all being in the same case and governing or governed by the same verb) and not less in the construction of words by apposition (*to him, a youth*). In short, were there excluded from Mr. Wordsworth's poetic compositions all, that a literal adherence to the theory of his preface *would* exclude, two-thirds at least of the marked beauties of his poetry must be erased. For a far greater number of lines would be sacrificed than in any other recent poet; because the pleasure received from Wordsworth's poems being less derived either from excitement of curiosity or the rapid flow of narration, the *striking* passages form a larger proportion of their value. I do not adduce it as a fair criterion of comparative excellence, nor do I even think it such; but merely as matter of fact. I affirm, that from no contemporary writer could so many lines be quoted, without reference to the poem in which they are found, for their own independent weight or beauty. From the sphere of my own experience I can bring to my recollection three persons of no every-day powers and acquirements, who had read the poems of others with more, and more unalloyed pleasure, and had thought more highly of their authors, as poets; who yet have confessed to me, that from no modern work had so many passages started up anew in their minds at different times, and as different occasions had awakened a meditative mood.

## CHAPTER XXII

*The characteristic defects of Wordsworth's poetry, with the principles from which the judgement, that they are defects, is deduced—Their proportion to the beauties—For the greatest part characteristic of his theory only.*

If Mr. Wordsworth have set forth principles of poetry which his arguments are insufficient to support, let him and those who have adopted his sentiments be set right by the confutation of these arguments, and by the substitution of more philosophical principles. And still let the due credit be given to the portion and importance of the truths, which are blended with his theory; truths, the too exclusive attention to which had occasioned its errors, by tempting him to carry those truths beyond their proper limits. If his mistaken theory have at all influenced his poetic compositions, let the effects be pointed out, and the instances given. But let it likewise be shown, how far the influence has acted; whether diffusively, or only by starts; whether the number and importance of the poems and passages thus infected be great or trifling compared with the sound portion; and lastly, whether they are inwoven into the texture of his works, or are loose and separable. The result of such a trial would evince beyond a doubt, what it is high time to announce decisively and aloud, that the *supposed* characteristics of Mr. Wordsworth's poetry, whether admired or reprobated; whether they are simplicity or simpleness; faithful adherence to essential nature, or wilful selections from human nature of its meanest forms and under the least attractive associations; are as little the *real* characteristics of his poetry at large, as of his genius and the constitution of his mind.

In a comparatively small number of poems he chose to try an experiment; and this experiment we will suppose to have failed. Yet even in these poems it is impossible not to perceive that the natural *tendency* of the poet's mind is to great objects and elevated conceptions. The poem entitled "Fidelity" is for the greater part written in language, as unraised and naked as any perhaps in the

two volumes. Yet take the following stanza and compare it with
the preceding stanzas of the same poem.

> There sometimes doth a leaping fish
> Send through the tarn a lonely cheer;
> The crags repeat the raven's croak,
> In symphony austere;
> Thither the rainbow comes—the cloud—
> And mists that spread the flying shroud;
> And sun-beams; and the sounding blast,
> That if it could would hurry past;
> But that enormous barrier binds it fast.

Or compare the four last lines of the concluding stanza with the
former half.

> Yes, proof was plain that since the day
> On which the traveller thus had died,
> The dog had watched about the spot,
> Or by his master's side
> *How nourish'd there through such long time*
> *He knows, who gave that love sublime,*
> *And gave that strength of feeling, great*
> *Above all human estimate!*

Can any candid and intelligent mind hesitate in determining,
which of these best represents the tendency and native character
of the poet's genius? Will he not decide that the one was written
because the poet *would* so write, and the other because he could
not so entirely repress the force and grandeur of his mind, but
that he must in some part or other of *every* composition write
otherwise? In short, that his only disease is the being out of his
element; like the swan, that, having amused himself, for a while,
with crushing the weeds on the river's bank, soon returns to his
own majestic movements on its reflecting and sustaining surface.
Let it be observed that I am here supposing the imagined judge,
to whom I appeal, to have already decided against the poet's theory, as far as it is different from the principles of the art, generally
acknowledged.

I cannot here enter into a detailed examination of Mr. Wordsworth's works; but I will attempt to give the main results of my
own judgement, after an acquaintance of many years, and re-

peated perusals. And though, to appreciate the defects of a great mind it is necessary to understand previously its characteristic excellences, yet I have already expressed myself with sufficient fulness, to preclude most of the ill effects that might arise from my pursuing a contrary arrangement. I will therefore commence with what I deem the prominent *defects* of his poems hitherto published.

The first *characteristic, though only occasional* defect, which I appear to myself to find in these poems is the INCONSTANCY of the *style*. Under this name I refer to the sudden and unprepared transitions from lines or sentences of peculiar felicity (at all events striking and original) to a style, not only unimpassioned but undistinguished. He sinks too often and too abruptly to that style, which I should place in the second division of language, dividing it into the three species; *first,* that which is peculiar to poetry; *second,* that which is only proper in prose; and *third,* the neutral or common to both. There have been works, such as Cowley's Essay on Cromwell, in which prose and verse are intermixed (not as in the Consolation of Boetius, or the Argenis of Barclay, by the insertion of poems supposed to have been spoken or composed on occasions previously related in prose, but) the poet passing from one to the other, as the nature of the thoughts or his own feelings dictated. Yet this mode of composition does not satisfy a cultivated taste. There is something unpleasant in the being thus obliged to alternate states of feeling so dissimilar, and this too in a species of writing, the pleasure from which is in part derived from the preparation and previous expectation of the reader. A portion of that awkwardness is felt which hangs upon the introduction of songs in our modern comic operas; and to prevent which the judicious Metastasio (as to whose exquisite *taste* there can be no hesitation, whatever doubts may be entertained as to his *poetic genius*) uniformly placed the ARIA at the end of the scene, at the same time that he almost always raises and impassions the style of the recitative immediately preceding. Even in real life, the difference is great and evident between words used as the *arbitrary marks* of thought, our smooth market-coin of intercourse, with the image and superscription worn out by currency; and those which convey pictures either borrowed from *one* outward object to enliven and particularize some *other;* or used allegorically to body forth the inward state of the person speaking; or such as are at least the exponents of his peculiar turn and unusual extent of faculty. So much so indeed, that in the social circles of private life we often find a striking use of the latter put a stop to the general flow of conversation, and by the excitement arising from concentered attention produce a sort of damp and interruption for some minutes after. But in the perusal of works of literary *art,* we *prepare* ourselves for such language; and the business of the writer, like that of a painter whose subject requires unusual splendor and prominence, is so to raise the lower and neutral tints, that what in a different style would be the *commanding* colors, are here used as the means of that gentle *degradation* requisite in order to produce the effect of a *whole.* Where this is not achieved in a poem, the metre merely reminds the reader of his claims in order to disappoint them; and where this defect occurs frequently, his feelings are alternately startled by anticlimax and hyperclimax.

I refer the reader to the exquisite stanzas cited for another purpose from the blind Highland Boy; and then annex, as being in my opinion instances of this *disharmony* in style, the two following:

> And one, the rarest, was a shell,
> Which he, poor child, had studied well:
> The shell of a green turtle, thin
> And hollow;—you might sit therein,
>     It was so wide, and deep.
>
> Our Highland Boy oft visited
> The house which held this prize; and, led
> By choice or chance, did thither come
> One day, when no one was at home,
>     And found the door unbarred.

Or page 172, vol. I.

> 'Tis gone—forgotten—*let me do*
> *My best.* There was a smile or two—
> I can remember them, I see
> The smiles worth all the world to me.

> Dear Baby, I must lay thee down:
> Thou troublest me with strange alarms;
> Smiles hast thou, sweet ones of thine own;
> I cannot keep thee in my arms;
> For they confound me: *as it is,*
> I have forgot those smiles of his!

Or page 269, vol. I.

> Thou hast a nest, for thy love and thy rest,
> And though little troubled with sloth
> Drunken lark! thou would'st be loth
> To be such a traveller as I.
> 　　Happy, happy liver!
> *With a soul as strong as a mountain river*
> *Pouring out praise to th' Almighty giver!*
> Joy and jollity be with us both!
> Hearing thee or else some other,
> 　　As merry a brother
> I on the earth will go plodding on
> By myself chearfully till the day is done.

The incongruity, which I appear to find in this passage, is that of the two noble lines in italics with the preceding and following. So vol. II. page 30.

> Close by a pond, upon the further side,
> He stood alone; a minute's space, I guess,
> I watch'd him, he continuing motionless:
> To the pool's further margin then I drew,
> He being all the while before me full in view.

Compare this with the repetition of the same image, in the next stanza but two.

> And, still as I drew near with gentle pace,
> Beside the little pond or moorish flood
> Motionless as a cloud the old man stood,
> That heareth not the loud winds as they call,
> And moveth altogether, if it move at all.

Or lastly, the second of the three following stanzas, compared both with the first and the third.

> My former thoughts returned; the fear that kills;
> And hope that is unwilling to be fed;

Cold, pain, and labour, and all fleshy ills;
And mighty poets in their misery dead.
But now, perplex'd by what the old man had said,
My question eagerly did I renew,
"How is it that you live, and what is it you do?"

He with a smile did then his words repeat;
And said, that gathering leeches far and wide
He travell'd; stirring thus about his feet
The waters of the ponds where they abide.
"Once I could meet with them on every side,
"But they have dwindled long by slow decay;
"Yet still I persevere, and find them where I may."

While he was talking thus, the lonely place,
The old man's shape, and speech, all troubled me:
In my mind's eye I seemed to see him pace
About the weary moors continually,
Wandering about alone and silently.

Indeed this fine poem is *especially* characteristic of the author. There is scarce a defect or excellence in his writings of which it would not present a specimen. But it would be unjust not to repeat that this defect is only occasional. From a careful reperusal of the two volumes of poems, I doubt whether the objectionable passages would amount in the whole to one hundred lines; not the eighth part of the number of pages. In the "Excursion" the feeling of incongruity is seldom excited by the diction of any passage considered in itself, but by the sudden superiority of some other passage forming the context.

The second defect I can generalize with tolerable accuracy, if the reader will pardon an uncouth and new-coined word. There is, I should say, not seldom a *matter-of-factness* in certain poems. This may be divided into, *first,* a laborious minuteness and fidelity in the representation of objects, and their positions, as they appeared to the poet himself; *secondly,* the insertion of accidental circumstances, in order to the full explanation of his living characters, their dispositions and actions; which circumstances might be necessary to establish the probability of a statement in real life, where nothing is taken for granted by the hearer; but appear superfluous in poetry, where the reader is willing to believe for his own sake. To this *accidentality* I object, as contravening the essence of poetry, which Aristotle pronounces to be σπουδαιότατον καὶ φιλοσοφώτατον γένος, the most intense, weighty and philosophical product of human art; adding, as the *reason*, that it is the most catholic and abstract. The following passage from Davenant's prefatory letter to Hobbs well expresses this truth. "When I considered the actions which I meant to describe, (those inferring the persons), I was again persuaded rather to choose those of a former age, than the present; and in a century so far removed, as might preserve me from their improper examinations, who know not the requisites of a poem, nor how much pleasure they lose, (and even the pleasures of heroic poesy are not unprofitable), who take away the liberty of a poet, and fetter his feet in the shackles of an historian. For why should a poet doubt in story to mend the intrigues of fortune by more delightful conveyances of probable fictions, because austere historians have entered into bond to truth? An obligation, which were in poets as foolish and unnecessary, as in the bondage of false martyrs, who lie in chains for a mistaken opinion. *But by this I would imply, that truth narrative and past is the idol of historians, (who worship a dead thing), and truth operative, and by effects continually alive, is the mistress of poets, who hath not her existence in matter, but in reason.*"

For this minute accuracy in the painting of local imagery, the lines in the Excursion, pp. 96, 97, and 98, may be taken, if not as a striking instance, yet as an illustration of my meaning. It must be some strong motive (as, for instance, that the description was necessary to the intelligibility of the tale) which could induce me to describe in a number of verses what a draughtsman could present to the eye with incomparably greater satisfaction by half a dozen strokes of his pencil, or the painter with as many touches of his brush. Such descriptions too often occasion in the mind of a reader, who is determined to understand his author, a feeling of labor, not very dissimilar to that, with which he would construct a diagram, line by line, for a long geometrical proposition. It seems to be like taking the pieces of a dissected map out of its box. We first look at one part, and then at another, then join and dove-tail them; and when the successive acts of attention have been com-

pleted, there is a retrogressive effort of mind to behold it as a
whole. The poet should paint to the imagination, not to the fancy;
and I know no happier case to exemplify the distinction between
these two faculties. Master-pieces of the former mode of poetic
painting abound in the writings of Milton, ex. gr.

> The fig-tree; not that kind for fruit renown'd,
> But such as at this day, to Indians known,
> In Malabar or Decan spreads her arms
> Branching so broad and long, that in the ground
> The bended twigs take root, *and daughters grow*
> *About the mother tree, a pillar'd shade*
> *High over-arch'd, and* ECHOING WALKS BETWEEN:
> *There oft the Indian Herdsman, shunning heat,*
> *Shelters in cool, and tends his pasturing herds*
> *At loop holes cut through thickest shade.*
>                    MILTON P. L. 9. 1100.

This is *creation* rather than *painting,* or if painting, yet such,
and with such co-presence of the whole picture flash'd at once
upon the eye, as the sun paints in a camera obscura. But the poet
must likewise understand and command what Bacon calls the
*vestigia communia* of the senses, the latency of all in each, and
more especially as by a magical *penna duplex,* the excitement of
vision by sound and the exponents of sound. Thus "THE ECHOING
WALKS BETWEEN," may be almost said to reverse the fable in tradition of the head of Memnon, in the Egyptian statue. Such may
be deservedly entitled the *creative words* in the world of imagination.

The second division respects an apparent minute adherence to
*matter-of-fact* in characters and incidents; *a biographical* attention
to probability, and an *anxiety* of explanation and retrospect. Under
this head I shall deliver, with no feigned diffidence, the results of
my best reflection on the great point of controversy between Mr.
Wordsworth and his objectors; namely, on THE CHOICE OF HIS
CHARACTERS. I have already declared and, I trust, justified, my
utter dissent from the mode of argument which his critics have
hitherto employed. To *their* question, Why did you chuse such a
character, or a character from such a rank of life? the poet might
in my opinion fairly retort: why with the conception of my char-

acter did you make wilful choice of mean or ludicrous associations not furnished by me, but supplied from your own sickly and fastidious feelings? How was it, indeed, probable, that such arguments could have any weight with an author, whose plan, whose guiding principle, and main object it was to attack and subdue that state of association, which leads us to place the chief value on those things in which man DIFFERS from man, and to forget or disregard the high dignities, which belong to HUMAN NATURE, the sense and the feeling, which *may* be, and *ought* to be, found in *all* ranks? The feelings with which, as Christians, we contemplate a mixed congregation rising or kneeling before their common Maker: Mr. Wordsworth would have us entertain at *all* times, as men, and as readers; and by the excitement of this lofty, yet prideless impartiality in *poetry*, he might hope to have encouraged its continuance in *real life*. The praise of good men be his! In real life, and, I trust, even in my imagination, I honor a virtuous and wise man, without reference to the presence or absence of artificial advantages. Whether in the person of an armed baron, a laurel'd bard, &c., or of an old pedlar, or still older leach-gatherer, the same qualities of head and heart must claim the same reverence. And even in poetry I am not conscious, that I have ever suffered my feelings to be disturbed or offended by any thoughts or images, which the poet himself has not presented.

But yet I object nevertheless and for the following reasons. First, because the object in view, as an *immediate* object, belongs to the moral philosopher, and would be pursued, not only more appropriately, but in my opinion with far greater probability of success, in sermons or moral essays, than in an elevated poem. It seems, indeed, to destroy the main fundamental distinction, not only between a poem and prose, but even between philosophy and works of fiction, inasmuch as it proposes *truth* for its immediate object, instead of *pleasure*. Now till the blessed time shall come, when truth itself shall be pleasure, and both shall be so united, as to be distinguishable in words only, not in feeling, it will remain the poet's office to proceed upon that state of association, which actually exists as *general*; instead of attempting first to *make* it what it ought to be, and then to let the pleasure follow. But here is unfortunately a small *Hysteron-Proteron*. For the communication of pleasure is the introductory means by which alone the poet must expect to moralize his readers. Secondly: though I were to admit, for a moment, *this* argument to be groundless: yet how is the moral effect to be produced, by merely attaching the name of some low profession to powers which are *least* likely, and to qualities which are assuredly not *more* likely, to be found in it? The poet, speaking in his own person, may at once delight and improve us by sentiments, which teach us the independence of goodness, of wisdom, and even of genius, on the favors of fortune. And having made a due reverence before the throne of Antonine, he may bow with equal awe before Epictetus among his fellow-slaves—

> and rejoice
> In the plain presence of his dignity.

Who is not at once delighted and improved, when the POET Wordsworth himself exclaims,

> O many are the poets that are sown
> By Nature; man endowed with highest gifts,
> The vision and the faculty divine,
> Yet wanting the accomplishment of verse,
> Nor having e'er, as life advanced, been led
> By circumstance to take unto the height
> The measure of themselves, these favor'd beings,
> All but a scatter'd few, live out their time
> Husbanding that which they possess within,
> And go to the grave unthought of. Strongest minds
> Are often those of whom the noisy world
> Hears least.
>
> EXCURSION, B. I.

To use a colloquial phrase, such sentiments, in such language, do one's heart good; though I for my part, have not the fullest faith in the *truth* of the observation. On the contrary I believe the instances to be exceedingly rare; and should feel almost as strong an objection to introduce such a character in a poetic fiction, as a pair of black swans on a lake in a fancy-landscape. When I think how many, and how much better books than Homer, or even than Herodotus, Pindar or Eschylus, could have read, are in the power of almost every man, in a country where almost every man is instructed to read and write; and how restless, how difficultly hidden, the powers of genius are; and yet find even in situations the most favorable, according to Mr. Wordsworth, for the formation of a pure and poetic language; in situations which ensure familiarity with the grandest objects of the imagination; but *one* BURNS, among the shepherds of *Scotland*, and not a single poet of humble life among those of *English* lakes and mountains; I conclude, that POETIC GENIUS is not only a very delicate but a very rare plant.

But be this as it may, the feelings with which

> I think of CHATTERTON, the marvellous boy,
> The sleepless soul, that perished in his pride;
> Of BURNS, that walk'd in glory and in joy
> Behind his plough upon the mountain-side—

are widely different from those with which I should read a *poem,* where the author, having occasion for the character of a poet and a philosopher in the fable of his narration, had chosen to make him a *chimney-sweeper;* and then, in order to remove all doubts on the subject, had *invented* an account of his birth, parentage and education, with all the strange and fortunate accidents which had concurred in making him at once poet, philosopher, and sweep! Nothing but biography can justify this. If it be admissible even in a *Novel,* it must be one in the manner of De Foe's, that were meant to pass for histories, not in the manner of Fielding's: in the life of Moll Flanders, or Colonel Jack, not in a Tom Jones, or even a Joseph Andrews. Much less then can it be legitimately introduced in a *poem,* the characters of which, amid the strongest individualization, must still remain representative. The precepts of Horace, on this point, are grounded on the nature both of poetry and of the human mind. They are not more peremptory, than wise and prudent. For in the first place a deviation from them perplexes the reader's feelings, and all the circumstances, which are feigned in order to make such accidents less improbable, divide and disquiet his faith, rather than aid and support it. Spite of all attempts, the fiction *will* appear, and unfortunately not as *ficti-tious* but as *false*. The reader not only *knows*, that the sentiments and language are the poet's own, and his own too in his *artificial* character, *as poet;* but by the fruitless endeavours to make him think the contrary, he is not even suffered to *forget* it. The effect is similar to that produced by an epic poet, when the fable and the characters are *derived* from Scripture history, as in the *Messiah* of *Klopstock*, or in *Cumberland's Calvary;* and not merely *suggested* by it, as in the Paradise Lost of Milton. That *illusion*, contra-distinguished from *delusion*, that *negative* faith, which simply permits the images presented to work by their own force, without either denial or affirmation of their real existence by the judgement, is rendered impossible by their immediate neighbour-hood to words and facts of known and absolute truth. A faith, which transcends even historic belief, must absolutely *put out* this mere poetic Analogon of faith, as the summer sun is said to extinguish our household fires, when it shines full upon them. What would otherwise have been yielded to as pleasing fiction, is repelled as revolting falsehood. The effect produced in this latter case by the solemn belief of the reader, is in a less degree brought about in the instances, to which I have been objecting, by the baffled attempts of the author to *make* him believe.

Add to all the foregoing the seeming uselessness both of the project and of the anecdotes from which it is to derive support. Is there one word, for instance, attributed to the pedlar in the "Ex-cursion," characteristic of a *pedlar?* One sentiment, that might not more plausibly, even without the aid of any previous explana-tion, have proceeded from any wise and beneficent old man, of a rank or profession in which the language of learning and refine-ment are natural and to be expected? Need the rank have been at all particularized, where nothing follows which the knowledge of that rank is to explain or illustrate? When on the contrary this information renders the man's language, feelings, sentiments, and information a riddle, which must itself be solved by episodes of anecdote? Finally when this, and this alone, could have induced a genuine *poet* to inweave in a poem of the loftiest style, and on subjects the loftiest and of most universal interest, such minute matters of fact, (not unlike those furnished for the obituary of a magazine by the friends of some obscure *ornament of society lately deceased* in some obscure town), as

> Among the hills of Athol he was born:
> There, on a small hereditary farm,
> An unproductive slip of rugged ground,
> His Father dwelt; and died in poverty;
> While he, whose lowly fortune I retrace,
> The youngest of three sons, was yet a babe,
> A little one—unconscious of their loss.
> But, ere he had outgrown his infant days,
> His widowed mother, for a second mate,
> Espoused the teacher of the Village School;
> Who on her offspring zealously bestowed
> Needful instruction.

> ——————

> From his sixth year, the Boy of whom I speak,
> In summer tended cattle on the hills;
> But, through the inclement and the perilous days
> Of long-continuing winter, he repaired
> To his step-father's school,—&c.

For all the admirable passages interposed in this narration, might, with trifling alterations, have been far more appropriately, and with far greater verisimilitude, told of a poet in the character of a poet; and without incurring another defect which I shall now mention, and a sufficient illustration of which will have been here anticipated.

Third; an undue predilection for the *dramatic* form in certain poems, from which one or other of two evils result. Either the thoughts and diction are different from that of the poet, and then there arises an incongruity of style; or they are the same and indistinguishable, and then it presents a species of ventriloquism, where two are represented as talking, while in truth one man only speaks.

The fourth class of defects is closely connected with the former; but yet are such as arise likewise from an intensity of feeling disproportionate to *such* knowledge and value of the objects described, as can be fairly anticipated of men in general, even of the most cultivated classes; and with which therefore few only, and

those few particularly circumstances, can be supposed to sympathize. In this class, I comprise occasional prolixity, repetition,
and an eddying, instead of progression, of thought. As instances,
see pages 27, 28, and 62 of the Poems, Vol. I. and the first eighty
lines of the Sixth Book of the Excursion.

Fifth and last; thoughts and images too great for the subject.
This is an approximation to what might be called *mental* bombast, as distinguished from verbal: for, as in the latter there is a
disproportion of the expressions to the thoughts, so in this there
is a disproportion of thought to the circumstance and occasion.
This, by the bye, is a fault of which none but a man of genius is
capable. It is the awkwardness and strength of Hercules with the
distaff of Omphale.

It is a well-known fact, that bright colors in motion both make
and leave the strongest impressions on the eye. Nothing is more
likely too, than that a vivid image or visual spectrum, thus originated, may become the link of association in recalling the feelings
and images that had accompanied the original impression. But if
we describe this in such lines, as

> They flash upon that inward eye,
> Which is the bliss of solitude!

in what words shall we describe the joy of retrospection, when the
images and virtuous actions of a whole well-spent life, pass before
that conscience which is indeed the *inward* eye: which is indeed
"*the bliss of solitude?*" Assuredly we seem to sink most abruptly,
not to say burlesquely, and almost as in a *medly*, from this couplet
to—

> And then my heart with pleasure fills,
> And dances with the *daffodils*.
> Vol. I. p. 320.

The second instance is from Vol. II. page 12, where the poet,
having gone out for a day's tour of pleasure, meets early in the
morning with a knot of *gypsies*, who had pitched their blanket-
tents and straw-beds, together with their children and asses, in
some field by the road-side. At the close of the day on his return
our tourist found them in the same place. "Twelve hours," says he,

> Twelve hours, twelve bounteous hours are gone, while I
> Have been a traveller under open sky,
> Much witnessing of change and cheer,
> Yet as I left I find them here!

Whereat the poet, without seeming to reflect that the poor tawny wanderers might probably have been tramping for weeks together through road and lane, over moor and mountain, and consequently must have been right glad to rest themselves, their children and cattle, for one whole day; and overlooking the obvious truth, that such repose might be quite as necessary for *them,* as a walk of the same continuance was pleasing or healthful for the most fortunate poet; expresses his indignation in a series of lines, the diction and imagery of which would have been rather above, than below the mark, had they been applied to the immense empire of China improgressive for thirty centuries:

> The weary SUN betook himself to rest:—
> —Then issued VESPER from the fulgent west,
> Outshining, like a visible God,
> The glorious path in which he trod!
> And now, ascending, after one dark hour,
> And one night's diminution of her power,
> Behold the mighty MOON! this way
> She looks, as if at them—but they
> Regard not her:—oh, better wrong and strife,
> Better vain deeds or evil than such life!
> The silent HEAVENS have goings on:
> The STARS have tasks!—but *these* have none!

The last instance of this defect (for I know no other than these already cited) is from the Ode, page 351, Vol. II., where, speaking of a child, "a six years' darling of a pigmy size," he thus addresses him:

> Thou best philosopher, who yet dost keep
> Thy heritage! Thou eye among the blind,
> That, deaf and silent, read'st the eternal deep,
> Haunted for ever by the Eternal Mind,—
> Mighty Prophet! Seer blest!
> On whom those truths do rest,
> Which we are toiling all our lives to find!
> Thou, over whom thy immortality

Broods like the day, a master o'er the slave,
A presence that is not to be put by!

Now here, not to stop at the daring spirit of metaphor which connects the epithets "deaf and silent," with the apostrophized *eye:* or (if we are to refer it to the preceding word, philosopher) the faulty and equivocal syntax of the passage; and without examining the propriety of making a "master *brood* o'er a slave," or the *day* brood *at all;* we will merely ask, what does all this mean? In what sense is a child of that age a *philosopher?* In what sense does he *read* "the eternal deep"? In what sense is he declared to be *"for ever haunted"* by the Supreme Being? or so inspired as to deserve the splendid titles of a *mighty prophet,* a *blessed seer?* By reflection? by knowledge? by conscious intuition? or by *any* form or modification of consciousness? These would be tidings indeed; but such as would presuppose an immediate revelation to the inspired communicator, and require miracles to authenticate his inspiration. Children at this age give us no such information of themselves; and at what time were we dipped in the Lethe, which has produced such utter oblivion of a state so godlike? There are many of us that still possess some remembrances, more or less distinct, respecting themselves at six years old; pity that the worthless straws only should float, while treasures, compared with which all the mines of Golconda and Mexico were but straws, should be absorbed by some unknown gulf into some unknown abyss.

But if this be too wild and exorbitant to be suspected as having been the poet's meaning; if these mysterious gifts, faculties, and operations, are *not* accompanied with consciousness; who *else* is conscious of them? or how can it be called the child, if it be no part of the child's conscious being? For aught I know, the thinking Spirit within me may be *substantially* one with the principle of life, and of vital operation. For aught I know, it might be employed as a secondary agent in the marvellous organization and organic movements of my body. But, surely, it would be strange language to say, that I construct my *heart!* or that I propel the finer influences through my *nerves!* or that I compress my brain, and draw the curtains of sleep round my own eyes! SPINOZA and

BEHMEN were, on different systems, both Pantheists; and among the ancients there were philosophers, teachers of the EN KAI ΠAN, who not only taught that God was All, but that this All constituted God. Yet not even these would confound the *part, as* a part, with the Whole, *as* the whole. Nay, in no system is the distinction between the individual and God, between the Modification, and the one only Substance, more sharply drawn, than in that of SPINOZA. JACOBI indeed relates of LESSING, that, after a conversation with him at the house of the poet, GLEIM (the Tyrtæus and Anacreon of the German Parnassus) in which conversation L. had avowed privately to Jacobi his reluctance to admit any *personal* existence of the Supreme Being, or the *possibility* of personality except in a finite Intellect, and while they were sitting at table, a shower of rain came on unexpectedly. Gleim expressed his regret at the circumstance, because they had meant to drink their wine in the garden: upon which Lessing in one of his half-earnest half-joking moods, nodded to Jacobi, and said, "It is *I,* perhaps, that am doing *that,*" i. e. *raining!* and J. answered, "or perhaps I"; Gleim contented himself with staring at them both, without asking for any explanation.

So with regard to this passage. In what sense can the magnificent attributes, above quoted, be appropriated to a *child,* which would not make them equally suitable to a *bee,* or a *dog,* or a *field of corn:* or even to a ship, or to the wind and waves that propel it? The omnipresent Spirit works equally in them, as in the child; and the child is equally unconscious of it as they. It cannot surely be, that the four lines, immediately following, are to contain the explanation?

> To whom the grave
> Is but a lonely bed without the sense or sight
> Of day or the warm light,
> A place of thought where we in waiting lie.

Surely, it cannot be that this wonder-rousing apostrophe is but a comment on the little poem, "We are seven?" that the whole meaning of the passage is reducible to the assertion, that a *child,* who by the bye at six years old would have been better instructed in most Christian families, has no other notion of death than that of lying in a dark, cold place? And still, I hope, not as in a *place of thought!* not the frightful notion of lying *awake* in his grave! The analogy between death and sleep is too simple, too natural, to render so horrid a belief possible for children; even had they not been in the habit, as all Christian children are, of hearing the latter term used to express the former. But if the child's belief be only, that "he is not dead, but sleepeth:" wherein does it differ from that of his father and mother, or any other adult and instructed person? To form an idea of a thing's becoming nothing; or of nothing becoming a thing; is impossible to all finite beings alike, of whatever age, and however educated or uneducated. Thus it is with splendid paradoxes in general. If the words are taken in the common sense, they convey an absurdity; and if, in contempt of dictionaries and custom, they are so interpreted as to avoid the absurdity, the meaning dwindles into some bald truism. Thus you must at once understand the words *contrary* to their common import, in order to arrive at any *sense;* and *according* to their common import, if you are to receive from them any feeling of *sublimity* or *admiration.*

Though the instances of this defect in Mr. Wordsworth's poems are so few, that for themselves it would have been scarce just to attract the reader's attention toward them; yet I have dwelt on it, and perhaps the more for this very reason. For being so very few, they cannot sensibly detract from the reputation of an author, who is even characterized by the number of profound truths in his writings, which will stand the severest analysis; and yet few as they are, they are exactly those passages which his *blind* admirers would be most likely, and best able, to imitate. But WORDSWORTH, where he is indeed Wordsworth, may be mimicked by Copyists, he may be plundered by Plagiarists; but he can not be imitated, except by those who are not born to be imitators. For without his depth of feeling and his imaginative power his *sense* would want its vital warmth and peculiarity; and without his strong sense, his *mysticism* would become *sickly*—mere fog, and dimness!

To these defects which, as appears by the extracts, are only occasional, I may oppose, with far less fear of encountering the dissent of any candid and intelligent reader, the following (for the most part correspondent) excellences. First, an austere purity of language both grammatically and logically; in short a perfect appropriateness of the words to the meaning. Of how high value I deem this, and how particularly estimable I hold the example at the present day, has been already stated: and in part too the reasons on which I ground both the moral and intellectual importance of habituating ourselves to a strict accuracy of expression. It is noticeable, how limited an acquaintance with the master-pieces of art will suffice to form a correct and even a sensitive taste, where none but master-pieces have been seen and admired: while on the other hand, the most correct notions, and the widest acquaintance with the works of excellence of all ages and countries, will not perfectly secure us against the contagious familiarity with the far more numerous offspring of tastelessness or of a perverted taste. If this be the case, as it notoriously is, with the arts of music and painting, much more difficult will it be to avoid the infection of multiplied and daily examples in the practice of an art, which uses words, and words only, as its instruments. In poetry, in which every line, every phrase, may pass the ordeal of deliberation and deliberate choice, it is possible, and barely possible, to attain that ultimatum which I have ventured to propose as the infallible test of a blameless style; its *untranslatableness* in words of the same language without injury to the meaning. Be it observed, however, that I include in the *meaning* of a word not only its correspondent object, but likewise all the associations which it recalls. For language is framed to convey not the object alone, but likewise the character, mood and intentions of the person who is representing it. In poetry it *is* practicable to preserve the diction uncorrupted by the affectations and misappropriations, which promiscuous authorship, and reading not promiscuous only because it is disproportionally most conversant with the compositions of the day, have rendered general. Yet even to the poet, composing in his own province, it is an arduous work: and as the result and pledge of a watchful good sense, of fine and luminous distinction, and of complete self-possession, may justly claim all the honor which belongs to an attainment equally difficult and valuable, and the more valuable for being rare. It is at *all* times the proper food of the understanding; but in an age of corrupt eloquence it is both food and antidote.

In prose I doubt whether it be even possible to preserve our style wholly unalloyed by the vicious phraseology which meets us everywhere, from the sermon to the newspaper, from the harangue of the legislator to the speech from the convivial chair, announcing a *toast* or sentiment. Our chains rattle, even while we are complaining of them. The poems of Boetius rise high in our estimation when we compare them with those of his contemporaries, as Sidonius Apollinarius, &c. They might even be referred to a purer age, but that the prose, in which they are set, as jewels in a crown of lead or iron, betrays the true age of the writer. Much however may be effected by education. I believe not only from grounds of reason, but from having in great measure assured myself of the fact by actual though limited experience, that, to a youth led from his first boyhood to investigate the meaning of every word and the reason of its choice and position, Logic presents itself as an old acquaintance under new names.

On some future occasion, more especially demanding such disquisition, I shall attempt to prove the close connection between veracity and habits of mental accuracy; the beneficial after-effects of verbal precision in the preclusion of fanaticism, which masters the feelings more especially by indistinct watch-words; and to display the advantages which language alone, at least which language with incomparably greater ease and certainty than any other means, presents to the instructor of impressing modes of intellectual energy so constantly, so imperceptibly, and as it were by such elements and atoms, as to secure in due time the formation of a second nature. When we reflect, that the cultivation of the judgement is a positive command of the moral law, since the reason can give the *principle* alone, and the conscience bears witness only to the *motive,* while the application and effects must depend on the judgement: when we consider, that the greater part of our success and comfort in life depends on distinguishing the similar from the same, that which is peculiar in each thing from that which it has in common with others, so as still to select the most probable, instead of the merely possible or positively unfit, we shall learn to

value earnestly and with a practical seriousness a mean, already
prepared for us by nature and society, of teaching the young mind
to think well and wisely by the same unremembered process and
with the same never forgotten results, as those by which it is
taught to speak and converse. Now how much warmer the
interest is, how much more genial the feelings of reality and
practicability, and thence how much stronger the impulses to imitation are, which a *contemporary* writer, and especially a contemporary *poet,* excites in youth and commencing manhood, has been
treated of in the earlier pages of these sketches. I have only to add,
that all the praise which is due to the exertion of such influence
for a purpose so important, joined with that which must be claimed
for the infrequency of the same excellence in the same perfection,
belongs in full right to Mr. Wordsworth. I am far however from
denying that we have poets whose *general* style possesses the same
excellence, as Mr. Moore, Lord Byron, Mr. Bowles, and, in all his
later and more important works, our laurel-honoring Laureate.
But there are none, in whose works I do not appear to myself to
find *more* exceptions, than in those of Wordsworth. Quotations or
specimens would here be wholly out of place, and must be left for
the critic who doubts and would invalidate the justice of this
eulogy so applied.

The second characteristic excellence of Mr. W's work is: a
correspondent weight and sanity of the Thoughts and Sentiments,
won—not from books, but—from the poet's own meditative observation. They are *fresh* and have the dew upon them. His muse, at
least when in her strength of wing, and when she hovers aloft in
her proper element,

> Makes audible a linked lay of truth,
> Of truth profound a sweet continuous lay,
> Not learnt, but native, her own natural notes!
>                                     S. T. C.

Even throughout his smaller poems there is scarcely one, which
is not rendered valuable by some just and original reflection.

See page 25, vol. 2nd.: or the two following passages in one of
his humblest compositions.

> O Reader! had you in your mind
> Such stores as silent thought can bring,
> O gentle Reader! you would find
> A tale in every thing;

and

> I've heard of hearts unkind, kind deeds
> With coldness still returning;
> Alas! the gratitude of men
> Has oftener left me mourning

or in a still higher strain the six beautiful quatrains, page 134.

> Thus fares it still in our decay:
> And yet the wiser mind
> Mourns less for what age takes away
> Than what it leaves behind.
>
> The Blackbird in the summer trees,
> The Lark upon the hill,
> Let loose their carols when they please,
> Are quiet when they will.
>
> With nature never do *they* wage
> A foolish strife; they see
> A happy youth, and their old age
> Is beautiful and free!
>
> But we are pressed by heavy laws;
> And often, glad no more,
> We wear a face of joy, because
> We have been glad of yore.
>
> If there is one, who need bemoan
> His kindred laid in earth,
> The household hearts that were his own,
> It is the man of mirth.
>
> My days, my Friend, are almost gone,
> My life has been approved,
> And many love me; but by none
> Am I enough beloved.

or the sonnet on Buonaparte, page 202, vol. 2; or finally (for a volume would scarce suffice to exhaust the instances) the last stanza of the poem on the withered Celandine, vol. 2, p. 212.

To be a prodigal's favorite—then, worse truth,
A miser's pensioner—behold our lot!
O man! that from thy fair and shining youth
Age might but take the things youth needed not.

Both in respect of this and of the former excellence, Mr. Wordsworth strikingly resembles Samuel Daniel, one of the golden
writers of our golden Elizabethan age, now most causelessly neglected: Samuel Daniel, whose diction bears no mark of time, no
distinction of age, which has been, and as long as our language
shall last, will be so far the language of the to-day and for ever,
as that it is more intelligible to us, than the transitory fashions of
our own particular age. A similar praise is due to his sentiments.
No frequency of perusal can deprive them of their freshness. For
though they are brought into the full day-light of every reader's
comprehension; yet are they drawn up from depths which few in
any age are priviledged to visit, into which few in any age have
courage or inclination to descend. If Mr. Wordsworth is not
equally with Daniel alike intelligible to all readers of average
understanding in all passages of his works, the comparative difficulty does not arise from the greater impurity of the ore, but from
the nature and uses of the metal. A poem is not necessarily obscure, because it does not aim to be popular. It is enough, if a
work be perspicuous to those for whom it is written, and

> Fit audience find, though few.

To the "Ode on the intimation of immortality from recollections
of early childhood" the poet might have prefixed the lines which
Dante addresses to one of his own Canzoni—

> Canzon, io credo, che saranno radi
> Che tua ragionne intendan bene,
> Tanto lor sei faticoso ed alto.

> O lyric song, there will be few, think I,
> Who may thy import understand aright:
> Thou art for *them* so arduous and so high!

But the ode was intended for such readers only as had been
accustomed to watch the flux and reflux of their inmost nature, to
venture at times into the twilight realms of consciousness, and to

feel a deep interest in modes of inmost being, to which they know
that the attributes of time and space are inapplicable and alien, but
which yet can not be conveyed save in symbols of time and space.
For such readers the sense is sufficiently plain, and they will be as
little disposed to charge Mr. Wordsworth with believing the Platonic pre-existence in the ordinary interpretation of the words, as
I am to believe, that Plato himself ever meant or taught it.

> Πολλά μοι ὑπ' ἀγκῶ-
> νος ὠκέα βέλη
> ἔνδον ἐντὶ φαρέτρας
> φωνᾶντα συνετοῖσιν· ἐς
> δὲ τὸ πᾶν ἑρμηνέων
> χατίζει. σοφὸς ὁ πολ-
> λὰ εἰδὼς φυᾷ.
> μαθόντες δέ, λάβροι
> παγγλωσσίᾳ, κόρακες ὥς,
> ἄκραντα γαρύετον
> Διὸς πρὸς ὄρνιχα θεῖον.

Third (and wherein he soars far above Daniel) the sinewy
strength and originality of single lines and paragraphs: the frequent *curiosa felicitas* of his diction, of which I need not here give
specimens, having anticipated them in a preceding page. This
beauty, and as eminently characteristic of Wordsworth's poetry,
his rudest assailants have felt themselves compelled to acknowledge and admire.

Fourth; the perfect truth of nature in his images and descriptions, as taken immediately from nature, and proving a long and
genial intimacy with the very spirit which gives the physiognomic
expression to all the works of nature. Like a green field reflected in
a calm and perfectly transparent lake, the image is distinguished
from the reality only by its greater softness and lustre. Like the
moisture or the polish or a pebble, genius neither distorts nor false-
colours its objects; but on the contrary brings out many a vein and
many a tint, which escapes the eye of common observation, thus
raising to the rank of gems what had been often kicked away by the
hurrying foot of the traveller on the dusty high road of custom.

Let me refer to the whole description of skating, vol. I., page 42 to 47, especially to the lines

> So through the darkness and the cold we flew,
> And not a voice was idle: with the din
> Meanwhile the precipices rang aloud;
> The leafless trees and every icy crag
> Tinkled like iron; while the distant hills
> Into the tumult sent an alien sound
> Of melancholy, not unnoticed, while the stars
> Eastward were sparkling clear, and in the west
> The orange sky of evening died away.

Or to the poem on the green linnet, vol. I. page 244. What can be more accurate yet more lovely than the two concluding stanzas?

> Upon yon tuft of hazel trees,
> That twinkle to the gusty breeze,
> Behold him perched in ecstasies,
>  Yet seeming still to hover;
> There! where the flutter of his wings
> Upon his back and body flings
> Shadows and sunny glimmerings,
>  That cover him all over.
>
> While thus before my eyes he gleams,
> A brother of the leaves he seems;
> When in a moment forth he teems
>  His little song in gushes:
> As if it pleased him to disdain
> And mock the form which he did feign,
> While he was dancing with the train
>  Of leaves among the bushes.

Or the description of the blue-cap, and of the noon-tide silence, page 284; or the poem to the cuckoo, page 299; or, lastly, though I might multiply the references to ten times the number, to the poem, so completely Wordsworth's, commencing

> Three years she grew in sun and shower, &c.

Fifth: a meditative pathos, a union of deep and subtle thought with sensibility; a sympathy with man as man; the sympathy indeed of a contemplator, rather than a fellow-sufferer or co-mate, (spectator, haud particeps) but of a contemplator, from whose view no difference of rank conceals the sameness of the nature; no injuries of wind or weather, or toil, or even of ignorance, wholly disguise the human face divine. The superscription and the image of the Creator still remain legible to *him* under the dark lines, with which guilt or calamity had cancelled or cross-barred it. Here the man and the poet lose and find themselves in each other, the one as glorified, the latter as substantiated. In this mild and philosophic pathos, Wordsworth appears to me without a compeer. Such he *is:* so he *writes.* See vol. I. page 134 to 136, or that most affecting composition, the "Affliction of Margaret —— of ——," page 165 to 168, which no mother, and, if I may judge by my own experience, no parent can read without a tear. Or turn to that genuine lyric, in the former edition, entitled "The Mad Mother," page 174 to 178, of which I cannot refrain from quoting two of the stanzas, both of them for their pathos, and the former for the fine transition in the two concluding lines of the stanza, so expressive of that deranged state, in which from the increased sensibility the sufferer's attention is abruptly drawn off by every trifle, and in the same instant plucked back again by the one despotic thought, bringing home with it, by the blending, *fusing* power of Imagination and Passion, the alien object to which it had been so abruptly diverted, no longer an alien but an ally and an inmate.

> Suck, little babe, oh suck again!
> It cools my blood; it cools my brain:
> Thy lips, I feel them, baby! they
> Draw from my heart the pain away.
> Oh! press me with thy little hand;
> It loosens something at my chest:
> About that tight and deadly band
> I feel thy little fingers prest.
> The breeze I see is in the tree!
> It comes to cool my babe and me.
> Thy father cares not for my breast,
> 'Tis thine, sweet baby, there to rest,
> 'Tis all thine own!—and, if its hue
> Be changed, that was so fair to view,
> 'Tis fair enough for thee, my dove!
> My beauty, little child, is flown,
> But thou wilt live with me in love;

> And what if my poor cheek be brown?
> 'Tis well for me, thou canst not see
> How pale and wan it else would be.

Last, and pre-eminently, I challenge for this poet the gift of IMAGINATION in the highest and strictest sense of the word. In the play of *Fancy*, Wordsworth, to my feelings, is not always graceful, and sometimes *recondite*. The *likeness* is occasionally too strange, or demands too peculiar a point of view, or is such as appears the creature of pre-determined research, rather than spontaneous presentation. Indeed his fancy seldom displays itself, as mere and unmodified fancy. But in imaginative power, he stands nearest of all modern writers to Shakespeare and Milton; and yet in a kind perfectly unborrowed and his own. To employ his own words, which are at once an instance and an illustration, he does indeed to all thoughts and to all objects

> add the gleam,
> The light that never was, on sea or land,
> The consecration, and the poet's dream.

I shall select a few examples as most obviously manifesting this faculty; but if I should ever be fortunate enough to render my analysis of imagination, its origin and characters, thoroughly intelligible to the reader, he will scarcely open on a page of this poet's works without recognising, more or less, the presence and the influences of this faculty.

From the poem on the Yew Trees, vol. I. page 303, 304.

> But worthier still of note
> Are those fraternal four of Borrowdale,
> Joined in one solemn and capacious grove:
> Huge trunks!—and each particular trunk a growth
> Of intertwisted fibres serpentine
> Up-coiling, and inveterately convolved,—
> Not uninformed with phantasy, and looks
> That threaten the profane;—a pillared shade,
> Upon whose grassless floor of red-brown hue,
> By sheddings from the pinal umbrage tinged
> Perennially—beneath whose sable roof
> Of boughs, as if for festal purpose decked

With unrejoicing berries, ghostly shapes
May meet at noontide—FEAR and trembling HOPE,
SILENCE and FORESIGHT—DEATH, the skeleton,
And TIME, the shadow—there to celebrate,
As in a natural temple scattered o'er
With altars undisturbed of mossy stone,
United worship; or in mute repose
To lie, and listen to the mountain flood
Murmuring from Glaramara's inmost caves.

The effect of the old man's figure in the poem of Resignation and Independence, vol. II. page 33.

While he was talking thus, the lonely place,
The old man's shape, and speech, all troubled me:
In my mind's eye I seemed to see him pace
About the weary moors continually,
Wandering about alone and silently.

Or the 8th, 9th, 19th, 26th, 31st, and 33d, in the collection of miscellaneous sonnets—the sonnet on the subjugation of Switzerland, page 210, or the last ode, from which I especially select the two following stanzas or paragraphs, page 349 to 350.

Our birth is but a sleep and a forgetting;
The soul that rises with us, our life's star,
Hath had elsewhere its setting,
    And cometh from afar.
Not in entire forgetfulness,
And not in utter nakedness,
But trailing clouds of glory do we come
From God, who is our home:
Heaven lies about us in our infancy!
Shades of the prison-house begin to close
    Upon the growing boy;
But he beholds the light, and whence it flows,
    He sees it in his joy!
The youth who daily further from the East
Must travel, still is nature's priest,
    And by the splendid vision
    Is on his way attended;
At length the man perceives it die away,
And fade into the light of common day.

And page 352 to 354 of the same ode.

> O joy that in our embers
> Is something that doth live,
> That nature yet remembers
> What was so fugitive!
> The thought of our past years in me doth breed
> Perpetual benedictions: not indeed
> For that which is most worthy to be blest;
> Delight and liberty, the simple creed
> Of childhood, whether busy or at rest,
> With new-fledged hope still fluttering in his breast:—    10
> Not for these I raise
> The song of thanks and praise;
> But for those obstinate questionings
> Of sense and outward things,
> Fallings from us, vanishings;
> Blank misgivings of a creature
> Moving about in worlds not realized,
> High instincts, before which our mortal nature
> Did tremble like a guilty thing surprised!
> But for those first affections,    20
> Those shadowy recollections,
> Which, be they what they may,
> Are yet the fountain light of all our day,
> Are yet a master light of all our seeing;
> Uphold us—cherish—and have power to make
> Our noisy years seem moments in the being
> Of the eternal silence; truths that wake
>      To perish never:
> Which neither listlessness, nor mad endeavour,
> Nor man nor boy,    30
> Nor all that is at enmity with joy,
> Can utterly abolish or destroy!
> Hence, in a season of calm weather,
> Though inland far we be,
> Our souls have sight of that immortal sea
> Which brought us hither;
> Can in a moment travel thither—
> And see the children sport upon the shore,
> And hear the mighty waters rolling evermore.

And since it would be unfair to conclude with an extract, which, though highly characteristic, must yet, from the nature of the thoughts and the subject, be interesting, or perhaps intelligible, to

but a limited number of readers; I will add, from the poet's last
published work, a passage equally Wordsworthian; of the beauty
of which, and of the imaginative power displayed therein, there
can be but one opinion, and one feeling. See "White Doe," page 5.

> Fast the church-yard fills;—anon
> Look again and they are gone;
> The cluster round the porch, and the folk
> Who sate in the shade of the prior's oak!
> And scarcely have they disappear'd,
> Ere the prelusive hymn is heard;—
> With one consent the people rejoice,
> Filling the Church with a lofty voice!
> They sing a service which they feel,
> For 'tis the sun-rise of their zeal;                           10
> And faith and hope are in their prime
> In great Eliza's golden time.
>
> A moment ends the fervent din,
> And all is hushed, without and within;
> For though the priest, more tranquilly,
> Recites the holy liturgy,
> The only voice which you can hear
> Is the river murmuring near.
> When soft!—the dusky trees between,
> And down the path through the open green,     20
> Where is no living thing to be seen;
> And through yon gateway, where is found,
> Beneath the arch with ivy bound,
> Free entrance to the church-yard ground;
> And right across the verdant sod,
> Towards the very house of God;
> Comes gliding in with lovely gleam,
> Comes gliding in serene and slow,
> Soft and silent as a dream,
> A solitary doe!                                           30
> White she is as lily of June,
> And beauteous as the silver moon
> When out of sight the clouds are driven
> And she is left alone in heaven!
> Or like a ship some gentle day
> In sunshine sailing far away—
> A glittering ship, that hath the plain
> Of ocean for her own domain.

*     *     *     *     *     *

> What harmonious pensive changes
> Wait upon her as she ranges              40
> Round and through this pile of state
> Overthrown and desolate!
> Now a step or two her way
> Is through space of open day,
> Where the enamoured sunny light
> Brightens her that was so bright;
> Now doth a delicate shadow fall,
> Falls upon her like a breath,
> From some lofty arch or wall,
> As she passes underneath.             50

The following analogy will, I am apprehensive, appear dim and fantastic, but in reading Bartram's Travels I could not help transcribing the following lines as a sort of allegory, or connected simile and metaphor of Wordsworth's intellect and genius.—"The soil is a deep, rich, dark mould, on a deep stratum of tenacious clay; and that on a foundation of rocks, which often break through both strata, lifting their back above the surface. The trees which chiefly grow here are the gigantic black oak; magnolia magni-floria; fraxinus excelsior; platane; and a few stately tulip trees." What Mr. Wordsworth *will* produce, it is not for me to prophecy: but I could pronounce with the liveliest convictions what he is capable of producing. It is the FIRST GENUINE PHILOSOPHIC POEM.

The preceding criticism will not, I am aware, avail to overcome the prejudices of those, who have made it a business to attack and ridicule Mr. Wordsworth's compositions.

Truth and prudence might be imaged as concentric circles. The poet may perhaps have passed beyond the latter, but he has confined himself far within the bounds of the former, in designating these critics, as too petulant to be passive to a genuine poet, and too feeble to grapple with him;—"men of palsied imaginations, in whose minds all healthy action is languid;—who, therefore, feed as the many direct them, or with the many are greedy after vicious provocatives."

Let not Mr. Wordsworth be charged with having expressed himself too indignantly, till the wantonness and the systematic and

malignant perseverance of the aggressions have been taken into
fair consideration. I myself heard the commander in chief of this
unmanly warfare make a boast of his private admiration of Wordsworth's genius. I have heard him declare, that whoever came into
his room would probably find the Lyrical Ballads lying open on
his table, and that (speaking exclusively of those written by Mr.
Wordsworth himself) he could nearly repeat the whole of them by
heart. *But* a Review, in order to be a saleable article, must be *personal, sharp,* and *pointed:* and, *since then,* the poet has made himself, and with himself all who were, or were supposed to be, his
friends and admirers, the object of the critic's revenge—how? by
having spoken of a work so conducted in the terms which it deserved! I once heard a clergyman in boots and buckskin avow, that
he would cheat his own father *in a horse*. A moral system of a
similar nature seems to have been adopted by too many anonymous
critics. As we used to say at school, in reviewing they *make* being
rogues: and he, who complains, is to be laughed at for his ignorance of *the game*. With the pen out of their hand they are *honorable men*. They exert indeed power (which is to that of the injured
party who should attempt to expose their glaring perversions and
misstatements, as twenty to one) to write down, and (where the
author's circumstances permit) to *impoverish* the man, whose
learning and genius they themselves in private have repeatedly
admitted. They knowingly strive to make it impossible for the man
even to publish* any future work without exposing himself to all
the wretchedness of debt and embarrassment. But this is all *in
their vocation:* and, bating what they do in their *vocation, "who
can say that black is the white of their eye?"*

So much for the detractors from Wordsworth's merits. On the
other hand, much as I might wish for their fuller sympathy, I dare
not flatter myself, that the freedom with which I have declared

---

* Not many months ago an eminent bookseller was asked what he thought
of——? The answer was: "I have heard his powers very highly spoken of by
some of our first-rate men; but I would not have a work of his if any one
would give it me: for he is spoken but slightly of, or not at all, in the
Quarterly Review: and the Edinburgh, you know, is decided to cut him
up!"

my opinions concerning both his theory and his defects, most of which are more or less connected with his theory, either as cause or effect, will be satisfactory or pleasing to *all* the poet's admirers and advocates. More indiscriminate than mine their admiration may be: deeper and more sincere it can not be. But I have advanced no opinion either for praise or censure, other than as texts introductory to the reasons which compel me to form it. Above all, I was fully convinced that such a criticism was not only wanted; but that, if executed with adequate ability, it must conduce, in no mean degree, to Mr. Wordsworth's *reputation*. His *fame* belongs to another age, and can neither be accelerated nor retarded. How small the proportion of the defects are to the beauties, I have repeatedly declared; and that no one of them originates in deficiency of poetic genius. Had they been more and greater, I should still, as a friend to his literary character in the present age, consider an analytic display of them as *pure gain*; if only it removed, as surely to all reflecting minds even the foregoing analysis must have removed, the strange mistake, so slightly grounded, yet so widely and industriously propagated, of Mr. Wordsworth's turn for SIM-PLICITY! I am not half so much irritated by hearing his enemies abuse him for vulgarity of style, subject, and conception; as I am disgusted with the gilded side of the same meaning, as displayed by some affected admirers, with whom he is, forsooth, a *sweet, simple poet!* and *so* natural, that little master Charles and his younger sister are *so* charmed with them, that they play at "Goody Blake," or at "Johnny and Betty Foy!"

Were the collection of poems, published with these biographical sketches, important enough, (which I am not vain enough to believe), to deserve such a distinction; EVEN AS I HAVE DONE, SO WOULD I BE DONE UNTO.

For more than eighteen months have the volume of Poems, entitled SIBYLLINE LEAVES, and the present volumes, up to this page, been printed, and ready for publication. But, ere I speak of myself in the tones, which are alone natural to me under the circumstances of late years, I would fain present myself to the Reader as I was in the first dawn of my literary life:

> When Hope grew round me, like the climbing vine,
> And fruits and foliage, not my own, seem'd mine!

For this purpose I have selected from the letters, which I wrote home from Germany, those which appeared likely to be most interesting, and at the same time most pertinent to the title of this work.

# ON THE
## PRINCIPLES OF GENIAL CRITICISM
### CONCERNING THE FINE ARTS,

MORE ESPECIALLY THOSE OF STATUARY AND PAINTING,
DEDUCED FROM THE LAWS AND IMPULSES WHICH GUIDE
THE TRUE ARTIST IN THE PRODUCTION OF HIS WORKS.

∽∽∽

#### ESSAY THIRD

[The opening paragraphs of this essay repeat, in almost identical language, the opening of Chapter X of the *Biographia Literaria*.]

. . . —Thus geometrical truths are all intuitive, or accompanied by an intuition. Nay, in order to express *"the many,"* as simply contra-distinguished from *"the one,"* I have hazarded the smile of the reader, by introducing to his acquaintance, from the forgotten terminology of the old schoolmen, the phrase, *multëity,* because I felt that I could not substitute *multitude,* without more or less connecting with it the notion of "a *great* many." Thus the Philosopher of the later Platonic, or Alexandrine school, named the triangle the first-born of beauty, it being the first and simplest symbol of *multëity in unity.* These are, I believe, the only liberties of this kind which I have found it necessary to attempt in the present essay: partly, because its object will be attained sufficiently for my present purpose, by attaching a clear and distinct meaning to the different terms used by us, in our appreciation of works of art, and partly because I am about to put to the press a large volume on the Logos, or the communicative intelligence in nature and in man, together with, and as preliminary to, a Commentary on the Gospel of St. John; and in this work I have labored to give real and adequate definitions of all the component faculties of our moral and intellectual being, exhibiting constructively the origin, development, and destined functions of each. And now with silent wishes that these explanatory prenotices may be attributed to their true cause, a sense of respect for the understanding of my reflecting readers, I proceed to my promised and more amusing task, that of establishing, illustrating, and exemplifying the distinct powers of the different modes of pleasure excited by the works of nature or of human genius with their exponent and appropriable terms. "Harum indagatio subtilitatum etsi non est utilis ad machinas farinarias conficiendas, exuit animum tamen inscitiæ rubigine, acuitque ad alia."—*Scaliger, Exerc.* 307, § 3.

AGREEABLE.—We use this word in two senses; in the first for whatever agrees with our nature, for that which is congruous with the primary constitution of our senses. Thus green is naturally agreeable to the eye. In this sense the word expresses, at least involves, a pre-established harmony between the organs and their appointed objects. In the second sense, we convey by the word *agreeable,* that the thing has by force of habit (thence called a second nature) been made to agree with us; or that it has become agreeable to us by its recalling to our minds some one or more things that were dear and pleasing to us; or lastly, on account of some after pleasure or advantage, of which it has been the constant cause or occasion. Thus by force of custom men *make* the taste of tobacco, which was at first hateful to the palate, agreeable to them; thus too, as our Shakspeare observes,

> Things base and vile, holding no quality,
> Love can transpose to form and dignity—

the crutch that had supported a revered parent, after the first anguish of regret, becomes agreeable to the affectionate child; and I once knew a very sensible and accomplished Dutch gentleman, who, spite of his own sense of the ludicrous nature of the feeling, was more delighted by the first grand concert of frogs he heard in this country, than he had been by Catalina singing in the compositions of Cimarosa. The last clause needs no illustrations, as it comprises all the objects that are agreeable to us, only because they are the means by which we gratify our smell, touch, palate, and mere bodily feeling.

The BEAUTIFUL, contemplated in its essentials, that is, in *kind* and not in *degree,* is that in which the *many,* still seen as many, becomes one. Take a familiar instance, one of a thousand. The frost on a window-pane has by accident crystallized into a striking resemblance of a tree or a seaweed. With what pleasure we trace the parts, and their relations to each other, and to the whole! Here is the stalk or trunk, and here the branches or sprays—sometimes even the buds or flowers. Nor will our pleasure be less, should the caprice of the crystallization represent some object disagreeable to us, provided only we can see or fancy the component parts each in relation to each, and all forming a whole. A lady would see an admirably painted tiger with pleasure, and at once pronounce it beautiful,—nay, an owl, a frog, or a toad, who would have shrieked or shuddered at the sight of the things themselves. So far is the Beautiful from depending wholly on association, that it is frequently produced by the mere removal of associations. Many a sincere convert to the beauty of various insects, as of the dragon-fly, the fangless snake, &c., has Natural History made, by exploding the terror or aversion that had been connected with them.

The most general definition of beauty, therefore, is—that I may fulfil my threat of plaguing my readers with hard words—Multëity in Unity. Now it will be always found, that whatever is the definition of the *kind,* independent of degree, becomes likewise the definition of the highest degree of that kind. An old coach-wheel lies in the coachmaker's yard, disfigured with tar and dirt (I purposely take the most trivial instances)—if I turn away my attention from these, and regard the *figure* abstractly, "still," I might say to my companion, "there is beauty in that wheel, and you yourself would not only admit, but would feel it, had you never seen a wheel before. See how the rays proceed from the centre to the circumferences, and how many different images are distinctly comprehended at one glance, as forming one whole, and each part in some harmonious relation to each and to all." But imagine the polished golden wheel of the chariot of the Sun, as the poets have described it: then the figure, and the real thing so figured, exactly coincide. There is nothing heterogeneous, nothing to abstract from: by its perfect smoothness and circularity in width, each part is (if I may borrow a metaphor from a sister sense) as perfect a melody, as the whole is a complete harmony. This, we should say, is beautiful throughout. Of all "the many," which I actually see, each and all are really reconciled into unity: while the effulgence from the whole coincides with, and seems to represent, the effluence of delight from my own mind in the intuition of it.

It seems evident then, first, that beauty is harmony, and subsists only in composition, and secondly, that the first species of the Agreeable can alone be a component part of the beautiful, that namely which is naturally consonant with our senses by the pre-established harmony between nature and the human mind; and thirdly, that even of this species, those objects only can be admitted (according to rule the first) which belong to the eye and ear, because they alone are susceptible of distinction of parts. Should an Englishman gazing on a mass of cloud rich with the rays of the rising sun exclaim, even without distinction of, or reference to its form, or its relation to other objects, how beautiful! I should have no quarrel with him. First, because by the law of association there is in all visual beholdings at least an indistinct subsumption of form and relation: and, secondly, because even in the coincidence between the sight and the object there is an approximation to the reduction of the many into one. But who, that heard a Frenchman call the flavor of a leg of mutton a beautiful taste, would not immediately recognize him for a Frenchman, even though there should be neither grimace or characteristic nasal twang? The result, then, of the whole is that the shapely (i. e. *formosus*) joined with the naturally agreeable, constitutes what, speaking accurately, we mean by the word beautiful (i. e. *pulcher*).

But we are conscious of faculties far superior to the highest impressions of sense; we have life and free-will.—What then will be the result, when the Beautiful, arising from regular form, is so modified by the perception of life and spontaneous action, as that the latter only shall be the object of our conscious *perception*, while the former merely acts, and yet does effectively act, on our feelings? With pride and pleasure I reply by referring my reader to the group in Mr. Allston's grand picture of the "Dead Man reviving from the touch of the bones of the Prophet Elisha," beginning with the slave at the head of the reviving body, then proceeding to the daughter clasping her swooning mother; to the mother, the wife of the reviving man; then to the soldier behind who supports her; to the two figures eagerly conversing: and lastly, to the exquisitely graceful girl who is bending downward, and whose hand nearly touches the thumb of the slave! You will find, what you had not suspected, that you have here before you a circular group. But by what variety of life, motion, and passion is all the stiffness, that would result from an obvious regular figure, swallowed up, and the figure of the group as much concealed by the action and passion, as the skeleton, which gives the form of the human body, is hidden by the flesh and its endless outlines!

In Raphael's admirable Galatea (the print of which is doubtless familiar to most of my readers) the circle is perceived at first sight; but with what multiplicity of rays and chords within the area of the circular group, with what elevations and depressions of the circumference, with what an endless variety and sportive wildness in the component figure, and in the junctions of the figures, is the balance, the perfect reconciliation, effected between these two conflicting principles of the FREE LIFE, and of the confining FORM! How entirely is the stiffness that would have resulted from the obvious regularity of the latter, *fused* and (if I may hazard so bold a metaphor) almost *volatilized* by the interpenetration and electrical flashes of the former.

But I shall recur to this consummate work for more specific illustrations hereafter: and have indeed in some measure offended already against the laws of method, by anticipating materials which rather belong to a more advanced stage of the disquisition. It is time to recapitulate, as briefly as possible, the arguments already advanced, and having summed up the result, to leave behind me this, the only portion of these essays, which, as far as the subject itself is concerned, will demand any *effort* of attention from a reflecting and intelligent reader. And let me be permitted to remind him, that the distinctions, which it is my object to prove and elucidate, have not merely a foundation in nature and the noblest faculties of the human mind, but are likewise the very groundwork, nay, an indispensable condition, of all *rational* enquiry concerning the Arts. For it is self-evident, that whatever may be judged of differently by different persons, in the very same degree of moral and intellectual cultivation, extolled by one and condemned by another, without any error being assignable to either, can never be an object of general principles: and *vice versâ*, that whatever can be brought to the test of general principles presupposes a distinct origin from these pleasures and tastes, which, for the wisest purposes, are made to depend on local and transitory fashions, accidental associations, and the peculiarities of individual temperament: to all which the philosopher, equally with the well-bred man of the world, applies the old adage, *de gustibus non est disputandum.* Be it, however, observed that "de gustibus" is by no means the same as "de gustu," nor will it escape the scholar's recollection, that taste, in its metaphorical use, was first adopted by the Romans, and unknown to the less luxurious Greeks, who designated this faculty, sometimes by the word αἴσθησις, and sometimes by φιλοκαλία—"ἀνδρῶν τῶν καθ᾽ ἡμᾶς φιλοκαλώτατος γεγονώς—i. e. endowed by nature with the most exquisite taste of any man of our age," says Porphyry of his friend, Castricius. Still, this metaphor, borrowed from the pregustatores of the old Roman Banquets, is singularly happy and appropriate. In the palate, the perception of the object and its qualities is involved in the *sensation,* in the mental taste it is involved in the *sense*. We have a *sensation* of sweetness, in a healthy palate, from honey; a *sense* of beauty, in an uncorrupted taste, from the view of the rising or setting sun.

RECAPITULATION. *Principle the First.* That which has become, or which has been *made* agreeable to us, from causes not contained in its own nature, or in its original conformity to the human organs and faculties; that which is not pleasing for its own sake, but by connection or association with some other thing, separate or separable from it, is neither beautiful, nor capable of being a component part of Beauty: though it may greatly increase the sum of our pleasure, when it does not interfere with the beauty of the object, nay, even when it detracts from it. A moss-rose, with a sprig of myrtle and jasmine, is not more *beautiful* from having been plucked from the garden, or presented to us by the hand of the woman we love, but is abundantly more delightful. The total pleasure received from one of Mr. Bird's finest pictures may, without any impeachment of our taste, be the greater from his having introduced into it the portrait of one of our friends, or from our pride in him as our townsman, or from our knowledge of his personal qualities; but the amiable artist would rightly consider it a coarse compliment, were it affirmed, that the *beauty* of the piece, or its merit as a work of genius, was the more perfect on this account. I am conscious that I look with a stronger and more pleasureable emotion at Mr. Allston's large landscape, in the spirit of Swiss scenery, from its having been the occasion of my first acquaintance with him in Rome. This may or may not be a compliment to *him*; but the true compliment to the picture was made by a lady of high rank and cultivated taste, who declared, in my hearing, that she never stood before that landscape without seeming to feel the breeze blow out of it upon her. But the most striking instance is afforded by the portrait of a departed or absent friend or parent; which is endeared to us, and more delightful, from some awkward position of the limbs, which had defied the contrivances of art to render it picturesque, but which was the characteristic habit of the original.

*Principle the Second.* That which is naturally agreeable and consonant to human nature, so that the exceptions may be attributed to disease or defect; that, the pleasure from which is contained in the immediate impression; cannot, indeed, with strict propriety, be called beautiful, exclusive of its relations, but one among the component parts of beauty, in whatever instance it is susceptible of existing as a part of a whole. This, of course, excludes the mere objects of the taste, smell, and feeling, though the sensation from these, especially from the latter when organized into touch, may secretly, and without our consciousness, enrich and vivify the perceptions and images of the eye and ear; which alone are true organs of sense, their sensations in a healthy or uninjured state being too faint to be noticed by the mind. We may, indeed, in common conversation, call purple a beautiful color, or the tone of a single note on an excellent piano-forte a beautiful tone; but if we were questioned, we should agree that a rich or delightful color; a rich, or sweet, or clear tone; would have been more appropriate— and this with less hesitation in the latter instance than in the former, because the single tone is more manifestly of the nature of a *sensation,* while color is the medium which seems to blend sensation and perception, so as to hide, as it were, the former in the latter; the direct opposite of which takes place in the lower senses of feeling, smell, and taste. (In strictness, there is even in these an ascending scale. The smell is less sensual and more sentient than mere feeling, the taste than the smell, and the eye than the ear: but between the ear and the taste exists the chasm or break, which divides the beautiful and the elements of beauty from the merely agreeable.) When I reflect on the manner in which smoothness, richness of sound, &c., enter into the formation of the beautiful, I am induced to suspect that they act negatively rather than positively. Something there must be to realize the form, something in and by which the *forma informans* reveals itself: and these, less than any that could be substituted, and in the least possible degree, distract the attention, in the least possible degree obscure the idea, of which they (composed into outline and surface) are the symbol. An illustrative hint may be taken from a pure crystal, as compared with an opaque, semi-opaque or clouded mass, on the one hand, and with a perfectly transparent body, such as the air, on the other. The crystal is lost in the light, which yet it contains, embodies, and gives a shape to; but which passes shapeless through the air, and, in the ruder body, is either quenched or dissipated.

*Principle the Third.* The safest definition, then, of Beauty, as well as the oldest, is that of Pythagoras: THE REDUCTION OF MANY TO ONE—or, as finely expressed by the sublime disciple of Ammonius, τὸ ἄμερες ὄν, ἐν πολλοῖς φανταζόμενον, of which the following may be offered as both paraphrase and corollary. *The sense of beauty subsists in simultaneous intuition of the relation of parts, each to each, and of all to a whole: exciting an immediate and absolute complacency, without intervenence, therefore, of any interest, sensual or intellectual.* The BEAUTIFUL is thus at once distinguished both from the AGREEABLE, which is beneath it, and from the GOOD, which is above it: for both these have an interest necessarily attached to them: both act on the WILL, and excite a desire for the actual existence of the image or idea contemplated: while the sense of beauty rests gratified in the mere contemplation or

intuition, regardless whether it be a fictitious Apollo, or a real
Antinous.

The Mystics meant the same, when they define beauty as the
subjection of matter to spirit so as to be transformed into a symbol,
in and through which the spirit reveals itself; and declare *that* the
*most* beautiful, where the most obstacles to a full manifestation
have been most perfectly overcome. I would that the readers, for
whom alone I write (*intelligibilia enim, non intellectum adfero*)
had Raphael's Galatea, or his School of Athens, before them! or
that the Essay might be read by some imaginative student, warm
from admiration of the King's College Chapel at Cambridge, or
of the exterior and interior of York Cathedral! I deem the sneers
of a host of petty critics, unalphabeted in the life and truth of
things, and as devoid of sound learning as of intuitive taste, well
and wisely hazarded for the prospect of communicating the pleasure, which to such minds the following passage of Plotinus will
not fail to give—Plotinus, a name venerable even to religion with
the great Cosmus, Lorenzo de Medici, Ficinus, Politian, Leonardo
da Vinci, and Michael Angelo, but now known only as a name to
the majority even of our most learned Scholars!—Plotinus, difficult
indeed, but under a rough and austere rind concealing fruit worthy
of Paradise; and if obscure, *"at tenet umbra Deum!"* Ὅταν οὖν καὶ
ἡ αἴσθησις τὸ ἐν σώμασιν εἶδος ἤδη συνδησάμενον καὶ κρατῆσαν τῆς
φύσεως τῆς ἐναντίας, καὶ μορφὴν ἐπ' ἄλλαις μορφαῖς ἐκπρεπῶς
ἐποχουμένην, συνελοῦσα ἀθρόον αὐτὸ τὸ πολλαχῇ ἀνήνεγκέ τε καὶ
ἔδωκε τῷ ἔνδον σύμφωνον καὶ συναρμόττον καὶ φίλον. A divine passage, faintly represented in the following lines, written many years
ago by the writer, though without reference to, or recollection of,
the above.

> O lady! we *receive* but what we *give*,
> And in *our* life alone does nature live!
> Ours is her wedding-garment, ours her shroud!
> And would we aught behold of higher worth,
> Than that inanimate cold world allow'd
> To the poor, loveless, ever-anxious crowd:
> Ah! from the soul itself must issue forth
> A light, a glory, a fair luminous cloud,
>       Enveloping the earth!

And from the soul itself must there be sent                    10
A sweet and powerful voice, of its own birth,
    Of all sweet sounds the life and element!
O pure of heart! thou need'st not ask of me,
What this strong music in the soul may be;
    What and wherein it doth subsist,
This light, this glory, this fair luminous mist,
    This beautiful, and beauty-making power!
Joy, O beloved! joy, that ne'er was given,
Save to the pure and in their purest hour,
Life of our life, the parent and the birth,                    20
Which, wedding nature to us, gives in dower
    A new heaven and new earth,
Undreamt of by the sensual and the proud—
*This* is the strong voice, this the luminous cloud!
    Our inmost selves rejoice:
And thence flows all that glads or ear or sight,
All melodies the echoes of that voice,
All colors a suffusion from that light,
And its celestial tint of yellow-green:
And still I gaze—and with how blank an eye!                    30
And those thin clouds above, in flakes and bars,
That give away their motion to the stars;
Those stars, that glide behind them or between,
Now sparkling, now bedimm'd, but always seen;
Yon crescent moon, that seems as if it grew
In its own starless, cloudless lake of blue—
I see them all, so excellently fair!
*I see, not feel, how beautiful they are.*
                                        S. T. C. MS. Poem.

SCHOLIUM. We have sufficiently distinguished the beautiful
from the agreeable, by the sure criterion, that, when we find an
object agreeable, the *sensation* of pleasure always precedes the
judgement, and is its determining cause. We *find* it agreeable.
But when we declare an object beautiful, the contemplation or
intuition of its beauty precedes the *feeling* of complacency, in
order of nature at least: nay, in great depression of spirits may
even exist without sensibly producing it.—

    A grief without a pang, void, dark, and drear!
    A stifled, drowsy, unimpassion'd grief,
        That finds no natural outlet, no relief
        In word, or sigh, or tear!

> O dearest lady! in this heartless mood,
> To other thoughts by yon sweet throstle woo'd!
> All this long eve, so balmy and serene,
> Have I been gazing at the western sky.

Now the least reflection convinces us that our sensations, whether of pleasure or of pain, are the incommunicable parts of our nature; such as can be reduced to no universal rule; and in which therefore we have no right to expect that others should agree with us, or to blame them for disagreement. That the Greenlander prefers train oil to olive oil, and even to wine, we explain at once by our knowledge of the climate and productions to which he has been habituated. Were the man as enlightened as Plato, his palate would still find that most agreeable to which it had been most accustomed. But when the Iroquois Sachem, after having been led to the most perfect specimens of architecture in Paris, said that he saw nothing so beautiful as the cook's shops, we attribute this without hesitation to savagery of intellect, and infer with certainty that the sense of the beautiful was either altogether dormant in his mind, or at best very imperfect. The Beautiful, therefore, not originating in the sensations, must belong to the intellect: and therefore we *declare* an object beautiful, and feel an inward right to *expect* that others should coincide with us. But we feel no right to *demand* it: and this leads us to that, which hitherto we have barely touched upon, and which we shall now attempt to illustrate more fully, namely, to the distinction of the Beautiful from the Good.

Let us suppose Milton in company with some stern and prejudiced Puritan, contemplating the front of York Cathedral, and at length expressing his admiration of its beauty. We will suppose it too at that time of his life, when his religious opinions, feelings, and prejudices most nearly coincided with those of the rigid Antiprelatists.—P. Beauty; I am sure, it is not the beauty of holiness. M. True; but yet it is beautiful.—P. It delights not me. What is it good for? Is it of any use but to be stared at?—M. Perhaps not! but still it is beautiful.—P. But call to mind the pride and wanton vanity of those cruel shavelings, that wasted the labor and substance of so many thousand poor creatures in the erection of this

haughty pile.—M. I do. But still it is very beautiful.—P. Think how many score of places of worship, incomparably better suited both for prayer and preaching, and how many faithful ministers might have been maintained, to the blessing of tens of thousands, to them and their children's children, with the treasures lavished on this worthless mass of stone and cement.—M. Too true! but nevertheless it is *very* beautiful.—P. And it is not merely useless; but it feeds the pride of the prelates, and keeps alive the popish and carnal spirit among the people.—M. Even so! and I presume not to question the wisdom, nor detract from the pious zeal, of the first Reformers of Scotland, who for these reasons destroyed so many fabrics, scarce inferior in beauty to this now before our eyes. But I did not call it *good,* nor have I told thee, brother! that if this were levelled with the ground, and existed only in the works of the modeller or engraver, that I should desire to reconstruct it. The GOOD consists in the congruity of a thing with the laws of the reason and the nature of the will, and in its fitness to determine the latter to actualize the former: and it is always discursive. The Beautiful arises from the perceived harmony of an object, whether sight or sound, with the inborn and constitutive rules of the judgement and imagination: and it is always intuitive. As light to the eye, even such is beauty to the mind, which cannot but have complacency in whatever is perceived as pre-configured to its living faculties. Hence the Greeks called a beautiful object καλόν quasi καλοῦν, i. e. *calling on* the soul, which receives instantly, and welcomes it as something connatural. Πάλιν οὖν ἀναλαβόντες, λέγωμεν τί δῆτα ἐστὶ τὸ ἐν τοῖς σώμασι καλόν. Πρῶτον ἔστι μὲν γάρ τι καὶ βολῇ τῇ πρώτῃ αἰσθητὸν γινόμενον, καὶ ἡ ψυχὴ ὥσπερ συνεῖσα λέγει, καὶ ἐπιγνοῦσα ἀποδέχεται, καὶ οἷον συναρμόττεται. Πρὸς δὲ τὸ αἰσχρὸν προσβαλοῦσα ἀνίλλεται, καὶ ἀρνεῖται καὶ ἀνανεύει ἐπ' αὐτοῦ οὐ συμφωνοῦσα, καὶ ἀλλοτριουμένη.—
PLOTIN: Ennead. I. Lib. 6.

## APPENDIX

"He, (Charles Brandon, Duke of Suffolk) knowing that learning hath no enemy but ignorance, did suspect always the want of it in those men who derided the habit of it in others, like the fox in the fable, who being.

by mischance or degeneracy, without a tail, persuaded others to cut theirs off as a burden. But he liked well the philosopher's division of men into three ranks; some who knew good and were willing to teach others.—These he said, were like gods among men; others who though they knew not much, yet were willing to learn and thankful for instruction.—These, he said, were like men among beasts; and some who knew not truth or good, and yet despised and maligned such as would teach them.—These he esteemed as beasts among men."—*Lloyd's State Worthies*, p. 33.

Thus, then, let us at once sum up and exemplify the whole. Its ambrosial odour renders the rose more agreeable to us, but it is not by this addition, that nature wrests the palm of beauty from the flower-pieces of Van Huysun. The patience, strength, and laboriousness of the Ox and the Ass, invaluable as we rightly deem them, can yet by no influence of association, bribe us to compare them in charm of form, and disposition of colors, with the fierce and untamable Zebra. The rough Sheep-dog is almost indispensable to the civilization of the human race. He appears to possess not Valuableness only, but even Worth! His various moral qualities, which seem above the effects of mere Instinct devoid of Will, compel our respect and regard, and excite our gratitude *to* him, as well as *for* him. Yet neither his paramount utility, no, nor even his incorruptible fidelity and disinterested affection, enable us to equal him, in outward beauty, with the cruel and cowardly panther, or leopard, or tiger, the hate and horror of the flock and of the shepherd.

But may not the sense of Beauty originate in our perception of the fitness of the means to the end in and for the animal itself? Or may it not depend on a law of Proportion? No! The shell of the Oyster, rough and unshapely, is its habitation and strong hold, its defence and organ of locomotion: the pearl, the beautiful ornament of the beautiful, is its disease. How charming the Moss Rose with its luxuriancy of petals! That moss, that luxuriancy, are the effects of degeneracy, and unfit the flower for the multiplication of its kind. Disproportion indeed may in certain cases preclude the sense of Beauty, and will do so wherever it destroys or greatly disturbs the wholeness and simultaneousness of the impression. But still proportion is not the positive cause, or the universal and necessary condition of beauty, were it only that proportion implies the perception of the coincidence of quantities with a pre-established rule of measurement, and is therefore always accompanied with an act of discursive thought. We declare at first sight the Swan beautiful, as it floats on with its long arching neck and protruding breast, which uniting to their reflected image in the watery mirror, present to our delighted eye the stringless bow of dazzling silver, which the Poets and Painters assign to the God of Love. We ask not what proportion the neck bears to the body;—through all the changes of graceful motion it brings itself into unity, as an harmonious part of an harmonious whole. The very word "part" imperfectly conveys what we see and feel; for the moment we look at it in division, the charm ceases. In this spirit the Lover describing the incidents of a walk on the riverbanks by moonlight is made by the poet to exclaim:

> The pairing swans have heard my tread,
> And rustle from their reedy bed.
> O beauteous birds! methinks ye measure
>    Your movements to some heavenly tune!
> O beauteous birds! 'tis such a pleasure
>    To see you move beneath the moon,
> I would it were your true delight
> To rest by day and wake all night.

The long neck of the ostrich is in exact and evident proportion to the height of the animal, and is of manifest utility and necessity to the bird, as it stoops down to graze and still walks on. But not being harmonized with the body by plumage or color, it seems to run along the grass like a serpent before the headless tall body that still stalks after it, inspiring at once the sense of the Deformed and the Fantastic.

I here close my metaphysical Preliminaries, in which I have confined myself to the Beauty of the Senses, and by the Good have chiefly referred to the relatively good. Of the supersensual Beauty, the Beauty of Virtue and Holiness, and of its relation to the ABSO-LUTELY GOOD, distinguishable, not separable (even such relation as that of color to the Light of Heaven, and as the Light itself bears to the Knowledge, which it awakens), I discourse not now, waiting for a loftier mood, a nobler subject, a more appropriate audience, warned from within and from without, that it is profanation to speak of these mysteries "τοῖς μηδέποτε φαντασθεῖσιν, ὡς καλὸν τὸ τῆς δικαιοσύνης καὶ σωφροσύνης πρόσωπον, καὶ ὡς οὔτε ἕσπερος οὔτε ἑῷος οὕτω καλά. Τὸν γὰρ ὁρῶντα πρὸς τὸ ὁρώμενον συγγενὲς καὶ ὅμοιον ποιησάμενον δεῖ ἐπιβάλλειν τῇ θέᾳ· οὐ γὰρ ἂν πώποτε εἶδεν ὀφθαλμὸς ἥλιον, ἡλιοειδὴς μὴ γεγενημένος, οὐδὲ τὸ καλὸν ἂν ἴδοι ψυχὴ μὴ γενομένη."

# LECTURES AND NOTES ON POETRY, DRAMA, SHAKESPEARE, AND OTHER CRITICAL NOTES

<hr>

### [Definition of Poetry, etc.]

Readers may be divided into four classes:

1. Sponges, who absorb all they read, and return it nearly in the same state, only a little dirtied.

2. Sand-glasses, who retain nothing, and are content to get through a book for the sake of getting through the time.

3. Strain-bags, who retain merely the dregs of what they read.

4. Mogul diamonds, equally rare and valuable, who profit by what they read, and enable others to profit by it also.

I adverted in my last lecture to the prevailing laxity in the use of terms: this is the principal complaint to which the moderns are exposed; but it is a grievous one, inasmuch as it inevitably tends to the misapplication of words, and to the corruption of language. I mentioned the word "taste," but the remark applies not merely to substantives and adjectives, to things and their epithets, but to verbs: thus, how frequently is the verb "indorsed" strained from its true signification, as given by Milton in the expression—"And elephants indorsed with towers." Again, "virtue" has been equally perverted: originally it signified merely strength; it then became strength of mind and valour, and it has now been changed to the class term for moral excellence in all its various species. I only introduce these as instances by the way, and nothing could be easier than to multiply them.

At the same time, while I recommend precision both of thought and expression, I am far from advocating a pedantic niceness in the choice of language: such a course would only render conversation stiff and stilted. Dr. Johnson used to say that in the most un-restrained discourse he always sought for the properest word,— that which best and most exactly conveyed his meaning: to a certain point he was right, but because he carried it too far, he was often laborious where he ought to have been light, and formal where he ought to have been familiar. Men ought to endeavour to distinguish subtilely, that they may be able afterwards to assimilate truly.

I have often heard the question put whether Pope is a great poet, and it has been warmly debated on both sides, some positively maintaining the affirmative, and others dogmatically insisting upon the negative; but it never occurred to either party to make the necessary preliminary inquiry—What is meant by the words "poet" and "poetry"? Poetry is not merely invention: if it were, Gulliver's Travels would be poetry; and before you can arrive at a decision of the question, as to Pope's claim, it is absolutely necessary to ascertain what people intend by the words they use. Harmonious versification no more makes poetry than mere invention makes a poet; and to both these requisites there is much besides to be added. In morals, politics, and philosophy no useful discussion can be entered upon, unless we begin by explaining and understanding the terms we employ. It is therefore requisite that I should state to you what I mean by the word "poetry," before I commence any consideration of the comparative merits of those who are popularly called "poets."

Words are used in two ways:—

1. In a sense that comprises everything called by that name. For instance, the words "poetry" and "sense" are employed in this manner, when we say that such a line is bad poetry or bad sense, when in truth it is neither poetry nor sense. If it be bad poetry, it is not poetry; if it be bad sense, it is not sense. The same of "metre": bad metre is not metre.

2. In a philosophic sense, which must include a definition of what is essential to the thing. Nobody means mere metre by poetry; so, mere rhyme is not poetry. Something more is required, and what is that something? It is not wit, because we may have wit where we never dream of poetry. Is it the just observation of human life? Is it a peculiar and a felicitous selection of words? This, indeed, would come nearer to the taste of the present age, when sound is preferred to sense; but I am happy to think that this taste is not likely to last long.

The Greeks and Romans, in the best period of their literature, knew nothing of any such taste. High-flown epithets and violent metaphors, conveyed in inflated language, is not poetry. Simplicity is indispensable, and in Catullus it is often impossible that more simple language could be used; there is scarcely a word or a line, which a lamenting mother in a cottage might not have employed. That I may be clearly understood, I will venture to give the following definition of poetry.

It is an art (or whatever better term our language may afford) of representing, in words, external nature and human thoughts and affections, both relatively to human affections, by the production of as much immediate pleasure in parts, as is compatible with the largest sum of pleasure in the whole.

Or, to vary the words, in order to make the abstract idea more intelligible:—

It is the art of communicating whatever we wish to communicate, so as both to express and produce excitement, but for the purpose of immediate pleasure; and each part is fitted to afford as much pleasure, as is compatible with the largest sum in the whole.

You will naturally ask my reasons for this definition of poetry, and they are these:—

"It is a representation of nature"; but that is not enough: the anatomist and the topographer give representations of nature; therefore I add:

"And of the human thoughts and affections." Here the metaphysician interferes: here our best novelists interfere likewise,— excepting that the latter describe with more minuteness, accuracy, and truth, than is consistent with poetry. Consequently I subjoin:

"It must be relative to the human affections." Here my chief point of difference is with the novel-writer, the historian, and all those who describe not only nature, and the human affections, but relatively to the human affections: therefore I must add:

"And it must be done for the purpose of immediate pleasure." In poetry the general good is to be accomplished through the pleasure, and if the poet do not do that, he ceases to be a poet to him to whom he gives it not. Still, it is not enough, because we may point out many prose writers to whom the whole of the definition hitherto furnished would apply. I add, therefore, that it is not only for the purpose of immediate pleasure, but—

"The work must be so constructed as to produce in each part that highest quantity of pleasure, or a high quantity of pleasure." There metre introduces its claim, where the feeling calls for it. Our language gives to expression a certain measure, and will, in a strong state of passion, admit of scansion from the very mouth. The very assumption that we are reading the work of a poet supposes that he is in a continuous state of excitement; and thereby arises a language in prose unnatural, but in poetry natural.

There is one error which ought to be peculiarly guarded against, which young poets are apt to fall into, and which old poets commit, from being no poets, but desirous of the end which true poets seek to attain. No: I revoke the words; they are not desirous of that of which their little minds can have no just conception. They have no desire of fame—that glorious immortality of true greatness—

> That lives and spreads aloft by those pure eyes,
> And perfect witness of all judging Jove;
>
> Milton's *Lycidas*.

but they struggle for reputation, that echo of an echo, in whose very etymon its signification is contained. Into this error the author of "The Botanic Garden" has fallen, through the whole of which work, I will venture to assert, there are not twenty images described as a man would describe them in a state of excitement. The poem is written with all the tawdry industry of a milliner anxious to dress up a doll in silks and satins. Dr. Darwin laboured to make his style fine and gaudy, by accumulating and applying all the sonorous and handsome-looking words in our language. This is not poetry, and I subjoin to my definition—

That a true poem must give "as much pleasure in each part as is compatible with the greatest sum of pleasure in the whole." We must not look to parts merely, but to the whole, and to the effect of that whole. In reading Milton, for instance, scarcely a line can be pointed out which, critically examined, could be called in itself good: the poet would not have attempted to produce merely what is in general understood by a good line; he sought to produce

glorious paragraphs and systems of harmony, or, as he himself
expresses it,

> Many a winding bout
> Of linked sweetness long drawn out.
>
> *L'Allegro*

Such, therefore, as I have now defined it, I shall consider the
sense of the word "Poetry": pleasurable excitement is its origin
and object; pleasure is the magic circle out of which the poet must
not dare to tread. Part of my definition, you will be aware, would
apply equally to the arts of painting and music, as to poetry; but
to the last are added words and metre, so that my definition is
strictly and logically applicable to poetry, and to poetry only,
which produces delight, the parent of so many virtues. When I
was in Italy, a friend of mine, who pursued painting almost with
the enthusiasm of madness, believing it superior to every other
art, heard the definition I have given, acknowledged its correct-
ness, and admitted the pre-eminence of poetry.

I never shall forget, when in Rome, the acute sensation of pain
I experienced on beholding the frescoes of Raphael and Michael
Angelo, and on reflecting that they were indebted for their preservation solely to the durable material upon which they were
painted. There they are, the permanent monuments (permanent
as long as walls and plaster last) of genius and skill, while many
others of their mighty works have become the spoils of insatiate
avarice, or the victims of wanton barbarism. How grateful ought
mankind to be, that so many of the great literary productions of
antiquity have come down to us—that the works of Homer, Euclid,
and Plato, have been preserved—while we possess those of Bacon,
Newton, Milton, Shakespeare, and of so many other living-dead
men of our own island. These, fortunately, may be considered
indestructible: they shall remain to us till the end of time itself—
till time, in the words of a great poet of the age of Shakespeare,
has thrown his last dart at death, and shall himself submit to the
final and inevitable destruction of all created matter.

A second irruption of the Goths and Vandals could not now
endanger their existence, secured as they are by the wonders of
modern invention, and by the affectionate admiration of myriads
of human beings. It is as nearly two centuries as possible since

Shakespeare ceased to write, but when shall he cease to be read?
When shall he cease to give light and delight? Yet even at this
moment he is only receiving the first-fruits of that glory, which
must continue to augment as long as our language is spoken.
English has given immortality to him, and he has given immortality to English. Shakespeare can never die, and the language in
which he wrote must with him live for ever.

Yet, in spite of all this, some prejudices have attached themselves to the name of our illustrious countryman, which it will be
necessary for me first to endeavour to overcome. On the continent,
we may remark, the works of Shakespeare are honoured in a
double way—by the admiration of the Germans, and by the contempt of the French.

Among other points of objection taken by the French, perhaps,
the most noticeable is, that he has not observed the sacred unities,
so hallowed by the practice of their own extolled tragedians. They
hold, of course after Corneille and Racine, that Sophocles is the
most perfect model for tragedy, and Aristotle its most infallible
censor; and that as Hamlet, Lear, Macbeth, and other dramas by
Shakespeare are not framed upon that model, and consequently
not subject to the same laws, they maintain (not having impartiality enough to question the model, or to deny the rules of the
Stagirite) that Shakespeare was a sort of irregular genius—that
he is now and then tasteful and touching, but generally incorrect;
and, in short, that he was a mere child of nature, who did not
know any better than to write as he has written.

It is an old, and I have hitherto esteemed it a just, Latin maxim,
*Oportet discentem credere, edoctum judicare;* but modern practice
has inverted it, and it ought now rather to stand, *Oportet discentem judicare, edoctum credere.* To remedy this mistake there
is but one course, namely the acquirement of knowledge. I have
often run the risk of applying to the ignorant, who assumed the
post and province of judges, a ludicrous, but not inapt simile:
they remind me of a congregation of frogs, involved in darkness
in a ditch, who keep an eternal croaking, until a lantern is
brought near the scene of their disputation, when they instantly
cease their discordant harangues. They may be more politely re-

sembled to night-flies, which flutter round the glimmering of a feeble taper, but are overpowered by the dazzling splendour of noon-day. Nor can it be otherwise, until the prevalent notion is exploded, that knowledge is easily taught, and until the conviction is general, that the hardest thing learned is that people are ignorant. All are apt enough to discover and expose the ignorance of their friends, but their blind faith in their own sufficiency is something more than marvellous.

Some persons have contended that mathematics ought to be taught by making the illustrations obvious to the senses. Nothing can be more absurd or injurious: it ought to be our never-ceasing effort to make people think, not feel; and it is very much owing to this mistake that, to those who do not think, and have not been made to think, Shakespeare has been found so difficult of comprehension. The condition of the stage, and the character of the times in which our great poet flourished, must first of all be taken into account, in considering the question as to his judgment. If it were possible to say which of his great powers and qualifications is more admirable than the rest, it unquestionably appears to me that his judgment is the most wonderful; and at this conviction I have arrived after a careful comparison of his productions with those of his best and greatest contemporaries.

If indeed "King Lear" were to be tried by the laws which Aristotle established, and Sophocles obeyed, it must be at once admitted to be outrageously irregular; and supposing the rules regarding the unities to be founded on man and nature, Shakespeare must be condemned for arraying his works in charms with which they ought never to have been decorated. I have no doubt, however, that both were right in their divergent courses, and that they arrived at the same conclusion by a different process.

Without entering into matters which must be generally known to persons of education, respecting the origin of tragedy and comedy among the Greeks, it may be observed, that the unities grew mainly out of the size and construction of the ancient theatres: the plays represented were made to include within a short space of time events which it is impossible should have occurred in that short space. This fact alone establishes, that all dramatic performances were then looked upon merely as ideal. It is the same with us: nobody supposes that a tragedian suffers real pain when he is stabbed or tortured; or that a comedian is in fact transported with delight when successful in pretended love.

If we want to witness mere pain, we can visit the hospitals: if we seek the exhibition of mere pleasure, we can find it in ball-rooms. It is the representation of it, not the reality, that we require, the imitation, and not the thing itself; and we pronounce it good or bad in proportion as the representation is an incorrect, or a correct imitation. The true pleasure we derive from theatrical performances arises from the fact that they are unreal and fictitious. If dying agonies were unfeigned, who, in these days of civilisation, could derive gratification from beholding them?

Performances in a large theatre made it necessary that the human voice should be unnaturally and unmusically stretched, and hence the introduction of recitative, for the purpose of rendering pleasantly artificial the distortion of the face, and straining of the voice, occasioned by the magnitude of the building. The fact that the ancient choruses were always on the stage made it impossible that any change of place should be represented, or even supposed.

The origin of the English stage is less boastful than that of the Greek stage: like the constitution under which we live, though more barbarous in its derivation, it gives more genuine and more diffused liberty, than Athens in the zenith of her political glory ever possessed. Our earliest dramatic performances were religious, founded chiefly upon Scripture history; and, although countenanced by the clergy, they were filled with blasphemies and ribaldry, such as the most hardened and desperate of the present day would not dare to utter. In these representations vice and the principle of evil were personified; and hence the introduction of fools and clowns in dramas of a more advanced period.

While Shakespeare accommodated himself to the taste and spirit of the times in which he lived, his genius and his judgment taught him to use these characters with terrible effect, in aggravating the misery and agony of some of his most distressing scenes. This result is especially obvious in "King Lear": the contrast of the Fool wonderfully heightens the colouring of some of the most painful situations, where the old monarch in the depth and fury of his despair, complains to the warring elements of the ingratitude of his daughters.

> . . . Spit, fire! spout, rain!
> Nor rain, wind, thunder, fire, are my daughters:
> I tax not you, you elements, with unkindness,
> I never gave you kingdom, call'd you children;
> You owe me no subscription: then, let fall
> Your horrible pleasure; here I stand, your slave,
> A poor, infirm, weak, and despis'd old man.
>
> *King Lear*, Act iii. Scene 2.

Just afterwards, the Fool interposes, to heighten and inflame the passion of the scene.

In other dramas, though perhaps in a less degree, our great poet has evinced the same skill and felicity of treatment; and in no instance can it be justly alleged of him, as it may be of some of the ablest of his contemporaries, that he introduced his fool, or his clown, merely for the sake of exciting the laughter of his audiences. Shakespeare had a loftier and a better purpose, and in this respect availed himself of resources, which, it would almost seem, he alone possessed.

## [Dramatic Illusion]

### DESULTORY REMARKS ON THE STAGE, AND THE PRESENT STATE OF THE HIGHER DRAMA

A theatre, in the widest sense of the word, is the general term for all places of amusement thro' the ear or eye in which men assemble in order to be amused by some entertainment presented to all at the same time. Thus, an old Puritan divine says: "Those who attend public worship and sermons only to amuse themselves, make a theatre of the church, and turn God's house into the devil's. *Theatra aedes diabololatricae.*" . . . The most important and dignified species of this genus is, doubtless, the STAGE (*res theatralis historionica*), which, in addition to the generic definition above given, may be characterized (in its *Idea,* or according to what it does, or ought to, *aim* at) as a combination of several, or of all the fine arts to an harmonious whole having a distinct end of its own, to which the peculiar end of each of the component arts, taken separately, is made subordinate and subservient; that, namely, of imitating reality (objects, actions, or passions) under a *semblance* of reality. Thus, Claude imitates a landscape at sunset, but only as a *picture;* while a forest-scene is not presented to the audience as a *picture,* but as a forest: and tho' in the *full* sense of the word we are no more *deceived* by the one than by the other, yet are our feelings very differently affected, and the pleasure derived from the one is not composed of the same elements as that afforded by the other, even on the supposition that the *quantum* of both were equal. In the former, it is a *condition* of all genuine delight, that we should *not* be deluded. See *Adam Smith's Posthumous Essays.*

In the latter, (inasmuch as its principal end is not in or for itself, as is the case in a picture, but to be an assistance and means of an end out of itself), its very purpose is to produce as much illusion as its nature permits. These and all other stage presentations are to produce a sort of temporary half-faith, which the spectator encourages in himself and supports by a voluntary contribution on his own part, because he knows that it is at all times in his power to see the thing as it really is. I have often noticed that little children are actually deceived by stage-scenery, never by pictures, tho' even these produce an effect on their impressible minds which they do not on the minds of adults. The child, if strongly impressed, does not indeed positively think the picture to be the reality; but yet he does not think the contrary. As Sir George Beaumont was shewing me a very fine engraving from Rubens, representing a storm at sea, without any vessel or boat introduced, my little boy (then about five years old) came dancing and singing into the room, and all at once (if I may dare use so low a phrase) *tumbled in* upon the print. He instantly started, stood silent and motionless, with the strongest expression first of wonder and then of grief in his eyes and countenance, and at length said, "And where is the ship? But that is sunk!—and the men all drowned!" still keeping his eye fixed on the print. Now what pictures are to little children, stage-illusion is to men, provided they retain any part of the child's sensibility, except that in the latter instance this suspension of the act of comparison, which permits this sort of negative belief, is somewhat more assisted by the will than in that of the child respecting a picture.

The subject of stage illusion is so important, and so many practical errors and false criticisms may arise, and indeed have risen, either from reasoning on it as actual delusion (the strange notion on which the French critics built up their theory and the French poets justify the construction of their tragedies), or from denying it altogether (which seems the butt of Dr. Johnson's reasoning, and which, as extremes meet, would lead to the very same consequences by excluding whatever would not be judged probable by us in our coolest state of feeling with all our faculties in even balance), that a short digression will, I hope, be pardoned, if it should serve either to explain or to illustrate the point.

It is a general but, as it appears to me, a mistaken opinion, that in our *ordinary* dreams we judge the objects to be real. I say, our *ordinary* dreams, because as to the nightmare, the opinion is to a considerable extent just. But the nightmare is not a mere dream, but takes place when the waking state of the brain is re-commencing, and most often during a rapid alternation, a *twinkling,* as it were, of sleeping and waking, while either from pressure, or from some derangement in the stomach or other digesting organs acting on the external skin (which is still in sympathy with the stomach and bowels) and benumbing it, the sensations sent up to the brain by double touch (*ex. gr.,* when my own hand touches my side or breast) are so faint as to be merely equivalent to the sensation given by single touch (when another person's hand touches me). The mind, therefore, which at all times, with and without our distinct consciousness, seeks for and assumes some outward cause for every impression from without, and which in sleep by aid of the imaginative faculty converts its judgements respecting the cause into a present image, as being the cause,—the mind, I say, in this case deceived by past experience, attributes the painful sensation received to a correspondent agent—an assassin, for instance, stabbing at the side, or a goblin sitting on the breast, etc. Add too that the impressions of the bed, curtains, room, etc., received by the eyes in the half-moments of their opening, blend with and add

vividness and appropriate distance to the dream-image, which returns when they close again: and thus we unite the actual perceptions, or their immediate reliques, with the phantoms of the inward
sense, and thus so confound the half-waking, half-sleeping, reasoning power, that we actually do pass a positive judgement for the
reality of what we see and hear, tho' often accompanied by doubt
and self-questioning, which, as I have myself experienced, will at
times become strong enough even before we awake, to convince us
that it is what it is—the nightmare.

-----

[1.] Illustration of principles [is] my main object; therefore [I
am] not so digressive as might appear.

2. With approved powers as a poet *Shakespeare* commences a
dramatist.

3. Finds the infant stage demanding an intermixture of ludicrous character, as imperiously as that of Greece the chorus, and
high language accordant.

4. Advantages of this—greater assimilation to nature; greater
scope of power (more truths, more feelings); effects of contrast,
Lear and the Fool; and that the true language of passion becomes
sufficiently elevated, by having before heard the lighter conversation of men, in the same piece, under no strong emotion.

5. Nakedness of the stage. Drama then something betwixt recitation and a re-presentation. No scenes. Consequently the laws of
unity of place and unity of time, the observance of which must
either confine the drama to as few subjects as might be counted
on the fingers, or involve gross improbabilities far more striking
than the violation [of the unities] would have been. Danger of a
false ideal, of aiming at more than what is possible on the whole.
[To] supermoralize [is to] demoralize. What play of the ancients,
taking their ideal [as the standard], does not hold out grosser absurdities than any in Shakespeare? On the Grecian [plan] a man
could be a poet, but rarely a dramatist; on the present a dramatist,
not a poet. Different states and degrees of delusion, partly shewn
by others before me.

6. Not only are we never deluded or anything like it; but the
highest possible degree of delusion to beings in their senses sitting

in a theatre is a gross fault, incident only to low minds, who feeling unconsciously that they cannot affect the heart or head permanently, endeavour to call forth the momentary affections. Pain [should be] no more than what is compatible with co-existing pleasure and to be amply repaid by thought; else onions or shaving the upper lip [may serve as satisfactory substitutes for tragedy.]

7. This leads us to what the drama should be. And first it is not *a copy* of nature; but it is an imitation. This is the universal principle of the fine arts. In every well-laid out grounds, what delight do we feel from that balance and antithesis of feelings and thought. "How natural!" we say; but the very wonder that furnished the *how* implies that we perceived art at the same moment. We catch the hint from nature itself. Whenever in mountains or cataracts we discover a likeness to anything artificial which we yet know was not artificial, what pleasure! So in appearances known to be artificial that appear natural. This applies in due degrees regulated by steady good sense, from a clump of trees to the *Paradise Lost* or the *Othello*. It would be easy to apply it to painting, and even, tho' with greater abstraction of thought and by more subtle tho' just analogies, even to music. But this belongs to others. Suffice it [to say] that one great principle is common to all, a principle which probably is the condition of all consciousness, without which we should feel and imagine only by discontinuous moments, and be plants or animals instead of men. I mean that ever-varying balance, or balancing, of images, notions, or feelings (for I avoid the vague word, idea) conceived as in opposition to each other; in short, the perception of identity and contrariety, the least degree of which constitutes *likeness*, the greatest absolute difference; but the infinite gradations between these two form all the play and all the interest of our intellectual and moral being, till it lead us to a feeling and an object more awful than it seems to me compatible with even the present subject to utter aloud, tho' [I am] most desirous to suggest it. For there alone are all things at once different and the same; there alone, as [in] the principle of all things, does distinction exist unaided by division—will and reason, succession of time and unmoving eternity, infinite change and ineffable rest.

Return, Alpheus! the dread voice is past
Which shrunk thy streams! . . .

. . . . .

. . . Thou honor'd flood,
Smooth-flowing Avon, crown'd with vocal reeds,
That strain I heard was of a higher mood.
But now my voice proceeds.

We may divide a dramatic poet's characteristics, before we enter into the component merits of any one work, and speaking only of those things which are to be the materials of all, into language, passion, and character, always bearing in mind, that these must act and react on each other—the language inspired by the passion, the language and passion modified and differenced by the character. To the production of the highest excellencies in these three, there are requisite in the mind of the author: 1. good sense, 2. talents, 3. sensibility, 4. imagination; and to the perfection of a work, two faculties of lesser importance, but yet necessary to the ornaments and foliage of the column or roof, we should add fancy and a quick sense of beauty.

Language. It cannot be supposed that the poet should make his characters say *all* that they would, or taking in his whole drama, that *each* scene or *paragraph* should be such as on cool examination we can conceive it likely that men in such situations would say, in that order and in that *perfection*. And yet, according to my feelings, it is a very inferior kind of poetry in which, as in the French tragedies, men are made to talk what few indeed even of the wittiest men can be supposed to converse in, and which both is, and on a moment's reflection appears to be, the natural produce of the hot-bed of vanity, namely an author's closet, who is actuated originally by a desire to excite surprise and wonderment at *his* superiority to other men, instead of having felt so deeply on certain subjects, or in consequence of certain imaginations, as make it almost a necessity of his nature to seek for sympathy,—no doubt, with that honorable desire of *permanent action* which distinguishes genius [?].

Where then [is] the difference? Each part [should be] proportionate, tho' the whole perhaps impossible: at all events, [it should be] compatible with a sound sense of logic in the mind of the poet himself.

Judging of books by books instead of referring what we read to our own experience, or making it a motive for observation—one great use of books.

Strong passions command figurative language and act as stimulants.

German bad tragedies ridiculed—in which the dramatist becomes a novelist *in his directions to the actors,* and degrades tragedy to pantomime.

Yet still the consciousness of the poet's mind must be diffused over that of the reader or spectator; but he himself, according to his genius, elevates us, and by being *always in keeping* prevents us from perceiving any strangeness, tho' we feel great exaltation. Very different kinds of style may be admirable, both in different men, and in different parts of the same poem. Instance of plain style in the story of the Falcon.

## [The Tempest]

Once more, tho' in a somewhat different and, I would fain believe, in a more instructive form, I have undertaken the task of criticizing the works of that great dramatist whose own name has become their best and most expressive epithet. The task will be genial in proportion as the criticism is reverential. Assuredly the Englishman who without reverence, who without a proud and affectionate reverence, can utter the name of Shakespeare, stands disqualified for the office. He wants one at least of the very senses, the language of which he is to employ, and will discourse at best [but as a blind man], while the whole harmonious creation of light and shade with all its subtle interchange of deepening and dissolving colors rises in silence to the silent fiat of the uprising Apollo. However inferior in ability to some who have followed me, I am proud that I was the first in time who publicly demonstrated to the full extent of the position, that the supposed irregularity and extravagances of Shakespeare were the mere dreams of a pedantry that arraigned the eagle because it had not the dimen-

sions of the swan. In all the successive courses delivered by me
since my first attempt at the Royal Institution, it has been and it
still remains my object to prove that in all points from the most
important to the most minute, the judgement of Shakespeare is
commensurate with his genius—nay, that his genius reveals itself
in his judgement, as in its most exalted form. And the more gladly
do I recur to the subject from the clear conviction that to judge
aright, and with the distinct consciousness of the grounds of our
judgement, concerning the works of Shakespeare, implies the
power and the means of judging rightly of all other works, those
of abstract science alone excepted.

We commence with *The Tempest* as a specimen of the romantic
drama. But whatever play of Shakespeare's we had selected there
is one preliminary point to be first settled, as the indispensable
condition not only of just and genial criticism, but of all consistency in our opinions. This point is contained in the words, probable, natural. We are all in the habit of praising Shakespeare or of
hearing him extolled for his fidelity to nature. Now what are we
to understand by these words in their application to the drama?
Assuredly not the ordinary meaning of them. Farquhar, the most
ably, and if we except a few sentences in one of Dryden's prefaces
(written for a particular purpose and in contradiction to the opinions elsewhere supported by him) first exposed the ludicrous absurdities involved in the supposition, and demolished as with the
single sweep of a careless hand the whole edifice of French criticism respecting the so-called unities of time and place. But a
moment's reflection suffices to make every man conscious of what
every man must have before felt, that the drama is an *imitation* of
reality, not a *copy*—and that imitation is contradistinguished from
copy by this: that a certain quantum of difference is essential to
the former, and an indispensable condition and cause of the pleasure we derive from it; while in a copy it is a defect, contravening
its name and purpose. If illustration were needed, it should be
sufficient to ask why we prefer a fruit view of Van Huysum's to a
marble peach on a mantel-piece, or why we prefer an historical
picture of West to Mrs. Salmon's wax-figure gallery. Not only
that we ought, but that we actually do, all of us judge of the drama

under this impression, we need no other proof than the impassive slumber of our sense of probability when we hear an actor announce himself as a Greek, Roman, Venetian, or Persian in good mother English. And how little our great dramatist feared awakening in it we have a lively instance in proof in Portia's answer to Nerissa's question, "What say you then to Falconbridge, the young baron of England?"—to which she replies, "You know I say nothing to him; for he understands not me, nor I him. He hath neither Latin, French, [n]or Italian, and you will come into the court and swear that I have a poor pennyworth in the English."

Still, however, there is a sort of improbability with which we are shocked in dramatic representation no less than in the narrative of real life. Consequently, there must be rules respecting it; and as rules are nothing but means to an end previously ascertained (the inattention to which simple truth has been the occasion of all the pedantry of the French school), we must first ascertain what the immediate end or object of the drama is. Here I find two extremes in critical decision: the French, which evidently presupposes that a perfect delusion is to be aimed at—an opinion which now needs no fresh confutation; the opposite, supported by Dr. Johnson, supposes the auditors throughout as in the full and positive reflective knowledge of the contrary. In evincing the impossibility of delusion, he makes no sufficient allowance for an intermediate state, which we distinguish by the term illusion.

In what this consists I cannot better explain than by referring you to the highest degree of it; namely, dreaming. It is laxly said that during sleep we take our dreams for realities, but this is irreconcilable with the nature of sleep, which consists in the suspension of the voluntary and, therefore, of the comparative power. The fact is that we pass no judgment either way: we simply do not judge them to be unreal, in consequence of which the images act on our minds, as far as they act at all, by their own force as images. Our state while we are dreaming differs from that in which we are in the perusal of a deeply interesting novel in the degree rather than in the kind, and from three causes: First, from the exclusion of all outward impressions on our senses the images in sleep become proportionally more vivid than they can be when the organs of sense are in their active state. Secondly, in sleep the sensations, and with these the emotions and passions which they counterfeit, are the causes of our dream-images, while in our waking hours our emotions are the effects of the images presented to us. (Apparitions [are] *so detectible*.) Lastly, in sleep we pass at once by a sudden collapse into this suspension of will and the comparative power: whereas in an interesting play, read or represented, we are brought up to this point, as far as it is requisite or desirable, gradually, by the art of the poet and the actors; and with the consent and positive aidance of our own will. We *choose* to be deceived. The rule, therefore, may be easily inferred. Whatever tends to prevent the mind from placing it[self] or from being gradually placed in this state in which the images have a negative reality must be a defect, and consequently anything that must force itself on the auditors' mind as improbable, not because it *is* improbable (for that the whole play is foreknown to be) but because it cannot but *appear* as such.

But this again depends on the degree of excitement in which the mind is supposed to be. Many things would be intolerable in the first scene of a play that would not at all interrupt our enjoyment in the height of the interest. The narrow cockpit may hold

> The vasty fields of France, or we may cram
> Within its wooden O the very casques
> That did affright the air at Agincourt.

And again, on the other hand, many obvious improbabilities will be endured as belonging to the groundwork of the story rather than to the drama, in the first scenes, which would disturb or disentrance us from all illusion in the acme of our excitement, as, for instance, Lear's division of his realm and banishment of Cordelia. But besides this dramatic probability, all the other excellencies of the drama, as unity of interest, with distinctness and subordination of the characters, appropriateness of style, nay, and the charm of language and sentiment for their own sakes, yet still as far as they tend to increase the inward excitement, are all means to this chief end, that of producing and supporting this willing illusion.

I have but one point more to add—namely, that tho' the excel-

lencies above mentioned are means to this end, they do not therefore cease to be themselves *ends,* and as such carry their own justification with them as long as they do not contravene or interrupt
the illusion. It is not even always or of necessity an objection to
them, that they prevent it from rising to as great a height as it
might otherwise have attained; it is enough, if they are compatible
with as high a degree as is requisite. If the panorama had been invented in the time of Leo X., Raphael would still have smiled at
the regret that the broom-twigs, etc., at the back of his grand pictures were not as probable trees as those in the panorama. Let me
venture to affirm that certain obvious, if not palpable, improbabilities may be hazarded in order to keep down a scene, [to keep it]
merely instrumental, and to preserve it in its due proportion of
interest. I now quit this subject for the time with less regret, because in my next lecture I shall have occasion to take it up again,
in application to Shakespeare's *historical* dramas.

*The Tempest,* I repeat, has been selected as a specimen of the
romantic drama; *i.e.,* of a drama, the interests of which are independent of all historical facts and associations, and arise from their
fitness to that faculty of our nature, the imagination I mean, which
owns no allegiance to time and place,—a species of drama, therefore, in which errors in chronology and geography, no mortal sins
in any species, are venial, or count for nothing.

The romance opens with a busy lively scene, admirably appropriate to the *kind* of drama, giving as it were the keynote.

---

Exquisite judgement—first the noise and confusion—then the
silence of a deserted island—and Prospero and Miranda. I have
often thought of Shakespeare as the mighty wizard himself introducing as the first and fairest [?] pledge of his so potent art, the
female character in all its charms, as if conscious that he first had
represented womanhood as a dramatist.

---

It addresses itself entirely to the imaginative faculty; and although the illusion may be assisted by the effect on the senses of
the complicated scenery and decorations of modern times yet this

sort of assistance is dangerous. For the principal and only genuine excitement ought to come from within,—from the moved and sympathetic imagination; whereas, where so much is addressed to the mere external senses of seeing and hearing, the spiritual vision is apt to languish, and the attraction from without will withdraw the mind from the proper and only legitimate interest which is intended to spring from within.

The romance opens with a busy scene admirably appropriate to the kind of drama, and giving, as it were, the keynote to the whole harmony. It prepares and initiates the excitement required for the entire piece, and yet does not demand anything from the spectators, which their previous habits had not fitted them to understand. It is the bustle of a tempest, from which the real horrors are abstracted;—therefore it is poetical, though not in strictness natural— (the distinction to which I have so often alluded)—and is purposely restrained from concentering the interest on itself, but used merely as an induction or tuning for what is to follow.

In the second scene, Prospero's speeches, till the entrance of Ariel, contain the finest example I remember of retrospective narration for the purpose of exciting immediate interest, and putting the audience in possession of all the information necessary for the understanding of the plot. Observe, too, the perfect probability of the moment chosen by Prospero (the very Shakespeare himself, as it were, of the tempest) to open out the truth to his daughter, his own romantic bearing, and how completely any thing that might have been disagreeable to us in the magician, is reconciled and shaded in the humanity and natural feelings of the father. In the very first speech of Miranda the simplicity and tenderness of her character are at once laid open;—it would have been lost in direct contact with the agitation of the first scene. The opinion once prevailed, but, happily, is now abandoned, that Fletcher alone wrote for women;—the truth is, that with very few, and those partial, exceptions, the female characters in the plays of Beaumont and Fletcher are, when of the light kind, not decent; when heroic, complete viragos. But in Shakespeare all the elements of womanhood are holy, and there is the sweet, yet dignified feeling of all that *continuates* society, as sense of ancestry and of sex, with a purity unassailable by sophistry, because it rests not in the analytic processes, but in that sane equipoise of the faculties, during which the feelings are representative of all past experience,—not of the individual only, but of all those by whom she has been educated, and their predecessors even up to the first mother that lived. Shakespeare saw that the want of prominence, which Pope notices for sarcasm, was the blessed beauty of the woman's character, and knew that it arose not from any deficiency, but from the more exquisite harmony of all the parts of the moral being constituting one living total of head and heart. He has drawn it, indeed, in all its distinctive energies of faith, patience, constancy, fortitude,— shown in all of them as following the heart, which gives its results by a nice tact and happy intuition, without the intervention of the discursive faculty,—sees all things in and by the light of the affections, and errs, if it ever err, in the exaggerations of love alone. In all the Shakespearian women there is essentially the same foundation and principle; the distinct individuality and variety are merely the result of the modification of circumstances, whether in Miranda the maiden, in Imogen the wife, or in Katharine the queen.

But to return. The appearance and characters of the super or ultranatural servants are finely contrasted. Ariel has in every thing the airy tint which gives the name; and it is worthy of remark that Miranda is never directly brought into comparison with Ariel, lest the natural and human of the one and the supernatural of the other should tend to neutralize each other; Caliban, on the other hand, is all earth, all condensed and gross in feelings and images; he has the dawnings of understanding without reason or the moral sense, and in him, as in some brute animals, this advance to the intellectual faculties, without the moral sense, is marked by the appearance of vice. For it is in the primacy of the moral being only that man is truly human; in his intellectual powers he is certainly approached by the brutes, and, man's whole system duly considered, those powers cannot be considered other than means to an end, that is, to morality.

In this scene, as it proceeds, is displayed the impression made by Ferdinand and Miranda on each other; it is love at first sight;—

> at the first sight
> They have changed eyes:—

and it appears to me, that in all cases of real love, it is at one moment that it takes place. That moment may have been prepared by previous esteem, admiration, or even affection,—yet love seems to require a momentary act of volition, by which a tacit bond of devotion is imposed,—a bond not to be thereafter broken without violating what should be sacred in our nature. How finely is the true Shakespearian scene contrasted with Dryden's vulgar alteration of it, in which a mere ludicrous psychological experiment, as it were, is tried—displaying nothing but indelicacy without passion. Prospero's interruption of the courtship has often seemed to me to have no sufficient motive; still his alleged reason—

> lest too light winning
> Make the prize light—

is enough for the ethereal connexions of the romantic imagination, although it would not be so for the historical. The whole courting scene, indeed, in the beginning of the third act, between the lovers is a masterpiece; and the first dawn of disobedience in the mind of Miranda to the command of her father is very finely drawn, so as to seem the working of the Scriptural command, *Thou shalt leave father and mother,* &c. O! with what exquisite purity this scene is conceived and executed! Shakspeare may sometimes be gross, but I boldly say that he is always moral and modest. Alas! in this our day decency of manners is preserved at the expense of morality of heart, and delicacies for vice are allowed, whilst grossness against it is hypocritically, or at least morbidly, condemned.

In this play are admirably sketched the vices generally accompanying a low degree of civilization; and in the first scene of the second act Shakspeare has, as in many other places, shown the tendency in bad men to indulge in scorn and contemptuous expressions, as a mode of getting rid of their own uneasy feelings of inferiority to the good, and also, by making the good ridiculous, of rendering the transition of others to wickedness easy. Shakspeare never puts habitual scorn into the mouths of other than bad men, as here in the instances of Antonio and Sebastian. The scene of

the intended assassination of Alonzo and Gonzalo is an exact counterpart of the scene between Macbeth and his lady, only pitched
in a lower key throughout, as designed to be frustrated and concealed, and exhibiting the same profound management in the
manner of familiarizing a mind, not immediately recipient, to the
suggestion of guilt, by associating the proposed crime with something ludicrous or out of place,—something not habitually matter
of reverence. By this kind of sophistry the imagination and fancy
are first bribed to contemplate the suggested act, and at length to
become acquainted with it. Observe how the effect of this scene
is heightened by contrast with another counterpart of it in low
life,—that between the conspirators Stephano, Caliban, and Trinculo in the second scene of the third act, in which there are the
same essential characteristics.

In this play and in this scene of it are also shown the springs of
the vulgar in politics,—of that kind of politics which is inwoven
with human nature. In his treatment of this subject, wherever it
occurs, Shakspeare is quite peculiar. In other writers we find the
particular opinions of the individual; in Massinger it is rank republicanism; in Beaumont and Fletcher even *jure divino* principles
are carried to excess;—but Shakspeare never promulgates any party
tenets. He is always the philosopher and the moralist, but at the
same time with a profound veneration for all the established institutions of society, and for those classes which form the permanent
elements of the state—especially never introducing a professional
character, as such, otherwise than as respectable. If he must have
any name, he should be styled a philosophical aristocrat, delighting
in those hereditary institutions which have a tendency to bind one
age to another, and in that distinction of ranks, of which, although
few may be in possession, all enjoy the advantages. Hence, again,
you will observe the good nature with which he seems always to
make sport with the passions and follies of a mob, as with an irrational animal. He is never angry with it, but hugely content with
holding up its absurdities to its face; and sometimes you may trace
a tone of almost affectionate superiority, something like that in
which a father speaks of the rogueries of a child. See the good-
humoured way in which he describes Stephano passing from the

most licentious freedom to absolute despotism over Trinculo and Caliban. The truth is, Shakspeare's characters are all _genera_ intensely individualized; the results of meditation, of which observation supplied the drapery and the colours necessary to combine them with each other. He had virtually surveyed all the great component powers and impulses of human nature,—had seen that their different combinations and subordinations were in fact the individualizers of men, and showed how their harmony was produced by reciprocal disproportions of excess or deficiency. The language in which these truths are expressed was not drawn from any set fashion, but from the profoundest depths of his moral being, and is therefore for all ages.

LECTURE VII, 1811–12 SERIES (J. P. COLLIER REPORT)

## [Romeo and Juliet]

In a former lecture I endeavoured to point out the union of the Poet and the Philosopher, or rather the warm embrace between them, in the "Venus and Adonis" and "Lucrece" of Shakespeare. From thence I passed on to "Love's Labours Lost," as the link between his character as a Poet, and his art as a Dramatist; and I shewed that, although in that work the former was still predominant, yet that the germs of his subsequent dramatic power were easily discernible.

I will now, as I promised in my last, proceed to "Romeo and Juliet," not because it is the earliest, or among the earliest of Shakespeare's works of that kind, but because in it are to be found specimens, in degree, of all the excellences which he afterwards displayed in his more perfect dramas, but differing from them in being less forcibly evidenced, and less happily combined: all the parts are more or less present, but they are not united with the same harmony.

There are, however, in "Romeo and Juliet" passages where the poet's whole excellence is evinced, so that nothing superior to them can be met with in the productions of his after years. The main distinction between this play and others is, as I said, that the parts are less happily combined, or to borrow a phrase from the painter, the whole work is less in keeping. Grand portions are produced: we have limbs of giant growth; but the production, as a whole, in which each part gives delight for itself, and the whole, consisting of these delightful parts, communicates the highest intellectual pleasure and satisfaction, is the result of the application of judgment and taste. These are not to be attained but by painful study, and to the sacrifice of the stronger pleasures derived from the dazzling light which a man of genius throws over every circumstance, and where we are chiefly struck by vivid and distinct images. Taste is an attainment after a poet has been disciplined by experience, and has added to genius that talent by which he knows what part of his genius he can make acceptable, and intelligible to the portion of mankind for which he writes.

In my mind it would be a hopeless symptom, as regards genius, if I found a young man with anything like perfect taste. In the earlier works of Shakespeare we have a profusion of double epithets, and sometimes even the coarsest terms are employed, if they convey a more vivid image; but by degrees the associations are connected with the image they are designed to impress, and the poet descends from the ideal into the real world so far as to conjoin both —to give a sphere of active operations to the ideal, and to elevate and refine the real.

In "Romeo and Juliet" the principal characters may be divided into two classes: in one class passion—the passion of love—is drawn and drawn truly, as well as beautifully; but the persons are not individualised farther than as the actor appears on the stage. It is a very just description and development of love, without giving, if I may so express myself, the philosophical history of it—without shewing how the man became acted upon by that particular passion, but leading it through all the incidents of the drama, and rendering it predominant.

Tybalt is, in himself, a common-place personage. And here allow me to remark upon a great distinction between Shakespeare, and all who have written in imitation of him. I know no character in his plays, (unless indeed Pistol be an exception) which can be called the mere portrait of an individual: while the reader feels all the satisfaction arising from individuality, yet that very individual is a sort of class character, and this circumstance renders Shakespeare the poet of all ages.

Tybalt is a man abandoned to his passions—with all the pride of family, only because he thought it belonged to him as a member of that family, and valuing himself highly, simply because he does not care for death. This indifference to death is perhaps more common than any other feeling: men are apt to flatter themselves extravagantly, merely because they possess a quality which it is a disgrace not to have, but which a wise man never puts forward, but when it is necessary.

Jeremy Taylor in one part of his voluminous works, speaking of a great man, says that he was naturally a coward, as indeed most men are, knowing the value of life, but the power of his reason enabled him, when required, to conduct himself with uniform courage and hardihood. The good bishop, perhaps, had in his mind a story, told by one of the ancients, of a Philosopher and a Coxcomb, on board the same ship during a storm: the Coxcomb reviled the Philosopher for betraying marks of fear: "Why are you so frightened? I am not afraid of being drowned: I do not care a farthing for my life."—"You are perfectly right," said the Philosopher, "for your life is not worth a farthing."

Shakespeare never takes pains to make his characters win your esteem, but leaves it to the general command of the passions, and to poetic justice. It is most beautiful to observe, in "Romeo and Juliet," that the characters principally engaged in the incidents are preserved innocent from all that could lower them in our opinion, while the rest of the personages, deserving little interest in themselves, derive it from being instrumental in those situations in which the more important personages develope their thoughts and passions.

Look at Capulet—a worthy, noble-minded old man of high rank, with all the impatience that is likely to accompany it. It is delightful to see all the sensibilities of our nature so exquisitely called forth; as if the poet had the hundred arms of the polypus, and had thrown them out in all directions to catch the predominant feeling. We may see in Capulet the manner in which anger seizes hold of everything that comes in its way, in order to express itself, as in the lines where he reproves Tybalt for his fierceness of behaviour, which led him to wish to insult a Montague, and disturb the merriment.—

> Go to, go to;
> You are a saucy boy. Is't so, indeed?
> This trick may chance to scath you;—I know what.
> You must contrary me! marry, 'tis time.—
> Well said, my hearts!—You are a princox: go:
> Be quiet or—More light, more light!—For shame!
> I'll make you quiet.—What! cheerly, my hearts!
> *Act I., Scene 5.*

The line
> This trick may chance to scath you;—I know what,

was an allusion to the legacy Tybalt might expect; and then, seeing the lights burn dimly, Capulet turns his anger against the servants. Thus we see that no one passion is so predominant, but that it includes all the parts of the character, and the reader never has a mere abstract of a passion, as of wrath or ambition, but the whole man is presented to him—the one predominant passion acting, if I may so say, as the leader of the band to the rest.

It could not be expected that the poet should introduce such a character as Hamlet into every play; but even in those personages, which are subordinate to a hero so eminently philosophical, the passion is at least rendered instructive, and induces the reader to look with a keener eye, and a finer judgment into human nature.

Shakespeare has this advantage over all other dramatists—that he has availed himself of his psychological genius to develope all the minutiae of the human heart: shewing us the thing that, to common observers, he seems solely intent upon, he makes visible what we should not otherwise have seen: just as, after looking at distant objects through a telescope, when we behold them subsequently with the naked eye, we see them with greater distinctness, and in more detail, than we should otherwise have done.

Mercutio is one of our poet's truly Shakespearian characters; for throughout his plays, but especially in those of the highest order, it is plain that the personages were drawn rather from meditation than from observation, the child of meditation. It is comparatively easy for a man to go about the world, as if with a pocket-book in his hand, carefully noting down what he sees and hears: by practice he acquires considerable facility in representing what he has observed, himself frequently unconscious of its worth, or its bearings. This is entirely different from the observation of a mind, which, having formed a theory and a system upon its own nature, remarks all things that are examples of its truth, confirming it in that truth, and, above all, enabling it to convey the truths of philosophy, as mere effects derived from, what we may call, the outward watchings of life.

Hence it is that Shakespeare's favourite characters are full of such lively intellect. Mercutio is a man possessing all the elements of a poet: the whole world was, as it were, subject to his law of association. Whenever he wishes to impress anything, all things become his servants for the purpose: all things tell the same tale, and sound in unison. This faculty, moreover, is combined with the manners and feelings of a perfect gentleman, himself utterly unconscious of his powers. By his loss it was contrived that the whole catastrophe of the tragedy should be brought about: it endears him to Romeo, and gives to the death of Mercutio an importance which it could not otherwise have acquired.

I say this in answer to an observation, I think by Dryden, (to which indeed Dr. Johnson has fully replied) that Shakespeare having carried the part of Mercutio as far as he could, till his genius was exhausted, had killed him in the third Act, to get him out of the way. What shallow nonsense! As I have remarked, upon the death of Mercutio the whole catastrophe depends; it is produced by it. The scene in which it occurs serves to show how indifference to any subject but one, and aversion to activity on the part of Romeo, may be overcome and roused to the most resolute and determined conduct. Had not Mercutio been rendered so amiable and so interesting, we could not have felt so strongly the necessity for Romeo's interference, connecting it immediately, and passionately, with the future fortunes of the lover and his mistress.

But what am I to say of the Nurse? We have been told that her character is the mere fruit of observation—that it is like Swift's "Polite Conversation," certainly the most stupendous work of human memory, and of unceasingly active attention to what passes around us, upon record. The Nurse in "Romeo and Juliet" has sometimes been compared to a portrait by Gerard Dow, in which every hair was so exquisitely painted, that it would bear the test of the microscope. Now, I appeal confidently to my hearers whether the closest observation of the manners of one or two old nurses would have enabled Shakespeare to draw this character of admirable generalisation? Surely not. Let any man conjure up in his mind all the qualities and peculiarities that can possibly belong to a nurse, and he will find them in Shakespeare's picture of the old woman: nothing is omitted. This effect is not produced by mere observation. The great prerogative of genius (and Shakespeare felt and availed himself of it) is now to swell itself to the dignity of a god, and now to subdue and keep dormant some part of that lofty nature, and to descend even to the lowest character—to become everything, in fact, but the vicious.

Thus, in the Nurse you have all the garrulity of old age, and all its fondness; for the affection of old-age is one of the greatest consolations of humanity. I have often thought what a melancholy world this would be without children, and what an inhuman world without the aged.

You have also in the Nurse the arrogance of ignorance, with the pride of meanness at being connected with a great family. You have the grossness, too, which that situation never removes, though it sometimes suspends it; and, arising from that grossness, the little low vices attendant upon it, which, indeed, in such minds are scarcely vices.—Romeo at one time was the most delightful and excellent young man, and the Nurse all willingness to assist him; but her disposition soon turns in favour of Paris, for whom she professes precisely the same admiration. How wonderfully are these low peculiarities contrasted with a young and pure mind, educated under different circumstances!

Another point ought to be mentioned as characteristic of the ignorance of the Nurse:—it is, that in all her recollections, she assists herself by the remembrance of visual circumstances. The great difference, in this respect, between the cultivated and the uncultivated mind is this—that the cultivated mind will be found to recal the past by certain regular trains of cause and effect; whereas, with the uncultivated mind, the past is recalled wholly by coincident images, or facts which happened at the same time. This position is fully exemplified in the following passages put into the mouth of the Nurse:—

> Even or odd, of all days in the year,
> Come Lammas eve at night shall she be fourteen.
> Susan and she—God rest all Christian souls!—
> Were of an age.—Well, Susan is with God;
> She was too good for me. But, as I said,
> On Lammas eve at night shall she be fourteen;
> That shall she, marry: I remember it well.
> 'Tis since the earthquake now eleven years;
> And she was wean'd,—I never shall forget it,—
> Of all the days of the year, upon that day;
> For I had then laid wormwood to my dug,
> Sitting in the sun under the dove-house wall:
> My lord and you were then at Mantua.—
> Nay, I do bear a brain:—but, as I said,
> When it did taste the wormwood on the nipple
> Of my dug, and felt it bitter, pretty fool,
> To see it tetchy, and fall out with the dug!
> Shake, quoth the dove-house: 'twas no need, I trow,
> To bid me trudge.
> And since that time it is eleven years;
> For then she could stand alone.

*Act I., Scene 3.*

She afterwards goes on with similar visual impressions, so true to the character.—More is here brought into one portrait than could have been ascertained by one man's mere observation, and without the introduction of a single incongruous point.

I honour, I love, the works of Fielding as much, or perhaps more, than those of any other writer of fiction of that kind: take Fielding in his characters of postillions, landlords, and landladies, waiters, or indeed, of any-body who had come before his eye, and nothing can be more true, more happy, or more humorous; but in all his chief personages, Tom Jones for instance, where Fielding was not directed by observation, where he could not assist himself by the close copying of what he saw, where it is necessary that something should take place, some words be spoken, or some object described, which he could not have witnessed, (his soliloquies for example, or the interview between the hero and Sophia Western before the reconciliation) and I will venture to say, loving and honouring the man and his productions as I do, that nothing can be more forced and unnatural: the language is without vivacity or spirit, the whole matter is incongruous, and totally destitute of psychological truth.

On the other hand, look at Shakespeare: where can any character be produced that does not speak the language of nature? Where does he not put into the mouths of his *dramatis personæ*, be they high or low, Kings or Constables, precisely what they must have said? Where, from observation, could he learn the language proper to Sovereigns, Queens, Noblemen or Generals? yet he invariably uses it.—Where, from observation, could he have learned such lines as these, which are put into the mouth of Othello, when he is talking to Iago of Brabantio?

> Let him do his spite:
> My services, which I have done the signiory,
> Shall out-tongue his complaints. 'Tis yet to know,
> Which, when I know that boasting is an honour,
> I shall promulgate, I fetch my life and being
> From men of royal siege; and my demerits
> May speak, unbonneted, to as proud a fortune
> As this that I have reach'd: for know, Iago,
> But that I love the gentle Desdemona,
> I would not my unhoused free condition
> Put into circumscription and confine
> For the sea's worth.
>
> *Act I., Scene 2.*

I ask where was Shakespeare to observe such language as this? If he did observe it, it was with the inward eye of meditation upon his own nature: for the time, he became Othello, and spoke as Othello, in such circumstances, must have spoken.

Another remark I may make upon "Romeo and Juliet" is, that in this tragedy the poet is not, as I have hinted, entirely blended with the dramatist,—at least, not in the degree to be afterwards noticed in "Lear," "Hamlet," "Othello," or "Macbeth." Capulet and Montague not unfrequently talk a language only belonging to the poet, and not so characteristic of, and peculiar to, the passions of persons in the situations in which they are placed—a mistake, or rather an indistinctness, which many of our later dramatists have carried through the whole of their productions.

When I read the song of Deborah, I never think that she is a poet, although I think the song itself a sublime poem: it is as simple a dithyrambic production as exists in any language; but it is the proper and characteristic effusion of a woman highly elevated by triumph, by the natural hatred of oppressors, and resulting from a bitter sense of wrong: it is a song of exultation on deliverance from these evils, a deliverance accomplished by herself. When she exclaims, "The inhabitants of the villages ceased, they ceased in Israel, until that I, Deborah, arose, that I arose a mother in Israel," it is poetry in the highest sense: we have no reason, however, to suppose that if she had not been agitated by passion, and animated by victory, she would have been able so to express herself; or that if she had been placed in different circumstances, she would have used such language of truth and passion. We are to remember that Shakespeare, not placed under circumstances of excitement, and only wrought upon by his own vivid and vigorous imagination, writes a language that invariably, and intuitively becomes the condition and position of each character.

On the other hand, there is a language not descriptive of passion, not uttered under the influence of it, which is at the same time poetic, and shows a high and active fancy, as when Capulet says to Paris,—

> Such comfort as do lusty young men feel,
> When well-apparell'd April on the heel
> Of limping winter treads, even such delight
> Among fresh female buds, shall you this night
> Inherit at my house.
>
> *Act I., Scene 2.*

Here the poet may be said to speak, rather than the dramatist; and it would be easy to adduce other passages from this play, where Shakespeare, for a moment forgetting the character, utters his own words in his own person.

In my mind, what have often been censured as Shakespeare's conceits are completely justifiable, as belonging to the state, age, or feeling of the individual. Sometimes, when they cannot be vindicated on these grounds, they may well be excused by the taste of his own and of the preceding age; as for instance, in Romeo's speech,

> Here's much to do with hate, but more with love:—
> Why then, O brawling love! O loving hate!
> O anything, of nothing first created!
> O heavy lightness! serious vanity!
> Misshapen chaos of well-seeming forms!
> Feather of lead, bright smoke, cold fire, sick health!
> Still-waking sleep, that is not what it is!
>
> *Act I., Scene 1.*

I dare not pronounce such passages as these to be absolutely unnatural, not merely because I consider the author a much better judge than I can be, but because I can understand and allow for an effort of the mind, when it would describe what it cannot satisfy itself with the description of, to reconcile opposites and qualify contradictions, leaving a middle state of mind more strictly appropriate to the imagination than any other, when it is, as it were, hovering between images. As soon as it is fixed on one image, it becomes understanding; but while it is unfixed and wavering between them, attaching itself permanently to none, it is imagination. Such is the fine description of Death in Milton:—

> The other shape,
> If shape it might be call'd, that shape had none
> Distinguishable in member, joint, or limb,
> Or substance might be call'd, that shadow seem'd,
> For each seem'd either: black it stood as night;
> Fierce as ten furies, terrible as hell,
> And shook a dreadful dart: what seem'd his head
> The likeness of a kingly crown had on.
>
> *Paradise Lost,* Book II.

The grandest efforts of poetry are where the imagination is called forth, not to produce a distinct form, but a strong working of the mind, still offering what is still repelled, and again creating what is again rejected; the result being what the poet wishes to impress, namely, the substitution of a sublime feeling of the unimaginable for a mere image. I have sometimes thought that the passage just read might be quoted as exhibiting the narrow limit of painting, as compared with the boundless power of poetry: painting cannot go beyond a certain point; poetry rejects all control, all confinement. Yet we know that sundry painters have attempted pictures of the meeting between Satan and Death at the gates of Hell; and how was Death represented? Not as Milton has described him, but by the most defined thing that can be imagined —a skeleton, the dryest and hardest image that it is possible to discover; which, instead of keeping the mind in a state of activity, reduces it to the merest passivity,—an image, compared with which a square, a triangle, or any other mathematical figure, is a luxuriant fancy.

It is a general but mistaken notion that, because some forms of writing, and some combinations of thought, are not usual, they are not natural; but we are to recollect that the dramatist represents his characters in every situation of life and in every state of mind, and there is no form of language that may not be introduced with effect by a great and judicious poet, and yet be most strictly according to nature. Take punning, for instance, which may be the lowest, but at all events is the most harmless, kind of wit, because it never excites envy. A pun may be a necessary consequence of association: one man, attempting to prove something that was resisted by another, might, when agitated by strong feeling, employ a term used by his adversary with a directly contrary meaning to that for which that adversary had resorted to it: it might come into his mind as one way, and sometimes the best, of replying to that adversary. This form of speech is generally produced by a mixture of anger and contempt, and punning is a natural mode of expressing them.

It is my intention to pass over none of the important so-called conceits of Shakespeare, not a few of which are introduced into his later productions with great propriety and effect. We are not to forget, that at the time he lived there was an attempt at, and an affectation of, quaintness and adornment, which emanated from the Court, and against which satire was directed by Shakespeare in the character of Osrick in Hamlet. Among the schoolmen of that

age, and earlier, nothing was more common than the use of conceits: it began with the revival of letters, and the bias thus given
was very generally felt and acknowledged.

I have in my possession a dictionary of phrases, in which the
epithets applied to love, hate, jealousy, and such abstract terms, are
arranged; and they consist almost entirely of words taken from
Seneca and his imitators, or from the schoolmen, showing perpetual antithesis, and describing the passions by the conjunction
and combination of things absolutely irreconcileable. In treating
the matter thus, I am aware that I am only palliating the practice
in Shakespeare: he ought to have had nothing to do with merely
temporary peculiarities: he wrote not for his own only, but for all
ages, and so far I admit the use of some of his conceits to be a
defect. They detract sometimes from his universality as to time,
person, and situation. . . .

FROM LECTURE XII, 1811–12 SERIES (J. P. COLLIER REPORT)

## [Hamlet]

. . . We will now pass to "Hamlet," in order to obviate some
of the general prejudices against the author, in reference to the
character of the hero. Much has been objected to, which ought to
have been praised, and many beauties of the highest kind have
been neglected, because they are somewhat hidden.

The first question we should ask ourselves is—What did Shakespeare mean when he drew the character of Hamlet? He never
wrote any thing without design, and what was his design when he
sat down to produce this tragedy? My belief is, that he always regarded his story, before he began to write, much in the same light
as a painter regards his canvas, before he begins to paint—as a
mere vehicle for his thoughts—as the ground upon which he was
to work. What then was the point to which Shakespeare directed
himself in Hamlet? He intended to pourtray a person, in whose
view the external world, and all its incidents and objects, were
comparatively dim, and of no interest in themselves, and which
began to interest only, when they were reflected in the mirror of

his mind. Hamlet beheld external things in the same way that a man of vivid imagination, who shuts his eyes, sees what has previously made an impression on his organs.

The poet places him in the most stimulating circumstances that a human being can be placed in. He is the heir apparent of a throne; his father dies suspiciously; his mother excludes her son from his throne by marrying his uncle. This is not enough; but the Ghost of the murdered father is introduced, to assure the son that he was put to death by his own brother. What is the effect upon the son?—instant action and pursuit of revenge? No: endless reasoning and hesitating—constant urging and solicitation of the mind to act, and as constant an escape from action; ceaseless reproaches of himself for sloth and negligence, while the whole energy of his resolution evaporates in these reproaches. This, too, not from cowardice, for he is drawn as one of the bravest of his time—not from want of forethought or slowness of apprehension, for he sees through the very souls of all who surround him, but merely from that aversion to action, which prevails among such as have a world in themselves.

How admirable, too, is the judgment of the poet! Hamlet's own disordered fancy has not conjured up the spirit of his father; it has been seen by others: he is prepared by them to witness its re-appearance, and when he does see it, Hamlet is not brought forward as having long brooded on the subject. The moment before the Ghost enters, Hamlet speaks of other matters: he mentions the coldness of the night, and observes that he has not heard the clock strike, adding, in reference to the custom of drinking, that it is

> More honour'd in the breach than the observance.
> *Act I., Scene 4.*

Owing to the tranquil state of his mind, he indulges in some moral reflections. Afterwards, the Ghost suddenly enters.

> *Hor.*          Look, my lord! it comes.
> *Ham.* Angels and ministers of grace defend us!

The same thing occurs in "Macbeth": in the dagger-scene, the moment before the hero sees it, he has his mind applied to some indifferent matters; "Go, tell thy mistress," &c. Thus, in both cases, the preternatural appearance has all the effect of abruptness, and the reader is totally divested of the notion, that the figure is a vision of a highly wrought imagination.

Here Shakespeare adapts himself so admirably to the situation— in other words, so puts himself into it—that, though poetry, his language is the very language of nature. No terms, associated with such feelings, can occur to us so proper as those which he has employed, especially on the highest, the most august, and the most awful subjects that can interest a human being in this sentient world. That this is no mere fancy, I can undertake to establish from hundreds, I might say thousands, of passages. No character he has drawn, in the whole list of his plays, could so well and fitly express himself, as in the language Shakespeare has put into his mouth.

There is no indecision about Hamlet, as far as his own sense of duty is concerned; he knows well what he ought to do, and over and over again he makes up his mind to do it. The moment the players, and the two spies set upon him, have withdrawn, of whom he takes leave with a line so expressive of his contempt,

> Ay so; good bye you.—Now I am alone,

he breaks out into a delirium of rage against himself for neglecting to perform the solemn duty he had undertaken, and contrasts the factitious and artificial display of feeling by the player with his own apparent indifference;

> What's Hecuba to him, or he to Hecuba,
> That he should weep for her?

Yet the player did weep for her, and was in an agony of grief at her sufferings, while Hamlet is unable to rouse himself to action, in order that he may perform the command of his father, who had come from the grave to incite him to revenge:—

>       This is most brave!
> That I, the son of a dear father murder'd,
> Prompted to my revenge by heaven and hell,
> Must, like a whore, unpack my heart with words,

And fall a cursing like a very drab,
A scullion.

*Act II., Scene 2.*

It is the same feeling, the same conviction of what is his duty, that makes Hamlet exclaim in a subsequent part of the tragedy:

How all occasions do inform against me,
And spur my dull revenge! What is a man,
If his chief good, and market of his time,
Be but to sleep and feed? A beast, no more. . . .
. . . . I do not know
Why yet I live to say—"this thing's to do,"
Sith I have cause and will and strength and means
To do't.

*Act IV., Scene 4.*

Yet with all this strong conviction of duty, and with all this resolution arising out of strong conviction, nothing is done. This admirable and consistent character, deeply acquainted with his own feelings, painting them with such wonderful power and accuracy, and firmly persuaded that a moment ought not to be lost in executing the solemn charge committed to him, still yields to the same retiring from reality, which is the result of having, what we express by the terms, a world within himself.

Such a mind as Hamlet's is near akin to madness. Dryden has somewhere said,

Great wit to madness nearly is allied,

and he was right; for he means by "wit" that greatness of genius, which led Hamlet to a perfect knowledge of his own character, which, with all strength of motive, was so weak as to be unable to carry into act his own most obvious duty.

With all this he has a sense of imperfectness, which becomes apparent when he is moralising on the skull in the churchyard. Something is wanting to his completeness—something is deficient which remains to be supplied, and he is therefore described as attached to Ophelia. His madness is assumed, when he finds that witnesses have been placed behind the arras to listen to what passes, and when the heroine has been thrown in his way as a decoy.

Another objection has been taken by Dr. Johnson, and Shakespeare has been taxed very severely. I refer to the scene where Hamlet enters and finds his uncle praying, and refuses to take his life, excepting when he is in the height of his iniquity. To assail him at such a moment of confession and repentance, Hamlet declares,

> Why, this is hire and salary, not revenge.
> *Act III., Scene 3.*

He therefore forbears, and postpones his uncle's death, until he can catch him in some act

> That has no relish of salvation in't.

This conduct, and this sentiment, Dr. Johnson has pronounced to be so atrocious and horrible, as to be unfit to be put into the mouth of a human being. The fact, however, is that Dr. Johnson did not understand the character of Hamlet, and censured accordingly: the determination to allow the guilty King to escape at such a moment is only part of the indecision and irresoluteness of the hero. Hamlet seizes hold of a pretext for not acting, when he might have acted so instantly and effectually: therefore, he again defers the revenge he was bound to seek, and declares his determination to accomplish it at some time,

> When he is drunk, asleep, or in his rage,
> Or in th' incestuous pleasures of his bed.

This, allow me to impress upon you most emphatically, was merely the excuse Hamlet made to himself for not taking advantage of this particular and favourable moment for doing justice upon his guilty uncle, at the urgent instance of the spirit of his father.

Dr. Johnson farther states, that in the voyage to England, Shakespeare merely follows the novel as he found it, as if the poet had no other reason for adhering to his original; but Shakespeare never followed a novel, because he found such and such an incident in it, but because he saw that the story, as he read it, contributed to enforce, or to explain some great truth inherent in human nature. He never could lack invention to alter or improve a popular narrative; but he did not wantonly vary from it, when he knew that, as it was related, it would so well apply to his own great purpose. He saw at once how consistent it was with the character of Hamlet, that after still resolving, and still deferring, still determining to execute, and still postponing execution, he should finally, in the infirmity of his disposition, give himself up to his destiny, and hopelessly place himself in the power, and at the mercy of his enemies.

Even after the scene with Osrick, we see Hamlet still indulging in reflection, and hardly thinking of the task he has just undertaken: he is all dispatch and resolution, as far as words and present intentions are concerned, but all hesitation and irresolution, when called upon to carry his words and intentions into effect; so that, resolving to do everything, he does nothing. He is full of purpose, but void of that quality of mind which accomplishes purpose.

Anything finer than this conception, and working out of a great character, is merely impossible. Shakespeare wished to impress upon us the truth, that action is the chief end of existence—that no faculties of intellect, however brilliant, can be considered valuable, or indeed otherwise than as misfortunes, if they withdraw us from, or render us repugnant to action, and lead us to think and think of doing, until the time has elapsed when we can do anything effectually. In enforcing this moral truth, Shakespeare has shown the fulness and force of his powers: all that is amiable and excellent in nature is combined in Hamlet, with the exception of one quality. He is a man living in meditation, called upon to act by every motive human and divine, but the great object of his life is defeated by continually resolving to do, yet doing nothing but resolve.

LECTURE III, 1813–14 SERIES (AS REPORTED IN THE *Bristol Gazette*)

[*Hamlet*]

The seeming inconsistencies in the conduct and character of Hamlet have long exercised the conjectural ingenuity of critics; and as we are always loth to suppose that the cause of defective apprehension is in ourselves, the mystery has been too commonly explained by the very easy process of supposing that it is, in fact, inexplicable, and by resolving the difficulty into the capricious and irregular genius of Shakespeare.

Mr. Coleridge, in his *third* lecture, has effectually exposed the shallow and stupid arrogance of this vulgar and indolent decision. He has shown that the intricacies of Hamlet's character may be traced to Shakespeare's deep and accurate science in mental philosophy. That this character must have some common connection with the laws of our nature, was assumed by the lecturer from the fact that Hamlet was the darling of every country where literature was fostered. He thought it essential to the understanding of Hamlet's character that we should reflect on the constitution of our own minds. Man was distinguished from the animal in proportion as thought prevailed over sense; but in healthy processes of the mind, a balance was maintained between the impressions of outward objects and the inward operations of the intellect: if there be an overbalance in the contemplative faculty, man becomes the creature of meditation, and loses the power of action. Shakespeare seems to have conceived a mind in the highest degree of excitement, with this overpowering activity of intellect, and to have placed him in circumstances where he was obliged to act on the spur of the moment. Hamlet, though brave and careless of death, had contracted a morbid sensibility from this overbalance in the mind, producing the lingering and vacillating delays of procrastination, and wasting in the energy of resolving the energy of acting. Thus the play of *Hamlet* offers a direct contrast to that of *Macbeth*: the one proceeds with the utmost slowness, the other with breathless and crowded rapidity.

The effect of this overbalance of imagination is beautifully illustrated in the inward brooding of Hamlet—the effect of a superfluous activity of thought. His mind, unseated from its healthy balance, is for ever occupied with the world within him, and abstracted from external things; his words give a substance to shadows, and he is dissatisfied with commonplace realities. It is the nature of thought to be indefinite, while definiteness belongs to reality. The sense of sublimity arises, not from the sight of an outward object, but from the reflection upon it; not from the impression, but from the idea. Few have seen a celebrated waterfall without feeling something of disappointment: it is only subsequently, by reflection, that the idea of the waterfall comes full into the mind, and brings with it a train of sublime associations. Hamlet felt this: in him we see a mind that keeps itself in a state of abstraction, and beholds external objects as hieroglyphics. His soliloquy, "Oh that this too, too solid flesh would melt," arises from a craving after the indefinite: a disposition or temper which most easily besets men of genius; a morbid craving for that which is not. The self-delusion common to this temper of mind was finely exemplified in the character which Hamlet gives of himself: "It cannot be, but I am pigeon-liver'd, and lack gall, to make oppression bitter." He mistakes the seeing his chains for the breaking of them; and delays action, till action is of no use; and he becomes the victim of circumstances and accident.

The lecturer, in descending to particulars, took occasion to defend from the common charge of improbable eccentricity, the scene which follows Hamlet's interview with the Ghost. He showed that after the mind has been stretched beyond its usual pitch and tone, it must either sink into exhaustion and inanity, or seek relief by change. Persons conversant with deeds of cruelty contrive to escape from their conscience by connecting something of the ludicrous with them, and by inventing grotesque terms, and a certain technical phraseology, to disguise the horror of their practices.

The terrible, however paradoxical it may appear, will be found to touch on the verge of the ludicrous. Both arise from the perception of something out of the common nature of things,—something out of place: if from this we can abstract danger, the uncommonness alone remains, and the sense of the ridiculous is excited. The close alliance of these opposites appears from the circumstance that laughter is equally the expression of extreme anguish and horror as of joy: in the same manner that there are tears of joy as well as tears of sorrow, so there is a laugh of terror as well as a laugh of merriment. These complex causes will naturally have produced in Hamlet the disposition to escape from his own feelings of the overwhelming and supernatural by a wild transition to the ludicrous,—a sort of cunning bravado, bordering on the flights of delirium.

Mr. Coleridge instances, as a proof of Shakespeare's minute knowledge of human nature, the unimportant conversation which takes place during the expectation of the Ghost's appearance: and he recalled to our notice what all must have observed in common life, that on the brink of some serious enterprise, or event of moment, men naturally elude the pressure of their own thoughts by turning aside to trivial objects and familiar circumstances. So in *Hamlet,* the dialogue on the platform begins with remarks on the coldness of the air, and inquiries, obliquely connected indeed with the expected hour of the visitation, but thrown out in a seeming vacuity of topics, as to the striking of the clock. The same desire to escape from the inward thoughts is admirably carried on in Hamlet's moralizing on the Danish custom of wassailing; and a double purpose is here answered, which demonstrates the exquisite judgment of Shakespeare. By thus entangling the attention of the audience in the nice distinctions and parenthetical sentences of Hamlet, he takes them completely by surprize on the appearance of the Ghost, which comes upon them in all the suddenness of its visionary character. No modern writer would have dared, like Shakespeare, to have preceded this last visitation by two distinct appearances, or could have contrived that the third should rise upon the two former in impressiveness and solemnity of interest.

Mr. Coleridge at the commencement of this lecture drew a comparison between the characters of Macbeth and Bonaparte— both tyrants, both indifferent to means, however barbarous, to attain their ends; and he hoped the fate of the latter would be like the former, in failing amidst a host of foes, which his cruelty and injustice had roused against him. At the conclusion of his lecture, he alluded to the successes of the Allies, and complimented his country on the lead she had taken, and the example she had set to other nations, in resisting an attack upon the middle classes of society; for if the French Emperor had succeeded in his attempts to gain universal dominion, there would have been but two classes suffered to exist—the high and the low. England, justly proud, as she had a right to be, of a Shakespeare, a Milton, a Bacon, and a Newton, could also boast of a Nelson and a Wellington.

LECTURE VI (1818)

[*Hamlet*] *

1. The significancy of the names of Shakespeare's plays, the "Twelfth Night," "Midsummer Night's Dream," "As You Like It," "Winter's Tale," when the total effect is produced by a co-ordination of the characters, by a wreath of flowers: but "Coriolanus," "Lear," "Romeo and Juliet," "Hamlet," "Othello, Moor of Venice," when the effect arises from the subordination of all to one, either as the prominent person or the principal object. "Cymbeline" is the only exception and even that has its advantages and prepares the audience for the chaos of time, place, and costume by throwing the date back into a [legendary] king's . . . [?] reign.

2. But as of more importance, so more striking is the judgement displayed by our truly *dramatic* poet as well as *poet* of the drama in the management of his first scenes. With the single exception of *Cymbeline* they either place before us in one glance both the past and the future in some effect which implies the continuance and full agency of its cause, as in the feuds and party spirit of the servants of the two houses in the first scene of *Romeo and Juliet,* or in the degrading passion for shews and public spectacles, and the overwhelming attachment for the newest successful war-chief in the Roman people, already become a populace, contrasted with the jealousy of the nobles, in *Julius Caesar;* or they at once commence the action so as to excite a curiosity for the explanation in the following [scenes], as in the storm of the wind, the waves, and the boatswain in the *Tempest,* instead of anticipating our curiosity, as in most other first scenes and in too many other first *acts;* or they act, by contrast of diction suited to the characters, at once to heighten the effect and yet to give a naturalness to the language and rhythm of the principal characters, either as that of

---

* See also the selections from *Table-Talk.*

Prospero and Miranda, in the last instance, by the appropriate lowness of the style, or as in *King John* by the equally appropriate stateliness of state harangue or official narration, so that the after blank verse seems to belong to the rank and quality of the speakers and not to the poet; or they strike at once the key-note, give the predominant spirit of the play, as in the *Twelfth Night* and in *Macbeth;* or the first scene comprizes all these advantages at once, as in *Hamlet.*

In all the best attested stories of ghosts and visions, as in that of Brutus, of Archbishop Cranmer, that of Benvenuto Cellini recorded by himself, and the vision of Galileo communicated by him to his favorite pupil Torricelli, the ghost-seers were in a state of cold or chilling damp from without, and of anxiety inwardly. It has been with all of them as with Francisco on his guard—alone, in the depth and silence of the night—" 'twas bitter cold and they were sick at heart"—and "not a mouse stirring." The attention to minute sounds,—naturally associated with the recollection of minute objects, and the more familiar and trifling, the more impressive from the unusualness of their producing any impression at all —gives a philosophic pertinency to this last image, but it has likewise its dramatic use and purpose, for its commonness in ordinary conversation tends to produce the sense of *reality,* and at once hides the poet and yet approximates the reader or spectator to that state in which the highest poetry will appear, and in its component parts, tho' not in whole composition, really is the language of nature. If I should not speak it, I feel that I should be thinking it; the voice only is the poet's, the words are my own. That Shakespeare meant to put an *effect* in the actor's power in the very first words, *"Who's there?"* is evident from the impatience expressed in the words that follow. "Nay, answer me: stand and unfold yourself." A brave man is never so peremptory, as when he fears that he is afraid.

The gradual transition from the silence and the recent habit of listening in Francisco's "I think I hear them," and the more cheerful call out, which a good actor would observe, in the "Stand ho! Who is there?" Bernardo's enquiry after Horatio, and the repetition of his name, and in his own presence, [indicate] *respect* or

eagerness . . . [?] that implies him as one of the persons who are
to appear in the foreground; and the scepticism attributed to him—

> Horatio says, 'tis but our phantasy;
> And will not let belief take hold of him—

preparing us for Hamlet's after eulogy on him as one whose blood
and judgement were happily commingled. The indefiniteness of
the first opening out of the occasion of this anxiety: "Welcome,
Horatio!" (gladness); "welcome, good Marcellus" (courtesy).

> M. What has *this thing* [appear'd again to-night?]

rising with the next speech into

> Touching this dreaded sight twice seen of us.

Horatio's confirmation of his disbelief—

> [Tush, tush, 'twill not appear]—

and the silence with which the scene opened again restored by the
narration. The solemnity of it and the exquisite proof of the narrator's deep feeling of what he is himself about to relate, [shown]
by his turning off from it, as from a something that is forcing him
too deep into himself, to the outward objects, the realities of nature
that had accompanied it—

> [Ber.] Last night of all,
> [When yond same star that's westward from the pole
> Had made his course to illume that part of heaven
> Where now it burns, Marcellus and myself,
> The bell then beating one,—]

seem to contradict the critical law that what is told makes a faint
impression compared with what is beheld, and do indeed convey
to the mind more than the eye can see; and [note] the interruption of the narration at the very moment when we are most intensely listening for the sequel, and have our thoughts diverted
from the dreaded sight in expectation of the desired, yet almost
dreaded, tale, thus giving all the suddenness and surprize of the
original appearance—

> Peace, break thee off! look where it comes again!

The judgement in having two of the persons present as having seen it twice before, hence naturally confirming their former opinions, while the sceptic is silent, and after [he has] twice been addressed by his friends, answers with two hasty syllables, "Most like," and confession of horror—

[it harrows me with fear and wonder.]

## NOTES ON *Lear*

Of all Shakespeare's plays Macbeth is the most rapid, Hamlet the slowest, in movement. Lear combines length with rapidity,—like the hurricane and the whirlpool, absorbing while it advances. It begins as a stormy day in summer, with brightness; but that brightness is lurid, and anticipates the tempest.

[I. i. 1–6.
*Kent.* I thought the king had more affected the Duke of Albany than Cornwall.
*Glou.* It did always seem so to us: but now, in the division of the kingdom, it appears not which of the dukes he values most; for equalities are so weighed that curiosity in neither can make choice of either's moiety.]

It was [not] without forethought, and it is not without its due significance, that the triple division is stated here as already determined and in all its particulars, previously to the trial of professions, as the relative rewards of which the daughters were to be made to consider their several portions. The strange, yet by no means unnatural, mixture of selfishness, sensibility, and habit of feeling derived from and fostered by the particular rank and usages of the individual; the intense desire to be intensely beloved, selfish, and yet characteristic of the selfishness of a loving and kindly nature—a feeble selfishness, self-supportless and leaning for all pleasure on another's breast; the selfish craving after a sympathy with a prodigal disinterestedness, contradicted by its own ostentation and the mode and nature of its claims; the anxiety, the distrust, the jealousy, which more or less accompany all selfish affections, and are among the surest contradistinctions of mere fondness from love, and which originate Lear's eager wish to enjoy his daughter's violent professions, while the inveterate habits of sovereignty convert the wish into claim and positive right, and the incompliance with it into crime and treason;—these facts, these passions, these moral verities, on which the whole tragedy is founded, are all prepared for, and will to the retrospect be found implied in, these first four or five lines of the play. They let us know that the trial is but a trick; and that the grossness of the old king's rage is in part the natural result of a silly trick suddenly and most unexpectedly baffled and disappointed. This having been provided in the fewest words, in a natural reply to as natural [a] question, which yet answers a secondary purpose of attracting our attention to the difference or diversity between the characters of Cornwall and Albany; the premises and data, as it were, having been thus afforded for our after-insight into the mind and mood of the person whose character, passions, and sufferings are the main *subject-matter* of the play;—from Lear, the *persona patiens* of his drama, Shakespeare passes without delay to the second in importance, to the main *agent* and prime mover—introduces Edmund to our acquaintance, and with the same felicity of judgement, in the same easy, natural way, prepares us for his character in the seemingly casual communication of its origin and occasion. From the first drawing up of the curtain he has stood before us in the united strength and beauty of earliest manhood. Our eyes have been questioning him. Gifted thus with high advantages of *person*, and further endowed by nature with a powerful intellect and a strong energetic will, even without any concurrence of circumstances and accident, pride will be the sin that most easily besets him. But he is the known and acknowledged son of the princely Gloster. Edmund, therefore, has both the germ of pride and the conditions best fitted to evolve and ripen it into a predominant feeling. Yet hitherto no reason appears why it should be other than the not unusual pride of person, talent, and birth, a pride auxiliary if not akin to many virtues, and the natural ally of honorable [impulses?]. But alas! in his own presence his own father takes shame to himself for the frank avowal that he is his father—has "blushed so often to acknowledge him that he is now braz'd to it." He hears his mother and the circumstances of his birth spoken of with a most degrading and licentious levity—described as a wanton by her own paramour, and the remembrance of the animal sting, the low criminal gratifications connected with her wantonness and prostituted beauty assigned as the reason why "the whoreson must be acknowledged." This, and the consciousness of its notoriety—the gnawing conviction that every shew of respect is an effort of courtesy which ·recalls while it represses a contrary feeling—this is the evertrickling flow of wormwood and gall into the wounds of pride, the corrosive virus which inoculates pride with a venom not its own, with envy, hatred, a lust of that power which in its blaze of radiance would hide the dark spots on his disk, [with] pangs of shame personally undeserved and therefore felt as wrongs, and a blind ferment of vindictive workings towards the occasions and causes, especially towards a brother whose stainless birth and lawful honors were the constant remembrancers of *his* debasement, and were ever in the way to prevent all chance of its being unknown or overlooked and forgotten. Add to this that with excellent judgement, and provident for the claims of the moral sense, for that which relatively to the drama is called poetic justice; and as the fittest means for reconciling the feelings of the spectators to the horrors of Gloster's after sufferings,—at least, of rendering them somewhat less unendurable (for I will not disguise my conviction that in this one point the tragic has been urged beyond the outermost mark and *ne plus ultra* of the dramatic)—Shakespeare has precluded all excuse and palliation of the guilt incurred by both the parents of the base-born Edmund by Gloster's confession that he was at the time a married man and already blest with a lawful heir of his fortunes. The mournful alienation of brotherly love occasioned by primogeniture in noble families, or rather by the unnecessary distinctions engrafted thereon, and this in children of the same stock, is still almost proverbial on the continent—especially, as I know from my own observation, in the south of Europe—and appears to have been scarcely less common in our own island before the Revolution of 1688, if we may judge from the characters and sentiments so frequent in our elder comedies—the younger brother, for instance, in Beaumont and Fletcher's *Scornful Lady,* on one side and the

Oliver in Shakespeare's own *As You Like It,* on the other. Need it be said how heavy an aggravation the stain of bastardy must have been, were it only that the younger brother was liable to hear his own dishonor and his mother's infamy related by his father with an excusing shrug of the shoulders, and in a tone betwixt waggery and shame.

By the circumstances here enumerated as so many predisposing causes, Edmund's character might well be deem'd already sufficiently explained and prepared for. But in this tragedy the story or fable constrained Shakespeare to introduce wickedness in an outrageous form, in Regan and Goneril. He had read nature too heedfully not to know that courage, intellect, and strength of character were the most impressive forms of power, and that to power in itself, without reference to any moral end, an inevitable admiration and complacency appertains, whether it be displayed in the conquests of a Napoleon or Tamerlane, or in the foam and thunder of a cataract. But in the display of such a character it was of the highest importance to prevent the guilt from passing into utter *monstrosity*—which again depends on the presence or absence of causes and temptations sufficient to *account* for the wickedness, without the necessity of recurring to a thorough fiendishness of nature for its origination. For such are the appointed relations of intellectual power to truth, and of truth to goodness, that it becomes both morally and poetic[ally] unsafe to present what is admirable—what our nature compels us to admire—in the mind, and what is most detestable in the heart, as co-existing in the same individual without any apparent connection, or any modification of the one by the other. That Shakespeare has in one instance, that of Iago, approached to this, and that he has done it successfully, is perhaps the most astonishing proof of his genius, and the opulence of its resources. But in the present tragedy, in which he [was] compelled to present a Goneril and Regan, it was most carefully to be avoided; and, therefore, the one only conceivable addition to the inauspicious influences on the preformation of Edmund's character is given in the information that all the kindly counteractions to the mischievous feelings of shame that might have been derived from co-domestication with Edgar and their common father, had been cut off by an absence from home and a foreign education from boyhood to the present time, and the prospect of its continuance, as if to preclude all risk of his interference with the father's views for the elder and legitimate son:

> He hath been out nine years, and away he shall again.

It is well worthy notice, that *Lear* is the only serious performance of Shakespeare the interest and situations of which are derived from the assumption of a gross improbability; whereas Beaumont and Fletcher's tragedies are, almost all, founded on some out-of-the-way accident or exception to the general experience of mankind. But observe the matchless judgement of Shakespeare! First, improbable as the conduct of Lear is, in the first scene, yet it was an old story, rooted in the popular faith—a thing taken for granted already, and consequently without any of the *effects* of improbability. Secondly, it is merely the canvas to the characters and passions, a mere *occasion*—not (as in Beaumont and Fletcher) perpetually recurring, as the cause and *sine qua non* of the incidents and emotions. Let the first scene of *Lear* have been lost, and let it be only understood that a fond father had been duped by hypocritical professions of love and duty on the part of two daughters to disinherit a third, previously, and deservedly, more dear to him, and all the rest of the tragedy would retain its interest undiminished, and be perfectly intelligible. The *accidental* is nowhere the groundwork of the passions, but the καθόλον, that which in all ages has been and ever will be close and native to the heart of man—parental anguish from filial ingratitude, the genuineness of worth, tho' coffered in bluntness, the vileness of smooth iniquity. Perhaps I ought to have added the *Merchant of Venice;* but here too the same remarks apply. It was an old tale; and substitute any other danger than that of the pound of flesh (the circumstance in which the improbability lies), yet all the situations and the emotions appertaining to them remain equally excellent and appropriate. Whereas take away from *The Mad Lover* the fantastic hypothesis of his engagement to cut out his own heart and have it presented to his mistress, and all the main scenes must go with it. . . .

[A LETTER ON SIR THOMAS BROWNE]

March 10th, 1804,
Sat. night, 12 o'clock.

MY DEAR———,

Sir Thomas Brown is among my first favorites, rich in various knowledge, exuberant in conceptions and conceits, contemplative, imaginative; often truly great and magnificent in his style and diction, though doubtless too often big, stiff, and hyperlatinistic: thus I might without admixture of falsehood, describe Sir T. Brown, and my description would have only this fault, that it would be equally, or almost equally, applicable to half a dozen other writers, from the beginning of the reign of Elizabeth to the end of Charles II. He is indeed all this; and what he has more than all this peculiar to himself, I seem to convey to my own mind in some measure by saying,—that he is a quiet and sublime enthusiast with a strong tinge of the fantast,—the humourist constantly mingling with, and flashing across, the philosopher, as the darting colours in shot silk play upon the main dye. In short, he has brains in his head which is all the more interesting for a little twist in the brains. He sometimes reminds the reader of Montaigne, but from no other than the general circumstances of an egotism common to both; which in Montaigne is too often a mere amusing gossip, a chit-chat story of whims and peculiarities that lead to nothing,—but which in Sir Thomas Brown is always the result of a feeling heart conjoined with a mind of active curiosity,—the natural and becoming egotism of a man, who, loving other men as himself, gains the habit, and the privilege of talking about himself as familiarly as about other men. Fond of the curious, and a hunter of oddities and strangenesses, while he conceived himself, with quaint and humourous gravity a useful inquirer into physical truth and fundamental science,—he loved to contemplate and discuss his own thoughts and feelings, because he found by comparison with other men's, that they too were curiosities, and so with a perfectly graceful and interesting ease he put them too into his museum and cabinet of varieties. In very truth he was not mistaken:—so completely does he see every thing in a light of his own, reading nature neither by sun, moon, nor candle light, but by the light of the faery glory around his own head; so that you might say that nature had granted to him in perpetuity a patent and monopoly for all his thoughts. Read his *Hydriotaphia* above all:—and in addition to the peculiarity, the exclusive Sir Thomas Brown-ness of all the fancies and modes of illustration, wonder at and admire his entireness in every subject, which is before him— he is *totus in illo;* he follows it; he never wanders from it,—and he has no occasion to wander;—for whatever happens to be his subject, he metamorphoses all nature into it. In that *Hydriotaphia* or Treatise on some Urns dug up in Norfolk—how earthy, how redolent of graves and sepulchres is every line! You have now dark mould, now a thigh-bone, now a scull, then a bit of mouldered coffin! a fragment of an old tombstone with moss in its *hic jacet;*— a ghost or a winding-sheet—or the echo of a funeral psalm wafted on a November wind! and the gayest thing you shall meet with shall be a silver nail or gilt *Anno Domini* from a perished coffin top. The very same remark applies in the same force to the interesting, though the far less interesting, Treatise on the Quincuncial Plantations of the Ancients. There is the same attention to oddities, to the remoteness and *minutiae* of vegetable terms,—the same entireness of subject. You have quincunxes in heaven above, quincunxes in earth below, and quincunxes in the water beneath the earth; quincunxes in deity, quincunxes in the mind of man, quincunxes in bones, in the optic nerves, in roots of trees, in leaves, in petals, in every thing. In short, first turn to the last leaf of this volume, and read out aloud to yourself the last seven paragraphs of Chap. v. beginning with the words "More considerables," &c. But it is time for me to be in bed, in the words of Sir Thomas, which will serve you, my dear, as a fair specimen of his manner. —"But the quincunx of heaven—(the Hyades or five stars about the horizon at midnight at that time)—runs low, and 'tis time we close the five ports of knowledge: we are unwilling to spin out our waking thoughts into the phantasmes of sleep, which often continueth praecogitations,—making cables of cobwebbes, and wildernesses of handsome groves. . . . To keep our eyes open longer were but to act our Antipodes. The huntsmen are up in America, and they are already past their first sleep in Persia." Think you, my dear Friend, that there ever was such a reason given before for going to bed at midnight;—to wit, that if we did not, we should be acting the part of our Antipodes! And then "the huntsmen are up in America."—What life, what fancy!—Does the whimsical knight give us thus a dish of strong green tea, and call it an opiate! I trust that you are quietly asleep—

> And that all the stars hang bright above your dwelling,
> Silent as tho' they watched the sleeping earth!

S. T. COLERIDGE

### SELDEN'S TABLE TALK

There is more weighty bullion sense in this book, than I ever found in the same number of pages of any uninspired writer.

### [Opinion]

Opinion and affection extremely differ. I may affect a woman best, but it does not follow I must think her the handsomest woman in the world. * * * Opinion is something wherein I go about to give reason why all the world should think as I think. Affection is a thing wherein I look after the pleasing of myself.

Good! This is the true difference betwixt the beautiful and the agreeable, which Knight and the rest of that πλῆθος ἄθεον have so beneficially confounded, *meretricibus scilicet et Plutoni.*

O what an insight the whole of this article gives into a wise man's heart, who has been compelled to act with the many, as one of the many! It explains Sir Thomas More's zealous Romanism, &c.

### [Parliament]

Excellent! O! to have been with Selden over his glass of wine, making every accident an outlet and a vehicle of wisdom!

### [Poetry]

The old poets had no other reason but this, their verse was sung to music; otherwise it had been a senseless thing to have fettered up themselves.

No one man can know all things: even Selden here talks igno-rantly. Verse is in itself a music, and the natural symbol of that union of passion with thought and pleasure, which constitutes the essence of all poetry, as contradistinguished from science, and dis-tinguished from history civil or natural. To Pope's Essay on Man, —in short, to whatever is mere metrical good sense and wit, the remark applies.

Ib.

Verse proves nothing but the quantity of syllables; they are not meant for logic.

True; they, that is, verses, are not logic; but they are, or ought to be, the envoys and representatives of that vital passion, which is the practical cement of logic; and without which logic must remain inert.

## FIELDING (1832)

### [*Notes on "Tom Jones"*]

Manners change from generation to generation, and with man-ners morals appear to change,—actually change with some, but appear to change with all but the abandoned. A young man of the present day who should act as Tom Jones is supposed to act at Upton, with Lady Bellaston, &c., would not be a Tom Jones; and a Tom Jones of the present day, without perhaps being in the ground a better man, would have perished rather than submit to be kept by a harridan of fortune. Therefore this novel is, and, in-deed, pretends to be, no exemplar of conduct. But, notwithstand-ing all this, I do loathe the cant which can recommend Pamela and Clarissa Harlowe as strictly moral, though they poison the imagination of the young with continued doses of *tinct. lyttæ*, while Tom Jones is prohibited as loose. I do not speak of young women;—but a young man whose heart or feelings can be injured, or even his passions excited, by aught in this novel, is already thoroughly corrupt. There is a cheerful, sun-shiny, breezy spirit that prevails everywhere, strongly contrasted with the close, hot, day-dreamy continuity of Richardson. Every indiscretion, every immoral act, of Tom Jones, (and it must be remembered that he is in every one taken by surprise—his inward principles remaining firm—) is so instantly punished by embarrassment and unanticipated evil consequences of his folly, that the reader's mind is not left for a moment to dwell or run riot on the criminal indulgence itself. In short, let the requisite allowance be made for the increased refinement of our manners,—and then I dare believe that no young man who consulted his heart and conscience only, without adverting to what the world would say—could rise from the perusal of Fielding's Tom Jones, Joseph Andrews, or Amelia, without feeling himself a better man;—at least, without an intense conviction that he could not be guilty of a base act.

If I want a servant or mechanic, I wish to know what he does: —but of a friend, I must know what he is. And in no writer is this momentous distinction so finely brought forward as by Fielding. We do not care what Blifil does;—the deed, as separate from the agent, may be good or ill;—but Blifil is a villain;—and we feel him to be so from the very moment he, the boy Blifil, restores Sophia's poor captive bird to its native and rightful liberty.

Book xiv. ch. 8.

> Notwithstanding the sentiment of the Roman satirist, which denies the divinity of fortune; and the opinion of Seneca to the same purpose; Cicero, who was, I believe, a wiser man than either of them, expressly holds the contrary; and certain it is there are some incidents in life so very strange and unaccountable, that it seems to require more than human skill and foresight in producing them.

Surely Juvenal, Seneca, and Cicero, all meant the same thing, namely, that there was no chance, but instead of it providence, either human or divine.

Book xv. ch. 9.—The Rupture with Lady Bellaston.

Even in the most questionable part of Tom Jones, I cannot but think, after frequent reflection, that an additional paragraph, more fully and forcibly unfolding Tom Jones's sense of self-degradation on the discovery of the true character of the relation in which he had stood to Lady Bellaston, and his awakened feeling of the dignity of manly chastity, would have removed in great measure any just objections,—at all events relatively to Fielding himself, and with regard to the state of manners in his time.

Book xvi. ch. 5.

That refined degree of Platonic affection which is absolutely detached from the flesh, and is indeed entirely and purely spiritual, is a gift confined to the female part of the creation; many of whom I have heard declare (and doubtless with great truth) that they would, with the utmost readiness, resign a lover to a rival, when such resignation was proved to be necessary for the temporal interest of such lover.

I firmly believe that there are men capable of such a sacrifice, and this, without pretending to, or even admiring or seeing any virtue in, this absolute detachment from the flesh.

### [*Notes on "Jonathan Wild"*]

Jonathan Wild is assuredly the best of all the fictions in which a villain is throughout the prominent character. But how impossible it is by any force of genius to create a sustained attractive interest for such a groundwork, and how the mind wearies of, and shrinks from, the more than painful interest, the μισητόν, of utter depravity,—Fielding himself felt and endeavoured to mitigate and remedy by the (on all other principles) far too large a proportion, and too quick recurrence, of the interposed chapters of moral reflection, like the chorus in the Greek tragedy,—admirable specimens as these chapters are of profound irony and philosophic satire. Chap. VI. Book 2, on Hats,—brief as it is, exceeds any thing even in Swift's Lilliput, or Tale of the Tub. How forcibly it applies to the Whigs, Tories, and Radicals of our own times.

Whether the transposition of Fielding's scorching wit (as B.III. c. xiv.) to the mouth of his hero be objectionable on the ground of *incredulus odi*, or is to be admired as answering the author's purpose by unrealizing the story, in order to give a deeper reality to the truths intended,—I must leave doubtful, yet myself inclining to the latter judgment. 27th Feb., 1832.

∾∾∾

## [The Ascending Scale of Creation]

Every rank of creatures, as it ascends in the scale of creation, leaves death behind it or under it. The metal at its height of being seems a mute prophecy of the coming vegetation, into a mimic semblance of which it crystallises. The blossom and flower, the acme of vegetable life, divides into correspondent organs with reciprocal functions, and by instinctive motions and approximations seems impatient of that fixure, by which it is differenced in kind from the flower-shaped Psyche, that flutters with free wing above it. And wonderfully in the insect realm doth the irritability, the proper seat of instinct, while yet the nascent sensibility is subordinated thereto—most wonderfully, I say, doth the muscular life in the insect, and the musculo-arterial in the bird, imitate and typically rehearse the adaptive understanding, yea, and the moral affections and charities, of man. Let us carry ourselves back, in spirit, to the mysterious week, the teeming work-days of the Creator; as they rose in vision before the eye of the inspired historian of *the generations of the heavens and of the earth, in the day that the Lord God made the earth and the heavens.* And who that hath watched their ways with an understanding heart, could, as the vision evolving still advanced towards him, contemplate the filial and loyal Bee; the home-building, wedded, and divorceless Swallow; and above all the manifoldly intelligent Ant tribes, with their commonwealths and confederacies, their warriors and miners, the husbandfolk, that fold in their tiny flocks on the honeyed-leaf, and the virgin sisters with the holy instincts of maternal love, detached and in selfless purity—and not say to himself, Behold the shadow of approaching humanity, the sun rising from behind, in the kindling morn of creation! Thus all lower natures find their highest good in semblances and seekings of that which is higher and better. All things strive to ascend, and ascend in their striving.

And shall man alone stoop? Shall his pursuits and desires, the reflections of his inward life, be like the reflected image of a tree on the edge of a pool, that grows downward, and seeks a mock heaven in the unstable element beneath it, in neighbourhood with the slim water weeds and oozy bottom-grass that are yet better than itself and more noble, in as far as substances that appear as shadows are preferable to shadows mistaken for substance! No! it must be a higher good to make you happy. While you labour for any thing below your proper humanity, you seek a happy life in the region of death. Well saith the moral poet—

Unless above himself he can
Erect himself, how mean a thing is man!

FROM ESSAYS ON HIS OWN TIMES

❧❧❧

*Conciones ad Populum,* OR *Addresses to the People*

[Introductory Address]

'Αεὶ γὰρ τῆς ἐλευθερίας ἐφίεμαι· πόλλα δὲ ἐν καὶ τοῖς
φιλελευθέροις μισητὰ, ἀντελεύθερα.*

When the wind is fair and the planks of the vessel sound, we may safely trust every thing to the management of professional mariners: in a tempest and on board a crazy bark, all must contribute their quota of exertion. The stripling is not exempted from it by his youth, nor the passenger by his inexperience. Even so, in the present agitations of the public mind, every one ought to consider his intellectual faculties as in a state of immediate requisition. All may benefit society in some degree. The exigences of the times do not permit us to stay for the maturest years, lest the opportunity be lost, while we are waiting for an increase of power.

Companies resembling the present will, from a variety of circumstances, consist *chiefly* of the zealous advocates for freedom. It will therefore be our endeavour, not so much to excite the torpid, as to regulate the feelings of the ardent; and above all, to evince the necessity of *bottoming* on fixed principles, that so we may not be the unstable patriots of passion or accident, nor hurried away by names of which we have not sifted the meaning, and by tenets of which we have not examined the consequences. The times are trying; and in order to be prepared against their difficulties, we should have acquired a prompt facility of adverting in all our doubts to some grand and comprehensive truth. In a deep and strong soil must that tree fix its roots, the height of which, is to "reach to heaven, and the sight of it to the ends of all the earth."

The example of France is indeed a "warning to Britain." A nation wading to their rights through blood, and marking the track of freedom by devastation! Yet let us not embattle our feelings

---

* For I am always a lover of liberty; but in those who would appropriate the title, I find too many points destructive of liberty and hateful to her genuine advocates. (C.)

against our reason. Let us not indulge our malignant passions under the mask of humanity. Instead of railing with infuriate declamation against these excesses, we shall be more profitably employed in developing the sources of them. French freedom is the beacon, which while it guides to equality, should shew us the dangers that throng the road.

The annals of the French revolution have recorded in letters of blood, that the knowledge of the few cannot counteract the ignorance of the many; that the light of philosophy, when it is confined to a small minority, points out the possessors as the victims, rather than the illuminators, of the multitude. The patriots of France either hastened into the dangerous and gigantic error of making certain evil the means of contingent good, or were sacrificed by the mob, with whose prejudices and ferocity their unbending virtue forbade them to assimilate. Like Samson, the people were strong—like Samson, the people were blind. Those two massive pillars of Oppression's temple, monarchy and aristocracy,

> With horrible convulsion to and fro
> They tugg'd, they shook—till down they came and drew
> The whole roof after them with burst of thunder
> Upon the heads of all who sat beneath,
> Lords, ladies, captains, counsellors, and priests,
> Their choice nobility!
>
> —MILTON. *Sam. Agon.*

There was not a tyrant in Europe, who did not tremble on his throne. Freedom herself heard the crash aghast!—

The Girondists, who were the first republicans in power, were men of enlarged views and great literary attainments; but they seem to have been deficient in that vigour and daring activity, which circumstances made necessary. Men of genius are rarely either prompt in action or consistent in general conduct: their early habits have been those of contemplative indolence; and the day-dreams, with which they have been accustomed to amuse their solitude, adapt them for splendid speculation, not temperate and practicable counsels. Brissot, the leader of the Gironde party, is entitled to the character of a virtuous man, and an eloquent speaker; but he was rather a sublime visionary, than a quick-eyed politician; and his excellence equally with his faults rendered him unfit for the helm, in the stormy hour of revolution. Robespierre, who displaced him, possessed a glowing ardour that still remembered the *end*, and a cool ferocity that never either overlooked, or scrupled, the *means*. What that *end* was, is not known: that it was a wicked one, has by no means been proved. I rather think, that the distant prospect, to which he was travelling, appeared to him grand and beautiful; but that he fixed his eye on it with such intense eagerness as to neglect the foulness of the road. If however his first intentions were pure, his subsequent enormities yield us a melancholy proof, that it is not the character of the possessor which directs the power, but the power which shapes and depraves the character of the possessor. In Robespierre, its influence was assisted by the properties of his disposition.—Enthusiasm, even in the gentlest temper, will frequently generate sensations of an unkindly order. If we clearly perceive any one thing to be of vast and infinite importance to ourselves and all mankind, our first feelings impel us to turn with angry contempt from those, who doubt and oppose it. The ardour of undisciplined benevolence seduces us into malignity: and whenever our hearts are warm, and our objects great and excellent, intolerance is the sin that does most easily beset us. But this enthusiasm in Robespierre was blended with gloom, and suspiciousness, and inordinate vanity. His dark imagination was still brooding over supposed plots against freedom —to prevent tyranny he became a tyrant—and having realized the evils which he suspected, a wild and dreadful tyrant.—Those loud-tongued adulators, the mob, overpowered the lone-whispered denunciations of conscience—he despotized in all the pomp of patriotism, and masqueraded on the bloody stage of revolution, a Caligula with the cap of liberty on his head.

It has been affirmed, and I believe with truth, that the system of terrorism by suspending the struggles of contrariant factions communicated an energy to the operations of the Republic, which had been hitherto unknown, and without which it could not have been preserved. The system depended for its existence on the general sense of its necessity, and when it had answered its end, it was soon destroyed by the same power that had given it birth—

popular opinion. It must not however be disguised, that at all times, but more especially when the public feelings are wavy and tumultuous, artful demagogues may create this opinion: and they, who are inclined to tolerate evil as the means of contingent good, should reflect, that if the excesses of terrorism gave to the republic that efficiency and *repulsive* force which its circumstances made necessary, they likewise afforded to the hostile Courts the most powerful support, and excited that indignation and horror, which every where precipitated the subject into the designs of the ruler. Nor let it be forgotten, that these excesses perpetuated the war in La Vendée and made it more terrible, both by the accession of numerous partizans, who had fled from the persecution of Robespierre, and by inspiring the Chouens with fresh fury, and an unsubmitting spirit of revenge and desperation.

Revolutions are sudden to the unthinking only. Political disturbances happen not without their warning harbingers. Strange rumblings and confused noises still precede these earthquakes and hurricanes of the moral world. The process of revolution in France has been dreadful, and should incite us to examine with an anxious eye the motives and manners of those, whose conduct and opinions seem calculated to forward a similar event in our own country. The oppositionists to "things as they are," are divided into many and different classes. To delineate them with an unflattering accuracy may be a delicate, but it is a necessary task, in order that we may enlighten, or at least beware of, the misguided men who have enlisted under the banners of liberty, from no principles or with bad ones: whether they be those, who

> admire they know not what,
> And know not whom, but as one leads the other:

or whether those,

> Whose end is private hate, not help to freedom,
> Adverse and turbulent when she would lead
> To virtue.

The majority of democrats appear to me to have attained that portion of knowledge in politics, which infidels possess in religion. I would by no means be supposed to imply, that the objections of both are equally unfounded, but that they both attribute to the system which they reject, all the evils existing under it; and that both, contemplating truth and justice "in the nakedness of abstraction," condemn constitutions and dispensations without having sufficiently examined the natures, circumstances, and capacities of their recipients.

The first class among the professed friends of liberty is composed of men, who unaccustomed to the labour of thorough investigation, and not particularly oppressed by the burthen of state, are yet impelled by their feelings to disapprove of its grosser depravities, and prepared to give an indolent vote in favour of reform. Their sensibilities unbraced by the cooperation of fixed principles, they offer no sacrifices to the divinity of active virtue. Their political opinions depend with weather-cock uncertainty on the winds of rumour, that blow from France. On the report of French victories they blaze into republicanism, at a tale of French excesses they darken into aristocrats; and seek for shelter among those despicable adherents to fraud and tyranny, who ironically style themselves constitutionalists.—These *dough-baked patriots* are not however useless. This oscillation of political opinion will retard the day of revolution, and it will operate as a preventive to its excesses. Indecisiveness of character, though the effect of timidity, is almost always associated with benevolence.

Wilder features characterize the second class. Sufficiently possessed of natural sense to despise the priest, and of natural feeling to hate the oppressor, they listen only to the inflammatory harangues of some mad-headed enthusiast, and imbibe from them poison, not food; rage, not liberty. Unillumined by philosophy, and stimulated to a lust of revenge by aggravated wrongs, they would make the altar of freedom stream with blood, while the grass grew in the desolated halls of justice. These men are the rude materials from which a detestable minister manufactures conspiracies. Among these men he sends a brood of sly political monsters, in the character of sanguinary demagogues, and, like Satan of old, "the tempter ere the accuser," ensnares a few into treason, that he may alarm the whole into slavery. He, who has dark purposes to serve, must use dark means—light would discover,

reason would expose him: he must endeavour to shut out both—
or if this prove impracticable, make them appear frightful by giving them frightful names: for farther than names the vulgar in-
quire not. Religion and reason are but poor substitutes for "church
and constitution;" and the sable-vested instigators of the Birmingham riots well knew, that a syllogism could not disarm a drunken
incendiary of his firebrand, or a demonstration *helmet* a philosopher's head against a brickbat. But in the principles, which this
apostate has, by his emissaries, sown among a few blind zealots for
freedom, he has digged a pit into which he himself may perhaps
be doomed to fall. We contemplate those principles with horror.
Yet they possess a kind of wild justice well calculated to spread
them among the grossly ignorant. To unenlightened minds, there
are terrible charms in the idea of retribution, however savagely it
be inculcated. The groans of the oppressors make fearful yet
pleasant music to the ear of him, whose mind is darkness, and into
whose soul the iron has entered.

This class, at present, is comparatively small—yet soon to form
an overwhelming majority, unless great and immediate efforts are
used to lessen the intolerable grievances of our poorer brethren,
and infuse into their sorely wounded hearts the healing qualities
of knowledge. For can we wonder that men should want humanity, who want all the circumstances of life that humanize? Can we
wonder that with the ignorance of brutes they should unite their
ferocity? Peace and comfort be with these! But let us shudder to
hear from men of dissimilar opportunities sentiments of similar
revengefulness. The purifying alchemy of education may transmute the fierceness of an ignorant man into virtuous energy—but
what remedy shall we apply to him, whom plenty has not softened, whom knowledge has not taught benevolence? This is one
among the many fatal effects which result from the want of fixed
principles. Convinced that vice is error, we shall entertain sentiments of pity for the vicious, not of indignation—and even with
respect to that bad man, to whom we have before alluded, although we are now groaning beneath the burthen of his miscon-
duct, we shall harbour no sentiments of revenge; but rather
*condole* with him that his chaotic iniquities have exhibited such a

complication of extravagance, inconsistency, and rashness as may *alarm* him with apprehensions of approaching lunacy!

There are a third class among the friends of freedom, who possess not the wavering character of the first description, nor the ferocity last delineated. They pursue the interests of freedom steadily, but with narrow and self-centering views: they anticipate with exultation the abolition of privileged orders, and of acts that persecute by exclusion from the right of citizenship. They are prepared to join in digging up the rubbish of mouldering establishments, and stripping off the tawdry pageantry of governments. Whatever is above them they are most willing to drag down; but every proposed alteration, that would elevate the ranks of our poorer brethren, they regard with suspicious jealousy, as the dreams of the visionary; as if there were any thing in the superiority of lord to gentleman, so mortifying in the barrier, so fatal to happiness in the consequences, as the more real distinction of master and servant, of rich man and of poor. Wherein am I made worse by my ennobled neighbour? Do the childish titles of aristocracy detract from my domestic comforts, or prevent my intellectual acquisitions? But those institutions of society which should condemn me to the necessity of twelve hours' daily toil, would make my *soul* a slave, and sink the *rational* being in the mere animal. It is a mockery of our fellow creatures' wrongs to call them equal in rights, when by the bitter compulsion of their wants we make them inferior to us in all that can soften the heart, or dignify the understanding. Let us not say that this is the work of time—that it is impracticable at present, unless we each in our individual capacities do strenuously and perseveringly endeavour to diffuse among our domestics those comforts and that illumination which far beyond all political ordinances are the true equalizers of men.

We turn with pleasure to the contemplation of that small but glorious band, whom we may truly distinguish by the name of thinking and disinterested patriots. These are the men who have encouraged the sympathetic passions till they have become irresistible habits, and made their duty a necessary part of their self-interest, by the long-continued cultivation of that moral taste which derives our most exquisite pleasures from the contemplation of possible perfection, and proportionate pain from the perception of existing depravation. Accustomed to regard all the affairs of man as a process, they never hurry and they never pause. Theirs is not that twilight of political knowledge which gives us just light enough to place one foot before the other; as they advance the scene still opens upon them, and they press right onward with a vast and various landscape of existence around them. Calmness and energy mark all their actions. Convinced that vice originates not in the man, but in the surrounding circumstances; not in the heart, but in the understanding; he is hopeless concerning no one —to correct a vice or generate a virtuous conduct he pollutes not his hands with the scourge of coercion; but by endeavouring to alter the circumstances would remove, or by strengthening the intellect, disarms, the temptation. The unhappy children of vice and folly, whose tempers are adverse to their own happiness as well as to the happiness of others, will at times awaken a natural pang; but he looks forward with gladdened heart to that glorious period when justice shall have established the universal fraternity of love. These soul-ennobling views bestow the virtues which they anticipate. He whose mind is habitually imprest with them soars above the present state of humanity, and may be justly said to dwell in the presence of the Most High.

> . . . . . . . . . . . . . . . . . . . . . would the forms
> Of servile custom cramp the Patriot's power?
> Would sordid policies, the barbarous growth
> Of ignorance and rapine, bow him down
> To tame pursuits, to indolence and fear?
> Lo! he appeals to nature, to the winds
> And rolling waves, the sun's unwearied course,
> The elements and seasons—all declare
> For what the eternal maker has ordain'd
> The powers of man: we feel within ourselves
> His energy divine: he tells the heart
> He meant, he made us to behold and love
> What he beholds and loves, the general orb
> Of life and being—to be great like him,
> Beneficent and active.
>
> —AKENSIDE.

Such is Joseph Gerald! Withering in the sickly and tainted gales of a prison, his healthful soul looks down from the citadel of his integrity on his impotent persecutors. I saw him in the foul and naked room of a jail—his cheek was sallow with confinement—his body was emaciated; yet his eye spoke the invincible purposes of his soul, and he still sounded with rapture the successes of freemen, forgetful of his own lingering martyrdom! Such too were the illustrious triumvirate whom as a Greek poet expresses it, it is not lawful for bad men even to praise. I will not say that I have abused your patience in thus indulging my feelings in strains of unheard gratitude to those who may seem to justify God in the creation of man. It is with pleasure that I am permitted to recite a yet unpublished tribute to their merit, the production of one who has sacrificed all the energies of his heart and head, a splendid offering on the altar of Liberty. . . .

Yes! there are those who have loved freedom with wise ardour, and propagated its principles with unshaken courage; For it was ordained at the foundation of the world, that there should always remain pure ones and uncorrupt, who should shine like lights in darkness, reconciling us to our own nature.

That general illumination should precede revolution, is a truth as obvious, as that the vessel should be cleansed before we fill it with a pure liquor. But the mode of diffusing it is not discoverable with equal facility. We certainly should never attempt to make proselytes by appeals to the selfish feelings—and consequently, should plead *for* the oppressed, not *to* them. The Author of an essay on political justice considers private societies as the sphere of real utility—that (each one illuminating those immediately beneath him,) truth by a gradual descent may at last reach the lowest order. But this is rather plausible than just or practicable. Society as at present constituted does not resemble a chain that ascends in a continuity of links.—There are three ranks possessing an intercourse with each other: these are well comprized in the superscription of a perfumer's advertisement, which I lately saw— "the Nobility, Gentry, and People of Dress." But alas! between the parlour and the kitchen, the tap and the coffee-room—there is a gulph that may not be passed. He would appear to me to have adopted the best as well as the most benevolent mode of diffusing truth, who uniting the zeal of the methodist with the views of the philosopher, should be *personally* among the poor, and teach them their *duties* in order that he may render them susceptible of their *rights*.

Yet by what means can the lower classes be made to learn their duties, and urged to practice them? The human race may perhaps possess the capability of all excellence; and truth, I doubt not, is omnipotent to a mind already disciplined for its reception; but assuredly the over-worked labourer, skulking into an ale-house, is not likely to exemplify the one, or prove the other. In that barbarous tumult of inimical interests, which the present state of society exhibits, *religion* appears to offer the only means universally *efficient*. The perfectness of future men is indeed a benevolent tenet, and may operate on a few visionaries, whose studious habits supply them with employment, and seclude them from temptation. But a distant prospect, which we are never to reach, will seldom quicken our footsteps, however lovely it may appear; and a blessing, which not ourselves but *posterity* are destined to enjoy, will scarcely influence the actions of *any*—still less of the ignorant, the prejudiced, and the selfish.

"Go, preach the GOSPEL to the poor." By its simplicity it will meet their comprehension, by its benevolence soften their affections, by its precepts, it will direct their conduct, by the vastness of its motives ensure their obedience. The situation of the poor is perilous: they are indeed both

> from within and from without
> *Unarm'd* to all Temptations.

Prudential reasonings will in general be powerless with them. For the incitements of this world are weak in proportion as we are wretched—

> The world is not *my* friend, nor the world's law.
> The world has got no law to make *me* rich.

They too, who live *from hand to mouth*, will most frequently become improvident. Possessing no *stock* of happiness they eagerly seize the gratifications of the moment, and snatch the froth from the wave as it passes by them. Nor is the desolate state of their families a restraining motive, unsoftened as they are by education, and benumbed into selfishness by the torpedo touch of extreme want. Domestic affections depend on association. We love an object if, as often as we see or recollect it, an agreeable sensation arises in our minds. But alas! how should *he* glow with the charities of father and husband, who gaining scarcely more, than his own necessities demand, must have been accustomed to regard his wife and children, not as the soothers of finished labour, but as rivals for the insufficient meal! In a man so circumstanced the tyranny of the *present* can be overpowered only by the tenfold mightiness of the *future*. Religion will cheer his gloom with her promises, and by habituating his mind to anticipate an infinitely great revolution hereafter, may prepare it even for the sudden reception of a less degree of amelioration in this world.

But if we hope to instruct others, we should familiarize our own minds to some fixed and determinate principles of action. The world is a vast labyrinth, in which almost every one is running a different way, and almost every one manifesting hatred to those who do not run the same way. A few indeed stand motionless, and not seeking to lead themselves or others out of the maze laugh at the failure of their brethren. Yet with little reason: for more grossly than the most bewildered wanderer does *he* err, who never aims to go right. It is more honourable to the head, as well as to the heart, to be misled by our eagerness in the pursuit of truth, than to be safe from blundering by contempt of it. The happiness of mankind is the *end* of virtue, and truth is the knowledge of the *means*; which he will never seriously attempt to discover, who has not habitually interested himself in the welfare of others. The searcher after truth must love and be beloved; for general benevolence is a necessary motive to constancy of pursuit; and this general benevolence is begotten and rendered permanent by social and domestic affections. Let us beware of that proud philosophy, which affects to inculcate philanthropy while it denounces every home-born feeling, by which it is produced and nurtured. The paternal and filial duties discipline the heart and prepare it for the love of all mankind. The intensity of private attachments encourages, not prevents, universal benevolence. The nearer we approach to the sun, the more intense his heat: yet what corner of the system does he not cheer and vivify?

The man who would find truth, must likewise seek it with an humble and simple heart, otherwise he will be precipitant and overlook it; or he will be prejudiced, and refuse to see it. *To emancipate itself from the tyranny of Association,* is the most arduous effort of the mind, particularly in religious and political disquisitions. The asserter of the system has associated with it the preservation of order, and public virtue; the oppugner imposture, and wars, and rapine. Hence, when they dispute, each trembles at the *consequences* of the other's opinions instead of attending to his train of arguments. Of this however we may be certain, whether we be Christians or Infidels, Aristocrats or Republicans, that our minds are in a state unsusceptible of knowledge, when we feel an eagerness to detect the falsehood of an adversary's reasonings, not a sincere wish to discover if there be truth in them;—when we examine an argument in order that we may answer it, instead of answering because we have examined it.

Our opponents are chiefly successful in confuting the theory of freedom by the practices of its advocates: from our lives they draw the most forcible arguments against our doctrines. Nor have they adopted an unfair mode of reasoning. In a science the evidence suffers neither diminution nor increase from the actions of its professors; but the comparative wisdom of political systems depends necessarily on the manners and capacities of the recipients. Why should all things be thrown into confusion to acquire that liberty which a faction of sensualists and gamblers will neither be able nor willing to preserve? "The simplicity of wants and of pleasures may be taken as the criterion of patriotism. Would you prove to me your patriotism? Let me penetrate into the interior of your house. What! I see your antechamber full of insolent lackies; they give you still those vain titles, which liberty treads under foot, and you suffer it and you call yourself a patriot! I penetrate a little further;—your ceilings are gilded—magnificent vases adorn your chimney-pieces—I walk upon the richest carpets—the most costly wines, the most exquisite dishes, cover your table—a crowd of servants surround it—you treat them with haughtiness;—No! you are not a patriot. The most consummate pride reigns in your heart, the pride of birth, of riches, and of talents. With this triple pride, a man never sincerely believes the doctrine of equality: he may repeat its dogmas, but efficient faith is not in him." *Preface to Brissot's Travels in America.*

You reply to Brissot, that these luxuries are the employment of industry, and the best means of circulating your property. Be it so. Renounce then the proud pretensions of democracy; do not profess tenets which it is impossible for you, surrounded by all the symbols of superiority, to wish realized. But you plead, it seems, for equalization of *rights,* not of *condition.* O mockery! All that can delight the poor man's senses or strengthen his understanding, you preclude; yet with generous condescension you would bid him exclaim "LIBERTY and EQUALITY!" because, forsooth, he should possess the same *right* to an hovel which you claim to a palace. This the laws have already given. And what more do *you* promise?

A system of fundamental reform will scarcely be effected by massacres mechanized into revolution. Yet rejected intreaty leads in its consequences to fierce coercion. And much as we deprecate the event, we have reason to conjecture that throughout all Europe it may not be far distant. The folly of the rulers of mankind grows daily more wild and ruinous: oppression is grievous—the oppressed feel and are restless. Such things *may* happen. We cannot therefore inculcate on the minds of each other too often or with too great earnestness the necessity of cultivating benevolent affections. We should be cautious how we indulge the feelings even of virtuous indignation. Indignation is the handsome brother of anger and hatred. The temple of despotism, like that of Tescalipoca, the Mexican deity, is built of human skulls, and cemented with human blood;—let us beware that we be not transported into revenge while we are levelling the loathsome pile: lest when we erect the edifice of freedom we but vary the style of architecture, not change the materials. Let us not wantonly offend even the prejudices of our weaker brethren, nor by ill-timed and vehement declarations of opinion excite in them malignant feelings towards us. The energies of mind are wasted in these intemperate effusions. Those materials of projectile force, which now carelessly scattered explode with an offensive and useless noise, directed by wisdom and union, might heave rocks from their base,—or perhaps (dismissing the metaphor) might produce the desired effect without the convulsion.

For this "subdued sobriety" of temper a practical faith in the doctrine of philosophical necessity seems the only preparative. That vice is the effect of error and the offspring of surrounding circumstances, the object therefore of condolence not of anger, is a proposition easily understood, and as easily demonstrated. But to make it spread from the understanding to the affections, to call it into action, not only in the great exertions of patriotism, but in the daily and hourly occurrences of social life, requires the most watchful attentions of the most energetic mind. It is not enough that we have once swallowed these truths—we must feed on them, as insects on a leaf, till the whole heart be coloured by their qualities and shew its food in every the minutest fibre.

Finally, in the words of an Apostle,

Watch ye! Stand fast in the principles of which ye have been convinced! Quit yourselves like men! Be strong! Yet let all things be done in the spirit of love.

*February, 1795.*

# SELECTIONS FROM *TABLE-TALK*

## ( 1 8 2 3 – 1 8 3 4 )

I have often told you that I do not think there is any jealousy, properly so called, in the character of Othello. There is no predisposition to suspicion, which I take to be an essential term in the definition of the word. Desdemona very truly told Emilia that he was not jealous, that is, of a jealous habit, and he says so as truly of himself. Iago's suggestions, you see, are quite new to him; they do not correspond with any thing of a like nature previously in his mind. If Desdemona had, in fact, been guilty, no one would have thought of calling Othello's conduct that of a jealous man. He could not act otherwise than he did with the lights he had; whereas jealousy can never be strictly right. See how utterly unlike Othello is to Leontes, in the Winter's Tale, or even to Leonatus, in Cymbeline! The jealousy of the first proceeds from an evident trifle, and something like hatred is mingled with it; and the conduct of Leonatus in accepting the wager, and exposing his wife to the trial, denotes a jealous temper already formed.

---

Hamlet's character is the prevalence of the abstracting and generalizing habit over the practical. He does not want courage, skill, will, or opportunity; but every incident sets him thinking; and it is curious, and, at the same time, strictly natural, that Hamlet, who all the play seems reason itself, should be impelled, at last, by mere accident, to effect his object. I have a smack of Hamlet myself, if I may say so.

---

In the very lowest link in the vast and mysterious chain of Being, there is an effort, although scarcely apparent, at individualization; but it is almost lost in the mere nature. A little higher up, the individual is apparent and separate, but subordinate to any thing in man. At length, the animal rises to be on a par with the lowest power of the human nature. There are some of our natural desires which only remain in our most perfect state on earth as means of the higher powers' acting.

---

I wish our clever young poets would remember my homely definitions of prose and poetry; that is, prose = words in their best order;—poetry = the *best* words in the best order.

---

I must acknowledge I never could see much merit in the Persian poetry, which I have read in translation. There is not a ray of Imagination in it, and but a glimmering of Fancy. It is, in fact, so far as I know, deficient in truth. Poetry is certainly something more than good sense, but it must be good sense, at all events, just as a palace is more than a house, but it must be a house, at least.

---

Arabian poetry is a different thing. I cannot help surmising that there is a good deal of Greek fancy in the Arabian Nights' Tales. No doubt we have had a great loss in the Milesian Tales. The Book of Job is pure Arab poetry of the highest and most antique cast.

Think of the sublimity, I should rather say the profundity, of that passage in Ezekiel, "Son of man, can these bones live? And I answered, O Lord God, thou knowest." I know nothing like it.

---

Shakspeare is the Spinozistic deity—an omnipresent creativeness. Milton is the deity of prescience; he stands *ab extra,* and drives a fiery chariot and four, making the horses feel the iron curb which holds them in. Shakspeare's poetry is characterless; that is, it does not reflect the individual Shakspeare; but John Milton himself is in every line of the Paradise Lost. Shakspeare's rhymed verses are excessively condensed,—epigrams with the point everywhere; but in his blank dramatic verse he is diffused, with a linked sweetness long drawn out. No one can understand Shakspeare's superiority fully until he has ascertained, by comparison, all that which he possessed in common with several other great dramatists of his age, and has then calculated the surplus which is entirely Shakspeare's own. His rhythm is so perfect, that you may be almost sure that you do not understand the real force of a line, if it does not run well as you read it. The necessary mental pause after every hemistich or imperfect line is always equal to the time that would have been taken in reading the complete verse.

---

I have no doubt whatever that *Homer* is a mere concrete name for the rhapsodies of the Iliad. Of course there was *a* Homer, and twenty besides. I will engage to compile twelve books with characters just as distinct and consistent as those in the Iliad, from the metrical ballads, and other chronicles of England, about Arthur and the Knights of the Round Table. I say nothing about moral dignity, but the mere consistency of character. The different qualities were traditional. Tristram is always courteous, Lancelot invincible, and so on. The same might be done with the Spanish romances of the Cid. There is no subjectivity whatever in the Homeric poetry. There is a subjectivity of the poet, as of Milton, who is himself before himself in every thing he writes; and there is a subjectivity of the *persona*, or dramatic character, as in all Shakspeare's great creations, Hamlet, Lear, &c.

---

Mrs. Barbauld once told me that she admired the Ancient Mariner very much, but that there were two faults in it,—it was improbable, and had no moral. As for the probability, I owned that that might admit some question; but as to the want of a moral, I told her that in my own judgment the poem had too much; and that the only or chief fault, if I might say so, was the obtrusion of the moral sentiment so openly on the reader as a principle or cause of action in a work of such pure imagination. It ought to have had no more moral than the Arabian Nights' tale of the merchant's sitting down to eat dates by the side of a well, and throwing the shells aside, and lo! a geni starts up, and says he *must* kill the aforesaid merchant, *because* one of the date-shells had, it seems, put out the eye of the geni's son.

I took the thought of *"grinning for joy,"* in that poem, from poor Burnett's remark to me, when we had climbed to the top of Plinlimmon, and were nearly dead with thirst. We could not speak from the constriction, till we found a little puddle under a stone. He said to me,—"You grinned like an idiot!" He had done the same.

---

The Pilgrim's Progress is composed in the lowest style of English, without slang or false grammar. If you were to polish it, you would at once destroy the reality of the vision. For works of imagination should be written in very plain language; the more purely imaginative they are the more necessary it is to be plain.

---

This wonderful work is one of the few books which may be read over repeatedly at different times, and each time with a new and a different pleasure. I read it once as a theologian—and let me assure you, that there is great theological acumen in the work—once with devotional feelings—and once as a poet. I could not have believed beforehand that Calvinism could be painted in such exquisitely delightful colours.

---

Rabelais is a most wonderful writer. Pantagruel is the Reason; Panurge the Understanding,—the pollarded man, the man with every faculty except the reason. I scarcely know an example more illustrative of the distinction between the two. Rabelais had no mode of speaking the truth in those days but in such a form as this; as it was, he was indebted to the King's protection for his life. Some of the commentators talk about his book being all political; there are contemporary politics in it, of course, but the real scope is much higher and more philosophical. It is in vain to look about for a hidden meaning in all that he has written; you will observe, that after any particularly deep thrust, as the Papimania, for example, Rabelais, as if to break the blow, and to appear unconscious of what he has done, writes a chapter or two of pure buffoonery. He every now and then flashes you a glimpse of a real face from his magic lantern, and then buries the whole scene in mist. The morality of the work is of the most refined and exalted kind; as for the manners, to be sure, I cannot say much.

---

Every man is born an Aristotelian or a Platonist. I do not think it possible that any one born an Aristotelian can become a Platonist; and I am sure no born Platonist can ever change into an Aristotelian. They are the two classes of men, beside which it is next to impossible to conceive a third. The one considers reason a quality, or attribute; the other considers it a power. I believe that

Aristotle never could get to understand what Plato meant by an idea. There is a passage, indeed, in the Eudemian Ethics which looks like an exception; but I doubt not of its being spurious, as that whole work is supposed by some to be. With Plato ideas are constitutive in themselves.

Aristotle was, and still is, the sovereign lord of the understanding;—the faculty judging by the senses. He was a conceptualist, and never could raise himself into that higher state which was natural to Plato, and has been so to others, in which the understanding is distinctly contemplated, and, as it were, looked down upon from the throne of actual ideas, or living, inborn, essential truths.

---

Yet what a mind was Aristotle's—only not the greatest that ever animated the human form!—the parent of science, properly so called, the master of criticism, and the founder or editor of logic! But he confounded science with philosophy, which is an error. Philosophy is the middle state between science, or knowledge, and sophia, or wisdom.

---

A poet ought not to pick nature's pocket: let him borrow, and so borrow as to repay by the very act of borrowing. Examine nature accurately, but write from recollection; and trust more to your imagination than to your memory.

---

Really, the metre of some of the modern poems I have read, bears about the same relation to metre properly understood, that dumb bells do to music; both are for exercise, and pretty severe too, I think.

---

"Most women have no character at all," said Pope, and meant it for satire. Shakspeare, who knew man and woman much better, saw that it, in fact, was the perfection of woman to be characterless. Every one wishes a Desdemona or Ophelia for a wife,—creatures who, though they may not always understand you, do always feel you, and feel with you.

---

The old definition of beauty in the Roman school of painting was, *il più nell' uno*—multitude in unity; and there is no doubt that such is the principle of beauty. And as one of the most characteristic and infallible criteria of the different ranks of men's intellects, observe the instinctive habit which all superior minds have of endeavouring to bring, and of never resting till they have brought into unity the scattered facts which occur in conversation, or in the statements of men of business. To attempt to argue any great question upon facts only is absurd; you cannot state any fact before a mixed audience, which an opponent as clever as yourself cannot with ease twist towards another bearing, or at least meet by a contrary fact, as it is called. I wonder why facts were ever called stubborn things: I am sure they have been found pliable enough lately in the House of Commons and elsewhere. Facts, you know, are not truths; they are not conclusions; they are not even premises, but in the nature and parts of premises. The truth depends on, and is only arrived at by, a legitimate deduction from *all* the facts which are truly material.

———'s face is almost the only exception I know to the observation, that something feminine—not *effeminate,* mind—is discoverable in the countenances of all men of genius. Look at the face of old Dampier, a rough sailor, but a man of exquisite mind. How soft is the air of his countenance, how delicate the shape of his temples!

All harmony is founded on a relation to rest—on relative rest. Take a metallic plate, and strew sand on it; sound a harmonic chord over the sand, and the grains will whirl about in circles, and other geometrical figures, all, as it were, depending on some point of sand relatively at rest. Sound a discord, and every grain will whisk about without any order at all, in no figures, and with no points of rest.

The clerisy of a nation, that is, its learned men, whether poets, or philosophers, or scholars, are these points of relative rest. There could be no order, no harmony of the whole, without them.

I regret to see that vile and barbarous vocable *talented,* stealing out of the newspapers into the leading reviews and most respectable publications of the day. Why not *shillinged, farthinged, tenpenced,* &c.? The formation of a participle passive from a noun is a license that nothing but a very peculiar felicity can excuse. If mere convenience is to justify such attempts upon the idiom, you cannot stop till the language becomes, in the proper sense of the word, corrupt. Most of these pieces of slang come from America.

---

Can dialogues in verse be defended? I cannot but think that a great philosophical poet ought always to teach the reader himself as from himself. A poem does not admit argumentation, though it does admit development of thought. In prose there may be a difference; though I must confess that, even in Plato and Cicero, I am always vexed that the authors do not say what they have to say at once in their own persons. The introductions and little urbanities are, to be sure, very delightful in their way; I would not lose them: but I have no admiration for the practice of ventriloquizing through another man's mouth.

---

I think Wordsworth possessed more of the genius of a great philosophic poet than any man I ever knew, or, as I believe, has existed in England since Milton; but it seems to me that he ought never to have abandoned the contemplative position, which is peculiarly, perhaps I might say exclusively, fitted for him. His proper title is, *Spectator ab extra.*

---

When a man mistakes his thoughts for persons and things, he is mad. A madman is properly so defined.

---

A loose, slack, not well-dressed youth met Mr. ——— and myself in a lane near Highgate. ——— knew him, and spoke. It was Keats. He was introduced to me, and stayed a minute or so. After he had left us a little way he came back, and said: "Let me carry away the memory, Coleridge, of having pressed your hand!"—"There is death in that hand," I said to ———, when Keats was gone; yet this was, I believe, before the consumption showed itself distinctly.

———————

Although Wordsworth and Goëthe are not much alike, to be sure, upon the whole, yet they both have this peculiarity of utter non-sympathy with the subjects of their poetry. They are always, both of them, spectators *ab extra*—feeling *for,* but never *with,* their characters. Schiller is a thousand times more *hearty* than Goëthe.

———————

In Ben Jonson you have an intense and burning art. Some of his plots, that of the Alchymist, for example, are perfect. Ben Jonson and Beaumont and Fletcher would, if united, have made a great dramatist indeed, and yet not have come near Shakspeare; but no doubt Ben Jonson was the greatest man after Shakspeare in that age of dramatic genius.

———————

In Shakspeare one sentence begets the next naturally; the meaning is all inwoven. He goes on kindling like a meteor through the dark atmosphere; yet, when the creation in its outline is once perfect, then he seems to rest from his labour, and to smile upon his work, and tell himself that it is very good. You see many scenes and parts of scenes which are simply Shakspeare's disporting himself in joyous triumph and vigorous fun after a great achievement of his highest genius.

———————

The collocation of words is so artificial in Shakspeare and Milton, that you may as well think of pushing a brick out of a wall with your forefinger, as attempt to remove a word out of any of their finished passages.

———————

A good lecture upon style might be composed, by taking on the one hand the slang of L'Estrange, and perhaps even of Roger North, which became so fashionable after the Restoration as a mark of loyalty; and on the other, the Johnsonian magniloquence or the balanced metre of Junius; and then showing how each extreme is faulty, upon different grounds.

It is quite curious to remark the prevalence of the Cavalier slang style in the divines of Charles the Second's time. Barrow could not of course adopt such a mode of writing throughout, because he could not in it have communicated his elaborate thinkings and lofty rhetoric; but even Barrow not unfrequently lets slip a phrase here and there in the regular Roger North way—much to the delight, no doubt, of the largest part of his audience and contemporary readers. See particularly, for instances of this, his work on the Pope's supremacy. South is full of it.

The style of Junius is a sort of metre, the law of which is a balance of thesis and antithesis. When he gets out of his aphorismic metre into a sentence of five or six lines long, nothing can exceed the slovenliness of the English. Horne Tooke and a long sentence seem the only two antagonists that were too much for him. Still the antithesis of Junius is a real antithesis of images or thought; but the antithesis of Johnson is rarely more than verbal.

The definition of good Prose is—proper words in their proper places—of good Verse—the most proper words in their proper places. The propriety is in either case relative. The words in prose ought to express the intended meaning, and no more; if they attract attention to themselves, it is, in general, a fault. In the very best styles, as Southey's, you read page after page, understanding the author perfectly, without once taking notice of the medium of communication; it is as if he had been speaking to you all the while. But in verse you must do more; there the words, the *media*, must be beautiful, and ought to attract your notice—yet not so much and so perpetually as to destroy the unity which ought to result from the whole poem. This is the general rule, but, of course, subject to some modifications, according to the different kinds of prose or verse. Some prose may approach towards verse, as oratory, and therefore a more studied exhibition of the *media* may be proper; and some verse may border more on mere narrative, and there the style should be simpler. But the great thing in poetry is, *quocunque modo*, to effect a unity of impression upon the whole; and a too great fulness and profusion of point in the parts will prevent this. Who can read with pleasure more than a hundred lines or so of Hudibras at one time? Each couplet or quatrain is so whole in itself, that you can't connect them. There is no fusion—just as it is in Seneca.

---

I could write as good verses now as ever I did, if I were perfectly free from vexations, and were in the *ad libitum* hearing of fine music, which has a sensible effect in harmonizing my thoughts, and in animating, and, as it were, lubricating my inventive faculty. The reason of my not finishing Christabel is not that I don't know how to do it—for I have, as I always had, the whole plan entire from beginning to end in my mind; but I fear I could not carry on with equal success the execution of the idea, an extremely subtle and difficult one. Besides, after this continuation of Faust, which they tell me is very poor, who can have courage to attempt a reversal of the judgment of all criticism against continuations? Let us except Don Quixote, however, although the second part of that transcendent work is not exactly *uno flatu* with the original conception.

---

In the Paradise Lost—indeed, in every one of his poems—it is Milton himself whom you see; his Satan, his Adam, his Raphael, almost his Eve—are all John Milton; and it is a sense of this intense egotism that gives me the greatest pleasures in reading Milton's works. The egotism of such a man is a revelation of spirit.

---

I quite agree with Strabo, as translated by Ben Jonson in his splendid dedication of the Fox, that there can be no great poet who is not a good man, though not, perhaps, a *goody* man. His heart must be pure; he must have learned to look into his own heart, and sometimes to look *at* it; for how can he who is ignorant of his own heart know any thing of, or be able to move, the heart of any one else?

---

How strange and awful is the synthesis of life and death in the gusty winds and falling leaves of an autumnal day!

---

The English affect stimulant nourishment—beef and beer. The French, excitants, irritants—nitrous oxyde, alcohol, champaign.

The Austrians, sedatives—hyoscyamus. The Russians, narcotics—opium, tobacco, and beng.

---

Dryden's genius was of that sort which catches fire by its own motion; his chariot wheels *get* hot by driving fast.

---

You may conceive the difference in kind between the Fancy and the Imagination in this way,—that if the check of the senses and the reason were withdrawn, the first would become delirium, and the last mania. The Fancy brings together images which have no connexion natural or moral, but are yoked together by the poet by means of some accidental coincidence; as in the well-known passage in Hudibras:—

> The sun had long since in the lap
> Of Thetis taken out his nap,
> And like a lobster boyl'd, the morn
> From black to red began to turn.

The Imagination modifies images, and gives unity to variety; it sees all things in one, *il più nell' uno*. There is the epic imagination, the perfection of which is in Milton; and the dramatic, of which Shakspeare is the absolute master. The first gives unity by throwing back into the distance; as after the magnificent approach of the Messiah to battle, the poet, by one touch from himself—

> —far off their coming shone!—

makes the whole one image. And so at the conclusion of the description of the appearance of the entranced angels, in which every sort of image from all the regions of earth and air is introduced to diversify and illustrate,—the reader is brought back to the single image by—

> He call'd so loud, that all the hollow deep
> Of Hell resounded.

The dramatic imagination does not throw back, but brings close; it stamps all nature with one, and that its own, meaning, as in Lear throughout.

---

What a master of composition Fielding was! Upon my word, I think the Œdipus Tyrannus, the Alchymist, and Tom Jones the three most perfect plots ever planned. And how charming, how wholesome, Fielding always is! To take him up after Richardson is like emerging from a sick-room heated by stoves into an open lawn on a breezy day in May.

## FROM ANIMA POETAE

The elder languages were fitter for poetry because they expressed only prominent ideas with clearness, the others but darkly . . . Poetry gives most pleasure when only generally and not perfectly understood. It was so by me with Gray's "Bard" and Collins' Odes. The "Bard" once intoxicated me, and now I read it without pleasure. From this cause it is that what I call metaphysical poetry gives me so much delight.

---

The nightingales in a cluster or little wood of blossomed trees, and a bat wheeling incessantly round and round! The noise of the frogs was not unpleasant, like the humming of spinning wheels in a large manufactory,—now and then a distinct sound, sometimes like a duck, and sometimes like the shrill notes of sea-fowl.

---

Slanting pillars of misty light moved along under the sun hid by clouds.

---

Leaves of trees upturned by the stirring wind in twilight,—an image of paleness, wan affright.

---

A child scolding a flower in the words in which he had been himself scolded and whipped, is poetry,—passion past with pleasure.

---

The thin scattered rain-clouds were scudding along the sky; above them, with a visible inter-space, the crescent moon hung, and partook not of the motion; her own hazy light filled up the concave, as if it had been painted and the colors had run.

---

A kind-hearted man who is obliged to give a refusal, or the like, which will inflict great pain finds a relief in doing it roughly and fiercely. Explain this and use it in *Christabel*.

---

The unspeakable comfort to a good man's mind, nay, even to a criminal, to be *understood*,—to have some one that understands one,—and who does not feel that, on earth, no one does? The hope of this, always more or less disappointed, gives the passion to friendship.

---

The sunny mist, the luminous gloom of Plato.

---

Nothing affects me much at the moment it happens. It either stupefies me, and I, perhaps, look at a merry-make and dance-the-hay of flies, or listen entirely to the loud click of the great clock, or I am simply indifferent, not without some sense of philosophical self-complacency. For a thing at the moment is but a thing of the moment; it must be taken up into the mind, diffuse itself through the whole multitude of shapes and thoughts, not one of which it leaves untinged, between not one of which and it some new thought is not engendered. Now this is a work of time, but the body feels it quicker with me.

---

The soul within the body—can I, anyway, compare this to the reflection of the fire seen through my window on the solid wall, seeming, of course, within the solid wall, as deep within as the distance of the fire from the wall. I fear I can make nothing out of it; but why do I always hurry away from any interesting thought to do something uninteresting? As, for instance, when this thought struck me, I turned off my attention suddenly and went to look for the copy of Wolff which I had missed. Is it a cowardice of all deep feeling, even though pleasurable? or is it laziness? or is it something less obvious than either? Is it connected with my epistolary embarrassments?

["The window of my library at Keswick is opposite to the fire-place. At the coming on of evening, it was my frequent amusement to watch the image or reflection of the fire that seemed burning in the bushes or between the trees in different parts of the garden."—*The Friend.*]

---

This evening, and indeed all this day, I ought to have been reading and filling the margins of Malthus.

I had begun and found it pleasant. Why did I neglect it? Because I ought not to have done this. The same applies to the reading and writing of letters, essays, etc. Surely this is well worth a serious analysis, that, by understanding, I may attempt to heal it. For it is a deep and wide disease in my moral nature, at once elm-and-oak-rooted. Is it love of liberty, of spontaneity, or what? These all express, but do not explain, the fact.

After I had got into bed last night I said to myself that I had been pompously enunciating as a difficulty a problem of easy and common solution,—viz., that it was the effect of association. From infancy up to manhood, under parents, schoolmasters, inspectors, etc., our pleasures and pleasant self-chosen pursuits (self-chosen because pleasant, and not originally pleasant because self-chosen) have been forcibly interrupted, and dull, unintelligible rudiments or painful tasks imposed upon us instead. Now all duty is felt as a *command,* and every command is of the nature of an offence. Duty, therefore, by the law of association being felt as a command from without, would naturally call up the sensation of the pain roused from the commands of parents and schoolmasters. But I awoke this morning at half past one, and as soon as disease permitted me to think at all, the shallowness and sophistry of this solution flashed upon me at once. I saw that the phenomenon occurred far, far too early; I have observed it in infants of two or three months old, and in Hartley I have seen it turned up and laid bare to the unarmed eye of the merest common sense. The fact is, that interruption of itself is painful, because, and as far as, it acts as *disruption.* And thus without any reference to, or distinct recollection of, my former theory I saw great reason to attribute the effect, wholly, to the streamy nature of the associative faculty, and the more, as it is evident that they labor under this defect who are most reverie-ish and streamy—Hartley, for instance, and myself. This seems to me no common corroboration of my former thought or the origin of moral evil in general.

———

I addressed a butterfly on a pea-blossom thus: "Beautiful Psyche, soul of a blossom, that art visiting and hovering o'er thy former friends whom thou hast left!" Had I forgot the caterpillar? or did I dream like a mad metaphysician that the caterpillar's hunger for plants was self-love, recollection, and a lust that in its next state refined itself into love? Dec. 12, 1804.

---

Title for a Medical Romance:—
The adventures, rivalry, warfare, and final union and partnership of Dr. Hocus and Dr. Pocus.

---

Idly talk they who speak of poets as mere indulgers of fancy, imagination, superstition, etc. They are the bridlers by delight, the purifiers; they that combine all these with reason and order—the true protoplasts—Gods of Love who tame the chaos.

---

To deduce instincts from obscure recollections of a preexisting state—I have often thought of it. "Ey!" I have said, when I have seen certain tempers and actions in Hartley, "that is I in my future state." So I think, oftentimes, that my children are my soul; that multitude and division are not [O mystery!] necessarily subversive of unity. I am sure that two very different meanings, if not more, lurk in the word One.

---

The drollest explanation of instinct is that of Mylius, who attributes every act to pain, and all the wonderful webs and envelopes of spiders, caterpillars, etc., absolutely to fits of colic or paroxysms of dry bellyache!

---

This tarantula-dance of repetitions and vertiginous argumentation *in circulo,* begun in imposture and self-consummated in madness!

---

The favorite object of all Oriental tales, and that which, whilst it inspired their authors in the East, still inspires their readers everywhere, is the impossibility of baffling Destiny. . . .

---

'T is one source of mistakes concerning the merit of poems, that to those read in youth men attribute all that praise which is due to poetry in general, merely considered as select language in metre. (Little children should not be taught verses, in my opinion; better not to let them set eyes on verse till they are ten or eleven years old.) Now, poetry produces two kinds of pleasure, one for each of the two master-movements and impulses of man,—the gratification of the love of variety, and the gratification of the love of uni- formity; and that by a recurrence delightful as a painless and yet exciting act of memory—tiny breezelets of surprise, each one de- stroying the ripplets which the former had made, yet all together keeping the surface of the mind in a bright dimple-smile. So, too, a hatred of vacancy is reconciled with the love of rest. These and other causes often make [a first acquaintance with] poetry an over- powering delight to a lad of feeling, as I have heard Poole relate of himself respecting Edwin and Angelina. But so it would be with a man bred up in a wilderness by Unseen Beings, who should yet converse and discourse rationally with him—how beautiful would not the first other man appear whom he saw and knew to be a man by the resemblance to his own image seen in the clear stream; and would he not, in like manner, attribute to the man all the divine attributes of humanity, though, haply, he should be a very ordinary, or even a most ugly man, compared with a hundred others? Many of us who have felt this with respect to women have been bred up where few are to be seen; and I acknowledge that, both in persons and in poems, it is well *on the whole* that we should retain our first love, though, alike in both cases, evils have happened as the consequence.

---

The Pine-Tree blasted at the top was applied by Swift to him- self as a prophetic emblem of his own decay. The Chestnut is a fine shady tree, and its wood excellent, were it not that it dies away at the *heart* first. Alas! poor me!

---

What a swarm of thoughts and feelings, endlessly minute frag- ments, and, as it were, representations of all preceding and embryos of all future thought, lie compact in any one moment! So, in a sin- gle drop of water, the microscope discovers what motions, what tumult, what wars, what pursuits, what stratagems, what a circle-dance of death and life, death-hunting life, and life renewed and invigorated by death! The whole world seems here in a many-meaning cypher. What if our existence was but that moment? What an unintelligible, affrightful riddle, what a chaos of limbs and trunk, tailless, headless, nothing begun and nothing ended, would it not be? And yet scarcely more than that other moment of fifty or sixty years, were that our all. Each part throughout infinite diminution adapted to some other, and yet the whole a means to nothing—ends everywhere, and yet an end nowhere.

---

The merry little gnats (*Tipulidœ minimœ*) I have myself often watched in an April shower, evidently "dancing the hayes" in and out between the falling drops, unwetted, or, rather, undown-dashed by rocks of water many times larger than their whole bodies.

---

If a man could pass through Paradise in a dream, and have a flower presented to him as a pledge that his soul had really been there, and if he found that flower in his hand when he awoke—Ay! and what then?

# ALLEGORIC VISION

A feeling of sadness, a peculiar melancholy, is wont to take possession of me alike in spring and in autumn. But in spring it is the melancholy of hope: in autumn it is the melancholy of resignation. As I was journeying on foot through the Apennine, I fell in with a pilgrim in whom the spring and the autumn and the melancholy of both seemed to have combined. In his discourse there were the freshness and the colours of April:

> Qual ramicel a ramo,
> Tal da pensier pensiero
> In lui germogliava.

But as I gazed on his whole form and figure, I bethought me of the not unlovely decays, both of age and of the late season, in the stately elm, after the clusters have been plucked from its entwining vines, and the vines are as bands of dried withies around its trunk and branches. Even so there was a memory on his smooth and ample forehead, which blended with the dedication of his steady eyes, that still looked—I know not, whether upward, or far onward, or rather to the line of meeting where the sky rests upon the distance. But how may I express that dimness of abstraction which lay on the lustre of the pilgrim's eyes like the flitting tarnish from the breath of a sigh on a silver mirror! and which accorded with their slow and reluctant movement, whenever he turned them to any object on the right hand or on the left? It seemed, methought, as if there lay upon the brightness a shadowy presence of disappointments now unfelt, but never forgotten. It was at once the melancholy of hope and of resignation.

We had not long been fellow-travellers, ere a sudden tempest of wind and rain forced us to seek protection in the vaulted doorway of a lone chapelry; and we sate face to face each on the stone bench along-side the low, weather-stained wall, and as close as possible to the massy door.

After a pause of silence: "even thus," said he, "like two strangers that have fled to the same shelter from the same storm, not seldom do Despair and Hope meet for the first time in the porch

seldom do Despair and Hope meet for the first time in the porch
of Death!" "All extremes meet," I answered; "but yours was a
strange and visionary thought." "The better, then, doth it beseem
both the place and me," he replied. "From a Visionary wilt thou
hear a Vision? Mark that vivid flash through this torrent of rain!
Fire and water. Even here thy adage holds true, and its truth is
the moral of my Vision." I entreated him to proceed. Sloping his
face toward the arch and yet averting his eye from it, he seemed
to seek and prepare his words: till, listening to the wind that
echoed within the hollow edifice, and to the rain without,

> Which stole on his thoughts with its two-fold sound,
> The clash hard by and the murmur all round,

he gradually sank away, alike from me and from his own purpose,
and amid the gloom of the storm and in the duskiness of that
place, he sat like an emblem on a rich man's sepulchre, or like
a mourner on the sodded grave of an only one—an aged mourner,
who is watching the waned moon and sorroweth not. Starting
at length from his brief trance of abstraction, with courtesy and
an atoning smile he renewed his discourse, and commenced his
parable.

"During one of those short furloughs from the service of the
body, which the soul may sometimes obtain even in this its mili-
tant state, I found myself in a vast plain, which I immediately
knew to be the Valley of Life. It possessed an astonishing diversity of soils: here was a sunny spot, and there a dark one, forming
just such a mixture of sunshine and shade, as we may have observed on the mountains' side in an April day, when the thin
broken clouds are scattered over heaven. Almost in the very
entrance of the valley stood a large and gloomy pile, into which
I seemed constrained to enter. Every part of the building was
crowded with tawdry ornaments and fantastic deformity. On
every window was portrayed, in glaring and inelegant colours,
some horrible tale, or preternatural incident, so that not a ray of
light could enter, untinged by the medium through which it
passed. The body of the building was full of people, some of
them dancing, in and out, in unintelligible figures, with strange
ceremonies and antic merriment, while others seemed convulsed

with horror, or pining in mad melancholy. Intermingled with these, I observed a number of men, clothed in ceremonial robes who appeared now to marshal the various groups, and to direct their movements; and now with menacing countenances, to drag some reluctant victim to a vast idol, framed of iron bars inter crossed, which formed at the same time an immense cage, and the shape of a human Colossus.

"I stood for a while lost in wonder what these things might mean; when lo! one of the directors came up to me, and with a stern reproachful look bade me uncover my head, for that the place into which I had entered was the temple of the only true Religion, in the holier recesses of which the great Goddess personally resided. Himself too he bade me reverence, as the consecrated minister of her rites. Awe-struck by the name of Religion, I bowed before the priest, and humbly and earnestly intreated him to conduct me to her presence. He assented. Offerings he took from me, with mystic sprinklings of water and with salt he purified, and with strange sufflations he exorcised me; and then led me through many a dark and winding alley, the dew-damps of which chilled my flesh, and the hollow echoes under my feet, mingled, methought, with moanings, affrighted me. At length we entered a large hall, without window, or spiracle, or lamp. The asylum and dormitory it seemed of perennial night—only that the walls were brought to the eye by a number of self-luminous inscriptions in letters of a pale sepulchral light, which held strange neutrality with the darkness, on the verge of which it kept its rayless vigil. I could read them, methought; but though each of the words taken separately I seemed to understand, yet when I took them in sentences, they were riddles and incomprehensible. As I stood meditating on these hard sayings, my guide thus addressed me—'Read and believe: these are mysteries.'—At the extremity of the vast hall the Goddess was placed. Her features, blended with darkness, rose out to my view, terrible, yet vacant. I prostrated myself before her, and then retired with my guide, soul-withered, and wondering, and dissatisfied.

"As I re-entered the body of the temple, I heard a deep buzz as of discontent. A few whose eyes were bright, and either pierc-

ing or steady, and whose ample foreheads, with the weighty
bar, ridge-like, above the eyebrows, bespoke observation followed
by meditative thought; and a much larger number, who were
enraged by the severity and insolence of the priests in exacting
their offerings, had collected in one tumultuous group, and with
a confused outcry of 'This is the Temple of Superstition!' after
much contumely, and turmoil, and cruel mal-treatment on all
sides, rushed out of the pile: and I, methought, joined them.

"We speeded from the Temple with hasty steps, and had now
nearly gone round half the valley, when we were addressed
by a woman, tall beyond the stature of mortals, and with a something more than human in her countenance and mien, which yet
could by mortals be only felt, not conveyed by words or intelli-
gibly distinguished. Deep reflection, animated by ardent feelings,
was displayed in them: and hope, without its uncertainty, and
a something more than all these, which I understood not, but
which yet seemed to blend all these into a divine unity of expression. Her garments were white and matronly, and of the
simplest texture. We inquired her name. 'My name,' she replied,
'is Religion.'

"The more numerous part of our company, affrighted by the
very sound, and sore from recent impostures or sorceries, hurried
onwards and examined no farther. A few of us, struck by the
manifest opposition of her form and manners to those of the
living Idol, whom we had so recently abjured, agreed to follow
her, though with cautious circumspection. She led us to an emi-
nence in the midst of the valley, from the top of which we could
command the whole plain, and observe the relation of the different parts to each other, and of each to the whole, and of all to
each. She then gave us an optic glass which assisted without
contradicting our natural vision, and enabled us to see far beyond
the limits of the Valley of Life; though our eye even thus assisted
permitted us only to behold a light and a glory, but what we
could not descry, save only that it was, and that it was most
glorious.

"And now with the rapid transition of a dream, I had over-
taken and rejoined the more numerous party, who had abruptly

left us, indignant at the very name of religion. They journeyed on, goading each other with remembrances of past oppressions, and never looking back, till in the eagerness to recede from the Temple of Superstition they had rounded the whole circle of the valley. And lo! there faced us the mouth of a vast cavern, at the base of a lofty and almost perpendicular rock, the interior side of which, unknown to them, and unsuspected, formed the extreme and backward wall of the Temple. An impatient crowd, we entered the vast and dusky cave, which was the only perforation of the precipice. At the mouth of the cave sat two figures; the first, by her dress and gestures, I knew to be Sensuality; the second form, from the fierceness of his demeanour, and the brutal scornfulness of his looks, declared himself to be the monster Blasphemy. He uttered big words, and yet ever and anon I observed that he turned pale at his own courage. We entered. Some remained in the opening of the cave, with the one or the other of its guardians. The rest, and I among them, pressed on, till we reached an ample chamber, that seemed the centre of the rock. The climate of the place was unnaturally cold.

In the furthest distance of the chamber sate an old dim-eyed man, poring with a microscope over the torso of a statue, which had neither basis, nor feet, nor head; but on its breast was carved Nature! To this he continually applied his glass, and seemed enraptured with the various inequalities which it rendered visible on the seemingly polished surface of the marble.—Yet evermore was this delight and triumph followed by expressions of hatred, and vehement railing against a Being, who yet, he assured us, had no existence. This mystery suddenly recalled to me what I had read in the holiest recess of the temple of Superstition. The old man spake in divers tongues, and continued to utter other and most strange mysteries. Among the rest he talked much and vehemently concerning an infinite series of causes and effects, which he explained to be—a string of blind men, the last of whom caught hold of the skirt of the one before him, he of the next, and so on till they were all out of sight; and that they all walked infallibly straight, without making one false step, though all were alike blind. Methought I borrowed courage from surprise, and asked him—Who then is at the head to guide them? He looked at me with ineffable contempt, not unmixed with an angry suspicion, and then replied, 'No one.' The string of blind men went on for ever without any beginning; for although one blind man could not move without stumbling, yet infinite blindness supplied the want of sight. I burst into laughter, which instantly turned to terror—for as he started forward in rage, I caught a glimpse of him from behind; and lo! I beheld a monster bi-form and Janus-headed, in the hinder face and shape of which I instantly recognised the dread countenance of Superstition—and in the terror I awoke."

*1811* *1811*

# LETTERS

❧

## I. FIVE AUTOBIOGRAPHICAL LETTERS
## TO THOMAS POOLE

*Monday, February, 1797*

My dear Poole,—I could inform the dullest author how he might write an interesting book. Let him relate the events of his own life with honesty, not disguising the feelings that accompanied them. I never yet read even a Methodist's Experience in the "Gospel Magazine" without receiving instruction and amusement; and I should almost despair of that man who could peruse the Life of John Woolman without an amelioration of heart. As to my Life, it has all the charms of variety,—high life and low life, vices and virtues, great folly and some wisdom. However, what I am depends on what I have been; and you, *my best Friend!* have a right to the narration. To me the task will be a useful one. It will renew and deepen my reflections on the past; and it will perhaps make you behold with no unforgiving or impatient eye those weaknesses and defects in my character, which so many untoward circumstances have concurred to plant there.

My family on my mother's side can be traced up, I know not how far. The Bowdons inherited a small farm in the Exmoor country, in the reign of Elizabeth, as I have been told, and, to my own knowledge, they have inherited nothing better since that time. On my father's side I can rise no higher than my grandfather, who was born in the Hundred of Coleridge in the county of Devon, christened, educated, and apprenticed to the parish. He afterwards became a respectable woollen-draper in the town of South Molton. (I have mentioned these particulars, as the time may come in which it will be useful to be able to prove myself a genuine *sans-culotte,* my veins uncontaminated with one drop of gentility.) My father received a better education than the others of his family, in consequence of his own exertions, not of his superior advantages. When he was not quite sixteen years old, my grandfather became bankrupt, and by a series of misfortunes was reduced to extreme poverty. My father received the half of his last crown and his blessing, and walked off to seek his fortune. After he had proceeded a few miles, he sat him down on the side of the road, so overwhelmed with painful thoughts that he wept audibly. A gentleman passed by, who knew him, and, inquiring into his distresses, took my father with him, and settled him in a neighbouring town as a schoolmaster. His school increased and he got money and knowledge: for he commenced a severe and ardent student. Here, too, he married his first wife, by whom he had three daughters, all now alive. While his first wife lived, having scraped up money enough at the age of twenty he walked to Cambridge, entered at Sidney College, distinguished himself for Hebrew and Mathematics, and might have had a fellowship if he had not been married. He returned—his wife died. Judge Buller's father gave him the living of Ottery St. Mary, and put the present judge to school with him. He married my mother, by whom he had ten children, of whom I am the youngest, born October 20, 1772.

These sketches I received from my mother and aunt, but I am utterly unable to fill them up by any particularity of times, or places, or names. Here I shall conclude my first letter, because I cannot pledge myself for the accuracy of the accounts, and I will not therefore mingle them with those for the accuracy of which in the minutest parts I shall hold myself amenable to the Tribunal of Truth. You must regard this letter as the first chapter of an history which is devoted to dim traditions of times too remote to be pierced by the eye of investigation.

Yours affectionately,
S. T. Coleridge

*Sunday, March, 1797*

My dear Poole,—My father (Vicar of, and Schoolmaster at, Ottery St. Mary, Devon) was a profound mathematician, and well versed in the Latin, Greek, and Oriental Languages. He published, or rather attempted to publish, several works; 1st, Miscellaneous Dissertations arising from the 17th and 18th Chapters of the Book of Judges; 2d, *Sententiæ excerptæ,* for the use of his own school; and 3d, his best work, a Critical Latin Grammar; in the preface to which he proposes a bold innovation in the names of the cases. My father's new nomenclature was not likely to become popular, although it must be allowed to be both sonorous and expressive. *Exempli gratiâ,* he calls the ablative the *quippe-quare-quale-quia-quidditive case!* My father made the world his confidant with respect to his learning and ingenuity, and the world seems to have kept the secret very faithfully. His various works, uncut, un-thumbed, have been preserved free from all pollution. This piece of good luck promises to be hereditary; for all *my* compositions have the same amiable *home-studying* propensity. The truth is, my father was not a first-rate genius; he was, however, a first-rate Christian. I need not detain you with his character. In learning, good-heartedness, absentness of mind, and excessive ignorance of the world, he was a perfect Parson Adams.

My mother was an admirable economist, and managed exclusively. My eldest brother's name was John. He went over to the East Indies in the Company's service; he was a successful officer and a brave one, I have heard. He died of a consumption there about eight years ago. My second brother was called William. He went to Pembroke College, Oxford, and afterwards was assistant to Mr. Newcome's School, at Hackney. He died of a putrid fever the year before my father's death, and just as he was on the eve of marriage with Miss Jane Hart, the eldest daughter of a very wealthy citizen of Exeter. My third brother, James, has been in the army since the age of sixteen, has married a woman of fortune, and now lives at Ottery St. Mary, a respectable man. My brother Edward, the wit of the family, went to Pembroke College, and afterwards to Salisbury, as assistant to Dr. Skinner. He married a woman twenty years older than his mother. She is dead, and he now lives at Ottery St. Mary. My fifth brother, George, was educated at Pembroke College, Oxford, and from there went to Mr. Newcome's, Hackney, on the death of William. He stayed there fourteen years, when the living of Ottery St. Mary was given him. There he has now a fine school, and has lately married Miss Jane Hart, who with beauty and wealth had remained a faithful widow to the memory of William for sixteen years. My brother George is a man of reflective mind and elegant genius. He possesses learning in a greater degree than any of the family, excepting myself. His manners are grave and hued over with a tender sadness. In his moral character he approaches every way nearer to perfection than any man I ever yet knew; indeed, he is worth the whole family in a lump. My sixth brother, Luke (indeed, the seventh, for one brother, the second, died in his infancy, and I had forgot to mention him), was bred as a medical man. He married Miss Sara Hart, and died at the age of twenty-two, leaving one child, a lovely boy, still alive. My brother Luke was a man of uncommon genius, a severe student, and a good man. The eighth child was a sister, Anne. She died a little after my brother Luke, aged twenty-one;

> Rest, gentle Shade! and wait thy Maker's will;
> Then rise *unchang'd,* and be an Angel still!

The ninth child was called Francis. He went out as a midshipman, under Admiral Graves. His ship lay on the Bengal coast, and he accidentally met his brother John, who took him to land, and procured him a commission in the Army. He died from the effects of a delirious fever brought on by his excessive exertions at the siege of Seringapatam, at which his conduct had been so gallant, that Lord Cornwallis paid him a high compliment in the presence of the army, and presented him with a valuable gold watch, which my mother now has. All my brothers are remarkably handsome; but they were as inferior to Francis as I am to them. He went by the name of "the handsome Coleridge." The tenth and last child was S. T. Coleridge, the subject of these epistles, born (as I told you in my last) October 20, 1772.

From October 20, 1772, to October 20, 1773. Christened Samuel Taylor Coleridge—my godfather's name being Samuel Taylor, Esq. I had another godfather (his name was Evans), and two godmothers, both called "Monday." From October 20, 1773, to October 20, 1774. In this year I was carelessly left by my nurse, ran to the fire, and pulled out a live coal—burnt myself dreadfully. While my hand was being dressed by a Mr. Young, I spoke for the first time (so my mother informs me) and said, "nasty Doctor Young!" The snatching at fire, and the circumstance of my first words expressing hatred to professional men—are they at all *ominous?* This year I went to school. My schoolmistress, the very image of Shenstone's, was named Old Dame Key. She was nearly related to Sir Joshua Reynolds.

From October 20, 1774, to October 20, 1775. I was inoculated; which I mention because I distinctly remember it, and that my eyes were bound; at which I manifested so much obstinate indignation, that at last they removed the bandage, and unaffrighted I looked at the lancet, and suffered the scratch. At the close of the year I could read a chapter in the Bible.

Here I shall end, because the remaining years of my life *all* assisted to form *my particular mind;*—the three first years had nothing in them that seems to relate to it.

*October 9, 1797*

My dearest Poole,—From March to October—long silence! But [as] it is possible that I may have been preparing materials for future letters, the time cannot be considered as altogether subtracted from you.

From October, 1775, to October, 1778. These three years I continued at the Reading School, because I was too little to be trusted among my father's schoolboys. After breakfast I had a halfpenny given me, with which I bought three cakes at the baker's close by the school of my old mistress; and these were my dinner on every day except Saturday and Sunday, when I used to dine at home, and wallowed in a beef and pudding dinner. I am remarkably fond of beans and bacon; and this fondness I attribute to my father having given me a penny for having eat a large quantity of beans on Saturday. For the other boys did not like them, and as it was an economic food, my father thought that my attachment and penchant for it ought to be encouraged. My father was very fond of me, and I was my mother's darling: in consequence I was very miserable. For Molly, who had nursed my brother Francis, and was immoderately fond of him, hated me because my mother took more notice of me than of Frank, and Frank hated me because my mother gave me now and then a bit of cake, when he had none, —quite forgetting that for one bit of cake which I had and he had not, he had twenty sops in the pan, and pieces of bread and butter with sugar on them from Molly, from whom I received only thumps and ill names.

So I became fretful and timorous, and a tell-tale; and the school-boys drove me from play, and were always tormenting me, and hence I took no pleasure in boyish sports, but read incessantly. My father's sister kept an *everything* shop at Crediton, and there I read through all the gilt-cover little books that could be had at that time, and likewise all the uncovered tales of Tom Hickathrift, Jack the Giant-killer, etc., etc., etc., etc. And I used to lie by the wall and *mope,* and my spirits used to come upon me suddenly; and in a flood of them I was accustomed to race up and down the churchyard, and act over all I had been reading, on the docks, the nettles, and the rank grass. At six years old I remember to have read Belisarius, Robinson Crusoe, and Philip Quarles; and then I found the Arabian Nights' Entertainments, one tale of which (the tale of a man who was compelled to seek for a pure virgin) made so deep an impression on me (I had read it in the evening while my mother was mending stockings), that I was haunted by spectres, whenever I was in the dark: and I distinctly remember the anxious and fearful eagerness with which I used to watch the window in which the books lay, and whenever the sun lay upon them, I would seize it, carry it by the wall, and bask and read. My father found out the effect which these books had produced, and burnt them.

So I became a *dreamer,* and acquired an indisposition to all bodily activity; and I was fretful, and inordinately passionate, and as I could not play at anything, and was slothful, I was despised and hated by the boys; and because I could read and spell and had, I may truly say, a memory and understanding forced into almost an unnatural ripeness, I was flattered and wondered at by all the old women. And so I became very vain, and despised most of the boys that were at all near my own age, and before I was eight years old I was a *character.* Sensibility, imagination, vanity, sloth, and feelings of deep and bitter contempt for all who traversed the orbit of my understanding, were even then prominent and manifest.

From October, 1778, to 1779. That which I began to be from

three to six I continued from six to nine. In this year [1778] I was admitted into the Grammar School, and soon outstripped all of my age. I had a dangerous putrid fever this year. My brother George lay ill of the same fever in the next room. My poor brother Francis, I remember, stole up in spite of orders to the contrary, and sat by my bedside and read Pope's Homer to me. Frank had a violent love of beating me; but whenever that was superseded by any humour or circumstances, he was always very fond of me, and used to regard me with a strange mixture of admiration and contempt. Strange it was not, for he hated books, and loved climbing, fighting, playing and robbing orchards, to distraction.

My mother relates a story of me, which I repeat here, because it must be regarded as my first piece of wit. During my fever, I asked why Lady Northcote (our neighbour) did not come and see me. My mother said she was afraid of catching the fever. I was piqued, and answered, "Ah, Mamma! the four Angels round my bed an't afraid of catching it!" I suppose you know the prayer:—

> "Matthew! Mark! Luke and John!
>   God bless the bed which I lie on.
>   Four angels round me spread,
>   Two at my foot, and two at my head."

This prayer I said nightly, and most firmly believed the truth of it. Frequently have I (half-awake and half-asleep, my body diseased and fevered by my imagination), seen armies of ugly things bursting in upon me, and these four angels keeping them off. In my next I shall carry on my life to my father's death.

God bless you, my dear Poole, and your affectionate

S. T. Coleridge

*October 16, 1797*

Dear Poole,—From October, 1779, to October, 1781. I had asked my mother one evening to cut my cheese entire, so that I might toast it. This was no easy matter, it being a *crumbly* cheese. My mother, however, did it. I went into the garden for something or other, and in the mean time my brother Frank *minced* my cheese "to disappoint the favorite." I returned, saw the exploit, and in an agony of passion flew at Frank. He pretended to have been seriously hurt by my blow, flung himself on the ground, and there lay with outstretched limbs. I hung over him moaning, and in a great fright; he leaped up, and with a horse-laugh gave me a severe blow in the face. I seized a knife, and was running at him, when my mother came in and took me by the arm. I expected a flogging, and struggling from her I ran away to a hill at the bottom of which the Otter flows, about one mile from Ottery. There I stayed; my rage died away, but my obstinacy vanquished my fears, and taking out a little shilling book which had, at the end, morning and evening prayers, I very devoutly repeated them—thinking at the *same time* with inward and gloomy satisfaction how miserable my mother must be! I distinctly remember my feelings when I saw a Mr. Vaughan pass over the bridge, at about a furlong's distance, and how I watched the calves in the fields beyond the river. It grew dark and I fell asleep. It was towards the latter end of October, and it proved a dreadful stormy night. I felt the cold in my sleep, and dreamt that I was pulling the blanket over me, and actually pulled over me a dry thorn bush which lay on the hill. In my sleep I had rolled from the top of the hill to within three yards of the river, which flowed by the unfenced edge at the bottom. I awoke several times, and finding myself wet and stiff and cold, closed my eyes again that I might forget it.

In the mean time my mother waited about half an hour, expecting my return when the *sulks* had evaporated. I not returning, she sent into the churchyard and round the town. Not found! Several men and all the boys were sent to ramble about and seek me. In vain! My mother was almost distracted; and at ten o'clock at night I was *cried* by the crier in Ottery, and in two villages near it, with a reward offered for me. No one went to bed; indeed, I believe half the town were up all the night. To return to myself. About five in the morning, or a little after, I was broad awake, and attempted to get up and walk; but I could not move. I saw the shepherds and workmen at a distance, and cried, but so faintly that it was impossible to hear me thirty yards off. And there I might have lain and died; for I was now almost given over, the ponds and even the river, near where I was lying, having been dragged.

But by good luck, Sir Stafford Northcote, who had been out all night, resolved to make one other trial, and came so near that he heard me crying. He carried me in his arms for near a quarter of a mile, when we met my father and Sir Stafford's servants. I remember and never shall forget my father's face as he looked upon me while I lay in the servant's arms—so calm, and the tears stealing down his face; for I was the child of his old age. My mother, as you may suppose, was outrageous with joy. [Meantime] in rushed a *young lady,* crying out, "I hope you'll whip him, Mrs. Coleridge!" This woman still lives in Ottery; and neither philosophy or religion have been able to conquer the antipathy which I *feel* towards her whenever I see her. I was put to bed and recovered in a day or so, but I was certainly injured. For I was weakly and subject to the ague for many years after.

My father (who had so little of parental ambition in him, that he had destined his children to be blacksmiths, etc., and had accomplished his intention but for my mother's pride and spirit of aggrandizing her family)—my father had, however, resolved that I should be a parson. I read every book that came in my way without distinction; and my father was fond of me, and used to take me on his knee and hold long conversations with me. I remember that at eight years old I walked with him one winter evening from a farmer's house, a mile from Ottery, and he told me the names of the stars and how Jupiter was a thousand times larger than our world, and that the other twinkling stars were suns that had worlds rolling round them; and when I came home he shewed me how they rolled round. I heard him with a profound delight and admiration: but without the least mixture of wonder or incredulity. For from my early reading of fairy tales and genii, etc., etc., my mind had been habituated *to the Vast,* and I never regarded *my senses* in any way as the criteria of my belief. I regulated all my creeds by my conceptions, not by my *sight,* even at that age. Should children be permitted to read romances, and relations of giants and magicians and genii? I know all that has been said against it; but I have formed my faith in the affirmative. I know no other way of giving the mind a love of the Great and the Whole. Those who have been led to the same truths step by step, through the constant testimony of their senses, seem to me to want a sense which I possess. They contemplate nothing but *parts,* and all *parts* are necessarily little. And the universe to them is but a mass of *little things.* It is true, that the mind *may* become credulous and prone to superstition by the former method; but are not the experimentalists credulous even to madness in believing any absurdity, rather than believe the grandest truths, if they have not the testimony of their own senses in their favour? I have known some who have been *rationally* educated, as it is styled. They were marked by a microscopic acuteness, but when they looked at great things, all became a blank and they saw nothing, and denied (very illogically) that anything could be seen, and uniformly put the negation of a power for the possession of a power, and called the want of imagination judgment and the never being moved to rapture philosophy!

Towards the latter end of September, 1781, my father went to Plymouth with my brother Francis, who was to go as midshipman under Admiral Graves, who was a friend of my father's. My father settled my brother, and returned October 4, 1781. He arrived at Exeter about six o'clock, and was pressed to take a bed there at the Harts', but he refused, and, to avoid their entreaties, he told them, that he had never been superstitious, but that the night before he had had a dream which had made a deep impression. He dreamt that Death had appeared to him as he is commonly painted, and touched him with his dart. Well, he returned home, and all his family, I excepted, were up. He told my mother his dream; but he was in high health and good spirits, and there was a bowl of punch made, and my father gave a long and particular account of his travel, and that he had placed Frank under a religious captain, etc. At length he went to bed, very well and in high spirits. A short time after he had lain down he complained of a pain in his bowels. My mother got him some peppermint water, and, after a pause, he said, "I am much better now, my dear!" and lay down again. In a minute my mother heard a noise in his throat, and spoke to him, but he did not answer; and she spoke repeatedly in vain. Her *shriek* awaked me, and I said, "Papa is dead!" I did not know of my father's return, but I knew that he was expected. How I came to think of his death I cannot tell; but so it was. Dead he was. Some said it was the gout in the heart;—probably it was a fit of apoplexy. He was an Israelite without guile, simple, generous, and taking some Scripture texts in their literal sense, he was conscientiously indifferent to the good and the evil of this world.

God love you and                                                    S. T. Coleridge

*February 19, 1798*

From October, 1781, to October, 1782.

After the death of my father, we of course changed houses, and I remained with my mother till the spring of 1782, and was a day-scholar to Parson Warren, my father's successor. He was not very deep, I believe; and I used to delight my mother by relating little instances of his deficiency in grammar knowledge,—every detraction from his merits seemed an oblation to the memory of my father, especially as Parson Warren did certainly *pulpitize* much better. Somewhere I think about April, 1782, Judge Buller, who had been educated by my father, sent for me, having procured a Christ's Hospital Presentation. I accordingly went to London, and was received by my mother's brother, Mr. Bowdon, a tobacconist and (at the same time) clerk to an underwriter. My uncle lived at the corner of the Stock Exchange and carried on his shop by means of a confidential servant, who, I suppose, fleeced him most unmercifully. He was a widower and had one daughter who lived with a Miss Cabriere, an old maid of great sensibilities and a taste for literature. Betsy Bowdon had obtained an unlimited influence over her mind, which she still retains. Mrs. Holt (for this is her name now) was not the kindest of daughters—but, indeed, my poor uncle would have wearied the patience and affection of an Euphrasia. He received me with great affection, and I stayed ten weeks at his house, during which time I went occasionally to Judge Buller's. My uncle was very proud of me, and used to carry me from coffee-house to coffee-house and tavern to tavern, where I drank and talked and disputed, as if I had been a man. Nothing was more common than for a large party to exclaim in my hearing that I was a *prodigy*, etc., etc., etc., so that while I remained at my uncle's I was most completely spoiled and pampered, both mind and body.

At length the time came, and I donned the *blue* coat and yellow stockings and was sent down into Hertford, a town twenty miles from London, where there are about three hundred of the younger Blue-Coat boys. At Hertford I was very happy, on the whole, for I had plenty to eat and drink, and pudding and vegetables almost every day. I stayed there six weeks, and then was drafted up to the great school at London, where I arrived in September, 1782, and was placed in the second ward, then called Jefferies' Ward, and in the under Grammar School. There are twelve wards or dormitories of unequal sizes, beside the sick ward, in the great school, and they contained all together seven hundred boys, of whom I think nearly one third were the sons of clergymen. There are five schools,— a mathematical, a grammar, a drawing, a reading and a writing school,—all very large buildings. When a boy is admitted, if he reads very badly, he is either sent to Hertford or the reading school. (N. B. Boys are admissible from seven to twelve years old.) If he learns to read tolerably well before nine, he is drafted into the Lower Grammar School; if not, into the Writing School, as having given proof of unfitness for classical attainments. If before he is eleven he climbs up to the first form of the Lower Grammar School, he is drafted into the head Grammar School; if not, at eleven years old, he is sent into the Writing School, where he continues till fourteen or fifteen, and is then either apprenticed and articled as clerk, or whatever else his turn of mind or of fortune shall have provided for him. Two or three times a year the Mathematical Master beats up for recruits for the King's boys, as they are called; and all who like the Navy are drafted into the Mathematical and Drawing Schools, where they continue till sixteen or seventeen, and go out as midshipmen and schoolmasters in the Navy. The boys, who are drafted into the Head Grammar School remain there till thirteen, and then, if not chosen for the University, go into the Writing School.

Each dormitory has a nurse, or matron, and there is a head matron to superintend all these nurses. The boys were, when I was admitted, under excessive subordination to each other, according to rank in school; and every ward was governed by four Monitors (appointed by the *Steward,* who was the supreme Governor out of school,—our temporal lord), and by four *Markers,* who wore silver medals and were appointed by the Head Grammar Master, who was our supreme spiritual lord. The same boys were commonly both monitors and markers. We read in classes on Sundays to our *Markers,* and were catechized by them, and under their sole authority during prayers, etc. All other authority was in the monitors; but, as I said, the same boys were ordinarily both the one and the other. Our diet was very scanty. Every morning, a bit of dry bread and some bad small beer. Every evening, a larger piece of bread and cheese or butter, whichever we liked. For dinner,—on Sunday, boiled beef and broth; Monday, bread and butter, and milk and water; on Tuesday, roast mutton; Wednesday, bread and butter, and rice milk; Thursday, boiled beef and broth; Saturday, bread and butter, and pease-porritch. Our food was portioned; and, excepting on Wednesdays, I never had a belly full. Our appetites were *damped,* never satisfied; and we had no vegetables.

# II. PASSAGES OF COMMENT
## ON CONTEMPORARY WRITERS

. . . after I had left you on the road between Ambleside and
Grasmere, I was dejected by the apprehension that I had been
unpardonably loquacious, and had oppressed you, and still more
Mrs. Sotheby, with my many words so impetuously uttered! But
in simple truth, you were yourselves, in part, the innocent causes
of it. For the meeting with you, the manner of the meeting, your
kind attentions to me, the deep and healthful delight which every
impressive and beautiful object seemed to pour out upon you;
kindred opinions, kindred pursuits, kindred feelings in persons
whose habits, and, as it were, walk of life, have been so different
from my own,—these and more than these, which I would but
cannot say, all flowed in upon me with unusually strong impulses
of pleasure,—and pleasure in a body and soul such as I happen to
possess "intoxicates more than strong wine." However, *I promise
to be a much more subdued creature when you next meet me,* for
I had but just recovered from a state of extreme dejection, brought
on in part by ill health, partly by other circumstances; and solitude
and solitary musings do of themselves impregnate our thoughts,
perhaps, with more life and sensation than will leave the balance
quite even. But you, my dear sir! looked at a brother poet with a
brother's eyes. Oh that you were now in my study and saw, what
is now before the window at which I am writing,—that rich mul-
berry-purple which a floating cloud has thrown on the lake, and
that quiet boat making its way through it to the shore!

We have had little else but rain and squally weather since you
left us till within the last three days. But showery weather is no
evil to us; and even that most oppressive of all weathers, hot, small
*drizzle,* exhibits the mountains the best of any. It produced such
new combinations of ridges in the Lodore and Borrowdale mountains on Saturday morning that I declare, had I been blindfolded

and so brought to the prospect, I should scarcely have known them again. It was a dream such as lovers have,—a wild and trans-figuring, yet enchantingly lovely dream, of an object lying by the side of the sleeper. Wordsworth, who has walked through Switzer-land, declared that he never saw anything superior, perhaps noth-ing equal, in the Alps.

The latter part of your letter made me truly happy. Uriel him-self should not be half as welcome; and indeed he, I must admit, was never any great favourite of mine. I always thought him a bantling of zoneless Italian muses, which Milton heard cry at the door of his imagination and took in out of charity. However, come as you may, *carus mihi expectatusque venies. De cœteris rebus si quid agendum est, et quicquid sit agendum, ut quam rectissime agantur omni meâ curâ; operâ, diligentiâ, gratiâ providebo.*

On my return to Keswick, I reperused the "Erste Schiffer" with great attention, and the result was an increasing disinclination to the business of translating it; though my fancy was not a little flattered by the idea of seeing my rhymes in such a gay livery.—As poor Giordano Bruno says in his strange, yet noble poem, "De Immenso et Innumerabili,"—

> Quam Garymedeo cultu, graphiceque venustus!
> Narcissis referam, peramarunt me quoque Nymphæ.

But the poem was too silly. The first conception is noble, so very good that I am spiteful enough to hope that I shall discover it not to have been original in Gesner,—he has so abominably maltreated it. First, the story is very inartificially constructed. We should have been let into the existence of the girl by her mother, through the young man, and after *his* appearance. This, however, is compara-tively a trifle. But the machinery is so superlatively contemptible and commonplace; as if a young man could not dream of a tale which had deeply impressed him without Cupid, or have a fair wind all the way to an island without Æolus. Æolus himself is a god devoted and dedicated, I should have thought, to the Muse of Travestie. His speech in Gesner is not deficient in fancy, but it is a girlish fancy, and the god of the wind, exceedingly disquieted with animal love, makes a very ridiculous figure in my imagination. Besides, it was ill taste to introduce Cupid and Æolus at a time which we positively know to have been anterior to the invention and establishment of the Grecian Mythology; and the speech of Æolus reminds me perpetually of little engravings from the cut stones of the ancients,—seals, and whatever else they call them. Again, the girl's yearnings and conversations with him are something between the nursery and the *Veneris volgivagæ templa, et libidinem spirat et subsusurrat, dum innocentiæ loquillam, et virginiæ cogitationis dulciter offensantis luctamina simulat.*

It is not the thought that a lonely girl could have; but exactly such as a boarding-school *miss*, whose imagination, to say no worse, had been somewhat stirred and heated by the perusal of French or German pastorals, would suppose her to say. But this is, indeed, general in the German and French poets. It is easy to clothe imaginary beings with our own thoughts and feelings; but to send ourselves out of ourselves, to *think* ourselves into the thoughts and feelings of beings in circumstances wholly and strangely different from our own, *hic labor hoc opus*; and who has achieved it? Perhaps only Shakespeare. Metaphysics is a word that you, my dear sir, are no great friend to, but yet you will agree with me that a great poet must be *implicité*, if not *explicité*, a profound metaphysician. He may not have it in logical coherence in his brain and tongue, but he must have the ear of a wild Arab listening in the silent desert, the eye of a North American Indian tracing the footsteps of an enemy upon the leaves that strew the forest, the touch of a blind man feeling the face of a darling child. And do not think me a bigot if I say that I have read no French or German writer who appears to me to have a *heart* sufficiently pure and simple to be capable of this or anything like it. I could say a great deal more in abuse of poor Gesner's poems, but I have said more than I fear will be creditable in your opinion to my good nature. I must, though, tell you the malicious motto which I have written in the first part of Klopstock's "Messias:"—

> Tale tuum carmen nobis, divine poeta!
> Quale sopor!

Only I would have the words *divine poeta* translated "verse-making divine." I have read a great deal of German; but I do dearly, dearly, dearly love my own countrymen of old times, and those of my contemporaries who write in their spirit.

William Wordsworth and his sister left me yesterday on their way to Yorkshire. They walked yesterday to the foot of Ulleswater, from thence they go to Penrith, and take the coach. I accompanied them as far as the seventh milestone. Among the last things which he said to me was, "Do not forget to remember me to Mr. Sotheby with whatever affectionate terms so slight an intercourse may permit; and how glad we shall all be to see him again!"

I was much pleased with your description of Wordsworth's character as it appeared to you. It is in a few words, in half a dozen strokes, like one of Mortimer's figures, a fine portrait. The word "homogeneous" gave me great pleasure, as most accurately and happily expressing him. I must set you right with regard to my perfect coincidence with his poetic creed. It is most certain that the heads of our mutual conversations, etc., and the passages, were indeed partly taken from note of mine; for it was at first intended that the preface should be written by me. And it is likewise true that I warmly accord with Wordsworth in his abhorrence of these poetic licenses, as they are called, which are indeed mere tricks of convenience and laziness. *Ex. gr.* Drayton has these lines:—

> Ouse having Ouleney past, as she were waxed mad
> From her first stayder course immediately doth gad,
> And in meandered gyres doth whirl herself about,
> *That, this* way, here and there, backward in and out.
> And like a wanton girl oft doubling in her gait
> In labyrinthian turns and twinings intricate, etc.

The first poets, observing such a stream as this, would say with truth and beauty, "it *strays;*" and now every stream shall *stray,* wherever it prattles on its *pebbled* way, instead of its bed or channel. And I have taken the instance from a poet from whom as few instances of this vile, commonplace, trashy style could be taken as from any writer [namely], from Bowles' execrable translation of that lovely poem of Dean Ogle's (vol. ii. p. 27). I am confident that Bowles good-naturedly translated it in a hurry, merely to give him an excuse for printing the admirable original. In my opinion, every phrase, every metaphor, every personification, should have its justifying clause in some *passion,* either of the poet's mind or of the characters described by the poet. But metre itself implies a passion, that is, a state of excitement both in the poet's mind, and is expected, in part, of the reader; and, though I stated this to Wordsworth, and he has in some sort stated it in his preface, yet he has not done justice to it, nor has he, in my opinion, sufficiently answered it. In my opinion, poetry justifies as poetry, independent of any other passion, some new combinations of language and *commands* the omission of many others allowable in other compositions. Now Wordsworth, *me saltem judice,* has in his system not sufficiently admitted the former, and in his practice has too frequently sinned against the latter. Indeed, we have had lately some little controversy on the subject, and we begin to suspect that there is somewhere or other a radical difference in our opinions. *Dulce est inter amicos rarissimâ dissensione condere plurimas consentiones,* saith St. Augustine, who said more good things than any saint or sinner that I ever read in Latin. . . .

### TO WORDSWORTH, MAY 30, 1815 [ON THE EXCURSION]

. . . But what did my criticism amount to, reduced to its full and naked sense? This, that *comparatively* with the *former* poem, "The Excursion," as far as it was new to me, had disappointed my expectations; that the excellencies were so many and of so high a class that it was impossible to attribute the inferiority, if any such really existed, to any flagging of the writer's own genius—and that I conjectured that it might have been occasioned by the influence of self-established convictions having given to certain thoughts and expressions a depth and force which they had not for readers in general. In order, therefore, to explain the *disappointment,* I must recall to your mind what my *expectations* were: and, as these again were founded on the supposition that (in whatever order it might be published) the poem on the growth of your own mind was as the ground plot and the roots, out of which "The Recluse" was to have sprung up as the tree, as far as [there was] the same sap in both, I expected them, doubtless, to have formed one complete

whole; but in matter, form, and product to be different, each not
only a distinct but a different work. In the first I had found
"themes by thee first sung aright,"

> Of smiles spontaneous and mysterious fears
> (The first-born they of reason and twin-birth)
> Of tides obedient to external force,
> And currents self-determin'd, as might seem,
> Or by some central breath; of moments awful,
> Now in thy inner life, and now abroad,
> When power stream'd from thee, and thy soul received
> The light reflected as a light bestowed;
> Of fancies fair, and milder hours of youth,
> Hyblæan murmurs of poetic thought                    10
> Industrious in its joy, in vales and glens
> Native or outland, lakes and famous hills!
> Or on the lonely highroad, when the stars
> Were rising; or by secret mountain streams,
> The guides and the companions of thy way;
> Of more than *fancy*—of the *social sense*
> Distending wide, and man beloved as man,
> Where France in all her towns lay vibrating,
> Ev'n as a bark becalm'd beneath the burst
> Of Heaven's immediate thunder, when no cloud         20
> Is visible, or shadow on the main!
> For Thou wert there, thy own brows garlanded,
> Amid the tremor of a realm aglow,
> Amid a mighty nation jubilant,
> When from the general heart of human kind
> *Hope* sprang forth, like a full-born Deity!
> Of that dear Hope afflicted, and amaz'd,
> So homeward summon'd! thenceforth calm and sure
> From the dread watch-tower of man's absolute self,
> With light unwaning on her eyes, to look             30
> Far on! herself a glory to behold,
> The Angel of the vision! Then (last strain)
> Of duty, chosen laws controlling choice,
> Action and Joy! *An Orphic song indeed,*
> *A song divine of high and passionate truths,*
> *To their own music chaunted!*

Indeed, through the whole of that Poem, με Αὔρα τις εἰσέπνευσε
μουσικωτάτη. This I considered as "The Excursion;" and the second, as "The Recluse" I had (from what I had at different times

gathered from your conversation on the Place [Grasmere]) anticipated as commencing with you set down and settled in an abiding
home, and that with the description of that home you were to
begin a *philosophical poem*, the *result* and fruits of a spirit so
framed and so disciplined as had been told in the former.

Whatever in Lucretius is poetry is not philosophical, whatever
is philosophical is not poetry; and in the very pride of confident
hope I looked forward to "The Recluse" as the *first* and *only* true
philosophical poem in existence. Of course, I expected the colours,
music, imaginative life, and passion of *poetry*; but the matter and
arrangement of *philosophy*; not doubting from the advantages of
the subject that the totality of a system was not only capable of
being harmonised with, but even calculated to aid, the unity (beginning, middle, and end) of a poem. Thus, whatever the length
of the work might be, still it was a *determinate* length; of the subjects announced, each would have its own appointed place, and,
excluding repetitions, each would relieve and rise in interest above
the other. I supposed you first to have meditated the faculties of
man in the abstract, in their correspondence with his sphere of
action, and, first in the feeling, touch, and taste, then in the eye,
and last in the ear,—to have laid a solid and immovable foundation
for the edifice by removing the sandy sophisms of Locke, and the
mechanic dogmatists, and demonstrating that the senses were living growths and developments of the mind and spirit, in a much
juster as well as higher sense, than the mind can be said to be
formed by the senses. Next, I understood that you would take the
human race in the concrete, have exploded the absurd notion of
Pope's "Essay on Man," Darwin, and all the countless believers
even (strange to say) among Christians of man's having progressed
from an ourang-outang state—so contrary to all history, to all religion, nay, to all possibility—to have affirmed a Fall in some sense,
as a fact, the possibility of which cannot be understood from the
nature of the will, but the reality of which is attested by experience
and conscience. Fallen men contemplated in the different ages of
the world, and in the different states—savage, barbarous, civilised,
the lonely cot, or borderer's wigwam, the village, the manufacturing town, seaport, city, universities, and, not disguising the sore

evils under which the whole creation groans, to point out, however, a manifest scheme of redemption, of reconciliation from this enmity with Nature—what are the obstacles, the *Antichrist* that must be and already is—and to conclude by a grand didactic swell on the necessary identity of a true philosophy with true religion, agreeing in the results and differing only as the analytic and synthetic process, as discursive from intuitive, the former chiefly useful as perfecting the latter; in short, the necessity of a general revolution in the modes of developing and disciplining the human mind by the substitution of life and intelligence (considered in its different powers from the plant up to that state in which the difference of degree becomes a new kind (man, self-consciousness), but yet not by essential opposition) for the philosophy of mechanism, which, in everything that is most worthy of the human intellect, strikes *Death,* and cheats itself by mistaking clear images for distinct conceptions, and which idly demands conceptions where intuitions alone are possible or adequate to the majesty of the Truth. In short, facts elevated into theory—theory into laws— and laws into living and intelligent powers—true idealism necessarily perfecting itself in realism, and realism refining itself into idealism.

Such or something like this was the plan I had supposed that you were engaged on. Your own words will therefore explain my feelings, viz., that your object "was not to convey recondite, or refined truths, but to place commonplace truths in an interesting point of view." Now this I suppose to have been in your two volumes of poems, as far as was desirable or possible, without an insight into the whole truth. How can common truths be made permanently interesting but by being *bottomed* on our common nature? It is only by the profoundest insight into numbers and quantity that a sublimity and even religious wonder become attached to the simplest operations of arithmetic, the most evident properties of the circle or triangle. I have only to finish a preface, which I shall have done in two, or, at farthest, three days; and I will then, dismissing all comparison either with the poem on the growth of your own support, or with the imagined plan of "The Recluse," state fairly my main objections to "The Excursion" as it is. But it would have been alike unjust both to you and to myself, if I had led you to suppose that any disappointment I may have felt arose wholly or chiefly from the passages I do not like, or from the poem considered irrelatively. . . .

### TO WORDSWORTH, SUMMER, 1810 [ON SCOTT]

I am sending Scott's Lady of the Lake, having had it on my table week after week till it cried shame to me for not opening it —But truly as far as I can judge from the first 98 pages my reluctance was not unprophetic—Merciful Apollo! what an easy pace dost thou jog on with thy unspurred yet unpinioned Pegasus! The movement of the Poem (which is written with exception of a multitude of Songs in regular 8 syllable iambics) is between a sleeping canter and a market woman's trot—but it is endless—I seem never to have made any way—I never remember a narrative poem in which I felt the sense of Progress so languid—There are (speaking of the first 90 pages) two or three pleasing Images— That of the Swan p. 25—is the best—the following seems to me to demand something more for its introduction than a mere description for description's sake supplies—

> With boughs that quaked at every breath!
> Gray Birch and Aspen wept beneath,
> Aloft the ash and warrior Oak
> Cast anchor in the rifted Rock—

I wish, there were more faults of this kind, if it be a *fault* yet I think if it had been a beauty, it would not have instantly struck a perplexed feeling in my mind, as it did, and continues to do—a doubt—I seem to feel that I could have used the metaphor; but not in that way, or without other images or feelings in line with it— That the Lady of the Lake is not without it's peccadillos against the 8th Commandment a la mode of Messieurs Scott and Campbell, this may suffice—

> Some feelings are to mortals given
> With less of Earth in them than Heaven.

In short, what I felt in Marmion I feel still more in the Lady of the Lake—viz.—that a man accustomed to cast words in metre, and familiar with descriptive Poets and Tourists, himself a Picturesque Tourist, must be troubled with a mental strangury, if he could not lift up his leg six times at six different corners, and each time p— a canto—I should imagine that even Scott's warmest admirers must acknowledge and complain of the number of prosaic lines—*prose in polysyllables,* surely the worst of all prose for chivalrous Poetry —not to mention the liberty taken with our articles, and pron. relatives, such as—

> And Malcolm heard his Ellen's scream
> *As faltered thro' terrific Dream.*
> Then Roderick plunged *in* sheath his sword,
> And veiled his wrath *in scornful word:*
> "Rest safe, till morning! Pity, were
> Such cheek should feel the midnight air.
> Then may'st thou to James Stuart tell
> Roderick will keep the Lake and Fell,
> Nor lackey, with his freeborn Clan,
> The pageant pomp of Earthly man!
> More would he of Clan Alpine know,
> Thou canst our strength and passes show—
> Malise, what ho!" his henchmen came—
> "Give our safe conduct to the Graeme!"
> Young Malcolm answered calm and bold,
> "Fear nothing for thy favourite hold—
> The spot an Angel deigned to grace,
> Is blessed, *though robbers haunt the place*:
> Thy churlish courtesy for those
> Reserve, who fear to be thy foes—
> As safe to me the mountain way
> At midnight, as in blaze of day,
> Tho' with his boldest at his back,
> Even Roderick Dhu *beset the track!*
> Brave Douglas—lovely Ellen—nay—
> Nought here of parting will I say—
> Earth does not hold a lonesome glen
> So secret, but we meet agen—
> Chieftain! we too shall find an hour—"
> He said, and left the sylvan bower—

On my word, I have not *selected* this stanza. I do not say that there are not many better, but I do affirm, that there are some worse, and that it is a fair specimen of the general style—But that you may not rely on my judgement I will transcribe the next stanza like-wise, the 36th—

> Old Allan followed to the Strand
> (Such was the Douglas's command)
> And anxious told, how, on the morn,
> The stern Sir Roderick *deep had sworn,*
> The Fiery Cross should circle o'er
> Dale, Glen, and Valley, Down and Moor—
> Much were the Peril to the Graeme
> From those, who to the signal came;
> Far up the lake 'twere *safest land,*
> Himself would row him to the Strand—
> He gave his counsel to the wind,
> While Malcolm did, unheeding, bind,
> Round Dirk and Pouch and broad sword rolled,
> His ample plaid in tightened *fold,*
> And stripped his limbs *to such array*
> As best might suit the watery way—
> Then spoke abrupt; "farewell to thee,
> Pattern of old Fidelity!"
> The minstrel's hand he kindly prest,—
> "O! could I *point a place* of rest!
> My Sovereign holds in ward my land,
> My uncle leads my vassal band;
> To tame his foes, his friends to aid,
> Poor Malcolm has but heart and blade"—

Poor Malcolm! a hearty Blade that I will say for him—The Poem commences with the poorest Paraphrase Parody of the Hart Leap Well—I will add but one extract more as an instance of the Poet's care for lyric harmony—Observe this a poem of the dark ages, and admire with me the felicity of aiding the imagination in its flight into the ages past, and oblivion of the present by—God Save the King! and other savory descants—

> Boat Song (Canto 2–19, p. 69).

> Hail to the Chief who in triumph advances,
> Honoured and blest be the evergreen Pine!
> Long may the Tree in his banner that glances,
> Flourish the shelter and grace of our line!
>   Heaven send it happy dew,
>   Earth lend it sap anew,

Gayly to bourgeon and broadly to grow,
    While every highland glen
    Sends our shouts back agen,
ⲣoderick Vich Alpine dhu, ho! *ieroe!*

Now, that will tell! that last Gaelic line is "a damned hard Hit"—
as Reynolds said of a passage in King Lear—I suppose, there is
some untranslatable Beauty in the Gaelic words, which has preserved this one line in each stanza unenglished, even as the old
Popish Translators left the Latin words and phrases of the Vulgate
sticking, like raisins in a pudding, in the English Text—

In short, my dear William!—it is time to write a Recipe for
Poems of this sort—(I amused myself a day or two ago on reading
a Romance in Mrs. Radcliffe's style with making out a scheme,
which was to serve for all romances a priori—only varying the proportions)—a Baron or Baroness ignorant of their Birth, and in
some dependent situation—Castle—on a Rock—a Sepulchre at some
distance from the Rock—Deserted Rooms—underground Passages
—Pictures—a Ghost, so believed—or—a written record—blood on it!
A wonderful cut-throat etc., etc., etc. Now I say, it is time to make
out the component parts of the Scottish Minstrelsy—The first
Business must be, a vast string of Patronymics, and names of
Mountains, Rivers, etc.—the most commonplace imagery the Bard
gave look almost as well as new by the introduction of Benvoirlich,
Namvar, or copse-wood Gray that *moaned* (?) *and wept* on *Loch
Achray* and mingled with the pine-trees *blue* on the bold cliffs of
Ben Venue—

How should the Poet e'er give o'er,
    With his eye *fixed* on Cambusmore—
    Need reins be tightened in Despair,
    When rose Benledis' crest *in air*
    Tho' not one image grace the Heath,
    It gain such charm from flooded Teith—
    Besides, you need not travel far,
    To reach the Lake of Vennachar—
    Or *ponder refuge* from your Toil
    By far Lochard or Aberfoil!

Secondly all the nomenclature of Gothic architecture, of Heraldry,
of Arms, of Hunting and Falconry—these possess the same power

of reviving the capat mortuum and rust of old imagery—besides, they will stand by themselves, stout substantives, if only they are strung together, and some attention is paid to the sound of the words—for no one attempts to understand the meaning, which indeed would snap the charm—3, some pathetic moralizing on old times, or anything else, for the head and tail pieces—with a *Bard* (that is absolutely necessary) and Songs of course— For the rest, whatever suits Mrs. Radcliffe, i.e. in the Fable, and the Dramatis Personae will do for the Poem—with this advantage, that however threadbare in the Romance shelves of the circulating Library it is to be taken as quite new as soon as told in rhyme—it need not be half as interesting—and the Ghost may be a Ghost, or may be explained—or both may take place in the same poem— Then the Poet not only may but must mix all dialects of all ages—and all styles from Dr. Robertson's to the Babes in the Wood—

I have read only two cantos out of six—it is not that it would be any act of self denial to send you the Poem, neither is it for the pain which, I own, I should feel, and shrink *at* but not *from* of asking Southey to permit me to send it—that I do not send you the Poem today—but because I think, you would not wish me to ask Southey, who perhaps would refuse, and certainly would grant it with reluctance and fear—and because I take for granted that you will have a copy sent you shortly. . . .

TO THOMAS ALLSOP, FROM HIGHGATE, APRIL 8, 1820 [ON SCOTT]

. . . But I chose an example in literature, as more in point for the subject of my particular remarks, and because every man of genius, who is born for his age, and capable of acting *immediately* and widely on that age, must of necessity *reflect* the age in the first instance, though as far as he is a man of genius, he will doubt- less be himself reflected by it reciprocally. Now I selected Scott for the very reason, that I do hold him for a man of *very extraordinary* powers; and when I say that I have read the far greater part of his novels twice, and several three times over, with undiminished pleasure and interest; and that, in my reprobation of the Bride of Lammermoor (with the exception, however, of the almost Shakespearian old witch-wives at the funeral) and of the Ivanhoe, I mean to imply the grounds of my admiration of the others, and the permanent nature of the interest which they excite. In a word, I am far from thinking that Old Mortality or Guy Mannering would have been less admired in the age of Sterne, Fielding, and Richardson, than they are in the present times; but only that Sterne, &c., would not have had the same *immediate* popularity in the present day as in their own less stimulated and, therefore, less languid reading world.

Of Sir Walter Scott's poems I cannot speak so highly, still less of the Poetry in his Poems; though even in these the power of presenting the most numerous figures, and figures with the most complex movements, and under rapid succession, in *true picturesque unity*, attests true and peculiar genius. You cannot imagine with how much pain I used, many years ago, to hear —————'s contemptuous assertions respecting Scott; and if I mistake not, I have yet the fragments of the rough draft of a letter written by me so long ago as my first lectures at the London Philosophical Society, Fetter Lane, and on the backs of the unused admission tickets.

One more remark. My criticism was *confined* to the one point of the higher degree of intellectual activity implied in the reading and admiration of Fielding, Richardson, and Sterne;—in moral, or, if that be too high and inwardly a word, in *mannerly* manliness of taste the present age and its *best* writers have the decided advantage, and I sincerely trust that Walter Scott's readers would be as little disposed to relish the stupid lechery of the courtship of Widow Wadman, as Scott himself would be capable of presenting it. And, that though I cannot pretend to have found in any of these novels a character that even approaches in genius, in truth of conception, or boldness and freshness of execution, to Parson Adams, Blifil, Strap, Lieutenant Bowling, Mr. Shandy, Uncle Toby and Trim, and Lovelace; and though Scott's *female* characters will not, even the very best, bear a comparison with Miss Byron, Clementina Emily, in Sir Charles Grandison; nor the comic ones with Tabitha Bramble, or with Betty (in Mrs. Bennet's Beggar Girl); and though, by the use of the Scotch dialect, by Ossianic mock-highland motley-heroic, and by extracts from the printed sermons, memoirs, &c., of the fanatic preachers, there is a good deal of *false effect* and stage trick: still the number of characters *so good* produced by one man, and in so rapid a succession, must ever remain an illustrious phenomenon in literature, after all the subtractions for those borrowed from English and German sources, or compounded by blending two or three of the old drama into one—*ex. gr.* the Caleb in the Bride of Lammermoor.

Scott's great merit, and, at the same time, his *felicity,* and the true solution of the long-sustained *interest* novel after novel excited, lie in the nature of the subject; not merely, or even chiefly, because the struggle between the Stuarts and the Presbyterians and sectaries, is still in lively memory, and the passions of the adherency to the former, if not the adherency itself, extant in our own fathers' or grandfathers' times; nor yet (though this is of great weight) because the language, manners, &c., introduced are sufficiently different from our own for *poignancy,* and yet sufficiently near and similar for sympathy; nor yet because, for the same reason, the author, speaking, reflecting, and descanting in his own person, remains still (to adopt a painter's phrase) in sufficient *keeping* with his subject matter, while his characters can both talk and feel interesting to *us* as men, without recourse to *antiquarian* interest, and nevertheless without moral anachronism (in all which points the Ivanhoe is so wofully the contrary, for what Englishman cares for Saxon or Norman, both brutal invaders, more than for Chinese and Cochin-Chinese?)—yet great as all these causes are, the essential wisdom and happiness of the subject consists in this,—that the contest between the loyalists and their opponents can never be *obsolete,* for it is the contest between the two great moving principles of social humanity; religious adherence to the past and the ancient, the desire and the admiration of permanence, on the one hand; and the passion for increase of knowledge, for truth, as the offspring of reason—in short, the mighty instincts of *progression* and *free agency,* on the other. In all subjects of deep and lasting interest, you will detect a struggle

between two opposites, two polar forces, both of which are alike
necessary to our human well-being, and necessary each to the
continued existence of the other. Well, therefore, may we contemplate with intense feelings those whirlwinds which are for
free agents the appointed means, and the only possible condition
of that equilibrium in which our moral Being subsists; while the
disturbance of the same constitutes our sense of life. Thus in the
ancient Tragedy, the lofty struggle between irresistible fate and
unconquerable free will, which finds its equilibrium in the Providence and the future retribution of Christianity. If, instead of a
contest between Saxons and Normans, or the Fantees and Ashan-
tees,—a mere contest of indifferents! of minim surges in a boiling
fish-kettle,—Walter Scott had taken the struggle between the men
of arts and the men of arms in the time of Becket, and made us
feel how much to claim our well-wishing there was in the cause
and character of the priestly and papal party, no less than in those
of Henry and his knights, he would have opened a new mine,
instead of translating into Leadenhall Street Minerva Library
sentences, a cento of the most common incidents of the stately self-
congruous romances of D'Urfe, Scuderi, &c. N. B. I have not read
the Monastery, but I suspect that the thought or element of the
faery work is from the German. I perceive from that passage in
the Old Mortality, where Morton is discovered by old Alice in
consequence of calling his dog Elphin, that Walter Scott has been
reading Tieck's Phantasies (a collection of faery or witch tales),
from which both the incident and name is borrowed. . . .

POSTSCRIPT, TO THE REV. H. F. CARY, FEBRUARY 6, 1818 [ON BLAKE]

P.S. I have this morning been reading a strange publication—viz.
Poems with very wild and interesting pictures, as swathing, etched
(I suppose) but it is said printed and painted by the author, W.
Blake. He is a man of Genius—and I apprehend a Swedenborgian
—certainly a mystic *emphatically*. You perhaps smile at *my* calling
another poet a *Mystic*; but verily I am in the very mire of common-
place common-place compared with Mr. Blake, apo- or rather—
ana-calyptic Poet, and Painter!

TO CHARLES AUGUSTUS TULK, 1818 [ON BLAKE]

. . . I return you Blake's poesies, metrical and graphic, with thanks. With this and the book, I have sent a rude scrawl as to the order in which I was pleased by the several poems. . . .

Blake's Poems.—I begin with my dypathies that I may forget them, and have uninterrupted space for loves and sympathies. Title-page and the following emblem contain all the faults of the drawings with as few beauties as could be in the compositions of a man who was capable of such faults and such beauties. The faulty despotism in symbols amounting in the title-page to the μισητὸν, and occasionally, irregular unmodified lines of the inani-mate, sometimes as the effect of rigidity and sometimes of exossa-tion like a wet tendon. So likewise the ambiguity of the drapery. Is it a garment or the body incised and scored out? The lumpness (the effect of vinegar on an egg) in the upper one of the two prostrate figures in the title-page, and the straight line down the waistcoat of pinky goldbeaters' skin in the next drawing, with the I don't-know-whatness of the countenance, as if the mouth had been formed by the habit of placing the tongue not contemptu-ously, but stupidly, between the lower gums and the lower jaw— these are the only *repulsive* faults I have noticed. The figure, how-ever, of the second leaf, abstracted from the *expression* of the countenance given it by something about the mouth, and the interspace from the lower lip to the chin, is such as only a master learned in his art could produce.

N. B. I signifies "It gave me great pleasure." I, "Still greater." II, "And greater still." O, "In the highest degree." O, "In the lowest."

Shepherd, I; Spring, I (last stanza, I); Holy Thursday, II; Laughing Song, I; Nurse's Song, I; The Divine Image, O; The Lamb, I; The little black Boy, O, yea O + O; Infant Joy, II (N. B. For the three last lines I should write, "When wilt thou smile," or "O smile, O smile! I'll sing the while." For a babe two days old does not, cannot smile, and innocence and the very truth of Nature must go together. Infancy is too holy a thing to be ornamented). "The Echoing Green," I, (the figures I, and of the second leaf, II); "The Cradle Song," I; "The School Boy," II; Night, O; "On another's Sorrow," I; "A Dream,"?; "The little boy lost," I (the drawing, I); "The little boy found," I; "The Blossom," O; "The Chimney Sweeper," O; "The Voice of the Ancient Bard," O.

Introduction, I; Earth's Answer, I; Infant Sorrow, I; "The Clod and the Pebble," I; "The Garden of Love," I; "The Fly," I; "The Tyger," I; "A little boy lost," I; "Holy Thursday," I; [p. 13, O; "Nurse's Song," O?]; "The little girl lost and found" (the ornaments most exquisite! the poem, I); "Chimney Sweeper in the Snow," O; "To Tirzah, and the Poison Tree," I—and yet O; "A little Girl lost," O. (I would have had it omitted, not for the want of innocence in the poem, but from the too probable want of it in many readers.) "London," I; "The Sick Rose," I; "The little Vagabond," O. Though I cannot approve altogether of this last poem, and have been inclined to think that the error which is most likely to beset the scholars of Emanuel Swedenborg is that of utterly demerging the tremendous incompatibilities with an evil will that arise out of the essential Holiness of the abysmal A-seity in the love of the Eternal *Person,* and thus giving temptation to weak minds to sink this love itself into *Good Nature,* yet still I disapprove the mood of mind in this wild poem so much less than I do the servile blind-worm, wrap-rascal scurf-coat of *fear* of the *modern* Saint (whose whole being is a lie, to themselves as well as to their brethren), that I should laugh with good conscience in watching a Saint of the new stamp, one of the first stars of our eleemosynary advertisements, groaning in wind-pipe! and with the whites of his eyes upraised at the *audacity* of this poem! Anything rather than this degradation I of Humanity, and therein of the Incarnate Divinity!

S. T. C.

O means that I am perplexed and have no opinion.
I, with which how can we utter "Our Father"?

# NOTES

# POETRY

Coleridge's own notes are indicated by the initial (C) and are printed without quotation marks.

### THE COMPLAINT OF NINATHÓMA (PAGE 4)

How long will ye roll around me, blue-tumbling waters of Ocean. My dwelling is not always in caves; nor beneath the whistling tree. My feast is spread in Torthoma's Hall. The youths beheld me in my loveliness. They blessed the dark-haired Nina-thomà. (C) The passage is quoted, with brief omissions, from *Ossian*.

### SONGS OF THE PIXIES (PAGE 4)

See note to page 11.

### IMITATIONS: AD LYRAM (PAGE 9)

If we except Lucretius and Statius, I know not of any Latin poet, ancient or modern, who has equalled Casimir in boldness of conception, opulence of fancy, or beauty of versification. The Odes of this illustrious Jesuit were translated into English about 150 years ago. . . . I have subjoined the third ode of the second book, which, with the exception of the first line, is an effusion of exquisite elegance. In the imitation attempted, I am sensible that I have destroyed the *effect of suddenness*, by translating into two stanzas what is one in the original.

Ad Lyram.

Sonori buxi Filia sutilis,
Pendebis alta, Barbite, populo,
   Dum ridet aer, et supinas
    Solicitat levis aura frondes:
Te sibilantis lenior halitus
Perflabit Euri: me iuvet interim
   Collum reclinasse, et virenti
    Sic temere iacuisse ripa.
Eheu! serenum quae nebulae tegunt
Repente caelum! quis sonus imbrium!
   Surgamus—heu semper fugaci
    Gaudia praeteritura passu!    (C)

Coleridge once planned to publish a volume of imitations of the modern Latin poets.

### PANTISOCRACY (PAGE 10)

Coleridge, Southey, and several friends planned an ideal society, to be called "Pantisocracy," which they hoped to establish by emigrating to America.

There has been some doubt of Coleridge's authorship of this sonnet. Southey attributed it to S. Favell, though he had received a copy of it directly from Coleridge, sent as his (Coleridge's) own. E. H. Coleridge was convinced that the poem is Coleridge's.

### TO THE AUTHOR OF *The Robbers* (PAGE 10)

One night in Winter, on leaving a College-friend's room, whom I had supped, I carelessly took away with me "The Robbers," a drama, the very name of which I had never before heard of:—A Winter midnight—the wind high—and "The Robbers" for the first time!—The readers of Schiller will conceive what I felt. Schiller introduces no supernatural beings; yet his human beings agitate and astonish more than all the *goblin* rout—even of Shakespeare. (C)

Coleridge translated Schiller's *Wallenstein* in 1800.

### TO A YOUNG ASS (PAGE 11)

Byron memorialized this poem and the *Songs of the Pixies* in *English Bards and Scotch Reviewers* (lines 255–264):

> Shall gentle Coleridge pass unnoticed here,
> To turgid ode and tumid stanza dear?
> Though themes of innocence amuse him best,
> Yet still obscurity's a welcome guest.
> If Inspiration should her aid refuse
> To him who takes a pixy for a muse,
> Yet none in lofty numbers can surpass
> The bard who soars to elegise an ass,
> So well the subject suits his noble mind,
> He brays the laureat of the long-ear'd kind.

12. *Which patient Merit: Hamlet,* III, i, 74.

### SONNETS ON EMINENT CHARACTERS (PAGE 12)

Other sonnets in this group were addressed to Erskine, Burke, Priestley, Pitt, Mrs. Siddons, Godwin, Southey, and R. B. Sheridan.

*IV. Lafayette:* La Fayette was in prison when this poem was written.

*V. Koskiusko:* Tadeusz Kosciuszko (1746–1817), Polish national leader, had, like La Fayette, assisted in the American War for Independence. He was captured by the Russians in 1794, not long before the composition of this sonnet.

*VII. To the Rev. W. L. Bowles:* William Lisle Bowles (1762–1850). To Mr. Bowles's poetry I have always thought the following remarks from Maximus Tyrius peculiarly applicable:—"I am not now treating of that poetry which is estimated by the pleasure it affords to the ear—the ear having been corrupted, and the judgment-seat of the perceptions; but of that which proceeds from the intellectual Helicon, that which is *dignified,* and appertaining to *human* feelings, and entering into the soul."—The 13th Sonnet for exquisite delicacy of painting; the 19th for tender simplicity; and the 25th for manly pathos, are compositions of, perhaps, unrivalled merit. Yet while I am selecting these, I almost accuse myself of causeless partiality; for surely never was a writer so equal in excellence! (C) Cf. *Biographia Literaria,* Chapter I, in which Coleridge describes his early enthusiasm for the poetry of Bowles.

### THE EOLIAN HARP (PAGE 14)

The Aeolian harp, named, obviously, from Aeolus, god of the winds, is an instrument that produces musical tones when placed in a strong current of air. It has generally eight or ten strings, stretched over a wooden sounding box. James Thomson describes it in *The Castle of Indolence* (lines 352–369):

> A certain music, never known before,
> Here lulled the pensive melancholy mind;
> Full easily obtained. Behoves no more,
> But sidelong to the gently-waving wind
> To lay the well-tuned instrument reclined;
> From which, with airy flying fingers light,
> Beyond each mortal touch the most refined,
> The god of winds drew sounds of deep delight:
> Whence, with just cause, the Harp of Aeolus it hight.

> Ah me! what hand can touch the strings so fine?
> Who up the lofty diapason roll
> Such sweet, such sad, such solemn airs divine,
> Then let them down again into the soul?
> Now rising love they fanned; now pleasing dole
> They breathed, in tender musings, through the heart;
> And now a graver sacred strain they stole,
> As when seraphic hands an hymn impart:
> Wild warbling nature all, above the reach of art!

The image was a favorite one with Coleridge for some years. Cf. the opening lines of the *Ode to the Departing Year,* and *Dejection: an Ode,* stanzas 1 and 7.

In several passages *The Eolian Harp* seems to anticipate Wordsworth's *Tintern Abbey.* Lines 26–33, which strikingly suggest Wordsworth, did not appear in Coleridge's poem until 1817, but lines 44–48 appeared in the original edition of 1796 and therefore preceded *Tintern Abbey.*

### REFLECTIONS ON HAVING LEFT A PLACE OF RETIREMENT (PAGE 16)

The cottage was at Clevedon on the coast near Bristol. Coleridge lived there for a few weeks after his marriage.

12. *Bristowa:* Bristol.

49. *Howard:* John Howard (1726–1790), a philanthropist and pioneer in the prison reform movement.

### RELIGIOUS MUSINGS (PAGE 19)

As any reader will guess, Coleridge did not write the entire poem in its present form on the Christmas Eve of 1794; there were many later alterations and additions.

89. *Passions:* Our evil Passions, under the influence of Religion, become innocent, and may be made to animate our virtue—in the same manner as the thick mist melted by the Sun, increases the light which it had before excluded. In the preceding paragraph, agreeably to this truth, we had allegorically narrated the transfiguration of Fear into holy Awe. (C)

133. *Supreme Reality:* If to make aught but the Supreme Reality the object of final pursuit, be Superstition; if the attributing of sublime properties to things or persons, which those things or persons neither do or can possess, be Superstition; then Avarice and Ambition are Super-

stitions: and he who wishes to estimate the evils of Superstition, should transport himself, not to the temple of the Mexican Deities, but to the plains of Flanders [the current seat of war], or the coast of Africa [center of the slave trade]. (C)

171–172. *That foul Woman:* Catherine II, Empress of Russia.

173. *And he:* That Despot who received the wages of an hireling that he might act the part of a swindler, and who skulked from his impotent attacks on the liberties of France to perpetrate more successful iniquity in the plains of *Poland.* (C) The reference is presumably to Frederick William II, King of Prussia.

180. *Soul-hardened:* The Father of the present Prince of Hesse Cassell supported himself and his strumpets at Paris by the vast sums which he received from the British Government during the American War[,] for the flesh of his subjects. (C)

192. *Lord of:* In this paragraph the Author recalls himself from his indignation against the instruments of Evil, to contemplate the *uses* of these Evils in the great process of divine Benevolence. In the first age, Men were innocent from ignorance of Vice; they fell, that by the knowledge of consequences they might attain intellectual security, i.e. Virtue, which is a wise and strong-nerv'd Innocence. (C)

215. *Priests:* I deem that the teaching of the gospel for hire is wrong; because it gives the teacher an improper bias in favour of particular opinions on a subject where it is of the last importance that the mind should be perfectly unbiassed. Such is my private opinion; but I mean not to censure all hired teachers, many among whom I know, and venerate as the best and wisest of men—God forbid that I should think of these, when I used the word PRIEST, a name, after which any other term of abhorrence would appear an anti-climax. By a Priest I mean a man who holding the scourge of power in his right hand and a bible (translated by authority) in his left, doth necessarily cause the bible and the scourge to be associated ideas, and so produces that temper of mind which leads to Infidelity—Infidelity which judging of Revelation by the doctrines and practices of established Churches honors God by rejecting Christ. (C)

234. *Patriot Sage:* Dr. Franklin. (C) The reference, of course, is to the lightning-rod.

304. *The fifth seal:* Rev. 6.

315. *Even now:* This passage alludes to the French Revolution: and the subsequent paragraph to the downfall of Religious Establishments. I am convinced that the Babylon of the Apocalypse does not

apply to Rome exclusively; but to the union of Religion with Power and Wealth, wherever it is found. (C)

323. *The abhorréd Form:* Rev. 17.

359. *Thousand Years.* The Millenium:—in which I suppose, that Man will continue to enjoy the highest glory, of which his human nature is capable.—That all who in past ages have endeavoured to ameliorate the state of man will rise and enjoy the fruits and flowers, the imperceptible seeds of which they had sown in their former Life: and that the wicked will during the same period, be suffering the remedies adapted to their several bad habits. I suppose that this period will be followed by the passing away of this Earth and by our entering the state of pure intellect; when all Creation shall rest from its labours. (C)

368–370. *He . . . wisest:* David Hartley. (C) Coleridge named his first child David Hartley, but his enthusiasm for the philosopher waned in the course of time. His second child was named after the philosopher Berkeley.

388. *Fiend:* The final Destruction impersonated. (C)

395. *Believe thou:* This paragraph is intelligible to those, who, like the Author, believe and feel the sublime system of Berkeley; and the doctrine of the final Happiness of all men. (C)

### MONODY ON THE DEATH OF CHATTERTON (PAGE 31)

The first version of this poem (1790) consisted of 90 lines. The whole was rewritten, revised, and expanded at various times until the year of Coleridge's death.

44. *Vales . . . Avon:* Bristol, Chatterton's birthplace, is situated on the River Avon.

159. *Susquehannah:* The site proposed for the colony that was to have established Pantisocracy.

### ON OBSERVING A BLOSSOM (PAGE 36)

12. *Bristowa's bard:* Chatterton, once more.

### SONNET COMPOSED ON A JOURNEY HOMEWARD (PAGE 37)

5–6. E. H. Coleridge quoted, with reference to these lines, a passage from an unpublished letter of Coleridge in which this sonnet and another on the same subject were enclosed:

Almost all the followers of Fénelon believe that men are degraded Intelligences who had all once existed together in a paradisiacal or perhaps heavenly state. The first four lines express a feeling which I have often had—the present has appeared like a vivid dream or exact similitude of some past circumstances.

## TO A YOUNG FRIEND (PAGE 38)

The poem is addressed to Charles Lloyd, a friend of Charles Lamb and a young man of many literary interests but very unstable temperament. For a few months he lived with the Coleridges as a boarder and informal pupil. By 1798 there had developed between pupil and teacher a bitter quarrel which not only ended their friendship but also for a time clouded Coleridge's friendship with both Southey and Lamb.

## ODE TO THE DEPARTING YEAR (PAGE 41)

The *Argument* was added by Coleridge in 1797. The divisions of the poem indicated there were later changed to the nine numbered stanzas of the present text. Their correspondence is as follows: Stanza I, originally Strophe I; II, Strophe II; III, Epode; IV, Antistrophe I; V, Antistrophe II; VI–IX, Epode II.

33. *Dread Name:* The Name of Liberty, which at the commencement of the French Revolution was both the occasion and the pretext of unnumbered crimes and horrors. (C, 1803)

40. A subsidiary Treaty had been just concluded; and Russia was to have furnished more effectual aid than that of pious manifestoes to the Powers combined against France. I rejoice—not over the deceased Woman (I never dared figure the Russian Sovereign to my imagination under the dear and venerable Character of WOMAN—WOMAN, that complex term for Mother, Sister, Wife!) I rejoice, as at the disenshrining of a Daemon! I rejoice, as at the extinction of the evil Principle impersonated! This very day, six years ago, the massacre of Ismail was perpetrated. THIRTY THOUSAND HUMAN BEINGS, MEN, WOMEN, AND CHILDREN, murdered in cold-blood, for no other crime than that their garrison had defended the place with perseverance and bravery. Why should I recal the poisoning of her husband, her iniquities in Poland, or her late unmotived attack on Persia, the desolating ambition of her public life, or the libidinous excesses of her private hours! I have no wish to qualify myself for the office of Historiographer to the King of Hell—! December 23, 1796. (C)

76. *Lampads seven:* The seven lamps of Rev. 4.

91. Gifts used in Scripture for corruption. (C) In some editions Coleridge printed "Senate" in place of "Synod." The reference is to the failure of Parliament to abolish the African slave-trade.

135. *Abandon'd of Heaven!:*

The Poet from having considered the peculiar advantages, which this country has enjoyed, passes in rapid transition to the uses, which we have made of these advantages. We have been preserved by our insular situation, from suffering the actual horrors of War ourselves, and we have shewn our gratitude to Providence for this immunity by our eagerness to spread those horrors over nations less happily situated. In the midst of plenty and safety we have raised or joined the yell for famine and blood. Of the one hundred and seven last years, fifty have been years of War. Such wickedness cannot pass unpunished. We have been proud and confident in our alliances and our fleets—but God has prepared the canker-worm, and will smite the *gourds* of our pride. (C) Coleridge followed this note with a long quotation from Nah. 3.

161. In later years Coleridge half apologized for the violence of this denunciation of England, though not for the rather smug concluding lines. E. H. Coleridge printed a manuscript note by the poet:

Let it not be forgotten during the perusal of this Ode that it was written many years before the abolition of the Slave Trade by the British Legislature, likewise before the invasion of Switzerland by the French Republic, which occasioned the Ode that follows [*France: an Ode*], a kind of Palinodia.

THIS LIME-TREE BOWER MY PRISON (PAGE 46)

The friends were William and Dorothy Wordsworth and Charles Lamb; the visit occurred in July, not in June. A letter of Coleridge to Southey explains the prosaic, if painful, disability: Mrs. Coleridge had accidentally "emptied a skillet of boiling milk" on her husband's foot.

8–20. This was a favorite scene with Coleridge. He had already described it in the poem *To a Young Friend on His Proposing to Domesticate with the Author.* Wordsworth, in a note to his *Lines Written in Early Spring* describes the place in prose:

Actually composed while I was sitting by the side of the brook that runs down from the Comb, in which stands the village of Alford, through the grounds of Alfoxden. It was a chosen resort of mine. The brook fell down a sloping rock so as to make a waterfall considerable for that country, and across the pool below had fallen a tree, an ash, if I rightly remember, from which rose perpendicularly, boughs in search of the light intercepted by the deep shade above. The boughs bore leaves of green that for want of sunshine had faded into almost lily-white; and from the underside of this natural sylvan bridge depended long and beautiful tresses of ivy which waved gently in the breeze that might poetically speaking be called the breath of the waterfall. This motion varied of course in proportion to the power of water in the brook. When, with dear friends, I revisited this spot, after an interval of more than forty years, this interesting feature of the scene was gone. To the owner of the place I could not but regret that the beauty of this retired part of the grounds had not tempted him to make it more accessible by a path, not broad or obtrusive, but sufficient for persons who love such scenes to creep along without difficulty.

17. *Weeds:* The *Asplenium Scolopendrium,* called in some countries the Adder's Tongue, in others the Hart's Tongue. . . . (C)

28. *Gentle-hearted Charles:* Lamb resented the epithet, jocularly but none the less genuinely. It usually means "poor-spirited," he wrote to Coleridge, and is fit only for a "green-sick sonneteer." He suggested instead "drunken dog, ragged-head, seld-shaven, odd-eyed, stuttering" —or anything else that had some truth.

74. Some months after I had written this line, it gave me pleasure to find that Bartram had observed the same circumstance of the Savanna Crane.

When these Birds move their wings in flight, their strokes are slow, moderate and regular; and even when at a considerable distance or high above us, we plainly hear the quill-feathers: their shafts and webs upon one another creek as the joints or working of a vessel in a tempestuous sea. (C)

The quotation is from Part I, Chapter 7, of William Bartram's *Travels,* a favorite book of both Coleridge and Wordsworth.

THE RIME OF THE ANCIENT MARINER (PAGE 49)

Many years later Wordsworth described the origin of this poem:

In reference to this poem, I will here mention one of the most noticeable facts in my own poetic history, and that of Mr. Coleridge. In the autumn of 1797 [Another version reads, "the spring of the year 1798." This is not the place to discuss such complex problems as the date of this and several other poems], he, my sister, and myself, started from Alfoxden pretty late in the afternoon, with a view to visit Linton, and the Valley of Stones near to it; and as our united funds were very small, we agreed to defray the expense of the tour by writing a poem, to be sent to the "New Monthly

Magazine," set up by Phillips, the bookseller, and edited by Dr. Aikin. Accordingly we set off, and proceeded, along the Quantock Hills, towards Watchet; and in the course of this walk was planned the poem of the "Ancient Mariner," founded on a dream, as Mr. Coleridge said, of his friend Mr. Cruikshank. Much the greatest part of the story was Mr. Coleridge's invention; but certain parts I suggested; for example, some crime was to be committed which should bring upon the Old Navigator, as Coleridge afterwards delighted to call him, the spectral persecution, as a consequence of that crime and his own wanderings. I had been reading in Shelvocke's Voyages, a day or two before, that, while doubling Cape Horn, they frequently saw albatrosses in that latitude, the largest sort of seafowl, some extending their wings twelve or thirteen feet. "Suppose," said I, "you represent him as having killed one of these birds on entering the South Sea, and that the tutelary spirits of these regions take upon them to avenge the crime." The incident was thought fit for the purpose, and adopted accordingly. I also suggested the navigation of the ship by the dead men, but do not recollect that I had anything more to do with the scheme of the poem. The gloss with which it was subsequently accompanied was not thought of by either of us at the time, at least not a hint of it was given to me, and I have no doubt it was a gratuitous after-thought. We began the composition together, on that to me memorable evening: I furnished two or three lines at the beginning of the poem, in particular—

> And listen'd like a three years' child;
> The Mariner had his will.

These trifling contributions, all but one, which Mr. C. has with unnecessary scrupulosity recorded, slipped out of his mind, as they well might. As we endeavoured to proceed conjointly (I speak of the same evening), our respective manners proved so widely different, that it would have been quite presumptuous in me to do anything but separate from an undertaking upon which I could only have been a clog. We returned after a few days from a delightful tour, of which I have many pleasant, and some of them droll enough, recollections. We returned by Dulverton to Alfoxden. The "Ancient Mariner" grew and grew till it became too important for our first object, which was limited to our expectation of five pounds; and we began to think of a volume which was to consist, as Mr. Coleridge has told the world, of poems chiefly on supernatural subjects, taken from common life, but looked at, as much as might be, through an imaginative medium. Accordingly I wrote *The Idiot Boy, Her Eyes Are Wild,* &c., and *We Are Seven, The Thorn,* and some others.

*The Ancient Mariner* was Coleridge's main contribution to the volume of *Lyrical Ballads,* the publication of which in 1798 has often been called the greatest landmark in the progress of Romanticism. Coleridge's account of the origin of this volume is given in Chap. XIV of *Biographia Literaria*. In its earlier form *The Ancient Mariner* showed very clearly the influence of the old popular ballads and of Chatterton's verse. Most of the archaisms, some other crudities, and a few realistic details were pruned away in later revisions. Originally, the sailors fed the albatross with "biscuit-worms." The crew of the phantom ship were not at first the symbolic forms of Death and Life-in-Death. The male phantom was described in the manner of the current Gothic romances:

> *His* bones were black with many a crack,
>> All black and bare, I ween;
> Jet-black and bare, save where with rust
> Of mouldy damps and charnel crust
>> They're patch'd with purple and green.
>> . . . .
> A gust of wind sterte up behind
>> And whistled thro' his bones;
> Thro' the holes of his eyes and the hole of his mouth
>> Half-whistles and half-groans.

The marginal gloss, which some readers consider to be as poetic as the poem itself, was not printed until 1817 but may have been written much earlier.

Coleridge's own comment on the moral of the poem will be found among the selections in this volume from his *Table-Talk*. All readers of *The Ancient Mariner* should at least dip into that great study of its imagery, Lowes's *The Road to Xanadu*. This work shows, among many other things, how closely even the most fantastic passages are anchored to known or supposed truth of natural phenomena.

103. *The fair breeze*: Originally "the breezes"—i.e., the trade winds.

104. Coleridge's determination to present natural phenomena as truthfully as possible, even in a tale of the supernatural, is shown in his alteration of this line. In 1817 he changed it to

> The furrow stream'd off free

and added the following note:

In the former editions the line was,

> The furrow follow'd free:

But I had not been long on board a ship, before I perceived that this was the image as seen by a spectator from the shore, or from another vessel. From the ship itself, the *Wake* appears like a brook flowing off from the stern.

The line of 1817 is indeed more exact; but it is more awkward and was later dropped.

225–226. For the last two lines of this stanza, I am indebted to MR. WORDSWORTH. It was on a delightful walk from Nether Stowey to Dulverton, with him and his sister, in the Autumn of 1797, that this Poem was planned, and in part composed. (C)

## CHRISTABEL (PAGE 70)

After his return from Germany in the summer of 1799, Coleridge undertook to finish Christabel, first for Southey's *Annual Anthology*, then for the second edition of the *Lyrical Ballads*. He succeeded in completing Part II, and it is not impossible that he may have composed something of Part III, though no trace of this survives. The fragment became famous long before its publication in 1816; manuscript copies were apparently circulated, and Coleridge read or recited it on various occasions. Scott heard it in 1801; *The Lay of the Last Minstrel* (1805) showed the influence of its meter. Some years later Byron heard the poem and in 1816 recommended it to his publisher, John Murray, who offered Coleridge £80 for it and £20 more for *Kubla Khan*. These were published together with *The Pains of Sleep*.

*Preface.* 1797: The date has been much disputed; it may well have been 1798.

*Cumberland:* Until after Coleridge's death, all editions of the preface contained the following passage, inserted after "Cumberland":

Since the latter date, my poetic powers have been, till very lately, in a state of suspended animation. But as, in my very first conception of the tale, I had the whole present to my mind, with the wholeness, no less than the liveliness of a vision; I trust that I shall be able to embody in verse the three parts yet to come, in the course of the present year.

Another comment by Coleridge on the fragmentary state of the poem will be found among the selections from *Table-Talk*.

There has always been speculation about how the story would have proceeded. Wordsworth doubted that Coleridge ever had any clear plan, though Coleridge himself said he had. Only one summary exists that has any claim to authority and even it is subject to many doubts. James Gillman, in whose house Coleridge lived from 1818 until his death, published the following account in his life of the poet:

The following relation was to have occupied a third and fourth Canto, and to have closed the tale.

"Over the mountains, the Bard, as directed by Sir Leoline, 'hastes' with his disciple; but in consequence of one of those inundations supposed to be common to this country, the spot only where the Castle once stood is discovered—the edifice itself being washed away. He determines to return. Geraldine being acquainted with all that is passing, like the Weird Sisters in *Macbeth,* vanishes. Reappearing, however, she waits the return of the Bard, exerting in the meantime, by her wily arts, all the anger she could rouse in the Baron's breast, as well as that jealousy of which he is described to have been susceptible. The old Bard and the youth at length arrive, and therefore she can no longer personate the character of Geraldine, the daughter of Lord Roland de Vaux, but changes her appearance to that of the accepted though absent lover of Christabel. Next ensues a courtship most distressing to Christabel, who feels—she knows not why—great disgust for her once favoured knight. This coldness is very painful to the Baron, who has no more conception than herself of the supernatural transformation. She at last yields to her father's entreaties, and consents to approach the altar with this hated suitor. The real lover, returning, enters at this moment, and produces the ring which she had once given him in sign of her betrothment. Thus defeated, the supernatural being Geraldine disappears. As predicted, the Castle bell tolls, the mother's voice is heard, and to the exceeding great joy of the parties, the rightful marriage takes place, after which follows a reconciliation and explanation between the father and daughter."

*Celebrated poets:* Scott and Byron.

16–19. Cf. Dorothy Wordsworth's Alfoxden Journal for January 31, 1798:

When we left home the moon immensely large, the sky scattered over with clouds. These soon closed in, contracting the dimensions of the moon without concealing her.

48–52. Cf. Dorothy Wordsworth's Journal entry for March 7, 1798:

William and I drank tea at Coleridge's. A cloudy sky. Observed nothing particularly interesting—the distant prospect obscured. One only leaf upon the top of a tree—the sole remaining leaf—danced round and round like a rag blown by the wind.

129–134. This particular bit of demonology has its moral symbolism: evil can enter the castle only with the help of those who dwell within. Whether the Lady Geraldine was witch, vampire, man supernaturally disguised, or other demon is still an open question. Coleridge takes pains, at any rate, in the subsequent lines, to mark her as some supernaturally evil being: she dare not praise the Virgin; the mastiff bitch is disturbed in sleep by her presence; and the dying fire leaps up as she passes by.

350. *Pike:* Peak.

351. *Ghyll:* Valley.

365. *Plight:* Probably plait.

408–426. These lines refer indirectly to the alienation between Coleridge and Southey, which had only recently ended when Part II was composed. Coleridge later described them as the "best and sweetest" lines he had ever written. Hazlitt also admired them, recalling no doubt his own broken friendship with their author.

589–612. This description of Christabel's unconscious imitation of the evil look of Geraldine may have been a psychological refinement upon another bit of demonology. In his notes to *Thalaba* (published in 1801 but completed earlier) Southey has a long account of vampires, in which he records the tradition that a vampire's victim becomes in turn another vampire.

## LINES TO W. L. (PAGE 90)

The lines are addressed to William Linley, Sheridan's brother-in-law.

## FIRE, FAMINE, AND SLAUGHTER (PAGE 91)

See the "Apologetic Preface" to this poem, pp. 172ff.

19. *Letters four:* The poem was an attack upon Pitt.

## FROST AT MIDNIGHT (PAGE 93)

7. *Infant:* Coleridge's son David Hartley.

13–15. The thin blue flame or "film" described here is more often noticed in a coal than in a wood fire. Coleridge described the superstition associated with it in a note: "In all parts of the kingdom these films are called *strangers* and supposed to portend the arrival of some absent friend."

24. *At school:* Christ's Hospital. Cf. Charles Lamb's famous essay on his childhood there.

37. *Stern preceptor:* Bowyer, master of the school, figures in an episode recorded in Coleridge's *Table-Talk* for May 27, 1830:

I had *one* just flogging. When I was about thirteen, I went to a shoemaker, and begged him to take me as his apprentice. He, being an honest man, immediately took me to Bowyer, who got into a great rage, knocked me down, and even pushed Crispin rudely out of the room. Bowyer asked me why I had made myself such a fool? to which I answered, that I had a great desire to be a shoemaker, and that I hated the thought of being a clergyman. "Why so?" said he.—"Because, to tell you the truth, sir," said I, "I am an infidel!" For this, without more ado, Bowyer flogged me,—wisely, as I think,—soundly, as I know. Any whining or sermonizing would have gratified my vanity, and confirmed me in my absurdity; as it was, I was laughed at, and got heartily ashamed of my folly.

Cf. also the first chapter of the *Biographia Literaria*.

42–43. *Sister:* Coleridge's favorite sister, Ann, who died in 1791.

### FRANCE: AN ODE (PAGE 96)

The occasion of this poem was the invasion of Switzerland by France in 1798. The ode was published in a newspaper, the *Morning Post*, with an editorial introduction:

The following excellent Ode will be in unison with the feelings of every friend to Liberty and foe to Oppression; of all who, admiring the French Revolution, detest and deplore the conduct of France towards Switzerland. It is very satisfactory to find so zealous and steady an advocate for Freedom as Mr. Coleridge concur with us in condemning the conduct of France towards the Swiss Cantons. Indeed his concurrence is not singular; we know of no Friend to Liberty who is not of his opinion. What we most admire is the *avowal* of his sentiments, and public censure of the unprincipled and atrocious conduct of France. The Poem itself is written with great energy. The second, third, and fourth stanzas contain some of the most vigorous lines we have ever read. The lines in the fourth stanza:—

> To scatter rage and trait'rous guilt
> Where Peace her jealous home had built,

to the end of the stanza are particularly expressive and beautiful.

Reprinted here from E. H. Coleridge's note.

In 1802 an Argument was added:

*First Stanza.* An invocation to those objects in Nature the contemplation of which had inspired the Poet with a devotional love of Liberty. *Second Stanza.* The exultation of the poet at the commencement of the French Revolution, and his unqualified abhorrence of the Alliance against the Republic. *Third Stanza.* The blasphemies and horrors during the domination of the Terrorists regarded by the Poet as a transient storm, and as the natural consequence of the former despotism and of the foul superstition of Popery. Reason, indeed, began to suggest many apprehensions; yet still the Poet struggled to retain the hope that France would make conquests by no other means than by presenting to the observation of Europe a people more happy and better instructed than under other forms of Government. *Fourth Stanza.* Switzerland, and the Poet's recantation. *Fifth Stanza.* An address to Liberty, in which the Poet expresses his conviction that those feelings and that grand *ideal* of Freedom which the mind attains by its contemplation of its individual nature, and of the sublime surrounding objects (see Stanza the First) do not belong to men, as a society, nor can possibly be either gratified or realised, under any form of human government; but belong to the individual man, so far as he is pure, and inflamed with the love and adoration of God in Nature. (C) In this ode Coleridge marked the first pronounced break from his faith in the French Revolutionary movement. At one time he christened the poem *The Recantation: an Ode*.

## LEWTI (PAGE 99)

47. *Lawny shroud:* In view of the indebtedness of Coleridge himself to Wordsworth in this poem, his manuscript note (published by E. H. Coleridge) is remarkable: "This image was borrowed by Miss Bailey in her Basil as the dates of the poems prove."

## FEARS IN SOLITUDE (PAGE 102)

Since the autumn of 1797 England had been alarmed by constant threats of an invasion from France. A manuscript comment on the poem by Coleridge was published by E.H.C.: "N. B. The above is perhaps not Poetry,—but rather a sort of middle thing between Poetry and Oratory—sermoni propriora.—Some parts are, I am conscious, too tame even for animated prose."

### THE NIGHTINGALE (PAGE 108)

13. *"Most musical, most melancholy"*: The quotation is from Milton's *Il Penseroso*, 62. Coleridge commented on 13–22:

This passage in Milton possesses an excellence far superior to that of mere description; it is spoken in the character of the melancholy Man, and has therefore a *dramatic* propriety. The Author makes this remark, to rescue himself from the charge of having alluded with levity to a line in Milton; a charge than which none could be more painful to him, except perhaps that of having ridiculed his Bible.

40. *My Friend:* Wordsworth and his sister Dorothy.

49–86. The castle of this passage is probably that of Enmore, seat of the Earl of Egmont. John Cruikshank, a friend of Coleridge (cf. the notes on *The Ancient Mariner*) was the Earl's agent at Stowey. The "gentle maid" may have been an Ellen Cruikshank, who seems to have lived at Enmore; but there is some uncertainty about her identity.

97–105. This incident was recorded, somewhat differently, by Coleridge in a notebook:

Hartley fell down and hurt himself—I caught him up crying and screaming—and ran out of doors with him.—The Moon caught his eye—he ceased crying immediately—and his eyes and the tears in them, how they glittered in the Moonlight!

### THE BALLAD OF THE DARK LADIÉ (PAGE 112)

See the notes to *Love*, below.

### KUBLA KHAN (PAGE 114)

*Preface:* Though many persons still accept as literal truth the statement of Coleridge that under the influence of opium, in a deep sleep, he dreamed the poem, both images and words, and afterwards wrote it down *verbatim* from memory, there are numerous reasons for doubting that he did so. Modern medical opinion does not confirm the traditional belief in the existence of "opium dreams" as a special *genre*, or even the belief that opium of itself produces dreams at all. In a note to an autograph copy of *Kubla Khan* that came to public notice only in 1934, Coleridge himself made a less sensational claim than in his published note; in the manuscript note he said only that the poem was composed in a "reverie" induced by opium. Other biographical

circumstances too complicated to be entered into here cast further doubt
upon the notion of a unique dream origin for the poem.

  *In the summer . . . 1797*: E.H.C. dates the poem 1798.
It may have been written in 1799 or even 1800.

  *Purchas's Pilgrimage*: The actual passage in Purchas is
slightly different:

In Xamdu did Cublai Can build a stately Palace, encompassing sixteene
miles of plaine ground with a wall, wherein are fertile meddowes, pleasant
Springs, delightfull Streames, and all sorts of beasts of chase and game, and
in the middest thereof a sumptuous house of pleasure, which may be removed from place to place.

  *Then all the charm . . . mirror*: These lines are quoted
from Coleridge's own poem *The Picture; or, The Lover's Resolution*.
  Σαμερον . . . ασω: Theocritus, *Idylls*, I, 132.

Since *Kubla Khan* has often been read as a piece of pure music or
pure magic without any rational meaning, it may not be out of place
to call attention here to what the poem actually says. The description
of the pleasure grounds is interrupted after line 36. The remaining
lines explain indirectly why the poet cannot complete the fragment:
he has lost his inspiration. In a vision, the lines say (when read literally
but carefully), the poet heard music which, if he could only revive it,
would by the joy it produced enable him to really recreate the scene
of Kubla's paradise into poetry truly immortal. He would then be
looked upon with awe as one of the inspired Great Ones, the Poet-
Prophets of the world. The last lines are a romanticized version of the
ancient Greek tradition concerning poetic inspiration. Cf. the *Ion* of
Plato and Coleridge's own *Dejection: an Ode*.

### THE DEVIL'S THOUGHTS (PAGE 118)

According to a later note by Coleridge, Southey's contribution consisted of Stanzas I, II, III, IX, XVI.

  20. *Death in the Revelation*: Rev. 6.

  27–28. *For I sate myself, like a cormorant*: This anecdote is related by that most interesting of the Devil's Biographers, Mr. John
Milton, in his *Paradise Lost*, and we have here the Devil's own testimony to the truth and accuracy of it. (C) Cf. *Paradise Lost*, Book IV.

  48. *Key*: Flag. (C) The allusion is to Archbishop Randolph con-
secrating the Duke of York's banners. (E.H.C.)

52 and 66. *Mr.* —— and *General* ——: It is not certain what, if any, names Coleridge had in mind. The "general" has been thought to be Gascoigne or Tarleton, but the poet's own note disclaimed any reference to an actual person:

If any one should ask who General —— meant, the Author begs leave to inform him, that he did once see a red-faced person in a dream whom by the dress he took for a General; but he might have been mistaken, and most certainly he did not hear any names mentioned. In simple verity, the author never meant any one, or indeed any thing but to put a concluding stanza to his doggerel.

### LOVE (PAGE 121)

The first version of this poem was published in *The Morning Post* under the title of *Introduction to the Tale of the Dark Ladie*, with the following prefatory letter to the editor:

SIR,
The following Poem is the introduction to a somewhat longer one, for which I shall solicit insertion on your next open day. The use of the Old Ballad word, *Ladie*, for Lady, is the only piece of obsoleteness in it; and as it is professedly a tale of ancient times, I trust, that "the affectionate lovers of venerable antiquity" (as Camden says) will grant me their pardon, and perhaps may be induced to admit a force and propriety in it. A heavier objection may be adduced against the Author, that in these times of fear and expectation, when novelties *explode* around us in all directions, he should presume to offer to the public a silly tale of old fashioned love; and, five years ago, I own, I should have allowed and felt the force of this objection. But, alas! explosion has succeeded explosion so rapidly, that novelty itself ceases to appear new; and it is possible that now, even a simple story, wholly unspired [? unspiced] with politics or personality, may find some attention amid the hubbub of Revolutions, as to those who have resided a long time by the falls of Niagara, the lowest whispering becomes distinctly audible.

S. T. COLERIDGE

The poem was composed shortly after Coleridge's first meeting with Sarah Hutchinson and is now thought to be a disguised reflection of his attachment to her.

### THE MAD MONK (PAGE 124)

These lines were written intentionally in the tradition of the Gothic romance, as the original subtitle shows—"An Ode in Mrs. Ratclif's Manner."

### TO ASRA (PAGE 126)

"Asra" was Sarah Hutchinson. According to E.H.C., this sonnet accompanied a manuscript copy of *Christabel* which Coleridge gave to Sarah Hutchinson in 1804.

### DEJECTION: AN ODE (PAGE 127)

The first version of this ode was addressed to Sarah Hutchinson. In subsequent versions the name was changed to "William" (Wordsworth), "Edmund," and eventually, as here, "Lady." The original poem was composed shortly after Wordsworth had written the first four stanzas of his *Ode on Intimations of Immortality*. The relation between the two poems is easily apparent though far from simple. In the revised version Coleridge omitted much personal matter and improved the whole structurally and poetically.

120. *Otway:* Originally "William." The story in lines 118–125 is that of Wordsworth's *Lucy Gray*.

### HYMN BEFORE SUN-RISE (PAGE 131)

On its first two appearances in print, Coleridge introduced the poem with a longer preface:

Chamouni is one of the highest mountain valleys of the Barony of Faucigny in the Savoy Alps; and exhibits a kind of fairy world, in which the wildest appearances (I had almost said horrors) of Nature alternate with the softest and most beautiful. The chain of Mont Blanc is its boundary; and besides the Arve it is filled with sounds from the Arveiron, which rushes from the melted glaciers, like a giant, mad with joy, from a dungeon, and forms other torrents of snow-water, having their rise in the glaciers which slope down into the valley. The beautiful *Gentiana major,* or greater gentian, with blossoms of the brightest blue, grows in large companies a few steps from the never-melted ice of the glaciers. I thought it an affecting emblem of the boldness of human hope, venturing near, and, as it were, leaning over the brink of the grave. Indeed, the whole vale, its every light, its every sound, must needs impress every mind not utterly callous with the thought—Who *would* be, who *could* be an Atheist in this valley of wonders! If any of the readers of the Morning Post have visited this vale in their journeys among the Alps, I am confident that they will not find the sentiments and feelings expressed, or attempted to be expressed, in the following poem, extravagant.

Coleridge himself had not seen Chamouni.

### THE PAINS OF SLEEP (PAGE 135)

Coleridge sent some lines of this poem in a letter to Thomas Poole on October 3, 1803, with an account in prose of his sufferings. He described his nightly torments, when he had fallen asleep though struggling to stay awake from fear of his appalling dreams. He would waken thankful even for his own "loud Screams" that had startled him out of those terrible dreams. His "Night-yells," he said, had made him a nuisance at home. "This is an unexaggerated tale," he assured Poole. "My Dreams become the Substances of my Life—."

This was written while Coleridge was attempting to break away from his slavery to opium. The mental and physical wretchedness that he described in *The Pains of Sleep* and in some of the letters is a typical experience of many persons when they are suddenly deprived of the drug or of an accustomed amount of it.

### TO WILLIAM WORDSWORTH (PAGE 137)

The occasion was that of Wordsworth's reciting from *The Prelude*.

21. *Hyblean:* Honeyed.

45. *Orphic song:* Probably a reference to the "Orphic Hymns" (translated in Coleridge's day by Thomas Taylor the Platonist) rather than to the legends more widely known in modern times, of Orpheus and Eurydice or of Orpheus charming the wild beasts with music.

### PSYCHE (PAGE 140)

1–2. In Greek Psyche is the common name for the soul and the butterfly. (C)

### A TOMBLESS EPITAPH (PAGE 141)

1. *Idoloclastes Satyrane:* Coleridge published some of his own letters from Germany under the title of Satyrane's *Letters* in *The Friend* (and again later in the *Biographia Literaria*), where this poem also first appeared. In Spenser's *Faerie Queene,* Satyrane "far abroad for straunge aduentures sought" (I, vi, 29). E. H. Coleridge suggests that Coleridge may have thought of Spenser's Satyrane as the anonym of Luther. *Idoloclast,* as Coleridge himself took care to note, is a "breaker of idols."

### THE MADMAN AND THE LETHARGIST (PAGE 142)

E. H. Coleridge called attention to the similarity in theme between these verses and the opening number of *The Friend* (1809):

Though all men are in error, they are not all in the same error, nor at the same time . . . each therefore may possibly heal the other . . . even as two or more physicians, all diseased in their general health, yet under the immediate action of the disease on different days, may remove or alleviate the complaints of each other.

### TIME, REAL AND IMAGINARY (PAGE 145)

Time was undoubtedly more imaginary than real to Coleridge if we are to judge by his blithe indifference to accuracy in dates. When this poem was first published in 1817 he described it as a "schoolboy poem" that he was publishing now only "at the request of the friends of my youth." E. H. Coleridge pointed out a passage in a notebook, probably written when Coleridge was nearly forty, which nevertheless seems to have preceded the composition of the poem:

How marked the contrast between troubled manhood and joyously-active youth in the sense of time! To the former, time like the sun in an empty sky is never seen to move, but only to have *moved*. There, there it was, and now 'tis here, now distant! yet all a blank between. To the latter it is as the full moon in a fine breezy October night, driving on amid clouds of all shapes and hues, and kindling shifting colours, like an ostrich in its speed, and yet seems not to have moved at all. This I feel to be a just image of time real and time as felt, in two different states of being. The title of the poem therefore (for poem it ought to be) should be time real and time felt (in the sense of time) in active youth, or activity with hope and fullness of aim in any period, and in despondent, objectless manhood—time objective and subjective. (*Anima Poetae*, 1895, pp. 241–242.)

When he published the poem Coleridge added an explanation of its title:

By imaginary Time, I meant the state of a school boy's mind when on his return to school he projects his being in his day dreams, and lives in his next holidays, six months hence; and this I contrasted with real Time.

### LIMBO (PAGE 149)

Probably a fragment. Parts were published separately during Coleridge's lifetime.

## NE PLUS ULTRA (PAGE 150)

E. H. Coleridge informs us that these lines were inscribed in a note-book immediately after *Limbo*.

18–21. *Lampads seven*: See note on the *Ode to the Departing Year*, 76.

## A CHARACTER (PAGE 155)

It has been suggested that the verses were written under the provocation of Hazlitt's essay on Coleridge in *The Spirit of the Age*. However this may be, the subject of the lines is of course not Hazlitt but the poet himself, the "bird" and "bard" accused of being a Jacobin-"bat" in disguise.

4. *Tit*: A titmouse or one of a number of other small birds.

19. *Cit*: Slang for *citizen*, used contemptuously with reference to Jacobins.

## CONSTANCY TO AN IDEAL OBJECT (PAGE 157)

9–10. *Like strangers*: Cf. the second paragraph of the *Allegoric Vision*.

30. *An image with a glory*: A phenomenon which had been scientifically explained in Coleridge's day and which Coleridge had seen and often referred to. Under certain atmospheric conditions a man's own shadow might be projected against mist, sometimes with a peculiar glow or "glory" about the head of the shadow. This appearance had given rise to numerous superstitions; ignorant of its cause, people had mistaken it for a spectre or wraith.

## EPITAPHIUM TESTAMENTARIUM (PAGE 158)

There is some error in Coleridge's Greek motto, but no one has determined precisely what the reading should be. As E. H. Coleridge said, the general intention is clear. The poet meant to imply that he was near the end of his life.

## COLOGNE (PAGE 159)

1. *Bones*: Of the eleven thousand virgin Martyrs. (C)

# PROSE

###### ❧❧❧

## THE WANDERINGS OF CAIN

P. 165. Prefatory Note. *The Death of Abel*: By Salomon Gessner, Swiss poet.

P. 167. *Canto II*: There was, of course, no Canto I, nor anything subsequent to Canto II.

P. 169, Par. 2. *The Shape . . . his brother Abel*: A fragmentary manuscript plan for this work indicates that the supposed Abel was not intended to be the real brother of Cain or his spirit but an evil spirit disguised, who endeavors by deception to lead Cain into sacrificing the child.

## APOLOGETIC PREFACE TO FIRE, FAMINE, AND SLAUGHTER

P. 172. See pages 91–93 for the poem. Though this "Preface" was probably composed more than fifteen years after the poem was written, the opening episode, according to E. H. Coleridge, probably occurred in 1803. Coleridge himself thought very highly of this piece of writing. A manuscript copy of *Sibylline Leaves* is said to contain this note by Coleridge: "With the exception of this slovenly sentence I hold this preface to be my happiest effort in prose composition." The "slovenly sentence is the one on p. 175, "What language Shakespear . . . stand here for Law."

## BIOGRAPHIA LITERARIA

P. 186. The work was originally intended as a kind of preface to the 1817 edition of Coleridge's poems, the *Sibylline Leaves*. The author intended, as Shawcross says, to "explain and justify his own style and practice in poetry." This purpose, however, led him into a discussion of Wordsworth's theories as differing from his own; and that in turn led to an analysis of the principles underlying all poetry, then to a discussion of imagination, and finally to a consideration of certain fundamental philosophical problems. The work became too long for its original purpose as a single volume but too short for independent publication in two volumes. Coleridge added the accounts of some experiences in Germany, *Satyrane's Letters* (published originally in *The Friend*), and some further discussion of Wordsworth's work, to fill up the volumes. The *Biographia Literaria* is thus in part a miscellaneous work, though the thread of its original intention holds much of it together.

For some additional comment on the *Biographia,* which is Coleridge's principal, if possibly not his best, critical work, see the Introduction to the present volume; for a full account, see the Introduction to Shawcross's edition.

P. 187. *In 1794:* Coleridge's date is wrong; the volume was published in 1796.

P. 200. . . . *second number of the monthly magazine:* Another inaccuracy. The "Higginbottom" sonnets appeared in November, 1797, in vol. 4 of the *Monthly Magazine.* This kind of error is so common in Coleridge's writing that there is little use in noting each instance of it. The *Biographia* is not to be read for its factual content.

P. 264. Chap. XIII. It need scarcely be said that the "friend" who wrote this letter was Coleridge himself. Shawcross called attention to Coleridge's own reference to "that letter addressed to myself as from a friend, at the close of the first volume of the *Literary Life,* which was written without taking my pen off the paper."

P. 268. The "critical essay on the uses of the Supernatural in poetry," which had been planned in 1801 or perhaps even earlier, in connection with the poem *Christabel,* never materialized.

P. 295–296. Wordsworth altered *The Thorn* a great deal in later editions; much of what Coleridge quotes here does not appear in the poem as it now stands. The same thing is true in greater or less degree of the other quotations from Wordsworth, especially those in Chap. XXII.

P. 344. The reference to the *Excursion,* "pp. 96," etc., is to Book III, 50ff.

P. 351. Coleridge's reference to "pages 27, 28, and 62" of Wordsworth's poems are intended to designate the *Anecdote for Fathers* and some other poem not certainly identifiable (page 62 in the edition used by Coleridge is blank). "The second instance" is from the poem *Gypsies.*

P. 358. *See page 25, vol. 2nd.* The poem referred to is *Star Gazers.*

P. 362. The description of skating is from the poem *Influence of Natural Objects* (also used in *The Prelude*). The "description of the blue-cap" occurs in *The Kitten and Falling Leaves.*

P. 363. *See vol. I, pages 134 to 136* refers to the poem *'Tis Said that Some Have Died for Love.*

P. 365. *Resignation and Independence* is *Resolution and Independence*.

### ON THE PRINCIPLES OF GENIAL CRITICISM

P. 372. These essays were first printed in *Felix Farley's Bristol Journal* in 1814, on the occasion of an exhibition of paintings by the American artist Washington Allston. Coleridge's correspondence explains his motive for publishing the essays on this subject in such an unusual place. "My motive was originally to serve poor Allston, who is now exhibiting his pictures in Bristol." Actually, the essays contain only the briefest reference to Allston, and Coleridge had other plans for them. He intended to increase the number to sixteen or twenty; and in offering them to Daniel Stuart for publication in the *Courier* he wrote: "I have no hesitation in declaring them the best compositions I have ever written." The series was never completed, and those that had appeared in Bristol were not reprinted during Coleridge's lifetime.

## LECTURES AND NOTES

P. 387. As T. M. Raysor has noted, Coleridge's lectures have in large measure "established the great tradition of English Shakespearean criticism." Their influence, as well as their intrinsic quality, has therefore made them mandatory reading for the student of literary criticism. The lectures survive, however, only in a fragmentary and imperfect state. Coleridge himself did not publish them, and in general his manuscripts yield notes rather than complete, polished lectures. Some lectures survive only in newspaper reports and notes (in shorthand or otherwise) taken by listeners.

For additional brief comments on the lectures, see the Introduction to this volume. A full and admirable discussion of those that relate to Shakespeare will be found in Professor Raysor's Introduction to Coleridge's *Shakespearean Criticism*.

## INTRODUCTORY LECTURE TO CONCIONES AD POPULUM

P. 446. This is the best known piece of Coleridge's early political prose writing.

## TABLE-TALK

P. 460. It should be borne in mind that the title of this work describes the contents literally. It is not, as in Hazlitt's *Table-Talk*, a title used conventionally for informal essays composed and *written down* by the author. The *Table-Talk* of Coleridge cannot be taken as an exact and complete record of his own words, for it was composed from notes made of his conversation.

## ANIMA POETAE

P. 472. The selections here are taken from Coleridge's notebooks. Unlike *Table-Talk,* they are literally his own words, though they were not published by himself and most of them were probably not intended for publication in their existing form.

## ALLEGORIC VISION

P. 478. A note of E. H. Coleridge records the history of this piece. An earlier version of 1795 was used by Coleridge as a preface to his first Theological Lecture on "The Origin of Evil." "Superstition" was the Church of England, and the feminine figure of "Religion," represented the poet's current leaning toward Unitarianism. In 1811 he rewrote the "Vision" for publication in the *Courier.* Here "Superstition" had become the Church of Rome, and the allegory as a whole was turned into an attack on the movement for Catholic Emancipation.

# Rinehart Editions